MMM

MARY MARGARET McBRIDE'S HARVEST OF AMERICAN COOKING

MARY

MARGARET

McBRIDE's

Illustrated by Adolar

G. P. PUTNAM'S SONS   NEW YORK

Harvest of American Cooking

WITH RECIPES FOR 1,000 OF AMERICA'S

FAVORITE DISHES

TO STELLA

whose book this is,
with love

Acknowledgments

Many have helped with this book, but I want to mention especially Estella Karn, Janice Devine, Helen Josephy Robison, and Gloria Marshall, whose wonderful efforts were far beyond the call of duty. Bless them.

Contents

THE SOUTH AND THE CARIBBEAN

THE HEARTLAND

THE MOUNTAINS AND THE SOUTHWEST

THE FAR WEST AND THE PACIFIC

1,000 SELECTED RECIPES

Introduction

When I was a young, green Middle Westerner newly come to New York and scared of my shadow, my intrepid friend Estella Karn —lately come, too, but from California—taught me to eat in twenty-eight languages. The woman actually knew restaurants in the city that served authentic food of that many countries.

I had plenty of misgivings at first but, almost before I knew it, began to take a reporter's interest if not unbounded eating pleasure in such unfamiliar items as sharkfin soup, grape leaves stuffed with pine nuts and currants, fried bean flour bread, sour cream soup, snails, broiled eels and tamales.

Since then, I've eaten my way appreciatively across America, collecting recipes discriminately and pounds rather less so. I treasure hundreds of ancient "receipts," mostly in spidery handwriting on yellowed bits of paper: Cousin Belle's Unfailing Rule for Green Tomato Ketchup handed down by her English great-grandmother; Mrs. Meredith's Moonshine (a dessert not a drink) that has descended from Welsh ancestors; Aunt Jacynthia's Dutch Flansjes.

Estella Karn kept insisting through the years that I ought to do a cookbook which would show the role of food in our history. I kept protesting, contending that I would rather show my appreciation of American food by eating it than writing about it. But because I have a weakness for trying anything once—even such atrocities as chicken fried in egg batter, and corn bread with sugar in it—I finally did begin the well-nigh impossible task of writing the history of America in its foods.

Four years later I realize that to do justice to the subject would consume not alone my lifetime but the lifetimes of a staff of researchers as well. The experience has also caused me to feel impassioned about the admirable men and women who came to this country to start life over again, bringing with them among their dearest possessions the recipes for the dishes of their homelands. And now, though I know some may scold me because of omissions they consider important, I am glad I have attempted to tell the story of America through its foods. However, I am not promising to teach how to cook in fifty or sixty languages. There are plenty of descriptions of odd, even outlandish dishes and gargantuan banquets that are fun to read about, but which I'm sure no cook in her right mind would want to reproduce in this diet-conscious, vitamin-aware age. Yet here I have tried to tell about those marvels of delight that each group has created out of a faraway past in the new, magnificent America that surrounded them.

When I did a television show from the 1956 Kitchen of Tomorrow, I found myself dialing for a recipe that was promptly flashed on a small screen in front of my eyes, drying dishes by sound waves, measuring ingredients by a "magic eye," viewing a push-button refrigerator which obligingly turned one side of itself outdoors so as to be convenient for the delivery boy. Later I saw an electric oven that bakes a layer cake in three minutes and cooks a five-pound roast of beef in thirty. And we are all bombarded constantly with news of dehydrated steaks, faster mixes, even food squeezed from tubes for the nurture of helmeted adventurers rocketing into outer space.

So you may ask: Why a cookbook at all in such times?

Well, I recently came on a consumer survey which reported that in the midst of this mad whirl of no-hands cooking, the sale of baking powder has increased substantially! Which proves what I have always believed—that nothing will ever surpass light-as-air biscuits made from scratch, served hot from the oven with butter melting in their tender little hearts, just as no satisfaction will ever equal the joy a woman finds in setting those biscuits and other delicious products of her own skill before her family.

So in the twenty-first century I predict that women will still be swapping recipes and pridefully bringing to their tables magnificent pies or cakes, at sight of which families and guests will gasp, "And to think you made it all yourself!"

THE INDIANS

PUYALLUPS
OBJIBWAS
SIOUX
MOHICANS
ALGONKIANS
POTOWATOMIS
HOPIS
PAWNEES
CHEROKEES
YUMAS
ZUÑIS
NAVAJOS
PIMAS
APACHES
COCOPAS
TEJAS

The Indians

TAMERS OF THE WILD

Three hundred years ago Mrs. Red Thunder took her ax and started into the deep forests of Wisconsin to cut the climbing bittersweet vines that had served her before in time of hunger. She found the vines, chopped them into chunks and boiled them until the spongy bark fell away from the stems. She dried the bark, ground it to powder and cooked it with water into a kind of soup.

It was an anonymous English traveler who gave his Potawatomi Indian hostess the name of Mrs. Red Thunder when he reported eating this curious soup by her fire. "One might not fatten on it," he observes, "still it would preserve life for a long time." His Journal and countless other old records and diaries like it have helped me piece together this first chapter of the story of America's food.

Rightly enough, we think of ourselves as scientific farmers, food producers, technologists. Yet over half the value of our farm produce depends upon plants that had already been domesticated

by the Indians when we got here. Here's the humbling statement
of two economics experts of the U.S. Department of Agriculture:
"The extent of the debt to the Indian is emphasized when we re-
call that the white man has not reduced to cultivation a single
important staple during the four hundred years he has dominated
the New World."

True, we have worked miracles in food preservation. But the
Zuñi Indians were freezing bread centuries ago. We have built
dams to make the desert flower. But as far back as the thirteenth
century, the vanished cliff-dwellers of the Southwest built an
irrigation system big enough to supply a quarter of a million people. Indians also invented pemmican, the dried pounded meat
mixed with fat which Explorer Robert E. Peary once pronounced
"the most satisfying food I know."

Indian women had many cookery tricks which we might do
well to try. They found that milkweed blossoms are a delicate
sweetener, and they used both blossoms and buds to flavor and
thicken their meat soups. When they gathered blueberries, they
lined their baskets with fresh sweet fern to preserve the wild
woods fragrance on the journey home. They sweetened wild strawberries by shaking the early morning dew from milkweed blossoms
over the sun-ripe berries.

Most of their calendar divisions were named for foods. In many
tribes June was the Month of the Strawberry Moon; the lush
nights of July were lighted by the Moon of the Blueberries; the
golden promise of the Harvest Moon was followed by the Moon
of the Hunters.

Nobody knows where or when two grasses were accidentally
crossed to become the ancestors of the Indian corn whose proper
name is maize. Some scientists believe it had its ancient birth in
Peru, others hold out for Mexico or Paraguay or Guatemala. But
wherever it came from, corn is helpless without man. It has to be
cultivated to survive. It must have taken centuries for corn to
travel north through America. Yet when the first Europeans arrived, they found all the varieties known to us—and some that
have been lost—growing in patches in the wilderness, in irrigated
plots across the plains, in secret valleys among the bare mountains
of the Southwest. One of the lost varieties had kernels so fat they
were eaten like grapes.

The first food reports to reach the outside world from North
America were probably brought by Eric the Red, who sailed his

dragon ship into the region of New England five centuries before Columbus and six hundred years ahead of the *Mayflower*. Historians who favor the Vikings as discoverers of America support their theories by pointing to descriptions in the Norse sagas of berries and fish indigenous to North America; and references to wild grapes, for which the new region was named Vineland.

Fishermen from England, Spain, Portugal and France ranged the coasts many years before the first white settlements were made. Nevertheless, it must have been a shock when that famous Indian, Squanto, greeted the arriving Pilgrims from the *Mayflower* in 1620 in their own language. Captured by the Spanish, Squanto had traveled to England and had been returned on a fishing boat in time to help make history. As every schoolchild knows, it was Squanto and Samoset who gave corn to the settlers during that first bitter winter, and it was due to Indian foods that we have that most American of holidays, Thanksgiving.

In the sixteenth century the Spanish, greedy and treacherous, cut a bloody path into America. But they left the first detailed reports of native foods, food which proved a greater treasure than the gold they sought. Castenada, recording the Coronado expedition in 1540, described birds in New Mexico with "great hanging chins," delicious when roasted. These were domesticated turkeys, and his "cows covered with frizzled hair which resembles wool" were buffalo, juicy steaks of which were to sizzle over many a pioneer's prairie fire.

The Spanish expeditions brought horses, cattle and pigs, many of which strayed off into the countryside to go wild or to be caught and domesticated by the Indians. The Spanish also had seeds and plants in such profusion that the food pattern of Florida, New Mexico and California became a blend of Indian, Spanish and Mexican before colonists from the East added their varied cuisine.

Along the coast of South Carolina and Georgia, peaches and figs were flourishing when the first English settlers came, probably planted by the priests who established the first Spanish missions in the 1500's. In those early days the Spanish did not come to colonize but rather to explore and to convert. By 1570 there were only 150 protesting Spaniards left in what is now St. Augustine, Florida. They had eaten all their horses and were dependent upon Cuba for food supplies. Their pioneer blood was thin and all they wanted was to go back home.

Was it a lean, desperate Puritan, I wonder, who first learned that the Indians put a fish in each corn hill to fertilize the soil? Did his homesick wife perhaps copy an Indian woman's technique of grinding corn and mixing it into an Indian pudding? Who first noticed corn and lima beans growing together in an Indian field and found that the two, boiled together, made a dish that sounded to alien ears like "succotash"? What forgotten Spaniard first trespassed on a Navaho wedding and discovered a thick, delectable porridge filling the bowls—cornmeal mush!

Jacques LeMoyne tells of sailing up the St. Johns River in the 1500's for his first astonished glimpse of Florida, which he said was "the fairest, fruitfullest and pleasantest country of all the world." The Indians brought him maize flour, smoked lizards and strange roots, and showed him how they stored their foods in palm-roofed granaries. Observing all this, he wrote wistfully: "No one fears being cheated. Indeed, it would be good if among Christians there were as little greed to torment men's minds and hearts."

There was plenty of greed, as our history books reveal all too clearly. But there must have been gentle exchanges, too, as Indian women showed the strangers how to make the clam into stew and chowder, how to bake a succulent pot of beans by sticking it in a hole in the ground, and how to fix cranberries and pumpkins a dozen ways.

Pumpkins were so much a part of the scene that one ditty of the 1630's ran:

> *We have pumpkins at morning and pumpkins at noon,*
> *If it were not for pumpkins, we should be undoon.*

They would have been "undoon," too, without the maples that grew green and magnificent over thousands of miles of the country. The Indians loved maple sugar and maple syrup. Some tribes burned tobacco as a thank-offering to the tree for giving its life blood. They boiled the sap and whisked off the foam with fresh brushes of spruce. Today children at sugaring-off parties in Vermont and New Hampshire trickle the waxy golden syrup into the snow and eat it, much as Indian children did.

One of the creations of Indians in New England was sweet corn and venison with maple, not unlike the German sweet-sour meats. Even after the arrival of salt in their region, the elders among the

Ojibway and neighboring tribes preferred maple sugar for seasoning.

Could an average American today exist for a week without his
customary food? Isolated in the woods or open country, miles from
civilization, could he live for a year without seeds and tools to
cultivate plants? Marion and G. L. Wittrock, in a survey for the
New York Botanical Garden, said that it certainly could be done
if the wandering citizen knew his Indian food lore. The Indians,
they found, ate the berries and fruits of nearly 300 different plants.

They fried the delicate redbud and boiled the buds of at least
fifteen other flowers, including marigold, clover and pokeweed.
They made jams and relishes from a dozen plants, ate at least 59
varieties of greens as we eat spinach.

Cattail sap was candy for Indians of Nevada, who also nibbled
happily on grasshopper cakes. Clara Beatty of the Nevada Historical Society writes: "The whites coming through relished grasshopper meal, it being quite tangy . . . until they found the legs
and wings in it."

Many a famished white trapper ate acorn and beechnut pancakes by Indian fires. In spare times, Indian women would walk
softly through the woods seeking the logs where the tiny deermouse had hidden his winter store of beechnuts, all carefully
shelled and packed away. An Indian woman who robbed the
cache of the deermouse always left a handful of corn as a thank-
you, just as she formally thanked the bear for guiding her to
edible berries, hidden rose haws and wild honey.

One important Indian food has come into its own as a luxury
dish today: wild rice. The Ojibway in Wisconsin call wild rice the
"good berry." They set up camps during the milk stage of the rice
and staked out preserves to protect their harvest rights. At harvest
time two women and one man would go out in a canoe to gather
enough rice for a small feast to precede the harvest work. The
final step, after the rice had been roasted, was to dig a hole and
sink a bucket for a threshing floor. A man wearing new moccasins
balanced himself with two poles as he trampled the grain. Finally
the chaff was blown away by filling shallow trays which women
shook up and down in a gentle breeze. Indians liked their wild
rice cooked in deer broth and seasoned with maple sugar.

A delicacy among Algonquian Indians was a dish of pine
lichens, boiled and stirred until they came together like scrambled

eggs. Another was wild gooseberries cooked with new sweet corn. Fresh-water fish were seasoned with wild ginger, and vinegar was made from soured maple sap and used in a stew of venison and young dandelion greens.

Almost everything that grew had a mystical meaning for the Navaho. Little sticks of oak blessed a new hogan, and mistletoe guarded it from lightning. Meadow rue, or Maid of the Mist, made a special tea to be drunk after the ceremony of the War Dance.

The yucca was a substitute for almost everything when the Navahos were on the move and far from their corn patches. They ate the fruit raw, they baked it in ashes, and from the ashes made a soap. On the sixth day of the Mountain Chant, appointed couriers washed themselves from head to foot in yucca suds. Yucca leaves made fearsome masks and children had skinny yucca dolls.

Today the Navahos are forgetting their ancient plant lore. Dr. Francis Elmore of the University of New Mexico, making a seven-year study, found that grass seeds are no longer harvested, the trading post stocks canned spinach instead of Rocky Mountain beeweed. In a few years, Dr. Elmore predicts, not many of the old customs will survive.

Along the Colorado River, where only pine, mesquite and pitayaha grow, Castenada found in 1540 that the Indians were making a bread from mesquite, which looked like cheese and "keeps good for a whole year."

Another Spaniard reported that "to know what manner of foods they had, I made a sign unto them that I would gladly eat, and they brought mee certaine cakes of maize and a loaf of mis-quiqui. . . ." Mesquite beans are still important on the menu of the Apache and Pima and other Indians of the Southwest, so much so that in the wild bottom lands a bunch of arrowweed is hung to a branch to signify that the mesquite tree is individually owned. The Yumas used to seal a marriage by giving the couple a bowl of mesquite gruel to share. A Cocopa Indian baby for four days after birth drank only a beverage made from the inner bark of the mesquite. The Pimas used the white mesquite gum for candy, and the Opata took a fungus from the mesquite tree and smoked it.

The fruit of the great organ-pipe cactus, green skinned and crimson within, was a highly prized delicacy. From the newly gathered pulp the Indians cooked up cactus jam in a pot presided over by the mother or mother-in-law of the household. Cactus pulp was dried on housetops and made into cakes and stored for many months. Flour was ground from a smaller cactus, the sahuaro, and combined with cornmeal for a sweet, oily gruel.

Indians knew how to make delectable dishes from tubers which the white man has never, even yet, recognized as edible, tubers which were cousins to our Irish potato. The so-called Irish potato, actually from South America, had to make five trans-Atlantic crossings before it landed for keeps in North America. Even then, it was at first so suspect that, like the tomato, it was grown in gardens only as an ornamental plant.

All during the colonial era the white potato struggled for recognition here, and in France the king even wore potato blossoms in his lapel in an effort to popularize the vegetable. When potatoes did begin to appear on American menus, they were often served with a sugar frosting, or cooked with dates, lemons, mace, cinnamon, sugar, nutmeg and grape juice!

All the same, the white potato was a valued plant thousands of years ago, when Indians living in what is now Peru and Bolivia developed it in a dozen different varieties, sizes and colors. They produced frost-resistant potatoes, a beetle-immune variety, as well as a type that was edible after freezing. Some of the ancient potatoes have been lost, but in Mexican and Peruvian markets you'll still find polka-dot and striped potatoes, as well as some with purple skins and yellow flesh.

Our own first settlers in North America converted the Indian name "batata" into "potato," but what they actually meant was the sweet potato they found flourishing in Indian gardens. A man named John Pory tasted one variety of what the Indians called "batata" in Virginia in 1621. He burned his tongue and commented indignantly: "I wouldn't give a farthing for a shipload."

An Indian somewhere in Chile found a strain of strawberries with both male and female parts in its flowers, and ever since plant hunters have been searching vainly for that original wild strain. It was a Frenchman who managed in 1714 to get five of the Chilean strawberry plants to France, where some of our own North American wild species had been taken. There the modern strawberry was born, and in a few years came home to America.

At least one other food had to take a trip to Europe to win respect. Some of the early explorers, before the *Mayflower*, found the Indians on Cape Cod growing patches of a tuber they called

"girasole." They noted that while the women tended the rest of
the garden crops, a girasole patch was cultivated only by men.
The explorers took a sample back to Spain and in a few years it
was popular all over Europe as the Jerusalem artichoke. It returned to the United States as an imported delicacy.

Indians had a trick of cooking meat and fish on a slab of wood
as the smartest restaurants do now with planked steaks and shad.

How many men were actually kept alive on the flowers, bark,
roots and leaves growing along the trails to the West will never
be known, but it is pretty sure that one small, acrid plant called
"Cigaga-wunj," or wild garlic, saved Marquette and his men from
starvation on their trip from Green Bay. At the end of the journey
they called the place of the wild garlic by their version of its
Indian name—"Chicago."

The desperate settlers who survived their first season in Utah
ate a lovely wild flower, the Mariposa Lily, which is the state
flower today.

The blue flowers of the Camass lily, treasured by the Prairie
Indians for the sugar-sweet bulbs, were discovered by hungry
settlers bound west. They created a Camass pie still fancied in
that part of the country. But the Yampa (John Fremont was enraptured of it with wild duck), growing along the Snake River in
Idaho and in meadows for miles around, has been forgotten as a
food. Breadroot, too, is neglected now, its winged blossoms no
longer made into cakes carried west by Lewis and Clark.

Even today, pigweed, when cooked right, tastes like the tenderest spinach. Then there's field sorrel to whisk into a creamy soup,
evening primrose for boiling or for salads, the asparaguslike cattail, hedge mustard, dock and jeweled sea plants that, M. F. K.
Fisher writes, make a delectable salad.

The *Round Valley Cookbook,* compiled by the Covelo Fed-
erated Church in Covelo, California, was sent me not long ago
by Edith V. A. Murphy of Wind River Reservation, Wyoming.
Some years ago, Mrs. Murphy won our radio program achieve-
ment award, partly for her work among the Indians. Among the
recipes in the Covelo book is acorn soup made with acorn meal.
In California's early days, acorns were soaked overnight until the
shells split open. The kernels were picked out by the old women
of the tribe, and the nuts spread in openwork baskets to dry, then
ground to flour in a stone mortar. After that the acorn meal was
spread on a frame of incense cedar twigs, and water was re-

peatedly poured through until the meal turned pink. Then it was dried. The Indians liked the spicy flavor the soaked cedar gave the meal.

During World War II, experts of the U.S. Department of Agriculture made a re-survey of neglected native foods, listing more than 1,000 native plants. Had rationing gone on, tightening our belts, we might have returned to at least part of our Indian food heritage. But the war ended and milk and honey flowed again. The produce of the world poured into our deep-freeze units, our markets. And the edible weeds blow in the wind, the berries ripen and fall in the woods, and the wild plant treasure of long ago is no more than a myth to the hurrying masses of Americans.

Yet it must be said that for nearly every native food we lost or discarded, there is another that we cherished and improved. For this we must thank devoted scientists, like Dr. Frederick V. Coville who spent half a century on botanical research for the government, chiefly on blueberries. He developed juicy, luscious varieties of this native American fruit, and at the close of a lifetime of work he wrote on his final report *Dixi*, the Latin word meaning "I am through." His last, plumpest blueberry is now known as the Dixi. And I am thankful that while such workers as Dr. Coville care about our agriculture, the story of American food will never be "dixi."

THE EAST

Maine

Vt.

N. H.

Mass.

N. Y.

Conn.

R. I.

Penn.

N. J.

SOUP

Del.

New York

A barn in the Catskill Mountains of New York state has been a fine place for the writing and editing of this story of America and her foods, even though I did burst into tears when I first glimpsed the farm. In the rain-soaked piggery, chicken house and other out-buildings that dismal day, I saw the dreary ghosts of rented farms in Missouri where my mother's superb cooking and her traveling pansy beds were the only bright touches.

I shuddered at the prospect of spending even a week end at the place. If anyone had told me then that I'd end up by living in the barn, I'm sure I'd have had hysterics. Yet I who sneered at idiots who make over old barns, now have a barn of my own, complete with 1761 beams which had to be kept intact (so my advisors said), no matter what else was sacrificed.

And I love it. I love the majesty of the view from my redwood-paneled living room—a view I never even saw on that first foggy Sunday. I can start a chicken frying on the stove (pink and push-button modern), then look out the great windows at forty miles of lake, with mountains piled up all around. I can pop corn in the vast bluestone fireplace after supper, with only the crackle of the fire and the pop of the corn to disturb the country quiet.

Down the hill from my barn is an old orchard full of what professional apple growers around here call "sentimental apples," meaning we don't spray or prune and the apples are not of commercial quality. But they make a fine, tart, cinnamon-flavored Catskill applesauce. In this region were once apple-holes, which farmers filled with fall apples to be dug up in spring.

Governor Peter Stuyvesant gets credit for the first grafted apple trees on these shores—time, 1647. The French Huguenots experimented with them, too, and the famed Prince Nursery in Flushing produced an apple called Newtown Pippin, so flavorful that Benjamin Franklin took a basketful to the royal court in London.

Which reminds me of a more recent discovery—"unconscious apples." Seems the apple people set out to find a way to store McIntoshes for months at a time without sacrificing prime eating qualities. A scientist at Cornell, who took on the project, pointed out that apples (as well as other plants) inhale oxygen and exhale carbon dioxide. It was discovered that when their oxygen supply is reduced to 3 per cent, McIntoshes go into a coma. Revived with fresh air months later, they are as flavor-fresh as the day they came off the tree.

It was apples that brought me, originally, to this lovely mountain region. Invited to Kingston to crown an Apple Blossom Queen, I fell in love with that old town and its steep-roofed stone houses. Some of them more than three hundred years old, they still look much as they did when Dutch housewives staged a tea strike of their own about the time Bostonians were dumping tea into the harbor.

When Dutch housewives managed to get sugar, they kept it in "bite and stir boxes" and hung the precious sugar lump over the table so everyone could take a tiny bite to sweeten tea, which was often flavored with saffron or peach leaves. In other parts of the colonies, women unused to tea sometimes brewed it, threw away the liquid and served the family a soggy dish of tea leaves sweetened and spiced.

Dutch settlers apparently agreed with Henry Hudson, who sailed up the river in 1609 and pronounced the section around Kingston "a pleasant land," for a few years later they were planting their first crops of maize, following the Indian custom of sowing when "the birch tree leaf was the size of a mouse's ear." They soon learned from the Indians to make *suppone*—a kind of cornmeal mush cooked each morning at sunrise and served with maple syrup and milk. They called their Indian neighbors "the wilden" and from them—in friendly interchange—learned how to use the wild plants, how to plant crops in cycles, where and when to fish.

After 1674 the Dutch in America celebrated a special Thanksgiving, with *hutspot* for the main dish. This was to give thanks for the saving of beleaguered Laidin in Holland, whose people had kept alive on a diet of dogs and cats while the Spanish laid siege to their city. When at last the enemy was forced to flee, starving Laidinese rushed into the deserted Spanish camps and found brimming kettles still simmering over the fires. The Spanish stew was christened hutspot. Ever since, wherever Dutchmen live, hutspot (which is tender beef simmered with carrots, onion and potatoes) reminds them of this occasion.

Eleven Fish, or shad, cooked on a birch bark plank over the embers of a woodfire, became another Dutch tradition. Shad was called Elft, or Eleven, because it then arrived on the eleventh of March, and the first shad was always presented to the governor.

The delicately flavored sea bass, with six stripes on each side, was called Der Twelft, and its season began on the twelfth of March. Thirteen Fish was the sturgeon, and the Dutch learned from the Indians how to make the first American caviar from sturgeon roe. Salmon was so plentiful that servants sometimes made it part of their contract that they should not have to eat it more than once a week.

A minor international feud arose over who owned the delicious hard-shell crabs of Manhattan—the Dutch or the English. The Dutch pointed proudly to the blue and white claws, their own Prince of Orange flag colors. But the claws turned red when boiled, which the English cited as proof that the crab gladly deserted the Dutch colors at the proper time.

Lobsters, by the way, were one of New York state's earliest war casualties. They didn't like the sound of cannonading. An English traveler named Eddis in his *Letters from America* reported in 1792 that "the vast lobsters" took flight from New York waters at the start of the Revolution, "not one having been taken or seen since the commencement of hostilities."

Each Dutch family had treasured recipes, especially for *caudle*
. . . a concoction of sweetened water, oatmeal, spices, raisins,
lemons and Madeira wine. This graced the center of company
tables, and ladies gathered for teatime used to serve themselves
from the big silver caudle bowl, which had tiny spoons hung round
its edge. Raisins and nuts enriched the *oly-koecks,* and almond
paste the wee *permoppen* cookies.

Izer cookies became so popular that their fame spread to New
Jersey and Pennsylvania, where they were called squeeze cakes.
They were made in special wedding-gift irons with the initials of
bride and bridegroom intertwined on top.

Every bride in colonial New York learned to make sack posset,
which combined sugar, Spanish sack, nutmeg, milk and twenty
eggs. As a rhymed recipe put it:

> *Stir them with steady hand and conscience prickin'*
> *To see the untimely fate of twenty chickens.*

Spices were precious everywhere in the colonies, and many
Dutch and English carried their own silver boxes with nutmeg
grater in one compartment and nutmeg in the other. While
colonial home cooking sounds delightful, we have only to read a
few of the old travel journals for a glimpse of what an eighteenth-
century tourist was in for at taverns of the day. Madame Sarah
Kemble Knight, in a tart record of a business trip from Boston to
New York in 1704, reported that she suspected a cabbage stew
of being made in a dye-pot, and averred that a dinner of mutton
turned out to be so pickled that she paid her sixpence for the
smell, and left the table. Traveler Charles Dickens, visiting Syra-
cuse, had "an old buffalo for dinner and an old pig for breakfast."

If these critical tourists had traveled along the New York-
Canadian border, they might have told a different story. So many
French-Canadians moved across to towns like Malone, Ogdens-
burg, Plattsburg and Cohoes that the cooking took on a delectable
French accent. There was cassoulet, an oven dish of white beans,
garlic and spices cooked with goose fat, pork and bits of roast goose
meat; onion soup, habitant style, with herb seasonings and onions
simmered pale gold in butter; hearty broths of black bean and
yellow pea; pot-au-feu; and venison chopped, rolled into balls and
served with a tomato and sour cream sauce.

Both French and Germans helped establish the great vineyards throughout upstate New York. The visiting Lafayette was toasted in local wine at Fredonia. But the truly elegant dishes of France made their New York appearance on the tables of wealthy *émigrés* of the 1830's. Joseph Bonaparte was one who hoped to establish a new France in this country, as well as an asylum for his brother, Napoleon. Joseph bought more than 160,000 acres in the Adirondacks and occasionally took picnic parties into the wilderness, serving them exquisite dinners of partridge, wild duck, caviar, *pâté* and such luxuries, on a gold "picnic" service.

It was a Frenchman also, C. B. Champlin, who started the production of fine champagne in the Hammondsport area. He built wine cellars in 1860, brought over a winemaker from Rheims and was soon turning out distinctive vintages . . . which came into their own with American gourmets almost a century later.

In Buffalo the most flavorful foreign touch today is Polish. There on wedding days and holidays, heirloom tablecloths emerge along with festive dishes such as plum *pierogi* (boiled dumplings made with potato dough and rich blue plum jam inside, with a spiced cream sauce poured over). The traditional wafer is broken at Christmastime, and some families cling to the custom of greeting a guest with bread and salt, and of putting on the table at Easter a special oatmeal soup, a crust of bread, and sausage.

A custom kept in Buffalo, by the Greek and Russian Orthodox church, is a colorful Easter service held a fortnight later than the American one, and followed by refreshments of tea served hot and strong from samovars, an array of fruit and cheese confections, also *kulitch*, a cake yeast-raised and rich with eggs and almonds.

In the city of Troy, during the War of 1812, a Samuel Wilson, nicknamed Uncle Sam, furnished beef for the soldiers at Watervliet arsenal. US stamped on the meat stood for United States, but the troops began calling their meat rations "Uncle Sams" . . . a term eventually translated by cartoonists into the tall, lanky figure which now symbolizes the nation.

New York state's maple products are so good that one resident of the traditional maple state of Vermont shocked his neighbors by sending across the border for his syrup supplies. As long ago as 1791, maple syrup was dreamed of as big business for New York by a promotor named Gerritt Boon, who bought 17,000 acres of woods near Utica for investors in Holland. A favorite pancake in that area today is buckwheat spread with melted butter and shavings of maple sugar, then maple syrup poured over.

Utica became a laboratory in the 1840's when a blight hit the potato crop and the Reverend Chauncey Goodrich sent to South America for new stock. His experiments resulted in more than two hundred varieties of potatoes.

Some of the best Swedish food in America is found in Jamestown, population about 60 per cent Swedish extraction. There on Lenten Tuesdays is eaten a wonderful bun pudding called *fastlagsbuller,* stuffed with almond paste, topped with whipped cream and accompanied by cups of hot, almond-flavored milk.

The baker's dozen is said to have originated in Albany. Baker Bass, a frugal gentleman, was finishing his New Year's baking when a hideous old woman entered his shop and bought a dozen raisin-stuffed cookies. She paid, then asked for one more. Bass refused. All that year Bass's bakery had bad luck. Bread either rose to the ceiling or fell flat. Near bankruptcy by the next New Year's, Bass was again finishing his baking when he spotted the old woman down the street. He muttered "Holy St. Nicholas—what shall I do?" and with that the door opened and St. Nicholas walked in.

"Since you ask," he said, "my answer is—give her the thirteenth cookie."

Bass did, and ever since a baker's dozen has been thirteen—and lucky.

The year 1825 in New York was called "The Year of the Great Cheese," because the milk of one hundred and fifty cows was turned into curd and produced a 1,400-pound cheese which went by canal boat to New York and thence to Washington, where it was presented to President Andrew Jackson. He saved it for Washington's birthday and then invited the public to a party. Thousands came and the White House reeked of cheese for weeks afterward.

Germans settled the Mohawk River section as early as 1735. The first earth and log huts built by Palatinate Germans in the Schoharie Valley date back to 1713. The settlers liked a gooseberry tart made, according to a 1794 cookbook, by laying "clean berries and sifting over them sugar . . . till a deep dish be filled, intermingling a handful of raisins" and baking "somewhat more than other tarts."

A cook in one of the fabulous summer homes at Saratoga Springs in the 1800's overdid her French-fried potatoes one day, but decided to serve them anyhow. Overnight the crisp delicacies became popular as Saratoga chips, ancestor of our potato chips.

Everything about Saratoga was elegant in the gilded nineties, when everybody who was anybody showed up in August for the racing. A Saratoga shortcake was soon being copied in kitchens all over the country . . . a dessert of sponge cake, uncrushed strawberries between the layers and a rich egg custard on top.

In New York City you can of course eat in almost every language. In the city's grocery stores you can find rose-petal jam from Egypt; a flat bread twenty-four inches in diameter, from Syria; the stuffed vine leaves of Greece; the heavy coffee of Turkey; the tongue-nipping curries of India.

But the millions of Italians who swarmed over New York's East Side brought a cuisine which permanently affected the national diet. From the Empire State to California, people eat pizza, make oil and vinegar dressings for green salads in the classic Italian fashion—and almost every amateur cook has a pet recipe for spaghetti sauce. New York City alone eats more spaghetti than Rome!

One of my special friends, Gene Leone, and his wife, Mary, often entertain ten thousand diners in an evening at their restaurant, started with a few tables by Mother Leone many years ago to support herself and her sons. The boys, as they grew up, got jobs, but used to rush home at night to help mother. She'd be very proud of Gene now. He has been listed by *Fortune* magazine as one of the great American success stories, yet every night he's in the kitchen making soups and sauces for the evening. I've been with him on expeditions to buy the many pounds of beans, potatoes, onions and more exotic vegetables he feeds to his thousands daily. We shelled peas, munched raw string beans, and he even made me bite into an ear of corn to see that the kernels were tender and juicy.

For dinner that night I had Leone antipasto—melon prosciutto, which is thin slices of honeydew melon wrapped in Italian ham; lumps of crabmeat sautéed in butter and then cooked in a casserole in a sauce of cream and sherry with a dusting of Parmesan cheese; then Jump-In-Your-Mouth Veal—a filet of veal in casserole, a layer of Mozzarella cheese, freshly ground black pepper, a layer of shaved Italian white truffles, a layer of Italian ham with drawn butter rubbed over it. There was a field salad with Gene's special dressing and finally a Sicilian pastry—very short and light, filled with ricotta cheese seasoned with nutmeg and cinnamon.

I was initiated into the mysteries of Chinese cookery by George Lee, whose sons and daughter—Calvin Bow Tong, Bow Lum and Lai Lai—are my godchildren. When their father died, Calvin at seventeen took over the restaurant in Chinatown, studying law by day, running the restaurant at night.

The tiffin dishes they make have been handed down from Grandfather Kung Lee's secret Cantonese recipes. Special cooks, who start work at four in the morning, do nothing but prepare tiffin specialties—half-moon pastries filled with mince meat, fried turnip pancakes, shrimp dumplings, steamed sponge cake, meat patties.

The first course in a typical New Year's feast with the Lees is shark's fin soup, and there are several later soups to clear the palate between courses. Then come lobster claws with a sauce of pork, egg, water chestnuts, black beans and garlic. The special Pekin duck, ordered three days before, is roasted, then smothered in a deep frying pan. One steamed fish is done with brown beans, ginger and seasoning; another fish with vegetables, shredded bamboo shoots, red dates, peas in pods and pork. Chicken is served with water chestnuts, bamboo shoots and fried almonds; shrimp is in tomato sauce and there are boneless spareribs sweet and sour, with green peppers and pineapple. At the end, some almond gruel, traditional Chinese finale to such a feast—and I usually wish we'd followed another tradition—that of taking a walk in the garden between courses.

I think the dish we lived on in my early impecunious days in Greenwich Village is as international as you can get. We took a can of tamales, removed them from their husks, mashed them up with a can of corn, some sliced, canned pimiento, rings of green pepper, mixed the whole business in a casserole, topped it with strips of bacon, served it with chile sauce and fittingly christened it Chaos.

When we did have a few extra dollars, nothing was more fun than going to a kosher delicatessen. I suspect that the delicatessen was born on the Lower East Side, and I know that in no other city in the United States do you find it in such mouth-watering glory as in New York. An army of salamis behind gleaming glass, warm pink rolls of beef, tongue, pastrami and frankfurters tinged with garlic; fresh-roasted turkey, corned beef, potato salad, half a dozen kinds of pickles and slaws, knishes and fragrant rye breads!

I came too late for the really gaudy days of Manhattan eating, but I loved the stories about Diamond Jim Brady and his horrendous meals at Delmonico's, Rector's and Bustanoby's. Once Leonard Jerome, August Belmont and William R. Travers staged an eating contest at Delmonico's. Nobody won because everybody ate so prodigiously, but the menu began with a canvasback duck aspic, and ended with truffled ice cream!

My favorite, storied dessert was served by Henri Charpentier on a hot August night. When the main courses were finished, the famous restaurateur led his guests to the garden. There stood a table covered with frosty-white linen, and at each place was a cool combination of sherbet and fresh fruit. The centerpiece was a mirrored platter rimmed with flowers and candles. Henri blew out the candles and there on the table gleamed the reflection of the full moon . . . the first time anybody actually got the moon on a platter for dessert.

Massachusetts

THE SACRED COD AND SATURDAY BEAN

To a true New Englander, clam chowder means clams or quahaugs, so fresh that the salty tang of the sea is still with them, minced with crisp bits of bacon, potatoes, onions simmered to pale gold, milk and cream, butter and more butter. Any other kind of chowder is unthinkable.

The great clam chowder controversy has been going on for years, and probably will continue as long as New Englanders and New Yorkers have breath to argue. Manhattan clam chowder is a concoction of water, clams and vegetables, with tomatoes predominating, and so obnoxious to New Englanders that a congressman went so far as to propose a bill making it illegal to put tomatoes into clam chowder.

Massachusetts claims its hordes of summer visitors are just as interested in a fine chowder and seafood as in the elm-shaded streets, the white-spired meetinghouses and the stately colonial homes. Yet the Pilgrims who landed at Plymouth in 1620 paid little attention to seafood. In that first desperate year, Governor William Bradford reported that the colony looked often "into the grim and grizzled face of starvation." Eventually, hunger taught them better.

There was a rumor around Plymouth in the 1620's that Governor Bradford drank water . . . though nobody exactly believed it. When they got sick, the Pilgrims blamed it on the water, and with some reason since they did nothing to prevent contamination of streams and springs. It was a dark day when women and children disembarked from the ship *Anne* in 1622 to find their men waiting on shore with nothing to offer in welcome except "lobster and a piece of fish—no bread—and only a cupful each of faire spring water." After a while they had cider and beer, and the law limited a man's beer consumption to five quarts a day. In fact, life in the Plymouth colony, and in the Bay colony of the Puritans, was probably not as drab as it is pictured in most schoolbooks.

Real tea was so rare and expensive then that the colonists' teapots frequently steamed with peculiar brews made from goldenrod, sage or blackberry leaves, and the coffee might be of corn and barley, rye, chestnut and dandelion roots.

Gradually the first housewives of Massachusetts learned to make do with the foods they found there. English hasty pudding took a turn for the better when it was done with cornmeal. Still, there *can* be too much of a good thing, and one visitor to Plymouth in the 1640's wrote in alarm that unless a man was careful he'd find himself eating three hundred and sixty-five hasty puddings a year.

Knives and spoons were the main eating implements, and forks were freakish novelties. Indeed when the first fork was imported for Governor Winthrop in 1633, people thought it downright comical. They couldn't see any need for it, especially since most of their meats were cut up and served in ragouts and stews. Recipes of the time call for meat to be "y-mynced," hewed on a gobbet, hacked, diced and "skerned." A few recipes included perfume—a canny method of dealing with meat that was no longer strictly fresh.

In its first year Plymouth had a five-day week—and price controls. Thursday was known as Lecture Day, when most people closed up shop and went to the village green to hear "edifying talks." Women liked to cook ahead for Lecture Day, and their families often had suppers of boiled pigeon or venison patty, with gooseberry tart for dessert. Price controls were mostly on food, so that butchers and bakers couldn't stage a pressure-group campaign to keep wages low and prices high. There are records of a good many men haled into court and fined for overcharging.

On the Sabbath, ordinary work ceased. Some inspired Puritan woman dealt with this crisis by cooking up dried beans on Saturday and serving them for variety in various forms on the Sabbath —hot, warm and cold. Thus was born that mainstay of New England, the Boston Baked Bean. Every family has its own recipe, but nearly all agree that the beans must be done with tender salt pork and a touch of dry mustard, that they must be sweet with molasses and brown sugar, and that they must cook all day, preferably in a brick oven. Finally, when they turn up at the Sunday breakfast table, a plate of steamy hot Boston brown bread must be there, too. Many families trooped home at nooning—the recess between morning and afternoon church services—to eat salt fish and cold rye-'n'-injun, half rye flour, half cornmeal.

Within a few decades life in general, and food in particular, had improved enormously. Mutton was so plentiful that Bostonians ate their fill of roasts and stews and had enough left over to ship to Barbados and the Caribbean. A favorite brew was called Cherry Bounce, made from five gallons of the best new rum and five gallons of fresh cherries, sealed in a keg for a year. Hedge-Hog pudding had no hedgehog, but "raisins of the sun," sweet cream and nutmeg, the whole boiled in a cloth in beef broth and garnished with butter and almonds, and for a dramatic finale, sugar thrown upon the dish. Curious little cakes called Wigs, "in Bigness as you see fit," were crowned with ginger and caraway seeds, sprinkled with rosewater after the dough had been raised with ale-yeast, and baked "quick" in an iron pan. A Salem recipe for wedding cake calls for seven dozen eggs and nine pounds of almonds, not to mention a ten-pound cone of sugar.

Despite such indications of prosperity, it is said that a Rockport fisherman got so sick of the corn bread and molasses his wife Anna served him, that he seized the mixing bowl one day, tossed flour and yeast into the cornmeal and molasses and baked the mixture, growling over and over as he worked, "Anna dam 'er, Anna dam 'er." Whether the story is true or false, Anadama bread became a standby, and in recent years a commercial product.

The sea was part of life along the Massachusetts coast. The

grateful settlers carved enchanting designs of grapevines and breadfruit—fruits brought in by their ships—as symbols of hospitality, over their mantels.

Lucy Larcom, who grew up in Beverly in the 1800's, wrote touchingly about the way "the pathos of the sea" haunted her whole town. Little Lucy also watched the barrels full of coconuts rolled about the streets. In every kitchen cupboard tamarinds, ginger-root and preserved tropical fruits were as common as cranberries. Holidays were bright spots in Lucy's childhood, especially Old Election, which came at the end of May when lilacs were in bloom. Her mother baked 'Lection cake which Lucy says was nothing but a kind of sweetened bread with a shine of egg and molasses on top . . . "but delicious."

In the middle 1800's Ephraim Bull came to the town of Concord on an exploring trip "to see what I can find among our wildings." What he "found" was the Concord grape which launched commercial grape production in this country. A shoot from the original vine he developed still clambers over the gambrel-roofed Ephraim Bull cottage. He never tried to make money from his Concord grape, and on the tombstone in Sleepy Hollow Cemetery where he lies in the company of the Alcotts, Hawthorne, Emerson and Thoreau, is the inscription: HE SOWED . . . OTHERS REAPED

Apple Slump, the house in Concord where Louisa May Alcott began writing *Little Women,* was named for a favorite dessert— a steamed pudding made from the juicy tart apples the Alcotts grew in their orchard. Slumps were also made with blackberries or blueberries, and served hot with nutmeg sauce.

Massachusetts is the only state I know which officially acknowledges its debt to food. On March 17, 1784, a painted wooden codfish, four feet eleven inches long, was hung in the old Boston State House "as a memorial to the importance of the codfishery to the welfare of this Commonwealth." The Sacred Cod has hung there ever since. Cape Cod children used to love to chew a Portuguese oddity known as Skully-Jo, which was a codfish cured in the sun "until it's hard enough to bend a lead pipe around."

Cape Cod guards the crops of its sandy soil jealously. In fact the town of Nawsett in 1667 ruled that no bachelor might marry until he had slain one dozen marauding blackbirds or three crows.

Cape Cod claims the cranberry and says that cranberry culture began at North Dennis in 1816, when natives noticed that a light sand blown over the bushes increased their growth. From the earliest days the "rules" and "receipts" collected by housewives included many cranberry dishes. But poor Joseph Lincoln, the writer, searched in vain for the kind of cranberry pie his grandmother used to make, a deep-dish pie "fat, puffy and inviting," sweetened with brown sugar, and spurting juice when cut.

Herbs grew in the colonial gardens of Massachusetts, and in addition to adding aroma to stews and puddings, several went along to church to keep worshipers awake during long prayers and sermons. Fennel, dill, caraway, coriander, cinnamon and lovage root were all used for meeting munching.

Corn and beans were put to an odd use on Martha's Vineyard. In an Edgartown election of 1671, freemen were instructed to use corn and beans for votes—"the corn to manifest election, the beanes contrary." A century later Vineyard Haven pioneered in eating frozen fish. A blizzard of 1778 coincided with a Tory raid which left the townspeople with virtually no food. The blizzard obligingly blew in a school of delectable sea bass, which froze in Lagoon Pond and were chopped out as needed. Baked sea bass is a Vineyard Haven delicacy to this day. Scootin-Long-The-Shore is a food name that has mystified visitors to the Vineyard. It is, however, only a boiled dinner, made with salt pork, potatoes and onions. Fishermen invented it and cooked it on the beach while they were scooting up and down tending their lines.

Out of sight below the horizon floats the faraway island of Nantucket, whose native families still refer to the rest of the United States as "the continent." Nantucket doughnuts and gingerbread were brought to perfection in the pitching galleys of whaling ships by intrepid wives of whaling captains, on epic voyages from Pitcairn Island to the Antarctic that sometimes lasted three years. Nantucket gingerbread was a traditional welcome-home for the whaling men, too. When the first ship was sighted, mixing bowls were whisked from cupboards, fires stirred up, and by the time the men landed, women and children were lined up on shore with plates of hot gingerbread.

In the village of Siasconset, where a sign pointing out to sea says *3,000 miles to Spain,* summer people have now settled in the little rose-covered cottages built by fishermen, and learned to cook up batches of beach-plum jelly in the miniature kitchens which the fishermen added as afterthoughts and always referred to as "warts." The visitors took to the Nantucket sword and blue fish and to the quahaug which they like to roast over hot coals on the miles of surf-swept beach. According to instructions left by old Peleg Folger, you take a few roasted quahaugs on a platter, add fresh butter, pepper and salt. You need nothing more except a pot of coffee, boiled on your driftwood fire, a soft sea wind and a friend or two with proper reverence for such fare.

George Washington's name gets into the food lore of New England by way of the first cattle show in America. Washington had studied cattle breeding and believed this country's food economy might well depend upon our beef and dairy cattle. So he encouraged his friend Elkanan Watson to put on a cattle show on the village green of Pittsfield in 1810.

Boston's famous Parker House is full of food legends, including a controversial one about the cook who lost his temper and tossed fistfuls of dough into the oven, thus creating the first batch of Parker House rolls. The same eating place claims the original Boston Cream pie, which isn't a pie at all but a cake with rich cream custard between layers and an icing on top.

Massachusetts cooks were always trying to outdo each other, and eaters profited. Edward Everett Hale, remembering a pie which was as permanent a fixture at Thanksgiving as the turkey, described it as "a sort of lemon pie—but each good housekeeper thinks her grandmother left a better receipt for Marlborough pie than anyone else did."

Pennsylvania

EATING IS SERIOUS BUSINESS

History claims that the pretzel was first made in ancient Rome. But try telling that to any Pennsylvania Dutchman. He knows that the pretzel, in all its crisp and salty wonder, is Pennsylvania born and bred. A pretzel hand-twisted and baked in Reading or Lititz is fat and gleams with big, authoritative crystals of salt. Pretzel dough must set overnight, and after it is twisted it must go on a wooden board to set some more. The Pennsylvanian likes it equally well with a heaping dish of homemade vanilla ice cream, a mug of birch beer tapped icy cold from the keg, or a stein of lager.

Pennsylvania Dutch cooking at its best is found in the ample farmhouses of Lancaster County, heart of the Pennsylvania Dutch district. Some also can be bought in the markets which twice weekly become treasure stores of everything the nearby farmers produce. Even in this day of the mix and the quick-freeze, people in the city of Lancaster still get up at six in the morning and tote old-fashioned market baskets down to the square, and around the handsome old colonial city hall, in the shadow of which stands the turreted market house. The farmers, in town before dawn, include Plain People from the Amish and Mennonite districts, who believe it is frivolous to be late. That is why so many clocks in Pennsylvania Dutch farmhouses are kept half an hour fast.

Eating is serious business to people in this part of the country. A successful banker or business executive will apply all his talents on market morning to choosing a shoofly pie of gingerbread spiciness, yet pie consistency—a requirement to be understood only when you bite into the almost-black, molasses-rich interior of this crumb pie so aptly named, because its sticky sweetness does compel the cook to keep shooing off flies.

Your knowing marketer, same big basket in hand that his grandfather carried, will head unerringly for the stand of a farmer whose butchering he respects and whose sausage and bologna lore he reveres. There he will choose links of a peculiar smoked sausage, mahogany in color, a bit too pungent for many palates. This smoked sausage is browned slowly in an iron skillet and put on the table with potatoes fried in fat slices so that they are crisp outside, mealy within. At the same stand he will have the farmer slice up a stack of Lebanon bologna, made with a secret blend of herbs and seasoning. He will add a pan of scrapple, made from scraps saved from butchering, plus cornmeal. This comes to the breakfast table on a frost-nipped morning, hot and crisp, ready to be doused with maple syrup or eaten just so.

The marketer knows which stall has his favorite dried corn, to be soaked to tenderness, cooked, drained and served with nothing but salt, butter, and freshly ground black pepper. He seeks out the hand-cheese made exactly as it was in Germany three hundred years ago, and the ball cheese, another colonial descendant, made from thick sour milk.

Next he heads for the horseradish man, who grinds it in eye-watering strength right there at the market stand. He alternates between two stalls, one presided over by an entire Amish family, the women and girls in their old-world bonnets and aprons, the men and boys in hook-and-eye suits; and nearby the stall of a small Mennonite lady in sprightly white net cap. Both offer bread loaded straight from the oven into the buggy that morning.

Of course, Pennsylvania "Dutch" are really Germans. They correctly described themselves as "Deutsch" which was quickly corrupted in this country to Dutch. No other group has clung more closely to its folkways than the Old Order or House Amish. These people do not believe in churches and they follow a way of life almost unchanged since the sixteenth century. The Amish live literally by the Bible, hard praying, hard working, devoted to their fertile fields and farmlands.

A Lancaster friend of mine once attended an Amish wedding, which began at dawn and lasted until after midnight, with a noon wedding feast which included forty chickens, five geese, forty loaves of homemade bread, two bushels of potato chips, not to mention seventy-five pies and twenty frosted layer cakes. The bride's table had a special roast turkey and a bowl of hearts of celery.

An old Pennsylvania cookbook lists a Barn Raising menu which began with four hundred "fat cakes" or doughnuts, and went on through a hundred lemon pies, gallons of applesauce, cornstarch puddings, stewed raisins—a favorite of the region—chicken, ham, bread, potatoes and two hundred light rolls.

New Order, or Church Amish, have accepted such twentieth-century conveniences as the automobile and the tractor. They hold meetings in simple frame meetinghouses, but the Sunday sessions are still long enough to warrant tucking a "preaching pie" in one's pocket. These are dried apple pies made in half-moon shapes, small enough and not juicy, so they may safely be toted to church.

Pennsylvania was a green and fertile asylum for the German sects—Amish, Dunkards, Mennonites, Schwenkfelders and half a dozen others—just as it was in earlier years for the Quakers. But a Swedish missionary first set the tone for tolerance and understanding in 1643 when he translated the Lutheran catechism into the

Lenni-Lenape Indian dialect, and changed the Lord's prayer to read: "And give us this day a plentiful supply of venison and corn."

The first Quaker housewives of Philadelphia were making tarts and pies of pink-gold peaches almost as soon as their kitchens were built. Peach trees left by the Spanish in Florida in the 1500's had spread north and the Indians were tending them in primitive orchards when the white men arrived. Philadelphia had the first botanical garden, and Philadelphians were eating with forks when the rest of colonial America was still impaling its meat on knife blades.

Fish House Punch has become world famous, but its home is the Fishing Company of the State in Schuylkill, founded in 1732 and claiming to be the oldest club in the country. Its membership, still limited to thirty, meets every two weeks and serves the renowned punch, major ingredient of which is peach brandy. Fish House clubmen also insist that they invented planked shad—or at least their special gourmet version of this dish.

I visited one home in Germantown, drowned in ivy and wistaria, which has been lived in by nine generations since 1690. Guests there through the years were served terrapin stew done in cream, and often the soup made famous in the City of Brotherly Love—Philadelphia pepperpot. A favorite Quaker way with chicken was to toss a tender young fryer into a skillet with minced green pepper and bread crumbs. Tiny reed birds, described as "lumps of sweetness," were often baked with oysters. There were clams and shad aplenty and the wild turkey came in great flights up the river.

Strath Haven Inn, where I have lingered overnight, is on land that was a Quaker farm, so wisely planted and cared for that the 150-year-old crabapple trees are still blossoming and bearing fruit. The little red crabapples in green leaves look like clumps of holly berries from a distance. Glazed, they are good with roast goose, and from them is made a rosy sauce, pies and tarts.

William Penn had an estate of three hundred acres at Pennsbury, where he set out orchards, vegetable and herb gardens, a greenhouse, vineyard and brewery. His cook made an omelet which has come down in history as the William Penn omelet, the only food on record which bears the Penn name.

Philadelphia likes to think of itself as the cradle of the ice cream industry, though of course, Alexander the Great was eating a version of it when he served fruit juice with sweetened milk, stirred in bowls surrounded by snow. Moreover, Nero imported snow and flavored it with fruit and honey. However, in 1851, one Pennsylvanian, Jacob Fussell, did become the first wholesale manufacturer of ice cream, and another, Robert N. Green, is credited with originating the ice cream soda. Mr. Green came to the Franklin Institute Exposition in Philadelphia in 1874 to demonstrate soda fountains. He served a popular concoction of sweet cream, syrup and carbonated water. One day he ran out of cream, hurriedly bought some vanilla ice cream, ladled a portion into a glass with syrup and soda—and there it was, the world's first ice cream soda.

An editor friend, a great food appreciator and a fine cook, guided me to a hotel in Pennsylvania Dutch country where the table was laid with the traditional seven sweets and seven sours. Seven is said to have a mystical significance lost in antiquity, but the only mystery for a visitor is how to sample all fourteen and still have room for the rest of the meal.

The sweets and sours sit in the center of the table in old-fashioned cut-glass bowls. They include: a corn salad that has the zing of dry mustard, vinegar and celery seed; beets spiced with ginger; watermelon pickles; artichokes with clove and mace; hard-boiled eggs turned scarlet with beet juice; green chow-chow with turmeric adding a subtle charm; piccalilli and homemade ketchup, pickled peaches, yellow tomato preserves, spiced crab-apples, the most delicate of red raspberry jam, pickled mushrooms and a smooth, rich tomato butter. So it takes restraint if justice is to be done to the ensuing tureens of golden chicken-corn soup, the roast chicken bursting with sage and bread-crumb stuffing, the fried country ham, the assortment of pies and cakes, and when the table has finally been cleared, the incredible finale of rich homemade ice cream flecked with vanilla bean.

Pennsylvania has many foods for special occasions. *Fastnachts*, for instance, are light, yeast-raised cakes cut in triangles, popped into deep fat to puff to final brown-gold perfection, dusted with powdered sugar . . . and served just once a year on Shrove Tuesday. It is said that a cook somewhere in Germany, centuries ago, wanted to use up the foods she wouldn't be permitted to serve during fast days. She put all the fat in a kettle, stirred up milk, flour, yeast, eggs, sugar, and just before midnight on Shrove Tuesday: behold the first Fastnacht!

Another authentic Pennsylvania Dutch delicacy is the *belsnickel* cookie, made to hand out to children who go from door to door before Christmas. Belsnickel originally meant "St. Nicholas in furs," but through the years he became a jolly character instead of a fellow who left bundles of switches for naughty children. The cookies are usually plain sand-tarts, but they may be gingersnaps or almost any other holiday cookie set aside for "belsnickeling" children.

In Bethlehem many of the old Moravian buildings still stand, just as do many of the time-honored customs. Moravian mints are part of Christmas here, and the secret of these cool-to-the-tongue candies is owned by a family that runs one of America's oldest drugstores, The Apothecary.

Schnitz House, with its green shutters and stucco mellowing over the log walls, looks much the same as it did in the 1700's when the sisters and brethren were allowed to mingle for one day in October to prepare *schnitz* . . . the name still used around there for dried apples. *Schnitz un Knepp* is an improbable-sounding but delicious combination of meat, dried apples and boiled dumplings.

Then there is the marvelous concoction with the doleful name of Funeral pie, so called because it is an invariable part of the big meal after a burying. Under its flaky crust are fat raisins with a sweet and winy sauce to swim in.

The women of Phoenixville in Chester County set out recently to prove that their town is as typical a melting pot as any place in the United States. For the benefit of their hospital they got up a food bazaar and included all the racial elements in their community. It was an interesting and flavorful affair, with Polish Czarina—a duck soup rich with dumplings; a Latvian salad of meat, eggs and sour pickles; English scones; Irish corned beef and cabbage; a Scandinavian smörgasbord; German strudel; French pastry; hot dogs and baked beans labeled US; Hungarian chicken paprika; Jewish lox and bagels; and Chinese lichee nuts.

Mary Kizis told me how one of her great-uncles came to this country and founded a little town in Pennsylvania to which many other Lithuanians came, and where they preserved all their national customs, festivals and food. Their Christmas starts with supper, begun as the first star of Christmas appears in the sky, and going on until the dawn of Christmas morning. The Christmas holidays—all feasting and visiting—last until January 13th.

the day of the arrival of the Three Wise Men. They usually
slaughter a pig just before Christmas and make all sorts of blood
puddings, sausages and headcheese. They fast forty days before
Christmas—one of their two such fasts per year. Mary remembered
one thirteen-course Christmas Eve supper and said that there is
always a suckling pig on Christmas Day, a custom dating back
to an ancient Norse period when the pig was considered the most
suitable sacrifice to the sun god.

The Alleghany Mountain country, where many Scotch-Irish
settled in the late 1700's, is proud of its wild life, and a good cook
up there has to know how to season a bear stew, and how to
braise a fresh deer liver in a broiling hot frying pan with a bit of
butter.

Down near Longwood and Westchester, mushroom nurseries
began a half century ago, and that section now grows more than
70 per cent of America's "snow apples," as the mushroom farmers
call their crop. Harvesters wear special headlamps as they work
in the moist, shadowy buildings.

Not many miles away is a town that smells like a candy bar and
is privately owned—Hershey, where the people pay no local taxes,
where Presidents come to play golf and eat at the sprawling
luxury-hotel. Milton Hershey was a young man who began by
cooking caramels and selling them on the streets of Lancaster. He
ended as a multimillionaire because of his chocolate.

There is even a farm in Pennsylvania that grows food for mice.
It is called, properly, the Mousery. Interestingly enough, foods for
a mouse include corn, oats, buckwheat, sunflower seeds, celery,
milk, bread—but no cheese!

Years ago in the town of McClure, some Civil War veterans
decided to have a reunion picnic, and to cook up a kettle of the
bean soup they'd eaten during their army service. Today that
small picnic has stretched into a two-day gathering the third Friday and Saturday in November, when more than 1,500 pounds
of beans and 1,600 pounds of beef furnish soup for twenty-five
thousand guests.

A fried chicken dinner at one of the country inns around Lititz
and Manheim is a favorite way to top off one of the state's loveliest
ceremonies—the paying of one red rose to a descendant of Baron
Stiegel, who gave the church a plot of ground in the 1770's,
stipulating the rose payment. On the second Sunday of June,
when the rent is paid, visitors crowd in and around the church to

watch the festivities. Part of the celebration is a big Sunday dinner, and the traditional dessert is a shortcake made of biscuit dough, split and buttered hot and heaped with sun-sweet June strawberries. Man-sized pitchers of cream come to the table along with a big soup plate for each serving of shortcake.

Another Pennsylvanian created quite a different sort of culinary tradition through material which at the time, 1888, was staggeringly expensive. The man, Charles Hall, talked to Pittsburgh capitalists about his ideas early in the twentieth century, and soon on the fringes of the town of New Kensington a factory appeared. Even Hall didn't dream that his first small aluminum plant would affect the cooking and eating habits of the world . . . in pots, pans, kitchen utensils, in wrappers for foods, in myriad products to ease and quicken housework.

In general, the Keystone State more than fulfilled the promise glimpsed by Peter Fithian, as he traveled the fair Juniata Valley in 1775 and noted wistfully: "Wilt not this, in some future time, be a vast, pleasant and very populous country? . . . I seem to wish to be transferred forward only one century. Great God! America will surprise the world!"

New Hampshire

MOLASSES AND INDEPENDENCE

Perhaps one of the last places you'd expect to be served Albanian bread is in New Hampshire. Yet Concord and Manchester have two of the oldest Albanian settlements in the United States, and observing the Law of Lek, which compels hospitality even to an enemy, you will be served something to eat when you enter an Albanian home.

Contrary to the melting-pot pattern, Albanians became proudly nationalistic after their arrival here. They preserve the customs and food of "The Land of the Eagle" and in their houses you often find bright, hand-woven rugs and gay wool blankets from the Old Country. They drink Albanian coffee, much like the Turkish, concocted of powdered coffee and sugar boiled to a froth three times and touched with rosewater. Their bread is made of whole wheat and potatoes, and their meat balls are flavored with mint. A sweet, rather sticky Turkish paste accompanies afternoon coffee, vegetables are cooked in oil, Greek style, lamb stew is flavored with okra, and rice mixed with raisins is served as a vegetable.

New Hampshire, almost entirely English and Scotch-Irish until a century ago, has lately been called the merriest of the Puritans, probably because now so many and such varied groups have settled within its rugged border.

French-Canadians teach their own language in parochial schools, and celebrate their feast-days. Processions march through the streets of Berlin to honor St. John the Baptist, and special dishes named for the saint include a creamy fish soup with dumplings and potatoes, and poached eggs with sauce Bernaise. Recipes for cream of pea soup are handed down from generation to generation, and so is the secret of a memorable little chestnut tart served with whipped cream.

Some Welsh families still make a pot of leek soup to honor St. David's Day, and on the Monday before Lent, collops (small pieces of bacon or other meat) and eggs are the traditional fare.

New Hampshire was rough country for pioneering. As a New Hampshire senator once said when taunted about the size of his state, "If you could iron it out, it would be bigger than Texas."

In one of the very un-ironed spots, high above Franconia Notch, is the state's own Plymouth Rock with the date 1652 on it, marking Governor Winthrop's claim that this land belonged to Massachusetts. Actually, New Hampshire was settled soon after the *Mayflower* landed, in the year 1623. It took courage to break trails through the White Mountains and plant the first patches of potatoes and winter squash. When a man left home he carried his own provisions with him, in the shape of bean porridge frozen into large cakes, fried pies, doughnuts, cheese and sausage.

On a chill Thanksgiving in the seventeenth century at Newport, New Hampshire, one family sat by the glow of firelight and bayberry candles, to eat a pie made of bear meat and dried pumpkin, seasoned with maple syrup and baked in a crust of cornmeal. As late as the 1870's and 90's some newcomers subsisted on baked acorns and considered beaver tails a luxury.

Hulled corn is still a New Hampshire favorite. It is corn boiled in lye, washed thoroughly when the shells have come off and re-boiled until it is "soft and good to eat." Mixed with maple sugar it was a dessert, fried in butter it was a breakfast dish, and served with milk it could be the main course for supper.

Blueberries hide deep in New Hampshire hills and for centuries they have been popped into everything from little hot biscuits to crusty deep-dish pies and blueberry slumps made with bits of airy dumplings. Shrewsbury cake had to be whisked to lightness "with your hand." Early recipes were often called Rules and carried such eloquent instruction as "beat like thunder" and "whip to a raging foam."

Molasses, which John Adams said was "an essential ingredient in American independence," went into the crispest of cookies, spiced with ginger and cinnamon, and into tender gingerbread— as well as into stout New England rum.

Up there, when they talk about a fresh cook, they mean one who goes light on salt, and when they say milk is "caught" they mean it's scorched. A woman who starts her dinner preparations later than she should is said to be "rubbing the time too close."

Pumpkin sauce predates the famed New England pumpkin pies, and John Jocelyn in his *New England Rarities Discovered* (1671) said "the housewife's manner is to slice them when ripe and cut them into dice and so fill a pot with them of two or three gallons and stew them upon a gentle fire for a whole day."

One recipe sent me by Helen McLaughlin, former home economics head at the state university, tells how they made pound cake in colonial times:

Take a pound of butter, beat it in an earthen pan with your own hand, till it is like a fine thick cream; then have ready twelve eggs, but half the whites; beat them well and beat them up with the butter, a pound of flour beat in it, a pound of sugar, and a few caraways. Beat it all well together for an hour with your hand, or a great wooden spoon, butter a pan and put it in, and then bake it an hour in a quick oven.

A hundred-year-old gingerbread recipe, modernized a bit, is still baked on Town Meeting Day when elders leave the meeting with a piece or two of the cake to take home to the children. On Election Day, New Hampshire women put out a version of Hartford Election Cake, yeast-raised and stuffed with raisins.

Samp, although still eaten today, isn't as socially important as it was to two lonely pioneer women whose husbands cleared land and built cabins separated by a gully and impassable woods. These women, pounding their samp in wooden mortars, worked out a sort of Morse code to talk to each other. When one was about to have a baby, she pounded out an SOS on her mortar, whereupon her friend set off on the long, roundabout trail and arrived in time to assist with the birth.

New Hampshire is probably the only place in the country where Guy Fawkes Night is celebrated. In Portsmouth it's called Pope's Night and in Newcastle it is Pork Night. Dr. B. A. Botkin, folklore specialist, says the significance of the day has been forgotten, but bonfires are still lighted amid blowing of horns and the carrying about of lighted pumpkin faces. Another unique holiday is the statewide observance of Fast Day, the last Thursday in April, when everybody takes down storm windows and serves for breakfast raised buckwheat cakes with maple syrup, bread dipped in maple syrup, cinnamon and egg and then fried to golden brown.

Dartmouth college, New Hampshire's pride, eats in civilized and vitamin-conscious style now, but in the late 1700's, reluctant students rejected "with an outcry" such dishes as peas and pork and "raised a hideous clamor when the pudding was not well salted."

First to see a future in the state's deep winter snowfalls were Norwegian settlers, who skied down the slopes of the White Mountains long before the average American knew what a slalom meant. Now the winter vacation business rivals the summer, and snow picnics have their own techniques, such as how to build a good fire on a frozen mountainside.

Many abandoned farms have been bought by city-weary writers, artists and businessmen, but the working farms still require a woman of stern mettle, just as they did when Sir John Crèvecoeur visited colonial America and noted: "What a useful requisition a good wife is to an American farmer. How small his chances of prosperity if he draws a blank in that lottery."

Maine

The strawberries you must pick wild from the semi-salt grassland of Casco Bay in Maine. The cream you must skim from milk given by island cows. The berries are crushed with a pine pestle, the cream laid on in thick yellow petals, and the concoction is put in a cool corner of the cellar to age for two days. Finally it is served with a stack of hot cream-of-tartar biscuits.

"That dish," said Robert P. Tristram Coffin, "did more to make a poet of me than any other one thing I can think of." Maybe having a mother able to "time a cake by the sunbeam creeping over the floorboards," as Poet Coffin says his mother did, also helped.

State of Maine food, while simple, seems to inspire writers to nostalgic prose as well as poetry. Sitting on a golden hillside in Italy, Writer Kenneth Roberts found himself almost insupportably homesick for Maine scenes and scents . . . his grandmother's lamplit kitchen, the meaty, fruity, steamy odors of the baked beans, served with her homemade, unsweetened ketchup, and a stack of rich, moist brown bread. Lemon pie topped with meringue was "as soothing to the palate as though scooped from a creamy white thundercloud hovering on the verge of sweet solidity."

The delight of hearing her mother singing hymns as she cooked in the sunny kitchen, its windows full of red geraniums, was part of Mary Ellen Chase's Maine childhood, and in her autobiography she harked back wistfully to "the warm, spicy smells of gingersnaps baking in the oven, of apple pies rich with cinnamon, and of countless doughnuts bobbing about on the surface of boiling lard."

A two-masted schooner came to Blue Hill when Mary Ellen was

small, bringing pilot bread, molasses, vinegar and oatmeal, and
best of all, white grapes in sawdust, oranges and bananas to hang
down cellar to ripen. High tides in April and May brought the
smelt runs, and men, women and children rushed out at three
in the morning to gather in the silvery little fish. Succulent clams
in that far-off day could be bought for ten cents a quart, and a
husky five-pound haddock for fifteen cents.

Beans in the home of Writer John Gould were hand-threshed
on Friday night, and the pot they were baked in was old enough
for its pores to be mellow. Jacob's cattle beans, speckled and
spotted, were best, but yellow-eyes and kidney beans would do,
just so the oven was heated by a hardwood fire. It helped, too,
John Gould believes, to tuck in a few other things to bake . . .
sheets of caraway cookies, say, and a loaf or two of potato yeast
bread.

The stewed chicken the Goulds had for Sunday dinner sounds
delicious, but not quite as alluring as Robert Coffin's description of his father's chicken and dumplings . . . "part flour, part
poetry" . . . the dumplings rolled with an empty bottle until
they were "as thin as the petals of wild roses and as shrinkingly
shy and alive to the touch."

Authors have been rhapsodizing about Maine for years—Long-
fellow, Whittier, Edna St. Vincent Millay, Gladys Hasty Carroll,
Edwin Arlington Robinson. As long ago as 1630, one reported
that Maine had "the smell of a garden." He was sailing past Mount
Desert Island on his way to Massachusetts Bay. It was June and
I know that heady summer fragrance, for I spent a holiday in a
borrowed house on that very island. It didn't make a poet of me,
but I have never been able to talk or write without excitement
about Maine.

Even Harriet Beecher Stowe succumbed to Maine magic. In
spite of a stove which "warms all but the floor, heats your head
and keeps your feet freezing," she managed to write much of
Uncle Tom's Cabin under the high-pitched roof of her Brunswick
house.

I remember Mama in Maine with extra nostalgia, and the
kitchen with a shiny black iron coal stove and rocking chair where
she used to sit, laughing at the sight of the stove and me squared
off for battle. She always came to my rescue, though, when the
stove blew hot and cold, threatening the ruin of an apple pie I'd
spent the whole morning putting together.

Mama arrived from early summer in Florida to find spring in bloom, an enchantment you can never forget once you have followed spring up the coast to its final flowery outpost in northern Maine. She took to the food—the earthy Aroostook potatoes, which baked superbly and did equally well in Mama's potato soup, a slow-simmered combination of potatoes and onions, innocent of flour, the hot milk, butter and seasonings stirred in at the last minute.

I was doing a reporting job for the State of Maine that summer, and Mama was as interested as I in the vast potato empire to the north. Aroostook County, bigger than all Connecticut, was growing potatoes long before Maine became a state in 1820, for Acadian refugees from the Evangeline country in Canada had found that the sun and soil were ideal. The railroad coming to Aroostook County in the 1890's made potatoes big business, and now at least thirty-eight states and a number of foreign countries use certified Maine potato seed.

A babble of provincial French enlivens towns like Fort Kent and Frenchville at harvest time, when the warehouses overflow and the talk, in whatever language, is about the prices this year's crop will bring. Descendants of Acadian refugees still relish their pea soup made habitant, or peasant, style, with mealy, yellow peas; their special onion soup with big rings sautéed pale gold in butter; their mysterious ragouts involving pigs' feet and innumerable herbs.

Mama was interested in the idea of cooking Maine lobster in seaweed, although she decided with her intuitive rightness where food was concerned that lobster is at its delicate best when broiled and served with drawn butter. She wanted to go along when I turned up in sou'wester, oilskins and hipboots, for an early start to the lobster traps located a few miles off our island.

My guides, veteran lobstermen, studied sky and water with weather-wise eyes. One whacking storm could wreck a trap that had set a man back three or four thousand dollars. Lobsters are no longer the free and easy catch they were in the early 1600's when fishermen from all over the world cruised along the Maine coast and feasted on crustaceans weighing up to fifteen and twenty pounds. It was not unusual then for the crew of one fishing boat to get fifty lobsters in a few hours, live-broiling them on a beach fire.

Many historians believe the Norsemen in their fast dragon

boats, almost a thousand years ago, were the first white men to fish off the Maine coast. By the year 1622, Governor Winslow reported thirty ships of different nationalities. Cod was the major catch and it went to all parts of Europe and the West Indies.

By the time I got round to pulling my own first lobster aboard, the State of Maine had laws governing every day of the creature's life, from the moment it emerges from a scientific lobster nursery until it descends into a caldron of boiling water or a sizzling broiler. The lobstermen who took me out could measure the shells by eye, gauging whether or not it was of legal size. Lobsters with V's stamped on their tails are females bearing eggs, and state officials may capture them for breeding. High-speed refrigerated carriers take millions of dollars' worth of lobsters out of Maine each season—a food business second only to potatoes.

When I came back from lobster fishing, drenched with sea spray and smelling of fish, Mama had worked her way through half a dozen New England cookbooks and was ready to tell me exactly how two or three of our larger lobsters should be diced, sautéed in butter and simmered in cream for a memorable stew. She was amused by old recipes calling for a dime's worth of salt—not meaning the amount you could buy, but the amount you could put on a dime!

She loved the doughnut recipe directing the cook to finish the batter by taking a big spoon and "giving her Hail Columbia for twenty seconds." Doughnuts got me into a lot of trouble that summer because I told on the air about an ingenious boy, Hanson Gregory, of Camden, Maine, who is said to have invented the doughnut in 1847. He was unhappy because his mother's fried cakes never got done in the center, so he poked his finger through one. That story caused a chorus of protest. My correspondents credited the doughnut to practically everybody, even the ancient Egyptians, and to almost every region on earth. Midway in this controversy they began to argue about when a doughnut ceases to be a doughnut and becomes a cruller, and whether a real doughnut is made of raised dough or sweet batter. The ultimate was a yarn from the Coffin family, which claimed a doughnut that could turn itself and jump out when done.

It was wonderful fun those days we spent on Goose Cove—"So different from Missouri," sighed Mama contentedly of our Maine summer.

New Jersey

THE GARDEN STATE

New Jersey's eight-lane turnpike spins airily above one of the most concentrated industrial areas on earth, and its Garden State Parkway swoops down the state to Atlantic City with its gargantuan shore dinners and tons of salt water taffy. The sightseer may drive the length of the state and see only the landscaped beauty of parkways. Or he may amble off on enchanting byways where, in summer and fall, fruit and vegetable stands offer sun-ripe tomatoes heaped in bushel baskets, winter apples, strings of red and green peppers, glasses of jewel-clear jelly, big orange pumpkins.

Towns called Double Trouble and Misery doze forgotten in the pine country, not drastically different from colonial times, when Jersey brides had the "free and unmolested right to do the white-washing" guaranteed them in the marriage contract. The sandy region now produces lush blueberries to enrich muffins, tarts, steamed puddings and butter cupcakes.

Corn grows well in New Jersey, and in the rich lands around Marksboro two yellow ears hung by the farmhouse door indicate that there has been an especially good crop. In the high valleys, onions, celery and lettuce thrive in the black-velvet soil. At famed Walker-Gordon farm, near Princeton, where I've often watched the cows being milked by Roto-Lactor, the first quart of certified milk in the country was produced in 1904.

Starting with Charles Newbold's invention of a cast-iron plow, New Jersey has, down the years, kept up with the latest methods in agriculture. At one experiment station, thirty thousand peach blossoms were pollinated by hand in an effort to find new and better types of fruit. Sure enough, among the magnificent peaches developed were the Golden Jubilee and the Cumberland. Experiments also produced strawberries so big that fifteen make a pound.

People all over the country have more chicken to eat, and more eggs, because of the research at Rutgers University Agriculture Experiment Station. The vaccine for destructive Newcastle disease, which once nearly wiped out the poultry business in New Jersey, now saves the chicken farmers of the nation more than $150,000,000 a year.

That's typical of the way Rutgers farmer-scientists work to improve our eating as well as to increase Jersey's fame as the Garden State. They developed the marvelous Rutgers tomato, perfected a compound which is giving us juicier, shinier, better-flavored apples, and introduced a brand-new sweet potato, the Jersey Orange.

Research to improve our food supply sometimes leads to unexpected laboratory miracles. Thus, in 1915, Selman Waksman, a Russian-born senior at Rutgers, started work on soil research. Proving what he himself described as "the infinitely great power of the infinitely small," Dr. Waksman's absorption with soil resulted in his discovery of the new wonder drug, streptomycin, for which he won the Nobel Prize.

I've gone story-hunting in most parts of New Jersey, tracking down old inns and houses where Washington is alleged to have slept, listening to tales about heroic housewives who fed our raggle-taggle Revolutionary troops. I remember one time when a group of women honored Molly Pitcher by serving a typical New Jersey meal on the 175th anniversary of the hot June day when Molly carried water to the wounded during the Battle of Monmouth. The menu included old-fashioned cream of potato soup with plenty of onions, turkey with corn-bread stuffing, mashed potatoes, peas, and for dessert a creamy rice pudding spread with currant jelly.

Most exciting of my New Jersey trips was to Seabrook Farms, which stretches over 90,000 acres in the southern part of the state and in two adjoining states. This is the world's largest vegetable factory. Farming as I knew it in Missouri was never like this: radio-equipped trucks moving into the fields so that less than an hour elapses between the moment a lima bean is picked until it's quick-frozen and packaged; a split-second schedule based on growth-units, so that fruits and vegetables will ripen on the exact day, even the exact hour, when the processing plant is ready to handle them. An overhead irrigation permits peas to be planted only seven inches apart. A special bureau experiments with rain-making and studies the inter-relationship of weather, soil and crops.

New Jersey is full of food "success stories," some sounding as fantastic as the saga of Stretch Garrison who in the 1880's is said to have trained two cows to plow, milked them into a churn at evening, then hung alfalfa hay just beyond their reach on a tread-mill so that by next morning they'd churned the butter.

A food experiment that affected the eating habits of millions was that of John T. Dorrance, a chemist who in 1897 went to work in the small Camden factory of Joseph Campbell and Abraham Anderson, at $7.50 a week. Dorrance had an idea for condensing soup. When he died, he was worth $117,000,000, and Campbell's had become a household word.

Pink lemonade originated in New Jersey, too, according to one Billie Griffiths, of Three Bridges, who was working for the circus when (he says) the lady acrobat's pink tights blew from the clothesline into his tub of lemonade—and changed the color.

Gloucester is famous for suppers featuring deep-dish oyster pie, and one restaurant there still knows the seventeenth-century technique of planking shad by tacking the fish on a piece of wood and baking it in front of an open fire. Other New Jersey regional dishes are Fort Morris' turtle soup, made of the rich red meat of the snapper; muskrat pot pie; and in spring, delicate roe of weakfish broiled with lemon, herbs and butter.

Straight back to Indian days goes the Salt Water Day celebration at Keyport on the second Saturday in August, when clambakes are held on the very beaches whereon Indians first taught the whites clambake technique.

In Middletown and Shrewsbury, drowsy villages with colonial houses surrounded by boxwood gardens and shaded by old elm trees, two churches are supported by pirate gold—conscience money left by a reformed privateer. The fund is augmented by church socials featuring homemade angel food with thin lemon frosting, soft molasses cookies, jelly and sauce from famous New Jersey cranberries. Cranberries, incidentally, were graduated from the wild state to a profitable crop after John Webb, a schoolteacher with a peg leg, drained a swamp in 1845 and got the idea of developing cranberry bogs. His first crop went aboard whaling ships to help prevent scurvy.

Irish in Bergen county eat *colcannon* at Hallowe'en and put a ring and key in the pot along with the onions, potatoes, beef broth and parsnips. The finder of the ring is headed for matrimony, and the key means a forthcoming journey.

From Civil War days to the turn of the century, Cape May was a favorite summer home of Presidents. Lincoln, Grant, Pierce, Buchanan and Harrison came there to breathe the clean salt air and eat sea bass, bluefish baked in wine and butter, oysters, lobster and crabs. When Henry Clay arrived for a holiday, Cape May women—so the story goes—chased him up the beach until they got close enough to snip off souvenir locks of his hair with their sewing scissors.

Jersey tomatoes were not always so respected as they are today. In the year 1830 the Salem county courthouse was the scene of a strange demonstration, when Robert Gibbon Johnson stood there and ate a tomato in public—to prove that the long-feared "love-apple" wasn't poisonous at all!

Connecticut

GOLD DUST FOR A PIE

One female pumpkin,
An iron kettle,
Salt and milk.

Mrs. George Israel Putnam wrote those items on the first page of a hand-made cookbook given me some years ago when we broadcast the three hundredth anniversary of the founding of Greenwich, Connecticut. Mrs. Putnam, a diminutive woman with white hair and bright blue eyes, told me that pumpkin bread made with female pumpkins has been a tradition in the Putnam family since colonial times.

Looking at the white-shingled house from which General Israel

Putnam escaped British capture in 1779 by dashing half-shaved into the courtyard, mounting his horse and plunging down a rocky precipice, I wondered whether he'd perhaps breakfasted on pumpkin bread before pulling off this legendary feat. One thing sure; pumpkin bread was part of the general's ration, and every Putnam bride who followed had to learn to make it. After cooking in the prescribed iron kettle, the mixture is settled in an iron crock overnight, then spooned into a pan to bake until crisply brown outside, moist within.

Another hand-me-down from colonial times is Scorched Cream . . . a dessert you iron. According to Mrs. Putnam's instructions, you make a rich custard, put a layer of sugar on top, and with a hot flatiron press until the sugar is glazed a golden-brown.

I am grateful to radio for making me aware of our American past. When I enjoyed assignments like the Greenwich tercentenary, history began to change from a series of dates and names, to the salt-box houses and village greens of New England, the columned plantations of the South, the Spanish missions in California, the ghost towns left from gold-rush days. Discovering history in the living countryside became more exciting than any page-one story of my newspaper days.

In Guilford I got to know the Reverend Lyman Beecher, father of Henry Ward Beecher, through a vivid record of his childhood kept during the 1770's. "We had wooden trenchers first, then pewter, and finally earthenware," he wrote. "Our living was very good. Rye bread, fresh butter, buckwheat cakes and pie for breakfast. After the dishes were washed, Annis and I helped Aunt milk. . . . Then they made cheese and spun till dinner. We dined on salt pork, vegetables and pies; corned beef also, and always on Sunday, a boiled Indian pudding. We made a stock of pies at Thanksgiving, froze them for winter's use and they lasted till March."

Connecticut land wasn't easy to farm, but within a century from its first colonization it was so productive that George Washington gratefully named it "The Provision State."

One of my favorite, though perhaps apocryphal, Washington stories concerns the time the great general, on his way to Cambridge, arrived late and hungry at Bridgeport, only to find no vacant seats at the Pixlee Tavern dinner table, and the waiters all occupied with serving the guests fried oysters. Washington is said to have remarked in a loud voice that "horses are very fond of oysters." When everybody stopped eating to argue this, he suggested that a dish be tried on his own horse, tethered outside. Most of the guests rushed outdoors to offer the horse oysters . . . while Washington sat down at a vacated place and made a leisurely meal!

Among Connecticut's 133 "firsts" is the first American silver-plated spoon, made in Spoonville in 1840. Seven years before, Amini Clark of Meriden got tired of the tedious hand-grinding of coffee, and invented the first coffee mill. Other Connecticut firsts which have affected our eating habits were the packaged garden seeds introduced by the Shaker colony at Enfield in 1802; W. W. Lyman's air-tight fruit jar with a spring-fastened top, in 1858; and the momentous first trip of Abijah Smith, Connecticut peddler, in 1807, bringing a bag of black stones that would burn. That was Connecticut's first anthracite coal, and it ushered in the era of cookstoves. By 1827, the fireplace was obsolete in all but "old-fashioned" country kitchens, and cookbooks had to be revised, including that of Amelia Simmons, the first American-printed cookbook published in Hartford in 1796.

Connecticut's first farm products got around almost as much as Connecticut peddlers did. Wethersfield onions went to the West Indies in the early 1700's and onions became such a quick-money crop that a historian of the time records women in silk dresses cultivating the onion fields. Washington Irving reported that the Dutch, who had been ousted from that region, couldn't look in the direction of the onion area without bitter tears in their eyes.

Seafood was a Connecticut specialty from Indian times, as witness the pre-colonial deposits of clam and oyster shells strewing the beaches. Milford claims the fattest and most flavorful clams in the state. Niantic's proud boast is small, sweet scallops, best when fried a delicate brown in deep fat. Shad once was so plentiful that farm hands around Hadden demanded a guarantee that they would not be served it more than five times a week.

Another food rebellion took place at Yale in its first years, when students kicked about salt pork, dry cod and stewed oysters for Sunday breakfast, and added a protest against having to shell their own peas for dinner. Yale rations were so meager that enterprising Lyman Beecher sold pies to the undergraduates and with the proceeds paid off a debt, bought a new suit and ended with $100 profit.

An anonymous rhymster of the time described Connecticut as

A land of notions, of apple sauce and greens,
A land of pumpkin pies, a land of pork and beans.

So renowned were Connecticut pumpkin pies that a homesick prospector in the gold rush of '49 wrote back that he'd trade his pile of gold dust for one good pumpkin pie.

The New England bean pot was used not only for beans but to simmer a stew of beef, onions, carrots, turnips and rolled oats, still known as a Bean-Pot Stew, and for making a cinnamon-spiced apple sauce that goes by the name of Bean-Pot Applesauce.

In colonial days, most housewives made Hallelujah, composed of boiled salt pork, onion and potatoes. Indian pudding was a stand-by, although P. T. Barnum's family seems to have been unusual in serving it as a first course, covered with molasses.

You might expect nutmeg to be sprinkled generously throughout early recipes of Connecticut, since it is called the Nutmeg State. But, in truth, the nickname comes not so much from the addiction of Connecticut cooks to nutmeg, as from the rumor that shrewd Yankee peddlers sold wooden nutmegs. Real spices were precious then, and those who had nutmegs often carried them in mono-grammed silver boxes containing a small silver grater.

Though there's plenty of Anglo-Saxon tradition in Connecticut, modern Yankee farmers may turn out to be German, Russian, Polish, Lithuanian, Magyar, French, Italian, Swiss, Czech, Austrian, Scandinavian, Greek or Armenian in background—for according to authorities, Connecticut, Rhode Island and Massachusetts have a greater proportion of foreign stock than any other states. This makes for a fine jumble of cookery and customs.

Many French Canadians who came to work in the textile mills cling with passionate tenacity to their own way. Their lamb stew is slow-cooked, then cooled so that every bit of fat can be skimmed from the top before the green beans, turnip, carrot, onion and tomato are added.

Once a year at Round Hill, near Greenwich, visitors to the Highland games may eat Scotch pies, small pastries filled with deviled mutton . . . while the bagpipes skirl and Scots in flashing tartans dance.

In New Britain in March the Ukrainians, who came to the so-called Hardware City in the early 1900's, honor their famous composer, Taras Shevchenko, at a festive concert at which they wear their native costumes. At Easter a suckling pig with a rose in its mouth and flowers in its ears is served on a table decked with pyramids of parsley, cress and herbs.

Roast goose comes to many tables in the Czech colony of Bridgeport on September 28th, St. Wenceslaus Day, and supper on Christmas Eve features boiled carp.

Danes opened bakeries, Greeks established coffeehouses, restaurants and candy stores, and Italians soon had Connecticut eating pizza pies. I ate one on a May afternoon in Greenfield Hills as we drove up a road lined with flowering dogwood to the white-steepled Congregational church on the town green. At the church food sale were ginger cookies made from an old "rule" which called for saleratus, water and butter, in a stoneware cup filled with molasses, the batter to be "beat like thunder till it foams" and the cookies to be cut with an oak-leaf cutter.

Then I was shown a hundred-year-old book called *The Young Housekeeper,* with advice from a certain William A. Alcott, who denounced lettuce and celery as "wholly indigestible" and warned New Englanders that "if eaten at all they should be eaten in the morning when the stomach is strongest."

After which I took another handful of Connecticut ginger cookies.

Vermont

VERMONT SUITS VERMONTERS FINE

On a certain March morning when the chemistry of early spring is at work, veteran Vermont maple farmers know the instant they awake that sugar weather has set in—fine and meltingly warm by day, frost-nipped at night. But New England weather is notoriously fickle, so the sugar farmer knows he'd better tap his trees before nature changes moods.

The first sugaring-off I ever saw was part of a junket for a Hollywood star in New Hampshire. But it was a Vermont farmer, looking remarkably like Calvin Coolidge, who taught me the lore of sugaring-off. We sat on a log near the weatherworn sugarhouse which leaned comfortably against a snowy hillside. The gathering sled, pulled by a knowing Morgan horse, drew up on the slope and men promptly began emptying the buckets of sap into vats. For maple sap is a delicate liquid. It must be boiled quickly, before sun and air can develop bacteria that will mar its sweetness and flavor.

Steam from the evaporator plumed into the cool, bracing air and two small boys hauled logs from the open woodshed to feed the firebox and keep the boil. My farmer described the modern power tapper, developed within his lifetime, to supplant the old bit brace and the earlier, primitive method of making an ax incision in the tree. Trees must be about forty years old to be good sugar-producers and they go right on for a century or more.

One towering maple in Vermont shows marks of well over a hundred years of tapping, starting with Indian sugar makers who used a reed spout and birchbark bucket. The scars on that tree tell the whole story of Vermont from Indian days on through the first settlements, when families made just enough sugar and syrup for their own use, up to our own time when some four million Vermont trees turn out their golden luxury products—maple sugar, maple syrup and maple sugar candy.

What I remember best about that morning is sugar-on-snow, classic part of every sugaring-off. One of the women set out big square pans of fresh snow and another brought a pitcher of hot syrup caught just before it reached the sugar stage. You ladle out the syrup and trail it from a spoon across the snow, where it turns to a waxy golden candy unlike any other confection on earth. Pickles, fresh unsweetened doughnuts, and mugs of steaming coffee are the invariable accompaniment to sugar-on-snow, and astonishingly, nobody ever seems to get indigestion.

When Champlain first saw Vermont in 1609, the Indians were using boiled maple sap to sweeten their cookery. The first settlers from western New England depended upon the maple, too, to see them through while they cleared land and set out farms.

Charles Siaz and his wife and ten children kept alive their first winter in Danville by combining maple syrup with wild game and berries. Later, when daily life settled into a degree of comfort, Vermonters had time to concoct such delights as maple divinity fudge and good tart apples baked in maple syrup and crowned with maple sugar. Vermont baked beans differ from the traditional New England variety in that maple syrup goes into the bean pot along with the salt pork and seasonings.

Vermont history is studded with fine resounding names like Remember Baker, Pardon Jones, Experience Davis and Mercy Twilight—names of the men and women who changed Vermont, as British General Burgoyne gloomily put it, "from a country un-peopled and almost unknown . . . to one abounding with the most active and rebellious race on the continent."

Those Vermonters didn't give up anything easily, whether it was an idea or an acre of land. Ethan Allen and his Green Moun-tain Boys, determined never to live under New York's feudal land-lord system, fought their way up and down Vermont and some-times survived for days on ground nuts and lily roots.

Allen was alternately hero-worshiped and denounced all over the country as an atheist, a patriot, a blasphemer, a hard-drinking dictator, a crusader and a man who regularly ate fire for lunch. Dorothy Canfield Fisher says a lot about her native state when she observes about Ethan: "We can see that he might not suit other people. He suits us fine."

And Vermont suits Vermonters, too. They are proud of the fat bronze turkeys, so famous that hotel and restaurant menus as well as poultry stores list Vermont turkeys to denote excellence.

They don't mind the old saw about Vermont having more cows than people. It was a Vermont cow, they claim, that inspired the first Red Flannel Hash, that zestful winter dish that combines tender chopped beef with beets and other vegetables and a final touch of cream and butter just before it comes well-browned from the frying pan.

Vermont cattle are the pride of the dozens of country fairs held all over the state, and these same aristocratically bred animals are the reason for the C. H. Dana Company, which manufactures accessories for the well-dressed cow: cow shampoo and coat dress-ing, monogrammed halters and blankets.

Vermont even celebrated Christmas when that holiday was banned from Puritan New England. Up there, tons of mince pies were baked and eaten while Puritans were denouncing that spicy delight, baked in manger-shaped tins, as pagan. It was evident from the start that anything as good as mince pie would not long remain in exile, but when it did creep back into New England's cuisine, the pie pan had become circular.

Veteran of World War II, Vrest Orton, had cashed in on American nostalgia. During the war he came upon a picture of an old country store. It looked like the store his father ran half a century before in the village of Calais, Vermont. Sick of war and of big cities, Vrest Orton began making lists of things he remembered from his boyhood: horehound drops, rock candy and licorice sticks in striped paper bags; yellow-eye beans and pork baked in his mother's brick oven; dandelion greens and the way they perked a fellow up in spring. . . . He remembered the hulled-corn man driving his wagon to the kitchen door and the 300 dishes his grandmother made from water-ground yellow cornmeal, and her way of cooking whole kernels of wheat overnight in a double boiler.

Orton thought there must be a lot of other people homesick for things of the past. When war ended he went to Weston, Vermont, and in 1945 hung out a shingle THE VERMONT COUNTRY STORE on a two-and-a-half-story frame building painted buttermilk red with white columns supporting its double-deck porches. Orton got the Vermont Guild to put an ancient water mill back into operation and to turn out thirteen different kinds of whole-grain grist, including samp—"no mushy liquid breakfast food this," he noted, "you can chew it."

Orton's Vermont Country Store is now famous all over the nation. He and his wife never give up their search for the long-ago things they loved. They found Bear's Paw popcorn, and they tell customers the Vermont way to pop it tender and fluffy, best when eaten in front of an open fire on a winter night.

They located a woman who could copy by hand an old-fashioned calico apron left to Mrs. Orton by her grandmother, and they found an 1860-type calico to make it from. They scoured the countryside for iron trivets, corncob pipes and the covered split-ash pie baskets which Vermonters still use for carrying cakes and pies to church suppers. When they remembered something and couldn't find it—old-time corn chowder, for instance—they made it.

I've had some charming and serene visits in Vermont, but I have not yet eaten at the Windham County Hotel and Jail, in Newfane. I intend to go there, because I'm sure it's the only place on earth where hotel guests and prisoners go in by the same door, register at the same desk and eat the same fine food! The county house sits on one side of the stately village green facing the 192-year-old courthouse with its white pillars and pointed bell tower.

The inn was opened in one end of the jail more than a century ago when personnel from the courthouse needed a place to eat and sleep. Since then it has been in Ripley's Believe-it-or-not, it has been used to promote a pancake flour and an automobile . . . but its elegant New England cuisine has survived all the fanfare.

I may, as Theodore Roosevelt is alleged to have suggested, commit some small crime there and then eat my way through the sentence in the barred section of this hostelry, which probably couldn't exist anywhere except in the delightful, contrary state of Vermont.

Delaware

THE BLUE HEN

The first log cabins and the first planked shad in America—Delaware claims them both. The Swedes, so-called (most of them were really Finns), built log cabins in Delaware in 1638, and they were widely copied in frontier settlements as well as by some Indian tribes. The Indians did bake fish on shingles, but it was the first white settlers in Delaware who brought their fish planks from the Old World and perfected the technique of nailing a split shad and its roe to a hardwood slab, to be browned before an open fire.

A seventeenth-century report on the Finns in New Sweden, as Delaware was then called, pointed out that they "despised above everything the idea of living upon the fruits of other people's labor"; that they seemed at home in the new land and knew how to use the wild fruit, fish and game they found. By the first spring their grain grew in small fields around the cabins. They ate four hearty meals a day and drank a punch called Meridian, made with rum, fresh spring water, lemon juice (when lemons could be had) and slices of hot toast floating on top.

The Swedish group preferred a mixture of beer, rum and sugar, called Manatham. Also, they are said to have introduced eggnog as the festive drink for New Year's and Easter.

The shores of Delaware Bay and the river provided "enough oysters to serve all England," as some writers recorded, and there were beef, venison, chicken, eggs, wild fowl, turnips, grapes, peaches and strawberries to keep the meals varied and nourishing.

Four-hundred-pound John Printz, who had lived for years in Finland, came to govern the colony, and on Tinicum Island built himself a log and brick castle, which later burned. Printz had a daughter, Armegot, whose size, appetite and disposition matched his. When he left the New World, before the invading Dutch led by Peter Stuyvesant, Armegot stayed on. She kept her maiden name, would not pay taxes, and tried to turn her island home into an independent kingdom.

Except for a few buildings like the famous Old Swedes Church in Wilmington, said to be the nation's oldest Protestant church in continuous use, little trace is left in Delaware of the Scandinavian settlers who used to drive their sleighs over the snowy country-side for Christmas Eve services. Every churchgoer was served sweetened rye bread and a piece of cold roast pork. In the homes on Christmas Day there was always a supply of the special holiday bread, braided loaves topped with glazed sugar and almonds.

When the Dutch came in, they named their principal town New Amstel, now New Castle. They lacked artisans and farmers, and as one chronicler put it, "the Dutch first built a town and then died for hunger and maladies of bad nutrition." Delaware's "lost colony" was Zwannendale, also a Dutch venture headed by one Gilles Hossett. At first the colony got on by bartering with the Indians a corn-persimmon beer in exchange for turkeys, ducks, fish and venison. But in a year no trace was left of the white settle-ment, except for a few bones . . . and some Indians walking around in European-cut jackets.

As so often happened in the colonies, when others failed, the English took over, and even though the Dutch regained the region for a few years it was the English cultural pattern which domi-nated life in Delaware, and to some extent, still does. Delaware girls began going to Philadelphia to study at Mrs. Goodfellow's

Cooking School, where among other things they learned to make "George Washington's soup," a rich blend of crabmeat, sweet cream, bacon, tiny meat balls and hard-boiled eggs.

A cookbook of the 1800's warned Delaware cooks never to wash a waffle iron, simply to clean it with coarse salt and brown paper and put it away in a paper bag. The book also specified that Irish bread should be cut with a string instead of a knife.

Delaware was growing good wheat and corn as early as 1680, venison was cheap, bear-meat cost nothing, kitchen gardens had every sort of herb as well as many vegetables. Three kinds of peaches grew in such profusion that they were left on the ground to rot, and William Penn advised housewives to dry the fruit. Delawarans made wine from cherries and from a vanished species of wild plum.

The memorable day I visited New Castle I had lunch in an ancient courthouse, remodeled for a restaurant, which featured broiled Delaware chicken and the region's favorite sour-milk biscuits with old-fashioned jelly roll for dessert. Then I walked along Front Street where clipper ships poked their prows almost into the front windows of the houses, and sat in a garden planted by a Quaker, to drink tea from thin, flower-sprigged cups brought from China in the 1700's.

Inns and motels line the super-highways, but in towns like New Castle you can still find quiet and cobbles and wonderful regional dishes—shrimp stewed over a pan of spiced vinegar and served with Tartare sauce; crab in the shell; local cauliflower cooked into a custard; creamed corn pudding garnished with parsley; and a fish stew called Muddle, made in a Dutch oven. Lemon butter, or lemon jelly, is a Delaware sandwich filling, and a favorite for picnics. Steamed crab is the highlight of suppers cooked on the beach.

Broiler chickens are Delaware's big agricultural product—the state's nickname is The Blue Hen. Modern broilers are not blue hens, however, for this species became extinct not long after a company of Delaware soldiers took a blue hen and her chicks to the Revolutionary War as mascots. The new broiler business has produced an annual festival and a nationwide contest for the best chicken recipes.

Ham smoked to a rich mahogany and aged at least a year has been a source of Delaware pride for nearly three centuries. Pigs down there can see the wind, according to a time-honored farm belief. Now science comes to the defense of the farmers, for Ida M. Mellen in her *Natural History of the Pig* says the ordinary sow exhibits apprehension of approaching high winds and is "the most accurate of living barometers."

The American food story was enormously affected by another Delaware product—cellophane—first loosed upon the world by the E. I. duPont de Nemours Company, one of the great corporations of the world and producer of more than 1,200 different products. So to Delaware goes the credit for handsome and protective food packaging . . . and perhaps the blame for some wrappings which defy anything less vigorous than a blowtorch to open.

One of the first great American inventors, Oliver Evans, came from a Delaware farm. The most prophetic of all his inventions was a system of conveyor belts for grist mills, designed to substitute machine for man. In the year 1787 a few adventurous wheat farmers brought their grain to Evans' "magic mill" and saw it changed to flour without any human intervention. But many farmers and millers thought the whole thing a lazy man's device, designed to destroy the virtue of hard work. They didn't dream that this first conception of the assembly line, the endless belt, would some day send a stream of packaged goods into American kitchens accompanied by the boast that they are "untouched by human hands."

Rhode Island

MONUMENT TO A CHICKEN

Rhode Island's famous little red hen was both the guest of honor and the main course at its own centennial celebration which began in the town of Little Compton, Rhode Island, during the fall of 1954. More than 3,000 people ate barbecued Rhode Island Red

chicken dinners and heard the romantic yarn of the farm-reared
sea captain who brought home from the Orient an exotic assortment of fowl called Shanghais, Malayas and Javas. Captain William Tripp stayed ashore long enough at Little Compton 100
years ago to cross some of the red and black plumaged birds with
domestic breeds. The result was the Rhode Island Red, the only
chicken I know which has a monument with a bronze marker in
its honor—at Adamsville, Rhode Island.

Those barbecue guests who stayed overnight discovered that
a favorite breakfast up there is creamy omelet, made from Rhode
Island Red eggs, eaten with hot Jonny-cake and tart red-plum
jam. They probably found, too, as I did when I first ventured
into Rhode Island, that you spell Jonny-cake without an "h."
Little Rhode Island has a flinty, unyielding attitude not only about
the spelling of Jonny-cake but also about making it. Thomas Robinson Hazard was quite clear in his famous "Jonny-Cake Papers"
as to the importance of white water-ground cornmeal from the
eastern coast of Rhode Island, a wooden mixing tray and a red oak
Jonny-cake board to balance in front of an open fire by means
of a heart-shaped flatiron. Every so often the cake must be pains-
takingly dressed with sweet golden-tinged cream.

Early Rhode Island inns evidently didn't suffer from painstaking
cookery. Madame Knight, who wrote with asperity about her
horseback trip from Boston to New York in 1704, says that at a
certain Rhode Island inn she got nothing for supper but a "dish
of pork and cabbage . . . the sauce of a deep purple which I
thought was boiled in a dye kettle."

My favorite Rhode Islander is William Blackstone, who left
Boston in 1635 because it was too crowded. A Cambridge graduate
and a solitary, Blackstone was living on what is now Beacon Hill
when the first colonists moved in. He sold them the whole of
Boston Peninsula, keeping out one acre for himself and his beloved
apple trees. But civilization was crowding in upon him, so collecting some apple cuttings and seedlings, he went off to Rhode
Island. There he built a house called Study Hill, near Providence,
and planted an orchard of "sweeting apple trees." Descendants
are the crisp, snappy Rhode Island apples you find in a famous
Blackstone pudding, mixed with white cornmeal and molasses,
slow-baked and served with hard sauce. When the first white
children arrived a few years later, Mr. Blackstone is said to have

ridden around the countryside on a cream-colored bull, handing out apples to any child he met.

Slaves, molasses and rum built the first Rhode Island fortunes. Later, after federal statute outlawed the slave trade for United States citizens, Rhode Island sea captains began to look to the Orient. One merchant, Metcalf Bowler, was intrigued by the shiny green apples he saw growing in the Far East. He brought back cuttings, and in a few years the state was famous for its greenings —which make as good a pie as I've eaten this side of Missouri, especially when combined with plenty of cinnamon, sugar and butter.

I like to think that one of Rhode Island's traditional desserts, Bristol peach slump, was bubbling fragrantly in the Dutch oven of the Reynolds kitchen in Bristol on the September day in 1778 that a young French officer knocked at the door. The best Narragansett clams had been brewed into a chowder, small, tender scallops from the bay were browning, the corn bread was perfection, because Mrs. Reynolds had just learned that Lafayette was to make his headquarters in her home. She dispatched the young officer to one of her lesser rooms. He came right down, politely asking for food, and poor Mrs. Reynolds had to put him at the table so carefully laid for Lafayette. He ate and ate, he talked, he lingered over his wine until the hostess finally had to remind him that she was expecting the general. The young man smiled and said not to worry—*he* was Lafayette.

I drove through Bristol to have a look at the Reynolds house and to hear the claims of some Bristolites that the place was visited by Norsemen in the year 1000, and that they were probably the first white men to taste a now-forgotten Indian bread concocted of crushed strawberries and cornmeal . . . a recipe I wish somebody would rediscover.

A Rhode Island friend of mine decided to stage a beach picnic with the same food the Indians had almost three and a half centuries ago. The menu included hominy, succotash, steamed clams, and swordfish baked on a plank over the driftwood fire.

Block Island is an enchanting setting for beach parties, with its seaside farms fenced in stone, its wind-silvered houses covered with honeysuckle, and its 365 shimmering ponds decked in water lilies and blue iris. There is no more succulent swordfish anywhere, and Block Islanders like it best cut in thick steaks and broiled, basted often with a blend of melted butter, white wine and tarragon, then served with lemon butter.

As early as 1760, a group of First Families ruled the Newport social seasons. They entertained at corn-husking festivals, but had slaves to do the husking.

I wondered why the old records contained so few recipes for meat and vegetable dishes until a friend whose family goes back to colonial times explained that her own grandmother believed every grown woman knew how to cook the "main dishes." You wrote down only such fancy creations as Newport spice cake, classic pound cake and the like. Exceptions were combinations such as the rice, eggs, fish and seasoning for a proper Wakefield Kedgeree; also the delicate timing for frying Narragansett clam fritters. Squantum, a steamed Indian pudding, was different in the Rule Book of each family, but I like best a sour-milk version with graham flour added.

For such a small state, Rhode Island has turned up some outrageous dinner parties. Godfrey Malbone, a Newport merchant who thought money could buy anything, used to reward his ship captains when they completed a profitable slave-trading voyage by inviting them to dinner and letting them break all the glasses and dishes after dessert. Mrs. Malbone, it is said, locked up her good china and glassware on these occasions.

Then there was the Dog's Dinner Party during Newport's preposterous age of extravagance, in the 90's. Harry Lehr, court jester for Mrs. Stuyvesant Fish, invited a hundred dogs and served them fricassee of bones, beef liver and rice, and a dessert of shredded dog biscuit. A dachshund ate so much he had to be carried from the table in a faint. Newport never had quite as much luster after the newspaper stories of that party, read by thousands who seldom had enough to eat. Today the baroque palaces along the Ten Mile Drive are becoming museum pieces. No society hostess now could —or would—set aside an entertainment budget of $300,000, as Mrs. Pembroke Jones did for a single Newport season. After one of Newport's three-hour dinners, served on golden plates with relays of rare wines and liqueurs, visiting Grand Duke Boris of Russia concluded that the Czars and all the Caesars put together couldn't match the magnificence of America's millionaires.

THE SOUTH AND THE CARIBBEAN

W. Va.

Md.

Va.

CIDER

Ky.

Tenn.

N. Car.

Ala.

S. Car.

Ark.

Miss.

Ga.

La.

Fla.

C a r i b b e a n

Maryland

TRADITION IN THE KITCHEN

White steps sparkling in the early morning sun, ponies pulling
carts heaped sky-high with garden greens, soft southern voices
chatting of thoroughbred horses, soft-shell crab and Chincoteague
oysters—in all the United States this could only be Baltimore.
Home of Lady Baltimore cake, almond bread and diamondback
terrapin, Baltimore manor houses have a long tradition of hospitality.

The cookery began with Indian corn, peas and beans. But Lord
Baltimore and his twenty gentlemen of fashion soon started building great shingle-roofed houses with orchards and gardens, cellars
full of imported wines, dining rooms furnished in Heppelwhite
and Chippendale, corner cupboards filled with pewter, china,
and in a few years, silver.

Chicken Maryland was probably born in the kitchen of the
1600's, when the hot corn bread came from the oven at the exact
moment that the floured, salted, peppered and fried golden-

brown chicken was ready. And so the two were put together and another southern classic was created. The corn bread must be made with white cornmeal, sliced in half and the fried chicken placed on top, the boat of rich cream gravy alongside.

The genius of the Negro cooks made things of beauty of Maryland omelets, browned in bacon fat and thickened ever so slightly with cornstarch so they could be warmed over and served with tender pink slices of Maryland ham. The famous black bean soup of the region the Negroes cooked with veal and seasoned with sherry and allspice. Dark amber Maryland consommé they flavored with sherry and caramelized sugar.

But the state's most famous dish is diamondback terrapin, so rare now that you almost have to wangle your way into private clubs to get it. In the old days, no matter how large her staff of cooks, the lady of the manor always went to the kitchen to make sure the terrapin came to the table with that elusive flavor that even gourmets have never adequately described. At Crisfield, which calls itself the Seafood Capital of the World, some terrapin —heifers, cows and bulls—are now being raised in special pounds to sell for as high as fifty dollars a dozen. Crisfield also has vast oyster-shucking houses and packing plants where hard crabs are steamed.

Eastern Shore food has interested me especially since I came to know Sophie Kerr. Sophie's novels and stories always have mouth-watering descriptions of favorite dishes, and to my delight the novelist, collaborating with June Platt a while ago, gathered all her treasured recipes in a book called *The Best I Ever Ate.* I remember her telling on my program about an Eastern Shore cook she knew in her childhood who casually whisked eggs, flour and milk into a batter with a bit of oyster liquor, dipped in the oysters, rolled them in fine-as-dust soda cracker crumbs and fried them in leaf lard, in an old iron frying pan. These, Sophie swears, were "such fried oysters as never were before and never will be again."

Sophie told, too, about Miss Lucy, whose pocketbook rolls were part inspiration, part instinct, and were known the length of the Eastern Shore; about Aunt Suzie's mustard pickle; and a lattice peach pie made with fresh, ripe peach halves cooked in cream.

Many culinary secrets of centuries are buried in the huge kitchens of manor houses in the green Tidewater country. Through their box hedges and sunken gardens, distinguished guests came to sample specialties of each house: blackberry flummery, Tipsy Squire, peach foam.

At Fair View, a yellow brick mansion with four ghosts, the *pièce de résistance* was rare canvasback duck cooked with wine brandy, and oyster pie with a crust that melted in the mouth. They say a beautiful ghost girl in hoopskirts haunts the old house to make sure that crab cakes have their proper quota of hard-boiled egg and parsley, that delicate rock-fish is butter-basted as it bakes in the big oven, and that Dorchester creamed oysters have the exact touch of lemon juice to make them perfect.

I suppose every little girl has dreamed of being a princess and living in a palace, but my friend Sally Weaver Van Buren came closest to doing it when her family bought Clynmalira, the great manor house built by Henry Carroll in the early 1800's on a land grant from Lord Baltimore of five thousand acres. Sally's family was only the second to own the house after the Carrolls themselves. It was almost a miniature village, and the Weavers even had their own cannery and at harvest time a troop of helpers arrived to put up huge supplies of fruits and vegetables.

Apple butter and beaten biscuits were made outdoors, the apple butter bubbling in an iron caldron over a wood fire while one of the cooks stirred it hours on end with a six-foot wooden pole. The beaten-biscuit table stood nearby and the dough was placed in a ball in the center and pounded with a wooden sledge hammer.

Sally's Christmas dinner always included sauerkraut, a custom she believes peculiar to that part of Maryland, and with the turkey there were invariably a roast duck, baked ham and pheasant or goose. Throughout the year, fried apples were a breakfast favorite and lunchtime usually found hominy among the dishes on the gleaming mahogany table. The family produced nearly everything they ate and slept under blankets made from the wool of their own sheep.

Henry Carroll, grandson of the Carroll for whom Clynmalira was built, was in 1956 still living at Duddington, the farm which is all that remains in the family name. He sent along some recipes from an heirloom cookbook. They sound luscious but leave something to the cook's imagination. For peach pudding, the recipe says:—

"Take a double handful of grated bread, a dredging box of flour, a tea cup chopped suet, three or four eggs, a quart of cut peaches and a quart of milk. Boil it three or four hours."

The less blue-blooded settlers who came along with the gentlemen of fashion cooked their humbler dishes with the same pride
and care—boiled poke and turnip greens, hog jowl and sweet
potato pie. They trimmed the Indian succotash with dumplings,
and there was one dish, now vanished, which an English traveler
ate in 1708—a rasher of broiled infant bear. In farmhouse and
manor house alike Merry Christmas has been said for two centuries not only with foaming cups of eggnog, but with Bay oysters
pickled according to a recipe handed down through the generations.

The nineteenth century lingers on in the comfortable houses
of Charles County. Even now, says Ethel Roby Hayden in the
Maryland Historical Magazine, you may be invited to tea when
your hostess really means supper, because years ago the ceremony
of afternoon tea grew so elaborate and the dishes so many that it
turned into an early supper. Rolled French omelet is a distinctive
dish down there, but the oddest is the ham eaten at Easter. It is
stuffed, according to Elizabeth Hayden, with a mixture of chopped
water cress, kale, cabbage sprouts and green garlic leaves wilted
in ham liquor and then poked into incisions in the ham. The whole
goes into a cloth bag and back into the kettle to boil some more.
When you cut the ham, the slices are striped red and green.

My favorite Maryland character is Mistress Margaret Brent,
spinster, who came alone to the Province of Maryland in 1638,
said she was "aged about thirty-eight" and proceeded to patent
her own lands, run her own manorial estates on St. Mary's and
Kent Islands, supervise the preparation of elaborate dinners, and
exercise power-of-attorney for her brother. She was considered
able enough to be appointed executrix for Governor Calvert's
estate, and this so set her up that on January 21, 1647, she became
the first woman in America to demand the right to vote. She was
so angry when refused that she moved to Virginia.

Louisiana

ALL THIS AND GUMBO TOO

The time was 1730. Barefooted Antoinette lifted high her Parisian skirts of brocaded satin and waded daintily into the mud of New Orleans' Vieux Carré. She was on her way to a party. By the light of a torch she rinsed her feet in the final puddle, and put on silk stockings and dancing shoes. The French government in 1728 brought out Antoinette and other Casket Girls (so-called from their trunks, which were shaped like caskets), hoping respectable women would tame roistering New Orleans. The Ursuline nuns who had arrived a year earlier reported primly that the new prospective brides were "ignorant about things concerning salvation, but not so about vanity."

Nor about food, the nuns might have added. The Casket Girls were so outraged by the diet in their new home that officials sent a hurry call to France, noting that "for corn the newcomers have a dogged aversion." From that dogged aversion grew the delectable cuisine of New Orleans and southern Louisiana, which includes—praise be—a dessert named for me by my friend Germaine Wells, who runs Arnaud's on Bienville Street. You'll find Germaine's way of making my peach flambee at the end of this chapter, along with three more of her specialties. Like my family recipes from Missouri, they do not conform to the standardized measurements our home economists have set up, so here they are, outside our regular recipe section, to charm and challenge the adventurous.

Somebody has said that if ever a good Louisianian died, went to heaven and found no gumbo there, he'd come straight back. Gumbo is New Orleans' unique contribution to American cookery. The early French bride found the Indians using a powder made

of sassafras leaves, appropriated it and named it *gumbo file.*
Gumbo file is the basis of all true gumbo. Descendants of the
Choctaw Indians still gather and sell it.

Gumbos vary with the cook. I have eaten superlative ones in
the Park Avenue home of my friends, Frances and Edward La-
Roque Tinker, who have, of course, a New Orleans cook. Some
cookbooks list as many as a dozen recipes, including Gumbo
Zheves made from seven greens and salt pork and bringing good
luck when eaten on Holy Thursday. There are gumbos with
shrimp and crabs, with chicken and oysters, with veal and herbs;
gumbos with *all* of these combined. Edward Tinker tells me that
the name derives from Kingombo, the African name for the okra
first brought to America by native Bantus. Later it became plain
gumbo.

The Creole cuisine includes the delicacy of the French cuisine,
the high-seasoned spiciness of Spanish cooking, the magic of the
Negro cook. Lowly cowpeas went into the pot with shrimps,
spices, herbs, rice and tomatoes to become jambalaya. Lima beans
found themselves dressed up with thyme, parsley, bay leaf, cream
and butter. Redfish, oysters, crabs, crawfish were glorified in concoctions that started with the French *roux*, a browned mixture of
pure sweet lard or butter, flour, onion, parsley, green pepper and
other seasonings.

Hotels, restaurants and homes outdo themselves for New Orleans' famed Mardi Gras Carnival. The celebration starts on January 6, Twelfth Night, with a twelve-egg brioche cake decorated
with *dragées* and surrounded by lighted candles, served just before the Carnival Ball.

The parade of good New Orleans food goes on all year round.
Creole coffee is the morning eye-opener, very hot, very full of
chicory, and served black or *au lait*—half hot milk.

The Calas Woman, as she has done for years, peddles her
baskets of hot fried rice cakes, light and delicious with powdered
sugar dusted over their brown tops.

"*Calas, Calas, tout chaud, tout chaud,*" she calls, offering from
the same basket, almond sticks and a warm, soft gingerbread
made with cane syrup. Other street vendors sell "poor-boy" sandwiches, mammoth combinations of meats and relishes heaped in
a split loaf of French bread.

Early French housewives, homesick for Paris almond candy,
made do with the pecans they found in Louisiana, and concocted

the brown-sugar confection called pralines. With typical French frugality, they also saved vegetable water and juices for the soup pot, and when they cooked chicken, the side product was pure golden consommé. (Legend has it that consommé was invented in France—because Louis VI had no teeth!)

Gourmets all over the world went into mourning half a century ago over the death of one of New Orleans' treasured cooks, Madame Begue. Her compatriot, Felix Kock, in the *Boston Cooking School Magazine* of 1906 grieved that there would be no more epicurean breakfasts in the Quartier Latin for the bon vivants of the nation . . . no more snails à la Creole . . . artichokes à la Begue; for, "the queer little two-story structure on the French market place . . . is silent and desolate." And although New Orleans is full of wonderful eating places, old-timers are united in the claim that there will never be anything to take the place of eleven o'clock "second breakfast" at Begue's: crawfish, omelet, tripe, fried chicken with boiled potatoes, cheese, apples with wine accompaniment, and, of course, many cups of black coffee with brandy.

St. Martinsville, settled by marquises and barons who fled the French Revolution, claims to make the finest court bouillon on earth, starting with a *roux* and going on through a procession of herbs and spices to the final tomatoes and slices of fresh-caught redfish or snapper. Here, just before 1800, visitors would come upon servants carrying great silver salvers of fruit in the streets, orchestras afloat on flower-decked barges, strolling noblemen in silk coats and velvet breeches, diamonds twinkling from their neck ruffs and buckles. The place lived up to its nickname, "Little Paris." A favorite dish was turkey stuffed with truffles.

Hundreds of tarpon are caught at the annual Rodeo on Grand Isle. Sheepshead, thought by some to be the king of all Gulf fish, is cooked here à la Creole, with mushrooms, oysters and shrimp. Red snapper forms the base for bouillabaise, and Louisiana pompano was once described by Mark Twain as "delicious as the less criminal forms of sin."

Louisiana honors its important food crops at a series of gay festivals and carnivals. Practically all of the sugar cane in the country grows in the "Sugar Bowl" of south-central Louisiana. Pale first-boil syrup is a must-spread for breakfast rice griddle cakes, waffles and flannel cakes in the section. Hominy is another first-meal-of-the-day regular at plantations such as The Shadows, pink-columned brick mansion in New Iberia, heart of the sugar region. Strawberries, which come north in a fragrant scarlet flood starting in March, are feted at Hammond with the crowning of a strawberry queen, and rival cooks vie for supremacy in short-cakes, strawberry pies and a dessert memorable for its flavor—sun-ripened strawberries that have stood in sugar syrup just long enough and are then served covered with whipped cream.

A big attraction for some years has been a rice-eating contest at Crowley in October, with parades by day and dancing by night. Here rice goes into rich pilafs, soufflés and puddings. Louisiana pecans grew wild in the bottomlands, and probably the first scientific cultivation was accomplished in 1846 by a Negro gardener named Antoine, who grafted sixteen trees at Oak Valley Plantation.

In the Cajun country, much of it hidden in the shadowy bayous, a French patois is spoken and coffee is so important that standard equipment in a pirogue (swift, narrow canoe) is a drip pot. Cajuns cook up coffee over twig fires wherever they stop. Their turtle stew is thick with rice, their bread is made at home in long, narrow loaves with crisp crusts, their creamy bisques are rich with oysters and shrimp.

The modern abundance of parties and fine food in Louisiana is nothing compared with the extravagance of plantation balls described by Louise Butler in the *Louisiana Historical Quarterly.* Three-story spiral staircases, garlanded with roses, "delightsome music" filling the air, midnight suppers with "cold meats, salads, salamis, gallantines quaking in jellied seclusion, an infinite variety of à-la's . . ." served from side tables, corsages at each plate, and on the carved oak sideboard "fruits, cakes in pyramids or layers or only solid deliciousness, iced and ornamented; custards, pies, jellies, creams, Charlotte Russes encircling a veritable Mont Blanc of whipped cream. . . ."

And at dawn when the dancing was finished, the guests each had "a plate of hot gumbo, a cup of black coffee and enchanting memories to sustain them on the long drive to their abodes."

WATER CRESS SALAD À LA GERMAINE

Chop celery fine, add olive oil, vinegar, mayonnaise, Philadelphia cream cheese, and a touch of saffron. Salt and pepper to taste. Mix well. Cut up a few pieces of Philadelphia cheese and celery, cut fine. Mix with water cress salad and serve.

CHICKEN FRICASSEE
À LA GERMAINE

Disjoint 1 2-pound drawn broiler. Brown slightly with butter in a skillet, seasoning with salt and pepper. Remove the chicken to a hot platter to keep it warm. Make a *roux* with flour, 1 egg yolk well beaten with cream. Sauté onions in butter until tender but not brown and mix with *roux*. Add chicken and wine, cover and steam, using low heat, until tender and done about 40 minutes. When it is ready to serve, sprinkle parsley over the chicken.

SHRIMP CANAPÉ À LA IRMA

Mince 1 bunch of shallots with 1 eye of garlic, fry in butter, brown. Add 2 tablespoons flour to make a *roux*. Add fish broth to thickness desired. Slice 2 pounds boiled shrimp fine, and put in sauce. Cook for about 20 minutes. Add 1 glass claret wine mixed with 4 yolks of eggs to tighten dressing. Season to taste. Spread on slice of trimmed toast, border with hard-boiled eggs and parsley minced fine. Top with bread crumbs and cheese and bake golden brown.

PEACH FLAMBEE,
MARY MARGARET McBRIDE

Place a scoop of vanilla ice cream in a small compote dish. Crush either macaroons or vanilla wafers and put on top of ice cream.

Dice 2 peach halves, put in Brulot bowl, add a lump of sugar and burn with rum.

While burning, pour over ice cream.

Kentucky

BURGOO AT THE DERBY

When I got up that first day in Louisville, redbud flamed in the river hills, blossoms tossed pink and white in the soft May air, voices had a bright edge of excitement . . . for it was Derby Day. Within a few hours some hundred thousand people from all over the world would be jammed into Churchill Downs to watch the event that's become a sort of Mardi Gras, New Year's Eve and horse race rolled into one.

If you're lucky enough to be a guest of one of Louisville's famous hostesses on these occasions, the food will be every bit as memorable as the race—more so if you didn't pick a winner. Derby breakfasts, held at 10:30 A.M. on Derby Day, include salad and dessert, heirloom silver agleam on antique lace tablecloths. An ancient and honored ritual is in progress as the host makes mint juleps in silver goblets, the outside glinting frostily, the contents lethal.

A Kentucky ham, which anyone in the Blue Grass country will tell you is superior to any other, comes to the table in an aura of sugar and spice, its meat a deep red. Sometimes it is baked whole and served cold, and sometimes fried with marvelous red gravy to pour over hot batter pudding. Accompanying are biscuits in relays that must be eaten before the oven heat can leave their tender hearts; dishes of pickled peaches, strawberry preserves, and salad bowls of endive, artichoke, tomato, cucumber. If anybody has room after all that, my favorite Derby hostess, Isabel McMeekin, likes a dessert of filled melon rings—golden ripe cantaloupe cut in circles, the centers filled with fresh pineapple sherbet decked with black cherries.

After the race, guests go on to a buffet at one of Louisville's spacious old houses, and on Sunday the guest-breakfast features traditional chicken hash, meltingly tender flannel cakes just off the griddle, sausages redolent with sage, and for dessert, individual puddin' pies or gingery little cookies coyly called Dollie Dimples.

A horse named Burgoo King, after that famous Kentucky dish, won the 1932 Derby. The colt was named for Colonel E. R. Bradley's burgoo cook, who was said to be unrivaled at preparing the stew. There are as many schools of thought about the ingredients of burgoo as there are about mint julep. Legend has it that when General John Morgan's cavalry troops were short on rations during the War Between the States, a soldier named Gus Jaubert shot some blackbirds and then gathered up all the meat and vegetables he could find, combining them with the birds in a great kettle . . . and creating the first burgoo.

One of the few points of agreement among burgoo *aficionados* is that it must be cooked and eaten outdoors; also, that squirrels go into the mixture, a dozen or so to every hundred gallons. Burgoo is never a small-time operation. One recipe calls for a ton of peeled, diced potatoes, six hundred pounds of soup meat, two hundred fat hens, and tomatoes, carrots, cabbage, corn and onions in proportion.

A world away from the lush Blue Grass, with its elegant food and sophisticated talk, is Ashland, where I am invited every June to eat shucky beans, yellow tomato preserves, and the famous "feudin' gingerbread"—foods which my friend Jean Thomas has ready for me. Jean is known as The Traipsin' Woman because she used to traipse horseback up Big Sandy Creek and down Peevish Hollow taking testimony in court cases. Jean got Rhody McCoy and America Hatfield, of the famous feuding families, to make me a patchwork quilt that's my special pride.

In the fall, Jean takes needle and thread and strings shucky beans in the pod, hanging them to dry on a rafter near her open fire. Then, says she: "When well dried, shuck them out and boil in an iron kettle two hours with a slab of sow belly and a table-spoon of salt. A quart of shucky beans will make a good mess for the whole family."

It was in 1756 that the first white woman stepped into Ken-tucky. She was Mary Inglis and she got there solely because she was a good cook. Mary was the prisoner of a party of Mingo Indians who captured her in Westmoreland County, Virginia. Her two children were carried off, her sister-in-law was murdered, but Mary's life was spared because she made even such simple dishes as hominy, venison and wild greens taste superlative. Maybe she fed her captors into a state of coma one night. At any rate she got away from them at what is now Big Boone Lick, Kentucky. For forty days she walked, climbed, forded streams, trying des-perately to follow the dim Indian trails and keep her directions straight. On the fortieth day she walked into her family's frontier cabin and calmly began stirring up the fire for supper!

By 1775 Kentucky's first school opened in a fort at Harrods-burg, and the teacher, Mrs. William Coomes, got her pay in buf-falo steak, jerked venison and corn. That same year a small boy was roasting a blue-wing duck he'd killed, when a gaunt man stumbled out of the woods and asked to share the meat. The child reported that "the man seemed half-starved and ate all of it." The man, who stayed and became leader of the local colony, turned out to be George Rogers Clark, of the famed Lewis and Clark Expedi-tion.

Soon after the first white women arrived, living began to be a bit more comfortable and inns sprang up. In 1781 laws were

passed forbidding an innkeeper to charge more than $10 for a gallon of shelled corn, $18 for a day's board, $6 for a featherbed, $4 for horses' keep . . . and not over $15 for a half pint of whiskey. But settlements grew and food became more plentiful, so that by 1816, Bright's Inn near Stanford was serving corn pone made in a Dutch oven, venison, pork and beef roasted on a spit, and for temperance guests, a cup of mitheglin, a drink of dark honey and vinegar. Total charge: twenty-five cents.

Even twenty-five cents was more than one family could afford when father, mother and two children reached Cloverport in 1816 to ferry across the Ohio. Col. David Murray, a boy at the time, remembered how "old Minerva, a colored slave, seeing the condition of the children, went into the house and came out with a plate heaped with slices of homemade bread and butter and a pitcher of milk . . . she seated the children on the steps of my father's house and fed them." This was the Lincoln family and one of the hungry children was Abraham, who no doubt sampled other regional fare including Kentucky oysters. The "oysters" are chitlin's (hog intestines), and a chitlin' feast includes potato salad and cider.

In ante-bellum Kentucky, young ladies often went into declines and were whisked away to places like Big Boone Lick to drink the sulphur water. I suspect such indispositions were sometimes caused by too much good food, too many meals of spiced black bean soup, potato rolls like those still turned out in Sam Mc-Meekin's Louisville home, fried chicken with cream gravy, and for dessert Moss Rose cake which tastes as much like poetry as it sounds. Beaten biscuits, Christmas fruit cake and a Tipsy Pecan cake were other items to abet the fashionable decline.

A lot of Blue Grass families agree today with the pronouncement of a pre-Revolutionary preacher to his congregation:

"Heaven is a Kentucky of a place."

Virginia

GINGERBREAD SAVES A HOME

"She touched the soil of Virginia with her little foot and the wilderness became home." That was Alyce Jordan's epitaph when she died on January 7, 1650 at Four Mile Tree Plantation, on the James River in Virginia. Almost certainly Alyce had discovered the hickory-smoked hams of Smithfield, because white men had learned from the Indians there how to cure the razorback hams. She probably baked the ham as Virginians still do, twenty minutes to the pound so that the fat is translucent amber, the meat dark-red, then sliced to paper thinness. A real Smithfield should never be desecrated with brown sugar, cloves, cider or even champagne . . . but served plain. These proud hams were supplied regularly to English royalty.

Not many miles from Smithfield is Wrenn's Mill, which has turned out water-ground white cornmeal since the 1600's. With it Alyce Jordan and her contemporaries made another classic Virginia food, spoon bread, baked slowly in a deep dish so that the fluffy dough under the golden-crisp crust is so soft it must be spooned to the plate. In lush plantation days, children of the household servants formed a brigade of runners to whisk the hot spoon bread from the outside kitchen ovens to the dining room.

Tansy pudding was born in an early Virginia kitchen, and this concoction, rich with eggs and cream, seasoned with spinach and tansy juice, wine and nutmeg, and cooked like an omelet, is still a company special.

The first fragrances to float from Virginia kitchens were created by the corn puddings, black-eyed peas and pumpkin fritters cooked by girls from the Brides' Ship of 1619, whose passages had been paid for in tobacco. Before that, the half-starving Jamestown

settlement had been saved by Captain John Smith, who persuaded
the Indians to give them corn and fish, and providentially then
"there came into the river a flight of fowl and sick men were
restored to health."

Once past the lean times, Virginians began skillfully combining
Indian fare with food from all over the world. Curiously enough,
peanuts came back to the New World on slave ships from Africa,
having journeyed to Spain with Columbus and from there to
Africa to trade for spices, gold and ivory. The little nut was put on
slave ships because it was the cheapest available food for the
cargo of human freight. So it was that a native American food
came home after circling half the world.

Treasured sugar was used only by elegant plantation families
in early Virginia days. The women of the house unlocked the
cupboard when need arose and with special shears snipped from
the cone enough for each meal. Salt in a huge bowl with a base
heavy enough to prevent its tipping over was the centerpiece of
many family tables, and Virginians followed the old English
custom of having important guests seated near the host at the
head of the table, or "above the salt."

Food in the 1600's apparently was a good deal better in homes
than in inns. At least there is on record a doleful comment from
a Reverend Jones who sat down to eat in a tavern in New Kent,
looked at the food, then offered this grace: "God bless the owl
that ate the fowl and left the bones for Mr. Jones."

To keep marauders out of their kitchen gardens, planted with
herbs brought from England, Virginians built ha-has—hidden
ditches at the edges of lawn and garden which worked as well as
garden walls and had the advantage of not spoiling the breath-
taking views from wide plantation verandas. Parsley and thyme
from the kitchen gardens added zest to a pie that was stranger
than the traditional four-and-twenty blackbirds. This one was
made of robins!

Sturgeon twelve feet long swam in Virginia waters. Arranged
on strawberry leaves and seasoned with parsley and sage, the fish
was baked with a bouquet sauce of wine and mushrooms. Trout
was so plentiful that often a housewife simply took her frying
pan to the stream and scooped up a mess to be cleaned and fried
for dinner.

Woodward says that a reasonably well-behaved traveler in

Virginia in the eighteenth century could live for a year without expense . . . just visiting. Old Dominion families tell of ancestors who rode along the highways, hoping to find suitable strangers who'd want to come to stay for a day or a week or even a month.

When Thomas Jefferson's father in Williamsburg acquired 400 acres of good Virginia land in exchange for "the Raleigh Tavern's biggest bowl of arrack punch," he joined a giddy company of Virginia gentlemen who, in colonial days, won and lost plantations at poker and dice. With arrack punch the inn served Tipsy cake, a sponge cake so light the cook didn't dare breathe on it when it came from the pan. The layers, sprinkled with sherry wine, were spread with strawberry jam, apricot jam, plum jelly, orange marmalade and almonds, and the whole smothered in whipped cream and brandy.

Williamsburg today is history come to life. Experts were so determined to be accurate that they even reconstructed a dog of a breed thought to have been lost for two centuries. The reconstructed dog was not, however, as successful as the sweetbreads and oysters, the ash cakes and bell fritters. He got mange, bit people and was finally presented to the United States Marines, to be replaced by a modern but amiable hound. The creature's ancient ancestors, however, helped guard the first flocks of sheep from wolves, so that Virginia plantations could have on table such items as Mutton à la Royal, with bacon, veal, "all sorts of sweet herbs and an onion stuck with cloves"; fricassee of lamb with shallots and wine; and succulent Virginia oysters dressed with brown butter.

Breads "hot and new" were part of every eighteenth-century Virginia meal, and so were thin beaten biscuits, cold. Travelers claimed that the early morning thump of cooks in plantation kitchens, beating out the biscuits, could be heard far down the road. Negro cooks argued heatedly over the number of thumps a good beaten biscuit should have. Nothing under 100 was tolerated, and company called for 300 to 500 strokes of the rolling pin or wooden thumper.

Almost every Virginia recipe of the 1700's and, in fact, almost all southern recipes of that era, had two versions—one plain, the other for company. Company recipes increased the eggs, butter and cream twofold in such desserts as Grateful pudding, which called for "cream in, instead of milk" when it was for company.

Of life in Virginia, William Byrd II wrote in 1726:

My doors are open to everybody . . . yet I have no bills to pay and half a crown will rest undisturbed in my pocket for many moons together . . . I live in a kind of independence of everyone but Providence.

Those restless settlers who picked up stakes and moved west found frontier life a far cry from Tidewater luxury. The wife of General George Martin had eighteen children to cook for while her brawny husband, his thick beard braided and tucked inside his shirt, marched off to fight Indians up and down the wild border regions. She gathered wild garlic and served it stewed with vinegar. All the small game birds her son shot were cooked at her fireplace in pot pie or in crusty cornmeal; black-eyed peas, wild persimmons and corn were often on the menu and later, when she came by enough molasses, a spicy soda cookie she called Cry Baby.

All over Virginia, from Tidewater to frontier, women made gingerbread, and there are as many recipes as there are First Family names in that state. But most famous of all was the one made by Sweet Molly, or Mary Ball Washington, mother of George. Her recipe for the gingerbread she served to so many of history's great, including Lafayette, has now become a modern mix. Sale of the recipe financed the reconstruction of her home in Fredericksburg . . . not a gingerbread house, perhaps, but a house that gingerbread saved.

Florida

FLAVORED WITH ORANGE BLOSSOMS

I remember many Florida meals with affection, but especially one dinner cooked outdoors in February, on the edge of a jungle full of chattering monkeys. Potatoes wrapped in paper were boiled in a big black pot of resin until they reached mealy perfection. With them came platters of just-caught fish from the nearby Indian River, fried over the open fire by a trio of silent, quick-moving Seminole Indians. From a kettle of deep, smoking fat came the hush-puppies, crisp and brown.

We ate in the flickering light of a campfire at a pine table on the edge of the jungle, and for dessert we were each handed sun-ripe oranges and the special sharp knife an orange grower always carries with him, stuck into a sheath at his belt. I am proud of having learned the technique of making one swift, unbroken cir-cular peel and then dissecting the fruit without breaking a fiber. It's not imagination that an orange picked and peeled that way has special sweetness and flavor.

Over hefty mugs of coffee our hosts told the story, now fairly well known, about the hush-puppy being created by a busy cook who was stirring up a batch of corn bread for a fish-fry. Half a dozen hungry puppies were frolicking around the kitchen floor, and to keep them quiet, the cook fried a few spoonfuls of the corn-meal batter in the fish kettle, tossing the crunchy morsels to the dogs with the admonition, "All right now, hush puppies."

My trip that year was a hectic one, with daily broadcasts up and down the state, from lakes, orange groves, sponge-diving villages and shiny resorts. Once a blackbird pie almost put my guest and me in jail. Marjorie Kinnan Rawlings had driven in from that de-lightfully unorthodox farm of hers, Cross Creek, and was on the air describing the blue crabs she traveled fifty miles into the scrub to get, hunting them by night in hidden jungle streams and then combining them with cream and butter for a superb Crab New-burgh. Suddenly she launched into a rhapsody on the subject of the blackbirds she shot in her orange grove and converted into a deep-dish pie. After the broadcast the station reported in alarm that the sheriff had been on the telephone, warning Marjorie that she was using my program to recommend a violation of the state game laws! So I never got to eat blackbird pie, but settled happily for a much more toothsome one made with Florida syrup and pecans.

Because Florida gave sunshine and sanctuary to my mother in her last years, it became as familiar to me as my native Middle West. When my family first moved there, I went down to see them in their little house near Orlando and had the rapturous experience of sleeping the moonlit night through in a grove of fragrant, flowering orange trees.

Another wonderful Florida experience is to explore the keys. If you like to fish from dawn to dusk, one of the smaller keys will suit you, but if you'd rather have your fish caught and cooked for you (I would), Key West is the place to head for. There they are proud of green turtle steak and turtle soup. The turtle-crawls (aquatic farms) ship the succulent green hawkbills and loggerheads all over the country, and can the soup, too.

The keys have been invaded through the years by pirates and wreckers, seafaring men from Spain and France, British colonials from the Bahamas, Cuban patriots, Tories from New England during the Revolution—and the cooking has inherited something from each. There is the Spanish influence, especially in *arroz con polo* . . . chicken with saffron rice. Cuban-style bread, with its tooth-challenging crust, is usually served in chunks two or three inches long. Other special Cuban dishes are roast beef stuffed with hard-boiled eggs, called *bolichi;* an elaborate beef stew— *alcoporado*—made with herbs, pepper, olives and raisins. Cuban bean soup is a rich dark-brown and can be a meal, followed by green coconut ice cream for dessert, or cream cheese with guava paste. Key coffee is so thick and strong that it is drunk *"un bochito"*—a sip at a time.

On the keys white sand blazes in the sun and clouds of mauve and pink are piled above a painted ocean. Almost as colorful are the fruits—Surinam cherries that make a spicy red preserve, delicately sweet Chinese limes, rose apples, tamarinds and purple star apples.

You could have a different fish, too, for nearly every day in the year . . . but not the electric rays which Marjorie Rawlings once fried up and ate with grits, believing they were flounder!

Rarest of Florida fishes is the pompano, which so delighted a railroad surveying engineer that he wrote the word on his map at the spot where he'd first tasted it, and the town has been Pompano ever since. Florida cooks are adept at encasing this delicately flavored fish in a paper bag along with plenty of herbs and seasoning, and bringing it forth in all its glory as Pompano en Papilotte.

Down in Pensacola's magnolia-shaded streets, where people still believe the old Spanish proverb, "the night is made for sleep and the day for rest," a favorite food is broiled red snapper . . .

caught that same morning, with the smell and taste of the sea still in it.

The Indian agriculturalists had fishbone hoes and cultivated their fields intensively for centuries before the first colonists, a group of French adventurers, arrived in the 1560's. These gay dogs paid little attention to Indian farming techniques, and as a result, nearly starving, had to send to Cuba for food. The arrival of the supply ships gave away the location of the one lone French colony, Fort Caroline, and it was promptly taken over by the Spanish.

Florida was virtually emptied of settlers three times during its years of being wrangled over by France, Spain and England. Yet there are traces of all three influences. Though the early French were no farmers, one of their number, André Michaux, did some rough pioneering along botanical lines and was the first to describe the pawpaw and call it "the melon that climbs a tree." He also reported, way back there, that papaya leaves would tenderize meat.

One of the oddest things that happens in Florida today is the butchering of an animal which the Florida State Legislature says does not exist—the razorback hog, those fierce beasts said to have descended from hogs brought in by the Spanish in the 1600's. The law was passed because persons suspected of stealing hogs frequently got off by claiming the animals under suspicion were wild razorbacks. So now there are butcherings every fall of the hog-that-doesn't-exist. The lard is tried out, the cracklings are combined with cornmeal to make crackling bread and the chitlin's with slabs of sowbelly to accompany the inevitable grits. Razorback hams and bacons fill many a larder.

The year of our Florida broadcasts, we drove from the neon glitter of Miami to the little gulf port of Tarpon Springs, where Greek sponge fishermen go to sea in a fleet of bright-sailed boats built exactly as they were for sponge-fishing 2,000 years ago. At Easter carloads of spring lamb arrive at the Springs, and Greek housewives stuff them with pecans and rice doused with olive oil. Airy golden honey puffs, with a hint of cinnamon and lemon, accompany the sweet, thick Greek coffee.

William R. Van Dersal in *The American Land* says citrus fruits first arrived in St. Augustine in 1579. Some oranges and limes went wild, but most remained in cultivation and newer, better species of orange, lemon, lime and grapefruit were developed. Until about fifty years ago, oranges were Christmas delicacies for millions of American children, and grapefruit was considered a freak in regions remote from citrus-growing states. In 1897 newspapers reported that a cluster of sixteen grapefruit sold in New York as a curiosity, with twenty-five boxes of them bid up to $156.25. Not long before that, a New York dealer who took a chance on buying a small shipment of grapefruit found a native Floridian to whom he offered the lot at any price because nobody else "knew what the darned stuff was."

Winter Haven, where I broadcast the story of citrus culture, now honors the orange at a week-long festival in January or February with some quarter of a million visitors watching the parades and sampling oranges in juice, sherbet, cakes and pies.

It seems incredible in this vitamin-conscious world that until nearly 1930, canned fruit juices were practically unknown. Grapefruit was the first of the canned juices, then tomato, orange and pineapple. Since Europe has had a tremendous effect on our eating, maybe it's only fair that our canned juices have made the only noticeable change in English and continental breakfasts in hundreds of years.

Now that its high Vitamin-C content has been discovered, Florida's guava may be coming into its own. The guava is another native American food that went traveling, being taken to India over four hundred years ago where it was used for making that wine-red, distinctively flavored jelly we now fancy with cream cheese and crackers.

A tiny crescent-shaped island named Estero furnishes another Florida specialty, coquinas . . . tiny clams no longer than half an inch that stand on their heads and burrow in the sand after each receding wave. The inhabitants of Estero have a Christmas of their own, with a barefoot Santa Clause who comes in a speedboat and greets the children under a huge palm tree, hands out gifts, and then whisks off in his boat.

South Carolina

MEMORABLE SUNDAY DINNERS

"They looked upon life gratefully and found it good."

Thomas R. Waring said that of South Carolinians in the golden era right after the Revolution. It is still true of many down there . . . or so it has seemed when I've gone visiting the galleried houses of Charleston and the fairy-tale gardens of old plantations.

Josephine Pinckney, descendant of one of South Carolina's founding families, was one of the first to delight me and my radio audience with descriptions of the state's food and customs. The traditional Sunday dinner at three is so fixed in Charleston that Josephine used it for the title of one of her distinguished novels. Children learn their manners at these family affairs, attended by all the relatives within driving distance, including "a clutch of cousins."

Afternoon sun slants through the slatted West Indian jalousies, and the family arranges itself in Heppelwhite chairs around a table set with heirloom blue India ware. A typical Pinckney Sunday dinner would start with delicate shrimp soup, prelude to the great silver platter of fricasseed chicken with side dishes of sweet potatoes, squash and macaroni. To finish off, peach ice cream, made that morning and served from a big china bowl, accompanied by layer cake on a glass pedestal.

These Sunday dinners have grown more restrained than when a visitor of the 1820's described a meal that ended with eight pies down one side of the table, six bowls of syllabub down the other, and in the center innumerable floating islands and three-foot-tall cakes. This was the sort of fare that made a historian hazard a guess that South Carolina had so many rich young widows because their husbands died of overeating. The ladies had to be more

moderate in order to get into the tiny-waisted crinolines they
wore, and so lived longer, the writer opined.

But for all the lavish hospitality, old Charleston houses still turn
their shoulders to the street and, in privacy, face their walled
gardens of heartsease and magnolia, heatherbell and hawthorn.
Their owners believe shrimp is best when you buy it in the early
morning from a peddler who cries:

> *"Ro-ro swimp, ro-ro swimp,*
> *Ro-ro-ro-ro-ro-ro swimp,*
> *Come and git yo swimp."*

They dip shrimp in egg and crumbs and fry it to pale gold in
deep fat, or use it for a stew with seasonings of garlic, thyme and
bay leaves. The plantation country is famous for baked shrimp
paste made of ground shrimp and biscuits, tartly seasoned, sliced
thin and served cold.

Records show that living was pretty thin in 1687, when the
colonists had "hardly overcome ye want of victuals." Each settler
at Charleston was rationed nine pounds of beef and fourteen of
dried peas. It was the old familiar story . . . strangers in a strange
land, going hungry in the midst of plenty. They tried farming,
but their first crops failed and they had to bribe the Indians to
bring them fish and venison to supplement the pint of peas
handed out each day. They faced near-starvation before their
crops improved and they discovered the oyster beds known for
centuries to the Indians. They imported cattle, hogs, corn and
flour from Virginia, too, and picked up some of the Indian techniques of hunting and fishing.

A later French Huguenot group arrived in 1685, after Louis XIV
revoked the privileges guaranteed them by the Edict of Nantes.
Charleston's sophisticated cuisine today is a flavorsome mixture of
French and English, with a dash of Spanish added by Sephardic
Jews who were among the city's first citizens, and later seasonings
of German and Italian . . . and a fillip from imaginative Negro
cooks.

Charleston she-crab soup, famous the world over, is made with
whipped cream, mace and sherry. Peddlers identify the she-crab
and charge more for it than the he-crab. The female of the South
Carolina cooter or terrapin is also preferred, and cooter stew is

made with quantities of fresh butter, sweet cream, hard-cooked eggs, nutmeg and wine.

Carolina oysters, so tiny that old recipes often call for one hundred or more, have been prized from the earliest days, but it was the Negro cooks who did them best in a stew gently seasoned with benne, or sesame seed. Legend has it that these exotic seeds were brought on slave ships for good luck. Anyway, modern South Carolina makes benne brittle with them, and thin benne cookies rich with brown sugar and butter.

In 1671 Charleston became the scene of a momentous historical accident. A sea captain enroute to London, blown off his course, put in there for a few days. He struck up an acquaintance with one Dr. Henry Woodward and gave him a present of a little bag of Madagascar rice which the doctor planted in his flower garden where it throve mightily. That little bag inaugurated the fabulous era of rice growing and plantation life, the importation of slaves on a large scale and the economy which failed so disastrously.

Although the economy was geared to rice, some plantation owners experimented with other crops. Thus in 1755 Henry Laurens succeeded in growing olives, capers, limes, ginger, blue and white grapes, French pears and Alpine strawberries on a four-acre tract. Planters had so many peaches that they were often fed to the hogs. Forty years after the Revolution a vineyard near Charleston turned out quality grapes for a fine local wine, and many plantations had figs, nectarines, pomegranates, apricots and sour oranges.

Trading ships carried chocolate, spices and rare wines to low-country plantation kitchens, where the chocolate went into Angel pie, a confection of sherry, beaten eggs, nutmeg, cream and chocolate.

When Lafayette landed in America to help the cause of freedom, he was entertained at the North Island plantation of Major Benjamin Huger. On the menu were the tiny ricebirds hunted by torch-carrying slaves and roasted in kitchen fireplaces until they were "sweet as new butter"; also wild pigeons in a flaky pie.

Beaufort County, which includes sixty-five islands, is filled with gracious historical houses that look like stage sets with their columns and gardens of wistaria, oleander and jessamine. A few cooks in the mellow old houses still make a rich yellow egg soup, with nutmeg and toasted bread crumbs afloat on top; a tender rice bread and a Confederate pudding perfected during the War Between the States . . . stacked-up slices of bread spread with jelly or jam, soaked in a milk and egg mixture and baked. Few people during that war could acquire the makings of the rich cream pie named Jeff Davis, nor the ingredients for a President Tyler pudding which is even richer, with eggs, brown sugar, cream, and fresh nutmeg grated on top.

Scotch-Irish Presbyterians came to Florence along with French Huguenots in the 1730's and Welsh Baptists arrived shortly after. All added contributions to the food pattern: Scotch shortbread, Welsh cold meat pies, the French breakfast of croissants and coffee with hot milk.

Upcountry, the mountain people ate poke salad, possum and potatoes, made velvet wine from dewberries, dried leather-breeches beans for winter, had peach leather for a favorite sweet.

One South Carolina custom that goes back to colonial days is the Dumb Supper. Girls get together and cook a special corn bread, using almost equal amounts of salt and cornmeal. Their young men stand by during the cooking, then all eat—in complete silence. At bedtime, if nobody has broken the silence, their dreams will disclose future husband or wife bringing a badly needed drink of water!

During the Revolution a British army officer came to discuss exchange of prisoners with Francis Marion, the famous Swamp Fox. The visitor saw soldiers eating roasted potatoes on pieces of bark and asked if that was their regular fare. Told that they had subsisted on it for weeks, he noted thoughtfully: "Such a people could not and ought not to be subdued."

Georgia

SYLLABUB AND JASMINE

The first roast pork dinner in America was probably eaten in 1540 in what is now Georgia. That was the year of the cross-country tour of De Soto's herd of pigs, from the Everglades to the Ozarks through a thousand wild and hostile miles of mountains, prairies, swamps, great rivers and plains. De Soto's footsore men, trailed by the reluctant pigs, halted, half-starved. No longer able to get food from the Indians, as a last resort they butchered the first of the pigs.

Georgia was almost two centuries away from settlement. The De Soto expedition went on to disaster. But like Cortez before him, De Soto left the nucleus for herds of both hogs and cattle, and by the time white men arrived to set up colonies, the Indians had learned to cure hams and to butcher both beef and pork.

Georgia's English colonists were mainly liberated inmates of debtors' prisons and almshouses for whom General James Oglethorpe planned a New World Utopia. They didn't want to farm, they didn't want to fight Indians. Although the ocean was full of seafood, and the woods of game, they lined up indolently at the public store for handouts of rice, cornmeal and salt fish.

Unwilling to give up his dream, General Oglethorpe sailed for Scotland and rallied 135 Highlanders who had been part of the 1715 Jacobite rebellion. They settled New Inverness, Georgia, arriving there in fine fighting mood, complete with plumes, kilts and family recipes for scones, collops and haggis. Haggis is the minced windpipe, pluck, skin and gristle of a sheep, mixed with broth and toasted oatmeal, sewed inside the sheep's paunch and boiled three hours, then served with a heated spoon to prevent chilling. For New Year's, turnips and potatoes go with it. Some of the Georgia Highlanders fought Indians, some farmed, some became cowherders in the upland country, profitably selling their beef to Oglethorpe.

Meantime, in Savannah—one of America's few planned cities— a daring experiment got underway when the trustees planted a ten-acre garden with apples, peaches, pears, olives, grapes, pomegranates, even coconut palms, pineapples, coffee and sugar cane, plantain and tropical nuts. Orange trees lined the garden walks, and orange growing was so successful that a large quantity of Georgia orange juice was exported to England in the 1760's.

But the dream of diversified agriculture was doomed. Georgia, set up as a non-slave state, could not hold out as the plantation system crept steadily southward. Eli Whitney, visiting a Georgia island in 1793, finally got his cotton gin perfected. Cotton growing and slavery seemed inevitable companions. No planter wanted to fool around with food crops when cotton meant quick and easy money.

The plantation system brought Negro cooks to create some of the memorable dishes of Georgia, such as whole hams boiled in tubfuls of tea and black molasses, basted with beer, coated with catsup and mustard and for the final half hour in the oven, brown sugar. They scorched sugar for a dessert called Burned Cream, which came to the table festooned with whipped cream and burnt almonds. They lavished eggs and cream on the delightfully named Serene Pudding. On company occasions, everyday biscuits had extra lard, butter and eggs added and became High Biscuits.

The amount of food and drink consumed by the average family in the early 1800's was prodigious. Historian W. E. Woodward pictures an 1807 dinner party given by Kitty Earle of Augusta. The wide hall and tall-ceilinged rooms of the porticoed mansion glowed with the light of sperm-oil lamps, and the dining table, set for twelve, twinkled with pink-shaded candles. The hostess, in a gown of yellow China silk, saw to it that everyone had sherry in the drawing room before the dinner, which consisted of turtle soup followed by brook trout fried in butter, then baked sweet potatoes and roast ham, wild turkey stuffed with walnuts and cornmeal, accompanied by dishes of rice, asparagus and green beans, with a cooling orange sherbet to give the guests a breather before they tackled the cold venison, stewed corn and cheese, and the dessert of corn fritters with syrup and sweet potato pie. Madeira wine, beer and milk were the beverages.

Oyster suppers, held outdoors by the light of a hunter's moon, are still as popular in the Savannah area as they were in plantation days. A huge sheet of tin covers the crackling fire, and the master of ceremonies spreads the small, delicately flavored bivalves with a rake, and at the precise moment they are ready, serves them with individual cups of melted butter mixed with lemon or Worcestershire. Hoppin' John (black-eyed peas and rice), green salad and quantities of strong black coffee complete the feast.

In the elegant homes of Savannah, guests discover such delights as crab soufflé seasoned with nutmeg and sherry, chicken pies with tiny mushrooms and hard-cooked eggs, corn bought from the "green cawn man" and made into creamy corn puddings, fried Georgia peach pie.

Savannahans still go home from the office at noon for lunch and a siesta. And many families still observe the bird's-eye pepper ritual, mashing the fresh-picked green peppers in the plate just before the soup is poured in. The peppers are so hot that all but the hardiest remove them from the soup before eating. Pompey's Head is another Georgia classic—ground beef, salt pork, spices and herbs molded into the shape of a bristly head.

There were many things Fanny Kemble hated about Georgia. The famous actress, who interrupted her career to marry and live on an island off the east coast, violently disapproved of slavery and recorded her convictions forthrightly. But she did write lovingly of the local shad which she said was "nothing like the animal you northerners devour," the mullet caught near her jasmine-draped island, and the mutton which she said seemed to be sweetened by the deep plantation grass, the peaches from trees that grew wild in the wake of the early Spanish missionaries.

Georgia's real peach romance, though, is the Elberta. It began, fittingly, in a white-columned mansion in Marshalville in 1857, when a gentleman living in Delaware sent an assortment of peach-tree buddings to Samuel Rumph. The trees flourished, and Mrs. Rumph dropped seeds from a few of the fruits into her sewing basket. More than ten years later her grandson, Samuel, decided to start an orchard of his own. Mrs. Rumph dug out the seeds, dry and old, and for fun, Samuel planted them.

An accidental cross-pollination took place, a casual miracle worked by the wind and the bees. When the time came for the first bearing of the trees, in 1870, they produced great golden peaches, a species brand-new in the fruit world. Samuel named the marvel Elberta for his wife. This was one of America's first valuable commercial peaches, and Samuel was one of the first orchardists to package his fruit attractively and to work out refrigeration for shipping.

Columbus took pimientos to Europe from the New World and they became so popular in Spain that pimiento growing was soon big business there. So it happened that practically all our pimientos were Spanish-imported until an enterprising Georgian brought in a packet of seeds and began experimenting. Now the pimiento is back home, and both growing and canning are done in the southeastern United States.

Peanuts and Georgia have had a close relationship ever since that genius and ex-slave, George Washington Carver, proved that goobers can turn into axle grease, shampoo, cooking oil and dozens of other profitable products. But most of all, Georgians are fond of peanuts for eating. The National Peanut Council in Atlanta has a collection of recipes that include a soup combining onions, peanut butter, and tomato juice; also something they call Shanghai Special: chopped peanuts and bite-size bits of pork browned in fat, simmered with celery, onions and seasonings and served with Georgia rice.

Syllabub is one of Georgia's most festive desserts, pure cream churned into a lather with a dash of sherry. I told on the air about a syllabub churn given me by a listener, and ever since people have been sending me syllabub recipes. I like best the centuries-old one that tells you to start by milking the cow straight into the churn. In Georgia it would probably be a Jersey cow, because Dr. Benjamin Hunt went all the way to the Isle of Jersey in the 1870's to select the cows that started profitable dairy-farming enterprises and restored many plantations.

Mississippi

The French *voyageurs,* exploring the upper Mississippi in the 1690's, set up trading posts in Indian towns. They ate the same food as the Indians and especially liked a cake from dried persimmons and a gruel called Coon'te, concocted from a brier root pounded in a mortar, strained and cooked.

When Pierre LeMoyne, Sieur d'Ilberville, descending the river from the north, established the first colony in 1699 along the Bay of Biloxi, his settlers discovered they could get chickens as well as fish and dried buffalo meat from the Indians. It is believed that the chickens came ashore from a ship wrecked off the coast four years earlier.

Biloxi brides from Paris were delighted with the fruit they found —apples, pears, peaches, wild grapes, cherries and melons. Within a few years they were developing such dishes as the famed Mississippi court bouillon, which starts with the traditional *roux* (shortening, flour and onion) and adds sliced redfish, green pepper, a substantial touch of garlic and assorted herbs.

From the earliest days, a good Mississippi kitchen always had its Soup Bunch. The modern version includes two carrots, celery, a quarter head of crisp cabbage, an onion and a ripe tomato, a handful of string beans and peas, a turnip, a potato, okra, and a sprig or two of parsley. The tomato would not have appeared in the Soup Bunch of pre-Revolutionary days because it was suspect then. But Mississippi helped give tomatoes to the nation as a food in the 1870's when N. Piazza brought seed from Italy and began scientific cultivation.

French brides planted honeysuckle and roses, trumpet vines and wistaria along with the crepe myrtle and camellia japonica which have made their gardens year-round delights. They discovered, too, the notable flavor of the small oysters still hawked in the early morning by the "oyster ma-an from Pass Christia-a-an."

All women worked hard in their new homes, but the French kept a certain grace even when they wore shoes made on their own plantations and clothes of homespun. John Bartram was surprised when in 1777 he saw a French planter leave his plow, walk gallantly to the edge of the field and offer his hand to a lady to help her across the furrows.

Ante-bellum days around Natchez saw the plantations and manor houses at their luxurious best. Coffee—hot, black and strong—was brought to guests before sunrise, mint juleps started the day, and late breakfasts were served on shaded balconies and verandas. Breakfast usually included three kinds of meat, an assortment of eggs, hominy grits, hot biscuits and waffles.

One far-sighted planter, John C. Jenkins, experimented with fruits and vegetables, producing a quince that weighed a pound and a half, new varieties of peas and assorted prize apples and pears. He foresaw modern marketing methods when he shipped a basket of his pears in an icebox to New York in the 1840's. In his own home he kept fresh fruit in good condition until late winter and loved to watch the faces of his guests when a servant appeared with a silver plate of juicy pears and peaches at Christmas time.

Biloxi, where the streets paved with oyster shells are shaded by moss-draped oaks, is famous for outdoor oyster bakes, and for the picturesque Blessing of the Shrimp Fleet, a three-day festival that includes the first Sunday in August. The gaily decorated shrimp boats proceed along the waterfront and there are street parades and a pretty Shrimp Queen.

New to northerners is chicken bread, made of flour, cornmeal, shortening, salt and milk, and baked in the frying pan the chicken was done in—much as Yorkshire pudding is prepared in beef drippings.

For a long while only the servants ate corn pone and pot liquor, but then a plantation mistress noticed that the colored children seemed healthier than her own. She decided that their habit of dipping the corn pone in the liquor left over from cooking turnip greens might have something to do with it, so she tried it on her own family. Experts know now that pot liquor brims with vitamins and minerals, but southerners relished it before the word vitamin entered our language and our consciousness.

During the tragic years of the Civil War the Confederacy was always hungry, and Mississippi women devised pie crusts from potatoes, salad oil from sunflower seed, a leavening for bread and cakes from corncob ashes. In besieged Vicksburg, one woman made soup from her pet jay bird, and in the market dressed rats were priced at two dollars and a half.

The South preserved a bitter humor at its plight. When Union soldiers arrived in Vicksburg, they found this menu:

Soup: mule-tail
Boiled mule bacon with polk greens
Roast saddle of mule
Entrees: Mule head stuffed, Reb fashion; mule beef jerk à la Yankee; mule liver hashed à la explosion
Dessert: Cotton berry pie on ironclad; china berry tart
Liquor: Mississippi water, vintage 1492—very inferior, $3.00, limestone water—Jeff Davis & Co., Props.

And a newspaper writer commented:

The laugh is about the cheapest thing to fatten on. Some can't even raise the price of that.

Arkansas

POSSUM IN THE PERSIMMON

My writer friend, Thyra Samter Winslow, claims that Arkansas is no longer "the state nobody knows." When hundreds of young men forsook their native state after World War II, Arkansas set up a commission to do some face-lifting. Towns imported shade trees and fringed outskirts with swimming pools, parks and playgrounds. The commission nudged the best hotels and restaurants into giving visitors a chance to discover what Arkansas can do with food and atmosphere.

One hotel built its eight floors against a mountainside, so that you can step from your room onto the cool greenery of a mountain trail. At another, you eat in a dining room with a flower-ringed fountain, and the specialty is Bing cherries molded around chicken salad.

Arkansans consider it practically illegal, Thyra points out, to serve cold light bread more than once a day, and so at every meal you get battalions of steaming corn dodgers, high, handsome hot biscuits or fresh-from-the-oven rolls. Hot breads accompany Arkansas-style chicken, which simmers in a skillet first, then goes into the oven where its juicy tenderness is blended with a Creole sauce.

In Eureka Springs, a hotel features a fifteen-foot salad table in its dining room. You mix your own and eat it while you wait for the remainder of the meal, choosing from bowls of fresh greens, tiny beets, sliced tomatoes, onions, green peppers, thin slices of cheese and three kinds of dressing.

Thus the food picture in Arkansas has changed dramatically from that pictured by the folk-singer of 1882, who complained:

> *"His bread it was corn dodgers, and beef I could not chaw,*
> *He charged me fifty cents a meal in the state of Arkansas."*

By the end of his stay, the singer got so thin on sage and sassafras that he was able to hide behind a straw.

In the 1840's, isolated farmers began experimenting with orchards and Arkansas apples began to win first prize at big-city exhibitions. These were the forerunners of the orchards that now in spring spread a fragrant drift of blossoms across the country-side between Bentonville and Fayetteville. Each year thousands of tourists make the apple-blossom pilgrimage, the good-food collectors stopping off at farms enroute where housekeepers gladly share recipes for deep-dish apple pies, cinnamon apple tarts, amber-gold jelly and a special tart-sweet applesauce made with lemon peel and a generous sprinkling of cinnamon and nutmeg.

Peaches are another of the state's food excitements. The Chero-kee Indians, forced north and west by greedy whites, brought the cuttings of peach trees originally planted in America by the Spanish. Peaches did not become a commercial crop, however, until Elbertas were introduced about 1900. Now the blossoms in all their spicy pink glory are honored by springtime tours, and cooks produce banner peach shortcakes, ice cream, pies, preserves and a marvelous golden peach butter.

Watermelons were a major Cherokee crop, too, but not until the white settlers took over did the competitions for the biggest and best melons start. However, when a Hempstead county farmer produced one weighing 195 pounds, the frenzy abated. People will stare at a 195-pound melon, but it's the ripe, juicy everyday size they buy. A well-thought-of Arkansas dessert is cubed watermelon with a little sherry poured over, chilled the entire day before serving. Watermelon must be picked ripe, and expert tappers know the right moment by the plunk.

Thyra Winslow says you can tell where you are in her native state by the food. In the bayou country, where cypresses shadow the coffee-colored water, plantation kitchens are lush with peach cobblers, roast wild duck, candied yams, fried chicken, fluffy biscuits. Around Texarkana, cattlemen in boots and Stetsons eat the typical baked pinto beans and barbecued beef of the Southwest.

Along the Arkansas River fried spoonbill catfish is accompanied by hot corn bread and cold buttermilk, or sweet young catfish is fried in cornmeal and served whole with baked potatoes and turnip greens. In the hills, the country folk still relish a meal such as Otto Rayburn describes in *The Ozark Country*—bacon with cracklin' corn bread, butter worked and shaped with a homemade cedar paddle, baked beans, lettuce wilted with bacon and vinegar, bread and apple jelly, and for dessert dried peaches and gingerbread.

The Ozark word for wild honey and sorghum is long-sweetnin'. Store-bought sugar is saved mostly for Christmas cakes and candies. The end of many meals is boiling-hot black coffee sweetened with wild honey, and fried pies—dried apples or peaches encased in lard pastry.

Arkansas pioneers really were great travelers. One family record shows the husband born in Florida, the wife in Tennessee, and four of the children in Kentucky. Forging west in their wagons, the settlers brought with them secrets of curing hams, roasting pork ribs before open fires, making soda biscuits and molasses cakes.

They also brought superstitions. To this day, when someone in a mountain household dies, it is the custom to tell the bees. The head of the family knocks on the hive and announces the name of the one who has died. Not to do this means, many believe, that the bees will desert the hive before the honey is ready. It is also considered bad luck to shake out a dinner cloth after dark, and Ozark housekeepers have a prejudice against letting their dishwater boil.

At hog-killing time everybody makes hog's-head cheese, sausage pungent with sage, and pig's stomach stuffed with bread crumbs and herbs. Roasted raccoon, roasted beaver-tail and baked opossum are Arkansas dishes about which there is a difference of opinion. Baked possum, however, has become such a famous regional dish that the Polk County Possum Club holds a festival every August. Persimmon trees, in which are perched live possums, line the streets. Possums baked with red peppers are dished out on mats of sassafrass twigs and eaten with baked sweet potatoes.

Venison and wild turkey are gourmets' delights in the sophisticated resort of Hot Springs, where expensive tastes have been indulged for more than a century. Hot Springs claimed that even the local stagecoach bandits were polite, and cited instances where they spread clean linen handkerchiefs by the roadside for the ladies to sit on, while they courteously removed money and jewels and wished the visitors "a pleasant good day."

Float fishing is a fine, lazy way to see some of Arkansas' handsome woods and streams. You can take a two-, four- or seven-day float, and unlikely as it may sound, you will float right back to the spot you started from. There is a camp at the end of each day's trip, and the floating trick is accomplished by following old waterways in a kind of circular course. The floats are flatboats, some equipped with motors and shaded by striped awnings. The fish you catch are fried over a campfire for supper.

Back from a recent Arkansas trip, Thyra Winslow reported that her favorite greens, mustard and beet and turnip tops, are now being canned by a firm in Springdale, although it's hard to find them in stores outside the Middle West. The only change in the food she remembers from her childhood is that hush-puppies are now being made finger-size and some are even quick-frozen. Out there a hush-puppy is highly seasoned with onion and when it comes out of the deep fat, it is crisp outside, but inside as soft and fluffy as good mashed potatoes.

In the best Arkansas shortcakes, she adds, the light, rich biscuit dough is buttered hot and then sprinkled with clover honey before the sliced (never mashed) peaches or strawberries are added. This shortcake, says Thyra (and I agree) is "no relation, none at all, to the shortcakes of the East . . . a cold piece of sponge cake covered with whipped cream and three or four anemic strawberries."

West Virginia

A FLOOD OF PUMPKINS

The Lilly family of West Virginia holds a record for kissing cousins. Everybody in the South is accustomed to claiming kin, even to the sixth and seventh cousin, but when the Lillys gather for two days in August to eat fried chicken and country ham, even the South is a bit startled, for 75,000 persons overflow the tiny mountain village of Flat Top. Nobody has to produce his family tree, either, to get a slice of pie made from wild huckleberries or a wedge of devil's food cake with seafoam frosting, for everybody knows that the Lillys have ample families and long lives. Example: "Father" Lilly was 114 when he died in 1810, and his wife lived to be 110.

West Virginia, with its contrast of porticoed plantation homes in the Panhandle and isolated cabins in the wild mountain gorges, has always been known for its rugged countryside and rugged people. When George II made it forbidden territory for settlers, the Germans explained that they could not read the edict, while the Scotch—who could—paid no attention at all and went right on establishing farms on cliffs so steep that stories arose of farmers who fell out of cornfields while plowing, and husbandmen who used ladders to climb to their apple orchards.

A mainstay of early frontier families was stewed squirrel, still a delicacy down there, cooked with wild garlic, onion, thyme and bacon. One pioneer killed twenty bears in a single autumn season to keep his family in fresh meat.

Medieval splendor attends the Riding Tournaments staged by residents of the Smoke Hole, when knights on horseback tilt at suspended rings. Tri-City Fairgrounds at Petersburg has the biggest of these tournaments, but the ancient game is played all through the mysterious gorge country where people still talk of "ham meat" and a "budget" of flour, "beastes" (farm animals), and "ghostes" in haunted houses. The few who penetrate these deep, shadowed gorges and follow first trails up the hollows will probably be invited to dine on home-cured ham and turnip greens, hoecakes, hominy grits, jam made from wild strawberries and raspberries.

In the West Virginia region's old-fashioned hotels, ruffled grouse and wild turkey are roasted over fires in wide stone fireplaces.

Richwood still has the swaggering air of a lumber town, and lumbermen call their cooks "stomick robbers." The omnipresent prunes are "log berries" and hot biscuits, part of every lumber camp's menu, are "cats' heads." In August, for three days, the town honors its two main products—potatoes and wood—at a Spud and Splinter Festival. Not far away, in Clay County, a marker commemorates the first Golden Delicious apple tree in America.

At Travelers Inn, where Daniel Boone stopped, food, lodging and entertainment were free on Sundays for more than forty years. The Sabbath-respecting proprietor charged on other days 16⅔ cents for a "warm diet dinner" and 10½ cents for a "cold diet dinner."

Salt bought from the local Kanawha Indians was responsible for an early American trust. The price dropped from ten cents a pound to four, and finally the salt men agreed to a meeting and formed a trust in 1817, fixing the price of salt and shipping it profitably to Ohio, Indiana, Illinois and Kentucky.

Around Mineral Wells and Salt Hills whole families still reap the green cane in autumn and boil it down to sorghum. The family mule, crowned with a bonnet of green leaves to keep off flies, plods in a circle, turning the sorghum mill. The kettles boil and bubble over fireplaces of stone and clay, and when the work is finished everybody flocks in for a "'lasses' lickin' "—scraping the kettles with little wooden paddles, and dancing, singing and courting. Sorghum, referred to as "they" and "them," pours in a golden stream all winter long over hot corn bread, hominy, biscuits and thick slices of freshly baked bread.

White Sulphur Springs, famous as a resort, is also renowned for what some scientists believe to be the oldest living plant—the box huckleberry, whose berries, sweetened by the sun, are made into muffins, pies and cakes. They have been picked in the summer woods for centuries, first by Indians and then by the dauntless women who, in 1796, were so determined to have a place of worship that they hauled limestone on horseback, four miles from the Greenbrier River, to build the Presbyterian church which stands there today.

Some West Virginians claim that a Bunyan-like character, a logger named Tony Beaver, achieved the first peanut brittle accidentally, by cooking up an extra supply of maple syrup and peanuts.

Get-togethers called "Soups" are a West Virginia specialty, held all over the state by church and civic organizations. The members contribute potatoes, onions and other makings, and the soup is cooked in gigantic kettles and served with plates of homemade bread, followed by ice cream and cake for dessert. Chicken-corn soup is a favorite.

At Harper's Ferry, haunted by tales of "God's Angry Man," John Brown, there was once a flood quite different from ordinary inundations. It was in 1753 and the swollen Potomac washed out the fields of the Indians, with the result that its waters swept down a flood of pumpkins that furnished Harper's Ferry that season with plenty of pumpkin butter, dried pumpkin for sweetening and pumpkin pies.

North Carolina
"WHEN EVENIN' IS APINKIN' UP"

Along the black waters of the Scuppernong River in North Carolina it was "day-down," as the natives still call the twilight hours. Two English gentlemen, far from home, were standing on the banks tasting honey-sweet white grapes from a wild vine. Then Philip Amadas and Arthur Barlow, elegant in their Elizabethan cloaks and breeches, dug up a young vine and carried it to the pleasant island they'd spotted earlier that day. They planted it at a spot named Manteo, for the "handsome and goodly" Indian they took back to England with them.

It was the summer of 1584 when they got home, and Amadas and Barlow told their queen that this new land was "the most plentiful, sweete, fruitful and wholesome of all the world." They did not exaggerate, for the waters of what is now Dare County brimmed with shad, channel bass, trout, bluefish and perch. In the woods were quail, wild duck and golden plover. Yet the doomed colony landed there by Sir Walter Raleigh in 1587—the second to attempt settlement—did not know how to keep itself alive on this wealth of food. Nobody is sure how the colony met its fate, whether by starvation, Indian massacre or a mysterious plague. When Raleigh sent investigators in 1591, all 116 men, women and children had vanished. They left one word carved on a tree—CROATOAN—the name of a powerful Indian chief.

Raleigh literally lost his shirt with the colony's failure, but tobacco, the white potato and Indian corn were introduced to England.

Today at Manteo, on Roanoke Island, one lordly scuppernong called "the mother vine" of Amadas and Barlow spreads its shade over more than an acre and the scuppernong grape goes into the most delicate of wines, as well as into jellies and pies. Along the shell-paved streets an occasional ox cart still rumbles by, and in the old houses women make the famous Roanoke hominy exactly as the Indians made it for those two English gentlemen.

Jonathan Daniel, chronicler of the American political scene, says there are really three, perhaps four, North Carolinas. And the food in each, from Tidewater to the border of Tennessee, is as distinctive as the people. North Carolina was rough country in colonial days. Members of the 1668 Assembly had to be told they "must wear shoes, if not stockings" and "must not throw chicken bones on the floor."

Hoppin' John was, and still is, a favorite wherever cowpeas grow. This historic dish is made with dried peas, salt pork and rice. Fish Muddle began in the early days, when many a cook saved herself work by combining all the fish from the day's catch in a big kettle with onions, potatoes and salt meat.

Almost a quarter of a century before the Revolution, the first band of Moravians arrived in the region of Winston-Salem, from Bethlehem, Pennsylvania. Today, two centuries later, they still make their famous citron pie, sugar cakes and cream cakes—the latter a light, white confection served without icing. On November 17th, Moravians at Winston-Salem bring out delicate wines and cakes topped with cream nut frosting, to mark the first Carolina Love Feast held there when the band found shelter and safety in 1753. Salem Tavern is in use now, looking as it did when Washington visited there in 1775, when God's Acre contained only seven graves instead of three thousand. At Eastertime special braided loaves of bread studded with raisins grace the breakfast table.

Blackbeard the pirate roistered through the eastern coastal region and legends about him persist. It's said that his favorite drink was pure juniper water from the interior of the Dismal Swamp. The water is the color of old Madeira wine, and for years it sailed the seven seas in casks, to be drunk by the sailors to preserve good health.

White cornmeal from the ancient McNeil's grist mill in Fayetteville, which has been standing for almost two hundred years, is a must for hoecakes and dodgers. One of the McNeils said: "The mill was here before the town was, and the mill will be here after the town ain't."

In the mountain country, descendants of Scotch-Irish settlers who arrived in the 1700's serve rich brandied cakes and scuppernong pies as their ancestors did. Descendants of Waldensians around Valoise favor a creamy cheese and egg dish, much like the French fondue. Another specialty is leaves of Swiss chard rolled around a mixture of bread crumbs, cheese, milk and eggs and baked in chicken broth. Roast partridge is served with zabaglione, the famous hot sauce (which also doubles as a dessert), made of Marsala wine, sugar and eggs. Fish is glorified with a sauce of capers, anchovies, chives and hard-boiled egg yolks piquant with vinegar and garlic. Green salad often has truffles and dry mustard in the dressing. Back home, the Waldensians used to deck a salad with edible Alpine flowers and call it "The Salad of the Twenty-Four Hours."

Motels sprawl along the Outer Banks, but there are still some isolated, primitive spots on this thin golden thread of sand cut into islands by rushing inlets. Through centuries of storm and shipwreck the Bankers have clung to their own speech and ways. Thus sunset is the time when "evenin' is a pinkin' up." Broiled salt-roe herring is the traditional Sunday breakfast, accompanied by one of what they call the "sober liquors"—tea, coffee or cocoa.

Dying out as hard-surface roads connect the outside world to the Banks is the picturesque Old Christmas Eve celebration on January 6th in the village of Rodanthe. Old Christmas is still observed in a few homes of St. Helena and Burgaw, but the younger generation is drifting away from it. Rodanthe, however, stakes its claim to fame on staging, annually, the world's biggest oyster roast.

There's a holiday oyster roast, too, in Wilmington, which every year lights a three-hundred-year-old live oak with thousands of firefly lights at Christmas. Wilmington cooks make a time-honored holiday dessert of angel cake crumbled into a rich custard and decked with candied cherries. Their black steamed fruit cake is packed with spices, pecans and fruit.

A favorite topic at beach parties is what happened to the *Deering*, a five-masted schooner which ran aground on Diamond Shoals in 1921—food still warm in the galley pots, and on the mess table coffeepot steaming, the only living creature aboard a cat!

Alabama

PARTY FOR A COW

Rumors trickled into Mexico in the late 1550's about a place to the north where "the people wore hats of solid gold." So about 1559 a Spaniard named Tristran de Luna rounded up a thousand adventurers and led them to what is now Mobile Bay. Around their little settlement there were no hats of gold, but corn grew fifteen and twenty feet high. Indians were cultivating patches of melons and squash, raising flocks of turkeys and chickens, catching fish and shooting game in great quantities.

As happened so often in the strange story of American food, the newcomers almost starved. In 1561, hungry, ragged and disillusioned, they trekked back to Mexico, and the first white settlement in Alabama history became a ghost town.

The reluctant French settlers who came next behaved in much the same way. When they arrived in the bay in 1702 with Jean Baptiste LeMoyne, Sieur de Bienville, their principal idea was to make some quick money and hurry home, but the government back in Paris suddenly became keen on colonization.

Two dozen orphan girls were hastily corralled and sent off to Fort Louis de la Mobile, each girl equipped with a small casette, or trunk. Within a month, twenty-three of the Casette Girls were married. The twenty-fourth was reported as "coy and hard to please," and history does not tell what her end was.

Slaves, who began to be unloaded on Dauphin Island in 1719, soon were adding their own sorcery of spices, seasonings and sauces to their mistresses' pet recipes. With easier living of later times, azaleas bloomed behind the lacy iron fences of Mobile gardens, dinner tables were graced with pale wine made from Alabama oranges, peaches flipped into sugary tarts, exotic honey from the melilotus, shad baked and stuffed, and an endless aromatic variety of soups and sauces. Reports went back home that a splendid new France was growing on the Gulf.

In the haunting shadow of live oak and Spanish moss, the Negro workers raised crops of summer squash to be candied or baked into puddings; partridges to be simmered into great deep-dish pies; tender turkeys to roast over open fires. And in domed and mirrored ballrooms, bowls flowed with champagne punch.

Cooks bought red snappers live from the cypress tanks of Mobile's market. Here they also laid in fresh supplies of the tiny sweet gulf shrimp for bisque, poulette and Jambalaya, still part of the French cuisine descended from Bienville. Molasses was so plentiful that one rich planter mixed it with sand and coated the twenty Ionic columns which still grace the front of the plantation's big-house.

From earliest times, Alabama's proudest food traditions have centered around the Mardi Gras in Mobile. The place for that most Gallic of celebrations, ushering in the Lenten season, was probably launched by a one-eyed, slightly drunken Pennsylvania Dutchman—on New Year's Eve. The bibulous German, Michael Krafft, rollicked out of Antoine La Tourette's café in the dawn of New

Year's Day, 1831, with two fellow celebrants. As they tried to find
their way home through the narrow cobbled streets, they noticed
a clerk opening a hardware store for the day's business. The group
gathered up cowbells, rakes and hoes and started an impromptu
parade, singing and shouting as they went. Instead of being
annoyed, the townspeople along their route invited them to have
refreshments. They serenaded the mayor—and he asked them in,
too. In fact, Mobile thought so well of the idea that they formed
the Cowbellion de Rakin Society, said to be the first mystic organ-
ization on record in this country.

Floats, which became a tradition of American street parades,
probably originated in Mobile's Mardi Gras, where the Mystics
of Time, the Maids of Mirth, Polka Dots and half a dozen other
groups compete to this day in glittering tableaux on wheels.

Much of my Alabama lore came from my manager, Estella Karn,
who knew more about more towns in the United States than any
other woman. Arriving in advance of the circus in all sorts of improbable places, Stella learned American food patterns by experience, both bitter and sweet. Being from De Soto Parish, Louisiana,
she was prejudiced in favor of the New Orleans Mardi Gras, but
she admitted that Mobile's Bon Secour oysters at Mardi Gras time
are as fat and delicately flavored as oysters can be, served on the
half-shell, or baked, fried, broiled or in bisques.

It is fun to eat practically anything during Mardi Gras week,
with the city of Mobile at its loveliest, sunshine slanting through
the great centuries-old live oaks, gardens afire with azaleas, and
delectable meals of red snapper baked with a sauce of tiny, sweet
shrimp, white wine, oysters and mushrooms à la Poulette, followed
by Pleasure Pudding, which isn't really a pudding but a light,
spicy almond cake with meringue between the layers, wine poured
over, and a crown of whipped cream.

Once in a radio interview I tentatively started talking about
southern food to Tallulah Bankhead, who grew up in Huntsville,
Alabama. I didn't expect that sleek and fabulous creature to have
gingham-apron memories of whipping up biscuits, fried chicken
and the like. But Tallulah, who specializes in the unexpected,
blithely described her favorite way of fixing veal cutlet with sour
cream, and told how to cook rice dry and fluffy, as Alabamans pre-
fer it, with the butter and fresh black pepper added at the last
minute. In another minute, if time had not run out, I might have
gotten out of her the famous recipe for Bienville white fruit cake,

one of the products . . . together with Tallulah . . . that Alabama is proudest of.

The Deep Sea Fishing Rodeo in Alabama brings sportsmen and tourists from all over the country to Dauphin Island, one of the jewels of the Gulf with its white sand dunes towering forty feet above the sapphire surf, and the piny fragrance of the air diluted with the aroma of broiling red fish, blue fish and pompano. The annual National Peanut Festival in Dothan includes a beauty queen, barbecues, parades, and a spirited peanut recipe contest among the women of the region.

Plantation gentlemen and their ladies still ride to the hounds, with elaborate hunt breakfasts to welcome back the hunters—broiled quail with rashers of crisp bacon, beaten biscuits, thin and bite-size, a rich chicken curry Mobile, platters of tender waffles, eggs stirred gently with cream and scrambled in butter, hominy grits.

Once in Alabama a plantation party was given for a cow. She was Lily Flag, a limpid-eyed Jersey beauty who won first prize as a butter producer at the 1893 Chicago Fair, for her owner, Samuel B. Moore. Samuel and Lily returned in triumph to the Moore plantation at Huntsville, a handsome white brick Georgian mansion with a ballroom big enough to accommodate an entire herd of Jerseys. Formal invitations to the ball went all over the United States, and when the guests assembled, there stood Lily Flag under a tower of roses, a garland around her neck. They toasted her in champagne, danced to the music of an imported European orchestra, and stayed for a midnight supper—which did not include roast beef.

Another historic Alabama party was George Steele's ox barbecue, postponed for four years. George announced his barbecue in honor of Martin Van Buren, but when Van Buren was defeated, he put the ox on a fattening diet and announced that the feast would be held after the *next* election. Sure enough, that time Van Buren won and 4,000 jubilant guests assembled in March of 1845 to eat the fatted calf. Barbecues and politics have been inseparable in Alabama for generations.

Alabama mountains were known to Indians and white hunters only, until the late 1700's when brave souls like Balaam Gaiter and his wife found South Carolina too crowded. Mrs. Gaiter set out for Alabama in a gray wool dress with white stripes she'd sewed on herself, and a poke bonnet. She smoked a pipe and chewed tobacco and "looked brave enough to tackle a den of wild cats."

Mrs. Gaiter made corn bread and baked ham with bread-crumb stuffing, and, as her descendants do today, cut firewood in the waning moon to be sure it would be quick-burning. She and generations after her kept two Christmases—December 26th and January 7th—but concentrating on January 7th when at first daybreak, an hour before sunrise, the animals rose, the pokeweed put out its first shoots, and the farmer started work for the year, even if it was only to plow a single furrow.

In the hill country there's not much store-bought food to this day; almost everything is home-raised and homemade. Ward Dorrance, writer, tells of asking one country storekeeper for onions. The man stared at him, then said: "What'd I be doin' with onions —folks raise stuff like that."

I suppose the time I'd have liked best of all to be in Alabama was that June day in 1880, in the elm-shaded town of Tuscumbia, when a little girl triumphantly counted the candles on her birthday cake. The child was Helen Keller, and that cake must have tasted sweet indeed to Anne Sullivan, the great teacher who led the little deaf, blind girl from darkness into light.

Tennessee

FOOD SET TO MUSIC

Venison and wild turkey were on the table and the only carpet in the State of Franklin was on the floor when Mrs. John Sevier, wife of the governor, entertained guests. When the company left, the carpet was carefully rolled up and put away.

The State of Franklin existed for about four years in what is now Tennessee. Its legislature functioned at Greenville until the government collapsed in 1884, and Franklin became a "lost state." During the brief years of its existence, the surrounding wilderness was changing gradually into frontier settlements.

The first permanent white settler in Tennessee is said to have been William Beane, who built a cabin on Boone's Creek in 1769 and was joined by a few families from North Carolina. These pioneers grew corn, grain and a little fruit. Some of the first mills, moss-covered but sturdy, are still standing and mountain boys bring in corn to be ground for hoecakes, corn pone and hot mush.

At Beane's tiny settlement, the women learned to make stews of possum and squirrel, and in the mountain regions today a stew get-together is as commonplace as a church sociable. Families are proud of their heirloom recipes. Counties have stew or barbecue kings who preside over the big iron kettles and graciously allow the women to wait on table.

After the Revolution, rovers in covered wagons swarmed over Daniel Boone's Wilderness Road. The families who stopped in the high mountain country and dug steep farms from the hillsides lived apart from the growing towns, and had a lore of their own about weather, crops and cooking. Mountain women today predict a fall of snow when the fire spits back at them. Many believe that you must never say thank-you for a gift of seed lest it perish in the ground. Onions must be planted at a respectable distance from potatoes, so that the potatoes won't have their eyes burned out. Most housewives wouldn't dream of putting lightning-struck wood in their stoves, and a man knows that he will reap a poor crop of peppers if he plants them while he's angry with his wife.

Some of the old horse-powered mills still grind cane for sorghum, and families come from miles around for the boiling and tasting.

Food was so important that it was often set to music. At Old Timers Day in Gatlinburg, held every June, and at the all-day singings in the East Tennessee region, you still hear the rollicking tunes of "Chicken in the Bread Tray," "Jimmy Crack Corn," "Possum Pie" and "Slop the Hogs." The cooks of Cheatham County are so famous for their chitlin's that there's a song called "When It's Chitlin' Time in Cheatham County."

A gift of a peck of clover seed, sent by the State Secretary of Agriculture to John Buck in the 1890's, grew into 50,000 fragrant crimson acres in Franklin County. The farm with the handsomest crop is chosen annually when the countryside turns out for the Clover Festival and a fried-chicken supper served out of doors.

There was a touch of elegance in the first frame house west of the Alleghanies, built by Governor William Blount on what later became a large plantation. The hunter's board in his dining room held decanters of imported wine and white china dishes heaped with grapes and peaches; his trestle table gleamed with silver and pewter, and turkeys rich with chestnut stuffing were borne in on china platters three feet long.

Tennessee hams have come out of the hills to rival Smithfields in the esteem of gourmets. They are cured in old-fashioned smokehouses, just as they were two hundred years ago, buried in salt for a month and smoked to a deep red. With the ham—fried with a dash of coffee in the fat --go red-eye gravy, hot biscuits, creamed potatoes and wilted lettuce.

Nashville's Market Square and the rambling red brick market house are as they have been for years, headquarters for farmers. One hundred and four tables are reserved for farm women to display their finest home-cured hams baked with brown sugar and cloves, golden loaves of egg bread, pies made from Nancy Hall sweet potatoes, jams from Humboldt strawberries, fried apple pies, pickled black walnuts.

In May every year West Tennessee celebrates at Humboldt with a three-day strawberry festival. Humboldt women's favorite strawberry desserts include deep-dish pies filled with sugared whole strawberries; sponge cakes with strawberry gelatine between each of the four layers and whipped cream on top; and a wonderful concoction consisting of paper-thin layers of buttered pastry spread with crushed berries and served hot.

The face of Tennessee changed slowly over the years. Then came TVA, the vast Tennessee Valley Authority, bringing electricity to transform isolated, primitive cabins into homes with telephones, radios, freezers, washing machines, lights and bathrooms. Tired land is being renewed to produce good crops again. Women who once bore the burden of dawn-to-dark work were old before thirty. Now they whisk meals together as quickly as their city sisters.

Not all of them wanted to give up their land to TVA. They were suspicious of the government, big business and change. TVA authorities sometimes seemed to understand and take this into account. An old householder said his hearth fire had been burning for three generations, and he didn't intend to let it go out. TVA considered the matter and then moved the whole fireplace with the crackling fire intact to a new home.

Puerto Rico and the Virgin Islands

KALALLOU IN THE MOONLIGHT

An improbable moon hung over the Caribbean. Our beach fire flared scarlet and gold against the sky, and an aromatic, mouth-watering fragrance filled the air; my first Kalallou in the Virgin Islands. The preparation for this mysterious stew starts with a soft sea wind, the haunting rhythm of a scratch band playing on instruments made from kerosene tins and gasoline cans, liberal dashes of moonlight and firelight and dozens of violet-colored land crabs. These exotic popeyed creatures must be caught by torchlight on beaches and marshes at least a week before the Kalallou time, and fed a steady diet of cornmeal.

The Kalallou ritual begins early in the morning, the chef often wearing a rosy-red straw hat of a shade called Flamboyant. Into the pot go such items as tania leaves, manbower (an island spinach), and a shrub named Papa Lolo. Assorted flavors are added by the crabs, diced okra, pork and a hambone, a salted conch, two kinds of pepper, a few sweet potatoes, spring onions —and a dried pig's tail. At the last minute, the cook plops in spoonfuls of *fungi*, a cornmeal mush to which fresh young okra is sometimes added. When the experienced host serves Kalallou, he sees to it that everybody gets a bit of the pig's tail.

One odd Virgin Islands dessert is Pudding-in-a-Bush, a corn-meal porridge to which practically anything can be added—ginger, cinnamon, fresh coconut milk, raisins, butter, sugar. The finished product is wrapped in green banana leaves, gay as a

Christmas present. If a Pudding-in-a-Bush is made with sweet potatoes instead of cornmeal, it isn't a dessert at all but part of the meat course.

The Virgin Islands supplied the setting for an idyllic off-beat vacation when I first went there, and although they have become popular with tourists now, I think they are still—as the natives say—the loveliest islands God ever made. At the turreted hilltop hotel called Bluebeard's Castle, you can sit down to a breakfast of Puerto Rican coffee, fresh roasted and served *con leche* (half coffee, half hot milk), with papayas or sugar-sweet West Indian oranges, descendants of the seedlings brought by Columbus on his second voyage. Then hot Spanish buns, spicy with cinnamon. Free with breakfast comes an incomparable view—the tumbled streets of the St. Thomas capital, Charlotte-Amalie, spread in a crazy-quilt of tile, tin roofs and flowering gardens, and beyond, the blue sweep of the bay fringed by soft green hills.

For lunch maybe you'll relish a tall glass of Almond Cream, made by pounding blanched almonds to a powder, with a little water and powdered sugar added, then strained and chilled. There is a jam I love, too, on hot corn bread, made with ripe bananas, oranges and limes.

In many island homes the women still cook on coal pots, portable units which burn charcoal and turn out delicious roasted peanuts and sweet potatoes, red pea soup, boiled fish with lime sauce, and a cornmeal-thickened stew called Mauffay, which has a song in its honor:

> *If you want to cook it right*
> *Soak the salt thing overnight*
> *Put it on until he biles*
> *Season, stir he for awhile*
> *No forget the tomato then*
> *Make the Mauffay taste like a hen*
> *Stir the flour pon the spot*
> *Mauffay done, take off the pot.*

An accompanying beverage called coca-tea is made of milk, cocoa, sugar, orange peel and cinnamon.

People from the United States have changed the islands' eating patterns in the bigger towns, but back-country they still call the first meal of the day "tea," the main meal at noon "breakfast" and a simple supper comes in late afternoon.

Island-hopping is a delightful part of any Caribbean holiday, but you're in perpetual peril of falling in love with a ruined sugar mill on the island of St. Croix, or a hilltop overlooking a palmy beach on St. John's, or perhaps a cliff-hanging cottage on St. Thomas. You may end up selling your return ticket and replanning your life. That's what happened to Jeanne Perkins, former *Life* magazine writer, who flew in to visit and stayed to marry a young Navy officer from the South, Harry Harmon. The Harmons started housekeeping on a boat, *The Love Junk*, and for a living they run glass-bottom boats and take out fishing parties.

Meat is scarce in St. Thomas and, as Jeanne Harmon discovered, you have to be introduced to a butcher before you can get even a small portion of beef, pork or lamb. You also have to find out what day animals are being slaughtered and the exact hour the meat arrives at the shop. After that your problem is to persuade the butcher to part with it.

Jeanne's parents have never stopped talking about a dinner they had in a small, ramshackle Charlotte-Amalie restaurant. Steve, the proprietor, did the cooking and serving and allowed no more than twelve guests in the place for a meal. Tomatoes stuffed with the islands' wonderful queen crabs were followed by chicken fried in olive oil and golden potatoes which Steve said were flavored with orange juice and mixed with chopped ham, onion, mushrooms and sweet potatoes. Cointreau, rum and thick cream made the frozen dessert.

St. Thomas fish venders haul their wares on small donkeys, and you have your choice of a rainbow-colored catch which includes pompano, a small rosy pink fish whose name I never did learn, blue Doctor Fish and one called Old Wife. From them you may make a Danish fish soup flavored with lime, popular in the islands, or maybe fish pudding.

On little St. John Island you either have too much fish or no fish at all. The fishermen come in with their bright-colored catch strung on a palm frond. You ask to buy a fish and the fisherman says "No, mum." You learn in time that he sells only the whole catch, called a strap of fish, and you must contract for it before he sets out. If you buy a strap of fifteen or twenty fish, there's not much to do but give a party.

The rule of Denmark ended in 1917 when the United States bought the Virgins for $25,000,000. However, there are many Danish echoes, in street names such as Dronningensgade, and in dishes like Herring Gundy and a sweet fruit bread made with almonds and spices. A Danish hard candy comes in doll shapes, perched on coconut palm sticks and known as Sugar Babies. The local gingerbread men, little fellows about four inches long, are called Long Cakes.

The most exciting food news in Caribbean history broke late in 1954 when the fruit of an ancient wild tree, the acerola, was found to be the richest source of natural Vitamin C known to man. Acerola trees have been growing in Puerto Rico for at least 2,000 years, but nobody paid much attention to them until Dr. Conrado F. Asenjo began to investigate claims made by the Indians that those who ate acerola fruit seemed immune to all the common island diseases.

One six-ounce glass of acerola juice has as much Vitamin C as fifty pounds of raw cabbage. It is fifty times richer in this important vitamin than orange juice. So Puerto Rico, which has to import at least half its food supply, may at last have found a food that will turn into a good cash crop. And it may not be long before mothers will be urging their children to "drink your acerola."

High spot of a visit to San Juan are the restaurants where an enormous native shrimp, called *camarones grande,* is the appetizer, followed by crayfish in a delicate wine sauce, and for dessert the lemon-ginger "Ice Cream of Our Ancestors."

A Puerto Rican outdoor pig roast includes suckling pig stuffed with herb-seasoned bread crumbs, basted with a peppery sauce and roasted a deep golden brown; with fried green plantain on the side.

Nicest compliment paid to the Caribbean was when Arthur Fairchild searched the world for the perfect place to live. He'd made all the money he needed in a Wall Street coup, and decided to take his sinus to a happier climate. Dividing up a global map, he sampled it in sections, eliminating as he went. He ended on top of the ridge overlooking Charlotte-Amalie, where he bought a ruined estate formerly the vacation spot of Danish royalty. He added all the land necessary to protect his superb view, and a few years ago gave back to the island a glittering stretch of beach. For beauty, serenity and health, the Virgins were his choice of the whole earth, and if it weren't for my Catskill barn-home, I'd agree with him.

THE HEARTLAND

N. Dak.

S. Dak.

Minn.

Wis.

Mich.

Neb.

Iowa

Ind.

Ohio

Kans

Mo.

Ill.

Okla.

Missouri

Missouri is not just a state to me. It is my childhood. Notably, it is one special summer on the Old Home Place, when I was six. That summer began with my mother singing in the kitchen of the farmhouse where she, too, had been a child, and where our family, after some very stormy financial times, was to have a brief season of content and plenty. Looking back now, it seems to me that never again did we recapture the charmed well-being we knew that whole, faraway year, from spring planting until harvest.

Even the food took on special enchantment. My mother was a truly great cook and so even on the bleakest of our prairie farms, everything we ate was seasoned with her rare skill as well as her love for us. But that summer on the Old Home Place her cooking art reached its zenith. Never were peas so green and succulent in their rich cream sauce with its flecking of black pepper. Little new potatoes, scraped so sparingly that the flavor of the brown earth stayed with them, came to the table floating in our own good butter. Small tender chickens went into the frying pan regularly, to emerge in crisp, brown perfection.

When Papa brought along for the noon dinner three or four neighbors with whom he was swapping work at haying or harvest time, there was often a whole ham on the table, crowned with cloves, basted with our own cider or molasses. Mama crisped the garden-fresh cucumber slices in cold, salted spring water, and then sliced them in vinegar with onions. There were great ponderosa tomatoes, and Mama's cole slaw drenched in her pale-gold boiled dressing.

In a family of good cooks, both the Craigs and the McBrides, my mother's biscuits were acknowledged the best, but that summer they came from the oven of the big iron range even more like puffs of cloud. And she took time to split them open and lavishly butter them hot.

Even if I knew exactly what we did to make that summer so happy, I suppose nobody could ever duplicate it, any more than I can take Mama's simple recipe for Charlotte Russe and emerge with anything as delectable as the crockfuls of creamy custard perfection that glorified all our birthdays. One ingredient in the happy formula, perhaps, was the good health of a six-year-old who ran barefooted and bareheaded from morning to night. Another may have been the quantities of milk expertly conveyed by my father straight from the cream-colored cow into my little silver mug. And finally there was the joy that fills a child when all is well with family and home.

Perhaps every human being in his lifetime cherishes one memorable period that stays clear and shining, its colors intermeshed, its fragrance unfaded. My memorable period is that summer on the Old Home Place.

If only I had set myself then to learn exactly what Mama did to glorify the simplest dishes. But I didn't nor shall I ever know now. Perhaps it takes a big, old-fashioned kitchen, steamy and rich with spice and sugar smells, to produce her hot peach cobbler, her sliced apple pie with its cinnamon, nutmeg, butter and brown sugar. More likely, though, it takes a baker who could listen to her bread, and when it stopped singing to itself, know that it was ready to take from the oven and cool in crusty golden loaves; a firemaker who could hear the crackle and spit of stovewood as it burned down and know more accurately than any thermometer

when the heat was right to cook pans of yellow corn pone or
fragile devil's food cake.

Mama knew long before laboratories proved it that corn must
be brought arunning from the garden, that each minute between
cornstalk and kettle of galloping water drains away a little more
of its youth and milk-sweet goodness. She didn't call them vitamins, but instinct told her to serve her family all the fresh, wild
greens she could find—new little shoots of dandelion, tender
turnip tops, mustard greens.

The yellow thickness of our Jersey cream certainly helped make
our homemade ice cream an exciting experience, but there was
more to it than taste: the fun of pounding fine in a sack the saw-
dust-covered ice from our icehouse; of taking turns at the frosty
freezer until it was time to pull out the dasher and lick off the
first luscious mouthful. Then there were our sun-ripened strawberries, crushed and mellowed in a yellow bowl, or our rosiest
peaches smelling of sun and deep summer. And finally, the end of
supper, ice cream time, when another blue and gold day was over
and we were a family, together, waiting in the cool, shadowy
kitchen while Mama served each of us.

I am sure that my mother would have taken in stride the magnificent short-cuts of the deep-freeze, the pressure cooker, the
electric stove, the mixers and blenders and infra-red broilers. But
she would have made them her own, just as she did her temperamental old cookstove, her pots and pans, her old egg beater and
battered mixing spoon. She would have known the exact heat she
needed, even on a streamlined push-button stove, for her incomparable potato soup, which smelled so good that only the
most iron-willed child could stay in the kitchen without swooning
from hunger while it cooked. After it came stacks of Mama's salt-
rising bread, and a bowl of her Damson plum preserves for dessert.

My Monroe County is a place of prairies and bluegrass. It was
settled by people like my great-grandparents who came there by
covered wagon from Kentucky and set up housekeeping in log
cabins. On the Old Home Place, the log cabin had become our
living room, with Great-Grandfather's split-bottom rocker in front
of the fireplace where he loved to sit and spin yarns of blood-
curdling escapes from wolves and Indians.

All through that region the cookery has the butter, egg and
cream lushness of the South, and the recipes are family treasures,
called Receipts. Auntie Mame's brown-sugar cake, with a

whipped, creamy caramel filling; Auntie Belle's plain omelet, which deserved some fancier adjective to hint at its delicate glory; Aunt Mary's transparent pie, which really was transparent like its name; Aunt Liza Buckner's pumpkin pie, with cream and vanilla, but not spices; Mother Blanton's corn dodgers, flipped hot and small from the griddle for a dredging of butter and sorghum molasses; Mama's cookies, which take dates and coconut and spices, and may not come out exactly the way they used to taste because she talked that recipe to me, and Mama was a "little of this" and a "pinch of that" kind of cook.

The family foods were an important part of this country child's life in the early part of the century. So was my Baptist preacher grandfather who drove seventy-five thousand miles in his long lifetime to serve his rural churches. And so was the county fair which brought out blooded cattle, prancing horses, scrubbed hogs, and counters heavy with ribbon-winning cakes, pies, jams, jellies, and fancy-work.

Until I went off to boarding school at eleven, that small part of Missouri was the whole world, and St. Louis was as remote as Europe. At school I found there were other Missourians with other ways of life. But I was to know a good deal about London and Paris and New York before I really got around to discovering my own state.

It was radio that took me back on an exciting trip to thank Lloyd Stark, then governor, and Mitchell White, editor of the *Mexico Ledger*, for Mary Margaret McBride Day, November 22nd. People came from all over the state and we all ate more than we should, of hickory-smoked ham, five years old, red ham gravy, mashed potatoes, mashed turnips, sweet potatoes candied with marshmallows. The toasts were in the same kind of creamy buttermilk I had poured from our cedar churn in the summer kitchen years ago.

I am looking right now at the map of my native state, with its delightful place names: Independence, Freedom, Liberty, Loyalty, Hurricane, Blue Eye, Dawn, Day. Its history lies there at the meeting of great rivers, the Missouri, Ohio and Mississippi, for they were the waterways of the French fur traders in the wake of Robert Cavalier de la Salle in the 1680's.

There is still an elegant French air about Ste. Genevieve, founded by seventeen Creole families in 1750, and the past is there in the old walled convent, the houses with their shaded

galleries and gardens, their faded rose brick walls, box hedges
and old-fashioned flowers.

The food, too, goes back: the thinnest and most exquisite of
crêpes, small sweet and bitter almond balls called *croquignoles*.
Christmas is magnificent, with turkey boned and cooked in an
extravaganza of spices, herbs and wine. On New Year's, old and
young go through the streets in masquerade, singing the ancient,
unwritten tune of La Guignole. On fast days a special soup is
brewed from dried peas, turnips, celery and onions, lightened with
sprigs of mint and thyme.

As a child, I never knew the vine-draped town of Bethel, the
picturesque flower gardens of Washington, the prim white houses
of Altenburg and Westphalia . . . part, too, of Missouri history.
Here and in half a dozen other neat German towns, they usher in
the New Year with herring salad, into which they have stirred
apples, beets, eggs, pickles, onions, spices and even chicken. They
say, too, that if you eat this dish you will never be in want. Cheesecake reaches heights of culinary glory in these German communities, as do raw potato pancakes fried thin and crisp in the lard of
the country.

Italians press the fragrant grapes for Missouri's Rosati wine, and
grapes—big, sun-sweet clusters of them—are given to visitors at
the early fall Grape Festival in St. James.

In Howard County's "Little Virginia" practically everyone is
kin, and the South is in their speech and in their cookery. There
sorghum has vintages, and each rival faction swears by its own
exalted "boil."

I am obliged to the American Guide Series book on Missouri
for making it clear at the start that we pronounced it "Mizz-our-
ah," and for this definition: "Missouri is many intangible things
. . . apple-blossom time at Marionville . . . a flaming July sunrise on the deep blue of Lake Taneycomo . . . firelight and un-
hurried talk of friends in a room, wind calling down the chimney
and wood smoke on the night air. It is living so that life tastes
good each day."

I like that, and I know that life tasted good, indeed, when I
could answer Mama's call to noon dinner—the meal I would choose
over any other, anywhere. I would want it on the old table in our
kitchen, spread with a red-checked cloth, the wood fire humming
softly in the old stove. And every single thing would be as my
mother did it:

Buttermilk biscuits so hot you can't pick them up and have to slather butter on their delicate insides by catch-as-catch-can method; mashed potatoes, hand-beaten with cream and butter until they are as fluffy as a cloud; baby chicken fried to crisp brownness and creamy gravy made in the skillet with all the little brown crumbs to give it color and flavor; tender young mustard greens cooked with side meat; and to finish off, apple dumplings rich with cinnamon, butter and brown sugar and thick country cream to pour over. . . .

That will always be Missouri and childhood and the best of life to me.

MISSOURI POSTSCRIPT

Here are my family recipes from Missouri. They can't go in the recipe section of this book because the domestic science experts don't know what to do with them.

"Where," asked Gloria Marshall in her most clinical voice, "are people going to find brown crocks? Right here you say a brown crock is important for your mother's Charlotte Russe."

Well, it is. Gloria belongs to the school of the level teaspoonful, the controlled oven temperature. The recipes she has supervised in this book will work, she says with assurance. Then with a visible shudder, she looks at my grandmother's way of cooking corn, which calls for "an iron spoon of lard." As for the corn dodgers which take "a little salt" and are "mixed with the hand to a stiff dough"—well—

"I'm afraid," said Gloria, "these can't go in the book at all."

But here they are, refugees from the test-kitchens—relics of a day when women knew what you meant by "butter the size of a walnut" and how to "cut a young chicken through the back" . . . and everybody had a brown crock.

MAMA'S CHARLOTTE RUSSE

Pour a custard mixture of one egg, one-half cup sugar and two cups milk in a double boiler. Add one tablespoon gelatine softened in one-fourth cup water. Cook until mixture coats the spoon. When custard begins to set, add one pint of cream which has been whipped and one teaspoon vanilla. Pour over sponge cake which has been sliced and used to line a brown crock. (The crock is very necessary if this is to taste exactly right.)

AUNT LIZA BUCKNER'S PUMPKIN PIE

One pint cooked pumpkin, one egg beaten, one tablespoon butter, one-half cup cream, one cup sugar, one-half teaspoon salt, flavor with vanilla. Beat mixture very hard and put it in pastry shell and bake.

MOTHER BLANTON'S CORN DODGERS

Take one pint of sifted cornmeal, half a cup sour milk, one-fourth teaspoon of soda, one heaping tablespoon lard, a little salt; mix with hand to stiff dough with hot water, mix thoroughly and make little dodgers and bake on a hot, greased griddle in a hot oven for 30 minutes.

GRANDMA'S WAY OF COOKING CORN

To 12 ears of corn, cut off, add one pint of half milk and half cream, season with salt, pepper and a little sugar. Put in skillet or baking pan with iron spoon of lard. Cook 30 or 40 minutes.

AUNTIE'S WHITE CAKE
(That won a blue ribbon for her at the fair)

Whites of six eggs, three-fourths cup of butter, one and one-half cups sugar, one cup milk, two and one-half cups of flour sifted three times with two heaping teaspoons baking powder, teaspoon vanilla. Cream butter and sugar until very light, add milk and flour alternately, beating each time well. Fold in whites of the egg which have been beaten stiff. Add vanilla. Bake in two layers about 40 minutes.

CHOCOLATE FILLING FOR AUNTIE'S WHITE CAKE

Three squares of chocolate melted, add two and one-half cups sugar and one cup cream. Mix well and cook to the soft-ball stage, let cool, and add teaspoon vanilla and beat until creamy.

MAMA'S COOKIES

Five cups flour, six eggs, three cups sugar, three scant cups shortening; one cup each chopped dates, nuts, raisins, one cup shredded coconut; one teaspoon each of ground allspice, cloves, cinnamon (or more according to taste); one teaspoon salt, one cup buttermilk; soda.

Sift flour several times with soda, salt and spices. Cream sugar and shortening thoroughly. Break one egg into this and beat. Continue beating in eggs separately until all are used. Into cup of buttermilk dissolve soda according to sourness of milk. Mix flour and milk alternately as when mixing cake. Mix in fruit at any time, a small amount at a time. Beat all together well at the last, then drop by teaspoonfuls on well-greased pan and bake in hot oven.

MAMA'S BUTTERMILK BISCUITS

Sift two full cups flour and one-half teaspoon salt. Add one-third cup shortening and three-quarters cup of buttermilk with one-half teaspoon soda dissolved in it, amount according to the sourness of the buttermilk. Mix, roll out on floured board, handling lightly. Cut out and turn over in melted shortening. Place in pan without crowding and bake in quick oven.

MAMA'S SOUTHERN CORN BREAD
(And no sugar in it, you may be sure)

Mix and sift three-quarters cup cornmeal, one and one-half teaspoons salt, five level teaspoons baking powder, one and one-fourth cups sweet milk, one well-beaten egg, two tablespoons lard. Beat well, turn in pan or muffin rings; bake 25 minutes.

MAMA'S BOILED DRESSING

Scald one cup of vinegar. Beat well two eggs into which beat one cup of sugar

and a piece of butter the size of a walnut. Pour hot vinegar over this, stirring constantly. Put back over flame. Let thicken, stirring constantly while it thickens. Set aside until thoroughly cold before pouring.

AUNT MARY'S SMOTHERED CHICKEN

Cut a young chicken through the back, salt and pepper well and put in pan with two large tablespoons butter and one pint boiling water. Put a cover over this and press with an iron. Set on back of stove and cook about one hour. Add more water if necessary.

AUNT BELLE'S PLAIN OMELET

To four egg yolks beaten, add six tablespoons cream, salt to taste; put in beaten egg whites, stirring all the time. Melt butter in frying pan, pour in egg mixture and set in oven; when cooked through, roll with knife on the platter and serve immediately.

AUNT MARY'S TRANSPARENT PIE

Take two cups sugar, one and a third cups butter, two tablespoons cream, four eggs. Cream butter and sugar, beat the yolks and add two of the whites to the cream. Make a meringue of two whites.

Illinois

"You transplanted Middle-Westerners are always bragging about the food you ate when young," a friend said accusingly.

It's true. In our memories, grandmothers, mothers and aunts wear culinary halos. And I think their food really was extraordinarily good, maybe because, since farm life was so limited then, the women simply had to create triumphant meals as a substitute for books, music, museums, travel, even for pretty clothes and furniture. And the best of them could hold their own with fine cooks anywhere.

Not long ago I came across a diary, kept near the turn of the century by a nameless Illinois farmwoman. It is a touching document, and could have been written by many of the women I knew in my childhood. Before 6:30 in the morning, she had fed her family, milked, strained the milk, packed her husband's dinner pail (he was working at a distance), turned the cows into the pasture, watered the horse, fed the pigs, cared for the young calves, put out feed and water for the chickens. . . .

Out of a whole harried day of this she takes for herself only a few minutes, soon after dawn."While the stove is getting hot," she confesses, "I go to my flower garden and gather a choice, half-blown rose and a spray of bride's wreath and arrange them in my hair. . . . There is little time for the higher life for myself . . . but my soul cries out for it."

So every time, now, that I speak longingly of the marvelous country food we had as children, I remember that Illinois woman and her one small gesture toward "the higher life"—the flowers in her hair. Then I feel grateful for the mixes and cans and deep-freezes, the radio and television, the mechanized harvest equipment that has nearly done away with the teams of workers and field hands who had to be fed by those overworked farmwomen.

Illinois, as an English traveler observed, was a hard country for women and cattle in the 1800's. When Illinois asked for statehood in 1818, Chicago was a mud village and the staple frontier diet was salt pork and parched barley "coffee." The Indians raised corn, pumpkins and beans along the banks of the Illinois, and in their villages stored maize and discs of dried pumpkin.

It was in the 1830–31 winter of the deep snow that the Lincoln family, thirteen of them, arrived in wagons from Indiana with almost nothing to eat. I like some of the food yarns about Lincoln, especially one from Carl Sandburg. Lincoln contemplated a cup of warmish brown liquid served him at a hotel.

"If this is coffee," he told the waiter, "then please bring me some tea. But if this is tea, please bring me some coffee."

Upon his first encounter with a strange new dessert, Mr. Lincoln is said to have remarked that he did not want to slander the hotel, "but this pudding is froze," a very apt description from one getting his first taste of ice cream.

Middle-Western women are used to making do with what they have. They brew sassafras and spice wood into spring tonics. In crisp fall weather, prairie chickens are roasted, fried and turned into deep-dish pies. Canned string beans go in the pot with ham hocks, and sometimes potatoes are added for a one-dish meal.

At a corn-husking in Modesta, five hundred pounds of Mississippi catfish went into the fry; ten thousand fruit pies finished off the feast. Saturday is still the big day in the river town of Cairo, when corn, apple and cotton farmers flock to town and eat, of all things for the Middle West, hot tamales! Evansville boasts a pork barbecue and a caramel candy made from a hundred-year-old recipe. Natives who have moved away make a ritual of getting these two delicacies when they come back to visit.

French families at Nauvoo built deep, cool cellars where they ripen an excellent blue cheese. Their vineyards produce a variety of wines, and these two products were honored for many years at a picturesque ceremony called the Wedding of the Wine and Cheese, when visitors could sip and sample on the house.

Cambridge features a Belgian game called *Rolle-Balle* at its county fair. Descendants of Belgian settlers still make the marvelous Walloon chicken of their grandmothers, an herb-fragrant dish in which veal and sweetbreads are added to the chicken.

Evanston was so strict in the 1890's that it was nicknamed

"Heavenston" and passed an ordinance forbidding the sale of ice cream sodas on Sunday. An enterprising merchant got around this by selling ice cream with syrup but no soda. In no time the soda-less soda became known as the Sunday soda, and eventually the Sundae.

Because the explorer Champlain thought China lay just across the lakes, the discovery of Lake Michigan was celebrated with the guest of honor, Jean Nicolet, in a robe of Chinese damask embroidered with brilliant flowers and birds. Champlain had ordered the robe and sent young Nicolet off in a canoe to confer with the Oriental potentate they expected to find. Nicolet donned his Chinese finery but was welcomed by Huron Indians who served him a banquet of beaver meat, venison and forest berries.

Chicago and meat-packing came almost two centuries later. Most of the meals I've had in Chicago, the meat center, were when I was covering political conventions, and it's difficult for even a good eater like me to enjoy her vittles when beset by fatigue and frazzled nerves. Nevertheless, I remember with pleasure a minted mound of fresh strawberries, pineapple and orange sections served in a bowl of shaved ice . . . which arrived just in time to save my sanity after two senators and a cabinet member failed to show up in time for a broadcast.

I also remember the blessed night a convention closed and we had a midnight supper in an air-cooled club, and while the rest ate inch-thick slices of rib roast, the chef did shrimp for me the way I like it best—sautéed tenderly in butter and accompanied by a sharp horseradish and tomato sauce.

I remember happily, too, a gala dinner with chunks of lamb set ablaze on shiny swords borne by beplumed waiters in velvet and satin; a luncheon beside a sparkling fountain that smelled of gardenias, with grapefruit and avocado salad; a late supper of German pancakes made with grated raw potato and onion, fried to crisp perfection on a sizzling griddle and served with German pot roast and gravy.

As you ride through miles of tottering wooden tenements to the roaring stockyards, and back to the glittering towers of the lakeside, you can well believe that this is the town that sprang from the prairie and, within fifty years, changed the eating habits of the nation—first by developing refrigerated meat cars in 1857, and eleven years later, refrigerated cars for fresh fruit.

Chicago still lives, talks and eats in a score or more languages, although the inevitable American standardizing process whittles away at the colorful heritages people brought with them from far places. Kitchens are redolent with garlic, bay leaf and caraway as Polish women cook the local lake fish in their own style, with carrots, lemon and a garnish of hard-boiled eggs and lemon juice; their rich beet soup which has in it tomatoes, cabbage and apple, lima beans and sour cream; their mashed potato dumplings and stuffed dough pockets; and their national dessert, sugar-glazed *babka* filled with nuts, raisins and candied fruit.

Italians, who came to Chicago from Sicily and the southern provinces, made all America conscious of the virtues of olive oil, tiny Italian tomatoes and an array of pastas, ranging from my favorite fettucini and the fragile *capellini d'angelo*, or angel's hair, to the more familiar spaghetti and macaroni. The pizza, that sizzling tomato-cheese pie which, to be at its best, must be baked in an open brick oven, soon captured the national imagination and has now become almost as common at roadside restaurants as the hamburger and the hot dog.

A world event in Chicago was the beginning of Rotary, when four businessmen met at Mme. Galli's restaurant in 1905. Since then millions of men have sung millions of choruses of "I Want a Girl Just Like the Girl That Married Dear Old Dad," and have eaten millions of tons of Chicken à la King in the name of Rotary International. Some diet experts even credit Rotary with reconciling men to fruit cocktails and salads.

One of the most dramatic chapters in our food history began in a field near El Paso, Illinois, in 1925, when Lester Pfister began tying paper bags around the tassels and ear shoots of his corn. Neighboring farmers thought it was a crazy idea, but Pfister mortgaged his farm and borrowed every cent he could wangle from the banks to prove that corn *could* be hybridized.

We have come a long way since the great Indian chief Black Hawk acknowledged defeat in 1833, thus: "Rock River was a beautiful country. I loved my towns, my cornfields and the home of my people. I fought for it. It is now yours. Keep it as we did."

In the ensuing century Chicago has been called Hog Butcher of the World and accused of materialism. All the same, it was hardheaded Chicago businessmen who in November, 1955, paid fifty dollars a plate for lobster and champagne in order to give a new lease on life to *Poetry Magazine*.

Indiana

Daniel Webster was an early victim of Hoosier hospitality. Wined and dined in Michigan City in 1837, he consumed so much good food and such a variety of beverages that his oration on the national debt foundered. Rising after dinner, he began bravely enough: "Ladies and gentlemen, the national debt . . . the national debt," he repeated, then after a weighty pause—"How much is the blankety-blank thing, anyway?"

His downfall probably involved something stronger than sorghum pumpkin pie, cold sliced pork dusted with nutmeg, venison haunch, succotash made with hull-out beans, but he'd probably had all these Indiana favorites in profusion.

Gone from the regional menu, and not deplored by anyone, is the bear-meat bacon of frontier days, as well as the ash cakes made of acorns, the substitute coffee made from seeds of wild rice and barley, and the bitter drink brewed from dried dandelion roots, said to be "of a soporific nature." The rugged woodsmen and flatboatmen drank hard cider, whiskey and applejack. Their disapproving womenfolk consented to bake applejack pies only after being convinced that the alcohol burned off in the oven heat.

Most picturesque of Indiana's food legends and traditions are from Vincennes, which was the sole white settlement in the early 1700's. Before then the region was known only to a scattering of traders, explorers and adventurers. Completely French, Vincennes was an exotic surprise to the New Englanders who went there. Here in the wilderness was a gay town with thatched, whitewashed cottages, neat streets and flourishing gardens. Garden produce came to town in two wheeled crates called caleches, and every year in whitewashed Creole kitchens, women baked the candy-decked Twelfth Night cake. The people sang and danced, gambled, celebrated feast-days and a giddy Mardi Gras. Women in beads and bright petticoats sang "L'Alouette" while cooking tender young hen smothered in herb bouquet, broth, bits of bacon and thin slices of lemon . . . or breast of chicken, à la Reine, with truffles, mushrooms and a touch of old Madeira. The town retained its Gallic atmosphere until Germans came in. Then the Frenchtown section began to dwindle, and German musical and cultural society, as well as food, became popular.

The elegance of early Vincennes cookery was in sharp contrast to the dried venison and salt pork diet of pioneers like Nancy and Thomas Lincoln. Abraham Lincoln's first Indiana home was a lean-to with a fire on the open side. That first winter of 1816, the Lincolns lived on water from melted snow, wild game and a bit of borrowed corn and wheat.

A woman's dearest possession was an iron skillet, and she baked cornmeal cakes on the end of a hoe over an open fire. Indiana hoecakes are still famous, though made now on a regular griddle.

By 1853 the inns along the Ohio River were providing fairly well for hungry travelers. The Beste family, eleven of them, popped out of an elegant covered wagon at Terre Haute, explaining that they were visitors from England. Mr. Beste wrote home about eating a brand-new food, corn bread . . . "very nice with plenty of molasses and butter" . . . a 6:30 A.M. breakfast which included "hot beefsteaks, roast and boiled chickens and various kinds of cold meat, little seed cakes, pancakes and fritters."

In the town of New Harmony, a communal Rappite society was tried, which included sharing everything down to the last slice of bread. Some years later Robert Owen tried creating another utopia there, and it was during this era that Frances Wright decided women ought to have something more spiritually nourishing than recipes for light rolls, pound cake and the like. She formed what is said to be the nation's first literary society in the 1820's. The same town's Minerva Club, 1859, claimed to be the first organized woman's club in the country.

Until recently New Harmony recalled its past at the Festival of the Golden Rain. Thousands of these trees, brought from China by Robert Owen, bloom in a shower of pure gold along the quiet old streets, and lucky festival visitors used to be treated to local specialties such as pickled perch with vinegar dressing and mince pies made with green tomatoes.

When the bagpipes skirl in the town of Bicknell, to honor Bobby Burns, the Clan Cameron gathers to eat shortbread, Scotch tea cakes and fruit dumplings, and drink nippy ginger wine.

Hungarians around South Bend still observe the gravely beautiful ceremony of blessing the wheat seed on March 24th. They cook by Old World recipes and the community is renowned for veal paprika, tiny toothsome dumplings and poppy-seed cakes.

Switzerland County is named for the immigrants who founded the town of Vevay in 1801. They made such excellent wine that Henry Clay used to send for it from Lexington, Kentucky. Meltingly delicious cheese fondues were also made in Vevay kitchens.

"Knee farmers," many of them Polish, Lithuanian and Hungarian, harvest the fat crops of onions. A favorite Hoosier delicacy is onion pie.

Around the late Wendell Willkie's town of Elwood grow the rich fields that provide reason for an annual tomato festival, and from towns like Austin and Franklin comes a scarlet flow of ketchup, soups, sauces and canned tomatoes.

William H. Wilson in *The Wabash* says Indiana "is the taste of crisp fried chicken and hot biscuits, of watermelons and cantaloupes, sweet roasting ears and homemade bread spread thick with yellow butter . . . it is women who wear aprons and sunbonnets and work miracles in their kitchens."

Indiana is also James Whitcomb Riley who immortalized the state "knee deep in June" with strawberries melting off the vine and sun lying on the winding roads "thick as butter on country bread."

Oklahoma

BLACK BLIZZARD CAKE

My part of Missouri was middle-aged and comfortable when the restless and the land-hungry began uprooting their wives from pleasant farmhouses to head west for the Sax and Fox country in what is now Oklahoma. Most of the women didn't dream what it would be like in that vast land of red dirt, rattlesnakes and swirling winds. They packed old English silver and sprigged china that had come with their mothers from Kentucky and Virginia. They took onion sets and packets of seeds. In their heads they carried southern secrets for burnt-sugar cakes and gingerbread, for swathing new butter in grape leaves to keep it cool and sweet.

When they camped out in tents and covered wagons, waiting for their men to return from the nightmare of The Run, families from Missouri found themselves overnight neighbors of crisp-voiced Yankees from Maine and Massachusetts, rosy-faced Pennsylvania Dutch, merry young wives of French adventurers. The newcomers shivered at tales like that of Bill Jones, of Paradise Valley, about living on grasshoppers for six weeks in the 1870's. They were pretty good, he said, but added that he wouldn't want to stay alive long enough to eat them three times a day again.

In a desperate duel for free land when the Cherokee Strip was opened, thousands of men took off on foot or on horseback. The stampede started at noon April 22, 1889, with the firing of the starting rifles, and by 12:15 that day Oklahoma City was rising from the dust. By night 10,000 persons were camped around a railroad boxcar set up as a station. Vendors sold cool water at ten cents a cup, lemonade at twenty. In wagons flaunting signs OKLAHOMA OR BUST . . . IN GOD WE TRUST, women scraped the bottoms of flour barrels to produce biscuits, invented a plainsman's stew of rabbit, turnips and flour-gravy.

In kettles over open fires dauntless pioneer women combined hard Spanish wheat with beef and called it Oklahoma stew, evolved pie fillings from the wild pecans—and Pioneer Pecan Pie is famous all over the state.

Melons grew first on Indian farms, and now the luscious red watermelons of Lamont have such a reputation that people come from miles around for Watermelon Day in September. Lamont housewives rescue the rinds to make clear, jewel-like preserves and pickles.

The rest of the United States and subsequently a large part of the world discovered Oklahoma in 1942. That year the curtain rose in a Broadway theater and a first-night audience held its breath at the impact of wide sky, shimmer of sunshine and the lilting tune, "Oh, What a Beautiful Morning." Thanks to the

Rodgers and Hammerstein musical, people got acquainted with the state where "the wavin' wheat can sure smell sweet when the wind comes right behind the rain." They got to know about herd-riding cowboys and box suppers where a young man can always figure out which lunch was packed by his best girl, and bids high to get it—because with it he gets the girl as a partner.

The Dust Bowl of the thirties gave a different picture. When the "Black Blizzard" descended upon them, farmwomen fought stubbornly—put milk, butter, water and all other liquids in covered fruit jars, mixed bread and biscuit dough in partly closed bureau drawers, with holes cut in cloth coverings for their hands to do the kneading. A cake made with sour cream and pecans evolved during the horror of dust and drought, to be known as Black Blizzard Cake.

Food in the hectic rush to the Oklahoma oil fields was likely to be as primitive as the fare of covered wagon days, and had strange names: Jamoka (coffee), cherries (beans), and cake which was really bread.

Barbecues and rodeos are a classic Oklahoma tradition. Texhoma's annual rabbit drive includes both, plus a wild-cow milking contest. There is a free buffalo-meat barbecue at Lake Holden-  ville on the Fourth of July, and four days of fun at Andarko's annual Indian get-together. The town of Guyman barbecues succulent buffalo steaks on its Pioneer Day, to celebrate the Panhandle's joining up with the rest of the state. A rip-snorting rodeo goes along with the barbecue. Oklahoma even stages a barbecue and rodeo at the state penitentiary near McAlester, believing it improves the morale of the inmates.

Coffee is strong and black on these occasions, though not quite up to chuckwagon standards, where they say a cowboy tosses a horseshoe into the pot, and if it floats the coffee passes muster.

Near El Reno, in the heart of the rich Canadian River valley, is the world's biggest quail hatchery, and these delicate-flavored birds are best liked in Oklahoma when they are wrapped in bacon and broiled over an open fire, then served with natural brown rice.

Oklahomans rather enjoyed it when "Alfalfa Bill" Murray campaigned for governor on a rat-cheese and cracker diet. Eschewing the traditional campaign luncheons and dinners, he rattled through the depression-ridden farm country in a Model-T Ford. Afterward he declared that "if a man is physically fit he can eat anything but whetstone and cordwood and it won't hurt him."

Murray came out for fat pork, too: "Nothing in the world is better for a man—it limbers up your system. . . ."

And finally, the governor won a devoted female following by declaring that "cooks could write as good a history any day as the sociologists and the militarists."

Kansas

LIBERAL PANCAKES

When the Mennonites arrived in Kansas in the 1870's they found the sunburnt prairies black with grasshoppers, and the farmers who had been depending on soft spring wheat, almost starving. Each Mennonite family carried a precious little package, the contents of which was to change the face of Kansas—enough Turkey Red Wheat to plant a tiny patch beside each cabin. The shrewd Mennonites believed that this hard winter wheat which throve on the steppes of Russia, where they had lived for years, would do well in the new land.

The Mennonites prospered and Kansas cooks began to learn from them exciting new delicacies such as *piroshki*—the flaky pastries filled with left-over meat and eaten with sour cream; suet pudding, buttermilk pie, cinnamon-flavored apple pie topped with buttered crumbs; the hot raised roll with smoked-sausage filling called *bubbat*.

On Saturday today, in any Mennonite home, the air is fragrant with freshly baked zwieback, some of which is saved especially for *faspa*, or Sunday lunch. Georgianna Smurthwaite, state home economics leader who treasures an old recipe for a sweet and airy "twin bun," says, "Some like them with jelly, others with butter, still others maintain they must be dunked. The only trouble is having enough to supply everyone." She also recommends meat roll, made with pounded strips of steak baked in a mixture of sour cream, browned onions, bacon and sweet pickle. *Pflaumenus* is a summer cooler—a soup of raisins, prunes and sugar in lightly thickened milk, served cold.

Not all the pioneers lived as bountifully as the Mennonites. Cora Skinner Ream, writing for the Kansas City *Star* about her childhood in the 70's, said, "Pancakes should decorate the coat of arms of the pioneers, for surely pancakes were the salvation of the early settlers—pancakes, sorghum and gravy." Mrs. Ream never tasted beef until she was twelve years old, and remembers vividly the dried buffalo meat she whittled off for between-meal snacks, the baked corn and pickled beaver-tail.

Kansas is famous for deep-dish apple pie now, but in the pioneer days, before apple orchards flourished, pies were made of sheep sorrel, dried currants and crackers treated with tartaric acid, which Cora Ream observes "looked like apple pie." Her family came west in a covered wagon train from Indiana in 1869. Their first house was a pen of cottonwood logs with a roof, but no door. She remembers watching herds of buffalo from the roof of a lean-to, and rolling popcorn balls with sorghum on a winter's night. Her mother made homemade noodles fried to deep gold with a rich gravy and bits of bacon sprinkled on top. Her sesame cakes were famous, and so were her jams and jellies of sandhill plums and chokeberries. Egg-butter was a creamy mixture of eggs and molasses, served with stacks of freshly baked bread.

Still visible on the unplowed prairies are the grass-grown ruts of wagon wheels, traces of ninety thousand people who poured westward in the exciting Gold Rush days of '49 and '50, in a variety of conveyances which included squarish carts equipped with sails and known as wind-wagons. On the Cimmaron Trail, with its fifty deadly miles of desert, travelers often had to drink the blood of their own oxen to survive.

The barbecue and the chuckwagon stew, still Kansas classics in the cattle country, were an important part of the rip-roaring days at Dodge City, when brawling cowboys brought droves of longhorns over the Texas Trail. The mayor of a few years back sent me an invitation to Dodge City's Pioneer Picnic at Wright Park. There are not too many of the real old-timers left, but sons and daughters carry on the picnic and bring baskets bulging with such Kansas specialties as Jonathan apple pie made with buttermilk pastry, and hamburger from Kansas beef, served with a hot barbecue sauce.

Kansans eat well today, but with considerably more restraint than in 1872, when a state luncheon was given at Topeka's Fifth

Avenue Hotel for Grand Duke Alexis of Russia, who came on a special train to go buffalo hunting. He was served one hundred and seven food items, including sage hen, black bear, curlew, roast opossum with persimmon jelly, coon chops, roast fawn, plover and two desserts I never heard of before—rose jelly cake and leopard cake. Pawpaw pies and persimmon pyramid are two other odd-sounding pioneer desserts.

At Lindsborg, Swedish families still eat Lenten dinners of baked brown beans, and serve the famous fast buns filled with almond paste and topped with whipped cream. The town of Cuba also has an old-world air, especially on Saturday nights when descendants of the first Bohemian settlers drive to town to drink Bohemian beer, eat highly spiced sausage produced on local farms and sing their native folk songs.

The little town of Liberal maintains a close tie with England through pancakes. Each year the pancake cooks of Liberal and those of Olney, England, sprint through the streets flipping pancakes. Last heard from, Liberal retained the championship and thus the right to call itself the Pancake Capital of the World.

For a while, some of the best food in Kansas was to be had in Franklin County, where Ernest Valeton de Bissiere set up a French socialistic colony in 1868 to raise silkworms. The Gallic farm wives concocted garlic-spiced sauces for the native quail, kept their soup kettles filled with rich black bean soup or gourmet stews of wild turkey and little new potatoes. But they soon found they could make more money at ordinary farming, and the silk industry gradually disappeared.

The world-famous editor William Allen White said, "There is just one way to stop progress in America, and that is to hire some hungry earthquake to come and gobble up Kansas."

And perhaps he was right.

Minnesota

THE BUTTER STATE

Theophilus Haecker used to tell his farm students at the University of Minnesota to "treat the cow kindly, boys. Remember, she's a lady—and a mother." The boys evidently obeyed, for in short order Minnesota became the Butter State. The dairyland sends its rich cream to the East, its butter and cheese all over the world.

Yet Minnesota was so untouched by "civilization" as late as 1860 that when Episcopal Bishop Wipple asked whether he might safely leave his valise in an Indian village for a few days, the Indians told him demurely: "Oh yes—there is no other white man in this part of the country."

To this land of lakes, soft hills and deep valleys, settlers came in colorfully costumed droves in the late 1800's from Sweden, Denmark, Norway and Finland, to acquire homesteads at a dollar and a quarter an acre. One Yankee farmer reported in alarm that his new neighbors were probably members of some evil secret society, because they went from their houses, wrapped in white, to small wooden buildings nearby from which then issued the loud hissing of steam. This was, of course, Finns taking steam baths, as they still do in the old-world community of Embarass. Finnish cookery adds a different flavor to Minnesota food—the pudding of rice, onion, grated liver and eggs, slightly sweetened, with raisins added, and served with melted butter, for instance; the cold fruit soups, the carrot custards, the filled crullers eaten with honey syrup on the first day of May. At butchering time the fresh pork blood is saved for distinctive blood pancakes and puddings.

On Shrove Tuesday all the Scandinavian communities eat special buns called *bollers*, or Shrovetide buns, filled with sweet whipped cream and coated with sugar and frosting. At Lenten meals they drink hot milk and eat thin pancakes rolled around a rich almond filling. Finnish Easter dinner traditionally ends with an orange-flavored porridge made of malt and rye flour and served with cream.

Proud and independent, Scandinavians felt at home in this new land where the hired hands sat down with the family and a caste system was unknown. The Danish Peoples Societies produced one of the world's earliest working co-operatives at Askov. This town has never had a jail, and never needed one. The Co-operative grew rutabagas, which were scorned at first as "Swede turnips," but as people tasted the delicate concoctions Swedish women made—such as crusty brown loaves of rutabaga bread—they began to buy the vegetable, and the Askov area now produces about a third of all the rutabagas in America.

On Midsummer Day, yellow-haired Swedish girls go off alone to pick flowers. When they have gathered nine different kinds, they start home, and if they get there still unescorted, they press the flowers under their pillows and dream of future husbands. On such festive occasions Swedish women bake great quantities of butter cookies and a special sweet pancake. The famous cinnamon-sprinkled rice pudding with one almond is served in most Scandinavian homes on Christmas, along with pitchers of rich country cream. Good luck or an early marriage is promised to whoever gets the almond.

The feminine pioneers who helped build Minneapolis and St. Paul were women of enormous courage and gaiety who managed to put together fine meals even with makeshift ingredients and utensils. Dried buffalo tongue is an example of their frontier delicacies. They scolded the Indians and fed them, battled to do away with whiskey and saloons, organized a sewing society and raised money for the first school; sent back East for books and magazines. These energetic creatures got up at dawn to bake bread and pies, but were on hand, fresh and glowing, for skating parties on the frozen river in winter, and for dances at any time of the year.

They welcomed fellow settlers from everywhere, and women from Ohio and Pennsylvania swapped recipes with Russian Mennonites, learned to enjoy the choir festivals with aftermaths of spiced borscht; found out how to make the succulent *porzelchen*

—raisin cakes fried in deep fat—still a specialty at New Year's Eve celebrations.

Minnesota is hospitable, with many festivals to entertain visitors. The oldest is Springfield's Sauerkraut Day, on the second Tuesday in August. This town wanted to serve a free community dinner and because so many of its citizens were of German origin, chose sauerkraut and wieners, buns and coffee for the menu. Now thousands arrive to watch the parade and sports, join in the street carnival—and eat on Springfield.

The town of Montgomery for many years observed Kolacky Day, named for the sweet turnover rolls filled with citron and topped with poppy seed. Czech homes can usually be spotted by bright poppies growing in the garden to supply seeds. On Easter Monday young boys go from door to door with a willow switch and basket to collect tinted Easter eggs from girls.

There used to be a melon festival in Atwater, and melons still grow there, but the mayor writes that the festival has been given up in favor of making his town "The Christmas Village," with the churches, parks, streets and private homes all twinkling with Christmas lights and displays.

Homecoming and Sugar Days find Chaska housewives turning out their best cakes and pies. Hopkins celebrates raspberry time, and Ortonville the ripening of the sweet corn. Milan's Scandinavians serve *lefse*, their standard salt fish, to all visitors in April, accompanied by good strong coffee. The ancient Rice Dance of the Indians in Milaca marks the harvesting of the wild rice.

Perhaps there will be a blue cheese celebration set up some time to honor the cave-ripened, Roquefortlike product of Minnesota that is fast winning gourmet approval. There ought to be some kind of commemoration, too, for a well-intentioned pioneer, Jacob Webster, who came to Caledonia in 1854, so hungry for greens that he sent back to New England and at great expense got himself some dandelions to plant!

The majestic Valley of the Mississippi is as irresistible today as when Mark Twain called it "tranquil and resposeful as dreamland . . . nothing this-worldly about it . . . nothing to hang a fret or a worry upon." Yet the life of one of my correspondents, Sue Mayo, could hardly be described as tranquil. She wrote to me from her home on Gunflint Trail, sixty-two miles from the nearest post office and store, six miles of the sixty-two across a lake, by boat in summer, by snowshoe in winter. She had been listening to me and an author on the air that day, talking about the modern housewife, who has practically nothing to do, what with mixes, deep-freeze, push-button cookery and so on. She then was baking five golden loaves of bread in an old wood stove and had just finished scrubbing a huge kitchen floor. Her water, she said, comes from a pump a hundred and fifty feet from her back door. But, she added: "What an exciting time it is to be home for the ice breakup in May—cut off from the world for three weeks—no one can get in or out. It is a hard life for a woman—but thrilling, every minute of it."

Ohio

JOHNNY APPLESEED WALKED HERE

Over a century ago a homesick young Bavarian in Wooster, Ohio, decided that Christmas was too somber a holiday in this new land. He went off into the woods, chopped a chipper young spruce and had the local blacksmith cut a metal star for its tip, then hung the branches with berries and paper flowers. So there in his candlelit home on December 25, 1847, glowed a Christmas tree which Wooster claims was the first in America. The new nation took the Christmas tree to its heart, along with German gingerbread men, thick sweet cookies called *pfeffernusse* and hard, anise-flavored *springerles*.

In the late 1700's and early 1800's, Ohio was a green lure for restless pioneers anxious to escape the "crowded" East. Farmlands bloomed and enthusiastic settlers declared the soil "needs only to be tickled with the hoe to laugh with the harvest."

In the Hocking Valley they brewed sassafras tea in spring and sipped cherry bounce, ate corn bread and mush, and steaming plates of *spex*, a German mixture of sauerkraut and pork.

There is still a Pennyroyal reunion in Guernsey County to commemorate the skill of natives who first distilled oils from that plant and from peppermint.

Most appealing of Ohio's frontier characters was a gentle young man from Massachusetts who walked out of the wilderness one day in 1801 leading a horse loaded with burlap bags. Near what is now the tiny village of Licking Creek, he found a clearing. Turning the soil he planted seeds from his burlap bag, fenced in the plot and went on. That is the first recorded Ohio visit of John Chapman, who described himself as "by occupation, a gatherer and planter of appleseeds."

A Swedenborgian by faith, he dedicated his life to setting out apple nurseries in the raw new lands where pioneer settlers would bless him and look after the fledgling orchards. For fifty years he floated down the Ohio, walked through wilderness trails, paddled up lonely creeks. Everywhere he left apple orchards. Shy and unworldly, he roamed the frontier wearing at one time a coffee sack and a cardboard hat. He loved all of nature's creatures and even put out campfires to prevent mosquitoes from getting singed! A legend in his lifetime, his death was sorrowfully reported in the Fort Wayne, Indiana, *Sentinel: Died in the neighborhood of this city, on Tuesday last, Mr. John Chapman, better known as Johnny Appleseed. . . .*

The three monuments Ohio built in his honor would please him less than the green and fragrant orchards pouring their harvest into cider, applesauce and big, old-fashioned pies. Ohio is famous for pies anyhow, including the succulent oyster pie which stars at church suppers, and an open tart of Ohio gooseberries with whipped sour cream.

In the lush Valley of God's Pleasure, another great food tradition grew as the devout Shakers established their model democracy and determined that the Kingdom of God should be set up on earth. In the four Ohio colonies, spacious kitchens were created for the Cooking Sisters. The Shakers possibly did the first commercial canning in this country, and the produce of their great Canning Kitchens grew so famous that outsiders clamored for Shaker corn salad and plump fruits and vegetables produced in experimental orchards and gardens.

The Shaker communities became highly inventive and soon produced an apple parer, a revolving oven, water-driven churn and a pea sheller. They also dreamed up quince pudding made with heavy cream and overtones of rose water, combined sour cream with eggs and ginger for Ginger Fluff, cooked the abundant Ohio catfish with parsley, carrot, turnip and onion. Herbs went into an aromatic Shaker soup, peaches into a fragrant relish and chestnuts into an exotic-sounding omelet.

For community fish fries, done the Ohio way, barrels of iced fish arrive from Lake Erie and the mayor of the town turns out in person at dawn to supervise the doings. A sheet of iron, scrubbed and rubbed with lard, is put atop a long brick oven and when the coals are right, on goes the fish, seasoned and rolled in cornmeal, to be eaten sizzling hot with fresh bread and butter and a succulent mountain of potato salad. Ice cream is made right there—fresh peach and vanilla the favorites—and eaten with prize layer cakes.

The rich black soil of Ohio farms produces twenty-five different kinds of pumpkin and squash. The town of Circleville, built on an earthworks believed to date back a thousand years to prehistoric Hopewell culture, celebrates its harvest with a pumpkin show in October. Local pies may be topped with a thin layer of maple-flavored whipped cream, flavored with a dash of coffee or topped with toasted coconut.

At the Geuga County maple festival in Chardon the best cooks serve continuous snacks at the local churches: corn fritters or pancakes with sausage and maple syrup; and night suppers of baked ham, hot biscuits and syrup. Local restaurants feature maple-barbecued spareribs, and ham and chicken dinners.

"The sweetest town on earth," Medina, got that way because a jewelry manufacturer bought a swarm of bees for a dollar back in 1865. Now his firm sends tons of packaged bees and queens by the thousands to beekeepers everywhere. Ohioans choose their honeys as carefully as connoisseurs do wine, and use them in delectable honey-raisin pies, honey cakes flavored with rose water and stored for a month before eating, honey-spiced baked country ham, and an angel food baked with honeyed egg whites.

Glendale, which might have been transplanted, green hills and all, from Massachusetts, bakes its beans in time-honored New England fashion with salt pork and molasses.

Dumplings made with sour milk, chicken pot pie, fudge cake with deep-piled boiled frosting and a host of other Yankee dishes mark the area along Lake Erie where homesick refugees from Connecticut settled after their homes were burned during the War of 1812. Town names are Norwalk, New London, Greenwich and New Haven.

It was the prairie schooner settlers from New England who began using bread stuffings for pork and beef. Today Ohio cooks have developed a special technique for putting pockets in all sorts of pork and beef cuts, filling them with a light, dry stuffing made of bread crumbs browned in butter and seasoned with onion, minced celery, salt, pepper and sage. They also like to wrap this stuffing in thin slices of meat and bake to a crusty brown.

The old-fashioned farms of Tuscarawas County turn out fine Swiss cheese which local cooks use to make *rigi-muchli*—a nut-brown Swiss cheese muffin—and *chunchel*, which is a rich cheese custard served in slices and topped with fruit.

Many settlers brought to Ohio their native customs and sometimes kept them intact, as in the Czech town of Taberville with its wonderful hand-carved birdhouses, close-huddled homes, rustic outdoor dining rooms and a town crier calling out the hours of 6 A.M. and 6 in the evening. Fish boiled with spices and served with a black sauce of prunes, almonds and raisins is a reminder of the old country, as is *milosti*, a pastry deep-fried and crisp, dredged in powdered sugar and flavored with local grape juice. Goose is served on St. Wenceslaus Eve, September 28th, while boiled carp is a must for Christmas Eve and boar's head often ushers in the New Year.

Sweitzer cheese, a German favorite, is still sold at Feundu, where Amish farmers hold a community sale two or three times a month, as well as at Farmerstown and other hamlets in this green and incredibly neat countryside.

Under the blazing blue skies of August, Syrians from all corners of the country come to the shady park at Carey for the Feast of the Assumption. Over outdoor fires the famous shish-kebab (skewered lamb) is broiled to juicy tenderness and eaten with Syrian pilaf, rice or barley. Rich shortbread cookies called *grabies* are served with tea.

When steel came to Cleveland, so did people from everywhere, and by the 1950's, forty languages could be heard within the city limits, and as many varieties of cooking graced the tables. One of the earliest and least known of the newcomers were the Manxmen. The first thirteen Manx families left their misty little island in May, 1826. When they arrived, Cleveland was a town of six hundred. The first arrivals took to agriculture, and for a good many years every farm for miles around Warrentown was owned by a family from the Isle of Man. Cleveland and Cuyhoga Counties are still Manx headquarters, and descendants of the islanders gather for picnics and festivals such as Midsummer Day. Manx recipes were handed down by word of mouth from pioneer women in hand-woven shawls and small caps—oaten cakes, griddle breads, sheepshead on herring.

Cincinnati sprouted after the War of 1812, and because of the quantities of meat shipped from there, was nicknamed Porkopolis. A visitor in the 1800's commented on "the elegance of the houses, the parade of servants, the display of furniture and more than all, the luxuries of the overloaded tables." A nineteenth-century hostess presided as a matter of course over a dinner of fish, roast chicken, beef, meat pie, tongue, baked ham, corn on the cob, potatoes and beans.

Oysters were the luxury food here, arriving by "oyster express" —an involved system which started in Baltimore, Maryland, with the oysters packed in straw soaked with sea water, then driven in light, fast wagons to Pittsburgh, where they were loaded on river boats. Arriving in Cincinnati, they were kept alive for weeks in tanks of salt water sprinkled with cornmeal. The oyster craze which swept this whole country from the 1830's on resulted in hundreds of fancy parlors devoted solely to oysters, raw, stewed, fried, baked and in pies. Rich people ate them the year round, even for breakfast.

Cincinnati's major food theme in the 1800's, however, was German. The effect of the hearty Teutonic eaters upon our American food pattern can be estimated from listing some words that are now part of our language: hamburger, sauerkraut, frankfurter, liverwurst and pumpernickel.

Nebraska

FIFTY MILES TO FUN

If the capital of the United States had been moved to Lincoln, Nebraska, in 1870, salt would have been the cause. A salt convention was held that year in Kansas City to urge the government to abandon Washington, D. C., in favor of the sprawling frontier town of Lincoln. The arguments were based on the discovery of the great salt flats of Lancaster County, Nebraska. Salt was so hard to come by that the government offered a bounty of two cents for each bushel refined. Businessmen, dreaming of fortunes to be made overnight, felt that the federal government ought to be as close as possible to the valuable salt deposits.

Washington remained the capital, but the salt deposits did bring prosperity to the Lincoln-Kearney section of the fledgling state. Settlers came from as far away as Des Moines, Iowa, swapping fruit and grain for the precious substance they needed for themselves and their livestock.

Nebraska had been a state for only three years when the salt convention was held, but none of the explorers, trappers and traders who came there in the early days was wise enough to really foresee the Nebraska of golden wheat fields. Indeed, military observer Major Stephen Long, who went through Nebraska in 1819, reported it "uninhabitable for people dependent upon agriculture for subsistence."

There have been times when later Nebraskans agreed. Rocky Mountain grasshoppers were the first plague they had to endure. The grasshoppers began swarming over the state in 1856, and during the next seventeen years reappeared six times. It was not uncommon to see a covered wagon bumping through Omaha's dusty streets with a sign on the back:

EATEN OUT BY GRASSHOPPERS. GOING BACK EAST
TO LIVE WITH WIFE'S FOLKS.

The Indians dealt with the crisis by grinding grasshoppers to
make meal. This never appealed to the white settlers, who lived
mostly on dried buffalo meat, or jerky, until they could plant crops
again.

Appleton Harmon, a Mormon pioneer, stood in his covered
wagon at the edge of the Platte River in 1847 and estimated that
he could count more than 10,000 buffalo in plain sight. But the
men who poured over the California and Oregon Trails by the
hundred thousand, with their families, soon wiped out the great
herds.

Mormons were among the first to realize that the immigrants
would be in the market for food and supplies by the time they hit
Nebraska and the last outfitting posts on the trail west. As a result,
Mormon farms became so prosperous that the settlers of the 1850's
were advised to "follow Mormons and prairie dogs, and find good
land." Those who chose the sandhill country instead of "following
Mormons" had rough going. Mari Sandoz, who grew up in this
region of violent storms and extreme weather, in her epic portrait
of her father recalls an abandoned shack with this grim verse
carved on its front door:

> 30 miles to water,
> 20 miles to wood,
> 10 miles to Hell,
> And I gone there for good.

The sandhill country is a strange, desolate region where
ranchers and farmers traveled fifty miles or more for a party, wearing the long fur robes that the first settlers designed for protection
from bitter winter cold. The parties were announced in the local
newspapers and everybody was urged to come for dinner, from
one to seven, with dancing, beds and breakfasts for all. Today's
parties usually break up by midnight, with a final snack of hickory-
smoked ham sandwiches on fragrant homemade bread, side dishes
of cole slaw, cucumber pickles, plenty of coffee and sometimes a
roast sandhill turkey.

People with "Methodist feet"—meaning those whose religion
forbade dancing—used to go to Play Parties, skip nimbly to old

folk tunes, eat popcorn balls sweetened with sorghum, and drink pitchers of nippy cherry cider.

The night in 1855 when Omaha citizens gave a grand ball for Territorial Governor Mark W. Izard, it was so cold that the scrub water froze on the ballroom floor of the City Hotel and dancers often fell flat. Refreshments on that occasion were thick bacon sandwiches, slabs of dried apple pie and coffee.

One of the earliest Omaha boardinghouses advertised "venison, fowl, bird or fish cooked in any manner you like," adding that "you may smoke in the parlor, put your heels on the sideboard—or spread your buffalo robe on the green grass."

Although Nebraska had only 2,732 inhabitants in 1854, it grew rapidly as settlers from other lands arrived. The first Bohemian, Charles Zulek, walked all the way back to Missouri to get provisions and carried them on his back to Humboldt. Maria Klodja came on foot from Wisconsin, driving her cattle. The Bohemian zest for cooking enlivens Nebraska menus with chicken paprika, goulash, tiny dumplings, holiday almond cakes. At the gala Bohemian fruit festival, halls are decked with grapes and a fine imposed on guests who eat the decorations. Everybody does, and the money goes to charity.

Swedes and Danes added to the Nebraska cuisine the Danish pear and barley porridge, red cabbage, pork pancakes, Swedish fish mousse, rye bread sweetened with molasses, and waffles made with snow for leavening and served with cherry jam.

In Nebraska, bachelors who managed to arrive at the home of a renowned cook exactly at mealtime were nicknamed "grub-line riders." They staked out kitchens famous for buttermilk spoon bread, yellow with cornmeal; raisin oatmeal bread, orange- and lemon-flavored cornmeal cookies, apple-bran rolls, toasted peaches with a crisp coating of butter and corn flakes. Many of these delicacies were invented by catalogue wives—the frontier label for wives obtained from matrimonial bureaus.

From early spring until late fall, the foods of Nebraska are feted at fairs, festivals and carnivals. Barbecues spice the air for miles around at Old Settlers' Reunions, Oregon Trail Days, Harvest Fairs, Pioneer Picnics, and descendants of frontier families gather for any reason at all to retell the stirring yarns of the past, meantime eating fried chicken, baked ham, corn bread, apple pie and layer cake.

There was the time biscuits saved a whole family. A reporter friend, Evelyn Wells, got the story from a Mrs. Tugwell, who came overland as a child, in a little covered wagon caravan. An Indian band swooped down on their camp one evening. Mrs. Tugwell's father looked at the war-painted riders and said calmly, "Mother, these boys look hungry . . . why not stir them up a batch of your biscuits?"

Mother did, while Father hurriedly milked the cows and started a rasher of bacon. The beaming Indians sat down to a prairie feast. While raids and killings went on almost within earshot, the Biscuit Caravan continued happily on its way, with the Indians dropping in at all hours and the cows on a most erratic milking schedule. The only fear was that the flour would give out before the Indians did. But the wagons rolled through the last mountain pass, and the green world of California welcomed the resourceful pioneers.

Iowa

HEAR THE CORN GROW!

When the August corn wind blows hot across Iowa, farmwomen search their shelves for the clearest glasses of jelly, get out their prize cake and pie recipes and begin baking for the Fair. The success of the Fair depends upon the crops. Corn, which has to be "knee-high by July" if it is to be a bumper crop, has given its golden harvest to Iowa since ancient Indian times. For more than 100 years the state's farmers have been bragging that corn grows taller there than anywhere.

In my Mid-Western childhood, I dreamed of living in New York and writing great novels. I inherited from my father the capacity for dreams, but his were always of land; deep, fertile midcontinental soil which was both a challenge and a satisfaction. He would have liked to own hundreds of acres of farmland in the rich corn belt.

I thought about Papa when a group of Soviet farmers came to

visit Iowa and found themselves warmly welcomed by country dwellers who had often been labeled isolationists. Some were surprised that the Russians' trip came off so well, but I understood, for I remember my father's absorbed face when he and another farmer—any farmer from anywhere—started to swap talk of weather, crops or market prices.

All the same, the Iowa farm of today would have awed my father just as much as it did the Russians. The great food freezers, the electric washing machines, clothes driers, television sets, shiny new automobiles—and most of all, the farm machinery that permits a man to operate a 150-acre farm almost single-handed—to my father, that sort of farm life would have been as improbable as a Jules Verne fantasy.

Corn is at least two thousand years old, and the Indians had developed many types of it before Marquette first invaded the prairies in 1673. But it was the trained experts of modern times who worked out Iowa's success formula—corn and hogs. Iowa's annual harvest of corn is a crop of appalling bulk. But 45 per cent of it reaches the market in the highly compressed and profitable form of meat. And this conversion often takes place on the farm where the corn is grown.

When the Russians arrived to study this miracle of the Middle West, they found the corn seven feet high and the farmers gloating over nights when the thermometer registered in the nineties, and you could, as we used to say, hear the corn grow—a soft, secret rustle in the hot dark. This is the time of year when a farmer anxiously watches the changeable face of nature, too. Tornadoes, hail and drought are threats to his family's well-being. All too vivid are his memories of the droughts of the thirties which, piled on top of the depression, almost put him out of business.

When nature is at her best, alfalfa grows purple-green in the meadows, in the fields are bumper crops of corn, wheat and oats, and in the barnyard, fat pigs grunt. The whirr of the machines in the fields is the signal for farmwomen to bring out all their cooking skills. When the men troop in, hungry, bronzed and sweating from the sun, long tables are ready, set with blue and white pitchers of milk and cream, glass jugs of cold cider, plates heaped with red and yellow tomatoes, bowls filled with cucumber and onions in vinegar, piccalilli, pickles, apple butter and spiced watermelon rind. Mountains of fresh bread accompany whole hams, roast chickens, pork and sauerkraut, clouds of mashed potatoes with butter melting in the center, baked beans, casseroles of macaroni with crusty browned cheese on top. And pies—raisin, custard, lemon, apple, gooseberry.

The whooee-whooeee of hog callers echoes across the state in early fall and, like the corn husking contests, is an excuse for picnics, community suppers and celebrations.

Iowa arrived at statehood in 1846, after being tossed casually from France to Spain and back again, then into the Territories of Louisiana, Indiana, Missouri, Michigan and Wisconsin. Its energetic people were freedom-seekers from Europe and the land-hungry from everywhere—New England, the South and the East.

Some Iowa towns have discovered that it's good publicity to preserve Old World flavor. Dutch settlers who came in 1847 built Pella into a city famous for its churches. Visitors by the hundreds come to eat the famous Pella sausages and soft Dutch spice cookies as big as saucers. On St. Nicholas Eve the old Dutch houses have straw men leaning against the door jambs, pockets filled with small gifts and sugary pastries cut into alphabet letters.

The so-called Hook and Eye Dutch founded the plain, prim town of Littleton, and there families sit on scrubbed benches drawn to home-built tables to eat their brown bean soup with onion, cabbage stuffed with sour apples and newly baked ginger cake made with ginger syrup, moist ginger and brown sugar.

The Amana Society came out of Germany to Iowa to establish a Community of True Inspiration in the 1800's. Amana hams, cured in village attics, are baked with cloves, vinegar and brown sugar, or sliced and fried thick to go with German fried potatoes and wilted greens. Amana bacon and dried beef are sought-after products as well. In the vine-covered bakery, famous Amana bread comes from the brick oven in great two-pound loaves. Amana housewives also make fluffs of apple fritters to serve hot with corn syrup.

All through the 1800's, the people came—Bohemians who still brew their tea with cinnamon, cloves and lemon; Scots who bake scones and assemble annually for the wild Sword Dance and Highland Fling; Germans who keep such pretty customs as the wearing of breakfast caps by housewives until the morning work is finished; Dunkards who build kitchens onto their churches and, instead of the usual ritual of communion, eat a full meal on the Sunday when they commemorate the Last Supper.

Food has its special days all over Iowa—Watermelon Day at

Leland; Pancake Day at Calumet; the taffy-pull at Brayton's molasses factory; and Corn Day at Waukon. Ten thousand people crowd into Ackley, whose normal population is about sixteen hundred, for Sauerkraut Day, and this has been going on for nearly fifty years.

But the best Iowa fun is the annual convention of Tourist Union No. 63, held every August in Britt. It began in 1900, when three energetic men, to get some publicity for their town, dreamed up a convention for hoboes. The stunt exceeded the press agents' wildest dreams, partly because August is a month known to newspaper people as the Silly Season, when some improbable stories get into print because there's nothing probable to take up space. So all the big city papers sent reporters, and front-page headlines hurtled Britt into nationwide fame. Canny businessmen saw a fine future in it, and Britt now attracts more than twenty thousand visitors for Hobo Day.

Want to know how to make a Mulligan? The Britt *News-Tribune* advises assembling twenty stew pots, or discarded lard cans if you're dining in true hobo style. In goes the following:

450	pounds of beef	10	pounds of parsnips
250	pounds of carrots	150	pounds of tomatoes
900	pounds of potatoes	3	pounds chili peppers
35	pounds of green and red peppers	25	pounds of rice
		60	pounds of celery
300	pounds of cabbage	1	pound bay leaves
100	pounds of turnips	25	gallons of mixed vegetables
	10 pounds of kitchen bouquet flavoring		

North Dakota

PEMMICAN, BANNOCKS AND *Skyr*

Visiting homes in North Dakota today, you could eat in at least a dozen languages, including Icelandic, and also celebrate Rama-

dan, the thirty-day fast of Syrian Moslems. Railroad promotion
agents, with tales of bonanza farms and fortunes to be made in
wheat, were responsible for the rush of such a colorful assortment
of human beings to North Dakota.

Before that the region was the stronghold of the great fur
companies, and the rugged white men who paddled the streams
adopted the food of the Indians. The most famous of all North
Dakotans, Vilhjalmur Stefansson, Arctic explorer and scholar, once
said on my radio program that it seems to have required "a famine
or other bit of tough luck to get colonists to go beyond tasting and
sneering at the special dishes of native America."

But in North Dakota, the trappers took to buffalo pemmican
enthusiastically. A pressed, concentrated food of dried lean meat
and rendered fat, pemmican was the invention of Plains Indians,
and it became such an important food that a war was named for it.
(The Pemmican War lasted from 1814 to 1821.) Without pemmican, the fur companies felt they faced ruin, because this pressed
light-weight food made possible their great transportation system.
These companies wanted to keep the country wild and the Indians healthy so that their supplies of buffalo and furs could continue. But farm-minded colonists shot the buffalo, fought the
Indians, pushed back the wilderness and fenced-in the land.

In 1812 a group of Scottish Highlanders, led by the Earl of
Selkirk, arrived in the Red River valley and set new food patterns,
stubbornly ignoring strange Indian items in favor of salt pork and
beef from England, oatmeal porridge, salt fish and shortbread.
You can still eat traditional Highland and Orkney food in the
Scottish homes of North Dakota, especially on gala occasions such
as the Highlanders Frolic at International Peace Gardens on the
Canadian border. In the nearby town of Dunseith descendants
of the first Scottish settlers to this day make steamed Free Kirk

pudding stuffed with spices, raisins and currants, little orange-
flavored cakes called *bannocks,* and an adaptation of Cream-
Crowdie—toasted oatmeal beaten into heavy sweetened cream
and served with fresh strawberries or raspberries.

Many families still have old Highland cookbooks containing
recipes like Hatted Kit, a frothy pudding which calls for warmed
buttermilk to be carried to the barn; then you "milk into it about
a pint of milk straight from a cow, having previously added to the
dish sufficient rennet for the whole." The recipe adds that Hatted
Kit "can quite well be made without milking the cow into it,

although the direct milking puts a better hat on the kit."

North Dakota has the chief Icelandic settlements in this country, at Hallron, Akra, Svols, Hensel and Gardas where they still like blueberries served with *skyr*, their version of yogurt which a few old-fashioned farmwomen still make at home with a special culture kept alive since the colonization of Iceland in the year 930. An Icelandic Christmas features such food names as *handikjot*, smoked mutton served cold with creamed green peas. Icelandic mutton is famous for the flavor acquired by pasturing the sheep on wild mountain herbs. Chopped, salted and laid down in barrels with brown sugar, it is called *saltkjotes*. *Kaefe* is fresh minced lamb cooked in a thick gravy with a bit of the heart added, then canned to be served all year round in thin slices as an hors d'oeuvres or sandwich filling. Even more exotic sounding is *riklinger*, sun-dried strips of halibut beaten soft with a stone sledge and served with butter.

When men went alone to explore, fight, trade or prospect for gold they settled for the food that was there when they arrived. But not so the women. Irene Paden, writing in *The Wake of the Prairie Schooner*, says women "were invariably prejudiced in favor of a better variety of food. They carried potatoes and squash, rice, preserves, pickles and eggs safely packed in cornmeal which would be used up on the way as the eggs vanished."

Finns who came to New Leipzig still bake at butchering time a mixture of beef blood, rye, wheat and oats which they cut into doughnut shapes and string on long sticks to harden before preserving in lime for year-round use.

The Moslem families who settled homesteads around Rosa still eat a sweet stew made of meat, vegetables and durum wheat which has been boiled, dried in the sun and then ground in a horse-powered mill.

The best food this side of Paris, they say, used to be served at the Marquis de Mores' twenty-eight-room château near Medora, where President Theodore Roosevelt in the 1880's, visiting North Dakota badlands, was often wined and dined. The marquis spent a fortune on agricultural experiments and a meat-packing plant that failed. But the state's great farms and meat-packing establishments today prove that the Frenchman's theories were sound, if a bit ahead of his time.

Another of the state's visionaries was Lawrence B. Waldron, genius of wheat. His Cerce variety, drouth and rust-resistant, a cross of Marquis wheat with Russian wheat brought to Fargo in 1903, has saved the state millions of dollars.

A famous North Dakotan pioneer was Fannie Heath, who came from Minnesota as a bride in 1881, to find that the tree-claim of her homestead was on barren alkaline soil. Fannie was determined to have a garden, and she was such a genius that forty years later her home was circled by box elder, cottonwood, ash and black walnut trees, and a thousand kinds of flowers and shrubs, among them the damask rose first planted by an ancestor of hers in Virginia in 1774. When Fannie died in 1931, the black raspberry she had developed was named for her, and today some of the best jellies, jams and pies in the state are made from Fannie Heath raspberries.

French Canadians who came to the Red River valley in the 1890's still serve such traditional dishes as *cassoulet*, made French fashion with pork, beans, goose and other good things; creamy vichyssoise, crescent-shaped breakfast rolls called *croissants*, with North Dakota wild honey to pour on.

In towns like Fargo, where the predominating population is Norwegian, the children in masks and costumes of Christmas Fools troop through the streets during the Yule season and are served coffee and pastries at each home visited. Christmas Angels, three specially trained and costumed girls who bless each house and sing a carol or two, tour German neighborhoods in the region.

Incidentally, North Dakota is the only state I know of which has a law to publicize flour. Every official state document has to be stamped BUY DAKOTA MAID FLOUR.

Michigan

A FESTIVAL A DAY

A tourist could eat his way up and down Michigan for a whole year just by keeping track of food festivals. Gay goings-on are held in honor of everything from smelts to cherries, from perch to peaches. But the town of Glenn puts on the festival to end all festivals. In a good-humored parody, it stages an annual Pancake fanfare to commemorate the day in December when the towns-people battled a blizzard with pancake turners. Railroad travelers were marooned there by the hundred, and when bread supplies ran out, Glenn housewives fed their involuntary guests pancakes. The Glenn Pancake Festival is held with mock solemnity and much fun, the last week in May—the date is part of the parody.

When the Peach Harvest Festival in Romeo begins, buses take loads of hungry tourists into the countryside and they eat their fill, free, of the pink and gold tree-ripened fruit. Most of them also buy peaches to take home, which is a practical aspect of the affair.

At Cherry Festival time, the kitchens of Traverse City turn out thousands of tart, juicy cherry pies and high, feathery angel-food cakes with cherry fillings. Roadside stands feature cherry cider and cherry cordials. In the twenties, when frosts and pests threatened the whole yield, orchardists instituted the Blessing of the Blossoms, with priest, rabbi and minister offering prayers for a rich harvest. Now more than 200,000 visitors come to Traverse City for three days of pageantry at blossom time.

The experiments of one man, B. J. Morgan, changed the face of the Grand Traverse Bay region and added to the eating pleasure of millions, for it was he who bought a few sandhills in the 1890's and found that tart red cherries flourished there. Today the area is one of the greatest fruit belts on earth.

Paw Paw is the heart of the grape country and in late October, when the countryside is spectacular with fall color, visitors are welcomed to the wineries and grape-pressing plants, where the blue Concord grape makes full-bodied juices, jams and wines, and where the more delicate Niagara White and Delaware Pink are also grown. A regional specialty is a grape upside-down cake served warm with unsweetened whipped cream.

My nicest link with Paw Paw is Radio Star Kathryn Roche, who did what I'm forever threatening to do—retire to the country to run a little business. Kathryn is happy with her gift shop on Blue-berry Hill and helps supervise the big business of blueberry growing. In season my mail brings cellophane-topped boxes of these prize berries, sweet, plump, purple-blue and ready to eat by the bowlful with a sprinkle of lemon juice, sugar, and plenty of cream.

Smelt, the silvery little fish which makes such a delicate pan-fry, is feted in a number of communities. Beulah, Escanaba and Sault Ste. Marie have festivals to mark the dramatic moment when the temperamental smelt decides to run. Smelt will not budge until the stream water is as cold as thirty-six degrees or below, and the urge to start usually comes around midnight. At a signal, lights are turned on and men and women go surging into the water with nets. As soon as the smelt supervisor decides they've caught enough, he turns the lights off and the fishermen retreat. The smelt run goes on undisturbed for another two hours, and then the waiting fishermen have another go at them. If the run is big enough, they get a final chance just before dawn. The smelt-dipper needs rubber hipboots, a hard dip net and warm clothing. The fish, delicious pan-fried with potatoes, has lent its name to the three villages of Smeltania, Middle Smeltania and Upper Smeltania.

Kalkaska claims to have the only National Trout Festival in the United States.

The famous Paint River Bass Festival came to an end about seven years ago because the bass developed a mysterious ailment. The mayor of Crystal Falls now reports that the epidemic is over, the streams are full of healthy fish . . . fine eating, too, for the lucky angler who lands a big one.

Perhaps best known of all Michigan fetes is the one at Holland in tulip-time. Every May, women begin to scrub down their city inch by inch. The town is fragrant with the smell of rich food—*speculas,* a spicy almond cookie cut in windmill shape; *weespermoppen,* cookies named for the Dutch city of Weesp, also almond-flavored and dropped from a spoon; crisp Dutch *sandtarts,* molasses cookies filled with nuts and raisins, all made from handed-down-for-generations recipes.

Holland is famous also for pea soup; *schniebonen,* pork simmered with potatoes and beans; red cabbage; fish cakes and pigs-in-a-blanket. Dutch sweets are *babalaars*—brown sugar and vinegar taffy; and *koffie* bonbons made by a three-century-old recipe. A favorite dessert is *flanajas,* made with rich milk, orange rind and egg.

Food-conscious in a slightly different way is Battle Creek. Bernice Love says there are children in Battle Creek who have never tasted pork or pepper, and undoubtedly adults who never in their lives have eaten meat. The community began to be concerned about health in 1855, when the Seventh Day Adventists migrated there from New York state. Water cures first made the place famous, but it remained for Dr. J. H. Kellogg to make Battle Creek known round the world when in 1897 he patented a method of making nut-meal and nut-butter. Later his brother added corn-flakes to the roster. Then came Postum and grapenuts, and the era or breakfast cereals that pop, crackle and crunch on millions of American tables.

At supper one night in the 1850's, guests at Burdick House in Kalamazoo encountered a strange green vegetable. A venturesome few tasted it, but weren't enthusiastic. James Taylor, the Scotsman who grew the first celery in his backyard, was so disappointed at the public reaction that he then and there gave up celery-growing. A Dutch farmer named DeBruin, less easily discouraged, sent his children from door to door selling the newcomer until the neighborhood gave in and accepted it. Now Kalamazoo is nationally noted for celery.

The French who piloted Indian canoes up and down Michigan's waterways in the seventeenth century raised only a few pears and apples and did not attempt any large-scale farming. They did, however, like a cider wine which Joseph Campau reported was made by these intricate instructions:

Take a tub with two heads in one and the upper one being a board full of holes then put on sticks to keep the flannel up then put in your flannel then put in one bushel of beach sand. Cover it with flannel then and 6^{11} of chalk 1^{11} of cinnamon 2^{11} of raisins. Cover the sand with flannel then put on waits to keep it down then pore in your cider and let it stand 24 hours tightly covered draw it off it will bee verry pleasant to make it stronger and more like port wine Add 2 gallons of brandy and sweten it with 8^{11} of shugur.

Elleine H. Stones sent me this recipe from the Detroit Public Library.

Michigan beans go into soup that is served in the United States Senate restaurant, and also make casseroles, salads and even sandwiches trimmed up with horseradish, onion, chopped ripe olives, mayonnaise and a dash of Tabasco. Before and just after the Civil War, dried apples were almost as important as beans in Michigan life. On the western prairies they filled the farm family's Thanksgiving or Christmas pie. In lumber camps they added the only touch of sweetness to frugal meals of potatoes, beans, and salt pork. They were even traded at the country store for gingham, red flannel, tea, coffee, spices and other items needed for the long winter months.

In the Upper Peninsula, Scandinavian settlers' distinctive foods are universally popular. The marvelous dishes of the smörgasbord: smoked salmon crowned with mayonnaise, Swedish salad of diced herring, meat, pickle, apple and potato with garnish of chopped hard-cooked eggs and pickled *bettes* (small, hot fish or meat balls); tiny potato puffs, anchovies, smoked herring. An Old World Christmas dinner in the region substitutes roast pork with chestnut dressing for turkey, glazed prunes for cranberry sauce and red cabbage with caraway for succotash. Roast goose has always been another Michigan Christmas dinner favorite.

Weddings in the Polish sections, especially Detroit's Hamtramck, bring out bright banners and streamers, and tables piled with stuffed suckling pigs, sauerkraut, partridges in vine leaves, herring in sour cream and pancakes, thin and delicate, stuffed with mixtures of cheese, or jams and jellies. The wedding day starts with breakfast, when the guests rattle spoons against plates and shout *"gouzko"* (bitter)—to warn that marriage may have its trials. The bride and bridegroom kiss each other to end the shouting and clatter. Toasts go on until dancing stops at midnight, when the bride's mother snips off a portion of the veil and puts it on her daughter's head as a matron's cap. Then the bride cuts the cake . . . and the guests dance until dawn.

It's all a part of the region which Pierre Radisson in 1658 described as "pleasant to the eye, the spirit and the belly"—Michigan.

South Dakota

A TOUCH OF THE SUBLIME

On a steep path along Grand River stands a monument to Hugh Glass that tells a good deal about the kind of people who built the state of South Dakota.

Glass was scouting ahead of a trading party in the summer of 1823 when a grizzly attacked him. By the time the party caught up with him, the bear was dead and Glass lay bleeding and unconscious. They decided after four days that he would die, and went away. Recovering consciousness, he could tell by the ashes of the fire and the remnants of cornmeal and salt pork that somebody had been and gone. This made him too angry to die. He clawed off enough bear meat to restore some of his strength, and with one broken leg, he began to crawl toward Fort Kiowa, a hundred miles away. After weeks, keeping alive by eating roots and berries, he made the fort, recovered, and then trailed by keelboat and on foot the men who had deserted him. He came upon one of them in a cabin at the mouth of the Big Horn, held his gun over the man who huddled in a corner, and said, "Get up and wag your tail. I wouldn't shoot a pup."

When he caught up with the other man, who had been his special friend, there was no more anger in Glass. The two looked long at each other and then shook hands. John C. Weihardt, the western poet who wrote a song about Hugh Glass, said that the end of this saga raised it from a story of endurance and revenge "to the level of sublimity."

There is a touch of the sublime, or at least of the capacity to endure bravely, in the whole story of South Dakota. Her people were marooned for months at a time by blizzards, often had to burn their precious corn to keep from freezing. As recently as 1949, the 5th Army had to organize an Operation Snowbound to dig out isolated ranch families during a twenty-one-day siege, while airplanes formed a haylift to drop feed for livestock.

But South Dakota has sturdily kept on growing.

Every year in the city of Mitchell, in the only Corn Palace in the world, a six-day festival climaxes the harvest season. Great pictorial panels are designed from 3,000 bushels of corn in ten shades, from flax, millet, oats and cane. One year the pictures told the South Dakota story, starting with an Indian roasting buffalo over a prairie fire and ending with sweeping fields of corn and a tractor standing beside a streamlined barn.

Settlers of many nationalities brought cattle, chickens and wheat to South Dakota. Long before the "coffee break" became fashionable in offices and factories, Scandinavians were having their coffee and cakes twice a day, mid-morning and mid-afternoon, often in the fields to which women hauled steaming coffeepots and baskets of almond cakes, yeast-raised crullers or spice cookies.

People come from miles around when the news gets out that there is to be a smörgasbórd at Beaver Valley Church. The Swedish cooks of the countryside are justly famed for the table they set: herring, sardines, anchovies, liver loaf, headcheese, vegetable salad, spiced ham, goat's milk cheese and twenty similar items. Then comes the famous herring-in-cream, with hot spicy meat balls. Bowlfuls of South Dakota strawberries with frozen whipped cream complete the picture.

Norwegians from the region of Hardanger, in Norway, still hold two-day wedding festivals at Baltic, Garretson, Colton and Canton, where the ceremonies end after two days with a tremendous banquet. A basket of shiny red apples is the centerpiece, flanked by American and Norwegian flags. The guests eat rutabaga, introduced to this country by the Swedes, served scalloped with apples, butter and brown sugar, or glazed and combined with sautéed mushrooms and green peas; roast mutton; four kinds of cheese; sliced bologna and creamed mush.

The Russo-German Mennonites, who fled Germany to Russia and thence to the farm region of South Dakota, brought recipes from every region they touched: poppyseed pies from the Slavic countries, and from Germany well-seasoned hamburger encased in pastry dough and fried in deep fat.

The Hutterites who founded Millerdale on a primitive plan for communal living, today have a deep-freeze, an electric bread slicer and other ultramodern devices to save work in their community kitchen. But the women still spin wool from their own sheep to make the family clothes.

In South Dakota, *gumbo* is the incredibly black soil of a desolate area north of the Black Hills where only a handful of humans have ever dared to make homes. Gumbo when dry wrinkles like an ancient face and when wet, rolls like a murky sea, so that neither man nor beast can move through it. Grass on the gumbo is so rich that gumbo-grazing lambs are known throughout the state for delicate flavor. A magnificent Sunday dinner dish is roast leg of gumbo lamb dusted with nutmeg, with Dakota potatoes sizzled in the hot fat until they are crusty brown outside, and buffalo-berry or chokeberry jelly.

In the eerie regions of the butte and badlands, and the ancient Black Hills, are found fossils of the 15-ton brontosaurus and the dinosaurs, beryllium for atomic energy, lithium for the hydrogen bomb, as well as bantomite, which looks and feels like butter when it is dug and among other uses, helps keep chocolate candy from melting.

But gold is still king in the Black Hills, and both the miners and ranchers of the Black Hills country are too busy to grow much food. So they drive to Upper Spearfish Valley, where a sprawling roadside market offers them the produce of the irrigated farms—apples for applesauce that accompanies a favorite South Dakota dinner of roast pork and baked sweet potatoes; rhubarb for pieplant pie; home-cured ham and bacon.

Visitors who hope to taste antelope steak or elk roast will have to eat elkburgers or buffaloburgers in State Legion Lake Park, because the brief hunting season for these animals is reserved for residents.

Most exotic of all the game birds is the Chinese ringneck pheasant at Huron. Hunters come by plane from all over the country to take more than three and a half million of these birds in a season. Many of the hotels and hunting lodges specialize in cooking pheasant to order, sometimes roasted, the breast covered with salt pork; sometimes braised with chopped liver and tangerine combined in a filling; or often in a casserole with onion, mushrooms and butter.

Old-time lamb and beef barbecues add to the excitement of the Days of '76 Celebration during the first week in August at Deadwood, the gold mining town.

South Dakota lemon drops are the symbol of the businessmen who form the Clown Band of the town of Lemmon, which marches and plays at state occasions and hands the candies to delighted children along the route.

Fish fries are Rapid City's specialty—trout hauled from the sparkling cold water and cooked on a 22-foot stove of logs and rock, with country-fried potatoes, biscuits, and pots of fragrant coffee. One of the strangest meals in the state's history was served when Rapid City topped its rival, Aberdeen, in population, and the Aberdeen Chamber of Commerce entertained the businessmen of Rapid City. The guests ate thick, juicy slices of Dakota prime ribs of beef, but the hosts solemnly chewed roast crow.

Wisconsin

A small boy named Ehrich Wales picked the lock of his mother's pastry cupboard and helped himself to a handful of oatmeal cookies and a piece of coffee cake topped with brown sugar and cinnamon. It was such a masterful job of lock-picking that though his mother knew the cakes were missing, she couldn't imagine how the theft was accomplished. She must have been aware of the culprit's identity, however, by the time Ehrich left Appleton, Wisconsin, to become world-famous as Harry Houdini, master-magician and escape artist.

Wisconsin food was pronounced superlative long before Houdini tried out his wizardry on his mother's cupboard. There are pre-Revolutionary records of enthusiastic consumers of trout, muskellunge, the now-rare sturgeon, and a dozen other kinds of fish drawn from the shining lakes to which Champlain sent an expedition in 1634.

Waves of settlers made Wisconsin a treasure-chest of fine regional cookery. When the state celebrated its centennial in 1948, the 4-H Clubs learned to cook the dishes of twenty different nationalities found among Wisconsin's people. At one meeting a beautiful Croatian woman showed how the dough for a good *odjabuka gibanica,* or apple strudel, has to be rested after kneading and then gently coaxed into tissue-paper thinness to be rolled around apples, nuts, sugar and cinnamon.

Apples fried to tawny gold in deep pork fat are the heart of old-fashioned breakfasts in Brussels, Wisconsin. In the 1850's when Brusselites arrived from Belgium, the first breakfast was at six in the morning, the second at eight. Then came dinner at noon —perhaps goose simmered with onions, carrots, eggs and cream, mixed herbs and spices, or Flemish *carbonnade,* a casserole of beef, herbs and boiled potatoes. At four there were dessert and coffee, and at seven, supper. Enormous fruit pies in those days, made with yeast dough, were baked outdoors.

Maypoles as gay as candy sticks still festoon the front lawns on May Day, and to eat there are stacks of Flemish waffles made with yeast and rich with cream and butter, to be sugared or served with Wisconsin honey, which lives up to Aristotle's description—"Dew distilled from the stars and the rainbow." Wisconsin's firewood honey is creamy white, that from clover has a touch of chartreuse, and buckwheat honey pours thick and amber-colored.

Visitors from all over the country drive through Door county in late May when miles of cherry orchards are in blossom. The cherries, mostly scarlet Montmorencies, have become a six-and-a-half-million-dollar crop and practically the entire harvest is quick-frozen or canned to help keep the nation supplied with its favorite cherry pie. Blossom week in the same region is a flowery promise of boiled apple dumplings served in a syrup of stick cinnamon, sugar and butter, dusted with nutmeg.

The breeze-swept wooded peninsula of Door county lures vacationists with fine fishing and boating and superb dinners of yellow perch. Fishermen now explore the same waters on which the *coureurs des bois* pushed their canoes three centuries ago, often broiling their fresh-caught black bass and great northern pike over campfires.

At Calumet County Courthouse women in the late 1800's were baking wonderful cheesecakes and putting up their best peach jam and cherry preserves to raise money to build a church. The men offered to help, provided the women would stop working for temperance. The women's answer was to bake more pies and cakes, keep right on preaching temperance—and finish the church themselves.

The women of Richland Center left their soup kettles—where frequently was simmering a Norwegian fruit soup, with sweet potato, prunes, raisins and brown sugar—to declare in 1882 that "it is a mistake to think all life for women is in marriage," and to hold what they called cultural gatherings, really suffrage meetings in disguise.

But in many sections feminine Wisconsiners hold to tradition even now. Thus at Ootsburg, where church services used to be in Dutch, women still cook all the food for Sunday on Saturday, the main dish often a heavy stew made of pork and vegetables, served with fried dumplings, sugared, raisin-stuffed coffee cake fried in deep fat, and the taffy-like candies called *babalaars*. Many housewives of Icelandic descent make for their families a special soup of milk and dried Icelandic moss. French Canadians in Wisconsin welcome Christmas with a hot turkey or pork pie for breakfast. And Norwegian descendants hold their annual *lutefisk* suppers. At Phillips, near the town of Boscobel, pioneer Bohemians brought their ancient recipes for *kolacky* (rounds of rich dough with a center of prune or apricot), their sauerkraut and their infinite variety of dumplings.

The cooks of Ozankee County are famous for tortes. Another special favorite is a thin, crisp pastry cut like noodles, deep fried and sprinkled with sugar.

At Watertown, German-born farmers were once so scholarly that they addressed each other in Latin when they met in town for the afternoon *gugelhopf*—a kind of coffee cake served about teatime. Their ample wives added to Wisconsin cookery hot potato salad, creamed cabbage accented with mustard, golden brown potato pancakes and an apple cake called *apfel kuchen*.

In the pleasant hill country where the Sugar River flows, you may hear the deep music of Swiss cowbells from the pastures. "We have Swiss kuchel at least once a week for supper," writes Mrs. Frank Schliesser of New Glarus, and adds that her family uses its own rich cream, soured, for Swiss cottage-cheese pie. The butcher in New Glarus makes *kalberwurst*—a peppery veal sausage—every Friday, which housewives serve with fried potatoes, Swiss style.

World War II gave a fillip to Wisconsin cheese-making. Milwaukee and Green Bay developed outstanding cheddars and an excellent *kummelkase*, or hand-cheese. Discovery of limestone caves near Milwaukee started production of a very good Wisconsin blue cheese. Visiting here shortly after the war, André Simon, president of the Wine and Food society, said our American cheese is the biggest improvement we've made in gastronomy.

THE MOUNTAINS AND THE SOUTHWEST

Mont.

Idaho

Wyo.

Nev.   Utah

Colo.

N. Mex.

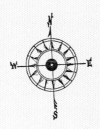

Ariz.

Texas

Texas

RABBIT FIRES ON THE HILLSIDES

It is Easter Eve and on the hillsides the Rabbit Fires are blazing. Excited children whisper to one another that this year the rabbits are busy cooking many bright eggs to hunt. Fredericksburg, Texas, the town where these children live, might have come straight from a Grimm fairy tale. The stone houses are soft amber in color, the roofs pitch steeply to the sky, and spicy little flower gardens are tucked in at the sides. The deep-toned ringing of the church bells can be heard all through the valley at 6 o'clock on Saturday evening, when work stops and families gather at the table for the tenderest of chicken, with golden dumplings afloat in rich broth, string beans cooked with vinegar and brown sugar, fresh-made milk bread, applesauce cake, and at least two kinds of pie—often lemon custard and red cherry.

The custom of the Rabbit Fires began in 1849, when the hundred-odd German settlers were threatened by Indians and their leader, John O. Meusebach, realized that a treaty must be made or the tiny town, tucked in the middle of this wild country, would be wiped out. He took a group of men to meet with the Indian chiefs. The Indians, fearing an ambush, built signal fires on the hills around the town. The children were terrified until one mother, remembering the old German legend of fairies dancing around fires of old wood, to make room for the new wood that would come in spring, comforted them with an adaptation of the old story suitable for frontier children. The fires were Easter fires, she said, tended by rabbits who were cooking and coloring eggs for Easter morning. By dawn the men returned, the treaty signed, and in gratitude the town vowed to kindle the fires as long as the treaty lasted. Fourth and fifth generations of pioneer families tend the fires today, and local Boy Scouts and other boys' clubs begin weeks before to carry kindling to the hilltops.

Almost as unusual as Fredericksburg is Scarborough Springs into which some 25,000 people crowd on Thanksgiving Eve for a possum hunt and a giant outdoor barbecue with sizzling possum, turkey, chicken, beef, pork, mutton and cracklin' bread.

Texas has towns named Seed Tick and Big Tussle, every kind of food, every kind of person and such a kaleidoscope of weather that it's said "only fools and strangers try to predict it." Pioneer women of Austin, who stirred their hog and hominy with wooden spoons and kept long rifles handy, coined a slogan: "Texas is heaven for men and dogs, but hell for women and oxen."

There was evidence to back this up. Women from France and Germany who trekked in ox carts to the Medina River were just in time for a drought so prolonged that mothers had to beat the bush for birds' eggs to feed their children, and some lived on rattlesnake meat. There were mothers like Mrs. Bunton who came to Wichita Falls with a half dozen children and set up housekeeping in a dugout. Her children went barefooted winter as well as summer, and wore clothes she made from tarpaulin. Legend says they hunted barehanded, climbed mesquite trees and jumped on the backs of bobcats to subdue them, then toted them home for dinner. Only the strong survived in this country, which as late as 1849 was so forbidding that Captain R. B. Macy said, "It is and must remain uninhabited forever."

Negro women brought Creole cookery to Fort Worth and it endured even when that city was, as a visitor reported, so dead during the 1873 panic that he saw a panther asleep and unmolested in the main street. Resolute Fort Worth ignored such comment and raised money to bring in the railroad—but ever since has called itself the Panther City.

Mexicans and Indians have also helped to season Texas cooking. Ears of boiled sweet corn are sold on the streets of San Antonio's Mexican section. There vendors offer a penny's worth of *dulces* (candy or cakes), or a live *abrito* (kid) to be turned into peppery barbecue. You hear the staccato rhythm of the *metates* as women grind corn for tortillas, the lighter, quicker sound of *molcajetes* as they prepare spices. Shredded leaves of the young prickly pear become salad. Chocolate, once the beverage of royalty (Montezuma drank fifty cups a day), is whirled to a froth and served with cinnamon. Candy is made from cactus or sweet potatoes, and unrefined sugar is a favorite sweet. Gay music pours from graveyards on the day of the dead, when Mexican residents go to visit relatives' graves and eat chicken mole and tortillas by flickering picnic fires.

There are still quilting bees where women bring roast turkey and haunches of venison for the ensuing supper. And the world's only Rattlesnake Derby is at McCamay.

The town of Cotulla was so tough that railroad conductors used to announce: "Cotulla—everybody get your guns ready."

Texas invented Mother-in-Law Day—as well as a crossbreed of buffalo and Brahma cattle called a "Cattalo." It developed, if it did not invent, the barbed-wire fence. Wolf hunts are still held—ranches still stretch to a million acres.

In Mount Pleasant, men "ride the ring," charging on horseback, armed with wooden lances, to catch the prize. Afterward they eat pot stew from washboilers filled with plump chickens and vegetables. Only a few miles away a gingerbread saloon flourished for years, serving nothing but hot gingerbread and homemade beer.

At Yoakum, the tomato-growing season is ushered in to the beat of tom-toms, and women swap recipes for green tomato pie, chili sauce and catsup. Turkeys parade in bronze and crimson splendor at Cuoro, destined to wind up in the annual Turkey Trot from which they are sent to markets all over the nation.

Amarillo, so called because its first substantial houses were yellow as the amaryllis, grew in half a century from a collection of hide huts to a tree-shaded modern city. A few miles from town the chuckwagons roll on the range and the first buckaroo to reach the coffeepot is supposed to take charge, filling tin cups to the brim and having to wait his turn for hot biscuits and lick, baked pinto beans, and beef—fried in butter, if it's tough, broiled over the embers if it's tender, or barbecued with a peppery sauce.

In the high-roofed houses of Castroville, with their dormer windows and arcaded galleries, New Year's Day is celebrated with gifts for parents and godparents of lightbread wreaths sugared and spiced. And in every home on that day, there is a big pot of baked frijoles. *Sucru garni,* an Alsatian sauerkraut creation with wedges of roast pork and an army of sausages and frankfurters, is another old-world survival in this town, where they also make curd cheese, wax tapers and lye soap just as they did a century ago.

Near Clairemont, Swedish families invite a guest to dinner and judge his manners by the resistance he shows to being dragged to the table. He must refuse to be seated, and the longer it takes to coax him, the politer he is deemed to be. Dinner is at noon, but the guest knows it is polite to stay right on for supper, too.

Perhaps oddest of all Texas oddities is the settlement of Wends at Serbin. Only about 80,000 of this ancient Slavic group are left in the world, and 7,000 of these made the pilgrimage from Saxony to Texas about 100 years ago. The Wends are proud of their full-flavored sausages, tart coleslaw, strong sweet coffee, and of the fact that they do not drink tea or beer. A few of the Wendish children still look out for the Moon Lady, who may turn them into imps. A few young men still break eggshells full of perfumed confetti on the heads of their chosen sweethearts. But old customs are fading in Texas, as elsewhere, and these days not many Wendish families cover the mirrors after a death or trudge to the barn solemnly to announce to the animals that someone in the house has died.

Contrary to much that motion pictures and fiction say of it, Texas spends more time assembling helpful data for middle-income families than it does catering to millionaires. The agricultural extension service experts have tested and distributed recipes for a browned beef liver and tomato-pepper sauce, and for Lone Star Favorite—an economical casserole of ground beef, peppers, rice, chili powder and tomatoes. To find the best corn bread they collected eighty-five different methods, tested them all . . . and concluded that only three can be called typical Texas corn breads, all made with sour milk.

One food that used to make fortunes for growers in the Rio Grande Valley was the Bermuda onion. About 1911, however, an onion grower in Mission Valley shipped his bumper crop to market and was so angry when he got back a check for twenty-five cents that he cashed it and nailed the quarter to a mesquite tree. Paper-shell pecans were tried next, to be replaced by citrus.

New Mission calls itself the "Home of the Grapefruit," and holds a citrus fiesta in late January, celebrating the courage and hard work of pioneers who refused to quit when their crops were ruined time and again by disastrous freezes. They stayed on, developing new and better types of fruit; their ambition was to see twelve million flourishing trees in the lower Rio Grande Valley. Fiestas and balmy climate combine to make the valley a popular vacation spot.

Even though it's not as fabulous as reports make it, the Texas of the oil millionaire does exist. Oil men really do commute to New York in their private planes to order caviar and imported wines. The terraced supper clubs of Houston's newest hotel offer such exotic dishes as breast of capon with thin-sliced mushrooms and smoked ham, in sherry and cream. In Dallas you can order quail quick-roasted with salt pork, stuffed with *foie gras* and doused with brandy set aflame as it comes to the table. Also you may still have pronghorn antelope steak for lunch, with hominy in casserole, done with cream, buttered crumbs and shredded almonds, as in the late 1800's.

On a ranch miles from nowhere, imported liqueurs at dinner may accompany a ginger parfait or a soufflé of fresh Texas figs. The house, built a year or so before, may be in the process of a $100,000 remodeling, and its mistress may, as one famed Dallas matron did, have fifteen coats of paint on a wall before she gets the shade she wants. Under the dining-room table there may be a $50,000 Persian rug; a guest or two may pull a six-shooter from a dinner jacket and start shooting at the ceiling. All this has happened.

My favorite Texas believe-it-or-not was told me on the air by Oklahoma-born Bob Duncan, writer and ballad singer. An oil field, he said, was discovered on the West Texas farm of Pearl and Henry Smith. A modest, aging couple, they were bewildered by the avalanche of money and anxious only to give it away. Soon engraved invitations went out to more than a hundred nearby families—for a cruise around the world. Henry happily sold the subsurface rights to his farm for a million and a half dollars, chartered a ship and set sail with his guests. Stopping in New

York City, the Smiths took their party on a shopping spree. A year later the travelers got back to Houston and ate up the Smith's last $2,000 at a gargantuan feast. Then Pearl and Henry went back to the farm and apparently lived happily ever after in the shadow of oil wells which no longer meant a wearisome fortune to them.

Montana

AWAY FROM IT ALL

Gary Cooper is a wonderful press agent for Montana. Asked to describe the best meal he ever ate, he told me: "There's nothing in the world that can compare with venison on a crisp Christmas Day, cooked camp style in the Montana woods . . . loin chops and steaks sizzling over the fire . . . and venison stew in a big iron pot. Maybe it was because I was doggone near starved . . . maybe it was the clear, cold air. All I know is—it was great."

In the high-rolling eighties the gold barons ruled Helena and the copper kings reigned in Butte. As in all get-rich-quick towns, they lived extravagantly. Coachmen in tall hats and livery drove elaborate vehicles through the dirt streets. In rococo mansions trimmed with Victorian gingerbread, guests dined on oysters from Baltimore, wine and champagne from France, pheasant and quail. Later they played poker—for $50,000 stakes.

Montana had been left pretty much to the Indians until gold and copper swept the frontier west from the Dakotas. Only a few trappers, a handful of Jesuit missionaries and daring traders, up to then invaded the wild canyons and high ridges of the Rockies. David Thompson, heading west in 1808, reported that the Indians fed his party moss bread "which gave us a bellyache," dried carp, muskrat and shoulder of venison.

In the heyday of the fur trader, Montana had millions of buffalo—doomed by gold and copper strikes, the coming of the railroad, the growth of vast sheep and cattle ranches. Toward the end of the buffalo's career, hunters frequently killed the animals just for the fur and tongue, considered a gourmet delicacy. An Indian named Walking Coyote realized that the buffalo was in danger of extinction, saved two males and two females, and from them came the protected herds in present-day Montana.

A man can still get away from it all in Montana, as Historian Stewart Holbrook discovered a few years ago when he spent a night in a cabin "in which lived a man who had seen but two motorcars since 1917 and but one motion picture." He was standing up well under this deprivation, too. For breakfast he served fried elk, and the guest slept under the hide of a bear which had been killed, skinned and tanned in the dooryard.

The cow center of Jordan once bragged that it was the lonesomest town in the world. Before 1935, when it got its first telephone, the inhabitants communicated with the outside world only by short-wave radio. Cowboys rode in from the range to eat antelope roast, as a change from their usual fare celebrated in an old ballad:—

Oh it's bacon and beans most every day.
I'd as soon be eatin' prairie hay.

Montana's ranches today stretch for miles into the valleys and up the slopes of the Gallatin Range. A Montanan will tell you that no steak on earth can compare with a "grasser," meaning beef from a two-year-old steer that has been fattened on sun-cured, vitamin-packed grass.

Loneliest of all Montanans are the sheepmen who throughout the Northwest spend months on the solitary high ranges with their flocks. In Montana a sheepman may be a Turk, a Russian, a Rumanian, a Basque, but if you came upon him in his canvas-top wagon at mealtime, chances are he'd be eating American beans, salt pork or sauerkraut.

The Russians, who grow potatoes, oats, flax, rye and barley on small farms around Flevna, serve their famous beet soup, borscht, in heirloom tureens, and a good dessert afterward is a cream cheese tart called *Vatroushki*. Just before Lent they make stacks of blinis . . . generous-sized buckwheat cakes over which they pour melted butter and sour cream. Very hot spiced tea is drunk from glasses, and when company comes dessert is often a pudding made of rye bread crumbs, Montana cherries and cinnamon, or it may be a pie called *Smettanick*, with a filling of cherry jam, almonds and sour cream.

Croats and Slavs brought their delightful old Yule customs to Butte, Great Falls and Anaconda. They observe Christmas on January 6, lighting the symbolic three logs and awaiting the first visitor after midnight mass, who comes into the house, sprinkles wheat over the family, kisses one of the logs and says "Christ is born." The family reply "Truly, He is born" and in turn sprinkle the visitor's head with wheat and give him a present. Holiday fare is likely to include a poppy-seed-stuffed pudding or the thinnest of pancakes rolled around tangy cherries with a dusting of sugar. Turkey comes to the table with an almond stuffing, cabbage is served with savory meat and rice, and finished off with a sour cream sauce. Usually some version of dumpling is on the menu —plum, cottage cheese or perhaps apple.

In the Scandinavian settlements, the Christmas fools frolic through the streets in antic costumes, and families eat porridge of rice and heavy cream, with a hidden almond which means that the boy or girl finding it will be first to marry. Thin griddle cakes made of flour and mashed potatoes, and the famous Swedish Christmas bread with its hearty touch of rye and molasses, help to enliven the holidays. Norwegians celebrate Midsummer Day and eat cold fruit soup and cookies they call "vanilla nonsense."

Golden bread is an Easter tradition in some of the older Irish familes—thick slices of homemade white bread dipped in egg and fried in butter, like French toast. Hot Cross buns with a cross of icing on top are baked for Good Friday—although a few traditionalists still keep "black fast" on that day, consuming nothing but tea. Eggs used to be exchanged as gifts on Easter Day and the old saying was "One egg for the true gentleman, two eggs for the gentleman, three eggs for the churl, four eggs for the lowest churl." The idea was apparently that the lowest churl was the most in need of eggs.

Montana Scotsmen cling more closely to their traditions than do the Irish, and many women insist upon stirring oatmeal with an heirloom wooden porridge stick. They have a light hand with scones and they fancy a rich Mulligatawny made from mutton and curry. Some admit that Montana barley broth is even better than in the Highlands because of the sweet, tender Montana carrots and the excellent split peas of the Northwest. At Christmas a lucky thimble is hidden in the plum pudding and each member of the family must stir it once.

Montana honey is white and perfumed with clover and sweet grasses, delicious on huckleberry nut bread. Montana farm cooks make a red rhubarb pudding, and in hunting season use leftover venison in browned venison balls served with hot spiced tomato sauce. They put venison in the Montana version of mincemeat, too, and use wild serviceberries for pies and summer drinks.

New Mexico

CENTURIES OF TORTILLAS

Every spring in New Mexico, on the morning when the first bluebirds appear, Indians leave their pueblos and begin to clear the *acequias*—ancient man-made waterways which have irrigated Indian fields since the memory of man. When the pussy willows bud along the banks it is time to dig furrows and plant corn, beans and melons. That day the pueblos are loud with laughter over the antics of odd leather balls filled with seeds. Men and boys kick and knock these balls through open doorways, and the object of the game, called "shinny," is to break as many of the balls as possible over the new furrows, thus guaranteeing a good harvest.

The average visitor seldom sees the primitive pueblos of the Rio Grande Valley. He may go to rather commercial fiestas in Santa Fe and Taos, burn his tongue on chili con carne, buy an Indian trinket or two. But while he may miss the color of the pueblos, he will have the magnificence of savage mountains and sun-baked desert and the benefit of a climate that permits a skiing party and a fishing derby on the same day.

Nowhere is the contrast of New Mexico as dramatically illustrated as in the dusty sun-filled pueblo of San Ildefonso, where women make beautiful black-glazed pottery and cook their pinto beans and tortillas just as they have been doing for centuries. It is hard to believe that a few miles from this place of silence and antiquity is Los Alamos where atomic scientists stir a witches' brew and the most elegant and sophisticated of food is served up from deep-freeze, pressure cooker and electric broiler.

Indian women still grind blue and white corn on *metates*, (stone slabs) for tortillas, although nutrition experts at the Illinois Institute of Technology, at the request of the Mexican government, have now developed a tortilla mix. I am amused to find that back on the farm in Missouri I was brought up on a form of tortilla. My Great-Aunt Cassie had a pat-a-cake method with corn cakes, later fried thin and crisp, which is pretty much the Indian way.

I've tried to figure out the differences between tacos, enchiladas and chalupas, but all I'm really sure of is that they're tortillas . . . some with meat, some with vegetables, mashed beans or cheese, variously flavored with sauces of chilis, herbs and spices.

Different from any other group in the United States, the Spanish-Americans of New Mexico, descendants of sixteenth-century Spanish colonists, live in isolated communities which once were part of vast Spanish land grants. In the fall, the adobe walls of their haciendas flame with drying chilis, wound by nimble-fingered women into strings and left to be sun-cured until the first flurry of snow. Many of these people still use goats and horses to thresh their grain as they did two and a half centuries ago.

New Mexican relishes are made with small red hot chilis, tiny green hot chilis, broad red hot chilis—and a few chilis that are euphemistically called sweet. Some cooks use five or six in a single sauce. Sometimes your tortilla is filled raw, folded over and fried in deep fat. Sometimes it is cooked first, then filled and toasted . . . or maybe only filled and not toasted; sometimes cooked on a griddle and then, while hot, buttered inside through splits in the top of the crust.

Since somebody is always making tortillas or tamales, it's no wonder New Mexican towns smell perpetually of corn, the way Spanish villages smell of olive oil. The tamale in its simplest form, sometimes colored red or green by the sauce used, is corn dough stuffed with bits of seasoned meat and wrapped in a corn husk to steam until the dough is cooked and the husk can be peeled off like a banana skin. Among the tamales I've had were some cinnamon-sprinkled, some stuffed with nuts, raisins, broken candies, and one bearded tamale—the beard belonging to a whole unpeeled shrimp inside the bundle of dough.

Other delicacies that I tried and relished were turkey fixed with a sauce of chili, spices, herbs, ground almonds and peanuts, fried bananas, toasted bread crumbs and black chocolate; knee fritters, shaped over the freshly scrubbed knee of the maker; little sour oranges eaten with salt and hot pepper, and thin corn flakes with hot caramel syrup. In the crooked streets of Santa Fe, women in graceful broomstick skirts and brilliant blouses shop for the same concho and blue corn from which sixteenth-century housewives made lye hominy and milled corn.

You could be dropped from the sky a mile from Sante Fe on any evening just after dark and know where you were by the pungent perfume of pinon fires burning in hundreds of patios and fireplaces (the word barbecue entered our language via New Mexico as did tortilla, chili and frijole). As in Spanish colonial days, they still prepare the pepper-hot meat balls with their fragrance of garlic, the pork strips cured in chile sauce and oregano, the rich stews mingling meat with green tops of onion and garlic, tiny squashes with squash blossoms, and corn on the cob.

The Palace of the Governors, built in 1609, commands the shady plaza in Sante Fe. It was a capital continuously for three hundred years, though under four flags. Those three centuries were important in New Mexico's historic cookery. Descendants of Spanish pigs became spicy sausage and dark red hams, which in turn went into garbanza stew—a pungent blend of chopped ham and sausage, with garlic and oregano. The same pumpkins the Spanish found—long-necked, green and yellow striped—go into preserves and candy. Bolito beans (frijoles) grow on the high mountains and cook better at high altitudes than the pinto bean. Lamb's quarter (the native green) is still fried with onions, beans and chili seeds, and the wild purslane is gently stewed with jerked meat, onion, sat pork and coriander seed.

New Mexico acquired its first Spanish accent with the coming of the Franciscan friars in the seventeenth century and the building of the missions which antedate California's by a century and a half. Most astonishing of these ancient churches is the Mission of the Pueblo of Acoma, set on a bare sandstone tableland four hundred feet above the plains and reached only by a trail cut into the treacherous cliff. There are no trees, not even grass or earth on that wind-torn tableland. Many Acoma families have homes in the nearby farming communities, but go regularly to their strange "city in the sky" for fiestas and special services.

The Mission of Zia Pueblo stands just as it did when Coronado, Oñate and De Vargas came there to visit, its adobe walls blending with the purple Sandias Mountains and the blue mist-hung peaks of the Jemez. There the tiny Virgin of the Assumption, possessed of several exquisite wardrobes, is carried through the pueblo on August 13th, her festival day, and the people fete her with special sweets, called *dulces,* made of pumpkin, squash, quince or green figs flavored with ginger root. These sweets take a full day to make.

August is the time to be in the Land of Enchantment, for in the last week, at Gallup, thirty tribes assemble for the greatest Indian show in the world. The Navahos, taking only what pleases them from the white man's civilization, have proved that the Indian can not only survive, but progress, in the modern world. At the turn of the century, only 10,000 Navahos remained; now there are more than 75,000.

Utah

WONDERFUL AND OUTRAGEOUS

> *The wind like fury here doth blow, that when we*
> *Plant or sow, sir,*
> *We place our foot upon the seed and hold it till*
> *It grows, sir.*

The pioneer who produced that rhyme about Utah winds was writing more truth than poetry.

Brigham Young, hunting for "a place on earth that nobody else wants," found Utah. Driven from Illinois, the Mormons in their famous 1847 exodus moved west to Salt Lake City and made to flower the arid desert of sand and canyons. Pioneer diaries show that the transformation wasn't easy. The first homes were often dirt dugouts and sapling lean-tos. And the occupants were sometimes reduced to a diet of roots and a kind of molasses made from Indian maize stalks. On a dim trail leading into a many-branched gorge, one party halted on Christmas Day and for their holiday dinner had a giant flapjack of flour and water baked in a frying pan. Other bands ate boiled sago lily bulbs and thistle greens, roasted owls, hawks and crows.

The famous Mormon Battalion made the longest sustained march in infantry history, 1,125 miles from Salt Lake City to San Diego, and on the return trip brought wheat to go into fragrant loaves of bread, California peas to eat new and green with the season's first lamb. While orchards were being nursed along and fields tenderly cultivated, Mormon women learned to cook the wild spinach, lambs-quarter, milkweed and wild lettuce with salt pork.

At Salt Lake City, buffalo and cattle hides were boiled to make glue for the great tabernacle organ. Chairs and tables were hollowed out of logs, mattresses were stuffed with dried cattails. If a neighborhood had only one pig, everyone saved scraps to feed it, and at butchering, the investors were given their share of fat, liver and bits of pork. Chewing gum from the juice of the milkweed and a sour-sweet jelly from the chokeberry enlivened the rather drab menus. When grasshoppers descended in a black storm, the Mormons, praying earnestly, were grateful—but not really surprised—to look up into the sky and find sea gulls flying to this spot 1,000 miles inland to eat up the grasshoppers and save the crops. This was just one of the dramatic events in Utah history.

As towns grew green and prosperous, cooks began creating the now famous home-cured ham with mustard sauce. Buttermilk biscuits were dipped in a Mormon gravy made with browned flour, ham grease, milk and black pepper. At Lion House, where Brigham Young's wives lived, Angie Earl evolved a pie crust of such richness and delicacy that the recipe has been handed down through the generations. After weeks on the trail, eating salt pork and biscuits, it was a treat for gold-seekers to find a Mormon dinner table offering roast beef and fried chicken, along with green peas, potatoes, cheese, bread, butter and tea.

Utah's spectacular past is being preserved today by women such as Kate Carter, who won an award for outstanding community service and came East to be on my radio program. Kate told about the dinners of Utah Pioneers to raise money for their Pioneer Memorial Building in Salt Lake City—there was Lumpy Dick, a rich soup with dumplings, baked ham with Mormon gravy, salt-rising bread, dried corn, salad of pigweed, beet tops and mustard greens with salt pickles on the side—and for dessert a Salt Lake City jelly layer cake, veiled bread pudding (bread crumbs browned with applesauce and cream), dried apple pie and Brigham Young tea, which is hot water, milk and sugar.

Mining days brought money enough for luxuries. A Mormon bride of the 1890's was awed at visiting a home in Silver Lode and discovering what fashionable living went on in that part of the world. Chinese-cooked wild duck with rice was served on gold-plated china, and the table was set with cut glass, fine silver and imported linens.

Utah is a great place for outdoor eating, and families haul their blackened coffeepots and campfire equipment off into the canyons on any mild week end. A favorite dish on such occasions is desert-broiled steak—three-inch slabs of steak smeared with lard, salt and pepper, grilled over glowing coals until a crisp crust forms.

Utah's latest lure is uranium and the new horde of prospectors searching the Colorado Plateau is developing Uranium-Rush cookery far different from the sourdough and salt pork diet of early mining days. Here in modern trailers you find instant coffee replacing the strong brew that boiled for hours over campfires, mixes for griddle cakes, waffles and biscuits, powdered milk, dehydrated soups. Women often go on these hunts for uranium and the eating is a good deal fancier than when a prospector's wife of '49 tried out shortening from a very fat bear to make pies.

Still, it's wild and exciting enough out there in the 45th state to justify the state guide's claim that "there is something wonderful and outrageous about Utah."

Wyoming

RAISED ON BUFFALO MILK

Esther Hobart Morris was very angry. Women should have the right to vote, to hold office, to control the money they earned, she was saying furiously to herself and to anybody else who would listen. On Election Eve in 1869 she invited to tea the two rival candidates for president of the First Territorial Legislative assembly of Wyoming. She beguiled them with feminine chatter and a luscious array of cakes, cookies, muffins and jam. Well-fed and content, the gentlemen asked what favor they might grant to show their appreciation. Whereupon Esther pinned them down to specific promises concerning the revolutionary law she wanted passed. And that's how it happened that Wyoming became the first state to give women the right to vote. Probably no tea party in history had such far-reaching effects as Esther Morris's.

To be sure, the majority of women didn't take advantage of their right to vote, and even the right to serve on juries was ended in Wyoming after three court terms. But the historic laws were there, and militant suffragettes took heart. Perhaps on the cue from Esther Morris's tea-party strategy, Susan B. Anthony began wooing the press by handing out homemade gingerbread to reporters.

Before Wyoming made world headlines with women's suffrage, it was the domain of fur trappers, mountain men and outlaws. Daniel Webster declared the whole "not worth a cent." The Missouri Fur Company chose a spot along the Green River for its annual rendezvous in 1825, when it's said that not since the days of Ghengis Khan were so many wild, tough men assembled in one place.

Strong men claimed to have been raised on buffalo milk. John Colter, who discovered Yellowstone Park and described it as

"hell," once walked one hundred miles naked to escape the Black-
foot Indians, and reported that he was delighted with the "acqui-
sition of a badger" to eat. These men obeyed no laws, swore no
loyalties. They came from everywhere, including Hawaii and the
Sandwich Islands.

By 1851, the wagon trains began rolling across Wyoming, heading west for gold. Women were in the minority. A train in Fort
Laramie that year consisted of more than 37,000 men, 5,700 cows
and only 803 women, one of whom left this touching plea carved
on a rock: *Remember me in mercy, O Lord.* The going was hard.
Salt pork and jerked venison, sourdough biscuits and beans were
a pretty monotonous diet, and a rare treat was fried deer liver.

In that year of 1851, four wagons started west from Cherry
Valley, Illinois. One of the women, a proud housekeeper, spread
an immaculate linen tablecloth for their first campfire dinner on
the trail, tucked linen napkins into rings and served her famous
fried chicken, corn bread and cherry pie as stylishly as though
she were back home in her own warm, lighted dining room. But
by the time they reached Independence Rock in western Wyoming, the tablecloth had vanished and cornmeal mush dished from
the pan was the daily fare.

Among the first white women to come to Wyoming, Mrs. Mar-
cus Whitman and Mrs. W. E. Spalding ate enthusiastically when
the Indians welcomed them in 1853 at what is now Rendezvous
Park. The venturesome brides, crossing the continent with their
missionary husbands, didn't know until afterward that they had
eaten roasted dogs.

The settlers lived on braised bear meat and venison steak,
hominy cooked with dried beef, rice with clover honey and cinnamon. Hunting lodges began to spring up, miniature empires whose
owners cared more for their wine cellars and blooded horses than
for their cattle. One Irish peer brought a hunting party overland
in six wagons, twenty-one carts, with a dozen yoke of cattle, one
hundred and twelve horses, fourteen dogs and forty servants!

Out on the range, cowboys lived a rugged, simple life, sang
lonesome songs and ate the classic chuckwagon beans and beef
with sometimes a camper's bread twist—biscuit dough twisted on
a stick, baked and filled with honey or jelly.

People came to Wyoming from all parts of the world—so many
that Rock Springs inaugurated an International Night with forty-
seven nationalities. A French bakery turned out brown fluffs of

croissants, and éclairs oozing creamy richness. The Greek candy shop was fragrant with baking almond cakes and Turkish delight, halvah and spice bars. In the Chinese restaurant, won-ton floated small and tender in its broth, pork sweet and sour came pungent from the kitchen, tiny teacups were filled again and again. Norwegians made cheesecake that night and Polish families served zesty cold fruit soup; the Germans, Wiener schnitzel.

Best Wyoming story of all is Lucy Morrison's of Dry Creek, the state's Sheep Queen. As a sickly child, Lucy was cured by drinking cow's milk prescribed by a passing stranger who turned out to be a notorious Spanish horse thief. Later, as wife and mother, she took over the flock when her husband became ill and tied her children to a sage bush while she went off with the sheep. In the lonely reaches of Copper Mountain, a wolf attacked the sheep and Lucy knew he would come back again and again until her flock was destroyed. She pounded up a glass bottle and "seasoned" the remains of one dead sheep with it. The wolf came back, but only once.

During the war between sheep- and cattle-men her wagon was burned and she lived in a tent until she could finish building a cabin. But Lucy never felt comfortable in a house and to the end of her days preferred living in her sheep wagon and serving up beans from an old Dutch oven.

Wyoming beans became such an important crop that the town of Basin organized a bean festival. Women made everything from beans—sandwich fillings, loaves, rarebit, breads, stuffings for green peppers, even cookies, and of course baked beans Wyoming style. These fascinating concoctions were served free on every street corner and for a finishing touch there were even pictures and plaques made of beans.

The town of Bevin conceived a novel way of celebrating the bean and potato crops by holding a festival at which guests dancing in one auditorium were served bowls of steaming bean soup, while at the party across the way the *pièce de résistance* was creamy potato soup.

Farming got its start in Wyoming more than a century ago, when a band of Mormons arrived in a wagon train at Fort Supply. They were well-fed pioneers, having brought herds of cattle, flocks of chickens and plentiful food supplies. Irrigation was started by Spaniards in the first gardens planted in 1855 at Fort Laramie.

While some women stayed properly by their home fires, others

rode the range. One, Anna Richey, put on overalls and boots and learned so much about cattle that she has the dubious distinction of being the only woman ever convicted of rustling.

In Wyoming, as throughout most of the West, frontier days are remembered today at scores of picnics, rodeos and pageants. The town of Big Piney has a huge Fourth of July barbecue, with beef served free to all the visitors who come for the Chuck Wagon Day celebration. At the Old Settlers Picnic at Devils Tower, everyone brings his own food and there is an imposing outlay of cold fried chicken, sandwiches and cakes with free coffee to wash it down.

From a treeless town of log cabins, Thermopolis has grown into a summer resort, with an international flavor to its food. There is good German cooking in the surrounding Dunkard farmland. The town is famous for real western dances to which families come from miles around and stay for several days.

Schoolhouse parties, attended by cattle growers and their families for miles around, are not very different from the typically western get-togethers described in *The Virginian*. Wives bring thick sandwiches of deviled eggs and ham, cream and chocolate layer cakes. They brew real cowboy coffee, black and strong. The fiddles and harmonicas play far into the night, babies doze placidly on a bundle of coats at the side of the room, and about midnight the parents gather up their families and start on the long drive home.

In the old days when the nearest snowdrift served as an icebox, three men wintering on Shell Creek in a dugout filled their snow refrigerator with buffalo, elk, antelope and bear and lived royally until the first thaw. Donald Hough, a writer friend and chronicler of Jackson Hole, says he once bargained for a furnished log cabin to include an elk steak cut two inches thick and delivered to him every week.

Jackson Hole probably has more wild animals per square mile than any comparable area in the country. Deer stroll casually through the town on winter afternoons and before the fencing-in of the U.S. Government Elk Reserve, the winter population of the town of Jackson was often half elk and half people. Also, according to Donald, elk often chased horses away and took over their food and warm stable quarters.

The traditional Thanksgiving dinner in the Jackson Hole region used to be wild goose, but the domesticated turkey has finally taken over and some farms are raising flocks of 3,000 and more—

none of your pampered non-walking birds, but big bronze fellows with a taste of the wild which gourmets insist is far better than the bland, all-white-meat varieties. Wild duck fattened on wild rice is another Wyoming delicacy, to be roasted or barbecued; smothered pheasant and partridge in cream are on many ranch tables in the hunting season.

Food expert Duncan Hines once wrote that the best meal he ever ate was in Wyoming. The man who has traveled several million miles in quest of notable food remembers best the meal he ate in 1899 when he was driving a Wells Fargo express wagon from Denver. Lost in a Wyoming blizzard, he wandered for two days without a bite to eat. When he staggered at last into Cheyenne he was guided to Harry Hynd's restaurant and there served the meal which was to be enshrined in his memory for over half a century. It was a platter of ham and eggs.

Nevada

CAMELS TO COMSTOCK

In Virginia City, Nevada, the ladies used to shake their hands above their heads for several minutes before their dinner guests arrived. This was so that they might perform their hostessly duties with hands that were elegantly pale.

During the dizzy days of the gold and silver rush in the 1860's parties in Virginia City sparkled with champagne that had crossed the ocean, rounded the Horn and been freighted over the high Sierras from California. Prospectors who struck it rich liked anything as long as it cost a lot. They served West Coast oysters, squab and strawberries, and imported silver and glass that gleamed under the light of great crystal chandeliers.

Young men from the East, expecting to live in rough outdoor clothing, took one look at elegant Virginia City society and sent home for dinner jackets and tails. Once Virginia City's swank

Ivy Social Club rounded up all the canaries in town, fed them their favorite food in the club cellar for a week, and then had a party with champagne drunk to canary song.

In 1849, men were crossing Nevada by the thousands, heading for California and gold. They didn't dream that the land under their creaking wagon wheels was filled with gold, silver, copper, lead, zinc, turquoise, quick-silver and fire-opals—a mineral treasure which in less than a century was to yield $1,600,000,000.

At first the Paiute Indians looked with kindly eyes upon the few white people who straggled west across the menacing mountains and the sun-blistered deserts. They showed white women how to crush the pulp of the barrel-cactus for a life-saving drink when there was no water, how to use the seeds of the salt bush as seasoning, and the finely ground fruit of the pine-nut tree as flour.

Grasshoppers were a Paiute delicacy, according to Clara Beatty, state historian, and when the insects got entangled in the sweet sap of the cattail, the Indians rolled the stuff into balls. Whites coming through liked it—until they found out what it was. They also liked grasshopper meal—until they discovered legs and wings in it.

The canny Mormons were the first to farm in Nevada. Brigham Young sent bands of his faithful followers to set up supply depots at strategic points where he anticipated that the headlong streams of gold seekers would be desperate for food.

Nevada's first town, Genoa, was only a roofless stockade in 1851. Historians believe that the first house in the state was a log cabin built about 1853 by Mormons John Reese and Jacob Dinsey. They brought seeds and cattle, and hungry immigrants were soon paying as much as a dollar apiece for turnips. Mormons had thirty cows and a small drove of hogs in Carson Valley, and although they were recalled to Utah within a few years, their methods of irrigating and of rotating crops set the pattern for agriculture. The Mormon policy, as opposed to that of some frontiersmen, was described by Frank Dellenbagh when he visited Nevada in the 1880's and noted that "the Mormons don't skim the cream off the country with a six-shooter and a whiskey bottle." Mormon grapes and melons, russet potatoes, corn, wheat and squash helped Nevada mining camps survive the hectic days of boom and bust.

By 1859 the rush was on in earnest. Prospectors got along fine on sourdough biscuits and sourdough bread, which descendants of pioneer families still bake, and claim are superior to any in the West. When women began arriving in the mining camps, they traded the recipes of their diverse native lands and developed a cuisine now regarded as typically Nevadan: tripe stewed with onion, celery and parsley, hot with mustard and Worcestershire; saffron cake, meat-stuffed Cornish pasties, potato-caramel cake.

When the going was rough in the early days, prospectors ate whatever came their way. Legend says that one gold-rush town lived an entire winter on nothing but whiskey. Results of this diet were likely to be disastrous, as witness the town which claimed seventy-five people were shot before anyone died a natural death.

Nobody knew at what moment a gleam of yellow would show up in a canyon or on a mountainside, and another man would become a millionaire. Once a cook dressing chickens for Sunday dinner found gold nuggets in their craws. During the silver fever of the 1860's, three men threw up a tiny rock house to shelter them in winter. Cooking their sage-hen stew one night, they noticed that the walls glittered. Investigation revealed they were full of silver and worth $75,000. They needed a fat income just to stay alive, though, for crackers at the time were worth seventy-five cents per handful.

One of the weirdest sights of gold-rush days was a string of camels lumbering through the sagebrush, carrying salt from Teel's Marsh to Comstock and Aurora. The camels were left-overs from an experiment of Jefferson Davis's. He bought them for the Army to use in the California desert, but by 1867 the beasts were auctioned off and driven to Nevada to form salt caravans for mining towns.

Oysters from the West Coast were fancied by newly rich miners. Oyster loaf was a delicacy, and oyster stuffing was used for quail. Nevada apples, developed in Pleasant Valley, became so famous that baskets of them were sent to England. Nevada women liked to tuck them into the mouths of juicy suckling pigs. They made cider, too, which was often left in the snow until it was nipped by frost.

In the days of tent cities and dugout houses, everybody ate outdoors when the weather permitted, and outdoor eating has remained a pleasant Nevada habit. The scenery is so melodramtic that guests sometimes neglect the charcoal-broiled steak to look at mountainsides purple, red, orange, blue and copper from minerals, at lakes glowing indigo-blue in the brilliant sunshine, at shifting mirages and gold and white poppies blooming on alpine meadows. Here a man may bring in his own mountain trout to sizzle over a campfire, or to bake, if it's a big one, in a barbecue pit filled with hot rocks. Here, too, he may get his quota of deer, mountain hare, grouse and partridge for a superb hunter's feast.

Picnic fare often includes the tender white meat of Fallon turkeys grown in Churchill County, famous Hearts of Gold cantaloupes from the same region, or open-face pies made of the big black gooseberries which grow wild in the hill country.

Seventeen of Nevada's sprawling counties are primarily cow country and the great roundups spring and fall find the ranch houses busy day and night. In recent years the picturesque chuckwagon, where cowboys ate while they were riding the range, has been getting scarcer. More and more roundups find the cowboys and bosses driving back to the ranch house at night for sourdough pancakes, strong coffee, beans and well-done beef. A characteristic story is one about the rancher who in New York ordered a steak, and when it came, charcoal on top, red and juicy within, he said, "Mister, I have saw steers hurt worse than this that got well."

The sheepmen are a lonely lot. Often they are Basques who enjoy the solitude and vast reaches of the mountain grazing land. A Basque sheepherder starts his day before sunup, with black coffee into which he crumbles bread and strong cheese. Nevada has adopted some of his native dishes, including the spicy *Paiella*, made of saffron rice, tiny hot sausages, herbs and chicken, with clams and shrimp added when available.

Probably the most glamorous dish to be had in all Nevada is roast pheasant, in its feathers, standing erect on a field of wild rice. This involves cooking the pheasant, then inserting it into the original feathered skin. Incubator pheasants are raised with meticulous care on large woodland farms, to supply this gourmet dish.

Nevadans are friendly people who believe their state should be as widely known for its food and scenery as for its gambling and easy divorce laws. The latter got off to an early start, though, when a miner proposed to a girl in 1854. They couldn't find a minister in all of Nevada, so they drew up this agreement:

By these presents we hereby certify in the presence of witnesses that we will from this time henceforth to the end of our lives, live together as man and wife, obeying all the laws of the United States as married persons. . . .

Nevertheless—whether he got tired of her cooking or she charged him with mental cruelty, we don't know—the bride took off for California and Nevada had its first, though unofficial, divorcée.

Arizona

ONE SMALL CLOUD

"I don't see what God Almighty made so much land for."

A Quaker forty-niner looked down the bleak miles of the Devil's Highway and said, all those years ago, what men today must often feel about this land of silence, solitude and sunshine—Arizona. Here among the blazing deserts, the forests turned to stone, the tiny towns hitched to the stars on the sheer sides of mountains, the food is as varied as the people and as dramatic as the landscape.

You used to be offered a free meal at a Yuma hotel any day the sun didn't shine, and I know a woman who got one. She spotted a tiny cloud in the sky and drove sixty miles to the hotel. Sure enough, the sun wasn't shining when she arrived and she had her meal on the house: chicken fricassee with rice, and for dessert an Arizona grapefruit pie.

Arizona's grapefruit and other citrus crops grow in man-made oases that date back to Indian times, when the first experiments with irrigation were for the benefit of beans and melons. Later the Spanish missionaries, and after that, the industrious Mormons, brought these oases to greater fertility. Growing around the sun-baked adobe missions today are descendants of wheat and fruit first brought north in 1692 from Mexico by Father Kino, a Spanish missionary. Some of the irrigation canals even go back as far as the prehistoric cliff dwellers. Our early pioneers used the canals until experts decided they were not at the right level. They began rerouting the irrigation system, only to find that the planners of five hundred years ago had been right after all.

Arizona is cow country and mining country, but also a lush producer of lettuce, melons, dates and citrus. It is so close to its recorded beginnings that less than 150 years have passed since it was airily dismissed by Major Stephen Long as "The Great American Desert."

The flavor of Spain and Mexico linger in little Arizona towns like Nogales and Morenci. Morenci mothers, because the town is built on a cliffside—so the story goes—often tether their children to keep them from falling off. Around there, the air is spicy with tamales and frijoles, and the patios ring with laughter and song.

In Nogales, where you can look across the fence into Mexico, children love to play at the Breaking of the Pinata. The Pinata is a big clay jar, dressed like a doll and crammed with cactus candy, Mexican sweets and other small presents. The Pinata is hung in the patio, where blindfolded children, armed with long poles, are given three chances each to break it.

Arizona cactus candy is made from the barrel cactus that, because of its stores of cool, sweetish juice in the tissues, is reported to have saved the lives of many desert travelers. Cactus for candy has first to be soaked in lye. Then it is washed, boiled, drained, boiled again, this time in sugar syrup, and after that soaked in sugar for at least a week.

Food on a dude ranch may not be very different from standard restaurant fare anywhere, but on a working ranch you will find such Arizona standbys as chicken-fried steak—a fairly tough piece of beef pounded and deep-fried in a milk and flour batter. Brown pinto beans are a must, baked with salt pork, and often there will be western-style potatoes, sliced thin with onions, and the whole fried slowly in oil or lard.

Over in the mining country, Old World foods and customs add a fairy-tale charm to the sunny days. Thus Christmas finds on Slavic tables the traditional roasted suckling pig, with a red apple in its mouth and a string of cranberries around its neck. As hosts born in Montenegro and Serbia play the *Gusla*—an instrument with goatskin sounding-board and horsehair strings—their guests may eat prairie chicken with spiced gravy, noodles baked with onions, plump dumplings and an assortment of poppy-seed tarts, sugar rolls and holiday cookies.

The copper town of Jerome, which dangles on a mountainside, skyrockets fifteen hundred feet into the air, and has some of its garages on rooftops. In other Jerome houses you climb three flights of stairs from the street to reach the basement kitchen! In many kitchens you could reach out the window and light a match on your neighbor's chimney.

Whether you eat filet mignon or bean stew in Jerome depends upon the price of copper. The town has known times when the finest food from the East and even Europe graced the tables of the mining kings. W. A. Clark, who brought the railroad there in the 1880's, used to serve pheasant, caviar, oysters and champagne in his private dining car.

The Slavic colony in Lowell still celebrates on January 27th a holiday unknown to most Americans—the birth of Saint Savam, twelfth-century monk who won independence from Constantinople for his Serbian Orthodox church. On his birthday the celebrants make wheat bread, cook wheat as gruel and place a tall candle in the center of a plate of wheat. Schoolchildren sing, play and recite Serbian poetry and everybody eats sour cream pies and crumb fritters.

Bakeries in Bisbee and Globe, in which live many Cornish— referred to as Cousin Jacks and Cousin Jennies—are kept busy turning out crisp-crusted Cornish pasties, small meat and potato pies.

Coffee with goat's milk, hot sourdough biscuits with lick (syrup), hot baked potatoes that come to the table on the bread plate along with homemade rolls, beans with every dinner even when the feature is broiled steak, are some of Arizona's food idiosyncrasies.

Anyone who has seen the Grand Canyon—anyone who has sat in the frosty glory of September to eat roast buffalo cooked outdoors—anyone who has been to Phoenix in May to share the Masque of the Yellow Moon Pageant, and dine on the hottest of chili, the crunchiest of tostados—anyone who has been to Arizona at all—is unlikely to get over it.

But one eighty-four-year-old woman did get over it. She and her husband had retired to California in the early 1900's. When he proposed going back to a ranch in Arizona, she grimly recalled the long years when she had to get out of bed at all hours of the night to cook up meals of beef and beans and biscuits, averting her eyes so that she would not recognize the outlaw guests her husband was about to feed. She'd stay in California alone, if need be, she added, but never, never would she go back to "that pesticated country."

Idaho

6,000-FOOT CAKE

Idaho, to quote one of its historians, has known women who could "pick up a deer by its heels and antlers and throw it down cellar, or murder a husband with an iron skillet, and never lose a night's sleep." Admittedly, Idaho was no place for delicate ladies in its explosive pioneer days when Bronco Maggie drove a freight wagon between Thompson Falls, Montana, and the mines of the Coeur d'Alene. One woman who came to Idaho with the idea of hiring out as a mining-camp cook resigned when she found that the miners didn't bother to wash their plates—simply swabbed them with bread and turned them upside down so the rats could only run over the tops.

The monotony of bread and beans was relieved by an occasional pie made of elderberries growing on a bush called the Tree of Music (because the wood was a favorite with Indian flute-makers). But the man known as the Great American Pie Eater of Bannack wasn't particular what was inside his pies. He was only interested in proving, for money, that he could bite through seven pies piled one on top of the other. He won all bets until a stranger paid the town baker to cook the contest pies in tins with bottoms that came out with the pies. By the time the Pie Eater got on to the hoax, the clever stranger, and the Pie Eater's gold, were headed west.

Idaho, the 43rd state, has as many extravagant contrasts in its food as in its scenery. The famous gourmet shops of Wallace furnish beluga caviar and imported cheeses, English biscuits and French *pâté* for the elegant dining rooms of the town's terraced homes. Yet a few miles away an old prospector will still be gathering the crisp leaves of the Oregon grape, which natives call Miner's Lettuce, to go with his stew.

The green and fertile land in which grows the Idaho potato celebrates each year on Spud Day in October. It might be a world away from that other Idaho to the north, where the River of No Return hurtles through a shadowed gorge, and Thunder Mountain sets the mood of a region where there are still unexplored lakes and silent forests which no ax has ever attacked.

The serrated peaks of the Seven Devils surround a wealth of gold, silver and copper which, because of the ruggedness of the country, is untouched, though only a few miles away at Mesa grows one of the biggest apple orchards in the world. At blossom time the air is perfume-drenched for miles around. In Idaho homes apples combine with ham for a casserole, and apple jelly is mixed with mayonnaise for a bland salad dressing. Cream and eggs with grated apples makes a favorite Idaho pie.

The soil and climate are given credit for the plump sweetness of Idaho prunes, and women in the region are proud of their prune butter, prune-whip pies and spicy prune puddings.

High-altitude cooking is a science in Idaho, and a 6,000-foot cake made with chocolate, nuts and spices is a specialty. The secret is the smaller amount of sugar, shortening and baking powder, worked out in a compromise with nature.

Vast irrigation systems have transformed the dusty sagebrush country into green fields. Where the desert once ruled is now the biggest potato flour mill in the world, the product of which goes into an unusual Idaho potato flour sponge cake, and into bread that stays fresh for a long time.

Deer are still plentiful in the forests, and in season, Idaho cooks stir up a wonderful sauce from the prickly wild currant to accompany venison. Huckleberries, darker and richer than the eastern variety, grow wild in the woods and make a hearty wine to go with charcoal-broiled elk steak.

Idaho's state flower, the Mariposa tulip, was admired by the Mormons who made the first permanent white settlement at Franklin in 1860—but not so much for its beauty. The ingenious Mormons dug up the bulb and found that it could be eaten steamed, seasoned and served with the duck and geese which were so plentiful that settlers described a nearby lake as the Market.

Idaho's famous white beans, baked with pimiento, bread crumbs and cheese, come from the fertile region around Filer where ten big bean plants operate. Idaho peas, for split-pea soup, thrive on the volcanic soil.

A few miles away, from a sparkling string of clear lakes come trout to sizzle crusty brown over a campfire. Next door to a fabulous gorge of the Snake River blooms the Hagermann Valley with blooded Guernsey that produce milk so thick you can spoon it out, also golden butter.

It is a far cry from the wheat fields and dairylands of Idaho to the rarefied luxury of the state's Sun Valley, where girls in bathing suits go skiing on costly snow, and imported chefs preside over an elegant cuisine. Still another world is that of the high mountains, where the loneliest men in the world, the sheepherders, tend their flocks. The sheepherder lives in a canvas-topped wagon on frugal fare. If he is a Basque—and many are—he celebrates when he comes down from the heights, on such specialties as *Tripakeschec,* tripe done in olive oil with tomatoes and onions; codfish in a highly seasoned tomato sauce, called *Makelou en Salsberdo;* a ham and bread-crumb omelet *Tortella;* and *Garbanzas,* which are Spanish chick-peas boiled with a soup bone.

Idaho still has a frontier feeling about its unexplored miles of wilderness. But visitors to the dude ranches have been educated by movies, television and travel to the ways of the West, so that they no longer exclaim, as did a young eastern lady in the 1870's upon seeing her first branded steer: "Oh look, look—a monogrammed cow!"

Colorado

FROM SNOW-CAP TO MINE-SHAFT

A house on Eleventh Street in New York's Greenwich Village was an odd place to get acquainted with Leadville, Colorado. In the firelit living room of Will and Inez Haynes Irwin, I spent magic evenings listening to Will as he described his childhood in that incredible mining town, and felt as if I knew the place.

Will Irwin was one of the greatest reporters of all times. When news of the earthquake in San Francisco reached him, he sat at his desk 3,000 miles away and dramatically recreated every corner of the stricken metropolis in "The City That Was." Years after that feat I, an awed cub reporter, listened while he told about the 30,000 wild-eyed gold hunters who swarmed into the pine flats of what was to be Colorado, and built a ragtag town of tents, huts roofed with sailcloth, saloons with no roofs. I could almost taste the five-cent oxtail soup at Smoothey's Restaurant, ingenious by-product of the man- and ox-exhausting trip across the plains to Leadville, perched 10,000 feet above sea level.

Except for the soup made from the unfortunate oxen, the food in Leadville tended to be a monotonous day-by-day repetition of salt pork, sourdough biscuits, beans and coffee. Any man who managed to haul a barrel of whiskey up the Arkansas Valley could make as much as $1,500 profit. One canny fellow, realizing what champagne would mean to prospectors who struck it rich, bought up old bottles and filled them with an explosive mixture of yeast and brown sugar, called Denver cider, which Leadville bars sold to celebrants too far gone to identify its component parts.

When half-starved men found gold or silver, they wined and dined at the swank Tontine, where chefs from New York whipped up hundred-dollar-a-plate banquets of oysters, caviar and pheasant. One overnight millionaire bought expensive clothes for his friends and invited the whole town to a champagne dinner with all the pretty girls he could round up in that rowdy he-man country of the 1880's.

Leadville died and was reborn half a dozen times. The gold strikes ended, silver prices crashed, then lead, manganese, zinc and later molybdenum and uranium brought in new generations of prospectors. The uranium prospector, his streamlined trailer stocked with mixes and canned, dehydrated and frozen foods, has never known the technique of sourdough cookery and campfire beans simmered with salt pork. He's probably healthier than his predecessors, although some old-timers hold that pancakes made with mix can't compare with the slightly acrid sourdough kind, stacked golden-brown on a tin plate with molasses poured over.

The covered-wagon trail from the Missouri River to Denver was so rugged that it was named the Unmarked Grave Route. As late as 1877, the wagons were still pushing west, and in one of them was a fifteen-year-old girl from Maine who surveyed the hungry transients and decided that a wayside inn was what the western end of the road needed.

At sixteen she married and with her husband opened the Twelve Mile House, where she accomplished herculean feats of cooking, turning out as many as thirty-six cakes at a baking, and on the same day churning butter, baking bread and roasting whole hams, sides of beef and roasts of pork, stirring up gallons of oyster stew and making buckets of coffee. The place became so famous that tally-hos drawn by prancing horses brought parties from Denver for dinner and dancing. When the railroad came through, she recorded one day when she baked a thousand biscuits for hungry crewmen.

Another famous Colorado camp started in Phantom Valley in the 1860's when a prospector named Squeaky Bob began baking and giving away wild-strawberry shortcakes and cooking trout fresh from the streams. Soon he was serving so many free meals that he had to put up four tents, and he prudently decided his guests had better start paying for their food. Eventually he made a good thing out of catering to rich Englishmen who came west to hunt elk and antelope. Antelope steaks were fried, elk was smoked over green aspen and willow branches, and as for bear, Squeaky Bob claimed "there was a meat for you . . . sweet . . . tasted very much like pork . . . and bear's lard biscuits . . . you just haven't tasted biscuits until you try them made with bear's lard."

The western cowboy, according to Bonnie and Ed Peplow in *Round-Up Recipes,* had his own biscuit and cake mixes. Before he started for the range he dumped flour, salt and leavening into a sack, tied the sack to his saddle, and when mealtime came, watered the mixture down to the right consistency and dropped it into a skillet greased with lard or bacon drippings.

The prospectors were after gold and silver, but they also helped Colorado become the important food-supply state it is today. One old fellow in 1858 turned his thin, exhausted oxen loose while he went off looking for gold. Next spring he recovered them, sleek and fat. Big-time cattle ranching dates from this inadvertent discovery that the plains provided good pasturage. Texas longhorns came north by the thousands and, later, the mountain slopes were turned into rich ranges for the cattle that eastern markets were bidding for.

Jesse Frazier, journeying west from Missouri to open a coal mine, took along some of his favorite apple seedlings. Apples now are such a major Colorado crop that festivals celebrate the snowy blossomings around Florence and Canon City.

Men managed fairly well with routine cooking, but until women invaded the western mountains, nobody could figure out how to make a good cake. Cakes didn't rise properly in the mountain heights, and at first pioneer women despaired when their treasured recipes failed to work. But before long, some sunbonneted easterner worked out the correct proportions of flour and leavening, and thus began the famous high-altitude cooking, which has produced some of the best cakes in America, including the famous Denver Red Chocolate Cake.

In the beginning, women accustomed to pretty china and silver and the comparative ease of life in the East and Middle West found the going pretty rough in Colorado. In the 1860's Central City had 4,000 people sleeping under pine-bough shelters and in tents. The grocery store was a board laid over some barrels, and customers paid in pinches of gold-dust, measured between thumb and finger like salt. On the same counter with jewelry and champagne were potatoes at $15.00 a bushel. Baltimore oysters cost $16.00 a gallon, and local beaver-tail soup became a gourmet's specialty at Denver's Delmonico's-of-the-West.

Some prospectors discovered that a good crop of grain and a few bushels of fruit brought them more gold than their frantic panning and digging. The prediction that Colorado farms would produce more riches than the mines began to come true when sugar beets were introduced into the South Platte Valley. This was after the sugar manufacturing plant designed by a Frenchman, to whom Napoleon awarded the Cross of Honor, was brought to America by the Mormons and failed to work in Utah, where the syrup turned out acid. The soil and climate of Colorado, however, proved felicitous for sugar beets, and soon beet seeds were being sold in quantity to growers there. Russians who came from the Volga regions to become beet farmers brought their favorite foods, including *Babbats*—savory sausages nestled in hot, rich biscuitlike shells; a special sponge cake made with lemon; cucumber salad with sour cream; meat baked in small tarts and called *Piroshki;* and *Golbutzi*, which are cabbage leaves rolled around a blend of sour cream, rice and chopped meat.

Mexicans came on the scene later to work in the sugar-beet fields and to add their spicy dishes to Colorado's menu, including such fiesta delicacies as *Pollo con Mole Poblano*, a chicken dish with chocolate in its seasonings. Local cooks learned from them the way to make tamale pie with a cornmeal mush topping, and a light, rich custard called *Flan*.

Rocky Ford, which the covered-wagon families named The Friendly Town because it was one of the few spots where they could safely cross the Arkansas River, has a Watermelon Day every year to commemorate the work of Senator G. W. Swink, who began experimenting with melons in 1877. The following year, with a fine juicy crop of melons on hand and nothing to do with them, he invited the countryside for a picnic. About twenty-five people came and he cut up watermelons on the door of a boxcar.

By 1854 the melon picnics had become an occasion, and women brought their best fried chicken, baked beans, pies and cakes to add to the gaiety. There were such crowds that eighty tons of watermelon were served, and many of the visitors stayed over to visit the zinnia fields, go on pheasant hunts and fish in the sparkling Holebrook lake for channel catfish, yellow perch and sunfish.

Lewis Gannett alarmed me a little when he reported in his New York *Herald Tribune* book review column that while he'd found some improvement in roadside food during his summer drive to California, he felt—alas—that our menus are becoming standardized.

"It seems extraordinary," he went on, "that Americans have so little local pride about food. Roadside stands sell wonderful peaches and melons in Colorado, but except for a superb apple pie in Fruit, Colorado, we found no dessert but ice cream in most restaurants."

Colorado, let's do something about this!

Alaska

THE FAR WEST AND THE PACIFIC

Wash.

Ore.

Calif.

Hawaii

Samoa

ADOLAR

California

MILLION-DOLLAR DISHWATER

Guests who dined at William Chapman Ralston's villa were not likely to forget the occasion. In all of lusty, dusty California, nobody tossed such a party as the Ralstons. By 1860, so many wings had been added to the sprawling mansion that 120 guests could sleep there overnight. Mr. Ralston made his first millions in the Comstock mines, doubled and trebled them in the Bank of California speculations, and spent fortunes on Oriental rugs, Turkish baths, stables paneled in mahogany, and Arabian Nights dinner parties.

He liked to load his four-in-hands with guests and drive down the peninsula to his Belmont villa after dark, when the place shimmered with thousands of gas lights. A hundred or more often came for dinner and he escorted them into the library where they sat in silence until a paneled wall rose, like a theater curtain, disclosing a great banquet hall with a pigtailed Chinese servant behind each chair. At one dinner the menu included salmon stuffed with trout

and cooked in rose water. At another the *pièce de résistance* was
hummingbirds filled with baked almonds and placed inside a lin-
net, which in turn was fitted into an English snipe, and that into
a goose. Two canvasback ducks were laid on top and crowned
with breast of goose. This chef's nightmare was soaked in raisin
wine for six days, larded and smoked over burning sandalwood,
and finally roasted on a spit with pork drippings.

Perhaps the food tastes especially wonderful in San Francisco
because everyone adores the city. I think that when you're in love
with a city, the food is always special. I've certainly never had a
finer dish than the wild strawberries and clotted cream I ate in a
treetop restaurant my first enraptured evening in Paris. Or a
fetuccini of such butter and garlic delicacy as that one in Rome
the spring I was in love with an Italian named Caesare; or an
apricot tart of such elusive flavor and fragile pastry as the one
served in a penthouse restaurant overlooking Central Park, on a
long-ago evening when New York City was still a giddy enchantment to me.

I was anti-San Francisco before I went there. In my early days
in New York most of my friends seemed to be fanatical San Fran-
ciscans. . . . The Irwins, the Haders, Stella Karn . . . all talking
incessantly about Fisherman's Wharf crab, pork done on a South
Seas barbecue, oyster loaf and fish cioppino, fresh lime sherbet.
But I hadn't been in San Francisco more than an hour before the
city began to get me. There is something about the dizzying cable-
car ride up Nob Hill that makes even a glass of iced tea taste
special—at least when you sip it underneath the spectacular
glassed-in roof of the Mark Hopkins, the harbor spread at your
feet glittering with sunshine or starred with night lights, Golden
Gate Bridge across the water, roller-coaster streets rising and
dipping among the city's hills.

The crab is as good as my friends bragged it would be, only
they forgot to mention the accompaniment of crisp French bread
that makes it even better. Brought in by the bright little boats of
the fishermen, the crab is cooked in big caldrons over open boxwood fires down on Fishermen's Wharf.

On that first San Francisco visit I was immediately whisked off
to Russian Hill to see the little houses hanging on the sides of the
cliff, where poets, painters and writers once lived in a West Coast
version of Greenwich Village . . . eating, if their tales are to be
believed, mostly succulent oyster loaves made of tiny Pacific

oysters crammed into hollowed-out loaves of buttered, paprikaed milk-bread, oven-toasted. The young adventurers kept old bath-tubs filled with flowers in front of their houses, and by placing boards on top of the tubs, made impromptu tables and staged progressive dinners, one serving the soup—pepper-red bean, probably —the next an oyster loaf; the third a dessert, often fresh green figs with heavy cream.

We went again to Fishermen's Wharf to see the sardine fleet set off in the dark of the moon to bring back tons of the small shining fish for canning. That time, protected by a huge bib, I ate fish cioppino, a hearty fish stew invented by the Italian fishermen.

Tall tales, it seems, always have come out of California. Indians who met the Spanish explorer, Fray Francisco de Escobar in 1682, told him about a tribe which lived "wholly on the odor of their food . . . not eating it at all." At that, probably some of the Spaniards, hungry and sun-bitten, *would* have enjoyed even the smell of a good meal. As late as 1776, the De Anza expedition was reduced to dining on toasted aconite, a wild iris which the Indians relished, but which the foreigners liked no better than they did acorn-meal cakes and toasted caterpillars.

The Spanish were out to find the treasure cities of Cibola and El Dorado. But the Franciscan fathers who came along with the expeditions brought a real and lasting treasure—the nucleus of California's great fruit industry. As Father Junipera Serra and his band of priests built their chain of missions north from San Diego to Sonoma, they also set out vineyards and tidy orchards of peach, apricot, apple and plum. They planted the first figs, olives and walnuts and even experimented with the most golden of all bonanzas, California oranges.

The fledgling United States didn't bother much about California in the years just before the Revolution, when rancheros were living in feudal magnificence on estates of 100,000 acres and more, raising cattle for hides and tallow, and roasting the meat at great outdoor barbecues. Guests thought nothing of riding 100 miles to attend such barbecues, which usually lasted three or four days. Today the tourist can still eat his way through countless barbecues and dance at as many fiestas as he can take. All over California meat sizzles out of doors . . . in private patios, in public parks, drive-in restaurants, at picnics and rodeos. At one Hollywood barbecue 70,000 picnickers ate twelve tons of beef and several carloads of beans and chili.

On St. John's Day the whole countryside comes to San Juan to pay tribute to Father Felipe Arroya, who rode muleback through this region, carrying a tinkling music box to lure Indian converts. The heart of the celebration is a service at Mission San Juan Batista, with its sweeping red tile roof, creamy adobe walls and, inside, an old redwood altar painted by Indians with mellow vegetable dyes. The inevitable barbecue follows the service.

Chili and enchiladas are peppery reminders of the era when Spain and Mexico ruled California. William Tecumseh Sherman, who came west as a young lieutenant in 1847, had occasion to visit the adobe ranch house of one Señor Gomez, where he was served a big helping of stewed hare and what he thought was "an abundant sauce of tomato." It turned out to be "liquid fire," Sherman wrote, adding "It nearly killed me."

The fascinating saga of a California colony under the flag of Russia was told me over a main dish of steaming hot *Kasha* (buckwheat) accompanied by sour cream. The Kasha was preceded by *Piroshkis* . . . small pastries with chopped meat and mushrooms rolled inside. Another feature of this meal was baked Benici peppers with a stuffing of calves' brain and cheese.

In 1806 the Russian settlers far to the north, at Sitka, were so near starvation that Count Nikolai Rezonov took off for San Francisco's Presidium to make a desperate appeal for food. The dark-eyed daughter of the governor, Doña Maria Concepcion Arguello, after one look at Count Rezonov persuaded her father to let him have the supplies. So the starving colony was fed because a girl fell in love. It's too bad the story doesn't end happily. Rezonov died on his way back to Russia to get the czar's permission to marry Doña Maria, and the poor girl, after keeping a long, hopeless vigil by the sea, retired to a convent to die.

A little building of sun-baked adobe at Mission San Gabriel, near Los Angeles, houses the oldest winery. The great gnarled Trinity Vine, which bore grapes for over 170 years, is there still, though now an endless tide of San Francisco commuters keeps the highways in a ferment, and new industries and housing developments are closing in around the relics.

This trend began way back when seafaring Yankee traders started to roam the seas from the Antarctic to China and the South Sea Islands, and clipper ship captains slipped into California harbors to trade cotton, silk, tea and spices for hides and furs. The Mexican governor in 1847 reported that "hordes of Yankee immigrants" were threatening the whole of California. The easy-going ranchers, humming Castillian tunes and putting off decisions until an indefinite tomorrow, were no match for the New Englanders, who industriously set about cultivating farms, planting vineyards, opening gristmills.

The Yankees took over just at the right time. On January 24, 1848, exactly a year after John V. Frémont became the first American governor, gold was discovered at Sutter's Mill on the American River. Food prices skyrocketed as gold hunters poured across the continent or were buffeted around the Horn. San Francisco became a town of tents, cloth houses, adobe huts and ramshackle gambling dens and saloons.

Men weary of salt pork were willing to pay almost anything for a change of diet. The harvest of a single peach tree brought $1,350, and a little plot of land bearing four apple trees was sold for $800, while four boxes of apples shipped from New England were auctioned off for $500. Pioneer settlers in Oregon and Washington shipped heavily salted butter in pine-bark firkins. A single slice of fairly fresh bread brought a dollar, but with a small blob of butter added, the price was two dollars. Potatoes were a dollar each, cooked. One man milked his cow twice a day and sold the milk for a dollar the whiskey-bottleful.

Hangtown Fry is a dish you're sure to get in San Francisco and vicinity, and also the tale that goes with it. Seems the Miner's Court, which meted out justice in lawless gold rush towns, once sentenced a man to death at what is now Placerville. At the foot of the hanging tree, the condemned man proposed a trade: a dish no one had ever tasted before, in exchange for a reprieve. The hungry miners decided to give him a chance. He brought from hiding a tin of oysters, a few precious eggs, a bit of butter and ham. He fried the oysters and the thin slices of ham, beat up the eggs and folded the whole thing into a sort of super-omelet. They never did hang him. Anything to do with food won friends in these days. Thus two great fortunes were made when in Placerville, Philip Armour opened a little butcher shop, and Mark Hopkins a grocery store.

Bacon, hardtack and coffee were standard items for the placer miners, and the coffee often was made from beans crushed in a sack between stones, and used over and over. They red up their tin plates and cups once a week, and it was while three newcomers were dish-washing in a creek that they noticed a pinprick of light in the water. So the famous Fifty Million Dollar stream was discovered by Jimmy Woods, Jack Rider and Charlie Bassett—in probably the most profitable dish-washing in American history.

The food miracles that have been wrought in California would take several fat volumes to record. At the top of the list of magicians goes the name of a mild-mannered New Englander, Luther Burbank, who developed a new potato on his Massachusetts farm and used the $150 he netted from it to go to Santa Rosa for a visit. Delighted with the gentle sun and rich soil, he stayed for fifty years, and during that half century he gave to California and to the world the Burbank cherry; the Climax, Wickson, Gold and Apple plums; the Burbank plum; three new varieties of prunes, including a stoneless one; countless varieties of fruits, vegetables, nuts, grasses, ferns and flowers. His garden tools still stand beside his greenhouse, and Burbank himself is buried under his favorite tree, a tall Deodar, "divine tree of the gods," sent to him from the Himalayas.

Three years after Burbank, Lyman Bruce arrived from Canada to try to improve his health in the golden climate of the Pacific coast. He started raising chickens, and horrified at the variety of ills they are heir to, began experimenting with diets and medicines. Before long Petaluma was known as the world's egg basket, and curious sightseers came there to see the only drugstore in the world devoted to prescriptions for chickens.

Judge J. H. Logan achieved an accidental hybrid from a wild blackberry and a red raspberry, and that is the loganberry. Rudolph Boysen crossed a loganberry, blackberry and raspberry, and got the boysenberry.

Every time you eat a Globe artichoke, you can thank the Italians who came to California in the late 1880's, bringing along their pet vegetable.

The first Chinese, two men and a woman, landed in San Francisco in 1848 and in the next ten years 25,000 more arrived, bringing with them a marvelous cookery in which texture is as important as taste. True, the most profound influence the Chinese have had upon American eating is represented by that un-Chinese dish, chow mein, and by chop suey, said to have been invented by Oscar of the Waldorf to honor the Chinese ambassador. Quick-frozen foods, including won-ton soup, fried rice and egg rolls, have added an Oriental touch to millions of American tables. But the elegant and subtle Chinese dishes remain the province of Chinese cooks:

Pekin duck, melon soups, chicken with walnuts Pekin style, and the intricate combinations of tender bits of meat with snow peas, bamboo and bean sprouts, lotus root, ginger and other special Chinese vegetables and fruits, that you can find in the pagodaed reaches of Grant Avenue in San Francisco.

A far cry from elegance are the cafeteria, the drive-in restaurant and the cheeseburger, but California borned them all. And straight from there, too, came the craze for outdoor barbecues which has put hordes of American males into chef's caps and aprons spattered with cute sayings.

I was pleased to find that a woman's curiosity gave us California navel oranges. As the story was told me, Eliza Tibbetts of Riverside heard that a new orange, seedless and full of juice, had been developed in Bahia, Brazil. She simply wrote to Washington and the government sent her the first two navel seedlings in 1875.

In mid-March San Bernardino stages a National Orange Show which goes on for ten days in a 135-acre park, with trout pool and midway. Features include a camel and ostrich race, a sports car exhibition, and eighty champion cooks lined up at eighty tables, flanked by eighty gas stoves. Forty of the cooks at a signal start mixing orange cakes and the other forty start whipping up lemon pies.

In August when the full moon rides over the channel, one of the most pleasant California fiestas takes place at Santa Barbara where pretty girls dance in the streets and you can eat lunch in a Santa Barbara patio, with the sea wind rustling the palms and the hibiscus in bloom. Your menu may be enlivened by chilled avocado on the half-shell with a dash of lemon, salt and fresh black pepper, abalone steak with butter sauce, a soufflé of summer squash, and for dessert an upside-down cake made of dried apricots and prunes.

Californians assure me that the grunions really exist, but my visits there have never coincided with the special night when these silvery little fish arrive on certain beaches to deposit their eggs. The grunion run is always on schedule, and people crowd the appointed beach hours ahead of time. The game is to catch the grunion literally between waves. Rules are rigorous; no tackle or nets, only bare hands. Afterwards you can stay on the beach and fry your grunion, or do it at home in a coating of oatmeal.

Judging by California's calendar of events, I figure you could spend almost every day of the year at some fiesta, barbecue, picnic or rodeo. Los Angeles alone lists 168 events, not counting the 47 Home State Picnics and the one called "the biggest picnic in the world, estimated attendance, 150,000." This is the Los Angeles that Captain Portola and Father Crespi came upon in 1769 and described as "a delightful place among the trees." The Indians greeted them with baskets of pinole and there were "wild grapes and an infinity of rosebushes in full bloom."

Southern California has contributed what the International Society of Epicures in Paris has declared "the greatest original dish to come out of the United States in the past 50 years"—Caesar salad.

Its originator, Caesar Cardini, a Beverly Hills food specialist, actually created his salad in a restaurant in Tijuana, Mexico, just across the border, on a Fourth of July week end when he ran out of supplies and scoured his pantry for something to feed his guests. The findings (eggs, romaine lettuce, stale bread and Romanello cheese) went into a garlic-rubbed bowl, the bread was soaked in olive oil, the eggs were coddled and stirred into a pear-vinegar and oil mixture, grated cheese and croutons were added—and the Caesar salad was born.

Alaska

LAND OF THE FATTENING MOON

A moose and her yearling stalked through the deep snow and peered into the window of Grace Filkin's log cabin. Grace, in her seventies, living alone on the edge of a vast virgin forest near Homer, Alaska, laughed aloud at the bemused curiosity on the two solemn faces.

This pioneer woman had a busy summer that year. The minute the snow melted, she laid out her garden and watched the woods for the wild fruits as they came in season. She knew where the squawberries grew thickest, where to find the wild rose hips for delicate preserves, how to pick the tiny mossberries that look like blue blobs of currant jelly and make a fine pie. Watermelonberry, blueberry, high and low bush cranberry, serviceberry and wild red currants, all these Grace canned or turned into sparkling jellies, jams and preserves that summer and fall.

She made chowder of some of the razorback clams and minced and canned others. It took her two weeks to get the meat of an 800-pound moose put down in brine, and just as the work was finished another minus tide brought the second of the clam harvests. She salted king salmon, canned silver salmon, helped dig a well and pour the concrete foundation for a school and home for the shy, dark-skinned Aleut children she adored.

All this pioneer living, as rugged as anything women ever knew in the days of covered wagons and log cabins, went on in the 1950's. Grace wrote about it in a series of letters I used on my radio program.

Alaska is still a land of frontiers, of room for homesteaders who can't breathe freely in cities. Little Jeannie Helmericks, who spent a good part of her early life with her explorer-parents in the Far North, pines for such a delicacy as *agutuk*, which is Eskimo ice cream made of warm bear's grease poured over whole cranberries and frozen.

"And of course, ALL children love raw frozen fish eyes," her father said casually, adding that you never have to coax a child to eat what's good for it in the polar lands.

Two other friends, Simeon Oliver, whose Aleutian name is Nutchuk, and his wife sent a little mimeographed cookbook compiled by Eskimo children in the day school of Sishmared, on the Seward Peninsula, 75 miles from East Siberia. Each child got home-recipes for such dishes as soured seal liver, cooked blubber, Incod ice cream, "seals bare feet" and *Suewok*, made with dried salmon eggs, seal oil and blackberries.

Side by side with ancient Eskimo foods are the exciting new products of Matanuska, whose families came as "cream-puff pioneers" in the depression years of the 1930's. Science went to work on these homesteads and the famed Matanuska potato is the result of agronomists' experiments with 155 different varieties. In summer when the sun shines twenty-two hours a day, Matanuska colonists can watch their grain shoot up as much as an inch a day. Thirty-five-pound cabbages, and strawberries the size of peaches are commonplace there.

Ghosts of the gold-rush days linger in fading records of eggs at eighteen dollars a dozen, condensed milk three dollars a can and sugar a hundred dollars a sack. They still dress Alaska lettuce salad with condensed milk mixed with Worcestershire and set sourdough regularly for pancakes. Old sourdough pots are as precious to Alaskans as Sheraton and Chippendale to New Englanders, and some veterans when they go outside on vacations freeze the batter so that their treasured starter will be ready when they get back.

When gold first lured 25,000 men to cross the desolate flats and mountain passes to Skagway in 1898, Harriet Pullen decided to leave her Wisconsin home for the North. Harriet was thirty-seven, a widow with four children. She took the four with her and arrived in Skagway with only seven dollars in her purse. She decided that what Skagway needed were the spicy apple pies she knew how to make. Five months later she'd saved enough money to have seven horses shipped north. The harbor was so full the ship couldn't dock, so out went Harriet in a rowboat. She had the horses walked off, one by one, on a wooden plank and towed them to shore. She trucked her goods up the trails and passes, opened a restaurant, ran a dairy and truck farm. Pullen House today is a memorial to her apple pies and her Wisconsin courage, with three of its rooms turned into a museum of the hectic 90's.

Alaskans say that the American West began around the strange volcanic islands of the Aleutians when the Russians came to Kodiak in 1792. On a memorable Alaskan trip a few years ago I went to Kodiak, which is anchored on a fleet of little islands that in summer look like flower gardens headed out to sea. Christmas still lasts twelve days up there, in the Russian Orthodox manner, with dancing for seven nights running and churchgoing for seven days. On the last three days groups troop through the streets carrying huge tinsel stars, singing carols and stopping at homes for glasses of strong, hot Russian tea and cookies.

In Sitka there are regal remnants of the days when the Russian fur-trader Baranoff built a great log castle and gave dinner parties for a hundred guests—officials in gold lace, bejeweled women in kid gloves and Paris gowns. There, if you're lucky, you may still eat a fine Koulibiak of Salmon, a rich Beef Stroganoff laced with spices, the famous Kasha with nuts and fruit stirred in, and at Easter, Paska.

My Alaska trip took me close to the Pribiloff Islands, foggiest spot on earth, where the seals have their own United States Coast Guards for protection. Seals are, of course, valued food among the Eskimos, but for us it is their precious fur that counts, and these small islands provide 90 per cent of the world's supply of seal pelts. On or about May 5th each year the males come roaring down to the beach to await the return of the females from southern waters. But, true to their sex, the females never get there on time. They've been known to be as much as five months late.

Food dominates the picturesque calendar of the Tlingit Indians. January is the Goose Moon, when there will be roast goose on Alaska tables, fragrant with sage and served with brown flour gravy and tart currant jelly. March is the month of the Sea Flower Moon, when the underwater life of the ocean begins to stir. Then it is time to think of concocting sweet sea pickles from kelp. Next comes the season of the sablefish, which is baked in a pie with pimiento and cheese. In June the Salmon Moon shines over the feverish run of the salmon as they fight their way upstream to breed and die. The big canneries of Alaska get ready then to process the pink and red fish which will go into salads, croquettes and casseroles in homes all over the nation.

Most interesting of all the months in the Tlingit calendar is August—month of the Fattening Moon, when everything in Alaska seems to be growing to gargantuan size. It is then that you can fly from Juneau to Glacier Bay, where a fortunate few will attend the birth of a baby glacier—a thunderous process called calving, when a mass of ice breaks away from the mother glacier and takes off on its own. The most entrancing part of this flight is a stop at Strawberry Island to eat juicy Alaskan strawberries almost as big as pears.

I know of one Alaskan farmer who homesteaded three islands. He lived and grew his vegetables on Forget-Me-Not. He kept his flock of sheep on Crooked Island and on Astrigan he grazed the cows, delivering the milk by boat.

Hawaii

THREE-FINGER POI

Once upon a time the men did all the cooking in Hawaii and a woman wasn't considered glamorous unless she was fat. Three hundred and fifty pounds was a favorite size. Nobody ever heard of corsets, either, and slim girls were given a special medicine to fatten them. The last of the great warrior kings of Hawaii had a bevy of some twenty curvaceous wives, none weighing less than two hundred and fifty, while the belle of them all had a ninety-two-inch waistline. Sometime in the 1820's, before the queen was swathed in Mother Hubbards by well-meaning missionaries, she tackled a meal which was later described by an awed sea captain. Flat on her stomach, she ate from a ring of bowls while servants fanned the flies away. The captain swore that her first installment was more than six men of his crew could eat. But at that point, a masseur entered, rolled her majesty over and gave her a vigorous workout, after which she started on another circle of bowls.

No doubt the queen was a three-finger poi woman. The business of one-, two- and three-finger poi has been explained to me repeatedly, but the only thing I'm sure of is that I don't like poi. It is taro root, washed, beaten and boiled with water until, in the opinion of some, it looks and tastes like library paste. Poi is one-finger when it is so thick you can lop up enough on one finger to twirl into a ball. The thinnest takes three fingers.

Poi goes along with a luau as inevitably as cranberry sauce with turkey. Luaus are fun and the ideal place for one is the big island of Hawaii, with its breath-taking mountain drives, its blazing white beaches and blue water, and the easy tempo of life turned to siestas and soft songs. The ingredients of a real luau are so distinctly Hawaiian that if you're anywhere else you might as well forget the whole idea and give a barbecue instead.

First, you need fresh, glossy green ti-leaves and lacy Hawaiian fern. These are your tablecloth. Your guests should all have leis, preferably of frilled purple and white Chinese pansies, ginger flowers or baby orchids. The *imu*, or outdoor oven, is a deep pit filled halfway with rocks heated to a glowing red. Some of these rocks are tucked into the scrubbed interior of a Kalua pig, and he is lowered into the pit along with dozens of *laulaus*. A laulau is simply the ti-leaf-wrapped bundle of food which is served along with the pork . . . usually a mixture of chicken, fish, red salt and chili peppers. Fresh wet ti-leaves are piled on top and the whole steams and simmers until luau-serving time. Roast Hawaiian sweet potatoes, fresh sugar-cane sticks, taro leaves in coconut milk—all these are part of the menu and the dishes are polished coconut shells. Add a royal Hawaiian moon and I'll tackle even three-finger poi.

The island of Lani is the place to be on that enchanted morning when the pineapple bursts into terraced miles of delicate blue flowers. The blossoms last just one day, opening in spirals as a pretty signal to growers that their golden harvest will be ready in about five months.

All over the world, Hawaiian pineapples have added to the pleasure of eating. But they aren't natives. The first known picture of a pineapple appeared in Seville, Spain, in 1535, and Columbus is credited with bringing the fruit from the island of Guadeloupe in the West Indies. Plant explorers now believe the fruit first grew in Brazil, and was carried to the far corners of the earth by traders and adventurers. Nobody knows when the first pineapple arrived in Hawaii, but small, sour ones were shipped to California during the Gold Rush, and according to the records, a Spanish physician, Don Francisco de Paula y Marin, had pineapples growing in his garden in 1813.

The real pineapple pioneer, however, was Captain John Kidwell, who brought slips of the Smooth Cayenne variety from Jamaica, and opened the first cannery in 1892. Although pineapples were destined to become a multimillion-dollar crop, the captain cared less for money than for his plant experiments, and in a few years sold his plantations and retired happily to his island gardens. It remained for James E. Dole to turn a tiny business—1,600 cases of canned pineapple in 1903—into a firm which produces that same amount in twelve minutes! Since World War II, quick-freezing has added a new delight in the form of golden pine-

apple chunks served with the frost still on them—a kind of glorified
sherbet.

Pineapples, sugar and cattle ranching have brought a fascinating variety of peoples to Hawaii and the food is as varied as
they. Hawaiians know and have long used at least forty varieties
of the delicately colored seaweed which nutritionists now tell us
could form a fine source of food, brimming with vitamins. Islanders make green papayas into a chowder with flecks of bacon
floating on top, use coconut milk in shrimp curry, simmer mullet
or whitefish in coconut milk, brown chicken in butter and simmer
it with spinach and coconut milk, bake ripe bananas in their skins
and serve hot with butter and salt, and make a ginger-milk sherbet
for dessert.

In the small Samoan community one may sample a memorable
dish of mashed, ripe bananas combined with lime juice, coconut
cream and water. An acquired taste is the Samoan breakfast of
boiled green bananas and fish.

The Portuguese in Hawaii like for breakfast fried cornmeal
mush to which water cress has been added, raised doughnuts
rolled in sugar and honey, and hot pickled codfish. The Koreans
eat sweet rice with cinnamon, dates and chestnut, and all the
classic Chinese and Japanese dishes are available, too, in Hawaii.
And in typical Cape Cod cottages shaded by coconut palms, tea
is poured from old Georgian silver services and the sandwiches
will be small and thin with crusts snipped off, English-style.

Soon I suppose there won't be a princess left in the islands, and
it's a pity. Armine von Tempski, writing of the good old days, tells
of going to a feast of truly regal magnificence, where the guest of
honor was "six feet tall, but as delicately boned as a gazelle . . .
eyes enormous, sparkling, fringed by outrageously long lashes
. . . richness enveloped her as if she had been born at high noon
in golden sunlight."

Oregon

PIE FROM A FLOWER

"She planted the apple seeds she had brought from Michigan." When Poet Edwin Markham wrote that about his mother, he was telling the story of Oregon. Settlers brought all kinds of seeds and plants over the terrifying passes of the Cascades or around the Horn on grueling ten-month voyages. William Meek and the Llewlyn brothers carried one hundred apple seedlings and grafted trees in their covered wagons. The first box of Oregon-grown apples brought $75 in the Portland market and in 1851, four boxes sold for $500 in San Francisco.

Oregon grew up overnight. Ezra Meeker crossed the plains in an ox-drawn wagon in 1852, and in his lifetime made the same trip by airplane. The first settlers ate a lot of boiled wheat and hominy, and learned to make clam chowder as the Indians did. They also invented a delicacy now virtually extinct—Fern pie—and from the roots of the blue camass flower concocted a pie which is still served in many Oregon homes. Flour for golden loaves of bread was first furnished by Jason Lee who brought his grist mill around Cape Horn and then by Chinook canoe to Salem. The mill was put together wrong at first and until it could be fixed, threw the wheat to the winds instead of grinding it.

Pioneer sourdough biscuits and pancakes are still eaten by fishermen and hunters, as well as another invention of gold-seekers, Prospector Soup made of flour, bacon fat, canned milk and onion. Plentiful game, however, provided the good shots among pioneers with gourmet dinners of wild duck, pheasant, venison and wild turkey.

On my last trip through the Northwest, as a matter of fact, I encountered excellent southern cooking and found that hundreds of veterans left the ruined South after the Civil War. They brought with them the tradition of hot bread, fried chicken, baked hams and hominy grits and they were among the first to make pioneer meat pancakes using leftover meat mixed with raisins, lemon pulp, eggs, milk, flour—fried first, then steamed.

Not far from Sutherlin is Aurora, settled by a German religious group experimenting in communal living. Many of the old weather-beaten buildings with fat chimneys at one end are still standing, and Aurora is famous for sage-fragrant sausage served with German fried potatoes and home-baked bread.

Progress in the form of the new dam has doomed the picturesque Salmon Feast held for many years in the beautiful Dalles. The falls and nearby Indian villages have vanished, but Oregonians learned the Indian way of cooking salmon outdoors by roasting a whole split fish on a sapling over glowing coals. Corn roasted in the shuck and potatoes in their skins complete the meal. Another Oregon delicacy: salmon cheeks dipped in egg and crumbs and deep-fried. In pre-pioneer days the Indians served salmon with great ceremony, laying the fish with its head upstream and salmon-berries in its mouth. The heart of a salmon, they believed, must never be buried, never eaten.

Oregon is justly proud of its seafood, sharing the succulent little Olympia oyster with Washington and liking it best in a flavorsome scappo or pan roast. Oregon crabmeat, also known as Donganese crab, can be creamed, barbecued or eaten cold with seasoned mayonnaise. A dish called Small Fry is the native whitebait, a miniature fish tossed in corn meal and fried whole, tails, heads, innards and all.

When W. F. Jewett arrived from Maine to found the town of Gardiner, he was determined that the place should look just like New England, and so it does—demure white houses, picket fences, lilacs, poplars, with, on the table good Down East fish chowder sharing honors with Boston baked beans.

Different is Jordan Valley, with stone houses like those in the heart of the Pyrenees, rooms painted bright red, green and yellow, Basque families dancing the Fandango to wild guitars and eating paella from great brown pottery casseroles. Paella combines saffron rice, highly spiced sausage, clams and shrimp with chicken. Sheep-herding Basques in Oregon spend solitary months tending their flocks. Many still speak the flowing tongue, analysis of which eludes experts. Oregon sheep-men celebrate at a Fall Lamb Show in Gold Beach, and for years barbecued lamb was served to all comers.

In stagecoach days outlaws and mule-skinners rubbed shoulders with gold miners, who came to town to eat Oregon huckleberry pie, made from the big blue huckleberries which still grow wild there, huckleberry griddle cakes, roast venison and plump little Columbia River smelt browned in butter and garlic.

In Oregon's rich dairyland, the cows graze knee-deep in yellow buttercups and the creamy milk pours into the cheese kitchens to be made into cream cheese and eaten in delicate cream cheese cake, pie and summer salads with Rogue River pears, plums, Bing cherries or strawberries. The cheese curd, by the way, squeaks when chewed.

Lebanon claims the world's biggest shortcake at the fragrant festival of strawberries and roses each year. This cake towers twelve feet in the air and measures fifteen feet in diameter. They cut it with a saw.

You have to climb up to the steep town of Hood River where a sea of blossoms spreads out for miles in spring and where the lush fruit harvest includes apples, pears, delicate red raspberries and loganberries as big as your thumb.

There have always been fine Oregon cooks to create such delights as McGinties, dried apple turnovers, apples mashed with brown sugar and spices and the turnover served hot with thick yellow cream.

Tillamook cheese has been justly famous ever since Peter McIntosh came many years ago and brought his secret of making fine cheddar, which is especially good in a sauce for broiled halibut.

Circled by the lovely Blue Mountains, the town of Milton-Freewater calls itself the Pea Capital of the World and until recently honored its profitable crop at a gala three-day festival. Millions of pounds of canned and frozen peas go to all parts of the country from the Walla-Walla Valley, while most of the peas for split pea soup come from the Inland Empire where a happy combination of soil and climate produces them in succulent profusion.

Golden Oregon prunes are descended from the first cuttings which journeyed from France in the 1850's. Cooks of the region like to make a prune stuffing for pheasant, wild ducks and geese.

All through Oregon, pioneer societies hold annual picnics and get-togethers. Towns like Weston and Brownsville make a big thing of remembering their adventurous past, with lamb or salmon barbecues. Oregonians agree with Rudyard Kipling who caught and ate a twelve-pound salmon in his first half hour of Oregon fishing, then wrote:

"I have lived . . . the American continent may now sink under the sea, for I have taken the best that it yields. . . ."

American Samoa and the Other Pacific Islands

A COCONUT BREAK

In Pago-Pago, capital of American Samoa, you find a Polynesian food pattern not always acceptable to white visitors. An exception is the tender browned chicken with coconut and spinach, and a dessert of yams, coconut and spices baked in a thatched outdoor oven called an Umu. It's puzzling to find the islanders eating half-ripened oranges, avocados and papaya, until someone explains that they developed a taste for unripe fruit because if left to ripen it was too often eaten by rats or other small animals.

American Samoa is actually three islands and a tiny coral atoll called Rose Island. There is a wild and flowery beauty to the region and in many out of the way villages the old and gentle ways of the Polynesians survive. Visiting chiefs may still be offered a baked, mashed breadfruit seasoned with sea water, mixed with coconut cream and laid out on fresh green leaves. Green bananas are mashed with coconut cream and baked in banana leaves. Whole fish, fresh from the sparkling Pacific, are baked in braided coconut fronds with a sauce of sea water, coconut milk and onions. The main green vegetable is seaweed boiled for a few minutes.

Almost all food is served slightly underdone and tasting of the Umu's wood smoke. The Samoans like it that way.

American trusteeship cuts a wide swath in the Pacific, across the Carolines, Marshalls and Mariannas. World War II hurtled many remote Pacific islands into the headlines and hundreds of easygoing islanders found themselves moved from the path of atom bomb tests as air bases and radio stations were set up. The American PX introduced them to Spam and candy bars, white flour, canned fruits and vegetables.

One of the most exciting food experiments was conducted on Midway Island, considered, though it is 1,000 miles from Honolulu, a suburb of Hawaii. There Pan American Airways began growing hydroponic vegetables to feed passengers and crews of planes which made overnight stops on the tiny, barren stretch of sand in mid-Pacific. Hydroponics is the growing of vegetables without soil, on a layer of pebbles to which is added a watery solution containing the necessary nutrients. Dr. W. P. Gericke developed the system at the University of California, and it stirred the imagination of conservationists alarmed at our dwindling world food supply. They had visions of the earth's arid regions turned into hydroponic garden spots.

But as planes flew higher and faster, flight kitchens improved and new techniques were worked out so that the need for hydroponics-produced vegetables vanished. Scientists now are not even sure that the technique is a good one because they do not know all the chemicals and substances required for good health—and how, then, can they guarantee that any nutrient solution duplicates good soil conditions? Hydroponic tomatoes may look big, red and juicy, beans crisp and green, strawberries lush and scarlet, but we cannot yet say for sure that we are successfully rivaling nature.

Across the water on the island of Guam, neon lights, deep freezes, bobby soxers and juke boxes have turned the principal town into a carbon copy of thousands of places in the States.

Guam is an odd little steppingstone to the Orient. When Magellan first spotted it in 1521, it was the wild, windy home of a primitive tribe called Chamorros, whose most prized food delicacy was the giant fruit bat. No trace of those people is left, except part of their language and a taste for fruit bats. The poor little island was occupied by the Japanese for almost three years, and when we got it back, many of the houses, most of the fish supply, the fruits and trees were destroyed.

The city of Agana, with its reinforced concrete houses anchored to defy the typhoons, has neon-lighted drug stores where you can get an American hamburger with a double malted, and similar typical delicacies.

You may also have your choice, on this dot of an island, of Guamish Guam food, American Guam, Oriental Guam or Spanish Guam. The natives, primarily of Micronesian stock, do not eat as much of their purely native food as in pre-war times, but at wedding feasts and special celebrations, they still serve suckling pig roasted on a spit and stuffed with a kind of hash-brown potatoes, dill pickle, celery and sausage meat.

Old Guamanian families still meet for Merienda, which might be called a "coconut break" as it is an afternoon snack of little, juicy dumplings made from green coconut, starch and sugar.

The island diet abounds in fried rice . . . in fact, rice in any form, including a gumbo-like concoction which is seasoned with achoti seeds to give it a gay orange color.

Guamanian kitchens have "hot lockers" where noodles, rice, salt and the like are kept warm and dry so they will not mold. There is no native bread, but during the war they made a bread substitute by grinding a palm tree fruit called fadang into a starchy substance. Tapo is the Guam version of poi, except it is cooked quite hard and served like sliced potatoes. Americans admit this is an acquired taste, and can take quite a time to develop.

Washington

A WORLD STILL NEW

It was an unwritten pioneer law that nothing worth less than a dollar a pound should be taken along in a covered wagon. But when nobody was looking, Louisa Denny ran back into her pretty

Illinois farmhouse and got her favorite mirror. That, and a bag of sweetbriar seeds from a friend's garden, went along with the four wagons west in 1851. The wagons took 108 days to reach Portland, Oregon, and from there the little group—seven men, four women, four children—boarded a small ship piloted by a Nantucket skipper, to sail into the mystery and silence of Puget Sound in a pouring rain. When Louisa's mother saw what awaited them . . . one tiny log cabin without a roof . . . she sat on a water-soaked stump and burst into tears. Her husband patted her shoulder and urged gently:—

"That's no way to start pioneering."

Later Louisa, when she and her bridegroom went to their new cabin, hung up her precious mirror, shooed her most valuable wedding presents—a hen and rooster—under the doorstep, and set up the rickety stove she'd bought from a ship's galley. On it she cooked her first meal—fried salt pork and potatoes.

Her sweetbriar flowered so luxuriantly that Seattle always called her the Sweetbriar Bride. Women brought all sorts of growing things to the West—one her favorite apples, another sweet red clover, and one misguided pioneer is said to have transported dandelions and planted them as carefully as the rarest flowers.

It wasn't long before the first Washington families were learning from the Indians how to eat the bountiful seafoods, the wild mint, minder's lettuce and service berries. Alta West, librarian of the State Historical Society, says that a favorite dish along the coast now is oyster pan-roast, made exactly as Captain Doane made it almost a century ago when he discovered the captivating Olympia oysters and tried simmering them in their own liquor with a brisk blend of catsup, cayenne, vinegar, Worcestershire and butter.

Jerry, a Puyallup Indian, was still cooking a fine kippered salmon when he was well past ninety years of age. Alta West first learned from him exactly how to season this delicacy, and also his method for baking the same fish for the annual celebration at Rown's Point. Jerry's method was to lay the salmon on sticks over a pit of hot alder coals, and cook for half an hour. The alder fire gives the salmon a special smoky flavor.

Washington is still close to frontier times. In his book on Puget Sound, Robert Walkinshaw remembers the day, in the 1930's, when a statue of Ezra Meeker was unveiled at Puyallup. Indians in full regalia formed a bright background for the ceremonies, and men and women were present who had crossed the continent in covered wagons. Finally Ezra Meeker himself arose, "the autumn sun falling on his white wind-blown hair . . . a man who in the summer of 1852 with his young wife and baby, had traveled for five months by ox-team over 2,000 miles of trail."

The wives of pioneers learned the Indian secrets of steaming hard-shell clams tender in a pit of hot rocks and coals. They found out how to go out at "minus" tide and dig deep for the fat deoduck clam, which they sliced and fried like chicken, also the rare Piddock clam which gives soup and stew such an exciting flavor.

Frontier families nursed the first apple, pear and peach trees to maturity and within their lifetime saw Washington fruit become world-famous. The Wanatchee and Yakima apple harvest grew into a six-week gala celebration, with women creating spicy apple crisps to serve hot with lemon sauce, apple meringues, apple butter to slather on hot biscuits and make into pies, and an apple candy they describe as "a sweet straight from fairyland."

They were and still are a "big" people. At Chahalis the farmers inaugurated an annual outing at Alexander Park and made it newsworthy by frying the world's biggest omelet over a blazing outdoor fire, using 7,200 eggs and greasing the 8-foot pan by fastening bacon to the feet of pretty girls who skated over the surface.

Tahola has an annual trout derby, and Indian guides still take venturesome visitors on a wild eight-hour trip through churning black and white water. Rainbow trout are best, the old-timers say, when rolled in cornmeal and cooked quickly in a frying pan, turned, when brown on one side, by an expert flip of the pan and served with hot flapjacks and coffee sweetened with maple sugar.

At Lynden where the Dutch grow golden miles of daffodils and rainbow fields of tulips, the specialty is thin pancakes called flensjes, with raspberry jam rolled inside. A few miles away at Burlington the crimson strawberry harvest is ushered in with a festival and great bowls of dewy fresh berries picked up by their green stems and dunked in sugar.

The coffee in the Greek coffee houses in Seattle is black and syrupy and served with a thin pastry called pilo. The international theme is continued by the suki-yaki of Japan, the bamboo shoots and Bombay duck of China . . . and sermons preached in Icelandic.

Enormous barbecues take whole pigs at a cooking. Salmon barbecues are almost ritualistic—the salmon cooked on slabs before an applewood beach fire and served with lemon-butter or hot sauce.

Toledo, in the heart of the logging country, serves free hot coffee and cheese sandwiches by the thousands at its June Cheese Days, when loggers roll into town along with crowds of tourists.

Tacoma is a city of terraces where a kitchen window may look out on the blue-gray reaches of Puget Sound framed in dark fir trees, or to snow-capped Mount Rainier. Here ocean rockfish are deep fried, honey in the comb is served with high, lightly browned biscuits, razorback clams make a famous hash and Washington apple pie comes to the table with a warm rum sauce.

In the noisy, colorful arcade markets of Seattle's Pike Place, horse radish is ground fresh, doughnuts are baked and sold hot, along with a famous cottage cheese and a local candy resembling Turkish Delight, made of Yakima apples and chopped walnuts.

A hint of the frontier still persists in the spring sailing of the S.S. *Victoria* for Alaska, the minute word arrives that the ice in Nome is breaking up. The frontier spirit lives on, too, in people like the 97-year-old woman who went on her honeymoon in a covered wagon in Wyoming and now lives as far from the city rush and bustle as possible, on a magic island in Puget Sound where she gathers the small, sweet shrimp for deep frying and makes jelly, emerald-clear, from wild mint. Urged by well-meaning relatives to come back to her native Pennsylvania, she wrote them in firm, rounded longhand:—

"You have been civilized far too long. Out here the world is still new. There is excitement, like a nip of frost, in this western air."

1000

SELECTED

RECIPES

Appetizers

HORS D'OEUVRES

NUTTY HORS D'OEUVRE

1 cup shelled pecans
1 cup shelled almonds
1 cup shelled filberts
2 tablespoons olive oil
2 drops garlic extract

Arrange nuts in shallow baking pan. Combine oil and garlic extract; let stand 20 minutes. Combine nuts and oil mixture; mix lightly. Bake in moderate oven (325° F.) 10 minutes. Makes 2 cups.

SALMON-CHEESE CANAPES

1 7-ounce can salmon
1 3-ounce package cream cheese
3 tablespoons mayonnaise
½ cup chopped celery
¼ teaspoon salt
½ teaspoon prepared mustard
2 tablespoons chopped parsley
16 slices bread
Parsley

Drain fish and flake. Blend cheese and mayonnaise. Stir in fish, celery and seasonings. Remove crusts from bread. Cut each slice into 3 strips and toast. Spread salmon on toast strips. Garnish with parsley. Makes 48.

BOLOGNA CANAPES

½ pound bologna
2 hard-cooked eggs, chopped
1 tablespoon chopped pimiento
2 tablespoons minced green pepper
Salad dressing
Toast rounds

Chop bologna; add eggs, pimiento, green pepper and enough salad dressing to moisten. Spread on toast rounds. Makes about 24.

MARINATED CAULIFLOWER

½ cup French dressing
2 tablespoons lemon juice
1 tablespoon grated onion
2 cups raw cauliflowerets

Combine dressing, lemon juice and onion. Add cauliflowerets and chill thoroughly. Drain. Makes about 18.

STUFFED EGG SPECIAL

6 hard-cooked eggs
2 tablespoons sour cream
¼ cup chopped liverwurst
⅛ teaspoon salt

Cut eggs in half, lengthwise, and remove yolks. Mash egg yolks with sour cream, liverwurst and salt. Fill whites with yolk mixture. Serve as appetizers. Makes 12 servings.

BROILED CHEESE APPETIZERS

1 cup grated American cheese
1 tablespoon chopped chives
2 tablespoons mayonnaise
Crackers

Combine cheese, chives and mayonnaise. Spread on crackers. Broil 3 or 4 inches from source of heat 3–5 minutes. Makes about 24.

GULF SHRIMP BALLS

2 cups sifted all-purpose flour
3 teaspoons baking powder
¼ teaspoon salt
⅛ teaspoon paprika
1 egg, beaten
1 cup milk
1½ cups cooked chopped shrimp

Sift flour with baking powder, salt and paprika. Combine egg and milk; add to sifted ingredients and mix until blended. Add shrimp and mix lightly. Drop by tablespoonfuls in deep hot fat (375° F.) and cook until browned on all sides. Drain on absorbent paper. Makes about 24.

BAKED ROLL-UPS

1 recipe plain pastry
1 cup grated sharp cheese
2 tablespoons chopped chives
⅛ teaspoon paprika
⅛ teaspoon salt

Roll pastry out on lightly floured surface to ⅛″ thickness. Cut into strips 1 x 4 inches. Combine cheese, chives, paprika and salt. Sprinkle cheese mixture over pastry and roll up jelly-roll fashion. Seal edges. Place on greased baking sheet. Bake in hot oven (400° F.) 10–12 minutes, or until slightly browned. Makes about 42.

HOT TUNA STICKS

1 cup flaked, cooked tuna
1 tablespoon grated onion
1 teaspoon Worcestershire sauce
Mayonnaise
4 slices buttered bread
¼ cup grated Swiss cheese

Combine tuna, onion, Worcestershire sauce and enough mayonnaise to moisten. Spread tuna mixture on bread slices. Top with cheese. Cut bread slices into 4 strips. Broil 3 or 4 inches below source of heat about 3 minutes, or until cheese is melted. Makes 16.

CHEESE AND PARSLEY BALLS

½ cup American cheese spread
2 tablespoons crumbled blue cheese
1 teaspoon grated onion
2 tablespoons chopped nuts
Mayonnaise
Chopped parsley

Combine cheeses, onion, nuts and enough mayonnaise to moisten. Shape into small balls and roll in parsley. Makes about 12.

HOT SWISS CANAPES

1 tablespoon all-purpose flour
1¼ cups grated Swiss cheese
⅛ teaspoon paprika
⅛ teaspoon salt
1 tablespoon chopped stuffed olives
2 tablespoons chopped walnuts
1 egg white

Combine flour, cheese, paprika, salt, olives and walnuts. Beat egg white until stiff and fold into cheese mixture. Shape into small balls. Fry in deep hot fat (370° F.) about 1–2 minutes, or until lightly browned on all sides. Drain on absorbent paper. Makes about 12.

ANCHOVY CANAPES

¼ cup cream cheese
1 tablespoon chopped parsley
Crackers
2 hard-cooked eggs, sliced
1 can anchovy fillets

Combine cheese and parsley. Spread cheese mixture on crackers. Top with egg slices and anchovies. Makes about 12.

TOMATO-OLIVE APPETIZERS

4 small tomatoes
¼ cup chopped stuffed olives
1 tablespoon salad oil
2 tablespoons vinegar
1 tablespoon chopped parsley
½ teaspoon salt

Remove stem ends from tomatoes. Scoop out pulp leaving shell about ¼″ thick. Combine tomato pulp, olives, oil, vinegar, parsley and salt. Fill tomato shells with olive mixture. Makes 4 servings.

STUFFED CELERY

1 3-ounce package cream cheese
1 tablespoon chili sauce
1 tablespoon sour cream
8 celery stalks (approx.)

Combine cream cheese, chili sauce and sour cream. Beat until light and fluffy. Fill celery stalks with cheese mixture. Chill. Cut into 2″ pieces if desired. Makes about 8 stalks.

STUFFED WALNUTS

¼ cup cream cheese
1 tablespoon chopped parsley
1 cup walnut halves

Combine cheese and parsley. Spread cheese mixture over half of walnuts. Top with remaining walnuts. Makes about 12.

SAUSAGE WITH OLIVES

1 can cocktail sausages
1 cup large stuffed olives (approx.)

Broil sausages 3 or 4 inches from source of heat for about 5 minutes, or until browned on all sides. Arrange sausages with olives on toothpicks. Makes about 12.

PICKLED HERRING

2 medium-sized salt herring
1 cup vinegar
½ teaspoon pepper
2 tablespoons sugar
6 peppercorns, crushed
¼ cup minced onion

Soak herring several hours. Drain and remove skin and bones. Add remaining ingredients and chill several hours. Makes 6 servings.

SWISS CHEESE CUBES

1 cup Swiss cheese cubes (½-inch cubes)
¼ cup salad dressing (approx.)
2 tablespoons chopped chives

Dip cheese cubes in dressing and roll in chives. Place on toothpicks. Makes about 18.

COCKTAIL OLIVES

1 cup stuffed olives
1 cup ripe olives
½ cup French dressing
1 clove garlic, peeled

Combine all ingredients. Cover and chill several hours. Drain and serve. Makes 2 cups.

ANCHOVY APPETIZERS

2 hard-cooked egg yokes, sieved
12 boneless anchovy fillets

Sprinkle egg yolks over anchovy fillets. Serve with shredded lettuce, as desired. Makes 4 servings.

PROSCIUTTO AND MELON

1 medium-sized cantaloupe
¼ pound thinly sliced prosciutto

Peel cantaloupe. Cut into slices ¼" thick.

Remove seeds. Arrange cantaloupe slices and prosciutto on serving plates. Makes 4 servings.

BOLOGNA CORNUCOPIAS

12 slices bologna
12 sweet gherkins

Roll bologna slices into cornucopias and fasten with toothpicks. Fill cornucopias with pickles. Makes 12.

SYRIAN SALAMI KABOBS

1 cup salami cubes (½-inch cubes)
½ cup small stuffed olives
½ cup pickled onions

Alternate salami, olives and onions on toothpicks. Makes about 12.

GARLIC RIPE OLIVES

1 can ripe olives
2 cloves garlic, peeled
¼ teaspoon salt

Combine olives, olive liquid, garlic and salt. Cover and chill several hours; drain.

SPREADS

LOX AND EGG SPREAD

½ pound smoked salmon, ground
2 hard-cooked eggs, chopped
1 tablespoon chopped chives
Salad dressing

Combine salmon, eggs and chives. Add enough salad dressing to moisten. Makes about 1½ cups.

LIVER AND MUSHROOM SPREAD

1 cup cooked chicken livers, chopped
½ cup cooked mushrooms, chopped
1 hard-cooked egg, chopped
2 tablespoons chopped parsley
Salad dressing

Combine livers, mushrooms, egg, parsley and enough salad dressing to moisten. Makes about 1½ cups.

MEXICAN CHEESE SPREAD

1 cup yellow cheese, grated
1 cup sour cream
¼ cup milk
2 tablespoons grated onion
1 tablespoon chopped parsley

Combine all ingredients and mix well. Makes about 2½ cups.

ONION AND EGG SPREAD

¼ cup chopped onion
4 hard-cooked eggs, chopped
¼ teaspoon salt
2 tablespoons chopped parsley
Mayonnaise

Combine onion, eggs, salt and parsley. Add enough mayonnaise to moisten. Makes about 1 cup.

ALMOND CHEESE SPREAD

1 3-ounce package cream cheese
¼ cup chopped toasted almonds
2 tablespoons salad dressing
¼ teaspoon salt

Combine all ingredients and mix well. Makes about 1¼ cups.

BLUE CHEESE-ONION SPREAD

1 cup crumbled blue cheese
2 tablespoons grated onion
2 tablespoons mayonnaise or sour cream

Combine all ingredients and mix well. Makes about 1¼ cups.

SARDINE-OLIVE SPREAD

1 4-ounce can sardines,
    drained and mashed
¼ teaspoon Worcestershire sauce
1 tablespoon lemon juice
2 tablespoon chili sauce
¼ cup chopped stuffed olives

Combine all ingredients and mix well. Makes about ¾ cup.

STUFFED OLIVE SPREAD

½ cup chopped stuffed olives
1 cup softened butter
⅛ teaspoon pepper
1 tablespoon grated onion
1 teaspoon vinegar
1 tablespoon chopped parsley

Combine all ingredients and mix well. Spread on hot French bread for appetizers, as desired. Makes about 1¼ cups.

PECAN APPETIZERS

⅓ cup cottage cheese
1 tablespoon mayonnaise
½ cup chopped pecans
⅛ teaspoon salt
⅛ teaspoon Tabasco
⅛ teaspoon onion salt

Combine all ingredients. Serve on crackers, as desired. Makes about ⅔ cup.

SALMON-PICKLE SPREAD

1 cup cooked, flaked salmon
2 tablespoons chopped parsley
¼ cup chopped mustard pickles
Mayonnaise

Combine salmon, parsley, pickles and enough mayonnaise to moisten. Makes about 1¼ cups.

AVOCADO-OLIVE SPREAD

1 cup mashed avocado
2 tablespoons lemon juice
½ teaspoon grated lemon rind
½ cup chopped stuffed olives

Combine all ingredients and mix well. Makes about 1½ cups.

CHEDDAR CHEESE SPREAD

1 jar Cheddar cheese spread
1 tablespoon grated onion
2 tablespoons mayonnaise
1 tablespoon chopped parsley

Combine all ingredients and mix well. Makes about ¾ cups.

TURKEY SPREAD

1 cup cooked ground turkey
¼ cup chopped celery
¼ cup chopped cucumber
French dressing

Combine turkey, celery, cucumber and enough dressing to moisten. Makes about 1½ cups.

WATER CRESS SPREAD

1 3-ounce package cream cheese
¼ cup chopped water cress
1 teaspoon grated onion
2 tablespoons mayonnaise

Combine all ingredients and mix well. Makes about ¾ cup.

DIPS AND DUNKS

AVOCADO DIP

1 medium-sized avocado
¼ cup chili sauce

1 tablespoon grated onion
1 tablespoon lemon juice

Cut avocado in half lengthwise. Remove pulp; reserve shells. Mash pulp and add chili sauce, onion and lemon juice. Fill shells with pulp mixture. Serve with crackers, as desired. Makes about 1 cup.

CHEESE AND CARROT DUNK

2 cups cottage cheese
¼ cup salad dressing
1 teaspoon Worcestershire sauce
½ cup grated carrots
2 tablespoons chopped green pepper
¼ cup grated radishes
¼ teaspoon salt

Combine all ingredients and chill. Makes about 2¾ cups.

CHIVE AND PARSLEY DUNK

1½ cups sour cream
½ cup chopped chives
¼ cup chopped parsley
½ cup chopped green pepper
2 tablespoons prepared horseradish
¼ teaspoon salt

Combine all ingredients and chill. Makes about 2¼ cups.

CLAM DIP

1 cup cottage cheese
1 7-ounce can minced clams, drained
2 tablespoons chopped chives
½ teaspoon paprika

Combine all ingredients and mix well. Serve with crackers and potato chips, as desired. Makes about 1½ cups.

CURRY CHEESE DIP

1 cup cottage cheese
½ cup grated cucumber, drained

⅓ cup salad dressing
2 tablespoons light cream
1 teaspoon curry powder
½ teaspoon salt

Combine all ingredients and chill. Makes about 1½ cups.

ROQUEFORT DIP

1 cup cottage cheese
½ cup Roquefort cheese
2 tablespoons grated onion
¼ cup sour cream

Combine all ingredients and mix well. Makes about 1¾ cups.

Beverages

COLD DRINKS

GINGER GRAPE JUICE

2 whole cloves
½ small stick cinnamon
3 tablespoons lemon juice
3 tablespoons sugar
1 quart grape juice
2 cups ginger ale

Tie spices in cheesecloth. Add lemon juice, sugar and grape juice and cook over low heat 15 minutes. Chill thoroughly. Just before serving, add ginger ale. Serve with ice. Makes 6–8 servings.

NECTAR PUNCH

½ cup sugar
¾ cup light corn syrup
1 cup water
⅛ teaspoon cinnamon
4 thin lemon slices
½ cup currant jelly
3 cups apricot nectar
⅔ cup lime juice

Boil sugar, syrup, water, cinnamon and lemon slices together 5 minutes. Remove from heat and remove lemon slices. Beat in jelly with rotary beater. Add nectar and lime juice, blending well. Chill. Serve in chilled glasses. Makes 4–6 servings.

ORANGE NOG

4 eggs, beaten
¼ cup sugar
1⅓ cups orange juice
2 cups milk
Nutmeg

Combine eggs, sugar and juice. Beat until well blended. Pour into 4 glasses. Fill glasses with milk. Sprinkle with nutmeg. Makes 4 servings.

GRAPEFRUIT-ORANGE SHAKE

2 cups orange juice
2 cups grapefruit juice
2 cups milk
¼ teaspoon salt
¼ teaspoon vanilla
¼ cup sugar
1 cup cracked ice

Combine all ingredients and shake until thoroughly blended. Serve immediately. Makes 6–8 servings.

SPICY BANANA MILK SHAKE

4 cups milk
4 bananas, mashed
2 tablespoons lemon juice
¾ teaspoon cinnamon
¼ teaspoon nutmeg
3 tablespoons sugar
1 pint vanilla ice cream

Combine ingredients; beat well. Pour into glasses and serve immediately. Makes 6–8 servings.

GOLDEN NECTAR

4 eggs, separated
3 cups grapefruit juice
1 cup orange juice
¼ cup honey
⅛ teaspoon salt

Beat egg yolks until thick. Gradually add fruit juices, beating constantly. Add honey and salt; beat well. Beat egg whites until stiff. Fold into grapefruit-juice mixture. Pour into chilled glasses. Makes 4–6 servings.

CONCORD GRAPE PUNCH

2 cups grape juice
2 cups water
⅓ cup lemon juice
½ cup orange juice
½ cup sugar

Mix ingredients. Allow to stand until sugar is dissolved. Serve over ice. Makes 6–8 servings.

RASPBERRY REFRESHER

2 cups sugar
3 cups boiling water
1½ cups red raspberries
2 cups orange juice

Dissolve sugar in water. Mash berries. Combine all ingredients and chill 2 hours. Strain and pour over ice. Makes 6–8 servings.

CHERRY BING

2 cups juice from canned Bing cherries
1½ cups water
½ cup orange juice

Mix ingredients. Pour over cracked ice in glasses. Makes 6 servings.

FRESNO APRICOT COOLER

2 cups apricot nectar
¾ cup orange juice
3 tablespoons lemon juice
2 tablespoons granulated sugar
2 cups ginger ale

Stir nectar, fruit juices and sugar together until sugar is dissolved. Chill. Just before serving, add ginger ale. Makes 6 servings.

ORANGE MILK SHAKE

1½ cups chilled orange juice
1 tablespoon lemon juice
¼ cup sugar
2 cups cold milk

Mix orange juice, lemon juice and sugar. Stir fruit-juice mixture slowly into milk. Shake and serve at once. Makes 4 servings.

HOT DRINKS

VERMONT MAPLE NOG

⅓ cup maple syrup
⅛ teaspoon salt
3 egg yolks, well beaten
2 cups milk
½ cup heavy cream, whipped
⅛ teaspoon ginger

Combine syrup, salt, egg yolks and milk. Beat until blended with rotary beater. Pour into glasses. Combine cream and ginger. Top each serving with cream. Makes 4 servings.

SAMARKAND HOT TEA PUNCH

½ cup sugar
½ cup water

1 2-inch stick cinnamon
2 teaspoons grated lemon rind
¼ cup orange juice
2 tablespoons lime juice
¼ cup pineapple juice
3 cups boiling water
3 tablespoons tea leaves

Combine sugar, water, cinnamon and lemon rind. Simmer 5 minutes. Remove cinnamon. Add fruit juices. Meanwhile pour boiling water over tea leaves; let stand 3 minutes. Strain tea into hot fruit-juice mixture. Serve hot. Makes 6–8 servings.

CAFÉ BRULOT

1-inch stick cinnamon
8 whole cloves
3 lumps sugar
3 jiggers brandy
3 cups strong coffee

Place cinnamon, cloves and sugar in chafing dish. Place brandy in large ladle; ignite brandy and pour over sugar mixture. Ladle until sugar is dissolved. Gradually add coffee, ladling until flames fade. Serve immediately. Makes 6–8 servings.

FIRESIDE CIDER CUP

1 quart cider
⅓ cup sugar
2 3-inch cinnamon sticks
12 whole cloves

Combine all ingredients. Heat to boiling point. Chill several hours. Remove spices. Heat and serve. Makes 6–8 servings.

heavy cream and fold in. Beat egg whites and fold in. Makes about 30 servings.

DRINKS

FOR A CROWD

GALA APPLE PUNCH

1½ quarts apple juice
2 quarts ginger ale
Lemon slices
Green and red maraschino cherries

Chill apple juice and ginger ale. Combine. Pour into punch bowl over ice cubes. Garnish with lemon slices and cherries. Makes 24 servings.

BOG CRANBERRY PUNCH

2½ cups fresh cranberries
2 cups water
1 cup sugar
2 cups apple juice, chilled
1 cup cranberry juice
½ cup lemon juice, chilled
1 cup canned pineapple cubes
1 quart ginger ale

Combine cranberries, water and sugar. Cook over low heat until tender. Strain and chill. Add cranberry mixture to remaining ingredients. Chill. Makes 25 servings.

EGG NOG

1 dozen eggs
2⅓ cups super fine sugar
2 cups brandy
1 cup Jamaica rum
1 cup peach brandy
1 quart milk
1 quart heavy cream

Separate eggs. Beat sugar into egg yolks. Slowly stir in liquors. Add milk. Beat

FESTIVAL PUNCH

2 quarts ginger ale
1 quart hulled strawberries
1 cup sliced bananas
2 cups pineapple juice
1 cup orange juice

Combine all ingredients. Serve over ice. Makes 18–20 servings.

FISHHOUSE PUNCH

1¾ cups sugar
2 quarts water
1 quart lemon juice
2 quarts rum
1 quart brandy
½ cup peach brandy

Combine sugar and 2 cups water. Stir until sugar is dissolved. Add remaining ingredients and mix well. Pour punch over ice. Makes about 42 servings.

PIE PLANT PUNCH

4½ cups diced rhubarb
1 quart water
¾ cup sugar
¼ cup orange juice
3 cups pineapple juice
12 fresh orange slices

Combine rhubarb and water. Simmer 20 minutes; strain. Add sugar and stir until sugar is dissolved. Add orange juice and pineapple juice. Chill thoroughly. Garnish with orange slices to serve. Makes 12 servings.

PINEAPPLE PUNCH

2 cups sugar
1 cup water
1 cup strong tea
2 cups pineapple syrup

¾ cup lemon juice
2 cups orange juice
2 cups pineapple juice
Ice water
½ cup pineapple chunks
½ cup maraschino cherries
1 quart ginger ale

Boil sugar and water 5 minutes; add tea, pineapple syrup and fruit juices. Let stand 30 minutes and add enough ice water to make 1½ gallons. Add pineapple, cherries and ginger ale. Serve in punch bowl. Makes 44 servings.

Soups

HOT SOUPS

ARIZONA BEAN SOUP

1 cup garbanzas (pinto beans)
1 quart cold water
2 green onions, chopped
1 clove garlic, chopped
2 teaspoons chili powder
1 teaspoon oregano
1 teaspoon salt
Dash cayenne pepper
1½ cups beef broth or bouillon

Soak garbanzas in water overnight. Drain and add cold water. Simmer 4–6 hours, adding water as needed, until garbanzas are tender. Add onions, garlic, chili powder, oregano, salt and cayenne pepper; cook until onions are tender. Rub through colander. Add broth or bouillon. Heat to serving temperature. Serves 6.

MANHATTAN CLAM CHOWDER

¼ pound salt pork, diced
2 medium-sized onions, chopped
2 carrots, diced
1 green pepper, chopped
2 large potatoes, diced
½ cup chopped celery
½ cup chopped parsley
1 10-ounce can minced clams
2½ cups tomatoes
2 cups water
2 teaspoons salt
½ teaspoon black pepper
½ teaspoon paprika

Fry salt pork in large kettle until crisp. Remove pork from kettle. Add onions, carrots, green pepper, potatoes, celery and parsley to pork drippings and cook until onions are tender. Add clams, saving the liquor. Add tomatoes, water and seasonings. Simmer 1 hour. Add clam liquor and heat to serving temperature. Serves 6.

STOCKYARD CHOWDER

¼ pound salt pork
½ pound veal, ground
½ pound beef, ground
2 carrots, chopped
½ cup diced celery
1 medium-sized onion, chopped
1½ cups tomato paste
1 teaspoon salt
⅛ teaspoon pepper
¼ cup rice
1½ quarts boiling water
2 cups cubed potatoes

Cook salt pork until browned. Remove pork. Brown veal and beef in pork fat. Add carrots, celery, onion, tomato paste, salt, pepper, rice, salt pork and water. Heat to boiling point. Simmer, covered, 1 hour. Add potatoes and cook, covered, 15–20 minutes or until potatoes are tender. Serves 6–8.

HARVEST GOLD SQUASH SOUP

1 cup light cream
4 cups milk
1 tablespoon chopped chives
1 bay leaf
2 cups cooked sieved squash
1 cup diced cooked celery
3 tablespoons butter or margarine
3 tablespoons all-purpose flour
1 teaspoon salt

Combine cream, milk, chives and bay leaf; heat to boiling point. Add squash and celery and mix well. Melt butter or margarine and blend in flour and salt. Gradually add milk mixture and cook over low heat, stirring constantly, until thickened. Remove bay leaf. Serves 6.

QUICK TOMATO BOUILLON

2½ cups tomato juice
1 tablespoon orange juice
1 teaspoon grated orange rind
½ teaspoon salt
⅛ teaspoon pepper
1 teaspoon grated onion
1 teaspoon chopped chives
¼ teaspoon Worcestershire sauce

Combine all ingredients and heat to serving temperature. Serves 4–6.

CHICKEN HAM CHOWDER

3 cups cooked, diced chicken
2 cups cooked, diced ham
1 large onion, chopped
3 tablespoons butter, melted
⅛ teaspoon thyme
2 tablespoons chopped parsley
1 quart water
2 quarts chicken stock
1 bay leaf, crushed
1 red pepper, chopped
2 teaspoons salt
2 cups cooked shrimp
1 tablespoon chili powder
1 cup cooked rice

Cook chicken, ham and onion in butter until onion is tender. Add thyme, parsley, water, chicken stock, bay leaf, red pepper and salt. Simmer, covered, for 1 hour. Add shrimp, chili powder and rice. Heat to serving temperature. Serves 8–10.

MONTANA BARLEY BROTH

½ cup barley
1 quart boiling water
2 quarts chicken broth
½ cup finely diced turnip
½ cup peas
½ cup diced celery
½ cup diced onions
½ cup diced carrots
2 teaspoons salt

Combine barley and water. Cover and cook over low heat until barley is tender.

Drain. Add remaining ingredients. Cover and cook over low heat until vegetables are tender. Serves 8.

JERSEY CREAM OF TOMATO SOUP

2 tablespoons butter
2 tablespoons all-purpose flour
2 cups milk
1 teaspoon celery seed
2 tablespoons chopped onion
2 cups tomato juice
1 teaspoon salt
Sour cream

Melt butter and blend in flour. Gradually add milk, and cook, stirring constantly, until thickened. Combine celery seed, onion and tomato juice. Heat to boiling point and strain. Gradually add tomato mixture to white sauce, stirring constantly. Add salt. Heat to serving temperature, stirring constantly. Pour into serving dishes. Top with sour cream. Serves 6–8.

TURTLE SOUP

1 medium-sized turtle
1 tablespoon butter
1 onion, chopped
2 cloves garlic
2 tablespoons all-purpose flour
1 No. 2 can tomatoes, drained
1 bay leaf
2 quarts boiling water
¼ teaspoon salt
¼ teaspoon black pepper
⅛ teaspoon cayenne pepper
3 sprigs parsley
1 tablespoon chopped dill
2 slices lemon
2 hard-cooked eggs

Clean turtle and cut in small pieces. Melt butter; add onion and garlic; brown. Add flour, stirring constantly. Add turtle meat, tomatoes and bay leaf. Stir constantly 10 minutes. Add boiling water, salt, black pepper and cayenne pepper. Cook over low heat about 2½ hours or until turtle meat is very tender. Add parsley, dill and lemon; continue cooking 10 minutes. Chop hard-cooked eggs in soup bowls, pour soup over eggs. Serves 8.

OLD NORTH OYSTER CHOWDER

1 quart oysters
2 cups diced cooked potatoes
1 cup diced cooked carrots
1 tablespoon grated onion
1 tablespoon butter or margarine
1 teaspoon celery salt
⅛ teaspoon pepper
3 cups milk
1 cup light cream
Pilot crackers

Cook oysters in oyster liquor until edges curl. Add potatoes, carrots, onion, butter or margarine, celery salt, pepper, milk and light cream. Heat to serving temperature, stirring occasionally. Pour into serving bowls. Top with crackers. Serves 6.

OYSTER PEPPER CHOWDER

1 pint oysters and liquor
1 cup tomato sauce
1 cup water
2 tablespoons catsup
2 tablespoons lime juice
2 tablespoons butter
½ green pepper, minced
Salt
Cayenne pepper

Heat oysters slowly in liquor. Heat tomato sauce, water, catsup, lime juice, butter and green pepper. Add oysters and liquor. Season with salt and cayenne pepper. Simmer only until oysters are plump. Serves 4.

NEW ENGLAND CLAM CHOWDER

1 quart clams, shelled or 3 cans minced
    clams (10 to 10½ ounces each)
Water
¼ pound salt pork or bacon, diced
1 medium onion, chopped
3 cups diced potatoes
½ teaspoon salt
⅛ teaspoon pepper
6 coarsely crushed soda crackers
3 cups milk
Paprika

Drain clams, measure liquid and add water to make two cups; chop clams. In large pan cook salt pork or bacon until lightly browned; add onion and cook until tender. Add clams, clam liquid, potatoes, salt and pepper; cover and cook about 15 minutes or until potatoes are tender. Combine crackers and milk, soak 5 minutes; add to potato mixture. Heat thoroughly. Pour into serving bowls; sprinkle with paprika. Serves about 6.

BAR HARBOR LOBSTER CHOWDER

2 small lobsters, cooked
1 cup cold water
3 cups milk
1 cup light cream
1 carrot, sliced thin
1 cup diced cooked potatoes
⅓ cup butter
2 crisp salted crackers, crumbled fine
1 teaspoon salt
¼ teaspoon black pepper
¼ teaspoon paprika
1 tablespoon minced chives

Remove lobster meat from shell and cut in cubes; cover shell with cold water, bring to boil, reduce heat and simmer 10 minutes; strain and reserve stock. Scald milk and cream with carrot and potatoes; strain. Cream butter and mix well

with cracker crumbs; add scalded milk and cream gradually, stirring until smooth. Add lobster and stock, salt, pepper, paprika and chives; heat thoroughly. Serves 4.

ROMANO EEL SOUP

2 tablespoons butter or oil
4 small leeks, sliced
2 small onions, sliced
5 cups boiling water
2 pounds small eels, skinned and cut into
    1½ inch pieces
2 cups chopped spinach
⅔ cup soft bread crumbs
3 egg yolks, beaten
⅔ cup light cream
1 teaspoon salt
¼ teaspoon pepper

Heat butter or oil; add leeks and onions and cook 3 minutes. Add water and eels. Boil 2 minutes. Reduce heat and cook 20 minutes. Remove eels and take out bones. Return eels to stock. Add spinach and cook 10 minutes over low heat. Stir in bread crumbs and remove from heat. Mix egg yolks and cream. Add salt and pepper. Blend well and stir gradually into eel mixture. Serve hot. Serves 4–6.

MARBLEHEAD FISH CHOWDER

1 4-pound haddock
2 cups water
4 slices salt pork, diced
1 medium-sized onion, sliced
4 cups diced potatoes
1 cup diced carrots
2 cups boiling water
2 teaspoons salt
⅛ teaspoon pepper
3 tablespoons butter
3 cups milk
1 cup light cream

Skin fish. Cut head and tail from fish. Remove fish from backbone and cut into 2" pieces. Break backbone in pieces. Place backbone, head and tail in 2 cups water. Heat to boiling point and cook 5 minutes. Brown salt pork lightly. Add onion and cook until onion is tender. Remove pork and onion. Add potatoes and carrots to pork drippings. Add boiling water and cook, covered, 5 minutes. Drain liquid from fish head and tail and add to potato mixture. Cook, covered, 15 minutes. Add pork, onion, salt, pepper, butter, milk and cream. Heat to serving temperature. Pour into serving bowls and top with crackers, as desired. Serves 8.

GASPÉ LEEK SOUP

2 bunches leeks
3 tablespoons butter or margarine
3 tablespoons all-purpose flour
2 quarts water
¼ teaspoon black pepper
¼ teaspoon salt

Wash and cut leeks in 1" pieces. Melt butter or margarine; add leeks and cook until tender and lightly browned. Stir in flour. Gradually add water, pepper and salt; simmer 1 hour. Serves 4.

REAL OLD-FASHIONED LENTIL SOUP

1 pound lentils
4 cups cold water
1 large onion, diced
1 large tomato, diced
2 carrots, diced
2 potatoes, diced
½ bay leaf
1 tablespoon chili sauce
1 tablespoon salt
Ham shank

Soak lentils several hours. Drain. Combine lentils, cold water and remaining ingredients. Simmer, covered, 2 hours. Remove ham shank. Dice ham and return to lentil mixture. Heat to serving temperature, stirring occasionally. Serves 6–8.

CAROLINA LIMA CHOWDER

2 slices bacon, diced
3 small onions, minced
4 potatoes, pared and diced
1 white turnip, diced
2 carrots, diced
2 cups cooked lima beans
1 teaspoon salt
¼ teaspoon pepper
Boiling water
2 cups medium white sauce

Cook bacon with onions until onions are tender. Add potatoes, turnip, carrots, lima beans, salt and pepper. Add enough boiling water to cover. Cover and cook until vegetables are tender. Add white sauce. Heat to serving temperature, stirring occasionally. Serves 6.

PROVENÇAL PEA SOUP

1 pound dried yellow peas
2 large onions chopped
½ pound salt pork
1 cup chopped frankfurters
¼ teaspoon salt
¼ teaspoon pepper

Soak peas several hours, drain. Cover peas, onions and salt pork with water. Simmer, covered, until peas are tender. Add frankfurters and heat to serving temperature. Season with salt and pepper. Garnish with parsley, if desired. Serves 8.

ALASKA SALMON BISQUE

¼ cup butter or margarine
½ cup chopped celery
¼ cup all-purpose flour
1 teaspoon salt
¼ teaspoon pepper
1 quart milk, scalded
1 cup diced cooked salmon
½ teaspoon onion salt
1 cup cooked corn

Melt butter or margarine; add celery and cook until tender. Blend in flour, salt and pepper. Gradually add milk and cook over low heat, stirring constantly, until thickened. Add remaining ingredients and heat to serving temperature, stirring occasionally. Serves 4–6.

FISHERMEN'S SCALLOP SOUP

1 pint scallops, chopped
1 tablespoon lime juice
1 cup cold water
4 cups milk
1 tablespoon butter
1 teaspoon salt
⅛ teaspoon pepper
2 tablespoons sherry

Sprinkle scallops with lime juice. Let stand 15 minutes. Add water and heat to boiling point. Add milk, butter and seasonings. Heat to serving temperature. Serves 4.

SEAFOOD CHOWDER

1 pound lean fish, cubed
4 large potatoes, sliced
2 large onions, sliced
6 cups hot water
⅓ cup rice
2 green peppers, diced
¼ cup diced bacon or salt pork
3 tablespoons minced parsley
1 cup diced carrots
1 cup diced tomato
Salt and pepper

Combine fish, potatoes, onions, water, rice, green peppers, bacon or salt pork, parsley, carrots and tomato. Simmer, covered, about 30 minutes or until vegetables are tender. Season to taste with salt and pepper. Heat to serving temperature. Serves 6–8.

CHARLESTON SHRIMP CHOWDER

¼ cup chopped onion
¼ cup melted bacon drippings
2 tablespoons butter
2 tablespoons all-purpose flour
1 quart milk
1 teaspoon salt
¼ teaspoon paprika
2 cups cooked, chopped shrimp
1 cup light cream

Cook onion in bacon drippings until tender. Melt butter and blend in flour. Gradually add milk and cook, stirring constantly, until thickened. Add onion, salt, paprika, shrimp and cream. Heat to serving temperature over low heat, stirring occasionally. Serves 4.

VEGETABLE SOUP PAYSAN

½ pound wax beans
1 small head cabbage
6 carrots
1 turnip
1 cup fresh lima beans
2 teaspoons salt
¼ teaspoon pepper
2 quarts water
6 link sausages
5 medium-sized potatoes, peeled and sliced

Cut beans into 1" pieces. Shred cabbage. Slice carrots. Cut turnip in quarters. Combine vegetables, salt, pepper and water. Heat to boiling and simmer, covered, 1½ hours. Add sausages and potatoes. Cook, covered, 30 minutes. Serves 6.

BAKED-BEAN SOUP PLYMOUTH

3 cups baked beans
4 cups water
2 tablespoons chopped onion
¼ cup chopped celery
½ cup diced salt pork
2 tablespoons all-purpose flour
2 cups chopped tomatoes
1 teaspoon salt
⅛ teaspoon pepper

Combine beans, water, onion and celery; cook over low heat 30 minutes. Force through a sieve. Brown salt pork and blend in flour. Add tomatoes, salt and pepper. Cook, stirring constantly, until slightly thickened. Combine bean mixture and tomato mixture. Cook over low heat 1 hour, stirring occasionally. Serves 8–10.

BLACK BEAN SOUP

2 cups black beans
2 quarts water
½ pound salt pork
2 cups beef stock
4 frankfurters, thinly sliced
⅛ teaspoon freshly ground pepper
1 tablespoon lemon juice
1 tablespoon sherry wine

Soak beans several hours; drain. Add water and salt pork. Cook, covered, until beans are tender. Force through a sieve. Add beef stock, frankfurters, pepper, lemon juice and wine. Heat to serving temperature, stirring occasionally. Pour soup into serving dishes. Serves 8–10.

ACROSS THE BORDER SOUP

2 tablespoons butter
1 cup chicken livers
⅓ cup chopped onions
1 tablespoon chopped chives
1 bay leaf
1 cup light cream
3 cups chicken broth
⅛ teaspoon salt
⅛ teaspoon black pepper

Melt butter; add chicken livers and onions. Cook over low heat until onions are tender. Force through a sieve. Add remaining ingredients and heat to serving temperature, stirring occasionally. Serves 6–8.

MATZOTH BALL SOUP

2 tablespoons chicken fat
2 eggs, well beaten
½ teaspoon salt
1 cup matzoth meal
1 quart boiling chicken broth

Soften fat. Add eggs, salt and enough matzoth meal to make a soft dough. Chill several hours. Shape into small balls. Drop into broth. Cook, covered, about 15 minutes. Serves 4.

MONTEREY MUSSEL SOUP

6 medium-sized onions, chopped
¼ cup butter, melted
3 cups cold water
1 tablespoon butter, melted
¼ cup all-purpose flour
2 cups scalded milk
1 quart mussel meat
1 teaspoon salt
Dash cayenne pepper

Cook onions in the ¼ cup butter until tender. Add water. Cover and cook over low heat 30 minutes. Press through a sieve. Melt the 1 tablespoon butter, stir in flour. Gradually add milk, stirring constantly. Add mussel meat and seasonings. Cook over low heat 5 minutes, stirring constantly. Add sieved onion stock. Heat to serving temperature. Serves 6–8.

CREAM OF POTATO SOUP

2 medium-sized onions, minced
2 tablespoons melted butter or margarine
6 cups cooked, sieved potatoes
1 teaspoon salt
¼ teaspoon pepper
3 cups potato water
1 cup heavy cream
Paprika

Cook onions in butter or margarine until tender. Add potatoes, salt, pepper, potato water and cream. Heat to serving temperature, stirring frequently. Pour into bowls. Sprinkle with paprika. Serves 6.

DAIRYLAND POTATO SOUP

3 medium-sized potatoes
2 cups boiling salted water
Milk
3 tablespoons butter
½ small onion, chopped
2 tablespoons all-purpose flour
1 teaspoon salt
⅛ teaspoon paprika
⅛ teaspoon cayenne pepper
2 cups grated American cheese
1 tablespoon chopped chives

Cook potatoes, covered, in boiling salted water until tender. Rub through a sieve. Measure the liquid and add enough milk to make 4 cups. Melt butter, add onion and cook until tender. Stir in flour and seasonings. Add potato milk. Cook 3 minutes and strain, if desired. Add cheese and beat until smooth. Add chives and serve hot. Serves 6.

RICE DUMPLING SOUP

⅔ cup cooked rice, mashed
2½ tablespoons all-purpose flour
1 teaspoon onion juice
1 teaspoon chopped parsley
1 egg
¼ teaspoon salt
¼ teaspoon Worcestershire sauce
⅛ teaspoon pepper
1 can beef consommé

Combine rice, flour, onion juice, parsley, egg, salt, Worcestershire sauce and pepper; mix well. Prepare consommé according to label directions. Heat to boiling point. Drop rice mixture by teaspoonfuls into consommé. Cover and cook 5 minutes. Serves 4.

QUEEN MARIE VEAL SOUP

1 medium-sized breast of veal
Water
¼ teaspoon paprika
2 tablespoons melted butter
½ cup chopped onions
1 cup diced carrots
2 cups diced potatoes
½ cup diced celery
½ cup dry white wine
2 teaspoons salt
1 cup sour cream

Cover breast of veal with water. Cover and cook over low heat until tender, about 1¼ hours. Combine paprika, butter, onions, carrots, potatoes, celery, wine and salt. Add to veal. Cover and cook over low heat about 20 minutes or until vegetables are tender. Serve topped with sour cream. Serves 6–8.

DUTCH PEA SOUP

1 pound dried peas
½ cup chopped onions
1 cup chopped celery
3 pounds pork shoulder
2 teaspoons salt
¼ teaspoon pepper
Water

Soak peas several hours; drain. Combine peas, onions, celery, pork, salt and pepper. Add enough water to cover. Cover and cook over low heat 3–4 hours, or until pork is tender. Serves 10–12.

KALAMAZOO CELERY CHOWDER

5 cups cooked diced celery
2 tablespoons chopped chives
2 tablespoons butter or margarine
½ teaspoon onion salt
1 teaspoon salt
1 cup diced cooked potatoes
3 cups milk
2 egg yolks, well beaten

Put celery through sieve. Combine celery, chives, butter or margarine, onion salt, salt, potatoes and milk. Heat to boiling point over low heat. Add a little of milk mixture to egg yolks and mix well. Cook over low heat, stirring constantly, 3 minutes. Serves 6.

CHICKEN ALMOND SOUP

1 cup chopped celery
½ cup shredded carrots
4 cups chicken bouillon
1 egg, beaten
1 cup light cream
⅛ teaspoon salt
½ cup ground almonds
Paprika

Cook celery and carrots, covered, in bouillon until tender. Combine egg and cream; mix well. Gradually add to celery mixture. Cook, over low heat, stirring constantly until thickened. Add salt and almonds. Heat to serving temperature. Pour into serving bowls and sprinkle with paprika. Serves 6.

CREAM OF CHICKEN SOUP

3 tablespoons rice
⅔ cup diced celery
3 cups hot chicken stock
2 tablespoons lemon juice
2 cups hot milk

Salt and pepper
8 slices lemon
Chopped chives

Boil rice and celery until tender, drain and rub through sieve. Combine with stock, lemon juice and milk; season to taste. Serve hot with lemon slices covered with chives. Serves 4.

VERMONT CORN CHOWDER

⅓ cup diced salt pork
1 small onion, thinly sliced
3 cups boiling water
3½ cups diced potatoes
2½ cups milk
2¼ cups corn, cooked or canned
1 teaspoon salt
⅛ teaspoon pepper
2 tablespoons chopped parsley

Brown salt pork. Remove pork from pan. Add onion to pork drippings and cook until tender. Add water and potatoes. Cook, covered, 15 minutes. Add pork, milk, corn, salt and pepper. Heat to serving temperature. Top with parsley. Serve with split pilot crackers, as desired. Serves 6.

CRAB SOUP CORTEZ

2 tablespoons butter
2 tablespoons all-purpose flour
3 cups milk
1 tablespoon Worcestershire sauce
1 teaspoon salt
⅛ teaspoon pepper
2 cups cooked, chopped crab meat
¼ cup sherry
Thin lemon slices

Melt butter and blend in flour. Gradually add milk and cook, stirring constantly, until thickened. Add Worcestershire sauce, salt, pepper, crab meat and sherry. Heat to serving temperature, stirring occasionally. Pour into serving bowls and garnish with lemon slices. Serves 4.

COUNTRY CABBAGE SOUP

1 3-pound soupbone
2 quarts cold water
2 teaspoons salt
¼ teaspoon pepper
1 bay leaf
1 medium-sized head cabbage, quartered
2 medium-sized onions, sliced
1 cup chopped celery
1 tablespoon butter

Cover bone with water. Add salt, pepper and bay leaf. Heat to boiling point. Cover and cook 1½ hours. Add remaining ingredients. Cover and simmer 1 hour. Remove meat from bone and return to cabbage mixture. Serves 8.

FRENCH CANADIAN CHOWDER

¾ cup chopped onions
¼ cup melted butter
3 cups flaked halibut
1½ cups cooked celery
1½ cups cooked carrots
2½ cups condensed tomato soup
2½ cups milk
1 teaspoon salt
½ teaspoon pepper

Brown onions slightly in butter. Combine halibut, vegetables, soup, milk and seasonings. Heat slowly to serving temperature. Serves 8.

NORWEGIAN HOLIDAY SOUP

2 tablespoons butter or margarine
2 tablespoons all-purpose flour
2 quarts bouillon
2 carrots, cubed
1 cup diced cooked potatoes
Dash cayenne pepper
2½ tablespoons sherry
1 tablespoon chopped parsley
½ teaspoon salt
12 small cooked meat balls

Melt butter. Stir in flour. Add bouillon slowly. Stir until slightly thickened. Add carrots and simmer until carrots are tender. Add potatoes, cayenne pepper, sherry, parsley, salt and meat balls. Heat to serving temperature. Serves 6.

VICKSBURG OKRA SOUP

1 ham bone
6 cups okra, cut in small pieces
2½ cups tomatoes
1 cup chopped green pepper
Salt to taste

Boil ham bone for 1 hour in enough water to cover. Add okra, tomatoes and green pepper. Simmer, covered, 3 hours. Season with salt. Serves 4.

CARIBBEAN ONION SOUP

1 cup shelled almonds
6 cups beef bouillon
1 cup sliced onions
1 cup croutons
½ cup grated Parmesan cheese
1 teaspoon lemon juice

Grind almonds; add bouillon and onions. Cook, covered, over low heat, 1 hour. Arrange croutons in serving bowls. Add soup. Top with cheese and lemon juice. Serves 4.

PARMESAN ONION SOUP

¼ cup butter
2 cups thinly sliced onions
2 quarts chicken stock or bouillon
1 teaspoon salt
⅛ teaspoon white pepper
Grated Parmesan cheese
Chopped parsley

Melt butter; add onions and cook until tender. Add stock or bouillon, salt and pepper. Cover and cook over low heat 1 hour. Pour into serving bowls. Top with cheese and parsley. Serves 8.

GEORGIA PEANUT BUTTER SOUP

½ cup butter
2 tablespoons minced onion
1 tablespoon all-purpose flour
1 cup peanut butter
1 quart chicken consomme
¼ teaspoon paprika
¼ teaspoon pepper
1 teaspoon salt
1 cup light cream
1 4-ounce can mushrooms, drained

Melt butter. Add onion and cook until tender. Blend in flour and peanut butter. Gradually add consomme and cook over low heat, stirring constantly, until thickened. Add remaining ingredients. Heat to serving temperature, stirring occasionally. Serves 8–10.

PHILADELPHIA PEPPERPOT

2 pounds fresh tripe
1 veal knuckle with meat
2 teaspoons salt
2 bay leaves
1 sweet red pepper, chopped
1 green pepper, chopped
4 medium-sized potatoes, diced
⅛ teaspoon cayenne pepper
½ cup chopped parsley

Clean and wash tripe. Simmer 4–5 hours in water to cover. Cook veal knuckle in water to cover until meat falls off bone. Cut tripe and veal into small pieces. Strain veal stock and add water to make 3 quarts. Add bay leaves, red pepper and green pepper. Simmer ½ hour. Add potatoes, cayenne pepper, parsley, veal and tripe. Simmer, covered, until potatoes are tender. Dumplings may be added, if desired. Serves 8.

CLASSIC OYSTER BISQUE

1 quart oysters
1 green pepper
¾ cup chopped celery
1 tablespoon butter
1 tablespoon all-purpose flour
1 quart milk
1 teaspoon Worcestershire sauce
1 teaspoon salt
⅛ teaspoon pepper
2 tablespoons chopped pimiento

Grind oysters, green pepper and celery. Melt butter and blend in flour. Gradually add milk, and cook, stirring constantly, until thickened. Add Worcestershire sauce, salt, pepper, oysters, green pepper, celery and pimiento. Heat to serving temperature. Serves 4–6.

OYSTER STEW CHABLIS

1 pint oysters
¼ cup butter, melted
3 cups chicken bouillon
1 cup Chablis wine
½ teaspoon salt
Parsley

Cook oysters in butter until oyster edges curl. Add chicken bouillon, wine and salt. Heat to serving temperature. Pour into serving bowls and garnish with parsley. Serves 6.

NUT CREAM SAN JUAN

½ pound almonds or cashews, ground
3 tablespoons all-purpose flour
3 tablespoons butter
2 cups milk
1 cup light cream
1 teaspoon salt

Combine all ingredients and cook over low heat, stirring constantly, until thickened. Serves 4.

OYSTER STEW U.S.A.

¼ cup butter
1 quart oysters
1 teaspoon salt
⅛ teaspoon pepper
¼ teaspoon celery salt
Dash cayenne pepper
4 cups light cream

Melt butter, add oysters and cook over low heat until edges curl. Add seasonings and cream. Heat to serving temperature. Serve at once. Serves 8.

SALT PORK PARSNIP CHOWDER

⅓ cup diced salt pork
4 medium-sized onions, sliced
2 cups pared, sliced parsnips
1 can tomato paste
2 cups boiling water
4 cups hot milk
3 tablespoons butter
Salt and pepper
½ cup cracker crumbs

Fry salt pork. Add onions and cook until brown. Add parsnips and tomato paste. Add water and cook, covered, until the vegetables are tender. Add milk, butter and seasonings. Add cracker crumbs. Heat to serving temperature. Serves 8.

TOMATO WHIP

2 tablespoons butter
1 teaspoon sugar
1 small onion, sliced
½ cup chopped celery
1 quart quartered tomatoes
1 tablespoon lemon juice
1 teaspoon pickling spices
1 teaspoon salt
¾ cup heavy cream, whipped
Croutons

Melt butter. Add sugar, onion and celery. Cook until tender. Add tomatoes, lemon juice and seasonings. Simmer 5 minutes. Rub through sieve. Heat to serving temperature. Add cream. Beat until frothy. Serve with croutons. Serves 6.

SOYBEAN SOUP

2 cups soybeans
1 cup diced celery
2 quarts cold water
2 small onions, thinly sliced
2 tablespoons melted butter
2 tablespoons all-purpose flour
1 teaspoon salt
⅛ teaspoon pepper
1 cup diced cooked carrots
2 hard-cooked eggs, sliced
1 lemon, cut into thin slices

Soak beans several hours. Drain. Add celery and cold water. Cook, covered, over low heat about 4 hours or until tender. Rub through sieve. Brown onion slightly in butter. Add flour, seasonings, bean stock and carrots. Heat to serving temperature, stirring occasionally; pour over eggs and lemon slices. Serves 6–8.

CRAB SOUP PIMLICO

1 pound crab meat, flaked
3 cups water
1 No. 2½ can tomatoes
2 cups okra, diced
2 stalks celery, diced
2 carrots, diced
2 onions, diced
2 teaspoons salt
½ teaspoon pepper
3 drops Tabasco
1 teaspoon Worcestershire sauce
1 bay leaf
½ teaspoon gumbo filé
2 tablespoons butter

Combine all ingredients and simmer 2 hours. Serves 8–10.

MICHIGAN NAVY BEAN SOUP

3 pounds navy beans
4 quarts water
1½ pounds ham hocks
½ cup chopped onions
2 tablespoons butter or margarine
2 teaspoons salt
¼ teaspoon pepper

Wash beans thoroughly. Add water, ham hocks and onions. Cover and cook over low heat about 3 hours. Add remaining ingredients and mix well. Serves 12.

CELESTIAL WATER CRESS SOUP

2 cups water
1 tablespoon salt
1 teaspoon diced leek
¼ cup bamboo shoots
¼ cup butter
2 cups chicken stock or bouillon
1 cup chopped water cress
1 egg, beaten

Simmer water, salt, leek, bamboo shoots and butter 20 minutes. Add stock or bouillon and simmer 20 minutes. Add water cress. Heat to boiling. Add egg and heat, stirring constantly, to serving temperature. Serves 6.

SHOKAN OXTAIL SOUP

1 oxtail
2 tablespoons butter
¼ cup chopped onion
6 cups beef broth or bouillon
½ cup carrot slices
½ cup chopped celery
1 bay leaf
1 cup chopped tomatoes
1 can tomato soup
1 tablespoon Worcestershire sauce
2 teaspoons salt
½ teaspoon pepper

Split oxtail into small joints. Melt butter and add oxtail and onion. Cook until onion is tender. Add remaining ingredients. Cook, covered, over low heat for 3–4 hours, or until meat is tender. Stir occasionally. Serves 6–8.

COLD SOUPS

SPICY SUMMER FRUIT SOUP

3 tablespoons quick-cooking tapioca
1½ cups boiling water
2 cups pineapple juice
2 cups orange juice
½ cup sugar
2 teaspoons lemon rind, grated
1 2"-stick cinnamon
1 cup strawberries, sliced
¼ cup white wine

Stir tapioca into water. Cook, until tapioca is clear, stirring constantly. Add pineapple and orange juices. Bring to boil. Add sugar, lemon rind and cinnamon. Cook, over low heat, 10 minutes. Remove from heat. Add strawberries and wine. Chill. Serves 6.

CHILLED SHRIMP BISQUE

1 quart buttermilk
1 teaspoon prepared mustard
⅛ teaspoon pepper
1 teaspoon salt
½ teaspoon paprika
1 tablespoon chopped chives
¼ cup grated cucumber
½ pound shrimp, cooked and chopped

Combine all ingredients. Chill thoroughly. Serves 6–8.

FARMERS' DILL SOUP

12 small potatoes
3 cups boiling water
2 tablespoons all-purpose flour
¼ cup cold water
1 cup sour cream
1 large bunch dill
1 bay leaf
2 egg yolks, slightly beaten
⅛ teaspoon salt

Cut potatoes into quarters. Cover with boiling water. Cook, covered, 20 minutes or until tender. Drain potatoes, saving them for another meal. Measure 2 cups of the potato water. Blend flour with cold water to make a smooth paste and add, with sour cream, to potato water. Chop dill. Add dill and bay leaf to cream mixture and cook, stirring constantly, until thickened. Stir a small amount of hot soup into egg yolks. Add to soup mixture, mixing well. Add salt. Chill. Serves 4.

NORWEGIAN FRUIT SOUP

1½ quarts blueberries
3 quarts water
¼ cup cornstarch
Cold water
½ cup sugar
1 teaspoon grated orange rind

Combine berries and water. Cover and cook over low heat until berries are soft. Put through sieve. Heat berries and juice to simmering point. Moisten cornstarch with water. Add to berry mixture and cook, stirring constantly, until thickened. Add orange rind. Chill thoroughly. Serves 6–8.

SCANDINAVIAN FRUIT SOUP

¾ pound dried peaches
1 3-inch stick cinnamon
1 cup sugar
3 quarts water
3 tablespoons tapioca

Cook peaches according to package directions. To cooked, drained peaches, add remaining ingredients and cook until tapioca is clear. Serve chilled. Serves 6–8.

VICHYSSOISE

4 leeks
⅓ cup chopped onions
3 tablespoons melted butter or margarine
5 medium-sized potatoes, pared and thinly sliced
4 cups chicken bouillon or stock
2 cups milk
1 cup light cream
Salt and pepper
Chopped chives

Cut leeks in thin slices. Brown leeks and onions lightly in butter or margarine. Add potatoes and bouillon or stock. Heat to boiling point. Cover and simmer 30 minutes or until potatoes are tender. Press through a sieve. Add milk and cream. Cook 10 minutes. Season to taste with salt and pepper. Chill thoroughly. Garnish with chopped chives. Serves 6–8.

JELLIED CHICKEN CONSOMMÉ

1 envelope unflavored gelatin
¼ cup cold water
3 cups chicken bouillon
2 tablespoons sherry
1 teaspoon lemon juice
¼ teaspoon nutmeg
Salt and pepper to taste

Soften gelatin in water. Heat chicken bouillon to boiling point; add gelatin and stir until dissolved. Add remaining ingredients and mix well. Chill thoroughly. Serves 6–8.

GOLDEN SUMMER SOUP

2 cups orange juice
1 teaspoon cornstarch
2 tablespoons cold water
½ cup sugar
1½ teaspoons grated orange rind
½ cup shredded coconut

Heat orange juice. Combine cornstarch and water. Stir into juice. Cook over low heat, stirring constantly, until thickened. Add sugar, orange rind and coconut. Chill. Serves 4.

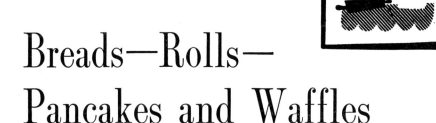

Breads—Rolls—
Pancakes and Waffles

BISCUITS

CAMPER'S BREAD TWISTS

1 cup all-purpose flour
1 teaspoon baking powder
⅛ teaspoon salt
1 tablespoon shortening
½ cup milk (approx.)
Green stick, ¾-inch thick, peeled
    part-way
Flour

Combine the 1 cup flour, baking powder and salt; cut in shortening. Add enough milk to make stiff dough. Heat stick and sprinkle with flour. Place ¼ of dough on stick in a spiral fashion. Hold about 6 inches away from coals to bake inside. Hold about 4 inches from coals until lightly browned. Turn continually. Remove from stick. Repeat with remaining dough. Makes 4 twists.

SOUR MILK BISCUITS

2 cups sifted all-purpose flour
2½ teaspoons baking powder
¼ teaspoon salt
¼ teaspoon baking soda
3 tablespoons shortening
1 cup sour milk

Sift dry ingredients together. Cut in shortening. Add milk and mix lightly. Turn out on lightly floured surface and knead lightly. Cut with floured cutter. Arrange on lightly greased baking sheet. Bake in hot oven (450° F.) 12–15 minutes. Makes about 12.

TOMATO CHEESE BISCUITS

2 cups sifted all-purpose flour
3 teaspoons baking powder
½ teaspoon salt
¼ cup shortening
⅔ cup tomato juice
½ cup grated American cheese

Sift flour, baking powder and salt to-gether. Cut in shortening. Add tomato juice and cheese; mix lightly. Turn out on lightly floured surface and knead 30 seconds. Pat out to ½-inch thickness. Cut with floured 2″ cutter. Place on greased baking sheet. Bake in hot oven (450° F.) 12–15 minutes. Makes about 18.

WHOLE WHEAT BISCUITS

1 cup sifted all-purpose flour
3 teaspoons baking powder
½ teaspoon salt
1 cup whole wheat flour
¼ cup shortening
⅔ cup milk

Sift all-purpose flour, baking powder and salt together. Add whole wheat flour and mix lightly. Cut in shortening. Add milk and mix lightly. Turn out on lightly floured surface. Roll out to ½-inch thick-ness. Cut with floured 2″ cutter. Place on greased baking sheet. Bake in hot oven (400° F.) about 15 minutes. Makes about 18.

CHEESE BISCUITS

2 cups sifted all-purpose flour
3 teaspoons baking powder
½ teaspoon salt
⅓ cup shortening
⅔ cup milk
1 cup small Swiss cheese cubes

Sift flour, baking powder and salt to-gether. Cut in shortening. Add milk and mix lightly. Turn out on lightly floured surface. Roll out to ½-inch thickness. Cut into diamond shapes and place on greased baking sheet. Press cheese cube lightly into center of each biscuit. Bake in hot oven (450° F.) 12–15 minutes. Makes about 18.

SOUTHERN YAM BISCUITS

2 cups sifted all-purpose flour
3 teaspoons baking powder
1 teaspoon salt
1 teaspoon brown sugar
¼ cup shortening
½ cup milk
1 cup mashed cooked yams

Sift together flour, baking powder, salt and sugar. Cut in shortening. Add milk and yams. Roll out on lightly floured surface. Cut with floured cutter. Bake in hot oven (450° F.) 12–15 minutes. Makes about 18.

MUFFINS

CHEESE MUFFINS

2 cups sifted all-purpose flour
3 teaspoons baking powder
½ teaspoon salt
¾ cup grated Cheddar cheese
1 egg, well beaten
1 cup milk
2 tablespoons melted shortening

Sift flour, baking powder and salt to-gether. Add cheese and mix lightly. Com-bine remaining ingredients. Add milk mixture to dry ingredients and mix only until ingredients are blended. Turn into greased muffin pans. Bake in hot oven (400° F.) 20–30 minutes, or until done. Makes about 12 medium-sized muffins.

SCOTCH OATMEAL MUFFINS

1 cup sifted all-purpose flour
1 teaspoon baking powder
½ teaspoon salt
½ teaspoon baking soda
1 cup sour milk
1 cup quick-cooking oats
1 egg, well beaten
⅓ cup firmly packed brown sugar
⅓ cup melted shortening

Sift flour, baking powder, salt and baking soda together. Pour milk over oats; add egg and brown sugar. Stir in sifted ingredients and shortening. Mix until ingredients are just blended. Fill greased muffin pans ⅔ full. Bake in hot oven (400° F.) 20–25 minutes. Makes about 12 medium-sized muffins.

SPICY BUTTERSCOTCH MUFFINS

3 tablespoons butter
⅔ cup brown sugar, firmly packed
2 cups sifted all-purpose flour
3 teaspoons baking powder
½ teaspoon salt
¼ teaspoon nutmeg
½ teaspoon cinnamon
¼ teaspoon ginger
1 egg
1 cup milk
2 tablespoons melted shortening

Grease 18 2½″ muffin cups and place ½ teaspoon butter and 1 teaspoon brown sugar in each cup. Sift flour, baking powder, salt and spices together. Beat egg; add milk, shortening and remaining brown sugar. Add to sifted dry ingredients, stirring only enough to dampen all

the flour. Fill muffin pan ¾ full, and bake in hot oven (425° F.) 20 minutes. Makes 18.

DATE AND NUT MUFFINS

2 cups sifted all-purpose flour
3 teaspoons baking powder
¼ teaspoon salt
1 tablespoon sugar
½ cup chopped dates
½ cup chopped walnuts
1 egg, slightly beaten
1 cup milk
⅓ cup melted shortening

Sift flour, baking powder, salt and sugar together. Add dates and walnuts; mix lightly. Combine remaining ingredients and add to date mixture. Mix only until ingredients are blended. Fill greased muffin pans ⅔ full. Bake in hot oven (400° F.) 20–25 minutes. Makes 12 medium-sized muffins.

CARROT-RAISIN MUFFINS

1 cup sifted all-purpose flour
3 teaspoons baking powder
2 tablespoons sugar
¼ teaspoon salt
1 cup whole wheat flour
⅓ cup raisins
1 egg, well beaten
1 cup carrot juice
¼ cup melted shortening

Sift flour, baking powder, sugar and salt together. Add whole wheat flour and raisins; mix lightly. Combine egg, carrot juice and shortening. Add to dry ingredients and mix until ingredients are just blended. Fill greased muffin pans ⅔ full. Bake in hot oven (400° F.) 20–25 minutes. Makes about 12 medium-sized muffins.

BANANA MUFFINS

1¾ cups sifted all-purpose flour
2 teaspoons baking powder
¼ teaspoon baking soda
¼ teaspoon salt
½ cup sugar
1 egg, well beaten
¼ cup melted shortening
1 cup mashed bananas

Sift flour, baking powder, baking soda, salt and sugar together. Combine egg, shortening and bananas; add to sifted ingredients and mix until just blended. Turn into greased muffin pans. Bake in hot oven (400° F.) 20–25 minutes. Makes 12 medium-sized muffins.

RAISIN BRAN MUFFINS

¾ cup sifted all-purpose flour
2 teaspoons baking powder
½ teaspoon salt
1 cup bran
½ cup raisins
2 tablespoons molasses
1 tablespoon melted shortening
½ cup milk
1 egg, well beaten

Sift together flour, baking powder and salt. Add bran and raisins. Combine molasses, shortening, milk and egg. Add to dry ingredients and stir just until flour is moistened. Bake in greased muffin pans in hot oven (400° F.) 20–25 minutes. Makes 12 medium-sized muffins.

HOLIDAY MINCE MUFFINS

2½ cups sifted all-purpose flour
¼ teaspoon salt
½ cup sugar
3 teaspoons baking powder
2 cups bran

2 eggs
1½ cups milk
⅓ cup melted shortening
½ cup chopped dates
½ cup mincemeat

Sift first 4 ingredients together and add bran. Beat eggs well; add milk, shortening, dates and mincemeat. Add to dry ingredients and stir until just blended. Fill greased muffin pans about ⅔ full and bake in hot oven (400° F.) about 25 minutes. Makes 18 medium-sized muffins.

CORN MUFFINS

2 cups cornmeal
2 teaspoons baking powder
½ teaspoon baking soda
½ teaspoon salt
½ teaspoon sugar (optional)
2 cups buttermilk
2 eggs
¼ cup melted butter

Sift meal with dry ingredients. Add buttermilk, eggs and butter. Beat with rotary egg beater. Pour batter into greased muffin pans. Bake in hot oven (400° F.) about 25 minutes. Makes about 12 medium-sized muffins.

HONEY MUFFINS

¼ cup honey
2 cups sifted all-purpose flour
3 teaspoons baking powder
¼ teaspoon salt
1 teaspoon nutmeg
¼ cup melted shortening
1 egg, well beaten
1 cup milk

Grease 12 2½″ muffin cups; place 1 teaspoon honey in each cup. Sift flour, baking powder, salt and nutmeg together. Add shortening, egg and milk.

Mix until ingredients are just blended. Fill muffin cups ⅔ full and bake in hot oven (400° F.) 20–25 minutes. Makes 12.

PEANUT BUTTER MUFFINS

½ cup peanut butter
3 tablespoons shortening
½ teaspoon salt
3 tablespoons sugar
1 egg, well beaten
1½ cups milk
2 cups sifted all-purpose flour
3 teaspoons baking powder

Cream peanut butter, shortening, salt and sugar until light and fluffy. Combine egg and milk. Sift flour with baking powder. Add milk mixture and sifted ingredients alternately to creamed mixture. Fill greased muffin pans ⅔ full. Bake in hot oven (400° F.) 20–25 minutes. Makes 12 medium-sized muffins.

BLUEBERRY MUFFINS KENNEBEC

2 cups sifted all-purpose flour
3 teaspoons baking powder
2 tablespoons sugar
¼ teaspoon salt
2 eggs, well beaten
1 cup milk
3 tablespoons melted shortening
¾ cup blueberries

Sift flour, baking powder, sugar and salt together. Combine eggs, milk and shortening. Add to sifted ingredients and mix until ingredients are just blended. Add blueberries; mix lightly. Fill greased muffin pans ⅔ full. Bake in hot oven (425° F.) 25–30 minutes. Makes about 18 small muffins.

POPOVERS, SCONES, OLD-FASHIONED DOUGHNUTS

SCOTCH CREAM SCONES

2 cups sifted all-purpose flour
3 teaspoons baking powder
½ teaspoon salt
⅓ cup butter
½ cup light cream

Sift flour, baking powder and salt. Cut in butter and add cream. Knead 5 minutes on lightly floured surface and roll out to ½-inch thickness. Cut into small triangles. Place on lightly greased baking sheet. Bake in hot oven (450° F.) 10–15 minutes or until light brown. Makes about 12.

POPOVERS

1 cup milk
¼ teaspoon salt
1 tablespoon melted butter or margarine
3 eggs, slightly beaten
1 cup sifted all-purpose flour

Combine milk, salt, butter or margarine and eggs. Add flour and beat until smooth. Fill greased baking cups ½ full. Bake in hot oven (425° F.) 40–45 minutes. Makes 6 large popovers.

OLD-FASHIONED DOUGHNUTS

2 cups sifted all-purpose flour
½ teaspoon baking soda
¼ teaspoon nutmeg
¼ teaspoon salt
2 tablespoons shortening
½ cup sugar
1 egg
½ teaspoon vanilla
½ cup sour milk

Sift flour, baking soda, nutmeg, salt together. Cream shortening and sugar until light and fluffy. Add egg and beat well. Blend in vanilla. Add sour milk and sifted ingredients alternately. Stir only until ingredients are blended. Roll dough out on a lightly floured surface ⅓ inch thick. Cut dough with floured 2½″ cutter and let stand 10 minutes. Fry in deep hot fat (365° F.) until lightly browned on all sides. Drain on absorbent paper. Makes 18.

COCONUT SCONES

2 cups sifted cake flour
3 teaspoons baking powder
¼ teaspoon salt
1 tablespoon sugar
¼ cup shortening
2 egg yolks
1 egg white
1 teaspoon grated orange rind
¼ cup shredded coconut
⅓ cup light cream

Sift flour, baking powder, salt and sugar together. Cut in shortening. Combine egg yolks, egg white, orange rind, coconut and cream. Beat well. Stir into flour mixture and mix lightly. Roll out on lightly floured surface to ½-inch thickness. Cut into triangles. Place on greased baking sheet. Bake in hot oven (450° F.) about 15 minutes. Makes about 18.

CORN BREADS

HARVEST CORN SQUARES

¾ cup sifted all-purpose flour
¾ cup cornmeal
3 teaspoons baking powder
¼ teaspoon salt
1 tablespoon sugar
1 egg, slightly beaten
¾ cup milk
¾ cup diced apples
3 tablespoons melted shortening

Sift together flour, cornmeal, baking powder, salt and sugar. Add egg and milk. Stir well. Add apples and shortening. Mix thoroughly. Pour into greased 8″ x 8″ baking pan. Bake in hot oven (425° F.) 25–30 minutes. Cool and cut into squares. Makes 8 servings.

CORN BREAD STICKS

1⅔ cups sifted all-purpose flour
¾ cup yellow cornmeal
3 teaspoons baking powder
2 tablespoons sugar
¼ teaspoon salt
1 egg, well beaten
1 cup milk
¼ cup melted shortening

Sift flour, cornmeal, baking powder, sugar and salt together. Combine egg, milk and shortening. Add to dry ingredients and mix until ingredients are just blended. Turn into greased cornstick pans. Bake in hot oven (425° F.) 20–25 minutes. Makes about 18.

BUTTERMILK SPOON BREAD

1 cup yellow cornmeal
2 cups boiling water
1 teaspoon salt
2 tablespoons salt pork drippings
2 eggs, separated
1 cup buttermilk
½ teaspoon baking soda
2 teaspoons baking powder

Gradually add cornmeal to water; cook over hot water 15 minutes. Cool. Add salt, drippings, egg yolks, buttermilk, baking soda and baking powder; mix thoroughly. Beat egg whites until stiff and fold into cornmeal mixture. Turn into greased 2-quart baking dish. Bake in moderate oven (350° F.) about 40 minutes. Serves 6.

CRACKLIN' BREAD

1½ cups cornmeal, white or yellow
2 tablespoons all-purpose flour
2 teaspoons sugar (optional)
½ teaspoon salt
3 teaspoons baking powder
1 egg, well beaten
1¼ cups milk
1⅓ cups cracklin's

Combine cornmeal, flour, sugar, salt, baking powder, egg and milk. Add cracklin's and beat thoroughly. Turn into well-greased 12″ x 9″ pan. Bake in hot oven (450° F.) about 20 minutes. Makes 12 servings.

TEXAS CORN BREAD

1 cup sifted all-purpose flour
½ teaspoon salt
1 teaspoon baking soda
¾ cup yellow cornmeal
2 eggs, well beaten
1 cup sour milk
¼ cup melted shortening

Sift flour, salt and baking soda together; add cornmeal and mix lightly. Combine remaining ingredients and add to dry ingredients. Beat until smooth. Turn into greased 8″ x 8″ pan. Bake in hot oven (425° F.) 30–35 minutes. Makes 8 pieces.

JONNY-CAKE

1 cup yellow cornmeal
1 teaspoon salt
¼ teaspoon baking soda
1 cup boiling water
½ cup light cream
2 tablespoons molasses

Combine cornmeal, salt and baking soda. Gradually add water and mix well. Add remaining ingredients and mix well. Shape into cakes and bake on greased griddle until well browned on both sides. Serves 6.

HUSH-PUPPIES

2 cups white cornmeal
½ teaspoon baking soda
1 teaspoon baking powder
1 tablespoon salt
1 egg
1½ cups buttermilk (about)

Mix dry ingredients. Add egg and milk to make a thick batter. Drop from spoon into deep hot fat (375° F.) and cook until golden brown. Drain on absorbent paper. Serve hot. Makes about 24 small hush-puppies.

BAKING POWDER

AND SODA BREADS

SOUTHERN ORANGE BREAD

2 cups sifted all-purpose flour
½ teaspoon salt
3 teaspoons baking powder
½ cup sugar
2 teaspoons grated orange rind
¾ cup orange juice
2 eggs, beaten
1 teaspoon almond extract
¼ cup melted shortening
2 tablespoons grated orange rind
½ cup sugar
1 teaspoon cinnamon
1 tablespoon butter or margarine

Sift flour, salt, baking powder and ½ cup sugar together. Add 2 teaspoons orange rind, orange juice, eggs, almond extract and shortening. Mix only until dry ingredients are moistened. Pour into waxed-paper-lined 8″ x 8″ pan. Combine remaining ingredients; sprinkle over batter. Bake in hot oven (400° F.) 30 minutes. Cut into squares. Serve hot. Makes 6–8 servings.

PECAN ROLLS

2 cups sifted all-purpose flour
2½ teaspoons baking powder
2 tablespoons sugar
½ teaspoon salt
⅓ cup shortening
¾ cup milk
¼ cup butter or margarine
¾ cup firmly packed brown sugar
½ cup pecans

Sift flour, baking powder, sugar and salt together. Cut in shortening. Add milk and mix lightly. Place 1 teaspoon butter or margarine, 1 tablespoon brown sugar and about 4 pecans in bottom of each greased muffin cup. Drop biscuit mixture into muffin pans. Bake in moderate oven (375° F.) 20–25 minutes. Turn out of cups immediately. Makes 12.

FRUIT SALLY LUNN

2 cups sifted all-purpose flour
3 teaspoons baking powder
¼ cup sugar
½ teaspoon salt
¼ cup shortening
⅓ cup chopped candied cherries
½ cup raisins
1 egg, beaten
¾ cup milk

Sift together flour, baking powder, sugar and salt. Cut in shortening. Add cherries and raisins; mix lightly. Combine egg and milk; add to shortening mixture and mix well until ingredients are just blended. Spread in greased 8″ x 8″ pan. Bake in moderate oven (350° F.) 25–30 minutes. Makes 6 servings.

ALMOND BREAD

3 cups sifted all-purpose flour
½ cup sugar
½ teaspoon salt
3 teaspoons baking powder
¾ cup chopped almonds
1½ cups milk
1 egg, well beaten
3 tablespoons melted shortening

Sift flour, sugar, salt and baking powder together; add almonds and mix lightly. Combine remaining ingredients and add to almond mixture. Mix until ingredients are blended. Turn into greased 9″ x 5″ x

3″ pan. Bake in moderate oven (375° F.) 60 minutes. Makes 1 loaf.

DATE AND NUT BREAD

¾ cup boiling water
1 cup pitted dates, cut in half
1¾ cups sifted all-purpose flour
1 teaspoon baking powder
½ teaspoon baking soda
¼ teaspoon salt
½ cup chopped pecans
1 tablespoon melted shortening
½ cup sugar
1 egg

Add water to dates and let stand 20 minutes. Sift flour, baking powder, baking soda and salt together; add pecans and mix lightly. Combine shortening, sugar and egg; beat well. Add dry ingredients alternately with date mixture to sugar mixture, beating well after each addition. Pour into greased 9″ x 5″ x 3″ pan. Bake in moderate oven (350° F.) 45–50 minutes. Makes 1 loaf.

APRICOT-PECAN LOAF

1 cup dried apricots
3 cups sifted all-purpose flour
¾ cup granulated sugar
4 teaspoons baking powder
1½ teaspoons salt
1 cup chopped pecans
1 egg, beaten
1½ cups milk
¼ cup melted shortening
2 tablespoons grated orange rind

Cover apricots with water and boil 15 minutes, or until tender. Cool, drain and chop. Sift together flour, sugar, baking powder and salt. Add pecans. Combine egg, milk, shortening and rind. Stir liquid mixture and apricots into dry mixture.

Turn into greased 9″ x 5″ x 3″ loaf pan. Let stand 15 minutes. Bake in moderate oven (350° F.) 1–1¼ hours. Makes 1 loaf.

APPLESAUCE-ALMOND BREAD

2 cups sifted all-purpose flour
¾ cup sugar
3 teaspoons baking powder
1 teaspoon salt
½ teaspoon baking soda
½ teaspoon cinnamon
½ teaspoon nutmeg
1 cup coarsely chopped blanched almonds
1 egg
1 cup applesauce
2 tablespoons melted shortening

Sift dry ingredients together. Add almonds. Beat egg; add applesauce and melted shortening. Add dry ingredients and stir until just blended. Pour into greased 9″ x 5″ x 3″ loaf pan and bake in moderate oven (350° F.) 1 hour. Makes 1 loaf.

BANANA BREAD

1¾ cups sifted all-purpose flour
2 teaspoons baking powder
¼ teaspoon baking soda
¼ teaspoon salt
⅓ cup shortening
⅔ cup sugar
2 eggs, well beaten
1 cup mashed bananas

Sift flour, baking powder, baking soda and salt together. Cream shortening and sugar until light and fluffy; add eggs and beat well. Add sifted ingredients and bananas alternately to creamed mixture, beating well after each addition. Turn into greased 9″ x 5″ x 3″ pan. Bake in moderate oven (350° F.) about 60 minutes. Makes 1 loaf.

BOSTON BROWN BREAD

½ cup cornmeal
½ cup whole wheat flour
½ cup rye flour or white flour
½ teaspoon salt
1 teaspoon baking soda
½ cup raisins
⅔ cup molasses
1 cup buttermilk

Blend together cornmeal, flours, salt and baking soda. Mix in raisins. Add molasses and buttermilk. Mix well. Turn into greased 5-cup mold. Cover tightly. Place mold on a rack in kettle. Pour boiling water into kettle to a depth of about 1 inch. Cover kettle tightly. Steam 4 hours. Add water as needed. Makes 1 large loaf.

PANCAKES

AND WAFFLES

SOURDOUGH PANCAKES

2 potatoes, cubed
1 cup water
½ package active dry yeast
½ cup warm, not hot, water
2 tablespoons sugar
1 cup all-purpose flour
1 egg, beaten
2 tablespoons butter or margarine
½ teaspoon baking soda
1 tablespoon hot water

Cook potatoes in the 1 cup water 25 min-

utes. Mash potatoes without draining. Cool to lukewarm. Dissolve yeast in the warm, not hot, water. Combine with lukewarm potato mixture. Add sugar and stir. Cover. Let stand 24 hours. Add flour, stir, cover, and let stand 24 hours. Add egg, butter or margarine. Dissolve soda in hot water. Add and stir well. Pour lightly on greased griddle. Brown on both sides. Serve with syrup, as desired. Serves 4–6.

VERMONT THINS

1 cup sifted all-purpose flour
1½ teaspoons baking powder
¼ teaspoon nutmeg
¼ teaspoon salt
1 tablespoon maple syrup
¼ teaspoon vanilla
1 egg, beaten
1 cup milk
3 tablespoons melted shortening

Sift flour, baking powder, nutmeg and salt together. Combine syrup, vanilla, egg and milk; add gradually to flour, mixing only until smooth. Add shortening. Bake on hot greased griddle. Makes about 10.

DUTCH BUCKWHEAT CAKES

1½ cups buckwheat flour
½ cup all-purpose flour
3 teaspoons baking powder
¼ teaspoon salt
2 tablespoons dark molasses
1 tablespoon melted butter or margarine
1½ cups light cream

Mix together buckwheat flour, all-purpose flour, baking powder and salt. Combine molasses, butter or margarine and light cream. Gradually add cream mixture to flour mixture; mix well. Drop by spoonfuls on greased griddle until browned on both sides. Serve with melted butter and shaved maple sugar, as desired. Serves 6.

CORN HOT CAKES

1¼ cups sifted all-purpose flour
1 teaspoon baking powder
1½ tablespoons sugar
¼ teaspoon salt
1 egg, well beaten
¾ cup milk
3 tablespoons melted shortening
1¼ cups whole kernel corn

Sift flour, baking powder, sugar and salt together. Combine egg, milk and shortening; add sifted ingredients and beat until smooth. Add corn and mix lightly. Drop by spoonfuls on hot greased griddle and brown on both sides. Makes about 12 4″ hot cakes.

HUCKLEBERRY GRIDDLECAKES

2 cups sifted all-purpose flour
3 teaspoons baking powder
¼ teaspoon salt
2 teaspoons sugar
1 egg, well beaten
1½ cups milk
1 cup huckleberries
   or blueberries

Sift flour, baking powder, salt and sugar together. Combine remaining ingredients and add to sifted ingredients. Mix until ingredients are blended. Drop by tablespoonfuls on hot greased griddle. Brown on both sides. Makes about 18 4″ pancakes.

SOUR MILK WAFFLES

2 cups sifted all-purpose flour
1 teaspoon baking soda
1 tablespoon sugar

¼ teaspoon salt
2 eggs, separated
2 cups sour milk
⅓ cup melted shortening

Sift flour, baking soda, sugar and salt together. Beat egg yolks and milk together; add sifted ingredients and shortening. Stir until smooth. Beat egg whites until stiff and fold into batter. Bake in heated waffle iron 3–4 minutes. Makes 6.

ALMOND PANCAKE

½ cup sifted all-purpose flour
¼ teaspoon salt
4 eggs, well beaten
½ cup light cream
1 teaspoon almond extract
2 tablespoons confectioners' sugar

Sift flour and salt together. Add eggs and cream alternately to flour mixture. Mix until smooth. Add almond extract. Turn into greased 10″ skillet. Bake in moderate oven (350° F.) about 25 minutes. Sprinkle with sugar. Serves 4.

BROWN SUGAR PANCAKES

1¼ cups sifted all-purpose flour
1¾ teaspoons baking powder
¼ teaspoon salt
1½ tablespoons brown sugar
⅛ teaspoon ginger
⅛ teaspoon nutmeg
1 egg, separated
¾ cup light cream
2 tablespoons butter

Sift flour, baking powder, salt, sugar and spices together. Beat egg yolk; add cream and mix well. Stir egg mixture into sifted ingredients. Beat egg white until stiff. Fold into flour mixture. Melt butter. Drop batter by tablespoonfuls onto buttered hot griddle. Cook over low heat until browned on both sides. Makes 6–8.

FLANNEL CAKES

2 cups sifted all-purpose flour
½ teaspoon salt
1 teaspoon baking soda
2 eggs
2 cups buttermilk
3 tablespoons melted butter

Sift flour with salt and baking soda. Beat eggs until light, add buttermilk and butter. Add to dry ingredients. Beat well. Drop from spoon on hot griddle and brown on both sides. Serve as dessert with melted butter, as desired. Makes about 20.

YEAST BREADS

ANADAMA BREAD

2 cups water
½ cup yellow cornmeal
2 tablespoons shortening
½ cup molasses
1½ teaspoons salt
1 package active dry yeast, or 1 cake compressed yeast
½ cup warm, not hot water (lukewarm for compressed yeast)
5 cups sifted enriched flour (about)

Boil water. Stir the cornmeal very slowly into the boiling water. When thoroughly mixed add the shortening, molasses and salt. Pour mixture into a large mixing bowl and cool to lukewarm. Sprinkle or crumble yeast into water (warm, not hot, water for active dry yeast; lukewarm water for compressed yeast). Stir until dissolved. When cornmeal-molasses mix-

ture is lukewarm, stir in dissolved yeast and enough flour to make a stiff dough. Turn dough out on a lightly floured board and knead until smooth and elastic, about 8–10 minutes. Place in a greased bowl; cover with a cloth and let rise in a warm place, free from draft, until doubled in bulk, about 1 hour. Turn out on a lightly floured board. Cut dough in half and form each half into a loaf. Place loaves in greased bread pans, 7½″ x 3½″ x 2¾″. Cover with a cloth. Let rise in a warm place, free from draft, until doubled in bulk, about 1 hour. Bake in a hot oven (400° F.) 50–60 minutes. Makes 2 loaves.

WHITE BREAD

1 package active dry yeast, or 1 cake compressed yeast
¼ cup warm, not hot, water (lukewarm for compressed yeast)
2 cups milk, scalded
2 tablespoons sugar
1½ teaspoons salt
1 tablespoon shortening
6 cups sifted all-purpose flour (approx.)

Dissolve yeast in water (active dry yeast in warm, not hot, water; compressed yeast in lukewarm water). Combine milk, sugar, salt and shortening; cool to lukewarm. Add yeast and 2 cups flour; mix well. Add enough of 4 cups flour to make stiff dough. Turn out on lightly floured surface and knead until smooth. Turn dough into greased bowl. Cover and let rise in warm place until doubled in bulk. Punch down. Cover and let rise until doubled in bulk. Divide dough in half and let stand 10 minutes. Shape into 2 loaves and place in 2 greased 9″ x 5″ x 3″ pans. Cover and let rise until doubled in bulk. Bake in hot oven (400° F.) 50–60 minutes. Makes 2 loaves.

FASTNACHTS

3 medium potatoes
¾ cup sugar
1 teaspoon salt
5 cups sifted all-purpose flour
1 package active dry yeast, or 1 cake
    compressed yeast
¼ cup warm, not hot, water (lukewarm
    for compressed yeast)
½ cup soft butter or margarine
2 eggs
½ teaspoon nutmeg

Peel potatoes and cook in 2 cups boiling salted water until tender. Drain off water reserving 1 cup. Pour water into a large mixing bowl. Stir in sugar, salt and 1 cup of the flour. Beat until smooth. Sprinkle or crumble yeast into the ¼ cup water (warm, not hot, water for active dry yeast; lukewarm water for compressed yeast). Stir until dissolved, then beat into batter. Cover with a cloth and let rise in a warm place, free from draft, until bubbly. Meanwhile, mash hot potatoes in pan in which they were cooked; measure 1 cup. Place in mixing bowl. Beat in margarine or butter, eggs, and nutmeg. When batter is full of bubbles, stir in potato mixture and remaining flour or enough to make a stiff dough. Turn dough out on a floured board and knead 8 to 10 minutes or until dough is smooth and elastic. Place in a greased bowl, and brush top of dough with soft or melted shortening. Let rise in a warm place, free from draft, until doubled in bulk. Punch down dough. Cut in half. Roll each half ⅛ of an inch thick on floured board. Cut with a doughnut cutter or into 2″ squares with a sharp knife. Place doughnuts on a floured board, cover with a cloth and let rise in a warm place until light and doubled in bulk. Slip doughnuts into deep fat heated to 365° F. As soon as they rise to the top, turn with a long-handled fork to brown on other side. Drain on absorbent paper toweling. Coat doughnuts with granulated sugar by shaking a few at a time in a paper bag containing about ½ cup sugar. Makes about 48.

CRULLERS

2 teaspoons sugar
½ cup warm, not hot, water (lukewarm for
    compressed yeast)
2 packages active dry yeast, or 2 cakes
    compressed yeast
½ cup milk
1 teaspoon salt
½ cup sugar
¼ cup shortening
2 eggs
4¼ cups sifted all-purpose flour
½ teaspoon mace
Fat for frying

Mix the 2 teaspoons sugar and water (warm, not hot, water for active dry yeast; lukewarm water for compressed yeast). Sprinkle or crumble in yeast and stir until dissolved. Scald milk. Stir in salt, the ½ cup sugar and the shortening. Cool to lukewarm. Add dissolved yeast to lukewarm milk mixture. Add eggs and mix thoroughly. Add half the flour and mace and beat until smooth. Add remaining flour and stir to mix thoroughly. Turn out on floured board and knead until smooth and elastic, about 8 minutes. Place in greased bowl. Cover and let rise in warm place until double in bulk (about 1 hour). Without punching down, turn out onto lightly floured board. Roll very thin. Cut dough into strips ½″ wide and 9″ long. Fold in half, twist and fasten ends. Place on lightly floured baking sheet; let rise uncovered in warm place until very light (about 1 hour). Fry in deep hot fat (350° F.) until golden, turning only once. Drain on absorbent paper, cool and roll in sugar. Makes about 48.

GUGELHOPH

½ cup milk
½ cup sugar
½ teaspoon salt
¼ cup butter or margarine
¼ cup warm, not hot, water
    (lukewarm for compressed yeast)
1 package active dry yeast, or 1 cake
    compressed yeast
2 eggs, beaten
2½ cups sifted all-purpose flour
14-16 whole blanched almonds
½ cup seedless raisins
½ teaspoon grated lemon rind

Scald milk. Stir in sugar, salt and butter or margarine. Cool to lukewarm. Measure water into a large mixing bowl (warm, not hot, water for active dry yeast; lukewarm water for compressed yeast). Sprinkle or crumble in yeast. Stir until dissolved. Stir in lukewarm milk mixture. Add eggs and flour. Beat vigorously, about 5 minutes. Cover. Let rise in a warm place, free from draft, until doubled in bulk, about 1 hour and 30 minutes. Sprinkle fine bread crumbs over sides and bottom of well-greased 1½-quart casserole or fancy mold. Arrange almonds on bottom of casserole or mold. Stir batter down. Beat thoroughly. Stir in raisins and lemon rind. Turn into prepared casserole or mold. Let rise in warm place, free from draft until doubled in bulk, about 1 hour. Bake in moderate oven (350° F.) about 50 minutes. Makes 1 cake.

CHEESE BREAD

1 cup milk
¼ cup sugar
1 tablespoon salt
2 packages active dry yeast, or 2 cakes
    compressed yeast
½ cup warm, not hot, water (lukewarm
    for compressed yeast)
5 cups sifted all-purpose flour (about)
2 cups grated sharp cheese

Scald milk. Add sugar and salt and stir in. Cool to lukewarm. Sprinkle or crumble yeast into water (warm, not hot, water for active dry yeast; lukewarm for compressed yeast). Stir until dissolved. Add lukewarm milk mixture. Add 2½ cups flour and beat until smooth. Add cheese and stir in. Add enough remaining flour to make a stiff dough. Turn dough out on lightly floured board and knead quickly and lightly 8 to 10 minutes or until smooth and elastic. Place in greased bowl; brush lightly with soft or melted shortening. Cover with cloth; let rise in a warm place, free from draft, until doubled in bulk, about 1 hour and 20 minutes. Punch down, pull sides into center and turn out on board. Divide into 2 equal portions. Shape into loaves. Place in greased bread pans (9″ x 5″ x 3″). Cover with cloth. Let rise in warm place, free from draft, until doubled in bulk, about 1 hour. Bake in a moderate oven (350° F.) about 35 minutes or until loaf sounds hollow when tapped. Turn out on cooling rack. Makes 2 loaves.

PARKERHOUSE ROLLS

½ cup milk
½ cup butter or margarine
⅓ cup sugar
½ teaspoon salt
¼ cup warm, not hot, water (lukewarm for
    compressed yeast)

1 package active dry yeast, or 1 cake
   compressed yeast
4 eggs
3½–4 cups sifted all-purpose flour
1 tablespoon sugar

Scald milk. Cool to lukewarm. Cream
butter or margarine thoroughly. Gradually cream in sugar and salt. Measure
water into a large mixing bowl (warm,
not hot, water for active dry yeast; lukewarm water for compressed yeast).
Sprinkle or crumble in yeast; stir until
dissolved. Stir in lukewarm milk and
creamed mixture. Separate one of the
eggs, adding yolk to yeast mixture and
putting egg white into a small bowl for
use later. Add remaining 3 whole eggs
and enough of the sifted flour to make
a very soft dough. Beat 10 minutes.
Cover. Let rise in a warm place, free
from draft, about 2 hours or until more
than doubled in bulk. Stir down. Beat
thoroughly. Cover tightly with waxed
paper or aluminum foil. Store in refrigerator overnight. Stir down and turn
out soft dough on floured board. Roll out
with floured rolling pin. Cut into rounds
with 2½″ cooky cutter. Crease with dull
edge of knife to one side of center. Brush
lightly with melted butter or margarine.
Fold larger side over smaller so edges
just meet. Seal. Place on greased baking
sheet about 1 inch apart. Cover. Let rise
in warm place, free from draft, until
doubled in bulk. Brush lightly with
melted butter or margarine. Bake in hot
oven (400° F.) about 15 minutes. Makes
about 24.

HOT CROSS BUNS

1 tablespoon sugar
¼ cup warm, not hot, water (lukewarm for
   compressed yeast)

1 package of active dry yeast, or 1 cake
   compressed yeast.
1 cup milk
1½ cups sifted all-purpose flour
¼ cup butter or margarine
¼ cup sugar
1 egg, well beaten
⅓ cup raisins
3¼ cups sifted all-purpose flour
½ teaspoon salt
1 teaspoon cinnamon
1 egg, slightly beaten
1 tablespoon water

Combine 1 tablespoon sugar and water
(warm, not hot water for active dry
yeast; lukewarm water for compressed
yeast). Dissolve yeast in sweetened
water. Scald milk and cool to lukewarm.
Combine yeast mixture, milk and 1½ cups
flour. Beat until smooth. Cover and let
rise about 1 hour. Cream butter or margarine and ¼ cup sugar. Add egg and
raisins. Mix well. Combine 3¼ cups flour,
salt and cinnamon; add yeast mixture and
raisin mixture. Turn out on lightly floured
surface and knead lightly. Place in
greased bowl. Cover and let rise until
doubled in bulk, about 2 hours. Shape
into medium-sized buns. Place about 2
inches apart in well greased shallow pan.
Cover and let rise until doubled in bulk,
about 1 hour. Combine slightly beaten
egg and water. Brush buns with egg-
water mixture. Bake in hot oven (425°
F.) 25–30 minutes. Decorate with confectioners' sugar glaze, as desired. Makes 24.

POPPY-SEED PASTE

1 cup ground poppy seed
½ cup water
1 tablespoon sugar
1 teaspoon flour

Combine ground poppy seed and water
and sugar. Cook over low heat to boiling

point, stirring constantly. Mix flour with
small amount of water to form smooth
paste and add to poppy-seed mixture.
Cool. Spread on Kolacke as directed
below.

KOLACKE

1½ cups milk
¾ cup butter
¼ cup shortening
½ cup sugar
4 egg yolks, beaten
2 packages active dry yeast, or 2 cakes
     compressed yeast
½ cup warm, not hot, water
     (lukewarm for compressed yeast)
1 teaspoon salt
¼ teaspoon mace

4–5 cups all-purpose flour (about)
Melted butter

Scald milk. Cool to lukewarm. Cream
butter and shortening; add sugar and
cream again. Add egg yolks. Dissolve
yeast in water (warm, not hot, for
active dry yeast; lukewarm for compressed yeast). Add lukewarm milk, salt
and mace and stir in enough of the flour
to make a soft dough. Cover, let rise
until bulk is doubled. Drop by spoonfuls
on floured board. Roll in balls and flatten
to ½ inch thickness. Dent tops with fingers, making 3 dents in each cookie.
Spread with poppy seed paste. Brush
with melted butter. Let rise until doubled
in size. Bake in hot oven (425° F.) about
20 minutes. Makes about 40.

Sandwiches

FILLINGS

AND SPREADS

OYSTER-CHICKEN SPREAD

1 cup cooked chopped oysters
1 cup cooked chopped chicken

1 tablespoon chopped parsley
1 tablesoon grated onion
¼ teaspoon salt
⅛ teaspoon pepper
Salad dressing

Combine oysters, chicken, parsley, onion,
salt and pepper; mix lightly. Add enough
salad dressing to moisten. Makes about
2 cups.

AMISH APPLE BUTTER SANDWICH SPREAD

½ cup apple butter
1 3-ounce package cream cheese, softened
2 tablespoons chopped peanuts
2 tablespoons chopped celery

Combine all ingredients and beat until well blended. Makes about 1¼ cups.

BACON-PECAN FILLING

1 3-ounce package cream cheese
2 tablespoons mayonnaise
¼ cup cooked crumbled bacon
2 tablespoons chopped pecans

Combine all ingredients; mix well. Makes about 1 cup.

BAKED BEAN SANDWICH FILLING

1 cup canned baked beans
¼ cup chopped celery
1 tablespoon minced onion
3 tablespoons chili sauce
⅛ teaspoon salt

Combine all ingredients and mix well. Makes about 1¼ cups.

CHEESE, EGG AND OLIVE SANDWICH SPREAD

1 cup cottage cheese
2 hard-cooked eggs, chopped
¼ cup chopped stuffed olives
2 tablespoons mayonnaise
⅛ teaspoon salt
1 tablespoon chopped parsley

Combine all ingredients; mix lightly. Makes about 1¾ cups.

CHEESE-OLIVE SANDWICH FILLING

1½ cups grated Cheddar cheese
¼ cup chopped stuffed olives
1 tablespoon grated onion
⅛ teaspoon salt
Mayonnaise

Combine cheese, olives, onion and salt; mix lightly. Add enough mayonnaise to moisten. Makes about 1¼ cups.

CREAM CHEESE-PINEAPPLE SANDWICH SPREAD

1 3-ounce package cream cheese with chives
½ cup canned crushed pineapple
2 tablespoons orange juice
½ teaspoon grated orange rind
⅛ teaspoon salt

Combine all ingredients and mix well. Makes about 1 cup.

SOUR CREAM-CHEESE SANDWICH SPREAD

1 cup sour cream
1 cup finely diced American cheese
2 tablespoons chopped green pepper
1 tablespoon minced onion
1 tablespoon lemon juice
½ teaspoon salt
⅛ teaspoon paprika
½ teaspoon Worcestershire sauce

Combine all ingredients; mix well. Makes about 2 cups.

SWISS CHEESE SANDWICH SPREAD

½ pound Swiss cheese, grated
2 tablespoons salad dressing
1 tablespoon chopped onion
2 tablespoons chopped pimiento
1 teaspoon Worcestershire sauce
¼ cup chili sauce
¼ teaspoon salt
⅛ teaspoon pepper

Combine all ingredients; mix well. Makes about 2 cups.

CORNED BEEF-HORSERADISH SANDWICH FILLING

1½ cups chopped, cooked corned beef
½ cup chopped green pepper
1 tablespoon horseradish
Salad dressing

Combine corned beef, green pepper and horseradish; add enough salad dressing to moisten; mix lightly. Makes about 2 cups.

DUBLIN SANDWICH FILLING

1 cup chopped, cooked corned beef
1 cup shredded cabbage
1 tablespoon chopped dill pickle
Salad dressing

Combine corned beef, cabbage and pickle with enough salad dressing to moisten. Makes about 2 cups.

HAM AND CHEESE SANDWICH SPREAD

1½ cups cooked, chopped ham
1½ cups grated American cheese
1 tablespoon grated onion
2 tablespoons chili sauce
Mayonnaise

Combine ham, cheese, onion and chili sauce. Add enough mayonnaise to moisten. Makes about 3 cups.

CREAMY SHRIMP SANDWICH SPREAD

1 5-ounce can shrimp, chopped
1 cup sour cream
2 tablespoons catsup
1 teaspoon lemon juice
¼ teaspoon grated lemon rind
¼ teaspoon salt
⅛ teaspoon pepper
1 teaspoon horseradish

Combine all ingredients and mix well. Makes about 1½ cups.

ALMOND-TUNA SANDWICH SPREAD

1 7¾-ounce can tuna
½ cup mayonnaise
½ cup chopped almonds
1 tablespoon chopped pimiento
Dash Tabasco
¼ teaspoon salt

Combine all ingredients and mix well; chill. Makes about 2½ cups.

SOUR CREAM-PIMIENTO SANDWICH SPREAD

1 cup cottage cheese
¼ cup cream cheese
3 tablespoons sour cream
2 tablespoons chopped pimiento
¼ teaspoon salt

Combine all ingredients; mix lightly. Makes about 1½ cups.

WATER CRESS-BACON SPREAD

1 3-ounce package cream cheese
2 tablespoons light cream
½ cup cooked crumbled bacon
½ cup chopped water cress

Combine all ingredients and beat until well mixed. Makes about 1 cup.

HAM FILLING HAWAIIAN

1½ cups cooked ground ham
¼ cup drained canned crushed pineapple
1 tablespoon brown sugar
2 tablespoons mayonnaise
1 teaspoon horseradish

Combine all ingredients and mix well. Chill thoroughly. Makes about 1¾ cups.

LIVER SAUSAGE SPREAD

½ pound liver sausage
½ cup chopped celery
2 tablespoons sweet pickle relish
1 tablespoon chopped onion
2 hard-cooked eggs, chopped
Salad dressing

Combine liver sausage, celery, pickle relish, onion, eggs and enough salad dressing to moisten. Makes about 1½ cups.

HOT SANDWICHES

DEVILED HAMBURGERS

1 pound ground beef
2 tablespoons chili sauce
1 tablespoon catsup
1 teaspoon prepared mustard
1 teaspoon horseradish
1 tablespoon grated onion
½ teaspoon salt
6–8 slices bread

Combine beef, chili sauce, catsup, mustard, horseradish, onion and salt. Mix well. Toast bread on one side. Spread untoasted sides with beef mixture. Broil 3 or 4 inches from source of heat 5–7 minutes. Serves 6–8.

BROILED TUNA SANDWICHES

1 tablespoon butter
1 tablespoon all-purpose flour
½ cup milk
1 cup grated American cheese
1 egg, well beaten
1 cup flaked canned tuna

¼ teaspoon salt
6 slices bread

Melt butter and blend in flour. Gradually add milk and cook, stirring constantly, until thickened. Add cheese and stir until melted. Add a little of hot mixture to egg and mix well. Add egg mixture to hot mixture and cook, stirring constantly, 2 minutes. Add tuna and salt. Remove from heat. Toast bread on one side. Spread untoasted sides with tuna mixture. Broil 3 or 4 inches from source of heat, 3–5 minutes, or until lightly browned. Serves 6.

APPLESAUCE AND CHEESE SANDWICH

4 slices buttered toast
½ cup applesauce
1 teaspoon cinnamon
6 slices American cheese

Spread toast with applesauce. Sprinkle cinnamon over applesauce. Top with cheese slices. Broil 3 or 4 inches from source of heat 3–5 minutes or until cheese is melted. Serves 4.

GRILLED CHEESE AND TOMATO SANDWICH

¼ cup butter or margarine, softened
½ teaspoon celery seed
6 slices bread
3 medium-sized tomatoes, sliced
6 slices processed Swiss cheese

Combine butter or margarine and celery seed. Toast bread on one side. Spread untoasted sides with celery seed mixture. Arrange tomato slices over celery seed mixture. Top with cheese slices. Broil 3 or 4 inches from source of heat about 5 minutes or until lightly browned. Serves 6.

HOT CORNED BEEF HASH SANDWICHES

1 cup corned beef hash
1 tablespoon chili sauce
1 tablespoon grated onion
1 tablespoon prepared mustard
4 slices bread
4 slices American cheese

Combine hash, chili sauce, onion and mustard. Toast bread on one side; spread untoasted side with corned beef mixture. Top with cheese slices. Broil 3 or 4 inches from source of heat about 5 minutes or until cheese is melted. Serves 4.

CHEESE PUFF SANDWICHES

6 slices bread
6 slices American cheese
⅛ teaspoon salt
3 eggs, separated
¼ cup mayonnaise

Toast bread on one side. Arrange cheese slices on untoasted side. Add salt to egg whites and beat until stiff. Combine mayonnaise and egg yolks. Beat until light. Fold yolk mixture into whites. Top cheese slices with egg mixture. Bake in moderate oven (350° F.) about 15 minutes or until lightly browned. Serve immediately. Serves 6.

HOT HAM SANDWICHES

¼ cup chopped onion
2 tablespoons melted butter or
    margarine
8 slices boiled ham
1 8-ounce can tomato sauce
4 slices buttered toast

Cook onion in butter or margarine until tender. Add ham and brown on both sides. Add tomato sauce and heat to serving temperature. Serve over toast. Serves 4.

BROILED VEGETABLE-CHEESE SANDWICHES

2 cups chopped fresh tomatoes
2 tablespoons chopped celery
1 tablespoon chopped green pepper
2 tablespoons grated onion
4 slices buttered toast
4 slices American cheese

Combine tomatoes, celery, green pepper and onion. Place vegetable mixture on toast. Top with cheese. Broil 3 or 4 inches from source of heat 4–5 minutes or until cheese is melted and lightly browned. Serves 4.

WESTERN SANDWICH

4 eggs, beaten
2 tablespoons minced onion
2 tablespoons chopped green pepper
¼ cup minced, cooked ham
⅓ cup milk
⅛ teaspoon salt
2 tablespoons melted butter or margarine
8 slices buttered bread

Combine eggs, onion, green pepper, ham,

milk and salt. Mix well. Cook over low heat in butter or margarine until set; arrange egg mixture on 4 slices bread. Top with remaining bread. Serves 4.

BROILED CRAB SANDWICHES

1 6½-ounce can crab meat, flaked
1 tablespoon chopped green pepper
1 tablespoon grated onion
¼ teaspoon salt
¼ cup mayonnaise
1 teaspoon lemon juice
1 teaspoon horseradish
4 slices bread
4 slices American cheese

Combine crab meat, green pepper, onion, salt, mayonnaise, lemon juice and horseradish; mix well. Toast bread on one side. Spread untoasted sides with crab meat mixture. Top crab meat mixture with cheese slices. Broil 3 or 4 inches from source of heat, about 5 minutes, or until lightly browned. Serves 4.

BAKED FRANKFURTER SANDWICHES

8 slices buttered bread
2 tablespoons prepared mustard
1 cup grated American cheese
4 frankfurters, sliced
2 tablespoons chopped onion
¼ teaspoon salt
⅛ teaspoon pepper
2 eggs, well beaten
¾ cup milk

Arrange 4 slices of the bread in greased 8″ x 8″ baking pan. Combine mustard, cheese, frankfurter slices, onion, salt and pepper. Top bread slices in baking pan with frankfurter mixture. Top with remaining bread slices. Combine eggs and milk; pour milk mixture over sandwiches. Bake in moderate oven (350° F.) 45 minutes. Serves 4.

KRAUT AND FRANKFURTER ROLLS

¼ cup softened butter or margarine
1 tablespoon prepared mustard
4 frankfurters
1 No. 2 can sauerkraut
4 frankfurter rolls

Combine butter or margarine and mustard; mix well. Broil frankfurters 3 or 4 inches from source of heat about 5 minutes or until browned on both sides. Heat sauerkraut to serving temperature; drain. Split rolls lengthwise and spread with mustard mixture. Arrange frankfurters on rolls; top with sauerkraut. Serves 4.

COLD SANDWICHES

TONGUE AND CHEESE SANDWICH

8 slices buttered bread
1 3-ounce package cream cheese, softened
8 slices tongue
¼ cup horseradish

Spread 4 slices of the bread with cream cheese; arrange tongue over cheese. Top with horseradish and remaining bread slices. Serves 4.

ROAST BEEF AND ONION SANDWICH

8 slices buttered pumpernickel bread
¼ cup mayonnaise
8 slices roast beef
1 Bermuda onion, thinly sliced

Spread 4 slices bread with mayonnaise. Arrange roast beef over mayonnaise. Top with onion slices and remaining bread slices. Serves 4.

OPEN VEGETABLE AND HAM SANDWICH

2 cups shredded cabbage
¼ cup grated carrot
1 cup cooked beets
¼ teaspoon salt
⅛ teaspoon pepper
Mayonnaise
4 slices ham
4 slices buttered toast

Combine cabbage, carrot, beets, salt and pepper. Add enough mayonnaise to moisten and mix lightly. Arrange ham slices on toast. Top with cabbage mixture. Serves 4.

CHICKEN LIVER-BACON SANDWICHES

½ pound chicken livers, cooked
½ cup cooked crumbled bacon
1 tablespoon chopped onion
Mayonnaise
8 slices buttered rye bread

Chop chicken livers; combine chicken livers, bacon and onion. Add enough mayonnaise to moisten and mix lightly. Chill thoroughly. Spread on 4 slices of the bread. Top with remaining bread. Serves 4.

CRAB MEAT SANDWICH SPECIAL

1 6½-ounce can crab meat, flaked
2 tablespoons chopped green pepper
¼ cup chopped cucumber
3 tablesoons mayonnaise
2 tablesoons chili sauce
1 teaspoon lemon juice

2 drops Tabasco
6 buttered frankfurter rolls

Combine crab meat, green pepper, cucumber, mayonnaise, chili sauce, lemon juice and Tabasco; mix lightly. Fill rolls with crab-meat mixture. Serves 6.

AVOCADO-CHEESE SANDWICH

½ cup mashed avocado
1 cup cottage cheese
1 tablespoon minced onion
⅛ teaspoon celery salt
⅛ teaspoon salt
1 teaspoon lemon juice
½ teaspoon Worcestershire sauce
8 slices buttered rye bread

Combine avocado, cheese, onion, celery salt, salt, lemon juice and Worcestershire sauce. Spread cheese mixture on 4 slices of the bread. Top with remaining bread. Serves 4.

CHEESE AND SALAMI SANDWICHES

8 slices buttered rye bread
1 tablespoon prepared mustard
4 slices Cheddar cheese
12 slices salami
1 medium-sized green pepper,
    cut in rings

Spread 4 slices of the bread with mustard. Arrange cheese, salami and pepper rings over mustard. Top with remaining bread slices. Serves 4.

TOMATO-PEANUT BUTTER SANDWICH

¾ cup peanut butter
¼ cup mayonnaise
⅛ teaspoon salt
8 slices buttered whole wheat bread
2 medium-sized tomatoes, thinly sliced

Combine peanut butter, mayonnaise and salt; mix well. Spread peanut butter mixture on 4 slices of the bread. Top with tomato slices and remaining bread. Serves 4.

BOLOGNA-BAKED BEAN SANDWICH

¼ pound bologna
1 1-pound can baked beans

1 tablespoon catsup
1 tablespoon prepared mustard
2 teaspoons grated onion
12 slices buttered bread

Chop bologna; add beans, catsup, mustard and onion. Mix well. Spread bean mixture on 6 slices of the bread. Top with remaining bread. Serves 6.

Eggs and Cheese

EGGS

SCOTCH WOODCOCK

2 tablespoons butter
1 tablespoon all-purpose flour
1 cup milk
4 hard-cooked eggs, chopped
1 tablespoon anchovy paste
¼ teaspoon salt
¼ teaspoon Worcestershire sauce
¼ teaspoon paprika

Melt butter; blend in flour. Gradually add milk and cook, stirring constantly, until thickened. Add remaining ingredients; heat to serving temperature. Serve over toast, as desired. Serves 4.

SCALLOPED EGGS WITH POTATO

2 tablespoons butter
2 tablespoons all-purpose flour
2 cups milk
2 tablespoons chopped parsley
1 teaspoon salt
6 medium-sized potatoes, cooked and sliced
6 hard-cooked eggs, sliced
1 cup cracker crumbs

Melt butter and blend in flour. Gradually add milk and cook, stirring constantly, until thickened. Add parsley, salt, potatoes and egg slices. Turn into greased 2-quart casserole. Top with crumbs. Bake in moderate oven (350° F.) 30–35 minutes. Serves 4–6.

BAKED EGGS ARKANSAS

4 slices Swiss cheese
8 slices bacon, cut in half
4 eggs
1 tablespoon minced scallions
½ teaspoon paprika
½ teaspoon salt
½ cup light cream

Arrange cheese slices in 4 greased individual baking dishes. Arrange bacon over cheese. Break eggs over bacon. Sprinkle scallions, paprika and salt over eggs. Pour 2 tablespoons cream over other ingredients. Bake in moderate oven (350° F.) about 15 minutes, or until eggs are set. Serves 4.

EGGS BAYOU

4 small tomatoes
½ teaspoon salt
⅛ teaspoon pepper
4 eggs
3 tablespoons butter
3 tablespoons all-purpose flour
1½ cups light cream
2 tablespoons chopped parsley
Dash Tabasco
4 slices toast

Remove stem ends from tomatoes and scoop out pulp. Sprinkle tomatoes with salt and pepper. Break 1 egg into each tomato. Place tomatoes in 4 greased baking cups. Bake in moderate oven (350° F.) 15–20 minutes, or until eggs are set. Melt butter and blend in flour. Gradually add cream and cook, stirring constantly, until thickened. Stir in parsley and Tabasco. Arrange tomatoes on toast slices and top with sauce. Serves 4.

GOLDEN EGG CROQUETTES

1 tablespoon minced onion
⅓ cup minced celery

3 tablespoons melted butter or margarine
⅓ cup all-purpose flour
1½ cups milk
2 cups cooked elbow macaroni
4 hard-cooked eggs, chopped
1 tablespoon chopped parsley
½ teaspoon salt
⅛ teaspoon pepper
¼ teaspoon poultry seasoning
Fine dry bread crumbs
3 tablespoons melted butter or margarine

Cook onion and celery in butter or margarine until tender. Blend in flour. Gradually add milk and cook, stirring constantly, until thickened. Add macaroni, eggs, parsley and seasonings. Chill thoroughly. Shape into croquettes and roll in bread crumbs. Cook in butter or margarine until browned on all sides. Serves 6.

NOVA SCOTIA POACHED EGGS

2 tablespoons butter
2 tablespoons all-purpose flour
1½ cups milk
1 teaspoon anchovy paste
1 teaspoon chopped pimiento
⅛ teaspoon Worcestershire sauce
4 slices smoked salmon
4 slices toast
4 poached eggs

Melt butter and blend in flour. Gradually add milk and cook, stirring constantly, until thickened. Add anchovy paste, pimiento and Worcestershire sauce. Arrange salmon on toast. Place poached eggs over salmon and top with anchovy sauce. Serves 4.

EGG POTATO PUFF

⅓ cup milk
1 cup mashed potatoes
1 teaspoon onion juice
½ teaspoon salt
⅛ teaspoon pepper

4 eggs, separated
¼ cup butter
12 slices cooked bacon

Combine milk, potatoes, onion juice, salt and pepper. Beat egg yolks and add potato mixture. Beat egg whites until stiff and fold into potato mixture. Melt butter and add potato mixture. Cook over low heat until browned on bottom. Broil 3 inches from source of heat until lightly browned. Serve with bacon. Serves 6.

EGGS SAN JOAQUIN

6 eggs, slightly beaten
½ teaspoon salt
⅛ teaspoon pepper
⅓ cup light cream
½ teaspoon Worcestershire sauce
¼ cup butter
1 medium-sized avocado, peeled and sliced
4 slices toast
8 slices cooked bacon

Combine eggs, salt, pepper, cream and Worcestershire sauce. Melt butter and cook until lightly browned. Add egg mixture and cook over low heat until eggs are set, stirring occasionally. Arrange avocado slices on toast. Top with eggs. Garnish with bacon. Serves 4.

BAKED CLAM OMELET

1 cup chopped clams
2 tablespoons melted butter
6 eggs, separated
½ teaspoon salt
2 tablespoons chopped parsley
½ cup light cream

Cook clams in butter 3 minutes over low heat. Beat egg yolks; add clam mixture, salt, parsley and cream. Beat egg whites until stiff and fold into clam mixture. Turn into well-greased skillet. Bake in moderate oven (350° F.) about 30 minutes. Serves 6.

IOWA MUFFIN PAN HASH

1 cup cooked, chopped beef
1 cup cooked, chopped potatoes
¼ cup chopped onion
1 teaspoon salt
⅛ teaspoon pepper
¼ cup beef broth
6 eggs

Combine beef, potatoes, onion, salt, pepper and broth. Mix thoroughly. Fill muffin pans ⅔ full with meat mixture. Bake in moderate oven (350° F.) 30 minutes. Break eggs over meat mixture and continue baking 10 minutes, or until eggs are set. Serves 6.

EGGS IN ISLANDS

4 slices bread
2 tablespoons butter
4 eggs

Remove centers from bread with small round cooky cutter. Melt butter. Add bread slices. Break eggs over bread so yolks fall in bread centers. Cook over low heat until eggs are set. Serves 4.

EGGS MARDI GRAS

⅓ cup chopped onion
⅓ cup chopped green pepper
2 tablesoons melted butter
1 No. 2 can tomatoes
2 cups water
1 cup rice
½ teaspoon salt
⅛ teaspoon pepper
6 eggs

Cook onion and green pepper in butter until tender. Add tomatoes and water. Heat to boiling point. Add rice, cover and cook over low heat until rice is tender. Add salt and pepper. Drop eggs over rice mixture. Cover and simmer until eggs are set. Serves 6.

DEVILED EGGS

4 hard-cooked eggs
2 tablespoons salad dressing
1 teaspoon grated onion
¼ teaspoon salt
⅛ teaspoon pepper

Cut eggs in half lengthwise. Remove yolks and mash. Combine yolks, salad dressing, onion, salt and pepper. Fill whites with yolk mixture. Top with chopped parsley, if desired. Serves 4.

EGGS ESPAGNOL

1 tablespoon butter
¼ pound dried beef, shredded
2 tablespoons grated American cheese
Dash of cayenne pepper
1 tablespoon chili sauce
1 cup cooked tomatoes
¼ teaspoon salt
4 eggs, well beaten

Melt butter, add beef and cheese. Toss lightly until beef is browned. Add remaining ingredients. Cook over low heat, stirring constantly, until thickened. Serves 4.

PIONEER EGG FRITTERS

1 cup cooked, minced tongue
1 cup cooked, minced ham
1 tablespoon chopped celery
1 tablespoon chopped stuffed olives
¼ teaspoon paprika
8 eggs, separated
¼ cup milk

Combine tongue, ham, celery, olives and paprika. Beat egg yolks well and add milk. Fold into tongue mixture. Beat egg whites until stiff and fold into tongue mixture. Drop by tablespoonfuls into hot fat, 1 inch deep. Cook about 2 minutes, or until browned on all sides. Drain on absorbent paper. Serves 8.

EGG-MUSHROOM SCRAMBLE

4 eggs
¼ cup light cream
Salt
½ teaspoon Worcestershire sauce
2 tablespoons melted butter
¼ cup mushrooms, chopped
3 strips crisp cooked bacon, crumbled

Beat eggs with cream, salt to taste. Add Worcestershire sauce. Heat butter and add mushrooms. Cook 3 minutes over low heat. Add bacon and eggs. Stir eggs lightly until done. Serves 4.

SHIRRED EGGS POPEYE

2 cups cooked spinach
¼ cup cooked, crumbled bacon
4 eggs
½ teaspoon salt
⅛ teaspoon pepper
2 tablespoons fine dry bread crumbs

Combine spinach and bacon. Turn into greased 1-quart casserole. Drop eggs over spinach mixture. Season with salt and pepper. Sprinkle crumbs over eggs. Bake in moderate oven (350° F.) 20–25 minutes, or until eggs are set. Serves 4.

MUSHROOM-OYSTER OMELET

3 tablespoons butter
3 tablespoons all-purpose flour
1 cup light cream
1 cup small oysters
1 4-ounce can mushrooms, drained
½ teaspoon salt
⅛ teaspoon pepper
4 eggs, slightly beaten
¼ cup light cream
2 tablespoons butter

Melt the 3 tablespoons butter and blend in flour. Gradually add 1 cup cream and cook, stirring constantly, until thickened. Add oysters and mushrooms, and cook over low heat until edges of oysters curl. Combine salt, pepper, eggs and ¼ cup cream. Melt the 2 tablespoons butter. Add egg mixture and cook over low heat until omelet is firm. Pour half of oyster mixture over omelet. Fold over and turn out on platter. Pour remaining oysters around omelet. Serves 4.

HOOSIER EGG CASSEROLE

¼ cup butter
¼ cup all-purpose flour
2 cups milk
1 tablespoon prepared mustard
2½ cups cooked green beans
4 hard-cooked eggs, chopped
Salt and pepper to taste
2 tablespoons buttered bread crumbs

Melt butter and blend in flour. Gradually add milk and cook, stirring constantly, until thickened. Add mustard, beans and eggs. Season with salt and pepper. Turn into greased 1½-quart casserole. Top with crumbs. Bake in moderate oven (350° F.) 30–40 minutes. Serves 6.

SUNDAY BREAKFAST OMELET

¼ cup butter
2 cups dry bread cubes
4 eggs, well beaten
1 tablespoon cream
1 teaspoon salt
Dash Tabasco
1 tablespoon chopped celery

Melt butter. Add bread cubes and cook over low heat until browned. Combine eggs, cream, salt, Tabasco and parsley. Pour over bread cubes and continue cooking until eggs are set. Serves 4.

DEEP SEA SCRAMBLED EGGS

6 eggs, slightly beaten
½ cup light cream
Salt and pepper to taste
1 tablespoon lemon juice
1 tablespoon chopped chives
1 cup diced cooked salmon
2 tablespoons melted butter

Combine eggs, cream, salt, pepper, lemon juice, chives and salmon. Cook in butter over low heat, stirring constantly, until eggs are set. Serves 4.

CHEESE

WELSH RABBIT

1 tablespoon butter
2 8-ounce packages natural Cheddar
    cheese, grated
½ to 1 cup ale or beer
1 teaspoon Worcestershire sauce
½ teaspoon dry mustard
⅛ teaspoon cayenne pepper
½ teaspoon salt

In chafing dish or double boiler over hot (not boiling) water, melt butter and cheese. As cheese begins to melt, gradually stir in ale or beer to make desired consistency. Cook only until smooth and hot. Stir in seasonings and serve on hot crisp toast or heated crackers. Serves 4–6.

CHEESE FONDUE

4 eggs, well beaten
2 cups milk
2 cups soft bread crumbs
2 cups grated American or Swiss cheese
1 tablespoon melted butter
½ teaspoon salt
⅛ teaspoon paprika

Combine all ingredients and mix lightly. Turn into greased 2-quart baking dish. Bake in moderate oven (350° F.) 30 minutes or until lightly browned. Serves 4.

CHEESE SOUFFLÉ

3 tablespoons butter or margarine
3 tablespoons flour
1 cup milk
¼ teaspoon salt
Dash of cayenne pepper
⅛ teaspoon dry mustard
1 cup grated cheese
4 eggs, separated

Melt butter or margarine. Stir in flour. Gradually add milk, stirring until well blended. Cook until sauce is thick. Add salt, cayenne, mustard and cheese; stir until cheese melts. Beat egg yolks, gradually add to cheese sauce stirring constantly. Cool. Beat egg whites until stiff but not dry. Fold egg yolk mixture into beaten egg whites. Pour into ungreased 1½-quart baking dish. Bake in a moderate oven (350° F.) 45 minutes. Serve immediately. Serves 4.

Fish

BAKED FLOUNDER

1 3-pound flounder, cleaned
1 teaspoon salt
⅛ teaspoon pepper
⅓ cup chopped onions
1 bay leaf, crushed
2 tablespoons chopped parsley
¼ teaspoon thyme
1 cup dry white wine
2 tablespoons butter
2 tablespoons all-purpose flour
6 medium-sized tomatoes, chopped
¼ teaspoon celery salt
¼ cup buttered cracker crumbs
Paprika

Sprinkle flounder with salt and pepper. Combine onions, bay leaf, parsley and

thyme. Spread onion mixture evenly over bottom of greased shallow baking pan. Place flounder over onion mixture. Pour wine over flounder. Bake in moderate oven (350° F.) 25 minutes. Melt butter. Add flour and brown. Add tomatoes and celery salt. Cook over low heat, stirring constantly, 10 minutes. Pour tomato mixture over flounder. Top with crumbs. Continue baking 10 minutes. Sprinkle with paprika. Serves 6.

BROILED SHAD

1 3-pound shad, cleaned and split
¼ cup melted butter
1 teaspoon salt
¼ teaspoon pepper

¼ cup chopped water cress
½ cup melted butter
2 tablespoons lemon juice

Brush shad with the ¼ cup butter. Broil, skin side down, 3 inches from source of heat 8–12 minutes, or until fish flakes easily when tested with a fork. Meanwhile, combine remaining ingredients. Heat to serving temperature. Pour over fish. Serves 6–8.

MINNESOTA BAKED PIKE

1 3-pound pike
Salt
2 cups soft bread crumbs
1 tablespoon melted bacon drippings
1 cup well-drained cooked tomatoes
1 teaspoon poultry seasoning
1 teaspoon salt
¼ teaspoon paprika
6 bay leaves
4 slices bacon
Lemon wedges
Parsley

Clean fish and rub with salt. Combine bread crumbs, bacon drippings, tomatoes, poultry seasoning, the 1 teaspoon salt and paprika. Stuff fish with tomato mixture and fasten with toothpicks. Place fish in greased baking pan. Top with bay leaves and bacon. Bake in moderate oven (350° F.) 45 minutes, or until fish flakes easily when tested with a fork. Garnish with lemon and parsley. Serves 6.

ISLANDERS' BAKED BASS

1 4-pound bass
1 cup olive oil
1 cup canned tomatoes
¼ cup chopped parsley
1 clove garlic, chopped fine
½ cup cracker meal

Clean, wash and salt fish. Place in a shallow baking pan. Mix olive oil, to-
matoes, parsley and garlic and spread part of this mixture over fish. Sprinkle fish with half of cracker meal, pour on rest of the sauce and cover with remaining cracker meal. Bake fish in hot oven (400° F.) about 1 hour, basting occasionally. Serves 4–6.

COD ANTIGUA

½ cup chives, chopped
2 cloves garlic, chopped
2 tablespoons olive oil
2 pounds cod, shredded
3 raw potatoes, sliced thin
2 tomatoes, peeled and sliced
1 green pepper, chopped
1 cup grated American cheese
Salt and pepper
1 cup water

Sauté chives and garlic in olive oil 5 minutes. Add cod and mix thoroughly. Place ½ of cod mixture in bottom of 2-quart casserole. Arrange potatoes, tomato slices, green pepper and cheese over fish. Season to taste with salt and pepper and cover with remaining fish. Add water; cover and bake in moderate oven (350° F.) 1 hour. Serves 6.

FISH FILLET CASSEROLE

1 medium-sized onion, thinly sliced
¼ cup melted butter or margarine
1½ pounds fish fillets
1 teaspoon salt
⅛ teaspoon pepper
½ cup buttered bread crumbs
2 tablespoons chopped parsley
½ cup cooked, crumbled bacon

Cook onion in butter or margarine until tender. Arrange fillets in a greased shallow baking dish. Arrange onion over fish. Add remaining ingredients. Bake in moderate oven (350° F.) 25–30 minutes. Serves 6.

BAKED SALMON PORTLAND

1 5-pound piece fresh salmon
Salt
Lemon juice
3 cups cracker crumbs, crushed
¼ cup melted butter or margarine
½ teaspoon salt
2 tablespoons vinegar
1 bay leaf, crushed
1 teaspoon Worcestershire sauce
2 tablespoons chopped chives
¼ teaspoon poultry seasoning

Rub fish inside and out with salt. Sprinkle with lemon juice. Combine remaining ingredients and pile into fish. Sew together. Place fish on rack in shallow pan. Bake, uncovered, in moderate oven (350° F.) about 1 hour. Serves 6–8.

FRESH SALMON CASSEROLE

2 pounds salmon steaks, cut 1-inch thick
2 teaspoons salt
Dash pepper
1½ cups chopped celery
½ cup onion rings
3 tablespoons chopped green pepper
¼ cup butter, melted
2 cups whole-kernel corn
2 tablespoons soy sauce

Sprinkle salmon on both sides with 1 teaspoon of the salt, and pepper. Place steaks in shallow well-greased casserole. Cook celery, onion and green pepper in butter until tender. Add corn and soy sauce; pour over salmon. Sprinkle with remaining salt, and bake, covered, in moderate oven (350° F.) for 25–30 minutes. Serves 6.

SALMON MOUSSE

2 egg yolks, slightly beaten
1 teaspoon salt
½ teaspoon dry mustard
¼ teaspoon paprika
¼ cup lemon juice
1 tablespoon butter
1 cup milk
1 envelope unflavored gelatin
¼ cup cold water
2½ cups cooked flaked salmon

Combine egg yolks, salt, mustard, paprika, lemon juice, butter and milk. Cook over low heat, stirring constantly, until thickened. Soften gelatin in water. Add gelatin to milk mixture and stir until dissolved. Chill until slightly thickened. Fold in salmon. Pour into 1-quart mold and chill until firm. Serves 4–6.

SHEPHERD SALMON PIE

1 1-pound can salmon
⅓ cup butter
⅓ cup all-purpose flour
½ teaspoon salt
¼ teaspoon paprika
Milk
1 tablespoon chopped onion
1 cup cooked mushrooms
3 cups seasoned mashed potatoes

Drain and flake salmon; reserve liquid. Melt butter and blend in flour, salt and paprika. Add enough milk to salmon liquid to make 2 cups. Gradually add milk mixture to butter mixture. Cook, stirring constantly, until thickened. Add onion and mushrooms. Line well-greased 9″ pie pan with 2 cups of the potatoes. Pour salmon mixture over potatoes. Top with remaining potatoes. Bake in hot oven (400° F.) 15–20 minutes, or until lightly browned. Serves 6.

BAKED STUFFED SMELTS

36 smelts
12 anchovies, skinned, boned and chopped
¾ cup fine dry bread crumbs
½ cup melted butter
½ teaspoon Worcestershire sauce

Remove head and backbone (if desired) from smelts. Place ½ of smelts in greased shallow baking pan. Top with anchovies. Top with remaining smelts. Sprinkle bread crumbs over smelts. Combine butter and Worcestershire sauce; pour over smelts. Bake in moderate oven (350° F.) 35–40 minutes, or until fish flakes easily when tested with a fork. Serves 6.

SOUTHERN RED SNAPPER

¼ cup minced onion
1 cup chopped green pepper
1 clove garlic, minced
2 tablespoons cooking oil
6 medium-sized tomatoes, chopped
½ cup chopped shrimp
4 pounds red snapper, cleaned
1 cup dry white wine
1 teaspoon salt
¼ teaspoon pepper
2 tablespoons chopped parsley

Cook onion, green pepper and garlic in oil until onion is tender. Add tomatoes and cook over low heat 20 minutes; stir in shrimp. Place red snapper in greased shallow baking pan. Pour wine over fish. Add tomato mixture. Sprinkle with salt, pepper and parsley. Bake in moderate oven (350° F.) 30 minutes, or until fish is tender. Serves 6.

CURRIED SOLE

2 pounds tomatoes, peeled
½ cup chopped onions
¼ teaspoon Worcestershire sauce
1 tablespoon curry powder
⅛ teaspoon pepper
¼ teaspoon salt
1 tablespoon chopped green pepper
1 tablespoon chopped pimiento
6 tablespoons butter
12 sole fillets
½ cup all-purpose flour
½ cup chopped parsley
½ cup light cream

Combine tomatoes, onions and Worcestershire sauce. Cook over low heat 1 hour. Add curry powder, pepper, salt, green pepper and pimiento. Melt butter. Dip fish in flour and cook in butter until browned on both sides. Sprinkle with parsley. Arrange on platter. Combine cream with tomato mixture. Heat to serving temperature. Pour over fish. Serves 6.

SAUTÉED STURGEON STEAK

1½ pounds sturgeon steak
2 tablespoons melted butter
½ cup lemon juice
½ teaspoon salt
⅛ teaspoon pepper
2 tablespoons horseradish
1 egg
2 tablespoons water
½ cup fine dry bread crumbs
¼ cup melted fat

Soak fish in hot water 5 minutes; drain. Combine butter, lemon juice, salt, pepper and horseradish; add fish and chill several hours. Beat egg with water. Drain fish and dip in egg mixture. Coat with crumbs. Cook in fat until browned on both sides and fish is tender. Serves 4.

WENDISH FISH HASH

1 salt herring
2 cups cooked cubed potatoes
2 tablespoons chopped onion
2 tablespoons melted butter
½ cup heavy cream
½ cup milk
⅛ teaspoon black pepper
⅛ teaspoon paprika
⅛ teaspoon celery salt

Clean herring and soak in cold water for several hours. Remove skin and bones. Cut in ½" cubes. Brown potatoes and onion in butter. Add herring and brown lightly. Add remaining ingredients and cook over low heat, stirring occasionally, until fish is tender. Serves 4.

TROUT DELICIOUS

1 cup blanched slivered almonds
¼ cup melted butter
3 tablespoons brown sugar
½ cup sherry
1 tablespoon chopped parsley
4 mountain trout
3 tablespoons melted butter

Add almonds to the ¼ cup butter and cook over low heat until lightly browned. Add brown sugar, sherry and parsley. Mix well and heat thoroughly. Cook trout in the 3 tablespoons butter until browned on both sides. Continue cooking until fish flakes easily when tested with a fork. Serve with almond sauce. Serves 4.

BAKED TROUT WITH TOMATO SAUCE

3 pounds lake trout
1 No. 2 can tomatoes
¼ cup chopped onion
¼ cup chopped celery
1 tablespoon butter
1 teaspoon salt
⅛ teaspoon pepper
1 tablespoon all-purpose flour
1 egg yolk
½ cup milk
⅛ teaspoon Tabasco

Arrange trout in greased shallow baking pan. Combine tomatoes, onion and celery. Pour tomato mixture over trout. Dot with butter. Sprinkle salt and pepper over tomato mixture. Bake in moderate oven (350° F.) 40 minutes, or until fish flakes easily when tested with a fork. Remove fish; strain tomato mixture. Combine flour, egg yolk, milk and Tabasco; mix well. Add flour mixture to tomato mixture and cook over low heat, stirring constantly, 5 minutes. Serve tomato sauce over trout. Serves 6.

PLANKED WHITEFISH

1 3-pound whitefish
⅓ cup butter or margarine
2 tablespoons lemon juice
1 teaspoon grated lemon rind
2 teaspoons salt
¼ teaspoon pepper
4 cups seasoned mashed potatoes

Clean fish and split down back. Remove bones. Place skin side down on preheated oiled plank. Combine butter or margarine, lemon juice and rind. Spread lemon mixture evenly over fish. Sprinkle with salt and pepper. Broil 3 inches from source of heat 5 minutes. Arrange potatoes around fish. Continue broiling about 5 minutes, or until potatoes are browned and fish flakes easily when tested with a fork. Serves 6.

SUNDAY CODFISH CAKES

2 cups cooked salt codfish
2 cups seasoned mashed potatoes
2 tablespoons melted butter
1 egg, well beaten
1 cup milk
⅛ teaspoon pepper
¼ cup melted bacon drippings

Combine fish, potatoes, butter, egg, milk and pepper. Chill several hours. Shape into cakes and cook in drippings until well browned on both sides. Serve with bacon, as desired. Serves 4.

FROGS' LEGS BIARRITZ

12 pairs frog's legs
1½ cups white wine
4 sprigs parsley
2 bay leaves
1 clove garlic, crushed
¼ cup all-purpose flour
1 teaspoon salt
⅛ teaspoon pepper
½ cup butter
¼ cup chopped shallots
3 tablespoons all-purpose flour
1 cup light cream
2 tablespoons minced parsley
Lemon quarters

Combine frogs' legs, wine, the 4 sprigs parsley, bay leaves and garlic. Let stand several hours. Remove frogs' legs. Combine the ¼ cup flour, salt and pepper. Coat frogs' legs with flour mixture. Melt butter; add frogs' legs and cook until lightly browned. Remove frogs' legs. Add shallots to butter and cook until lightly browned. Blend in the 3 tablespoons flour. Gradually add cream and cook until thickened, stirring constantly. Strain wine mixture; add to cream mixture and heat to serving temperature, stirring constantly. Garnish frogs' legs with minced parsley and lemon quarters. Serve with wine sauce. Serves 4.

HALIBUT-BEET HASH

¾ cup flaked cooked halibut
¾ cup chopped cooked potatoes
2 cooked medium beets, chopped
1 tablespoon minced onion
1 tablespoon minced parsley
½ teaspoon salt

⅛ teaspoon black pepper
1 teaspoon soy sauce
3 tablespoons milk
1½ tablespoons butter

Mix all ingredients except butter. Cook in butter, stirring until hot; then press lightly with pancake turner and cook until underside is well browned. Fold. Serves 4–6.

STUFFED HALIBUT STEAKS

2½ cups soft bread cubes
1 teaspoon salt
¼ cup grated onion
⅓ cup melted butter
2 tablespoons chopped parsley
1 can tomato soup
1 cup grated Cheddar cheese
2 1-pound halibut steaks

Combine bread cubes, salt, onion, butter, parsley, soup and cheese; mix well. Place 1 halibut steak in a greased shallow baking pan. Cover with tomato mixture. Place remaining halibut steak over tomato mixture. Bake in moderate oven (350° F.) 1 hour, or until fish flakes easily when tested with a fork. Serves 6.

FISHERMAN'S HALIBUT HASH

2 cups cooked flaked halibut
2 cups diced cooked potatoes
2 tablespoons minced onion
1 egg, beaten
1 teaspoon salt
⅛ teaspoon pepper
¼ cup chopped celery
¼ cup melted bacon drippings

Combine halibut, potatoes, onion, egg, salt, pepper and celery. Mix well. Cook in bacon drippings until well browned on both sides. Serves 4.

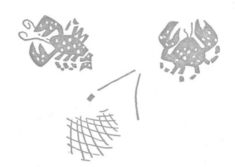

Shellfish

ABALONE CASSEROLE

2 eggs
2 tablespoons water
2 pounds abalone, sliced
1½ cups cracker crumbs
⅓ cup melted fat
1 cup water
¼ cup chopped onion
⅔ cup tomato juice
2 tablespoons lemon juice
1 teaspoon salt
⅛ teaspoon pepper

Beat eggs with the 2 tablespoons water. Dip fish in egg mixture and coat with crumbs. Cook in fat until browned on both sides; arrange in greased baking dish. Combine remaining ingredients with fish drippings and cook 10 minutes. Pour over fish. Bake in moderate oven (350° F.) 1 hour, or until fish is tender. Serves 6.

OREGON CLAM CAKES

2 cups ground clams
2 eggs, well beaten
½ cup fine dry bread crumbs
½ teaspoon salt
¼ teaspoon thyme
¼ cup grated onion
Fine dry bread crumbs
2 tablespoons melted fat

Combine clams, eggs, the ½ cup crumbs, salt, thyme and onion. Chill and shape into cakes. Coat with crumbs. Cook in fat over low heat until browned on both sides. Serves 4.

CLAM AND CORN CASSEROLE

1 7-ounce can minced clams
Milk
3 eggs, well beaten
1¼ cups canned cream-style corn
2 tablespoons grated onion
2 tablespoons finely chopped parsley
1 tablespoon melted butter
¼ teaspoon salt
⅛ teaspoon pepper

Drain clams; reserve liquid. Add enough milk to clam liquid to make 1 cup. Add clams and remaining ingredients. Mix well and turn into greased 1½-quart casserole. Bake in moderate oven (350° F.) about 50 minutes. Serves 4–6.

CLAMS GUILFORD

1 cup soft bread crumbs
2 cups chopped clams
1 teaspoon salt
¼ teaspoon paprika
2 tablespoons chopped parsley
2 tablespoons chopped onion

¼ cup light cream
½ cup clam juice
1 tablespoon butter

Alternate layers of bread crumbs and clams in a greased 1-quart casserole. Season with salt and paprika. Sprinkle parsley and onion over clam mixture. Pour cream and clam juice over clam mixture. Dot with butter. Bake in moderate oven (350° F.) 30 minutes. Serves 4.

ALASKAN CLAM PIE

1 7-ounce can minced clams
⅓ cup butter
⅓ cup all-purpose flour
Water
½ teaspoon Worcestershire sauce
1 tablespoon chopped parsley
1 cup milk
¼ teaspoon salt
⅛ teaspoon black pepper
1 9″ baked pastry shell
2 tablespoons melted butter
½ cup fine dry bread crumbs

Drain clams and reserve liquor. Melt the ⅓ cup butter and blend in flour. Add enough water to clam liquor to make 1 cup. Add clam liquor, Worcestershire sauce, parsley and milk to flour mixture. Cook over low heat, stirring constantly, until thickened. Add salt, pepper and clams and mix well; pour into pastry shell. Combine the 2 tablespoons butter and crumbs; sprinkle over clam mixture. Bake in hot oven (400° F.) 12–15 minutes. Serves 6.

CLAM EGGPLANT CASSEROLE

1 medium-sized eggplant
2 tablespoons chopped onion
2 tablespoons butter or margarine, melted
2 7-ounce cans minced clams
2 cups fine cracker crumbs
1 teaspoon salt

⅛ teaspoon pepper
1 tablespoon butter or margarine
¼ cup light cream
½ teaspoon Worcestershire sauce

Peel and cube eggplant. Cook, covered, in small amount of boiling water 10 minutes; drain. Cook onion in melted butter or margarine until tender. Drain clams; reserve liquor. Alternate layers of eggplant, clams and cracker crumbs in greased 1½-quart casserole. Sprinkle layers with salt and pepper. Dot with butter or margarine. Combine clam liquor, cream and Worcestershire sauce. Pour over other ingredients. Bake in moderate oven (350° F.) 40 minutes. Serves 4–6.

MARBLEHEAD CLAM FRITTERS

2 cups sifted all-purpose flour
2 teaspoons baking powder
¼ teaspoon salt
2 eggs, well beaten
½ cup milk
½ cup clam liquor
2 tablespoons chopped parsley
2 cups cooked chopped clams

Sift flour, baking powder and salt together. Combine eggs, milk and clam liquor; add to sifted ingredients and mix until blended. Add parsley and clams; mix lightly. Drop by tablespoonfuls into deep, hot fat (365° F.) and fry until browned on all sides. Drain on absorbent paper. Serves 6.

EASTERN SHORE SOFT-SHELLS

¼ cup melted butter
3 tablespoons lemon juice
Salt and pepper
¼ teaspoon cayenne pepper
6 soft-shell crabs
Flour
Parsley

Combine butter, lemon juice, salt, pepper and cayenne pepper. Roll crabs in butter mixture. Roll in flour. Broil over hot coals 8 minutes, turning once. Garnish with parsley. Serves 6.

CRAB-STUFFED AVOCADO

3 large avocados
3 tablespoons lime juice
1 teaspoon salt
3 tablespoons butter
6 tablespoons flour
⅛ teaspoon paprika
⅛ teaspoon black pepper
1½ cups milk
¾ cup cooked sliced celery
¼ cup minced pimiento
1 cup cooked crab meat

Cut avocados lengthwise into halves and peel. Sprinkle with lime juice and ½ teaspoon of the salt. Melt butter, blend in flour, add remaining seasonings and milk; cook until thickened, stirring constantly. Add celery, pimiento and crab meat. Fill avocados with crab meat mixture. Place in baking pan, pour in water to depth of ½ inch and bake in moderate oven (350° F.) 15 minutes. Serves 6.

CRAB WITH NOODLES

2 tablespoons butter
¼ cup chopped green pepper
¼ cup chopped pimiento
3 tablesoons all-purpose flour
1 teaspoon prepared mustard
1 cup cooked tomatoes
½ pound Swiss cheese, grated
1 egg, well beaten
¾ cup milk
1½ cups cooked, flaked crab meat
Salt and pepper to taste
4 cups cooked noodles

Melt butter, add green pepper and pimiento, and cook 5 minutes. Blend in flour and mustard. Add tomatoes and cook until thickened, stirring constantly. Add cheese and egg. Stir until smooth. Add milk and crab meat. Season with salt and pepper. Serve with noodles. Serves 4.

CRAB SUPREME

3 cups cooked flaked crab meat
Salad greens
1 cup salad dressing
⅓ cup heavy cream, whipped
⅓ cup catsup
¼ cup chopped green pepper
¼ cup grated onion
¼ cup chopped sweet pickles
¼ teaspoon salt
1 tablespoon lemon juice

Arrange crab meat on salad greens. Combine remaining ingredients and pour over crab meat. Serves 4.

PAELLA

1 frying chicken, cut up
4 hot sausages
⅓ cup olive oil
1 clove garlic
1 cup rice
1 cup boiling water
2 cups peas
½ bay leaf
Pinch of saffron
Salt and pepper
4-ounce can pimiento
½ pound shrimp, cleaned
6–8 clams in shell, scrubbed

In a large skillet, brown chicken and sausages in olive oil. Add garlic and rice, cook about 5 minutes. Add boiling water and remaining ingredients. Cover and cook until rice has absorbed all the water and is fluffy and tender. Stir frequently during cooking. Turn into casserole or serve from skillet. Serves 4.

CRAB CAKES MARYLAND

1 pound crab meat, flaked
1 egg yolk
1 teaspoon salt
¼ teaspoon pepper
1 teaspoon dry mustard
2 teaspoons Worcestershire sauce
1 tablespoon mayonnaise
1 tablespoon chopped parsley
1 teaspoon lemon juice
1 tablespoon melted butter
Fine dry bread crumbs
2 tablespoons melted butter

Combine crab meat, egg yolk, salt, pepper, mustard, Worcestershire sauce, mayonnaise, parsley, lemon juice and the 1 tablespoon butter. Shape into cakes and coat with crumbs. Cook in the 2 tablespoons melted butter over low heat until browned on both sides. Serves 6.

SHRIMP CROQUETTES

1 pound shrimp
1 tablespoon lemon juice
1 tablespoon Worcestershire sauce
1 tablespoon butter
⅛ teaspoon nutmeg
1 teaspoon salt
⅛ teaspoon pepper
2 tablespoons melted fat

Peel shrimp and remove black vein. Grind shrimp and combine with lemon juice, Worcestershire sauce, butter, nutmeg, salt and pepper. Chill thoroughly. Shape into patties. Cook patties in fat over low heat until browned on both sides. Serves 4.

SHRIMP CURRY, HAWAIIAN STYLE

6 tablespoons butter
2 teaspoons onion, finely chopped
6 tablespoons flour
2 cups milk
2 cups shredded coconut
1¼ teaspoons salt
3 teaspoons curry powder
2 teaspoons chopped preserved ginger
1½ pounds fresh shrimp, shelled and cleaned
1 tablespoon lime juice

Melt butter, add onion and cook about 2 minutes; stir in flour. Gradually add milk, stirring constantly, and cook until thickened. Add coconut, salt, curry powder and ginger. Cook over low heat about 30 minutes. Add shrimp and cook, stirring constantly, about 5 minutes or until shrimp are cooked. Stir in lime juice. Serve with rice, as desired. Serves 4–6.

PAPILLON FRIED SHRIMP

2 pounds shrimp
2 eggs, eaten
½ teaspoon celery salt
⅛ teaspoon pepper
1½ cups cracker crumbs

Peel shrimp and remove black vein. Combine eggs, celery salt and pepper. Dip shrimp in egg mixture and coat with crumbs. Fry in deep hot fat (375° F.) until lightly browned on all sides. Drain on absorbent paper. Serves 6.

DEVILED CRABS

¼ cup minced onion
3 tablespoons melted butter
2 tablespoons all-purpose flour
1 cup milk
¼ teaspoon salt
1 teaspoon prepared mustard
1 tablespoon lemon juice
1 tablespoon Worcestershire sauce
1 egg, beaten
1 pound crab meat
½ cup buttered cracker crumbs

Cook onion in butter until tender. Blend in flour. Gradually add milk and cook, stirring constantly, until thickened. Add salt, mustard, lemon juice, Worcestershire sauce, egg and crab meat. Mix well. Turn into 6 greased individual baking dishes. Top with crumbs. Bake in moderate oven (350° F.) 20 minutes, or until lightly browned. Serves 6.

SHRIMP FRICASSEE OVER RICE

2 pounds shrimp, cooked
2 cups chopped fresh tomatoes
2 tablespoons chopped onions
1 bay leaf
¼ cup chopped green pepper
¼ cup butter or margarine
¼ cup all-purpose flour
2 cups tomato juice
Salt and pepper to taste
Cooked rice

Combine shrimp, tomatoes, onions, bay leaf and green pepper. Melt butter or margarine and blend in flour. Remove from heat, gradually add tomato juice and cook until thickened, stirring constantly. Add shrimp mixture and heat to serving temperature, stirring occasionally. Season with salt and pepper. Remove bay leaf. Serve over rice. Serves 6.

MARDI GRAS SHRIMP

¼ cup chopped onion
¼ cup chopped green pepper
¼ cup chopped celery
1 clove garlic, minced
¼ cup melted butter
3 tablespoons all-purpose flour
½ teaspoon chili powder
1 bay leaf
⅛ teaspoon pepper
1 No. 2 can tomatoes
1½ pounds shrimp, cooked and cleaned
4 cups cooked hot rice

Cook onion, green pepper, celery and garlic in butter until onion is tender. Blend in flour and seasonings. Gradually

add tomatoes, and cook, stirring constantly, over low heat until thickened. Add shrimp and heat just to serving temperature. Remove bay leaf. Arrange rice on serving platter. Top with shrimp mixture. Serves 6.

GOURMET SHRIMP

⅓ cup sherry
2 tablespoons chopped chives
⅓ cup chopped parsley
1 clove garlic, minced
1 cup chopped mushrooms
4 medium-sized tomatoes, peeled and diced
1 cup beef bouillon
1 teaspoon chili powder
1 teaspoon salt
⅛ teaspoon pepper
½ teaspoon Worcestershire sauce
¼ cup chopped green pepper
1 cup tomato sauce
3 pounds shrimp
½ cup melted butter

Combine all ingredients except shrimp and butter. Cover and cook over low heat, 30 minutes. Peel shrimp and remove black vein. Cook shrimp in butter until firm and pink, about 5 minutes. Serve with sauce. Serves 6–8.

SHRIMP JAMBALAYA

2 tablespoons butter
2 tablespoons all-purpose flour
2 cups cooked tomatoes
1 small onion, sliced
¼ teaspoon thyme
½ cup chopped green pepper
1 tablespoon chopped parsley
1 teaspoon salt
⅛ teaspoon pepper
⅛ teaspoon paprika
1 teaspoon Worcestershire sauce
1 red pepper, chopped
4 cups water

1 cup rice
3 cups cleaned shrimp

Melt butter in large saucepan; blend in flour. Add tomatoes. Cook over low heat, stirring constantly, 3 minutes. Add remaining ingredients except shrimp and cook, covered, over low heat 25–30 minutes or until water is absorbed. 10 minutes before cooking time is up, arrange shrimp on surface, cover and continue cooking. To serve, stir shrimp into rice mixture. Serves 6.

SHRIMP LOUISIANA

½ cup French dressing
¼ cup horseradish
¼ teaspoon chili powder
1 tablespoon dry mustard
¼ teaspoon thyme
1½ pounds cooked cleaned shrimp

Combine French dressing, horseradish, chili powder, mustard and thyme. Beat until thoroughly blended. Add shrimp. Chill several hours. Drain and serve. Serves 4.

OYSTERS ROCKEFELLER

¼ cup melted butter
¼ cup cooked chopped spinach
3 tablespoons minced onion
2 tablespoons minced lettuce
1 tablespoon minced celery
¼ cup fine dry bread crumbs
¼ teaspoon anchovy paste
¼ teaspoon salt
⅛ teaspoon pepper
2 dozen oysters on half shells

Combine butter, spinach, onion, lettuce, celery, bread crumbs, anchovy paste, salt and pepper. Cook over low heat, stirring occasionally, 5 minutes. Remove oysters from shells. Clean shells thoroughly. Place an oyster in each shell. Broil 4

inches from source of heat 5 minutes. Top oysters with spinach mixture. Continue broiling 2–5 minutes. Serves 4–6.

BILOXI SCALLOPED OYSTERS

⅓ cup melted butter
1½ cups cracker crumbs
1 pint oysters
1 teaspoon salt
⅛ teaspoon pepper
2 tablespoons oyster liquor
¼ cup light cream

Combine butter with crumbs. Alternate layers of crumb mixture and oysters in greased 1-quart casserole. Sprinkle with salt and pepper. Pour oyster liquor and cream over other ingredients. Bake in moderate oven (350° F.) 30 minutes. Serves 4.

SKEWERED OYSTERS

1½ cups fine bread crumbs
½ cup finely minced celery
¼ cup minced parsley
¼ teaspoon salt
⅛ teaspoon black pepper
⅛ teaspoon paprika
36 large oysters, shucked
2 eggs, slightly beaten
4–6 slices bacon, cut in 1″ pieces
3 tablespoons melted butter
½ teaspoon Worcestershire sauce
Toast

Mix crumbs, celery, parsley and seasonings. Drain oysters; dip into eggs, then in crumb mixture until well covered. Place oysters and bacon on skewers, allowing 6 oysters to each. Mix butter with Worcestershire sauce. Broil oysters 4 inches from source of heat until browned on both sides. Baste with butter mixture. Serve hot on toast. Serve with remaining butter mixture. Serves 6.

OYSTER-STUFFED POLLOCK

1 4-pound pollock
Salt
2 cups finely chopped oysters
½ cup cracker crumbs
½ cup milk
¼ teaspoon salt
⅛ teaspoon pepper
⅛ teaspoon cayenne pepper
1 tablespoon melted butter
¼ cup chopped parsley

Clean pollock and rub with salt. Combine remaining ingredients and mix lightly. Stuff pollock with oyster mixture and fasten with skewers or cord. Place in greased shallow baking pan. Add enough water to cover bottom of pan. Bake in moderate oven (350° F.) 40 minutes, or until fish flakes easily when tested with a fork. Serves 6.

SEA FOOD COCKTAIL SAUCE

1 cup catsup
2 tablespoons chili sauce
2 tablespoons vinegar
1 tablespoon horseradish
1 tablespoon minced celery
1 tablespoon grated onion
½ teaspoon salt
1 teaspoon Worcestershire sauce
Dash Tabasco

Combine all ingredients; chill thoroughly. Serve with sea foods, as desired. Makes about 1¼ cups.

MARINATED SCALLOPS

¼ cup lemon juice
1 tablespoon olive oil
1 teaspoon salt
¼ teaspoon pepper
1 quart scallops
⅓ cup finely shredded soft bread crumbs
¼ cup cooked minced ham
1 teaspoon minced chives
1 egg, slightly beaten

Combine lemon juice, olive oil, salt and pepper. Pour oil mixture over scallops and let stand 1 hour. Drain scallops. Combine bread crumbs, ham and chives. Dip scallops in egg and coat with crumb mixture. Fry in deep hot fat (375° F.) until browned on all sides. Serves 4–6.

SCALLOP MUSHROOM KABOBS

1 pound scallops
1 pound small mushrooms
½ cup melted butter
1 cup cracker meal
1 teaspoon salt
½ teaspoon celery seed
¼ teaspoon thyme
Lemon wedges

Dip scallops and caps of mushrooms in butter. Combine cracker meal, salt, celery seed and thyme. Roll scallops in meal mixture. Alternate scallops and mushroom caps on skewers. Broil 3 inches from source of heat 3 minutes. Turn and continue broiling 3–4 minutes or until golden brown. Serve with lemon wedges. Serves 4–6.

SCALLOP SAUTÉ MONTAUK

¼ cup all-purpose flour
½ teaspoon salt
⅛ teaspoon pepper
1 pound scallops
¼ cup melted fat
2 tablespoons melted butter
2 tablespoons lemon juice
1 teaspoon lemon rind
1 tablespoon chopped parsley

Combine flour, salt and pepper. Coat scallops with flour mixture. Cook scallops in fat over low heat until lightly browned on all sides and tender. Combine butter, lemon juice, rind and parsley. Heat to serving temperature. Pour over scallops. Serves 4.

OLYMPIA OYSTER PAN ROAST

2 cups small oysters
⅓ cup butter or margarine, melted
1½ teaspoons lemon juice
Salt and pepper

Cook oysters in butter or margarine until edges curl. Remove from heat. Sprinkle with lemon juice, salt and pepper. Serves 4–6.

BROILED OYSTERS

12 large oysters
½ cup melted butter
¼ teaspoon salt
Dash cayenne pepper
¾ cup fine dry bread crumbs
4 slices buttered toast
Lemon slices

Dip oysters in butter and sprinkle with salt and cayenne pepper. Roll in bread crumbs. Broil 3–4 inches from source of heat until browned on both sides, brushing occasionally with remaining butter. Arrange oysters on toast. Serve with lemon slices. Serves 4.

CASCO BAY LOBSTER

¼ cup butter or margarine, melted
1 teaspoon Worcestershire sauce
¼ teaspoon salt
⅛ teaspoon pepper
1 tablespoon lemon juice
1 tablespoon prepared mustard
2 cups cooked diced lobster
4 slices buttered toast

Combine butter or margarine, Worcestershire sauce, salt, pepper, lemon juice, mustard and lobster. Cook over low heat, stirring, until thoroughly heated. Serve over toast. Serves 4.

LOBSTER CROQUETTES

¼ cup butter
¼ cup all-purpose flour
1 cup milk
1 egg yolk, beaten
2 cups cooked diced lobster
1 tablespoon chopped parsley
1 tablespoon catsup
½ teaspoon salt
2 eggs, beaten
Fine dry bread crumbs

Melt butter and blend in flour. Gradually add milk and cook, stirring constantly, until thickened. Add a little of hot mixture to egg yolk and mix well; stir into hot mixture and cook, stirring constantly 2 minutes. Remove from heat; add lobster, parsley, catsup and salt. Chill thoroughly. Shape into croquettes. Dip in eggs and coat with crumbs. Fry in deep, hot fat (375° F.) until browned on all sides. Drain on absorbent paper. Serves 6.

LOBSTER NEWBURG

2½ cups cooked, diced lobster
5 tablespoons butter
2 tablespoons sherry
2 tablespoons all-purpose flour
¼ teaspoon salt
⅛ teaspoon paprika
⅛ teaspoon cayenne pepper
¼ teaspoon nutmeg
2 cups light cream
2 egg yolks, slightly beaten
4 slices toast

Heat lobster with 3 tablespoons of the butter. Add sherry. Melt remaining 2 tablespoons butter and blend in flour and seasonings. Gradually add cream and cook over low heat, stirring constantly, until thickened. Stir a little of sauce into egg yolks and mix well. Stir into sauce and continue cooking, stirring constantly, 2 minutes. Add lobster mixture and mix well. Serve over toast. Serves 4.

LOBSTER STEW

3 cups diced cooked lobster
1 quart milk
2 cups clam broth
2 tablespoons butter or margarine
⅛ teaspoon cayenne pepper
1½ teaspoons salt

Combine all ingredients and heat to serving temperature, stirring occasionally. Serves 6.

CURRIED MUSSELS

1 pint mussels
3 tablespoons minced onion
2 tablespoons butter, melted
½ cup dry white wine
1 tablespoon chopped parsley
¼ teaspoon celery seed
1 teaspoon curry powder
¼ cup sour cream
⅛ teaspoon pepper

Drain mussels and reserve liquid. Cook onion in butter until tender. Add mussel liquid, wine, parsley, celery seed and curry powder. Simmer 5 minutes. Add mussels, sour cream and pepper. Heat to serving temperature, stirring constantly. Serves 4.

OYSTERS AND BACON ON SHELL

24 oysters in shells
4 slices bacon, diced
Salt
Pepper
2 tablespoons chopped parsley

Remove oysters from shells and drain. Place oysters on half shells and top with bacon. Sprinkle salt, pepper and parsley over bacon. Bake in very hot oven (450° F.) about 10 minutes. Serves 4–6.

BAKED OYSTERS

2 dozen large oysters in shells
1 egg, beaten
¼ teaspoon salt
⅛ teaspoon pepper
1 tablespoon water
1 cup dry bread crumbs
2 tablespoons butter

Remove oysters from shells. Combine egg, salt, pepper and water. Dip oysters in egg mixture and roll in crumbs. Place oysters in shells. Dot with butter. Bake in hot oven (400° F.) 15–20 minutes. Serves 6.

MAINE BAKED LOBSTER

2 cups cracker crumbs
¼ teaspoon salt
⅛ teaspoon pepper
¼ cup butter or margarine, melted
¼ cup milk
2 cups cooked flaked crab meat
4 2-pound lobsters, cleaned and split
½ cup melted butter or margarine
¼ cup grated Parmesan cheese

Combine crumbs, salt, pepper, the ¼ cup butter or margarine, milk and crab meat. Mix lightly. Stuff lobsters with crab-meat mixture. Pour the ½ cup butter over stuffing and sprinkle with cheese. Bake in hot oven (400° F.) 20–25 minutes. Serves 4.

BOILED LOBSTER

Salt
Boiling water
4 lobsters
1 cup melted butter
¼ cup lemon juice

Add 1 tablespoon salt to each quart boiling water. (There should be enough water to cover lobsters.) Drop lobsters, head first, one at a time into water. Let water come to boiling point after each

lobster is added. Cover and cook 20 minutes. Combine butter and lemon juice. Heat to serving temperature and serve with lobster. Serves 4.

Poultry

CHICKEN TETRAZZINI

½ pound spaghetti, cooked
½ pound mushrooms, sliced
4 tablespoons butter or margarine
1 teaspoon lemon juice
2 tablespoons all-purpose flour
2 cups milk
2 tablespoons sherry
1 teaspoon salt
2 cups diced cooked chicken
2 tablespoons grated Parmesan cheese

Arrange half of spaghetti in shallow baking dish. Cook mushrooms in 2 tablespoons of the butter or margarine until tender; add lemon juice. Arrange mushroom mixture over spaghetti in baking dish. Melt remaining 2 tablespoons butter or margarine; blend in flour. Gradually add milk and cook, stirring constantly, until thickened. Add sherry, salt and chicken. Pour chicken mixture over mushroom mixture. Top with remaining spaghetti. Sprinkle with cheese. Bake in hot oven (400° F.) about 20 minutes, or until lightly browned. Serves 4.

SUNDAY SUPPER CHICKEN LOAF

¼ cup butter or margarine
¼ cup all-purpose flour
1 cup chicken stock
½ cup milk
2 tablespoons chopped onion
2 tablespoons chopped green pepper
¼ cup chopped celery
2 tablespoons melted butter or margarine
3 cups soft bread crumbs
4 cups chopped cooked chicken
1 teaspoon salt

Melt the ¼ cup butter or margarine; blend in flour. Gradually add stock and milk. Cook, stirring constantly, until thickened. Remove from heat. Cook onion, green pepper and celery in the 2 tablespoons butter or margarine until onion is tender. Combine sauce, vegetable mixture, crumbs, chicken and salt; mix lightly. Turn into greased 9″ x 5″ x 3″ baking pan. Bake in moderate oven (350° F.) 1½ hours, or until firm. Serves 6.

SAVOY CHICKEN

1 5-pound fowl
2 carrots
2 stalks celery
1 medium-sized onion, chopped
1 bay leaf
½ teaspoon black pepper
1 teaspoon salt
4 sprigs parsley
¼ cup butter
¼ cup all-purpose flour
2 cups chicken stock
½ cup dry white wine

Cover fowl with hot water, add remaining ingredients. Simmer, covered, about 2 hours or until chicken is tender. Remove skin from chicken and cut into serving pieces. Strain stock and reserve. Melt butter and blend in flour. Gradually add chicken stock, and cook, stirring constantly, until thickened. Add wine and cook 3 minutes, stirring constantly. Add chicken and heat to serving temperature, stirring occasionally. Serve with rice or noodles, as desired. Serves 6.

SMOTHERED CHICKEN CHARLESTON

1 3-pound chicken
½ cup all-purpose flour
1 teaspoon salt
⅛ teaspoon pepper
¼ cup melted butter or margarine
½ cup sliced onions
1 cup chicken stock
½ cup light cream
2 tablespoons melted butter or margarine
2 tablespoons all-purpose flour

Cut chicken into serving pieces. Combine the ½ cup flour, salt and pepper; coat chicken with flour mixture. Brown chicken on all sides in the ¼ cup butter or margarine. Add onions, stock and cream.

Cover and simmer about 45 minutes, or until chicken is tender. Remove chicken. Combine the 2 tablespoons butter or margarine and the 2 tablespoons flour. Add to chicken liquid and cook, stirring constantly, until thickened; strain. Serve gravy over chicken. Serves 4.

CHICKEN SOUFFLÉ

¼ cup butter or margarine
½ cup all-purpose flour
2 cups milk
1 cup chicken stock
½ cup soft bread crumbs
3 cups chopped cooked chicken
1 tablespoon chopped parsley
2 tablespoons chopped celery
1 teaspoon salt
4 eggs, separated

Melt butter or margarine; blend in flour. Gradually add milk and stock; cook, stirring constantly, until thickened. Remove from heat. Add crumbs, chicken, parsley, celery and salt. Beat egg yolks until thick and fold into chicken mixture. Beat egg whites until stiff; fold into chicken mixture. Turn into greased 2½-quart baking dish. Bake in moderate oven (350° F.) about 1¼ hours, or until firm. Serves 6.

SOUTHERN CHICKEN AND DUMPLINGS

1 5-pound stewing chicken
1 medium onion
2 stalks celery
3 tablespoons salt
½ teaspoon pepper
2 cups sifted all-purpose flour
1 teaspoon salt
1½ teaspoons baking powder
2 tablespoons shortening
2 eggs, beaten slightly
1 cup milk (about)

Cover chicken with boiling water. Add onion, celery, the 3 tablespoons salt and pepper. Cover and cook until tender, about 3 hours. Remove chicken, reserve stock. While chicken is cooking, prepare dumplings. Sift together flour, salt and baking powder. Cut in shortening. Stir in eggs and enough milk to make a soft dough. Turn out on floured board and roll dough very thin. Cut into strips 1½″ wide and about 3″ long. Drop dough strips one at a time into boiling stock. Cook about 15 minutes. Serve with chicken. Makes 6–8 servings.

CHICKEN TIMBALES

3 tablespoons butter or margarine
3 tablespoons all-purpose flour
1½ cups light cream
3 eggs, well beaten
3 cups ground cooked chicken
1 tablespoon minced onion
1 tablespoon chopped parsley
½ teaspoon salt
⅛ teaspoon pepper

Melt butter or margarine; blend in flour. Gradually add cream and cook, stirring constantly, until thickened. Add a little of hot mixture to eggs and mix well. Stir into remaining hot mixture and cook, stirring constantly, 2 minutes. Add remaining ingredients and mix well. Turn into greased individual baking cups. Place cups in pan of hot water. Bake in moderate oven (350° F.) 25–30 minutes, or until firm. Serve with tomato or mushroom sauce (pages 325, 330), as desired. Serves 6.

CHICKEN TURNOVERS

¼ cup butter or margarine
¼ cup all-purpose flour
1 cup milk

2 cups minced cooked chicken
1 teaspoon grated onion
½ teaspoon salt
⅛ teaspoon pepper
1 recipe plain pastry

Melt butter or margarine; blend in flour. Gradually add milk and cook, stirring constantly, until thickened. Add chicken, onion, salt and pepper; mix lightly. Roll pastry out to ⅛″ thickness on lightly floured surface. Cut into 6″ squares; top with chicken mixture. Fold over to form triangles and seal edges. Prick tops. Place on baking sheet. Bake in hot oven (400° F.) 25–30 minutes or until lightly browned. Serve with mushroom sauce (page 325), if desired. Serves 4–6.

GOOSE FARM STYLE

8-pound domestic goose
2 onions, sliced
2 heads cabbage, chopped fine
1 medium-sized apple, cored and chopped
Salt and pepper to taste

Cut goose into serving pieces. Place on rack in roasting pan and bake in slow oven (325° F.) until almost tender, about 2½ hours. Pour off fat. Cook onions in fat. Add cabbage and apple. Cook 10 minutes; season. Arrange goose over cabbage. Cover and cook 1 hour or until goose is tender. Serves 6.

ROAST GOOSE

1 8-pound domestic goose
2 teaspoons salt

Stuff goose as desired. Sprinkle with salt. Place on rack in roasting pan. Bake in slow oven (325° F.) about 3½ hours, or until tender. Drain off fat occasionally during baking period. Baste with drippings frequently. Serves 6–8.

NEW MEXICO BAKED CHICKEN

3 cups diced cooked chicken
1 cup cooked rice
2 tablespoons chopped green olives
2 tablespoons chopped pimiento
1 teaspoon salt
3 eggs, slightly beaten
1½ cups chicken stock
½ cup corn cereal flakes

Combine chicken, rice, olives, pimiento, salt, eggs and stock; mix well. Turn into greased 8″ x 8″ baking pan. Top with cereal flakes. Place in pan of hot water. Bake in moderate oven (350° F.) about 40 minutes, or until firm. Serves 6.

BARBECUED CHICKEN MEXICALI

2 medium-sized broiling chickens
¼ cup melted butter
1 tablespoon sugar
1 tablespoon all-purpose flour
¼ teaspoon dry mustard
⅛ teaspoon cayenne pepper
1 teaspoon salt
1 cup vinegar
1 cup water
1 cup chili sauce

Cut chickens in quarters; brown on all sides in butter. Place in shallow baking pan and sprinkle with sugar, flour, mustard, cayenne pepper and salt. Mix vinegar, water and chili sauce and pour over chicken. Bake in moderate oven (350° F.) 1 hour or until chicken is tender. Baste occasionally during baking period. Serves 6.

BROWNED CHICKEN WITH COCONUT AND SPINACH

1 cup shredded coconut
1 cup milk
2 tablespoons peanut oil
2½-pound chicken, boned and cut into 1½″ cubes
2 teaspoons salt
½ cup water
1½ pounds spinach, cooked
3 tablespoons butter
⅛ teaspoon nutmeg

Combine coconut and milk. Bring to boil, remove from heat. Let stand 30 minutes. Press very thoroughly through wire strainer (you don't use the pulp). Heat oil. Add chicken cubes and brown on all sides. Add salt and water. Cook, covered, over low heat 20 minutes or until chicken is tender. Drain. Combine chicken with spinach, butter, nutmeg, and coconut milk. Cook over low heat 5 minutes. Serves 4.

CHICKEN CACCIATORE

1 3½-pound frying chicken
½ cup cooking oil
½ cup thinly sliced onions
1 No. 2½ can tomatoes
1 can tomato paste
1 bay leaf
1 clove garlic, minced
1 teaspoon salt
¼ teaspoon pepper
2 tablespoons chopped parsley
½ cup white wine

Cut chicken into serving pieces. Brown chicken on all sides in oil. Add remaining ingredients. Cover and cook over low heat 45–50 minutes, or until chicken is tender. Serves 4.

CREAMED CHICKEN AND AVOCADO

3 tablespoons butter or margarine
3 tablespoons all-purpose flour
2 cups milk
½ teaspoon salt
2 tablespoons chopped parsley

2 cups diced cooked chicken
2 tablespoons lemon juice
3 avocados, cut in halves
1 tablespoon chopped pimiento

Melt butter or margarine; blend in flour; gradually add milk and cook, stirring constantly, until thickened. Add salt, parsley and chicken; heat to serving temperature. Brush lemon juice over avocados. Sprinkle with pimiento. Serve chicken mixture over avocados. Serves 6.

ARROZ CON POLLO

1 medium-sized frying chicken
½ cup cooking oil
1 cup rice
¼ cup chopped onion
½ cup chopped green pepper
1 clove garlic, minced
1 cup tomato sauce
1 No. 2½ can tomatoes
1 teaspoon salt
1½ teaspoons chili powder
¼ teaspoon oregano
¼ cup chopped stuffed olives

Cut chicken into serving pieces; brown on all sides in oil; remove chicken; add rice, onion, green pepper and garlic. Cook, stirring occasionally, until rice is lightly browned. Add remaining ingredients and chicken; cover and cook over low heat about 30 minutes or until chicken is tender. Serves 4.

CHICKEN À LA KING

⅓ cup butter or margarine
⅓ cup all-purpose flour
1 cup chicken stock
2 cups light cream
2 egg yolks, slightly beaten
¼ cup chopped green pepper
½ cup sliced mushrooms
1 teaspoon minced onion
2 tablespoons melted butter or margarine
3 cups diced cooked chicken

¼ cup chopped pimiento
½ teaspoon salt
4 slices buttered toast

Melt the ⅛ cup butter or margarine; blend in flour. Gradually add stock and cream and cook, stirring constantly, until thickened. Add a little of hot mixture to egg yolks and mix well. Add to sauce and cook 2 minutes, stirring constantly. Remove from heat. Cook green pepper, mushrooms and onion in the 2 tablespoons butter or margarine until pepper is tender. Combine sauce, green pepper mixture, chicken, pimiento and salt. Heat to serving temperature, stirring constantly. Serve over toast. Serves 4.

CHICKEN CROQUETTES

¼ cup butter or margarine
⅓ cup all-purpose flour
1 cup milk
½ cup chicken stock
½ cup chopped mushrooms
3 cups ground cooked chicken
1 tablespoon minced onion
2 tablespoons chopped parsley
½ teaspoon salt
⅛ teaspoon pepper
¼ teaspoon nutmeg
1 egg, slightly beaten
1 tablespoon water
Fine dry bread crumbs
Deep hot fat

Melt butter or margarine; blend in flour. Gradually add milk and stock. Cook, stirring constantly, until thickened. Add mushrooms, chicken, onion, parsley, salt, pepper and nutmeg; chill thoroughly. Shape into croquettes. Combine egg and water. Dip croquettes in egg mixture and roll in crumbs. Fry in deep hot fat (350° F.) about 4–5 minutes, or until browned on all sides. Drain on absorbent paper. Serves 4–6.

DEVILED CHICKEN WITH MUSHROOMS

1 4-pound frying chicken
1 teaspoon salt
½ teaspoon pepper
½ cup melted butter or margarine
2 tablespoons all-purpose flour
1 cup chicken bouillon
1 cup chopped mushrooms
1 tablespoon prepared mustard
1 tablespoon chili sauce
½ teaspoon paprika
½ cup dry white wine
2 cups seasoned mashed potatoes
Paprika

Cut chicken into serving pieces; sprinkle with salt and pepper. Brown chicken on all sides in butter or margarine; remove chicken. Blend flour into chicken drippings; add chicken bouillon and cook, stirring constantly, until thickened. Add mushrooms, mustard, chili sauce, paprika and wine. Add chicken and cook, covered, over low heat about 45 minutes or until chicken is tender. Arrange potatoes over chicken mixture. Broil 3 or 4 inches from source of heat 3–5 minutes or until potatoes are lightly browned. Sprinkle with paprika. Serves 4.

VIENNESE CHICKEN DIVAN

1 package frozen broccoli, cooked
4 chicken breasts, cooked
2 tablespoons butter or margarine
2 tablespoons all-purpose flour
1 cup chicken stock
2 egg yolks, well beaten
2 tablespoons sherry
½ teaspoon salt
2 tablespoons grated Parmesan cheese

Arrange broccoli and chicken in greased shallow baking pan. Melt butter or margarine; blend in flour. Gradually add stock and cook, stirring constantly, until thickened. Add a little of hot mixture to egg yolks and mix well. Stir into hot mixture and cook 2 minutes, stirring constantly. Add sherry and salt; pour over broccoli-chicken mixture. Top with cheese. Bake in moderate oven (350° F.) 25–30 minutes, or until lightly browned. Serves 4.

CHICKEN AND LIGHT DUMPLINGS

1 5-pound fowl
1 medium-sized onion, chopped
1 carrot, finely chopped
1 teaspoon salt
½ teaspoon paprika
Water
1 cup sifted all-purpose flour
1½ teaspoons baking powder
¼ teaspoon salt
½ cup milk

Cut fowl into serving pieces. Place in kettle with onion, carrot, the 1 teaspoon salt, paprika and enough water to cover. Cover and simmer about 2 hours, or until fowl is tender. Sift flour, baking powder and the ¼ teaspoon salt together. Add milk and mix only until ingredients are moistened. Drop by tablespoonfuls into boiling chicken liquid. Cover and cook over low heat 20 minutes. Serves 4.

CHICKEN LIVERS EN BROCHETTE

1 pound chicken livers
6 slices bacon
½ pound mushrooms
1 teaspoon salt
¼ teaspoon pepper

Cut chicken livers in quarters. Cut bacon into 1″ pieces. Alternate livers, bacon and mushrooms on skewers. Sprinkle with salt and pepper. Broil 3 or 4 inches from source of heat 5 minutes. Turn and broil 3–5 minutes, or until bacon is crisp. Serves 4–6.

CHICKEN MARYLAND

3 broiling chickens, cut into quarters
2 tablespoons salad oil
¾ cup all-purpose flour
1 teaspoon salt
⅛ teaspoon black pepper
3 slices salt pork, finely chopped
2 cups light cream

Brush chicken quarters with oil and dredge with flour, salt and pepper. Fry salt pork until brown. Add chicken, cook until browned on all sides. Add 1 cup cream. Cook uncovered until cream is thickened, about 5 minutes. Add remaining cream. Cover and cook over low heat about 15 minutes, or until tender. Serve with cream gravy. Serves 6–8.

CHICKEN PAPRIKA BUDAPEST

2 medium-sized broiling chickens
2 tablespoons all-purpose flour
1 teaspoon salt
¼ cup melted butter
1 large onion, chopped
1 cup chicken stock
2 teaspoons paprika
1 cup sour cream

Cut chickens into serving pieces. Combine flour and salt and coat chicken with flour mixture. Brown chicken on all sides in butter. Add onion and cook until tender. Add stock and simmer, covered, 30 minutes or until chicken is tender. Stir paprika into chicken liquid. Add sour cream. Heat to serving temperature. Serve with wide noodles or dumplings, as desired. Serves 4.

SAUTERNE SIMMERED CHICKEN

1 medium-sized frying chicken
½ cup all-purpose flour
1 teaspoon salt

¼ teaspoon paprika
¼ teaspoon pepper
¼ cup olive oil
¾ cup white wine
2 tablespoons chopped parsley

Cut chicken into serving pieces. Combine flour, salt, paprika and pepper. Sprinkle flour mixture over chicken. Brown chicken in oil. Add wine and parsley. Cover and cook over low heat about 30 minutes, or until chicken is tender. Serves 4.

CURRIED CHICKEN LIVERS

1 pound chicken livers, ground
1 cup light cream
½ teaspoon curry powder
6 eggs, slightly beaten
2 tablespoons chopped parsley
¼ teaspoon salt
⅛ teaspoon pepper
3 cups cooked noodles

Combine all ingredients, except noodles, and mix well. Turn into greased 9″ ring mold. Place mold in pan of hot water. Bake in moderate oven (350° F.) about 1 hour, or until firm. Unmold and fill center with noodles. Serves 6.

SAUTÉED CHICKEN LIVERS

1½ pounds chicken livers
1 teaspoon salt
⅛ teaspoon pepper
¼ cup all-purpose flour
¼ cup melted butter or margarine
6 slices buttered toast
¼ cup chopped parsley

Sprinkle livers with salt, pepper and flour. Cook in butter or margarine about 10 minutes, or until browned on all sides. Arrange livers on toast. Pour liver drippings over livers. Sprinkle with parsley. Serves 6.

KENTUCKY FRIED CHICKEN

1 5-pound roasting chicken
2 teaspoons salt
1 cup fine dry bread crumbs
    (approx.)
3 eggs, slightly beaten
3 tablespoons water
Deep hot fat

Cut chicken into serving pieces, sprinkle with salt. Arrange chicken in skillet; add enough water to cover bottom of pan. Cover and cook over low heat about thirty minutes or until chicken is tender. Chill chicken. Roll chicken pieces in crumbs; combine eggs and water; dip chicken in egg mixture and coat with crumbs. Fry in hot deep fat (350° F) about 8 minutes or until browned on all sides. Drain on absorbent paper. Serves 4.

CHICKEN LIVER BALLS

2 slices dry white bread
¼ cup milk, approx.
4 eggs, slightly beaten
2 tablespoons chopped parsley
½ teaspoon salt
2 tablespoons melted butter or margarine
1 cup chopped cooked chicken livers
1 quart chicken stock

Crumble bread; add enough milk to cover and let stand 5 minutes. Combine bread mixture, eggs, parsley and salt. Cook in butter or margarine until thickened, stirring constantly. Add livers and cool. Shape into balls; heat stock to boiling point; add liver balls and cook, covered, over low heat 25 minutes. Serves 4.

BAKED CHICKEN WITH OYSTERS

1 broiling chicken, split
½ cup all-purpose flour
1 teaspoon salt
⅛ teaspoon pepper
½ teaspoon nutmeg
1 cup chicken stock or bouillon
1 cup light cream
¼ cup melted butter or margarine
2 cups oysters

Sprinkle chicken with flour, salt, pepper and nutmeg. Arrange chicken in greased shallow baking pan. Pour stock or bouillon over chicken. Cover and bake in moderate oven (350° F.) about 1 hour, or until chicken is tender. Add cream, butter or margarine, and oysters. Cover and bake about 10 minutes, or until oyster edges curl. Serves 4–6.

BAKED CHICKEN IN SCALLOP SHELLS

1 tablespoon melted butter or margarine
1 teaspoon lemon juice
¼ pound mushrooms, sliced
2 cups diced cooked chicken
1 can condensed cream of mushroom soup
6 greased scallop shells or ramekins
Salt and pepper to taste
2 tablespoons fine dry bread crumbs
6 tablespoons diced bacon

Combine butter or margarine, and lemon juice. Add mushrooms and cook until tender. Add chicken and soup; mix well. Turn into scallop shells or ramekins. Sprinkle with salt and pepper. Top with crumbs and bacon. Bake in moderate oven (350° F.) 25–30 minutes. Serves 6.

BARBECUED TURKEY WINGS

4 medium-sized turkey wings
2 tablespoons brown sugar
½ teaspoon chili powder
1 teaspoon salt
2 tablespoons lemon juice
1 tablespoon Worcestershire sauce

⅓ cup chili sauce
1 cup water

Combine all ingredients and mix lightly. Cover and cook over low heat about 1½ hours or until turkey wings are tender. Serves 4.

CAROLINA TURKEY WITH BISCUITS

2 tablespoons butter or margarine
2 tablespoons all-purpose flour
1 cup milk
1 cup turkey gravy
½ teaspoon salt
2 cups diced cooked turkey
1 cup cooked peas
4 hot baking powder biscuits

Melt butter or margarine; blend in flour. Gradually add milk and cook, stirring constantly, until thickened. Add gravy, salt, turkey and peas. Heat to serving temperature. Split biscuits and top with turkey mixture. Serves 4.

TURKEY MUSHROOM HASH

2 cups cooked diced turkey
1 cup potatoes, diced
1 egg
2 tablespoons chopped onion
½ cup chopped mushrooms
Salt and pepper
¼ cup melted butter

Combine turkey, potatoes, egg, onion and mushrooms. Salt and pepper to taste. Brown in butter on both sides over low heat. Serves 4.

BAKED TURKEY CROQUETTES

¼ cup butter or margarine
¼ cup all-purpose flour
1 cup milk

1 egg, beaten
1½ cups ground, cooked turkey
¼ cup chopped pecans
1 cup seasoned mashed potatoes
2 tablespoons grated onion
2 tablespoons minced pimiento
½ teaspoon salt
⅛ teaspoon pepper

Melt butter or margarine; blend in flour; gradually add milk and cook, stirring constantly, until thickened. Add a little of hot mixture to egg and mix well; stir into hot mixture and cook, stirring constantly 1 minute. Add remaining ingredients and mix lightly. Chill thoroughly. Shape into croquettes and arrange in greased shallow baking pan. Bake in moderate oven (350° F.) 25–30 minutes or until lightly browned. Serves 4.

DE LUXE CREAMED TURKEY

½ pound mushrooms, sliced
¼ cup melted butter or margarine
¼ cup all-purpose flour
½ teaspoon salt
⅛ teaspoon pepper
1 tablespoon grated onion
1 cup light cream
1 cup chicken bouillon
2½ cups diced cooked turkey
2 tablespoons chopped green pepper
¼ cup chopped pimiento
2 tablespoons sherry
½ cup cooked small white onions

Cook mushrooms in butter or margarine until tender; blend in flour, salt, pepper and onion. Gradually add cream and bouillon; cook, stirring constantly, until thickened. Add remaining ingredients and mix well. Turn into greased 1½-quart baking dish. Bake in moderate oven (350° F.) 35–40 minutes, or until lightly browned. Serves 4.

SQUAB IN CASSEROLE

4 squabs
½ cup melted butter or margarine
1 teaspoon salt
2 cups cooked potato balls
2 cups cooked peas
2 cups sliced cooked carrots
1 cup small white onions, cooked

Arrange squabs in shallow baking pan. Brush with butter or margarine and sprinkle with salt. Cover and bake in moderate oven (350° F.) 40 minutes. Arrange remaining ingredients around squabs. Bake, uncovered, 15–20 minutes,

or until vegetables are thoroughly heated. Serves 4.

ROAST SQUAB

4 squabs
1 teaspoon salt
½ cup melted butter or margarine
¼ cup melted currant jelly

Arrange squabs on rack in shallow baking pan. Sprinkle with salt and brush with butter or margarine. Brush with jelly. Bake in moderate oven (350° F.) about 45 minutes, or until tender. Brush frequently with drippings during baking period. Serves 4.

Stuffings

BAYOU SHRIMP STUFFING
(for Turkey or Fish)

2 slices bacon
1 cup chopped celery
½ cup chopped onions
2 cups chopped cooked shrimp
2 eggs, slightly beaten
3 cups cracker crumbs
¼ cup sherry
1 teaspoon salt
¼ teaspoon pepper

Cook bacon until crisp; drain on absorbent paper and crumble. Add celery and onion to bacon drippings and cook until tender. Combine all ingredients and mix lightly. Makes about 6 cups.

APPLE-ORANGE STUFFING
(for Game)

½ cup chopped salt pork
1½ cups chopped celery
½ cup chopped onions
4 cups diced apples
1 cup sugar
2 cups fine dry bread crumbs
1 teaspoon salt
¼ teaspoon pepper
1 tablespoon grated orange rind

Cook salt pork until crisp; remove pork. Add celery, onions and apples. Cover and cook until tender. Add remaining ingredients and salt pork; mix lightly. Makes about 5 cups.

MUSHROOM STUFFING
(for Meat or Fish)

1 cup chopped mushrooms
¼ cup melted butter or margarine
1 cup fine dry bread crumbs
1 tablespoon minced parsley
½ teaspoon salt
⅛ teaspoon pepper
½ teaspoon sage
½ teaspoon marjoram

Cook mushrooms in butter or margarine until tender. Add remaining ingredients and mix lightly. Makes about 2 cups.

ORANGE-CRANBERRY STUFFING
(for Poultry or Crown Roast of Pork)

2 cups ground cranberries
½ cup melted butter or margarine
⅓ cup sugar
8 cups soft bread cubes
1 teaspoon salt
⅛ teaspoon pepper
1 tablespoon sage
½ cup chopped celery
1 cup water
2 tablespoons grated orange rind

Cook cranberries in butter or margarine 5 minutes; add sugar and mix well. Add remaining ingredients and cook over low heat, stirring constantly, 10 minutes. Makes 6 cups.

OYSTER STUFFING
(for Turkey)

1½ pints oysters
¾ cup melted butter or margarine
¼ cup chopped parsley
2 tablespoons chopped onion
2½ quarts soft bread crumbs
½ teaspoon poultry seasoning
½ teaspoon celery seed
⅛ teaspoon garlic salt
2 teaspoons salt

Cook oysters in butter or margarine until edges curl; remove oysters. Add parsley and onion to butter or margarine and cook until onion is tender. Add remaining ingredients and oysters. Mix lightly but thoroughly. Makes enough for 10–12 pound turkey.

PEACH PECAN STUFFING
(for Duck)

2 cups fine dry bread crumbs
½ cup melted butter or margarine
½ cup chopped stewed dried peaches
½ cup chopped pecans
1 teaspoon salt
⅛ teaspoon pepper
¼ teaspoon poultry seasoning

Combine all ingredients and mix lightly. Makes about 2½ cups.

PYRENEES BROWN RICE PUDDING
(for Poultry)

2 cups brown rice, cooked
2 tablespoons grated onion
1 cup finely chopped mushrooms, cooked
3 slices crisp bacon, crumbled
2 tablespoons melted butter or margarine
1 poultry giblet, cooked and chopped
½ teaspoon poultry seasoning
⅛ teaspoon pepper
⅛ teaspoon paprika

Combine all ingredients and mix lightly. Makes about 6 cups.

EGG STUFFING
(for Fish)

1 cup soft whole wheat bread crumbs
2 tablespoons melted butter or margarine
2 hard-cooked eggs, chopped
1 tablespoon minced chives
Salt and pepper

Combine all ingredients and mix lightly. Makes about 1½ cups.

CELERY STUFFING
(for Goose)

¾ cup chopped parsley
1 cup chopped onions
½ cup melted butter or margarine
2 quarts soft bread crumbs
3 cups chopped celery
1 teaspoon celery seed
½ teaspoon poultry seasoning
2 teaspoons salt
¼ teaspoon pepper

Cook parsley and onions in butter or margarine until onions are tender. Add remaining ingredients and mix lightly. Makes enough for 10–12-pound goose.

BROWNED STUFFING BALLS
(for Poultry or Fish)

1 loaf whole wheat bread
2 eggs, beaten
¼ cup melted butter or margarine
1 teaspoon salt
2½ cups chicken stock
1 tablespoon minced chives
¼ teaspoon freshly ground pepper
½ teaspoon poultry seasoning
⅛ teaspoon paprika

Crumb bread. Add eggs and butter or margarine; mix well. Add salt, stock, chives, pepper, poultry seasoning and paprika. Shape into balls. Arrange in greased shallow pan. Bake in hot oven (400° F.) 25 30 minutes. Serve with poultry or fish. Serves 6–8.

OLD-FASHIONED BREAD STUFFING
(for Chicken)

3 cups soft bread crumbs
½ teaspoon salt
¼ teaspoon pepper
¼ teaspoon sage
2 tablespoons chopped onion
1 tablespoon chopped raisins
⅓ cup melted butter or margarine

Combine all ingredients and mix lightly. Makes enough for 5-pound chicken.

OZARK CORN BREAD STUFFING
(for Chicken)

1 cup chopped celery
2 tablespoons chopped parsley
2 tablespoons chopped onion
⅓ cup melted butter or margarine
4 cups corn bread crumbs
¼ teaspoon thyme
1 teaspoon salt
⅛ teaspoon pepper

Cook celery, parsley and onion in butter or margarine until onion is tender. Add remaining ingredients and mix lightly. Makes enough for 5-pound chicken.

CORN AND BACON STUFFING
(for Poultry)

6 slices bacon, diced
1 cup chopped onions
1 cup chopped celery
1 cup fine dry bread crumbs
4 cups cooked corn
½ teaspoon poultry seasoning
1 teaspoon salt
¼ teaspoon pepper
½ cup milk

Cook bacon until crisp; remove bacon and drain on absorbent paper. Cook onions and celery in bacon drippings until tender. Add remaining ingredients and bacon; mix lightly. Makes about 5 cups.

AVOCADO STUFFING
(for Fish)

¼ cup butter
½ cup chopped mushrooms
1 tablespoon chopped chives
1 ripe avocado, peeled and mashed

2 tablespoons chopped pimiento
2 tablespoons all-purpose flour
½ cup lemon juice
½ cup beef stock or bouillon
1 teaspoon poppy seeds
2 egg yolks

Heat butter. Add mushrooms and chives; sauté until tender. Add avocado, pimiento and flour; mix well. Cook over low heat 3 minutes. Add lemon juice, beef stock or bouillon and poppy seeds; mix well. Cook 10 minutes over low heat or until thickened, stirring occasionally. Add egg yolks gradually. Cook, stirring constantly, until thickened. Makes about 4 cups.

Meat

BEEF

CHILI CON CARNE

1 pound ground beef
¼ cup chopped onion
¼ cup chopped green pepper
2 tablespoons melted butter or margarine
1 No. 2 can kidney beans, drained
2 cans tomato soup
1 cup water
2 tablespoons chili powder
1 teaspoon salt
Dash cayenne pepper

Cook beef, onion and green pepper in butter or margarine until onion is tender. Add remaining ingredients and mix well. Cook, covered, over low heat 1 hour, stirring occasionally. Serves 4–6.

LONE STAR FAVORITE CASSEROLE

½ cup chopped green pepper
½ cup sliced onions
3 tablespoons melted salt pork drippings
¾ pound ground round steak
2 tablespoons chopped parsley
¼ teaspoon sugar
3 cups cooked tomatoes
1 teaspoon Worcestershire sauce
2 cups cooked rice
½ teaspoon chili powder
1 teaspoon salt
⅛ teaspoon freshly ground pepper

Cook green pepper and onions in drippings until tender. Add ground round steak and brown. Add remaining ingredients and mix lightly. Turn into greased 2-quart baking dish. Bake in moderate oven (350° F.) 30 minutes. Serves 4–6.

CORNED BEEF WITH
MUSTARD SAUCE

4 pounds corned beef
¼ cup butter or margarine
2 tablespoons chopped onion
3 tablespoons all-purpose flour
½ teaspoon salt
⅛ teaspoon pepper
¼ cup prepared mustard
1½ cups milk
2 egg yolks, well beaten
3 tablespoons lemon juice

Cover corned beef with cold water.
Cover and simmer 3½–4 hours or until
tender. Drain. Melt butter or margarine;
add onion and cook until tender. Blend
in flour, salt, pepper and mustard. Gradually add milk and cook over low heat,
stirring constantly, until thickened. Add
a little of hot mixture to egg yolks and
stir well. Stir into hot mixture and cook
1 minute, stirring constantly. Remove
from heat; stir in lemon juice. Serve sauce
with corned beef. Serves 8.

GOULASH BOHEMIAN

2 pounds round beef
¼ cup chopped onion
2 tablespoons butter or margarine
⅛ teaspoon cloves
1 small onion, thinly sliced
1 teaspoon sugar
1 cup water
¼ cup chili sauce
1 teaspoon salt
⅛ teaspoon pepper

Cut beef into ½-inch cubes. Cook onion
in butter or margarine until tender; add
beef and brown. Add remaining ingredients and cook, covered, over low heat
about 1 hour, or until beef is tender. Add
more water during cooking period, if
necessary. Serves 6.

MEAT BALLS À LA DENMARK

3 slices bread
1 cup cold water
½ pound ground beef
½ pound ground veal
1 tablespoon chopped chives
1 teaspoon salt
⅛ teaspoon pepper
¼ teaspoon nutmeg
1 egg
⅓ cup all-purpose flour
¼ cup butter, melted
1 cup hot beef stock or bouillon

Soak bread in cold water, squeeze dry.
Add beef, veal, chives, salt, pepper, nutmeg and egg; mix well. Shape into 1"
balls. Coat with flour. Brown on all sides
in butter. Add beef stock or bouillon.
Cover, and cook over low heat 30 minutes. Serves 6.

BARNYARD BARBECUE

1 pound round steak, cubed
1 pound pork, cubed
¼ cup melted shortening
½ cup sliced onions
½ cup chopped celery
1½ cups chili sauce
1 No. 2 can tomatoes
1 teaspoon salt
¼ teaspoon pepper
1 teaspoon chili powder

Cook beef and pork in shortening until
well browned on all sides. Add remaining
ingredients and mix well. Cover and cook
over low heat about 1½ hours, or until
meat is tender. Uncover and cook 1 hour.
Serves 6.

NEW ENGLAND BOILED DINNER

Boiling water
4 pounds corned beef
1 medium-sized head cabbage,
       cut in quarters

6 medium-sized carrots, scraped
6 medium-sized onions, peeled
6 medium-sized potatoes, peeled
1 medium-sized turnip, peeled and cubed

Add enough boiling water to cover corned beef. Cover and cook over low heat 3–4 hours or until meat is tender. Add cabbage, carrots, onions, potatoes and turnip. Cover and cook about 30 minutes or until vegetables are tender. Serves 6–8.

SHORT RIBS OF BEEF

2 pounds short ribs
3 tablespoons melted shortening
1 medium-sized onion, thinly sliced
2 tablespoons melted butter or margarine
2 tablespoons lemon juice
1 tablespoon brown sugar
½ cup chili sauce
1 tablespoon Worcestershire sauce
1 tablespoon prepared mustard
½ cup water
1 cup chopped celery
1 teaspoon salt
¼ teaspoon pepper

Brown short ribs on all sides in shortening. Combine remaining ingredients and heat to boiling point. Pour sauce over short ribs; cover and cook over low heat 1½–2 hours or until meat is tender. Serves 4–6.

STEAK MANDARIN

1 pound top round steak, cut 1 inch thick
½ cup sliced onions
1 cup cooked bamboo sprouts
2 tablespoons melted shortening
1 small clove garlic, crushed
1½ teaspoons sugar
1 teaspoon salt
⅛ teaspoon pepper
1 tablespoon soy sauce
1 cup beef bouillon
1 tablespoon cornstarch
¼ cup cold water

Cut meat into thin strips. Cook meat, onions and bamboo sprouts in shortening until meat is cooked; add garlic, sugar, salt, pepper, soy sauce and bouillon. Cover and cook over low heat 10 minutes. Combine cornstarch and cold water. Add to meat mixture and cook, stirring constantly, until thickened. Serves 4–6.

IOWA BEEF STEW

1 pound beef chuck, cut in 1 inch pieces
3 tablespoons melted shortening
¼ cup chopped onion
1 clove garlic, minced
1 No. 2 can tomatoes
1 teaspoon salt
⅛ teaspoon pepper
1 cup canned lima beans
1 cup canned whole kernel corn

Brown beef on all sides in shortening. Add onion, garlic, tomatoes, salt and pepper. Cover and cook over low heat 1½–2 hours or until meat is tender. Add lima beans and corn. Heat to serving temperature. Thicken liquid, as desired. Serves 4.

BEEF STROGANOFF

1 pound beef round, cut in 1 inch cubes
2 tablespoons melted shortening
2 cups chopped onions
½ teaspoon salt
1 teaspoon celery seed
3 cups noodles
1 4-ounce can mushrooms
½ cup sour cream
3 cups tomato juice
1 tablespoon Worcestershire sauce

Cook beef in shortening until it is well browned on all sides. Add onions and cook until tender. Add salt and celery seed. Add noodles and mushrooms. Combine remaining ingredients and pour over beef mixture. Cover and simmer 30 minutes. Serves 4.

FLEMISH CARBONADE

2½ pounds boneless beef chuck,
    cut in cubes
½ cup all-purpose flour
2 teaspoons salt
½ teaspoon pepper
2 tablespoons shortening
¼ cup butter or margarine
4 medium onions, sliced
1 12-ounce can or bottle beer
1 clove garlic, peeled
3 sprigs parsley
1 bay leaf
¼ teaspoon dried thyme
2 2-inch pieces celery

Dredge meat with flour, then sprinkle with salt and pepper. Heat shortening in a Dutch oven or heavy skillet until very hot. Add meat and brown on all sides. Meanwhile, melt butter or margarine in a skillet and sauté onion slices until tender. Add sautéed onions, beer and garlic clove speared with a wooden pick. Place parsley, bay leaf and thyme in the curve of one piece of celery. Cover with second piece of celery. Tie securely with a white string. Add to carbonade. Cover and cook over low heat 1¼ hours, or until tender. Discard garlic and celery mixture. Skim off the surface fat. Serves 4–6.

CLASSIC MEAT LOAF

1 pound ground beef
½ pound ground pork
2 cups fine dry bread crumbs
1 egg, well beaten
1 cup milk
½ cup chopped onions
1 teaspoon salt
1 tablespoon Worcestershire sauce

Combine all ingredients and mix well. Pack into greased 9″ x 5″ x 3″ baking pan. Bake in moderate oven (350° F.) 1½ hours. Serves 6–8.

BEEF CHOW MEIN

½ cup sliced onions
½ cup chopped mushrooms
1½ cups diced celery
3 tablespoons melted butter or margarine
1½ tablespoons all-purpose flour
1 cup beef stock
2 cups diced, cooked beef
1 cup sliced water chestnuts
¼ teaspoon salt
¼ teaspoon soy sauce
Chinese noodles

Separate onion slices into rings; cook onion rings, mushrooms and celery in butter or margarine until tender. Blend in flour. Gradually add stock and cook, stirring constantly, until thickened. Add beef, water chestnuts, salt and soy sauce. Heat to serving temperature. Serve over noodles. Serves 4.

SAUERBRATEN

1 clove garlic, cut in half
3 pounds beef round
1 tablespoon salt
¼ teaspoon pepper
2 cups vinegar
2 cups water
½ cup sliced onions
1 bay leaf
1 teaspoon peppercorns
¼ cup sugar
3 tablespoons melted shortening

Rub cut side of garlic over meat. Sprinkle meat with salt and pepper. Combine vinegar, water, onions, bay leaf, peppercorns and sugar; heat to boiling point. Pour over meat and chill at least 4 days. Drain meat and reserve liquid. Brown meat well in shortening. Add half of liquid. Cover and simmer 2½–3 hours or until meat is tender. Add more liquid during cooking period if necessary. Serves 6–8.

ROAST BEEF HASH

¼ cup chopped onion
1 cup diced celery
2 tablespoons melted shortening
1½ cups ground, cooked roast beef
1 cup diced, cooked potatoes
½ cup fine dry bread crumbs
2 tablespoons chopped parsley
1 teaspoon salt
1 cup milk

Cook onion and celery in shortening until tender. Add remaining ingredients and mix well. Turn into greased shallow baking pan. Bake in hot oven (400° F.) 25 minutes. Serves 6.

GOURMET PORTERHOUSE STEAK

1 3-pound porterhouse steak,
    cut 1½ inches thick
½ cup crumbled blue cheese
¼ cup light cream
1 tablespoon grated onion
1 teaspoon lemon juice
1 teaspoon Worcestershire sauce
⅛ teaspoon salt

Broil steak 3 or 4 inches from source of heat 15–20 minutes (depending upon desired degree of doneness), turning once. Combine blue cheese with remaining ingredients and spread over steak. Broil until cheese melts. Serves 4.

SAVORY SWISS STEAKS

2 pounds round steak, cut
    1½ inches thick
1½ cups all-purpose flour
2 tablespoons melted shortening
¼ cup sliced onion
1 cup tomato juice
1 cup tomato sauce
¼ cup lemon juice
1 teaspoon sugar
½ teaspoon dry mustard

½ teaspoon chili powder
1 teaspoon salt
¼ cup sliced stuffed olives

Cut steak into serving pieces; coat with flour. Brown meat on both sides in shortening. Combine remaining ingredients and pour over meat. Cover and simmer 2–2½ hours or until meat is tender. Serves 6.

RED FLANNEL HASH

1½ cups cooked chopped corned beef,
    or 12-ounce can
¼ teaspoon salt
2½ cups cooked chopped potatoes
1 cup cooked chopped beets
½ cup finely chopped onions
1 tablespoon chili sauce
2 tablespoons butter or margarine

Combine all ingredients and mix lightly. In skillet melt butter or margarine; add corned-beef mixture, spread evenly. Cook over low heat until lightly browned on under side. Serves 4.

LAMB

POTATO LAMB HASH

2 cups ground, cooked lamb
2 tablespoons grated onion
2 tablespoons chopped pimiento
2 cups mashed potatoes
2 tablespoons chili sauce
1 teaspoon salt
3 tablespoons melted shortening

Combine lamb, onion, pimiento, potatoes, chili sauce and salt. Mix well. Cook in shortening over low heat until well browned on both sides. Serves 4.

CURRIED LEG OF LAMB

1 tablespoon fat
2 onions, sliced
1 bay leaf
1½ teaspoons salt
1 4-pound leg of lamb
1 tablespoon curry powder
1½ cups light cream
¼ cup lemon juice

Melt fat in iron kettle. Add onions, bay leaf and salt. Brown meat on all sides; cover and cook 10 minutes. Add curry powder, cream and lemon juice. Cover and cook over low heat about 1½ hours, or until lamb is tender. Serves 6–8.

PICNIC LAMB LOAF

1½ pounds ground lamb shoulder
2 cups cooked rice
½ cup canned tomatoes
2 eggs, slightly beaten
¼ cup chopped onion
1 teaspoon celery seed
1 tablespoon prepared mustard
1 tablespoon chili sauce

Combine all ingredients and mix lightly. Pack into greased 9" x 5" x 3" pan. Bake in slow oven (325° F.) about 1½ hours. Serves 6.

APRICOT-MINT LAMB ROAST

1 4-pound leg of lamb
½ teaspoon salt
⅛ teaspoon pepper
1 teaspoon ginger
¼ teaspoon nutmeg
1 cup apricot nectar
1 tablespoon mint jelly

Place lamb on rack in shallow baking pan. Combine remaining ingredients; pour over lamb. Bake in slow oven (325° F.) 2 hours, or until done. Baste frequently during baking with apricot mixture. Serves 6–8.

BRAISED LAMB SHANKS

2 pounds lamb shanks
¼ cup melted shortening
1 tablespoon Worcestershire sauce
1 teaspoon salt
¼ teaspoon pepper
2 cups water
1 cup diced carrots
1 cup diced potatoes
½ cup chopped celery
¼ cup grated onion

Brown lamb shanks in shortening. Add Worcestershire sauce, salt, pepper and water. Cover and simmer 1½ hours. Add vegetables. Cover and cook about 25 minutes, or until vegetables are tender. Thicken stock as desired. Serves 4.

DUBLIN LAMB STEW

2 pounds lamb shoulder
Boiling water
1 cup diced turnip
2 cups cubed potatoes
½ cup sliced onions
1 cup diced carrots
1 teaspoon salt
⅛ teaspoon pepper
1 bay leaf

Cut meat in small pieces. Add enough boiling water to cover. Cover and cook over low heat about 2 hours. Add remaining ingredients and cook, covered, about 25 minutes, or until vegetables are tender. Thicken as desired. Serve with dumplings, as desired. Serves 6.

SHISH KABOB

1½ pounds lean lamb, cut in 1 inch cubes
2 medium-sized tomatoes, cut in wedges
¼ pound mushrooms, cut in halves
2 small onions, cut in ¼-inch slices
2 tablespoons oil
1 teaspoon salt
⅛ teaspoon pepper

Alternate lamb, tomato wedges, mushrooms, and onions on skewers. Brush with oil and sprinkle with salt and pepper. Broil 3 or 4 inches from source of heat 10 minutes on each side. Serves 6.

PORK AND HAM

SWEET AND SOUR SPARERIBS

3 pounds spareribs
¼ cup melted shortening
¼ teaspoon ginger
2 teaspoons salt
¼ teaspoon pepper
1 tablespoon sugar
1 cup white vinegar
3 tablespoons soy sauce
¼ cup chopped onion
1 orange, thinly sliced

Brown spareribs in shortening. Combine ginger, salt, pepper, sugar, vinegar and soy sauce. Heat to boiling point. Pour over spareribs. Top with onion and orange slices. Cover and simmer 1–1½ hours, or until meat is tender. Serves 4.

GLORIA'S HAM AND YAM CASSEROLE

2 cups diced, cooked ham
2 cups cooked green beans
1 can condensed cream of mushroom soup
4 medium-sized yams, cooked and peeled
¼ teaspoon nutmeg
¼ teaspoon cinnamon
¼ teaspoon salt
1 tablespoon butter or margarine

Combine ham, beans and soup. Turn into greased 1½-quart baking dish. Mash yams and beat until light and fluffy. Fold in spices, salt, and butter or margarine. Pile yam mixture over ham mixture. Bake in moderate oven (350° F.) 30–35 minutes. Serves 6.

PORK CANTONESE

½ cup all-purpose flour
½ teaspoon salt
⅛ teaspoon pepper
1 pound pork, cut in 1-inch cubes
1 egg, slightly beaten
2 tablespoons melted shortening
3 tablespoons water
1 tablespoon cornstarch
¼ cup sugar
¾ cup chopped green pepper
¾ cup canned pineapple chunks
¾ cup pineapple juice
3 cups cooked, hot rice

Combine flour, salt and pepper. Dip pork into flour mixture, then in egg. Coat with flour mixture. Brown on all sides in shortening. Add water and cook over low heat, covered, 20 minutes. Cook, uncovered, 10 minutes. Combine cornstarch and sugar; add green pepper, pineapple and pineapple juice. Cook over low heat, stirring constantly, until thickened. Add pork. Serve over rice. Serves 4.

CELERY-STUFFED PICNIC SHOULDER

1 5-pound smoked ham shoulder,
   with bone
2 tablespoons chopped onion
1 cup diced celery
2 tablespoons melted butter or margarine
1 cup fine dry bread crumbs
½ teaspoon salt
⅛ teaspoon pepper

Cover ham shoulder (also called picnic shoulder) with water. Cover and simmer 2–2½ hours or until tender. Cool thoroughly. Remove bone and skin. (Or return meat to butcher and ask him to remove bone so that cavity can be stuffed.) Cook onion and celery in butter or margarine until tender. Add bread crumbs, salt and pepper; mix lightly. Stuff shoulder with bread-crumb mixture. Fasten with skewers. Place on rack in shallow baking pan. Bake in moderate oven (350° F.) 30 minutes. Serves 8.

MUSHROOM AND PORK TETRAZZINI

¾ cup sliced mushrooms
2 tablespoons chopped onion
1 tablespoon chopped pimiento
¼ cup melted butter or margarine
3 tablespoons all purpose flour
¼ teaspoon salt
⅛ teaspoon pepper
2½ cups milk
2 cups cooked, diced pork
1 8-ounce package egg noodles, cooked

Cook mushrooms, onion and pimiento in butter or margarine until onion is tender. Blend in flour; add salt and pepper. Gradually add milk and cook over low heat, stirring constantly, until thickened. Add pork and mix well. Turn noodles into greased shallow baking dish. Top with pork mixture. Bake in hot oven (400° F.) about 15 minutes. Serves 6.

SCHNITZ UN KNEPP

2 cups dried apples
1 3½–4 pound ham butt
¼ cup firmly packed brown sugar
1 cup sifted all-purpose flour
1 teaspoon baking powder
⅛ teaspoon salt
⅓ cup milk
2 tablespoons melted butter or margarine
1 egg, well beaten

Soak apples in enough water to cover several hours. Cook ham butt, covered, in enough water to cover over low heat until almost tender. Add apples and brown sugar and cook, covered, 30 minutes. Sift flour, baking powder and salt together; add remaining ingredients and mix well. Drop by tablespoonfuls into ham mixture. Cover and simmer 15–20 minutes. Serves 6.

FRESH HAM WITH APPLE STUFFING

1 6½-pound fresh ham
1 No. 2½ can sauerkraut
¼ cup finely chopped onion
2 small apples, cored, pared and chopped
Salt and pepper

Ask butcher to remove bone from ham so that bone area can be stuffed. Drain sauerkraut. Combine sauerkraut, onion and apples; mix well. Stuff ham with sauerkraut mixture. Fasten with skewers. Score rind and sprinkle with salt and pepper. Place fat side up on rack in shallow baking pan. Bake in moderate oven (350° F.) 3–3½ hours or until tender. Serves 8–10.

DELUXE HAM FRITTERS

1 cup sifted all-purpose flour
1 teaspoon baking powder
½ teaspoon salt
⅛ teaspoon pepper
2 cups ground cooked ham
2 cups cooked peas
2 eggs, separated
¼ cup melted shortening

Sift flour, baking powder and salt together. Add pepper, ham and peas. Beat egg yolks well and add to ham mixture. Mix lightly. Beat egg whites until stiff and fold into ham mixture. Drop by tablespoons into shortening and cook until well browned on both sides. Serves 6.

SAUSAGE PATTIES

4 medium-sized potatoes, peeled,
   cooked and chopped
½ pound sausage, ground
1 tablespoon grated onion
2 eggs, slightly beaten
2 tablespoons chopped parsley
½ teaspoon salt
⅛ teaspoon pepper
½ cup fine dry bread crumbs
3 tablespoons melted shortening

Combine potatoes and sausage. Add onion, eggs, parsley, salt and pepper. Mix well. Shape into 8 patties. Coat with bread crumbs. Cook in shortening over low heat 10 minutes; turn patties and cook 10–15 minutes. Serves 4.

BRAISED PORK AND KRAUT

1 cup sliced onions
¼ cup melted butter or margarine
1½ pounds pork tenderloin,
   cut in 1-inch cubes
2 cups sauerkraut
1 teaspoon salt

¼ teaspoon nutmeg
1 cup sour cream

Cook onions in butter or margarine until tender. Remove onions from pan. Add pork to pan and brown well on all sides. Add onions, sauerkraut and salt. Cover and cook over low heat 40 minutes. Add nutmeg and sour cream and mix lightly. Heat to serving temperature, stirring occasionally. Serves 4–6.

SPARERIBS ORCHARD STYLE

2 onions, chopped
6 tart apples, chopped
¼ cup firmly packed brown sugar
1 cup toasted bread crumbs
3 pounds spareribs, in 2 parts
¼ teaspoon salt
⅛ teaspoon black pepper

Combine onions, apples, sugar and crumbs. Cover 1 part of ribs with stuffing. Place other section on top and season with salt and pepper. Bake, uncovered, in moderate oven (350° F.) until tender, about 1½ hours. Serves 6.

PORK CHOP SKILLET

4 loin pork chops
2 tablespoons melted shortening
¾ cup rice
2 medium-sized tomatoes, cut in halves
1 green pepper, cut in thin strips
1 teaspoon salt
¼ teaspoon pepper
1 can beef bouillon

Brown chops on both sides in shortening. Turn into greased 2-quart casserole. Arrange rice, tomatoes and pepper strips over chops. Sprinkle with salt and pepper. Pour bouillon over other ingredients. Cover and bake in moderate oven (350° F.) 45–50 minutes. Serves 4.

APPLE-HAM CASSEROLE

3 cups diced cooked ham
2 tablespoons prepared mustard
2 apples, cored and sliced
2 tablespoons lemon juice
½ cup brown sugar, firmly packed
1 teaspoon grated orange rind

Arrange ham in greased shallow baking dish. Spread mustard over ham. Arrange apple slices over ham mixture and brush with lemon juice. Combine sugar and orange rind; sprinkle over ham mixture. Bake in moderate oven (350° F.) 30–35 minutes. Serves 4.

BEAN AND SAUSAGE CASSEROLE

4 cups cooked navy beans
½ cup chili sauce
1 tablespoon prepared mustard
1 tablespoon prepared horseradish
1 cup firmly packed brown sugar
3 tablespoons chopped onion
1 pound pork sausage links

Combine beans, chili sauce, mustard, horseradish, sugar and onion. Turn into greased 1½-quart baking dish. Arrange sausage links over bean mixture. Bake in moderate oven (350° F.) 50 minutes. Serves 6.

HAM STEAK WAIKIKI

4 ½-pound ham steaks
4 slices canned pineapple
2 tablespoons toasted almonds
2 tablespoons honey
1 cup orange juice
½ cup white wine
½ cup crushed pineapple

Grease large heated skillet with a piece of fat trimmed from ham steak. Brown ham steaks in skillet. Add pineapple slices, almonds, honey, orange juice, wine and crushed pineapple. Cover and simmer until ham is tender, about 30 minutes. Serves 4.

CITY SCRAPPLE

1 cup white corn meal
1 quart boiling water
1 teaspoon salt
1 pound pork sausage
¼ teaspoon thyme
¼ teaspoon sage

Gradually add cornmeal to boiling water. Add remaining ingredients and mix well. Cook over hot water, covered, 1½ hours, stirring frequently. Pour into loaf pan and chill until firm. Serves 6.

HAM LOAF

1 pound ground ham
1 pound ground pork
1 cup crushed wheat cereal flakes
2 eggs, slightly beaten
1 cup milk
½ teaspoon salt
⅛ teaspoon pepper

Combine all ingredients and mix well. Pack into 9″ x 5″ x 3″ pan. Bake in moderate oven (350° F.) about 1½ hours. Serves 6–8.

BROILED HAM AND BEANS AU GRATIN

1 slice ham, cut 1-inch thick
1 No. 2 can green beans, drained
1 cup grated Swiss cheese

Broil ham 3 inches from source of heat 10 minutes. Turn ham and broil 8 minutes. Arrange beans over ham; top with cheese. Broil 4 or 5 inches from source of heat about 3 minutes, or until cheese is melted. Serves 4.

LIVER, HEART, KIDNEY, SWEETBREADS, TRIPE AND TONGUE

TORY BEEF AND KIDNEY STEW

2 pounds round steak
¼ cup all-purpose flour
2 tablespoons melted shortening
1 beef kidney
3 cups water
1 teaspoon salt
1 teaspoon Worcestershire sauce
2 cups sliced carrots
½ cup sliced onions
2 tablespoons chopped parsley

Cut round steak into 1″ cubes. Coat with flour. Brown well in shortening. Remove membrane and fat from kidney. Cut into ½″ cubes. Combine beef, kidney, water, salt and Worcestershire sauce. Cover and cook over low heat 1½ hours. Add remaining ingredients; cook covered about 20 minutes, or until vegetables are tender. Serves 6.

CALF'S LIVER CHIANTI

1 pound calf's liver, thinly sliced
3 tablespoons melted butter
¼ teaspoon salt

⅛ teaspoon pepper
¼ cup chopped celery
¼ cup chopped chives
½ cup red wine

Brown liver on both sides in butter. Add remaining ingredients. Cover and bake in slow oven (325° F.) 25–30 minutes. Serves 4.

SAUTÉED LIVER PATTIES

1 pound beef liver
1 small onion
1 tablespoon all-purpose flour
1 egg, slightly beaten
½ teaspoon salt
1 teaspoon Worcestershire sauce
½ cup fine dry bread crumbs
3 tablespoons melted butter or margarine

Cut liver into thin slices. Cover liver with boiling water and cook over low heat 10 minutes. Drain. Put liver and onion through meat grinder; add flour, egg, salt and Worcestershire sauce. Mix well. Shape into 4 patties. Coat with crumbs. Cook patties in butter or margarine over low heat until well browned on both sides. Serves 4.

SAVORY TONGUE DIVAN

½ cup vinegar
2 teaspoons salt
2 tablespoons sugar
2 bay leaves
1 teaspoon whole cloves
½ cup sliced onions
4 quarts boiling water
1 5-pound tongue

Combine all ingredients. Cover and simmer 3½–4 hours, or until tongue is tender.

Drain and remove outer skin. Slice diagonally to serve. Serves 6–8.

SWEETBREADS À LA POULETTE

1 pair sweetbreads
1 tablespoon vinegar
1 teaspoon salt
1 quart boiling water
2 cups diced, cooked veal
¼ cup butter or margarine
3 tablespoons all-purpose flour
2 cups milk
⅛ teaspoon pepper
¼ teaspoon salt

Soak sweetbreads in ice water 20 minutes; drain. Add vinegar and the 1 teaspoon salt to boiling water and add sweetbreads. Cook, covered, over low heat, 30 minutes. Drain and place again in ice water. Drain. Separate sweetbreads. Remove fat and connecting tissue and fine membrane. Dry. Break sweetbreads into pieces and combine with veal. Melt butter or margarine and blend in flour; gradually add milk and cook, stirring constantly, until thickened. Add veal, sweetbreads, pepper and the ¼ teaspoon salt. Heat to serving temperature. Serves 4.

PHILADELPHIA TRIPE CAKES

1 pound boiled tripe
1 egg
½ cup dry bread crumbs
1 teaspoon onion juice
1 teaspoon lemon juice
1 teaspoon salt
⅛ teaspoon black pepper

Grind tripe and combine with remaining ingredients. Shape into patties and fry in greased skillet until browned on both sides. Serves 4.

VEAL

BUDAPEST CABBAGE ROLLS

½ pound ground veal
½ pound ground pork
2 tablespoons chopped onion
2 tablespoons melted butter or margarine
1 cup soft bread crumbs
¼ cup beef bouillon
2 egg yolks, slightly beaten
8 large cabbage leaves, blanched
2 cups cooked tomatoes
½ teaspoon salt

Combine veal, pork, onion, butter or margarine, bread crumbs, bouillon and egg yolks. Mix well. Spread meat mixture over cabbage leaves. Roll up and fasten with toothpicks. Arrange cabbage rolls in greased shallow baking pan; pour tomatoes over cabbage rolls. Sprinkle with salt. Bake in moderate oven (350° F.) 1 hour. Serves 4.

VEAL PAPRIKA

1 cup grated carrots
¼ cup melted butter
½ teaspoon salt
1 teaspoon paprika
½ teaspoon pepper
2 pounds veal shoulder, diced
2 cups beef stock or bouillon
1 tablespoon all-purpose flour
½ cup sour cream

Cook carrots in butter until tender. Add salt, paprika, pepper, veal and stock or bouillon. Cover and cook over low heat about 1 hour, or until veal is tender. Combine flour and sour cream. Add to veal mixture and cook, stirring constantly, until mixture boils. Serve with dumplings if desired. Serves 6–8.

FRENCH HAM AND VEAL LOAF

2½ pounds ground veal
½ pound ground ham
1 cup soft bread crumbs
¾ cup chopped mushrooms
½ cup finely chopped green pepper
2 tablespoons prepared horseradish
1 tablespoon prepared mustard
1 tablespoon Worcestershire sauce
Dash of Tabasco
1 egg, well beaten

Combine all ingredients and mix well. Pack into greased 9″ x 5″ x 3″ pan. Bake in slow oven (325° F.) 1½–2 hours. Serves 6.

VEAL STEW CHAMPIGNON

2 pounds boneless veal shoulder,
   cut in 1-inch cubes
3 tablespoons melted shortening
1½ teaspoons salt
⅛ teaspoon pepper
¼ teaspoon paprika
2 cups water
1 4-ounce can mushrooms, drained
1 package frozen mixed vegetables
3 tablespoons all-purpose flour
½ cup water

Brown meat in shortening. Add salt, pepper, paprika and 2 cups water. Cover and cook over low heat 1½ hours. Add mushrooms and vegetables. Cover and cook about 15 minutes or until vegetables are tender. Combine flour and ½ cup water; add to meat mixture and cook, stirring constantly, until thickened. Serves 6–8.

VEAL SCALLOPINI

¼ cup all-purpose flour
1 teaspoon salt
¼ teaspoon pepper
1½ pounds veal cutlet, thinly sliced
⅓ cup olive oil
¼ cup minced onion
¼ cup chopped green pepper
1½ cups tomato sauce
¼ cup water

Combine flour, salt and pepper. Coat veal with flour mixture. Heat olive oil; add onion and green pepper and cook until tender. Remove onion and pepper; reserve drippings. Brown meat on both sides in drippings. Combine tomato sauce and water. Pour over veal. Add onion and green pepper. Cook, covered, over low heat 15–20 minutes. Serves 6.

VEAL FRICASSEE

2 pounds veal rump, cut in 1-inch cubes
¼ cup all-purpose flour, approx.
3 tablespoons melted shortening
½ cup hot water
½ cup sliced onions
1 cup diced celery
2 cups cubed potatoes
1 cup sliced carrots
1 teaspoon salt
¼ teaspoon pepper

Coat veal with flour; brown on all sides in shortening. Add water; cover and cook over low heat about 40 minutes. Add remaining ingredients; cover and cook 20–25 minutes, or until vegetables are tender. Serves 6.

VEAL CHOPS WITH PINEAPPLE

6 shoulder veal chops
¼ cup melted shortening
1 teaspoon salt
6 slices canned pineapple
1 cup pineapple juice

Brown chops on both sides in shortening; sprinkle with salt. Arrange pineapple slices over chops. Add pineapple juice. Cover and simmer 45–50 minutes or until chops are tender. Serves 4.

BRAISED VEAL LYON

1 3-pound veal shoulder, boned and rolled
2 tablespoons melted shortening
1 teaspoon salt
⅛ teaspoon pepper
1 medium-sized orange, thinly sliced
¾ cup orange juice

Brown veal shoulder on all sides in shortening. Season with salt and pepper; arrange orange slices over veal. Add orange juice. Cover and cook over low heat about 2½ hours, or until veal is tender. Serves 6.

DRIED BEEF, FRANKS

SPANISH FRANKFURTERS

½ cup finely chopped onions
¼ cup chopped celery
¼ cup chopped green pepper
3 tablespoons melted butter or margarine
1 can condensed tomato soup
1 tablespoon brown sugar
2 tablespoons Worcestershire sauce
2 tablespoons vinegar
1 tablespoon prepared mustard
8 frankfurters

Cook onions, celery and green pepper in butter or margarine until onions are tender. Add soup, sugar, Worcestershire sauce, vinegar and mustard. Mix well. Cook over low heat, stirring occasionally, 10 minutes. Add frankfurters and heat to serving temperature. Serves 4.

FRANKFURTER-POTATO CASSEROLE

1 pound frankfurters, cut in 1-inch pieces
2 tablespoons chopped onion
¼ cup chopped green pepper
½ cup chopped celery
¼ cup melted butter or margarine
3 tablespoons all-purpose flour
1¼ cups milk
1 teaspoon salt
⅛ teaspoon pepper
2 cups mashed, seasoned potatoes

Cook frankfurters, onion, green pepper and celery in butter or margarine until onion is tender; blend in flour. Gradually add milk and cook, stirring constantly, until thickened. Add salt and pepper. Turn into greased 1½-quart casserole. Arrange potatoes over frankfurter mixture. Bake in moderate oven (350° F.) 35 minutes. Serves 4.

OLIVE-CHIPPED BEEF CASSEROLE

¼ pound chipped beef
3 tablespoons melted butter or margarine
2 tablespoons all-purpose flour
2 cups milk
1 cup chopped celery
½ cup sliced ripe olives
½ cup grated American cheese
2 cups cooked egg noodles

Cook beef in butter or margarine 5 minutes. Blend in flour. Gradually add milk and cook, stirring constantly, until thickened. Add remaining ingredients and mix lightly. Turn into greased 1½-quart baking dish. Bake in moderate oven (350° F.) 30 minutes. Serves 6.

Macaroni and Spaghetti

MACARONI

NEAPOLITAN MACARONI SALAD

1 8-ounce package elbow macaroni, cooked
1 cup diced celery
2 tablespoons grated onion
¼ cup chopped green pepper
¼ cup sweet pickle relish
1 cup grated carrot
¼ teaspoon garlic salt
1 teaspoon Worcestershire sauce
2 tablespoons vinegar
½ cup salad dressing
2 hard-cooked eggs, chopped

Combine all ingredients, mix lightly. Chill thoroughly. Serves 6.

QUICK SAUCEPAN MACARONI AND CHEESE

1 tablespoon salt
3 quarts boiling water
2 cups elbow macaroni (8 ounces)
¼ cup butter or margarine
2 cups grated processed American cheese (about ½ pound)
¼ cup finely chopped onion
Salt and pepper to taste
Pimiento-stuffed green olives

Add 1 tablespoon salt to rapidly boiling water. Gradually add macaroni so that water continues to boil. Cook uncovered, stirring occasionally, until tender. Drain in colander. Combine macaroni, butter or margarine, cheese, onion and salt and pepper to taste. Cook over low heat until cheese is melted. Serve immediately, garnished with olives, as desired. Serves 4–6.

MACARONI AND GREEN PEPPER AU GRATIN

3 medium-sized green peppers
1 tablespoon salt
3 quarts boiling water
2 cups elbow macaroni (8 ounces)
1 cup light cream
2 cups grated, processed American cheese (about ½ pound)
1 teaspoon Worcestershire sauce
1 teaspoon prepared mustard
Salt and pepper to taste

Quarter peppers and remove seeds and membranes. Cover and cook in small amount of boiling salted water until tender, about 10 minutes. Drain. Add the 1 tablespoon salt to rapidly boiling water. Gradually add macaroni so that water continues to boil. Cook uncovered, stirring occasionally, until tender. Drain in colander. Combine cream and cheese. Cook over low heat until cheese is melted, stirring constantly. Add peppers, macaroni and remaining ingredients. Mix well and turn into greased 2-quart casserole. Bake in moderate oven (350° F.) 30 minutes. Serves 4–6.

BOHEMIAN MACARONI

1 1-pound jar pickled red cabbage
2 medium-sized onions, thinly sliced
1 tablespoon butter or margarine
1 cup grated processed Swiss cheese,
    (about ¼ pound)
1 tablespoon salt
3 quarts boiling water
2 cups elbow macaroni (8 ounces)
Salt and pepper to taste

Combine cabbage, onions, butter or margarine and cheese. Cook over medium heat until cheese is melted, stirring occasionally. Add the 1 tablespoon salt to rapidly boiling water. Gradually add macaroni so that water continues to boil. Cook uncovered, stirring occasionally, until tender. Drain in colander. Combine macaroni and cabbage mixture; toss lightly. Season to taste with salt and pepper. Serves 4–6.

MACARONI CHEESE LOAF

1 tablespoon salt
3 quarts boiling water
2 cups elbow macaroni (8 ounces)
1 14½-ounce can evaporated milk

2 cups grated Cheddar cheese
    (about ½ pound)
1 4-ounce can pimientos, drained
    and chopped
½ cup chopped parsley
1 tablespoon grated onion
1½ teaspoons salt
Freshly ground pepper

Add 1 tablespoon salt to rapidly boiling water. Gradually add macaroni so that water continues to boil. Cook uncovered, stirring occasionally, until tender. Drain in colander. Combine macaroni and remaining ingredients. Mix lightly but thoroughly. Turn into greased 9″ x 5″ x 3″ loaf pan. Place in pan of hot water. Bake in slow oven (325° F.) 45–50 minutes, or until firm. To serve, unmold and slice. Serves 4–6.

VEGETABLE-MACARONI MEDLEY

¼ pound elbow macaroni, cooked
1 cup cooked green beans
2 onions, chopped
2 green peppers, chopped
½ cup diced cooked carrots
2 cups canned tomatoes
1 cup diced American cheese
½ cup cracker crumbs
1 teaspoon salt
¼ teaspoon pepper

Alternate layers of macaroni, vegetables and cheese in greased 1½-quart casserole. Top with crumbs. Add salt and pepper. Bake in moderate oven (375° F.) 35–40 minutes. Serves 6.

DEEP-SEA MACARONI

1 clove garlic, minced
1 cup sliced mushrooms
½ cup melted butter
½ cup chopped parsley
¾ cup diced shrimp
¾ cup diced oysters

¼ teaspoon salt
1 8-ounce package shell macaroni, cooked

Combine garlic, mushrooms, butter and parsley. Cover and cook over low heat 15 minutes. Add shrimp, oysters and salt; cook 5 minutes. Arrange macaroni on serving platter and top with shrimp-oyster mixture. Serves 4.

NOODLES

LYONNAISE NOODLES

1 tablespoon salt
3 quarts boiling water
8 ounces medium egg noodles
    (about 4 cups)
¼ cup butter or margarine
¼ cup finely chopped onion
1½ teaspoons paprika
2 tablespoons chopped chives

Add the 1 tablespoon salt to rapidly boiling water. Gradually add noodles so that water continues to boil. Cook uncovered, stirring occasionally, until tender. Drain in colander. Meanwhile, melt butter or margarine over low heat; add onion and cook until tender. Add paprika and mix thoroughly. Combine noodles, and butter or margarine mixture; mix thoroughly. Sprinkle with chopped chives. Serve with pot roast, as desired. Serves 6.

NUTTY NOODLES

2 tablespoons blanched slivered almonds
1 tablespoon melted butter
1½ cups cooked, diced beef
1 beef bouillon cube
½ cup hot water

1 teaspoon salt
8 ounces medium egg noodles, cooked
1 cup sour cream

Cook almonds in butter until lightly browned. Add beef and brown. Combine bouillon cube and water; stir until dissolved. Add bouillon, salt and noodles to beef mixture. Cook over low heat, stirring occasionally, 10 minutes. Add sour cream and mix lightly. Heat to serving temperature. Serves 4.

NOODLES WITH CLAMS

1 10½-ounce can minced clams
½ cup diced celery
3 tablespoons butter or margarine
½ cup chopped onions
1 small clove garlic, finely chopped
3 tablespoons all-purpose flour
1½ cups milk
2 cups grated sharp Cheddar cheese
    (about ½ pound)
1 No. 303 can peas, drained
Salt and pepper to taste
1 tablespoon salt
3 quarts boiling water
8 ounces medium egg noodles
    (about 4 cups)

Combine clams and celery; heat to boiling point and cook 10–15 minutes, or until celery is tender. Melt butter or margarine over low heat. Add onions and garlic and sauté 5 minutes. Add flour and blend. Gradually add milk and clam mixture and cook until thickened, stirring constantly. Add cheese and stir until cheese is melted. Add peas and salt and pepper to taste. Meanwhile, add the 1 tablespoon salt to rapidly boiling water. Gradually add noodles so that water continues to boil. Cook uncovered, stirring occasionally, until tender. Drain in colander. Serve sauce over noodles. Serves 4–6.

NOODLE AND LETTUCE TOSS

1 tablespoon salt
3 quarts boiling water
8 ounces medium egg noodles
    (about 4 cups)
¼ cup butter or margarine
6 cups shredded lettuce (1 medium-sized
    head)
¼ cup grated Parmesan cheese
Salt and pepper

Add the 1 tablespoon salt to rapidly boiling water. Gradually add noodles so that water continues to boil. Cook uncovered, stirring occasionally, until tender. Drain in colander. Meanwhile, melt butter or margarine and add lettuce. Cook over low heat 5 minutes, tossing lightly. Combine lettuce, noodles and cheese; season with salt and pepper. Toss lightly but thoroughly. Serves 4–6.

LAMB AND NOODLE LOAF

4 ounces egg noodles
2 cups cooked, ground lamb
¼ cup chopped green pepper
2 tablespoons grated onion
1 teaspoon salt
⅛ teaspoon pepper
1 tablespoon chopped pimiento
1 cup light cream

Cook noodles according to package directions. Drain. Add remaining ingredients and mix lightly. Turn into greased 9″ x 5″ x 3″ pan. Bake in moderate oven (350° F.) 1¼ hours. Serves 4–6.

SAUTÉED NOODLES AND ALMONDS

6 tablespoons butter or margarine
8 ounces medium egg noodles
    (about 4 cups)
1 large onion, thinly sliced
⅔ cup chopped, toasted almonds
3 cups milk
Salt and pepper to taste

Melt butter or margarine and add noodles, onion and almonds. Cook over medium heat, stirring occasionally, until noodles are browned. Add milk and cook, stirring occasionally, 15–20 minutes, or until noodles are tender. Season with salt and pepper. Serves 4.

NOODLE CHEESE DESSERT

8 ounces egg noodles, cooked
4 eggs, beaten
2 cups cottage cheese
¾ cup sugar
2 teaspoons cinnamon
½ teaspoon nutmeg
¼ teaspoon ground ginger
1 cup crushed salted almonds
½ cup melted butter

Combine all ingredients and mix lightly. Turn into greased 1½-quart baking dish. Bake in moderate oven (350° F.) 20–30 minutes, or until lightly browned. Serves 6.

TURKEY NOODLE BAKE

6 tablespoons butter or margarine
6 tablespoons all-purpose flour
3 cups milk
3 cups cooked noodles
¼ cup grated onion
1 cup cooked peas and carrots
2 cups diced cooked turkey
½ cup grated cheddar cheese
¼ cup buttered cracker crumbs

Melt butter or margarine; blend in flour; gradually add milk and cook, stirring constantly, until thickened. Add noodles, onion, peas and carrots, turkey and cheese; mix lightly. Turn into greased 2-quart casserole. Top with crumbs. Bake in moderate oven (350° F.) about 1 hour. Serves 6.

NOODLES WITH
TOASTED NUTS

3 tablespoons butter
½ cup chopped Brazil nuts
3 cups cooked noodles
1 tablespoon chopped chives

Melt butter. Add nuts. Cook until lightly browned. Pour butter mixture over noodles. Sprinkle with chives Serves 4.

SPAGHETTI

SPAGHETTI WITH TOMATO AND
MUSHROOM SAUCE

2 tablespoons olive or salad oil
2 large onions, chopped
2 cloves garlic, finely chopped
1 pound button mushrooms
1 No. 2½ can tomatoes
1 No. 2 can tomato juice
⅓ cup tomato paste
⅓ cup water
1½ teaspoons salt
¼ teaspoon pepper
2 tablespoons salt
4–6 quarts boiling water
1 pound spaghetti
Grated Parmesan cheese

Heat oil over medium heat. Add onions and garlic and cook until tender. Add mushrooms; cover and cook over low heat 20 minutes, stirring occasionally. Add tomatoes, tomato juice, tomato paste and water. Heat to boiling point over high heat. Reduce heat and cook 1 hour, stirring occasionally. Add the 1½ teaspoon salt and pepper. Add the 2 tablespoons salt to rapidly boiling water about 10 minutes before sauce is done. Gradually add spaghetti so that water continues to boil. Cook uncovered, stirring occasionally, until tender. Drain in colander. Serve sauce over spaghetti. Sprinkle with grated cheese, if desired. Serves 8.

NEAPOLITAN SPAGHETTI SAUCE

1 pound ground beef
1 cup sliced mushrooms
1 small clove garlic, minced
½ cup chopped onions
¼ cup melted butter or margarine
⅛ teaspoon oregano
⅛ teaspoon basil
1 No. 2½ can tomatoes
1 can tomato paste
½ teaspoon salt
⅛ teaspoon pepper

Cook beef, mushrooms, garlic and onions in butter or margarine until onions are tender. Add remaining ingredients and simmer 1–2 hours. Serve with spaghetti, as desired. Makes about 6 cups.

SPAGHETTI WITH CHICKEN LIVERS

1 clove garlic, minced
¼ cup cooking oil
¼ cup minced chives
1 cup chopped chicken livers
1 cup cooked tomatoes
¼ cup sliced mushrooms
½ cup white wine
½ teaspoon salt
⅛ teaspoon pepper
½ teaspoon Worcestershire sauce
1 pound spaghetti, cooked
¼ cup butter or margarine

Cook garlic in oil 5 minutes. Add chives and chicken livers; cook 5 minutes. Add tomatoes, mushrooms, wine, salt, pepper and Worcestershire sauce. Simmer 20 minutes. Combine hot spaghetti and butter or margarine; serve chicken liver sauce over spaghetti. Serves 4.

PARSLEY SPAGHETTI

1 tablespoon salt
3 quarts boiling water

8 ounces spaghetti
¼ cup butter or margarine
3 tablespoons finely chopped onion
½ cup finely chopped parsley
¼ teaspoon sweet basil
1 teaspoon salt

Add the 1 tablespoon salt to rapidly boiling water. Gradually add spaghetti so that water continues to boil. Cook uncovered, stirring occasionally, until tender. Drain in colander. While spaghetti is cooking, melt butter or margarine over low heat; add onion, parsley, basil and the 1 teaspoon salt. Cook over low heat 10 minutes. Remove from heat and pour over spaghetti; mix lightly. Serves 4–6.

Gravies and Sauces

CAPER SAUCE PESCADERO

2 tablespoons butter or margarine
2 tablespoons all-purpose flour
2 cups chicken stock or bouillon
1 teaspoon lemon juice
¼ teaspoon salt
½ cup capers

Melt butter or margarine; blend in flour. Gradually add stock or bouillon and cook, stirring constantly, until thickened. Add remaining ingredients and heat to serving temperature, stirring constantly. Serve with fish, as desired. Makes about 2½ cups.

BARBECUE SAUCE

¼ cup chopped onions
1 tablespoon butter, melted
1½ cups chili sauce
1½ cups water
3 tablespoons lemon juice
1 tablespoon brown sugar
1½ tablespoons Worcestershire sauce
1 tablespoon prepared mustard
1 teaspoon salt
1 cup minced celery

Combine all ingredients and simmer over low heat until celery and onion are tender. Serve with hamburgers, as desired. Makes about 4 cups.

HOLLANDAISE SAUCE

¼ cup butter or margarine
2 tablespoons lemon juice
3 egg yolks, well beaten
⅛ teaspoon salt
¼ cup butter or margarine
¼ cup butter or margarine
Dash cayenne pepper

Combine ¼ cup butter or margarine, lemon juice, egg yolks and salt in top of double boiler. Cook over hot water, beating constantly, until butter melts. Add the second ¼ cup butter or margarine and continue cooking, beating constantly, until mixture begins to thicken. Add remaining ¼ cup butter or margarine and cayenne pepper; cook, stirring constantly, until thickened. Serve immediately, with fish and vegetables, as desired. Makes about ¾ cup.

HORSERADISH BUTTER SAUCE

½ cup butter or margarine
3 tablespoons horseradish
⅛ teaspoon salt
Dash of cayenne

Combine all ingredients. Cook over low heat, stirring constantly, until butter melts. Serve with steaks and chops, as desired. Makes about ⅔ cup.

SAUCE DIABLE

¼ cup melted butter or margarine
2 tablespoons water
¼ cup chili sauce
2 teaspoons sugar
½ clove garlic, minced
1 tablespoon Worcestershire sauce
½ teaspoon salt
⅛ teaspoon Tabasco

Combine all ingredients and heat to serving temperature. Serve with lobster or crab. Makes about ½ cup.

EGG AND ANCHOVY SAUCE

3 hard-cooked eggs, chopped
3 anchovies, chopped
1 tablespoon chopped stuffed olives
1 teaspoon grated onion
2 egg yolks
1½ teaspoons prepared mustard
¼ teaspoon salt
3 tablespoons white vinegar

Combine all ingredients and beat until well blended. Chill thoroughly. Serve with fish, as desired. Makes about ¾ cup.

GAME SAUCE

3 tablespoons butter
¼ cup chopped mushrooms
3 tablespoons all-purpose flour
1 cup beef stock
1 cup water
½ teaspoon salt
⅛ teaspoon paprika
2 tablespoons chopped chives
2 tablespoons red wine

Melt butter, add mushrooms and cook until tender. Blend in flour. Gradually add stock and water. Cook over low heat, stirring constantly, until thickened. Add remaining ingredients and heat to serving temperature, stirring constantly. Makes about 3 cups.

ANCHOVY BUTTER SAUCE

⅓ cup butter or margarine
1 tablespoon chopped parsley
¼ teaspoon salt
⅛ teaspoon pepper
1 teaspoon anchovy paste
½ teaspoon prepared mustard
1 tablespoon lemon juice
1 teaspoon Worcestershire sauce

Melt butter or margarine; add remaining ingredients and heat to serving temperature. Serve with fish, as desired. Makes about ⅓ cup.

BROWN GRAVY

¼ cup all-purpose flour
¼ cup melted meat or poultry drippings
2 cups meat or vegetable stock
¼ teaspoon salt
⅛ teaspoon pepper

Blend flour into drippings and cook over low heat until browned. Gradually add stock and cook, stirring constantly, until thickened. Season with salt and pepper. Serve with meat and poultry, as desired. Makes about 2 cups.

RAISIN SAUCE

½ cup raisins
1 cup water
¼ teaspoon cloves
¾ cup firmly packed brown sugar
2 teaspoons cornstarch
⅛ teaspoon salt
1 tablespoon butter or margarine
1 tablespoon lemon juice
1 tablespoon orange juice

Combine raisins, water and cloves. Cook over low heat ten minutes. Combine sugar, cornstarch and salt. Add cornstarch mixture to raisin mixture, and cook, stirring constantly, until thickened. Add remaining ingredients and heat to serving temperature, stirring constantly. Serve with ham or tongue, as desired. Makes about 2 cups.

FLEMISH CARROT SAUCE

¼ cup butter or margarine
¼ cup all-purpose flour
1 cup chicken stock
1 cup light cream
¾ cup grated carrots
¼ teaspoon salt
¼ teaspoon paprika

Melt butter or margarine; blend in flour. Gradually add stock and cream and cook, stirring constantly, until thickened. Add remaining ingredients. Heat to serving temperature, stirring constantly. Serve with fish and vegetables, as desired. Makes about 2¾ cups.

BRUSSELS MUSHROOM SAUCE

½ cup sliced mushrooms
¼ cup melted butter or margarine
¼ cup all-purpose flour
1 cup milk
1 cup light cream
2 tablespoons chopped parsley
¼ teaspoon salt

Cook mushrooms in butter or margarine until tender. Remove mushrooms. Blend in flour. Gradually add milk and cream and cook, stirring constantly, until thickened. Add mushrooms, parsley and salt. Serve with meats, fish, poultry and vegetables, as desired. Makes about 2 cups.

ALMOND SAUCE

⅓ cup slivered blanched almonds
½ cup melted butter
2 tablespoons lemon juice
⅛ teaspoon garlic salt

Cook almonds in butter until lightly browned. Add remaining ingredients and heat to serving temperature. Serve with game, fish, or vegetables, as desired. Makes about 1 cup.

VELOUTE SAUCE

2 tablespoons butter or margarine
2 tablespoons all-purpose flour
1 cup chicken stock
¼ cup light cream
¼ teaspoon salt
⅛ teaspoon pepper

Melt butter or margarine; blend in flour. Gradually add stock and cream and cook, stirring constantly, until thickened. Season with salt and pepper. Serve with poultry, vegetables and fish, as desired. Makes about 1 cup.

FRENCH VINAIGRETTE SAUCE

½ cup French dressing
1 tablespoon chopped green pepper
1 teaspoon grated onion
1 tablespoon chopped parsley
1 tablespoon chopped dill pickle

Combine all ingredients and beat well. Serve with meats and vegetables, as desired. Makes about ¾ cup.

WINE SAUCE

1 tablespoon butter
½ cup currant jelly
2 tablespoons lime juice
Dash cayenne pepper
½ cup water
1 teaspoon salt
½ cup sherry wine

Combine butter, jelly, lime juice, cayenne pepper, water and salt. Simmer 5 minutes. Add sherry wine. Heat to serving temperature. Serve with game, or tongue. Makes about 1½ cups.

ALL-PURPOSE CHEESE SAUCE

3 tablespoons butter or margarine
3 tablespoons all-purpose flour
1½ cups milk
1 cup grated Cheddar or American cheese
1 tablespoon Sherry
⅛ teaspoon salt

Melt butter or margarine; blend in flour. Gradually add milk and cook, stirring constantly, until thickened. Add remaining ingredients and stir until cheese is melted. Serve with meat, fish and vegetables, as desired. Makes about 3 cups.

DANISH CREAM CHEESE SAUCE

1 8-ounce package cream cheese
2 egg yolks
¼ cup lemon juice
⅛ teaspoon salt
⅛ teaspoon pepper

Soften cream cheese and blend in remaining ingredients. Cook over low heat, stirring constantly, until thoroughly heated. Serve with green vegetables and fish, as desired. Makes about 1½ cups.

BOG CRANBERRY SAUCE

4 cups cranberries
1½ cups water
2 cups sugar
⅛ teaspoon salt
1 tablespoon lemon juice

Wash cranberries. Add ¾ cup of the water and cook until cranberries are very tender. Press through sieve. Combine sugar, salt, lemon juice and remaining ¾ cup water; cook 10 minutes. Add strained cranberries and cook 10 minutes. Strain and pour into molds. Chill until firm. Serve with fowl and meat. Makes about 4 cups.

PINEAPPLE CHUTNEY SAUCE

½ cup pineapple jam
2 tablespoons chopped cucumber pickles
¼ cup sherry
1 tablespoon butter or margarine
1 teaspoon chopped pimiento

Combine all ingredients and heat to serving temperature, stirring constantly. Serve with lamb and ham, as desired. Makes about ¾ cup.

DINARD CUCUMBER ONION SAUCE

½ cup chopped cucumber, drained
2 tablespoons grated onion
1 tablespoon vinegar
½ cup heavy cream, whipped
¼ teaspoon salt

Combine cucumber, onion and vinegar. Fold in cream and salt. Chill thoroughly. Serve with fish, as desired. Makes about 1¼ cups.

CHATEAUBRIAND SAUCE

2 tablespoons butter
1 tablespoon lime juice
½ teaspoon salt
1 teaspoon minced parsley
2 cups tomato sauce
Dash Tabasco

Combine butter, lime juice, salt and parsley. Add tomato sauce and Tabasco. Heat to serving temperature. Serve with steak or roast beef. Makes about 2 cups.

HORSERADISH SAUCE FOR SHRIMP

1 cup catsup
1 tablespoon horseradish
2 tablespoons chili sauce
2 tablespoons white vinegar
Dash Tabasco

Combine all ingredients and chill. Makes about 1¼ cups.

INDONESIAN CURRY SAUCE

1 tablespoon chopped onion
2 tablespoons melted butter or margarine
2 tablespoons all-purpose flour
1 tablespoon curry powder
2 cups chicken stock
¼ teaspoon salt

Cook onion in butter or margarine until tender. Blend in flour and curry powder. Gradually add stock and cook, stirring constantly, until thickened. Season with salt. Serve with meats, fish and poultry, as desired. Makes about 2 cups.

WHITE WINE SAUCE

3 tablespoons butter or margarine
3 tablespoons all-purpose flour
¾ cup water
¼ cup dry white wine
1 cup light cream
1 tablespoon Sherry
¼ teaspoon salt

Melt butter or margarine; blend in flour. Gradually add water, white wine, cream, Sherry and salt. Cook, stirring constantly, until thickened. Serve with fish, as desired. Makes about 1¼ cups.

PARISIENNE PARSLEY BUTTER SAUCE

¼ cup butter or margarine
¼ teaspoon garlic salt
¼ teaspoon celery salt
¼ teaspoon paprika
2 tablespoons chopped parsley

Combine all ingredients and cook, stirring occasionally, until butter or margarine melts. Serve with green vegetables, as desired. Makes about 1 cup.

FROZEN HORSERADISH SAUCE

½ cup horseradish
1 tablespoon sugar
¼ teaspoon salt
½ cup salad dressing
1 cup heavy cream, whipped

Combine horseradish, sugar, salt and salad dressing. Fold in cream. Turn into refrigerator tray and freeze until firm. Serve with cold meats, as desired. Makes about 2 cups.

CANTONESE LOBSTER SAUCE

½ cup sliced mushrooms
3 tablespoons melted butter or margarine
2 tablespoons all-purpose flour
1⅓ cups beef stock
½ cup chopped, cooked lobster
¼ teaspoon salt

Cook mushrooms in butter or margarine until tender. Remove mushrooms. Blend in flour. Gradually add stock and cook, stirring constantly, until thickened. Add mushrooms, lobster and salt. Heat to serving temperature, stirring constantly. Serve with fish croquettes and loaves, as desired. Makes about 2 cups.

SAUCE MOULIN

4 onions, sliced
2 tablespoons melted butter
2 tablespoons all-purpose flour
1 cup beef stock
1 tablespoon dry white wine
1 tablespoon chili sauce
¼ teaspoon paprika
Salt and pepper to taste

Cook onions in butter until browned. Remove onions. Stir in flour. Gradually add stock, wine and remaining ingredients and cook until thickened, stirring constantly. Serve with meats or sea food. Makes about 1½ cups.

SOUR CREAM GRAVY

2 tablespoons butter or margarine
2 tablespoons all-purpose flour
½ cup meat or vegetable stock
¾ cup sour cream
¼ teaspoon black pepper
¼ teaspoon salt
¼ teaspoon nutmeg
1 tablespoon chopped parsley

Melt butter or margarine; blend in flour. Gradually add stock and cook over low heat, stirring constantly, until thickened. Add remaining ingredients and heat to serving temperature, stirring constantly. Serve with beef and veal. Makes about 1½ cups.

STEAK SAUCE

½ cup butter or margarine
1 tablespoon Worcestershire sauce
1 tablespoon prepared mustard
2 tablespoons chili sauce
½ teaspoon paprika
2 tablespoons vinegar

Combine all ingredients and heat to serving temperature, stirring occasionally. Serve with steak, as desired. Makes about ¾ cup.

MARSHALL'S SWEET AND SOUR GRAPE SAUCE

1 teaspoon cornstarch
⅔ cup water
½ cup grape jelly
1 tablespoon onion juice
2 tablespoons horseradish
2 tablespoons butter or margarine
⅛ teaspoon salt

Combine cornstarch and water; add remaining ingredients and cook, stirring constantly, until thickened. Serve with meats, as desired. Makes about 1¼ cups.

TOMATO SAUCE

1 No. 2 can tomatoes
¼ teaspoon salt
⅛ teaspoon pepper
1 bay leaf
1 tablespoon chopped onion
2 tablespoons butter or margarine
2 tablespoons all-purpose flour

Combine tomatoes, salt, pepper, bay leaf and onion. Cook over low heat ten minutes; remove bay leaf. Force tomato mixture through sieve. Melt butter and blend in flour. Gradually add tomato mixture and cook, stirring constantly, until thickened. Serve with meat, fish and vegetables, as desired. Makes 1 cup.

OYSTER CHIVE SAUCE

¼ cup butter
¾ cup oysters
¼ cup all-purpose flour
2 cups milk
2 tablespoons sherry
1 tablespoon chopped chives
¼ teaspoon salt

Melt butter, add oysters and cook until edges curl, about 2 minutes. Remove oysters. Stir in flour. Gradually add milk and cook, stirring constantly, until thickened. Add oysters and remaining ingredients and heat to serving temperature, stirring constantly. Serve with fish. Makes about 2½ cups.

MINT SAUCE

⅓ cup finely chopped mint leaves
2 teaspoons powdered sugar
½ cup white vinegar

Combine all ingredients and stir until sugar is dissolved. Let stand thirty minutes. Serve with lamb, as desired. Makes about ¾ cup.

HUNTERS ORANGE SAUCE

2 tablespoons butter or margarine
2 tablespoons all-purpose flour
1¼ cups orange juice
¼ teaspoon grated orange rind
⅛ teaspoon salt
1 teaspoon sugar

Melt butter or margarine and blend in flour. Gradually add orange juice and cook, stirring constantly, until thickened. Add remaining ingredients and heat to serving temperature, stirring constantly. Serve with game and poultry, as desired. Makes about 1¼ cups.

MUSTARD SAUCE

1 tablespoon butter or margarine
1 tablespoon all-purpose flour
2 tablespoons dry mustard
1 tablespoon sugar
¼ teaspoon salt
⅓ cup boiling water
⅓ cup vinegar
½ teaspoon Worcestershire sauce

Melt butter or margarine; blend in flour, mustard, sugar and salt. Remove from heat and gradually add remaining ingredients. Cook over low heat, stirring constantly, until thickened. Serve with meats and fish, as desired. Makes about 1 cup.

MUSHROOM GRAVY

¾ cup chopped mushrooms
¼ cup melted meat or poultry drippings
3 tablespoons all-purpose flour
2 cups meat, poultry or vegetable stock
2 tablespoons chopped parsley
¼ teaspoon salt

Cook mushrooms in drippings until tender. Blend in flour. Gradually add stock and cook, stirring constantly, until thickened. Add parsley and salt. Heat to serving temperature, stirring constantly. Serve with meat or poultry, as desired. Makes 2 cups.

SWEET AND SOUR CURRANT SAUCE

½ cup currant jelly
½ cup prepared mustard
½ teaspoon horseradish

Melt jelly over low heat. Add remaining ingredients and cook, stirring constantly, until thoroughly heated. Serve with meats or game, as desired. Makes about 1½ cups.

NEWBURGH SAUCE

1 tablespoon butter or margarine
1 tablespoon all-purpose flour
1 cup milk
1 egg yolk
1 tablespoon Sherry
⅛ teaspoon salt
⅛ teaspoon paprika

Melt butter or margarine; blend in flour. Gradually add milk and cook, stirring constantly, until thickened. Add a little of hot mixture to egg yolk and mix well. Stir into hot mixture and cook, stirring constantly, 1 minute. Add Sherry, salt and paprika. Serve with fish, as desired. Makes about 1 cup.

AUSTRIAN POPPY SEED SAUCE

½ cup butter or margarine
2 tablespoons lemon juice
½ teaspoon grated lemon rind
1 teaspoon poppy seed
⅛ teaspoon salt

Combine all ingredients and cook, stirring occasionally, until butter or margarine melts. Serve with green vegetables, as desired. Makes about ½ cup.

MARINARA SAUCE

1 No. 2½ can tomatoes
¾ cup water
2 tablespoons butter or margarine
½ teaspoon garlic salt
½ teaspoon oregano

Combine all ingredients and simmer 1 hour. Serve with spaghetti and macaroni. Makes about 3 cups.

CREOLE TOMATO SAUCE

2 tablespoons chopped onion
2 tablespoons chopped green pepper
1 tablespoon salad oil
1 can condensed tomato soup
¼ cup water
1 teaspoon chili powder
¼ teaspoon salt

Cook onion and green pepper in oil until onion is tender. Add remaining ingredients and heat to serving temperature, stirring frequently. Serve with meat, fish and vegetables, as desired. Makes about 1½ cups.

MISSOURI CREAM GRAVY

¼ cup all-purpose flour
¼ cup melted chicken drippings
1 cup chicken or vegetable stock
1 cup light cream
¼ teaspoon salt
⅛ teaspoon pepper

Blend flour into drippings and cook over low heat until browned. Gradually add

stock and cream; cook, stirring constantly, until thickened. Season with salt and pepper. Serve with chicken. Makes about 2 cups.

TARTARE SAUCE

2 tablespoons chopped parsley
1 teaspoon capers
¼ cup sweet pickle relish
1 cup salad dressing

Combine all ingredients; chill. Serve with fish, as desired. Makes about 1¼ cups.

TURKEY GIBLET GRAVY

½ cup all-purpose flour
1½ cups melted turkey drippings
3½ cups turkey or vegetable stock
Turkey giblets, cooked
1½ teaspoons salt
⅛ teaspoon pepper

Blend flour into drippings. Gradually add stock and cook, stirring constantly, until thickened. Add remaining ingredients and heat to serving temperature, stirring constantly. Serve with turkey, as desired. Makes about 4 cups.

ONION GRAVY

½ cup chopped onions
¼ cup melted meat or poultry drippings
¼ cup all-purpose flour
2 cups meat, poultry or vegetable stock
¼ teaspoon salt
⅛ teaspoon pepper

Cook onions in drippings until tender. Blend in flour. Gradually add stock and cook, stirring constantly, until thickened. Season with salt and pepper. Serve with meats or poultry, as desired. Makes 2 cups.

Vegetables

ASPARAGUS VINAIGRETTE

1 package frozen asparagus
1 tablespoon vinegar
½ teaspoon prepared mustard
3 tablespoons melted butter or margarine
¼ teaspoon paprika
¼ teaspoon salt
1 teaspoon grated onion
1 hard-cooked egg, chopped

Cook asparagus according to package directions. Drain and chill. Combine remaining ingredients and mix well. Pour vinegar mixture over asparagus. Serves 4.

ARTICHOKES, ITALIAN STYLE

3 small artichokes
2 tablespoons olive oil
½ teaspoon salt
⅛ teaspoon pepper
3 tablespoons water
6 eggs, slightly beaten
1 tablespoon grated Parmesan cheese

Wash artichokes and trim. Remove tough upper portions of petals. Cut in half and remove chokes. Cut petals into thin lengthwise strips. Cook in oil until wilted. Add salt, pepper and water. Cover and cook over low heat 15–20 minutes, or until tender. Add eggs and cook until firm, stirring occasionally. Sprinkle with cheese. Serves 6.

BOSTON BAKED BEANS

1 quart pea beans
Water
½ pound salt pork
1 teaspoon salt
2 tablespoons brown sugar
⅛ teaspoon ginger
¼ cup molasses
½ teaspoon dry mustard
Boiling water

Wash beans; soak overnight in water to cover. Without draining, simmer 2 to 3 hours until skins wrinkle. Cut pork into thin slices. Alternate layers of undrained beans and pork in bean pot. Add salt, sugar, ginger, molasses and mustard. Add enough boiling water to cover. Cover and bake in slow oven (250° F.) about 6 hours, or until beans are tender. Add boiling water during baking period as needed to cover beans. Uncover for last half hour of baking. Serves 8–10.

BAKED BEAN CROQUETTES

2 cups baked beans
2 tablespoons minced onion
½ teaspoon salt
⅛ teaspoon pepper
1 teaspoon molasses
1 egg, slightly beaten
1 tablespoon water
Fine dry bread crumbs

Mash beans with onion, salt, pepper and molasses. Shape into croquettes. Combine egg and water. Dip croquettes in egg mixture and roll in bread crumbs. Fry in deep hot fat (375° F.) 1½–2 minutes, or until browned on all sides. Drain on absorbent paper. Serves 4.

JERUSALEM ARTICHOKES

1 pound Jerusalem artichokes
⅓ cup melted butter or margarine
3 tablespoons lemon juice
2 tablespoons chopped parsley
¼ teaspoon salt

Wash and pare artichokes. Cook, covered, in small amount of boiling salted water 15–25 minutes or until tender. Drain. Add remaining ingredients and heat to serving temperature, stirring frequently. Serves 4–6.

BAKED BEETS WITH ORANGE

6 medium-sized beets, sliced
½ cup water
½ teaspoon salt
1 tablespoon orange juice
1 teaspoon grated orange rind
1 tablespoon butter
Dash of pepper

Combine all ingredients and turn into greased 1-quart casserole. Bake, covered, in moderate oven (350° F.) 45 minutes, or until beets are tender. Serves 4.

BEET GREENS WITH CREAM

3 cups cooked chopped beet greens
1 tablespoon grated onion
½ cup light cream
1 tablespoon prepared mustard
2 tablespoons prepared horseradish
½ teaspoon salt
⅛ teaspoon pepper

Combine all ingredients and heat to serving temperature, stirring frequently. Serves 6.

GREEN BEANS WITH CELERY

1 cup chopped celery
½ cup chopped green pepper
3 tablespoons melted butter or margarine
3 cups green beans
1 teaspoon salt
½ cup water

Cook celery and green pepper in butter or margarine until tender. Add beans and salt. Turn into greased 1½-quart casserole. Pour water over other ingredients. Cover and bake in moderate oven (375° F.) about 20 minutes or until beans are tender. Serves 6.

SOUR CREAM LIMA BEANS

¼ cup chopped onion
2 tablespoons melted butter
½ cup sour cream
2 tablespoons chopped pimiento
¼ teaspoon salt
⅛ teaspoon pepper
2 cups cooked hot lima beans
½ teaspoon paprika

Cook onion in butter until tender. Add sour cream, pimiento, salt and pepper. Cook, stirring constantly, until thoroughly heated. Arrange beans in serving dish. Pour sour-cream mixture over beans. Sprinkle with paprika. Serves 4.

CARROT FLUFF

4 cups mashed cooked carrots
⅛ teaspoon pepper
¼ teaspoon salt
¼ teaspoon paprika
2 tablespoons butter, melted
¼ cup hot milk

Combine all ingredients. Beat until light. Serves 6.

SWEET AND SOUR CARROTS

4 cups sliced carrots
2 tablespoons melted fat
1 cup boiling water
3 tablespoons vinegar
3 tablespoons sugar
1 teaspoon salt
2 tablespoons cornstarch
¼ cup water
¼ teaspoon soy sauce

Cook carrots in fat three minutes, stirring constantly. Add boiling water, vinegar, sugar and salt; simmer for 10 minutes. Mix cornstarch with water and soy sauce; add to carrots and cook, stirring constantly, until thickened. Serves 6.

BAKED CAULIFLOWER

1 large head cauliflower, cooked
3 eggs, well beaten
¼ cup chopped onion
¼ cup chopped parsley
1 small clove garlic, minced
1 cup canned tomatoes
¼ cup cooking oil
1 teaspoon salt
¼ teaspoon pepper
1 cup grated sharp cheese

Separate cauliflower into flowerets. Arrange in greased 2½-quart casserole. Combine remaining ingredients and pour over cauliflower. Bake in moderate oven (350° F.) 35–40 minutes. Serves 6.

CARROT POTATO BALLS

4 medium-sized carrots, grated
4 medium-sized potatoes, grated
3 tablespoons all-purpose flour
¼ cup milk
1 tablespoon onion, grated
¼ teaspoon salt
⅛ teaspoon pepper
¼ cup melted shortening

Combine carrots, potatoes, flour, milk, onion, salt and pepper. Shape into small balls. Cook in shortening over low heat, about 10 minutes, or until browned on all sides. Serves 4–6.

CARROTS WITH HONEY

¼ cup honey
¼ cup butter or margarine
½ teaspoon grated orange rind
⅛ teaspoon salt
12 medium-sized carrots, cooked

Combine honey, butter or margarine, orange rind and salt. Heat to boiling point, stirring constantly. Simmer 5 minutes. Pour honey mixture over carrots. Serves 4.

CANDIED CARROTS

12 medium-sized carrots, cooked
½ cup water
1 cup firmly packed brown sugar
3 tablespons melted butter or margarine
⅛ teaspoon salt

Arrange carrots in greased shallow baking pan. Combine remaining ingredients and cook over low heat until sugar melts, stirring constantly. Pour sugar mixture over carrots. Bake in moderate oven (350° F.) 20–25 minutes. Serves 4.

CHEESE CRUMBED CAULIFLOWER

⅓ cup butter
½ cup cracker crumbs
1 teaspoon grated onion
½ cup grated Swiss cheese
⅛ teaspoon salt
1 medium-sized cauliflower, cooked

Melt butter; add crumbs, onion, cheese and salt. Cook over low heat, stirring until cheese is melted. Pour over cauliflower. Serves 6.

COTTAGE CHEESE STUFFED BEETS

8 medium-sized beets, cooked
¼ cup chopped onion
1 tablespoon chili sauce
½ teaspoon lemon juice
½ cup cottage cheese
½ teaspoon salt
⅛ teaspoon pepper

Remove centers from beets, leaving a shell about ¼ inch thick. Chop beet pulp and add remaining ingredients. Mix lightly. Fill shells with cheese mixture. Place in greased shallow baking pan. Add enough water to cover bottom of pan. Bake in moderate oven (375° F.) about 20 minutes. Serves 4.

HARVARD BEETS

⅓ cup sugar
¼ teaspoon salt
1 tablespoon cornstarch
½ cup vinegar
1 tablespoon butter or margarine
1 tablespoon grated onion
3 cups diced cooked beets

Combine sugar, salt and cornstarch; gradually add vinegar and cook over low heat, stirring constantly, until thickened. Add remaining ingredients and cook, stirring frequently, 15 minutes. Serves 4.

BROCCOLI PARMESAN

1 package frozen chopped broccoli
2 tablespoons butter or margarine
1 small clove garlic, minced
1 tablespoon grated Parmesan cheese

Cook broccoli according to package directions; drain. Melt butter or margarine; add garlic and cook until lightly browned. Pour over broccoli and mix lightly. Sprinkle with Parmesan cheese. Serves 4.

BRAISED BRUSSELS SPROUTS

¼ cup chopped onion
3 tablespoons butter or margarine
¼ cup chicken stock
4 cups Brussels sprouts
½ teaspoon salt
2 tablespoons chopped chives

Cook onion in butter or margarine until tender. Add stock, Brussels sprouts and salt. Cook over low heat, stirring occasionally, 8–10 minutes or until liquid has evaporated and sprouts are tender. Sprinkle with chives. Serves 6.

BRUSSELS SPROUTS WITH CHESTNUTS

4 cups Brussels sprouts
¼ cup chopped onion
½ cup chopped, cooked chestnuts
½ cup chopped celery
1½ cups beef bouillon
2 tablespoons butter or margarine
½ teaspoon salt
1 tablespoon lemon juice

Arrange Brussels sprouts in greased 1½-quart casserole. Combine onion, chestnuts, celery and bouillon. Heat to boiling point and cook 10 minutes. Add remaining ingredients and mix well. Pour over Brussels sprouts. Bake in moderate oven (350° F.) 15–20 minutes or until sprouts are tender. Serves 6.

CABBAGE WITH SOUR CREAM

1 medium-sized head of cabbage,
    finely shredded
¼ cup melted butter or margarine
1 egg, slightly beaten
1 cup sour cream
1 tablespoon sugar
2 tablespoons lemon juice
½ teaspoon salt
⅛ teaspoon pepper

Cook cabbage in butter or margarine over low heat about 15 minutes or until tender. Combine remaining ingredients and mix well. Pour sour-cream mixture over cabbage and heat to serving temperature, stirring constantly. Serves 6.

CHINESE CABBAGE

1 medium-sized head Chinese cabbage, sliced
1 cup boiling water
½ teaspoon salt
¼ cup light cream
2 tablespoons butter or margarine
2 tablespoons minced parsley

Combine cabbage, boiling water and salt. Cook, covered, 7 minutes. Drain and add remaining ingredients. Heat to serving temperature. Serves 4.

CELERIAC HOLLANDAISE

4 celery roots
1 cup Hollandaise sauce (page 323)

Cut leaves and root fibers from celery roots. Pare and dice. Cook, covered, in boiling salted water 15–25 minutes or until tender. Serve with Hollandaise sauce. Serves 4–6.

WAX BEANS WITH DILL AND EGG

½ cup finely chopped onion
2 tablespoons melted butter or margarine
4 cups cooked, diced wax beans
½ teaspoon salt
⅛ teaspoon pepper
1 tablespoon chopped dill
1 hard-cooked egg, chopped

Cook onion in butter or margarine until lightly browned. Add remaining ingredients and heat to serving temperature, stirring frequently. Serves 6.

BRAISED CELERY

1 large bunch celery
¼ cup butter or margarine
¼ cup water
1 teaspoon salt
⅛ teaspoon pepper
¼ teaspoon nutmeg

Cut celery stalks in 2″ lengths. Melt butter or margarine; add celery and cook until lightly browned. Add remaining ingredients, cover and cook over low heat 10–15 minutes or until celery is tender. Serves 6.

BAKED CELERY

3 medium-sized bunches celery
1 chicken bouillon cube
1 cup boiling water
¼ cup butter or margarine
½ teaspoon salt
⅛ teaspoon pepper

Cut celery stalks in 2″ lengths and place in greased, shallow baking pan. Combine remaining ingredients and stir until bouillon cube is dissolved. Pour over celery. Cover and bake in moderate oven (350° F.) about 45 minutes or until celery is tender. Serves 4.

SWISS CHARD AND EGGS CHINESE

1 clove garlic, minced
2 tablespoons peanut oil
2 eggs, beaten
2 tablespoons milk
½ teaspoon salt
⅛ teaspoon pepper
3 cups cooked chopped Swiss chard

Cook garlic in peanut oil 1 minute. Combine remaining ingredients and add to garlic. Cook over low heat, stirring occasionally, until eggs are set. Serves 4.

BUTTERED SWISS CHARD

1 pound Swiss chard
½ teaspoon salt
⅛ teaspoon pepper
3 tablespoons melted butter or margarine

Wash Swiss chard thoroughly; cook, covered, with water that clings to leaves 10–12 minutes or until tender. Drain if necessary. Add remaining ingredients and mix lightly. Serves 4.

BACON, CORN AND TOMATOES

8 slices bacon
¼ cup chopped onion
¼ cup chopped green pepper
1 No. 303 can whole kernel corn, drained
1 No. 2 can tomatoes
1 teaspoon salt
¼ teaspoon sugar
⅛ teaspoon pepper

Cook bacon until crisp, reserving bacon dripping. Drain bacon on absorbent paper; crumble. Cook onion and green pepper in 3 tablespoons bacon drippings until onion is tender. Add corn, tomatoes, salt, sugar, pepper and bacon. Heat to serving temperature. Serves 6–8.

SOUTHERN CORN PUDDING

3 eggs, well beaten
2 cups cooked corn, cut from cob
2 tablespoons melted butter
2 cups milk
1 teaspoon salt
⅛ teaspoon pepper
½ teaspoon sugar
2 tablespoons fine dry bread crumbs

Combine eggs, corn, butter, milk, salt, pepper and sugar. Pour into greased 1½-quart baking dish. Sprinkle with crumbs. Bake in slow oven (325° F.) 40 minutes, or until firm. Serves 6.

CORN SCALLOP

1 No. 303 can whole kernel corn
Milk
2 tablespoons butter
2 tablespoons all-purpose flour
1 tablespoon chopped pimiento
2 tablespoons minced onion
1 teaspoon salt
⅛ teaspoon pepper
2 eggs, beaten
¼ cup buttered bread crumbs

Drain corn. Add enough milk to corn liquid to make one cup. Melt butter and blend in flour. Gradually add milk mixture and cook, stirring constantly, until thickened. Add pimiento, onion, salt and pepper. Add a little of hot mixture to eggs and mix well. Add egg mixture to hot mixture and mix well. Turn into greased 1-quart casserole. Sprinkle crumbs over top. Bake in moderate oven (350° F.) 45 minutes. Serves 4.

CORN FRITTERS

1 cup sifted all-purpose flour
1 teaspoon baking powder
½ teaspoon salt
2 cups grated fresh corn
2 eggs, separated
Fat

Sift flour, baking powder and salt together. Add grated fresh corn and mix well. Beat egg yolks well and stir into corn mixture. Beat egg whites until stiff and fold into batter. Drop by tablespoonfuls into deep hot fat (360° F.) and fry until browned on all sides. Drain on absorbent paper. Serves 4–6.

CORN CHEESE CASSEROLE

2 cups fresh corn
¼ cup light cream
2 tablespoons minced onion

2 tablespoons chopped green pepper
2 tablespoons chopped pimiento
¼ cup cooked crumbled bacon
1½ cups of soft bread crumbs
1 cup grated Cheddar cheese
2 tablespoons melted butter
1 teaspoon salt
⅛ teaspoon pepper

Combine all ingredients and mix lightly. Turn into greased 1½-quart casserole. Bake in moderate oven (350° F.) 40 minutes, or until lightly browned. Serves 6.

CORN CREOLE

1 green pepper, diced
1 small onion, diced
1 tablespoon melted butter
2 cups fresh corn
3 tomatoes, chopped
½ teaspoon salt
Dash cayenne pepper
1 teaspoon sugar

Cook pepper and onion in butter five minutes. Add remaining ingredients and cook, covered, ten minutes. Serves 4.

CORN AND ONION SCALLOP

1 No. 2½ can creamed style corn
1 cup small white onions, cooked
1 teaspoon salt
⅛ teaspoon pepper
1 cup buttered cracker crumbs

Combine corn, onion, salt and pepper. Turn into greased 1½-quart baking dish. Top with crumbs. Bake in moderate oven (350° F.) 25–30 minutes. Serves 6.

GERMAN RED CABBAGE

4 cups shredded, cooked red cabbage
2 tablespoons melted bacon drippings
2 tablespoons chopped onion
¼ cup vinegar
1 teaspoon sugar

Cook cabbage in bacon drippings, tossing lightly, until thoroughly heated. Add remaining ingredients and heat to serving temperature. Serves 6.

DANDELION GREEN BAKE

2 pounds dandelion greens, chopped
⅓ cup all-purpose flour
⅓ cup melted butter or margarine
1 cup milk
½ teaspoon salt
⅛ teaspoon pepper
½ cup grated Swiss cheese
½ cup cracker crumbs

Arrange greens in layers in greased 1½-quart baking dish, sprinkling flour between layers. Combine butter or margarine, milk, salt and pepper. Pour over greens. Combine cheese and crumbs. Sprinkle over top. Bake in moderate oven (350° F.) 35 minutes. Serves 6.

CHEESE EGGPLANT CASSEROLE

1 medium-sized eggplant
3 tablespoons melted shortening
¼ cup chopped onion
½ chopped green pepper
2 medium-sized tomatoes, sliced
1 teaspoon salt
⅛ teaspoon pepper
½ cup grated Cheddar cheese

Peel eggplant and cut in ½″ slices. Brown eggplant slices in shortening on both sides. Arrange eggplant slices in greased 1-quart casserole. Top with onion, green pepper, tomato slices, salt and pepper. Cover and bake in moderate oven (350° F.) about 40 minutes. Uncover and sprinkle cheese over other ingredients. Continue baking 10 minutes, or until cheese is browned. Serves 4.

ARMENIAN EGGPLANT

1 large eggplant
2½ cups diced, cooked lamb
1 clove garlic, cut in half
¼ cup olive oil
2 tablespoons minced onion
¼ cup chopped green pepper
1 cup cooked tomatoes
1 cup cooked rice
2 tablespoons pinola nuts
½ teaspoon salt
⅛ teaspoon pepper
¼ cup water

Cook eggplant, covered, in boiling salted water 20 minutes. Drain. Cut eggplant in half lengthwise. Scoop out pulp, leaving a shell about ¼ inch thick. Cook lamb and garlic in olive oil until lamb is well browned. Remove garlic. Add onion, green pepper, tomatoes, rice, nuts, salt, pepper, water and eggplant. Mix well. Fill eggplant shells with lamb mixture. Bake in moderate oven (350° F.) 45 minutes. Serves 6.

OKRA WITH LEMON BUTTER

1 pound okra
¼ cup melted butter
½ teaspoon salt
2 tablespoons lemon juice

Cook okra, covered, in a small amount of boiling salted water 8–10 minutes or until tender. Combine remaining ingredients and heat to serving temperature. Drain okra. Pour lemon mixture over okra. Serves 4.

ONION AND CARROT SAUTÉ

4 medium-sized onions
4 medium-sized carrots
¼ cup melted butter or margarine
½ teaspoon salt
⅛ teaspoon pepper

Cut onions in ¼″ slices. Cut carrots in ⅛″ slices. Add onions and carrots to butter or margarine and cook, covered, over low heat 20 minutes, or until vegetables are tender. Stir occasionally. Season with salt and pepper. Serves 4.

BAKED ONIONS

4 medium-sized onions
1 tablespoon butter
½ cup beef bouillon
½ cup buttered bread crumbs

Peel onions and cut in half crosswise. Place in shallow baking pan. Dot with butter. Pour beef bouillon over onions. Cover and bake in moderate oven (350° F.) 40 minutes, or until tender. (Add more bouillon during baking period, if necessary.) Sprinkle crumbs over onions. Continue baking, uncovered, until lightly browned. Serves 4.

DUTCH ONION CASSEROLE

2 tablespoons butter
2 tablespoons all-purpose flour
1 cup milk
¼ cup butter
4 medium-sized onions, sliced
8 hard-cooked eggs, sliced
1 teaspoon salt
¼ teaspoon paprika
¼ cup buttered cracker crumbs

Melt the two tablespoons butter and blend in flour. Gradually add milk and cook, stirring constantly, until thickened. Melt the ¼ cup butter and add onions. Cook until onions are tender. Arrange onions and egg slices alternately in a greased 1½-quart casserole. Pour white sauce over onion-egg mixture. Sprinkle with salt and paprika. Top with crumbs. Bake in moderate oven, (350° F.) 20–30 minutes. Serves 6.

MORMON STEW

2 tablespoons butter or margarine
2 tablespoons all-purpose flour
3 medium-sized tomatoes, finely chopped
2 cups diced cooked eggplant
¼ cup chopped green pepper
2 tablespoons grated onion
1 cup diced cooked potatoes
½ cup diced cooked carrots
1 teaspoon sugar
1 teaspoon salt
⅛ teaspoon pepper
½ cup grated Cheddar cheese

Melt butter or margarine and blend in flour. Add tomatoes and cook over low heat, stirring constantly, until thickened. Add eggplant, green pepper, onion, potatoes, carrots, sugar, salt and pepper. Turn into greased 1½-quart baking dish. Sprinkle cheese over vegetable mixture. Bake in moderate oven (350° F.) 30–35 minutes. Serves 4–6.

ESTELLA'S KOHLRABI

4 medium-sized kohlrabi
2 tablespoons butter or margarine
2 tablespoons all-purpose flour
1 teaspoon grated lemon rind
1 cup milk
½ teaspoon salt

Remove leaves from kohlrabi; wash and pare. Cut into ½″ cubes. Cook, covered, in a small amount of boiling salted water 25 to 30 minutes or until tender. Drain. Melt butter or margarine; blend in flour. Gradually add milk. Add lemon rind and salt. Cook, stirring constantly, until thickened. Serve with kohlrabi. Serves 4.

DUTCH WILTED LETTUCE

1 head lettuce
8 slices bacon
½ cup vinegar
1 tablespoon sugar
¼ cup water
1 teaspoon salt
1 hard-cooked egg, sliced

Clean lettuce and separate leaves. Fry the bacon until crisp and remove from pan. Reserve drippings. Drain bacon on absorbent paper and crumble. Sprinkle half of bacon over lettuce. Add vinegar, sugar, water and salt to drippings. Heat to boiling point and pour over lettuce. Mix thoroughly. Sprinkle remaining bacon over top and garnish with hard-cooked egg slices. Serves 4–6.

CREAMED KALE AND ONIONS

2 pounds kale
3 tablespoons butter
3 tablespoons all-purpose flour
1½ cups milk
¾ cup cooked small white onions
1 teaspoon salt
⅛ teaspoon pepper

Cook kale, covered, in a small amount of boiling water 10–15 minutes, or until tender; drain. Meanwhile, melt butter and blend in flour. Gradually add milk and cook, stirring constantly, until thickened. Add onions, salt and pepper. Heat to serving temperature. Serve onion sauce over kale. Serves 6.

MUSHROOM WITH ONION

1 pound small mushrooms, chopped
¼ cup chopped onion
¼ cup butter
½ cup sour cream
½ teaspoon salt
⅛ teaspoon pepper

Cook mushrooms and onion in butter until onion is tender. Add remaining ingredients and cook, stirring occasionally, until thoroughly heated. Serves 4.

EGGPLANT PUFF

1 large eggplant
2 cups grated Cheddar cheese
2 cups soft bread crumbs
1 tablespoon chili sauce
2 tablespoons minced onion
½ teaspoon salt
2 eggs, separated

Cut eggplant in half lengthwise and scoop out pulp. Cook pulp, covered, in a small amount of boiling water 10 minutes, or until tender. Drain. Mash pulp. Combine eggplant pulp, cheese, crumbs, chili sauce, onion and salt. Beat egg yolks until thick and add to eggplant mixture. Beat egg whites until stiff and fold into eggplant mixture. Fill shells with eggplant mixture. Place in greased shallow baking pan. Bake in moderate oven (350° F.) about 40 minutes, or until firm. Serves 4.

GREEN BEAN-TOMATO BAKE

2 tablespoons minced onion
2 tablespoons chopped green pepper
2 tablespoons melted butter or margarine
3 cups cooked green beans
2 cups diced tomatoes
1 teaspoon salt
⅛ teaspoon pepper
¼ cup cracker crumbs
¼ cup grated American cheese

Cook onion and green pepper in butter or margarine until tender. Add beans, tomatoes, salt and pepper. Turn into greased 1½-quart baking dish. Top with crumbs and cheese. Bake in moderate oven (350° F.) 20–25 minutes. Serves 6.

GOLDEN MARRON BALLS

2 cups hot mashed chestnuts
¼ cup butter
2 eggs, slightly beaten

Salt and pepper to taste
¼ teaspoon sage
1 tablespoon minced onion
1 egg, slightly beaten
Dry bread crumbs

Combine chestnuts, butter, the 2 eggs, salt, pepper, sage and onion. Shape into croquettes. Dip in the slightly beaten egg and roll in crumbs. Fry in deep hot fat (375° F.) until browned on all sides. Drain on absorbent paper. Serve with gravy or sauce, as desired. Serves 4.

PEPPERS WITH MUSHROOMS

6 medium-sized green peppers
1 cup chopped mushrooms
¼ cup melted butter
2 cups fine dry bread crumbs
2 tablespoons butter
2 tablespoons all-purpose flour
1 cup milk
1 teaspoon salt
⅛ teaspoon pepper

Remove stem ends, seeds and membrane from peppers. Cook in boiling salted water 5 minutes; drain. Combine mushrooms, the ¼ cup butter and crumbs. Melt the 2 tablespoons butter and blend in flour. Gradually add milk and cook, stirring constantly, until thickened. Add mushroom mixture, salt and pepper; mix lightly. Fill peppers with mushroom mixture. Place in shallow baking pan. Add enough water to cover bottom of pan. Bake in moderate oven (350° F.) 40–50 minutes, or until peppers are tender. Serves 6.

FRIED GREEN PEPPER RINGS

3 large green peppers
1 egg, slightly beaten
1 tablespoon water
½ cup dry bread crumbs
½ teaspoon salt

Remove stem end from peppers and cut into rings. Remove seeds and membrane. Combine egg and water. Combine crumbs and salt. Dip pepper rings in egg mixture and coat with crumb mixture. Fry in deep hot fat (375° F.) 3–4 minutes or until brown. Drain on absorbent paper. Serves 4–6.

ORIENTAL PEA SOUFFLÉ

¼ cup butter
¼ cup all-purpose flour
2 cups milk
3 eggs, separated
1 tablespoon grated onion
No. 303 can peas, drained
¼ cup chopped bean sprouts
½ teaspoon salt
⅛ teaspoon pepper

Melt butter and blend in flour. Gradually add milk and cook over low heat, stirring constantly, until thickened. Add a little of hot mixture to egg yolks and mix well. Stir into hot mixture and cook, stirring constantly, until thickened. Remove from heat; add onion, peas, bean sprouts, salt and pepper. Beat egg whites until stiff and fold into peas mixture. Turn into 1½-quart baking dish. Bake in moderate oven (350° F.) 40–50 minutes, or until firm. Serves 6.

SAUTÉED CUCUMBERS

4 medium-sized cucumbers
½ cup all-purpose flour, approx.
¼ cup melted butter or margarine
1 teaspoon salt
⅛ teaspoon pepper

Cut cucumbers into quarters; cook, covered, in small amount of boiling salted water 5 minutes. Drain. Coat with flour. Cook in butter or margarine until lightly browned. Sprinkle with salt and pepper. Serves 4–6.

PARSNIP SCALLOP

2 cups sliced cooked parsnips
3 tablespoons butter
3 tablespoons all-purpose flour
1½ cups milk
½ cup grated Cheddar cheese
¼ cup buttered cracker crumbs

Arrange parsnips in greased 1½-quart casserole. Melt butter and blend in flour. Gradually add milk and cook, stirring constantly, until thickened. Add cheese and stir until cheese melts. Pour cheese mixture over parsnips. Sprinkle crumbs over cheese. Bake in moderate oven (350° F.) 30 minutes. Serves 4.

MINTED PEAS DENVER

1 package frozen peas
2 tablespoons chopped mint
3 tablespoons butter or margarine
½ teaspoon salt
⅛ teaspoon pepper

Cook peas according to package directions; drain. Add remaining ingredients and stir until butter or margarine is melted. Serves 4.

FRENCH FRIED ONION RINGS

2 large sweet onions
⅔ cup milk
½ cup all-purpose flour
½ teaspoon salt
¼ teaspoon pepper
Deep hot fat

Peel onions and cut in crosswise slices ½ inch thick. Separate into rings. Pour milk over onions and let stand 30 minutes. Combine flour, salt and pepper. Coat onion rings with flour mixture. Cook in deep hot fat (365° F.) 1–2 minutes, or until lightly browned. Drain on absorbent paper. Serves 4.

STUFFED PEPPERS

6 medium-sized green peppers
1 pound ground meat
2 tablespoons melted butter
Salt and pepper to taste
1 cup cooked rice
1 8-ounce can tomato sauce

Remove stem ends from peppers; remove seeds and membrane. Brown beef in butter. Season with salt and pepper and add rice. Stuff peppers with meat mixture. Place peppers in greased baking dish. Pour tomato sauce over peppers. Bake in moderate oven (350° F.) 40 minutes. Serves 6.

MONTEREY STUFFED PIMIENTOS

1 can pimientos, drained
1 cup grated Swiss cheese
Fine dry bread crumbs
¼ cup melted butter

Fill pimientos with cheese; roll in crumbs. Cook in butter over low heat until browned on both sides. Serves 4.

BAKED POTATO CAKE

8 potatoes
1 tablespoon grated onion
3 eggs, beaten
1 cup milk, scalded
⅓ cup butter, melted
1 teaspoon salt

Peel and grate potatoes. Add remaining ingredients; mix well. Pour into a well-greased, shallow baking dish. Bake in a moderate oven (350° F.) 1 hour. Serves 6.

BAKED STUFFED POTATOES

6 medium-sized potatoes, baked
½ teaspoon salt
2 tablespoons chopped parsley

2 tablespoons butter or margarine
3 tablespoons light cream
1 teaspoon grated onion

Cut potatoes in half lengthwise and scoop out. Add remaining ingredients and beat until light and fluffy. Fill shells with potato mixture; bake in hot oven (400° F.) about 5 minutes, or until lightly browned. Serves 6.

POTATO CHEESE CASSEROLE

¼ cup butter
¼ cup all-purpose flour
2 cups milk
6 medium-sized potatoes, thinly sliced
1 teaspoon salt
⅛ teaspoon pepper
1 cup grated Cheddar cheese

Melt butter and blend in flour. Gradually add milk and cook, stirring constantly, until thickened. Add potatoes and heat to boiling point. Add salt and pepper. Alternate layers of potato mixture and cheese in greased 1½-quart casserole. Cover and bake in moderate oven (350° F.) 30 minutes. Uncover and continue baking 10 minutes or until potatoes are tender. Serves 6.

CREAMED POTATOES

3 cups diced raw potatoes
2 tablespoons chopped onion
½ cup light cream
⅔ cup milk
1 teaspoon salt
⅛ teaspoon pepper
2 tablespoons butter

Combine potatoes, onion, cream, milk, salt and pepper in top of double boiler. Cook, covered, over simmering water about 40 minutes, or until potatoes are tender. Add butter and stir until melted. Serves 4.

DUCHESS POTATOES

2 cups hot mashed potatoes
2 tablespoons butter
2 eggs, separated
½ teaspoon salt

Combine potatoes and butter. Beat egg yolks and add to potatoes. Season with salt. Force through pastry tube onto greased baking sheet, forming 1″ balls. Or drop by teaspoonfuls onto greased baking sheets. Beat egg whites slightly and brush over potatoes. Bake in very hot oven (450° F.) 5–10 minutes, or until browned. Serves 6.

BASQUE POTATO HASH

4 medium-sized potatoes, peeled and
    sliced
¼ cup melted fat
4 eggs, slightly beaten
1 teaspoon salt
¼ teaspoon pepper
1 teaspoon chopped chives
2 tablespoons chopped parsley
¼ teaspoon thyme

Cook potatoes in fat over low heat until tender, turning occasionally. Pour eggs over potato mixture and mix lightly. Add remaining ingredients and cook over low heat until eggs are set, stirring occasionally. Serves 4.

OVEN FRENCH FRIES

6 medium-sized potatoes
¾ cup butter or margarine
½ teaspoon salt

Do not peel potatoes; cut into eighths. Place in shallow baking pan; dot with butter or margarine and sprinkle with salt. Bake in moderate oven (350° F.) about one hour or until tender. Stir occasionally during baking period. Serves 6.

STEAMED POTATOES AND ONIONS

6 medium-sized potatoes, thinly sliced
4 medium-sized onions, thinly sliced
1 teaspoon salt
⅛ teaspoon pepper
2 tablespoons chopped parsley
⅓ cup butter or margarine
1 cup boiling water

Alternate layers of potatoes and onions in greased 1½-quart casserole. Sprinkle salt, pepper and parsley over vegetables. Dot with butter or margarine. Pour water over ingredients. Bake in hot oven (400° F.) 40–50 minutes, or until potatoes are tender. Serves 6.

POTATO STEW CALAIS

6 large potatoes, cooked
⅓ cup butter
2 cups milk
2 tablespoons minced onion
1 teaspoon salt
⅛ teaspoon pepper

Cut potatoes into ½″ cubes. Combine remaining ingredients and heat to boiling point. Add potatoes and cook over low heat, stirring occasionally, until slightly thickened. Serves 6.

POTATOES IN TOMATO SAUCE

4 cups thinly sliced potatoes
¼ cup chopped onion
2 cups tomato sauce
1 clove garlic, minced
¼ cup chopped green pepper
1 teaspoon salt
⅛ teaspoon pepper

Arrange potatoes and onion in greased 2-quart casserole. Combine remaining ingredients and pour over potato mixture. Cover and bake in moderate oven (350° F.) 1¼ hours, or until potatoes are tender. Serves 6.

SAVORY POTATO ROAST

6 medium-sized potatoes
½ cup all-purpose flour
¼ teaspoon salt
¼ teaspoon pepper
2 tablespoons butter
½ teaspoon thyme
1 teaspoon onion salt
1 bay leaf

Peel potatoes. Roll in flour. Sprinkle with salt and pepper. Place in greased shallow baking pan. Top with remaining ingredients. Cover and bake in hot oven (400° F.) 45–60 minutes. Remove bay leaf. Serves 6.

POTATO SCALLOP

4 cups thinly sliced potatoes
1 egg, beaten
1⅓ cups light cream
1 teaspoon salt
¼ teaspoon black pepper
½ teaspoon nutmeg
2 tablespoons grated onion

Place potatoes in greased 1½-quart casserole. Combine remaining ingredients; pour over potatoes. Bake in hot oven (400° F.) 1 hour, or until potatoes are tender. Serves 6.

POTATO CURRY

2 cups cooked, diced potatoes
1 pint sour cream
2 teaspoons curry powder
¼ cup butter
1 teaspoon salt
½ teaspoon cloves
¼ teaspoon ginger
¼ cup beef bouillon

Combine all ingredients and heat to serving temperature, stirring frequently. Serves 4.

DUTCH POTATO PANCAKES

2 cups grated raw potatoes
¼ cup milk
1 egg, slightly beaten
½ teaspoon salt
⅛ teaspoon pepper
2 tablespoons all-purpose flour
2 tablespoons grated onion
3 tablespoons melted shortening

Combine potatoes, milk, egg, salt, pepper, flour and onion; mix well. Drop by tablespoonfuls into shortening. Brown well on both sides. Serves 4.

WESTERN STYLE POTATOES

¼ cup bacon drippings
4 cups thinly sliced potatoes
½ cup thinly sliced onions
1 teaspoon salt
⅛ teaspoon pepper

Melt bacon drippings over low heat. Add potatoes, onions, salt and pepper. Cover and cook about 15 minutes, or until browned on bottom. Turn and continue cooking, covered, 15 minutes, or until potatoes are tender. Serves 6.

RICED POTATOES

6 medium-sized cooked hot potatoes, cut in halves
1 tablespoon butter
1 teaspoon salt
⅛ teaspoon pepper

Force potatoes through ricer. Add butter, salt and pepper. Serves 4.

SOUTHERN BLACK-EYED PEAS

2 cups dried black-eyed peas
1½ teaspoons salt
⅛ teaspoon pepper
¼ cup bacon drippings
2 tablespoons molasses

Soak peas in water several hours; drain. Cover peas with cold water and add remaining ingredients. Cook, covered, 40–45 minutes, or until tender. Serves 4–6.

NEW ENGLAND BAKED PUMPKIN

1 3-pound pumpkin
½ cup melted butter
2 tablespoons chopped fresh ginger
1 teaspoon cinnamon
½ cup firmly packed brown sugar
¼ teaspoon salt

Cut pumpkin into serving pieces; remove seeds. Combine remaining ingredients. Place pumpkin in greased shallow baking pan. Top with sugar mixture. Bake in moderate oven (350° F.) about 1½ hours, or until tender. Baste occasionally during baking period. Serves 8.

PUMPKIN VEGETABLE SKILLET

4 cups diced pumpkin
¼ cup melted bacon drippings
½ cup onion slices
1 clove garlic, minced
½ cup chopped green pepper
1 cup chopped tomatoes
2 cups cut green beans
1 cup whole kernel corn
½ cup chicken stock
½ teaspoon chili powder
1 teaspoon salt
¼ teaspoon pepper

Cook pumpkin in bacon drippings 5 minutes. Add remaining ingredients and cook over low heat, covered, 30–35 minutes, or until vegetables are tender. Serves 6.

ESCAROLE WITH LEMON

2 pounds escarole
¼ cup melted butter or margarine
1 medium-sized lemon thinly sliced

Cook escarole, covered, in small amount of boiling salted water 10–12 minutes, or until tender. Drain and add butter or margarine. Top with lemon slices. Serves 4–6.

LEMON BUTTERED ONIONS

12 medium-sized onions, peeled
⅓ cup melted butter
2 tablespoons lemon juice
¼ teaspoon grated lemon rind
¼ teaspoon salt
⅛ teaspoon pepper

Cook onions, covered, in a small amount of boiling salted water, 30–40 minutes, or until tender. Drain. Combine remaining ingredients and heat to serving temperature. Pour over onions. Serves 4.

ONION RAISIN MEDLEY

2 pounds small white onions, peeled
¼ cup seedless white raisins
¼ cup sugar
1 cup water
¼ cup lemon juice
½ cup tomato paste
3 tablespoons melted butter
1 teaspoon salt

Combine all ingredients. Cover and cook over low heat about 35 minutes, or until onions are tender. Serves 8.

CREAMY SPINACH AND EGG

1½ pounds spinach, cooked and chopped
2 hard-cooked eggs, chopped
2 tablespoons butter or margarine
½ cup heavy cream
1 teaspoon salt
⅛ teaspoon pepper

Combine all ingredients and heat to serving temperature, stirring occasionally. Serves 4.

RED RHUBARB PUDDING

2 cups diced rhubarb
1 cup raisins, chopped
¼ teaspoon cinnamon
¼ cup chopped candied fruits
1 teaspoon grated lemon rind
¼ cup sugar
2 tablespoons butter, melted
2 eggs
1¼ cups sifted all-purpose flour
1½ teaspoons baking powder
⅛ teaspoon salt
½ cup milk

Combine rhubarb, raisins, cinnamon, candied fruits and lemon rind. Turn into greased shallow baking dish. Cream sugar with butter until light. Add eggs and mix well. Sift flour, baking powder and salt together. Add sifted ingredients and milk alternately to sugar mixture. Mix well after each addition. Place batter over rhubarb mixture. Bake in moderate oven (350° F.) about 35–40 minutes. Serves 4.

LEMON BUTTER SALSIFY

1 tablespoon vinegar
1 quart cold water
1½ pounds salsify
⅓ cup melted butter or margarine
1½ tablespoons lemon juice
1 tablespoon chopped chives
½ teaspoon salt
⅛ teaspoon pepper

Combine vinegar and cold water. Wash and scrape salsify; slice and drop into vinegar-water mixture. Drain. Cook, covered, in a small amount of boiling salted water about 20 minutes or until tender. Drain. Combine remaining ingredients and heat to serving temperature, stirring occasionally. Pour lemon mixture over salsify. Serves 4.

FRIED SPINACH BALLS

2 cups cooked chopped spinach
1 tablespoon melted butter
2 tablespoons grated American cheese
½ teaspoon salt
⅛ teaspoon pepper
1 egg
1 cup fine dry bread crumbs
1 egg, slightly beaten
2 tablespoons water
Fine dry bread crumbs
Deep hot fat

Combine spinach, butter, cheese, salt, pepper, egg and the 1 cup bread crumbs. Mix well and chill 1 hour. Shape spinach mixture into 1″ balls. Combine slightly beaten egg with water. Dip spinach balls in egg mixture and roll in bread crumbs. Fry in deep hot fat (365° F.) 3–4 minutes, or until well browned on all sides. Drain on absorbent paper. Serve with a tomato sauce, as desired. Serves 4.

WILTED SPINACH

4 slices bacon
3 cups chopped spinach
3 tablespoons all-purpose flour
1½ cups water
1 tablespoon brown sugar
3 tablespoons vinegar
½ teaspoon salt
⅛ teaspoon pepper
1 hard-cooked egg, chopped

Cook bacon until crisp. Reserve drippings. Drain bacon on absorbent paper and crumble. Combine bacon and spinach. Blend flour into drippings. Gradually add water and cook, stirring constantly, until thickened. Add sugar, vinegar, salt, pepper and egg; mix well. Add spinach mixture and heat to serving temperature, tossing lightly. Serves 4–6.

SPINACH RING WALLOON

3 cups cooked chopped spinach
½ cup fine dry bread crumbs
1 tablespoon minced onion
2 tablespoons chopped celery
⅛ teaspoon nutmeg
½ teaspoon salt
⅛ teaspoon pepper
2 tablespoons melted butter
3 eggs, well beaten
2 cups hot diced cooked carrots

Combine spinach, crumbs, onion, celery, nutmeg, salt, pepper, butter and eggs; mix well. Turn into well-greased 9″ ring mold. Place in pan of hot water. Bake in moderate oven (350° F.) about 50 minutes, or until firm. Unmold and fill center with carrots. Serves 6.

SUMMER SQUASH PUDDING

1 pound small yellow squash
⅓ cup butter, melted
½ cup light cream
1 teaspoon salt
⅛ teaspoon pepper
¼ cup buttered cracker crumbs

Cut squash into quarters; cook in butter until lightly browned. Turn squash into greased 1-quart casserole. Pour cream over squash. Sprinkle with salt and pepper. Top with crumbs. Bake in moderate oven (350° F.) about 30 minutes, or until squash is tender. Serves 4.

SUMMER SQUASH SOUFFLÉ

1 tablespoon butter
1 tablespoon all-purpose flour
⅛ teaspoon salt
⅛ teaspoon pepper
½ cup milk
3 eggs, separated
1 cup mashed, cooked summer squash

Melt butter, stir in flour, salt and pepper. Remove from heat and gradually add milk. Cook 3 minutes over low heat, stirring constantly. Add beaten egg yolks. Stir. Add squash. Fold in stiffly beaten egg whites. Turn into ungreased casserole. Bake in slow oven (325° F.) 30–35 minutes. Serves 4.

BAKED ACORN SQUASH

2 medium-sized acorn squash
1 tablespoon minced chives
1 tablespoon minced celery
2 tablespoons melted butter or margarine
¾ cup grated American cheese
1¼ cups soft bread crumbs
½ teaspoon salt
⅛ teaspoon pepper

Cut squash in half lengthwise; remove seeds and stringy portion. Place cut side down in buttered baking pan. Bake in hot oven (400° F.) 25 minutes. Turn cut side up and continue baking 20–25 minutes or until tender. Scoop out pulp leaving a shell about ¼ inch thick. Mash pulp and add remaining ingredients. Stuff squash with bread-crumb mixture. Bake in moderate oven (350° F.) about 10–20 minutes, or until lightly browned. Serves 4.

ROSY RADISH SAUTÉ

2 medium-sized bunches radishes
2 tablespoons melted butter or margarine
⅓ cup light cream
½ teaspoon salt
⅛ teaspoon pepper

Cook radishes, covered, in small amount of boiling, salted water 10 minutes. Drain. Add radishes to butter or margarine and cook over low heat 10 minutes. Add remaining ingredients and heat to serving temperature. Serves 4–6.

SYRIAN BAKED EGGPLANT

1 medium-sized eggplant
¼ cup all-purpose flour (approx.)
3 tablespoons melted butter or margarine
1 teaspoon salt
⅛ teaspoon pepper
6 slices mild cheese

Peel eggplant and cut into slices ½ inch thick; coat eggplant slices with flour. Brown on both sides in butter or margarine. Sprinkle with salt and pepper. Alternate layers of eggplant and cheese in greased 2-quart casserole, ending with cheese. Bake in moderate oven (375° F.) about 20 minutes. Serves 4.

SUCCOTASH

2 cups cooked lima beans
2 cups cooked corn
2 tablespoons melted butter
½ cup light cream
½ teaspoon salt
⅛ teaspoon pepper
¼ teaspoon sugar

Combine all ingredients and heat to serving temperature. Serves 4.

TURNIPS WITH EGG SAUCE

3 tablespoons butter or margarine
3 tablespoons all-purpose flour
1½ cups milk
1½ teaspoon salt
⅛ teaspoon pepper
Dash cayenne pepper
2 hard-cooked eggs, chopped
4 cups diced, cooked yellow or white turnips

Melt butter or margarine; blend in flour. Gradually add milk and cook, stirring constantly, until thickened. Add remaining ingredients and heat to serving temperature, stirring constantly. Serves 6.

BAKED TOMATOES IN CREAM

6 medium-sized tomatoes
¼ cup chopped green pepper
¼ cup chopped pimiento
¼ cup chopped onion
1 teaspoon salt
⅛ teaspoon pepper
⅛ teaspoon oregano
2 tablespoons melted butter or margarine
1 cup light cream

Remove stem ends from tomatoes. Arrange tomatoes in greased shallow baking pan. Combine remaining ingredients and pour over tomatoes. Bake in moderate oven (350° F.) about 45 minutes, or until tomatoes are tender. Baste with cream mixture occasionally during baking period. Serves 6.

COUNTRY FRIED TOMATOES

6 medium-sized tomatoes
Flour
3 tablespoons melted butter
2 tablespoons all-purpose flour
1 cup light cream
Salt and pepper

Cut tomatoes into ½" slices. Dip in flour. Cook in butter until lightly browned on both sides. Remove tomatoes. Add 2 tablespoons flour to butter and stir until browned. Gradually add cream and cook, stirring constantly, until thickened. Season with salt and pepper. Add tomato slices and heat to serving temperature. Serves 6.

STEWED TOMATOES WITH ONIONS

1 cup sliced onions
2 cups chopped fresh tomatoes
½ teaspoon salt
⅛ teaspoon pepper
½ cup dry bread cubes
1 tablespoon butter or margarine

Combine onions, tomatoes, salt and pepper. Cover and cook over low heat 25–30 minutes, or until onions are tender. Add remaining ingredients. Stir until butter or margarine melts. Serves 4.

TOMATO-CORN FARM STYLE

8 medium-sized tomatoes
¼ cup butter
1 teaspoon salt
⅛ teaspoon pepper
½ teaspoon sugar
1 No. 303 can whole kernel corn

Remove stem ends from tomatoes. Cut tomatoes into quarters. Combine tomatoes, butter, salt, pepper and sugar. Cook, covered, over low heat 30 minutes. Add corn and heat to serving temperature. Serves 6–8.

BROILED OLIVE TOMATOES

4 medium-sized tomatoes
½ cup chopped stuffed olives
3 tablespoons butter or margarine
Pepper

Remove stem ends from tomatoes. Cut tomatoes into crosswise halves. Top with olives and dot with butter or margarine. Sprinkle lightly with pepper. Broil 3 or 4 inches from source of heat 10–15 minutes, or until tomatoes are tender. Serves 4.

FRIED SWEET POTATOES

4 cups thinly sliced sweet potatoes
½ cup thinly sliced onions
¼ cup melted fat
1 teaspoon salt
⅛ teaspoon pepper

Cook sweet potatoes and onions in fat, covered, 15 minutes. Turn and add salt

and pepper. Continue cooking, covered, 15 minutes or until potatoes are tender. Serves 4–6.

OLD-FASHIONED SWEET POTATO PONE

½ cup all-purpose flour
½ teaspoon cinnamon
¼ teaspoon freshly grated nutmeg
¾ teaspoon salt
4 cups grated, raw sweet potatoes
1 egg
¾ cup corn syrup
3 tablespoons melted butter
1 cup milk

Sift flour and seasonings. Add remaining ingredients. Pour into greased 1½-quart baking dish. Bake in slow oven (325° F.) for 2¼ hours, stirring occasionally during first hour. Serves 8.

DE SOTO PARISH SWEET POTATOES

3 cups cubed cooked sweet potatoes
½ cup chopped green pepper
½ cup chopped onions
1 tablespoon chopped pimiento
⅛ teaspoon salt
⅓ cup melted bacon drippings

Combine sweet potatoes, green pepper, onions, pimiento and salt; mix lightly. Cook vegetable mixture in bacon drippings over medium heat until browned. Serves 4.

SWEET POTATOES WITH APPLES

3 sweet potatoes
3 apples
3 tablespoons butter
1 teaspoon salt
½ cup firmly packed brown sugar

Peel and cut sweet potatoes into ¼" slices. Peel, core and slice apples. Melt butter; add potatoes and apples. Season with salt, and sprinkle with sugar. Cook, covered, over low heat about 30 minutes or until tender, turning occasionally. Serves 6.

CANDIED SWEET POTATOES

4 medium-sized cooked, peeled sweet
   potatoes
1 cup firmly packed brown sugar
3 tablespoons butter
2 tablespoons cornstarch
1 cup water
¼ teaspoon salt
½ teaspoon nutmeg

Cut sweet potatoes in half lengthwise. Arrange sweet potatoes in greased shallow baking pan. Combine remaining ingredients and cook, stirring constantly, over low heat until thickened. Pour sugar mixture over sweet potatoes. Bake in moderate oven (350° F.) 30 minutes. Baste occasionally during baking period. Serves 4.

COMPANY BAKED YAMS

6 medium-sized yams, cooked and peeled
1 No. 2 can crushed pineapple
1 cup firmly packed brown sugar
1 tablespoon butter
½ teaspoon salt
½ cup chopped pecans
8 marshmallows

Cut yams in half lengthwise. Arrange yams in greased 8" x 8" pan. Combine pineapple, sugar, butter, salt and pecans; heat to boiling point, stirring constantly. Simmer 5 minutes. Pour pineapple mixture over yams. Top with marshmallows. Bake in moderate oven (350° F.) 30 min-

utes. Baste occasionally during baking period. Serves 6.

YAM AND PRUNE CASSEROLE

4 medium-sized yams, cooked and peeled
1 cup cooked prunes
½ cup firmly packed brown sugar
1 teaspoon salt
2 tablespoons orange juice
2 tablespoons lemon juice
½ teaspoon nutmeg
¼ cup melted butter

Cut yams into ¼" slices. Arrange yams and prunes alternately in greased 1½-quart casserole. Sprinkle each layer with sugar. Combine remaining ingredients and pour over yam mixture. Bake in moderate oven (350° F.) 40 minutes. Serves 6.

BAKED TURNIP WITH PARSLEY

4 cups cooked, mashed white or yellow
   turnip
3 tablespoons melted butter or margarine
3 tablespoons chopped parsley
½ teaspoon salt
1 egg, well beaten
½ cup grated American cheese

Combine turnip, butter or margarine, parsley and salt. Turn into greased 1½-quart baking dish. Pour egg over turnip mixture. Top with cheese. Bake in hot oven (400° F.) 20–25 minutes. Serves 4.

ZUCCHINI WITH TOMATO

3 medium-sized zucchini
2 tablespoons minced onion
2 tablespoons melted butter or margarine
1 No. 2 can tomatoes
1 teaspoon salt
⅛ teaspoon pepper

Cut zucchini into ½″ slices, cook, covered, in small amount boiling salted water about 5 minutes or until tender. Drain. Cook onion in butter or margarine until tender; add tomatoes, salt and pepper. Simmer 5 minutes. Add zucchini and heat to serving temperature. Serves 6.

LOMPOC ZUCCHINI WITH MUSHROOMS

1 pound zucchini
1 pound mushrooms, sliced
¼ cup melted butter or margarine

3 tablespoons all-purpose flour
1 cup light cream
1 teaspoon salt
⅛ teaspoon pepper

Cut zucchini into 1″ slices. Cook, covered, in a small amount of boiling salted water until tender; drain. Cook mushrooms in butter or margarine until tender. Remove mushrooms. Blend flour into butter or margarine. Gradually add cream and cook, stirring constantly, until thickened. Add salt, pepper, mushrooms and zucchini. Heat to serving temperature, stirring occasionally. Serves 4.

Fruit

HOT APPLE SAUCE

3 medium-sized apples
1½ cups water
1 tablespoon vinegar
½ cup firmly packed brown sugar
1½ tablespoons cornstarch
1 teaspoon dry mustard
¼ teaspoon cinnamon
¼ teaspoon salt
3 tablespoons butter

Pare and core apples; cut into thin slices. Heat water to boiling point; add vinegar and apples and cook 1 minute. Remove apples. Combine sugar, cornstarch, mustard, cinnamon and salt. Gradually add to water and mixture and cook over low heat, stirring constantly, until thickened.

Add butter and apples. Heat to serving temperature, stirring occasionally. Serve with ham and beef, as desired. Makes about 2 cups.

GLAZED APPLE RINGS

4 large tart apples
1½ cups water
1 cup sugar
2 tablespoons cinnamon candies
⅛ teaspoon salt

Core apples and cut into ½″ slices. Combine remaining ingredients and heat to boiling point. Add apple slices and simmer about 10 minutes, or until apples are tender. Serve with meat. Serves 6.

BAKED APPLE SURPRISE

6 medium-sized tart apples
⅓ cup chopped pecans
⅓ cup sugar
2 tablespoons butter or margarine
1 cup orange juice

Core apples and place in greased shallow baking pan. Combine pecans and sugar. Fill apple centers with pecan mixture. Dot with butter or margarine. Pour orange juice over apples. Bake in moderate oven (350° F.) 35–40 minutes, or until apples are tender. Baste apples with orange juice occasionally during baking period. Serves 6.

APPLE CRISP

6 cups sliced tart apples
1 cup sifted all-purpose flour
½ cup firmly packed brown sugar
1 teaspoon cinnamon
½ teaspoon nutmeg
⅓ cup butter

Arrange apples in greased 2-quart casserole. Combine flour, sugar, cinnamon and nutmeg. Cut in butter. Sprinkle sugar mixture over apples. Bake in moderate oven (350° F.) about 30 minutes, or until apples are tender. Serve with cream as desired. Serves 6.

BANANAS GLACÉ

¼ cup butter
6 bananas, peeled
¼ cup currant jelly
1 tablespoon orange juice
½ cup apricot nectar

Melt butter; add bananas. Cook until bananas are lightly browned. Add remaining ingredients. Continue cooking until bananas are tender. Baste often with sauce. Serves 6.

MINCEMEAT STUFFED APPLES

6 medium-sized tart apples
1 cup mincemeat
2 tablespoons butter
1 cup sugar
1½ cups water
1 tablespoon brandy

Core apples and arrange in greased shallow baking pan. Fill apple centers with mincemeat. Dot with butter. Combine sugar, water and brandy; pour over apples. Bake in moderate oven (350° F.) 30–45 minutes, or until apples are tender. Serves 6.

BLUEBERRY SLUMP

4 cups blueberries
3 cups water
2 cups sugar
1½ cups sifted all-purpose flour
⅛ teaspoon salt
1½ teaspoons baking powder
½ cup light cream

Combine berries, water and sugar. Cook over low heat until berries are soft. Sift flour, salt and baking powder together. Add cream and mix lightly. Drop by tablespoonfuls into blueberry mixture. Cover and cook 15 minutes. Serves 6.

GLAZED ORANGES

4 seedless oranges
½ cup sugar
⅓ cup water
2 tablespoons light corn syrup
4 whole cloves

Peel and section oranges. Combine remaining ingredients and heat to boiling point. Add orange sections and simmer 5 minutes. Serves 4.

SPICY BANANA BAKE

6 firm bananas
¼ cup melted butter
¼ cup lemon juice
½ cup sugar
½ teaspoon cinnamon
½ teaspoon nutmeg

Peel bananas and cut in half lengthwise. Arrange bananas in greased shallow baking pan. Combine remaining ingredients and pour evenly over bananas. Bake in moderate oven (350° F.) 15 minutes, or until bananas are tender. Serves 6.

COLD FRUIT COUP

2 pounds sweet cherries, pitted
2 cups sugar
3 quarts water
2 teaspoons grated lemon rind
¾ pint sherry

Combine cherries, sugar and water. Cook over low heat until mixture boils, stirring frequently. Cool. Add lemon rind and sherry. Chill thoroughly. Serves 6.

FRIED PEARS OREGON

1 cup sifted all-purpose flour
1 teaspoon baking powder
¼ teaspoon salt
1 tablespoon sugar
3 eggs, well beaten
1 cup milk
6 large pears, cored and peeled
Fat
¼ cup confectioners' sugar

Sift flour, baking powder, salt and the 1 tablespoon sugar together. Add eggs and milk to sifted ingredients; stir until smooth. Dip pears into egg mixture. Fry in deep hot fat (350° F.) 2–3 minutes, or until browned on all sides. Drain on absorbent paper. Sprinkle with confectioners' sugar. Serves 6.

SAUTEED PEACHES

6 medium-sized peaches
¼ cup firmly packed brown sugar
2 tablespoons butter

Peel peaches; cut in half and remove pits. Sprinkle peaches with sugar. Melt butter; add peaches and cook over low heat 10 minutes, or until peaches are tender. Serves 6.

QUICK SPICED PEACHES

1 No. 2½ can peach halves
1 cup firmly packed brown sugar
½ cup vinegar
2 3″ sticks cinnamon
1½ teaspoons whole cloves

Drain peaches and reserve syrup. Combine peach syrup, sugar, vinegar, cinnamon and cloves. Simmer 5 minutes. Add peaches and simmer 5 minutes. Chill 24 hours. Serve with meat or poultry. Serves 8.

STEWED PEACHES

¾ cup sugar
1 cup water
12 fresh peaches, peeled

Combine sugar and water. Heat to boiling point. Add peaches and simmer about 20 minutes, or until tender. Chill thoroughly. Serves 6.

PEARS IN WINE

4 fresh pears
¾ cup sugar
½ cup sherry or port wine
1 tablespoon butter

Cut pears in half and remove cores. Place cut side down on greased shallow baking pan. Combine remaining ingredients and heat to boiling point. Pour wine mixture over pears and make in moderate oven

(350° F.) 15 minutes. Turn pears and baste with sauce. Continue baking 15 minutes. Serves 4.

DELUXE BLUEBERRY FRUIT CUP

1 cup blueberries
1 cup diced peaches
½ cup diced pears
1 cup strawberries
½ cup water
½ cup light corn syrup
1 tablespoon lemon juice
1 teaspoon grated lemon rind
¼ teaspoon cinnamon
¼ teaspoon nutmeg

Combine fruits and mix lightly. Combine remaining ingredients. Heat to boiling point and simmer 10 minutes. Cool. Add syrup to fruits and mix lightly. Chill thoroughly. Serves 6.

BAKED PEACHES

1 tablespoon grated orange rind
¼ cup sugar
¼ cup orange juice
6 fresh peaches
¼ cup melted butter
2 cups crushed corn flakes

Combine orange rind, sugar and juice. Peel peaches; cut in half, removing pits. Dip peach halves in orange mixture, then butter and roll in corn flakes. Place peaches in greased 7" x 11" baking pan. Bake in moderate oven (350° F.) about 30 minutes, or until peaches are tender. Serves 6.

CRANBERRY-ORANGE COMPOTE

2 cups raw cranberries
1 cup orange sections
5 whole cloves
2 cups diced fresh pears
1 cup light corn syrup

Combine all ingredients and turn into greased 1½-quart baking dish. Bake in moderate oven (350° F.) 30 minutes, or until pears are tender. Serves 6.

HONEY GINGER PEARS

¼ cup honey
¼ cup sugar
½ teaspoon ginger
1 tablespoon grated lemon rind
1 tablespoon lemon juice
½ cup water
8 pears

Combine honey, sugar, ginger, lemon rind, lemon juice and water. Heat to boiling point and cook 5 minutes. Arrange pears in greased shallow baking pan. Pour lemon mixture over pears. Cover and bake in moderate oven (350° F.) 30 minutes, or until pears are tender. Serves 8.

PRUNES IN CLARET

1 cup claret wine
¾ cup water
2 dozen dried prunes
⅓ cup sugar
¼ teaspoon vanilla

Combine wine and water; add prunes and let stand several hours. Cook 25 minutes, or until prunes are tender. Add sugar and continue cooking 5 minutes. Stir in vanilla. Chill. Serves 6.

GINGER PRUNES CATHAY

3 cups dried prunes
5 cups water
3 lemons, thinly sliced
2 cups sugar
⅓ cup sliced preserved ginger

Combine all ingredients, and cook over low heat, covered, 1¼ hours. Chill thoroughly before serving. Serves 6–8.

SHERRY GRAPEFRUIT BROIL

2 grapefruits, cut in half
¼ cup firmly packed brown sugar
½ teaspoon nutmeg
¼ teaspoon cinnamon
1 tablespoon butter or margarine
¼ cup sherry

Section grapefruits. Combine sugar and spices. Sprinkle sugar mixture over grapefruit sections. Dot with butter or margarine. Broil 3 or 4 inches from source of heat about 5 minutes, or until lightly browned. Pour sherry over grapefruit. Serve hot. Serves 4.

ISABEL'S MELON RINGS
(Kentucky)

Peel 1 medium-sized cantaloupe, remove seeds and cut into 1-inch slices. Arrange cantaloupe rings on serving plates. Fill centers with diced pineapple, using about 1 cup. Centers may be filled with fruit sherbet, if desired. Serves 4.

ORANGE AND GRAPEFRUIT CUP

½ cup diced orange sections
1 cup diced grapefruit sections
¼ cup chopped maraschino cherries
2 tablespoons lime juice

Combine all ingredients and chill. Serve with Custard Sauce, if desired. Serves 4.

STRAWBERRY-MELON BALL CUP

1 package frozen crushed strawberries
1 package frozen melon balls
¼ cup chopped mint

Thaw strawberries and melon balls. Arrange in serving dishes. Top with mint. Serves 8.

Salads

FRUIT SALADS

APPLE-ONION SALAD

2 cups diced apples
2 tablespoons chopped onion
¼ cup salad oil
¼ cup vinegar
½ teaspoon salt
Salad greens

Combine apples, onion, oil, vinegar and salt. Mix lightly and arrange on greens. Serve immediately. Serves 4.

WALDORF SALAD

4 unpeeled red apples, cubed
3 tablespoons lemon juice
2 cups diced celery
½ cup chopped walnuts
Mayonnaise
Salad greens

Combine apples, lemon juice, celery and walnuts with enough mayonnaise to moisten. Arrange on greens. Serves 4.

GELATIN

AND FROZEN SALADS

APPLE-STRAWBERRY DESSERT SALAD

2 packages strawberry-flavored gelatin
3½ cups hot apple juice
¼ cup lemon juice
2 cups diced apples
1 cup chopped celery
½ cup chopped pecans
½ cup salad dressing
Salad greens

Dissolve gelatin in apple juice. Add lemon juice. Pour into ring mold and chill until firm. Combine apples, celery, pecans and salad dressing. Unmold gelatin; fill center with apple mixture. Garnish with greens. Serves 6–8.

FROZEN DATE AND HONEY SALAD

¼ cup honey
1 8-ounce package cream cheese

1 cup canned crushed pineapple
2 tablespoons chopped pecans
½ cup chopped dates
½ cup heavy cream, whipped

Combine honey and cheese. Beat until well blended. Add pineapple, pecans and dates. Fold in cream. Turn into refrigerator tray. Freeze until firm. Serve with salad greens, if desired. Serves 6.

MOLDED FRUIT SALAD

1 envelope unflavored gelatin
⅓ cup cold water
⅓ cup boiling water
⅓ cup lemon juice
1 cup ginger ale
½ cup chopped pecans
½ cup blueberries
½ cup diced peaches
Salad greens

Soften gelatin in cold water. Add boiling water and stir until dissolved. Add lemon juice and ginger ale. Chill until slightly thickened. Fold in pecans, blueberries and peaches. Turn into 1-quart mold and chill until firm. Unmold and garnish with greens. Serve with French dressing, as desired. Serves 4–6.

RIO GRANDE LIME SALAD

1 package lime-flavored gelatin
1 cup boiling water
1 No. 2 can crushed pineapple
1 cup cottage cheese
2 tablespoons chopped pimiento
1 3-ounce package cream cheese
2 tablespoons mayonnaise
2 tablespoons lemon juice
Salad greens

Combine gelatin and water; stir until gelatin is dissolved. Chill until slightly thickened. Fold in pineapple, cottage cheese and pimiento. Turn into 8″ x 8″

pan and chill until firm. Combine cream cheese, mayonnaise and lemon juice. Beat until light and fluffy. Cut lime mixture into squares and arrange on greens. Top with cream-cheese mixture. Serves 6–8.

MINTED APPLE SALAD

2 cups diced apples
¼ cup lemon juice
2 cups diced celery
Salad dressing
¼ teaspoon salt
1 tablespoon finely chopped mint
Salad greens

Combine apples, lemon juice, celery and enough salad dressing to moisten. Add salt and mint; toss lightly. Arrange on greens. Serves 6.

CRANBERRY-ORANGE SALAD

2 cups cranberries
1 orange, quartered
1 cup sugar
2 large apples, cored and diced
2 tablespoons lemon juice

Grind cranberries and orange. Add sugar and chill. Add apples and lemon juice; mix well. Serve with salad greens, if desired. Serves 6.

BOG CRANBERRY-PEAR SALAD

1 3-ounce package cream cheese with chives
¼ cup cranberry sauce
¼ cup chopped pecans
1 No. 2 can pear halves, well drained

Combine cheese, cranberry sauce and pecans. Beat until thoroughly blended. Top pear halves with cheese mixture. Serve with salad greens, if desired. Serves 4.

HOLIDAY SALAD

1 package lemon-flavored gelatin
2 cups cranberries, ground
½ cup drained canned crushed pineapple
1 cup diced apples
½ cup orange sections
¼ teaspoon salt
Salad greens
Salad dressing

Prepare gelatin according to package directions. Chill until slightly thickened. Fold in cranberries, pineapple, apples, orange sections and salt. Pour into 8″ x 8″ pan and chill until firm. Cut salad into squares and arrange on greens. Top with salad dressing. Serves 6.

APPLE RING SALAD

2 red apples, cored and sliced
¼ cup lemon juice
1 3-ounce package cream cheese
2 tablespoons light cream
½ cup chopped dates
2 tablespoons chopped walnuts
Salad greens
French dressing

Brush apple slices with lemon juice. Combine cheese, cream, dates, and walnuts. Arrange apple slices on greens. Top with cheese mixture. Serve with French dressing. Serves 4.

FRUIT SALAD BOWL

1 small head lettuce
2 cups watermelon balls
2 cups cantaloupe balls
1 cup white grapes
French dressing

Separate lettuce into leaves; line salad bowl with lettuce leaves. Arrange fruits over lettuce; add enough French dressing to moisten. Serves 4.

EGG-SHRIMP ASPIC

2 packages unflavored gelatin
1 cup cold water
2 10½ ounce cans (2½ cups) consommé
3 tablespoons lemon juice
¼ cup sherry
1 pound cooked shrimp
8 eggs, poached
Mayonnaise

Soften gelatin in water. Heat consommé to boiling point; add gelatin and stir until dissolved. Add lemon juice and sherry; chill until slightly thickened. Arrange shrimp in 8 individual molds. Add enough gelatin mixture to cover shrimp. Add eggs. Pour remaining gelatin mixture over eggs. Chill until firm. Serve with mayonnaise. Serves 8.

GULF SHRIMP SALAD MOLD

1 package lemon-flavored gelatin
1¾ cups boiling water
1 cup cooked chopped shrimp
1 cup diced celery
½ cup chopped stuffed olives
¼ cup chopped sweet pickles
¼ teaspoon salt
Salad greens
Salad dressing

Add gelatin to water and stir until dissolved. Chill until slightly thickened. Add shrimp, celery, olives, pickles and salt. Turn into 1½-quart mold and chill until firm. Unmold and garnish with greens. Serve with dressing. Serves 4–6.

TOMATO-AVOCADO MOLD

1 envelope unflavored gelatin
¼ cup cold water
1¾ cups tomato juice
1 bay leaf
3 whole cloves
¼ cup minced onions
½ teaspoon salt
⅛ teaspoon pepper
1 cup diced avocado
1 cup diced celery
Salad greens

Soften gelatin in cold water. Combine tomato juice, bay leaf, cloves, onions, salt and pepper. Simmer 5 minutes; strain. Add gelatin and stir until dissolved. Chill until slightly thickened. Fold in avocado and celery. Turn into 1½-quart mold and chill until firm. Unmold and garnish with greens. Serve with French dressing, as desired. Serves 6.

DILL TOMATO ASPIC

1 envelope unflavored gelatin
¼ cup cold water
1 8-ounce can tomato sauce
¾ cup water
¼ teaspoon dill seeds
2 tablespoons vinegar
1 teaspoon horseradish
½ teaspoon salt
⅛ teaspoon pepper
½ teaspoon sugar

Soften gelatin in cold water. Combine tomato sauce and water; heat to boiling point. Add gelatin and stir until dissolved. Add remaining ingredients and mix well. Turn into 2-cup mold. Chill until firm. Unmold and garnish with salad greens, as desired. Serves 4.

STRAWBERRY-FRUIT SALAD

1 pint strawberries, cleaned
1 cup honeydew melon balls
1 grapefruit, peeled and sectioned
1 cup canned pineapple chunks
Mayonnaise

Combine fruits with enough mayonnaise to moisten; serve on salad greens, if desired. Serves 6.

MEAT, FISH, AND CHEESE SALADS

GOURMET SWISS CHEESE SALAD

½ pound Swiss cheese, diced
6 hard-cooked eggs, chopped
½ cup sour cream
1 tablespoon prepared mustard
2 teaspoons chopped sweet pickle
½ teaspoon salt
¼ teaspoon pepper
1 teaspoon chopped chives

Combine all ingredients and mix lightly. Serve with lettuce, romaine or chicory, as desired. Serves 6.

HOT CHICKEN SALAD DELAWARE

3 cups diced, cooked chicken
1 cup diced celery
1 tablespoon grated onion
½ cup chopped almonds
1 tablespoon lemon juice
1 teaspoon grated lemon rind
1 cup grated Cheddar cheese
½ teaspoon salt
⅛ teaspoon pepper
Mayonnaise
1 cup crushed potato chips

Combine chicken, celery, onion, almonds, lemon juice, lemon rind, cheese, salt and pepper. Add enough mayonnaise to moisten; turn into greased individual baking dishes. Top with potato chips. Bake in moderate oven (350° F.) 25–30 minutes, or until lightly browned. Serves 4–6.

CRAB MEAT SALAD À LA REINE

4 cups cooked flaked crab meat
1 tablespoon chopped pimiento
¼ cup chopped green pepper
1 tablespoon grated onion
1 teaspoon salt
⅛ teaspoon pepper
3 hard-cooked eggs, chopped
French dressing
Salad greens

Combine crab meat, pimiento, green pepper, onion, salt, pepper and eggs; mix lightly. Add enough French dressing to moisten. Arrange on greens. Serves 6.

CHOPPED HERRING SALAD PARISIENNE

2 cups grated cabbage
⅔ cup grated carrot
2 tablespoons grated onion
¼ cup chopped green pepper
¼ cup chopped marinated herring
2 tablespoons lemon juice
½ cup sour cream
¼ teaspoon sugar

Combine all ingredients; mix lightly. Serve with salad greens, if desired. Serves 4.

HAM AND POTATO SALAD

2 cups diced, cooked ham
2 cups diced, cooked potatoes
1 cup chopped celery
¼ cup chopped green pepper
4 hard-cooked eggs, chopped
½ cup salad dressing
2 tablespoons prepared mustard
1 tablespoon vinegar
1 teaspoon salt
⅛ teaspoon pepper

Combine all ingredients; mix lightly. Serve with salad greens, if desired. Serves 6.

CHICKEN-APPLE SALAD NEW YORK

2 cups diced cooked chicken
1 cup diced apple
2 tablespoons lemon juice
¼ cup chopped celery
¼ cup chopped green pepper
1 teaspoon salt
Salad dressing
Salad greens

Combine chicken, apple, lemon juice, celery, green pepper and salt; mix lightly. Add enough salad dressing to moisten. Arrange chicken mixture on greens. Serves 4.

CHICKEN SALAD CAPRI

2 cups cooked, cubed chicken
1 cup French dressing
3 cups shredded lettuce
6 poached eggs, chilled
½ cup mayonnaise
2 cups cooked chilled asparagus tips

Combine chicken and French dressing; let stand 1 hour. Arrange lettuce on serving plates. Arrange chicken mixture over lettuce and cover with eggs. Top with mayonnaise. Surround eggs with asparagus tips. Serves 6.

VEGETABLE SALADS

ASPARAGUS SALAD BOWL

1½ pounds fresh asparagus, cooked
3 hard-cooked eggs, chopped
1 cup thin cucumber slices

3 tomatoes, cut in wedges
½ cup chopped green pepper
½ cup onion rings
1 medium-sized head lettuce, broken in
     bite-size pieces

Cut asparagus in 1″ pieces. Add remaining ingredients and toss lightly. Serve with French dressing or mayonnaise, as desired. Serves 6–8.

LAMB AND CELERY SALAD

2½ cups diced cooked lamb
3 tablespoons chili sauce
2 tablespoons chopped dill pickle
1 hard-cooked egg, chopped
1½ cups chopped celery
½ cup chopped water cress
1 teaspoon salt
⅛ teaspoon pepper
Mayonnaise

Combine lamb, chili sauce, pickle, egg, celery, water cress, salt and pepper; mix lightly. Add enough mayonnaise to moisten. Serve with salad greens, as desired. Serves 6.

SALMON SALAD ALASKA

2 cups cooked flaked salmon
¾ cup chopped celery
1 cup cooked peas
3 hard-cooked eggs, chopped
2 teaspoons capers
1 cup mayonnaise
1 teaspoon salt
⅛ teaspoon pepper

Combine all ingredients; mix lightly. Chill thoroughly. Arrange salmon mixture on salad greens, as desired. Serves 4.

SARDINE-PEA SALAD

½ cup mashed sardines
1 tablespoon lemon juice
⅓ cup salad dressing

1 cup cooked peas
½ cup chopped celery
1 tablespoon chopped onion
2 hard-cooked eggs, chopped
¼ teaspoon salt
⅛ teaspoon pepper

Combine all ingredients and mix lightly. Serve on salad greens, if desired. Serves 4.

VEAL PEPPER SALAD

2 cups diced, cooked veal
1 cup chopped green pepper
1½ cups chopped celery
3 hard-cooked eggs, chopped
⅓ cup chopped dill pickles
Salad dressing

Combine veal, pepper, celery, eggs and pickles. Add enough salad dressing to moisten. Serve with salad greens, if desired. Serves 6.

VEGETABLE MEAT SALAD

2 cups shredded cabbage
1 cup cooked diced green beans
1 cup grated carrots
¼ cup onion rings
1 cup thin luncheon meat strips
1 cup thin Cheddar or American cheese
    strips
1 cup French dressing
Salt and pepper to taste
Salad greens

Combine vegetables, meat, cheese and French dressing. Season with salt and pepper. Serve on greens. Serves 6.

ASPARAGUS-ALMOND SALAD

16 cooked asparagus spears
4 green pepper rings
Salad greens
½ cup toasted slivered almonds
½ cup French dressing

Arrange asparagus and green pepper rings on greens. Combine almonds and French dressing; pour dressing over salad. Serves 4.

AVOCADO ROMAINE SALAD

1 head romaine
1 head lettuce
1 tomato, cut in wedges
1 avocado, peeled and sliced
2 tablespoons sweet pickle relish
¼ cup onion rings
French dressing

Tear romaine and lettuce in bite-size pieces. Combine romaine, lettuce, tomato, avocado, pickle relish, onion rings and enough French dressing to moisten. Serves 6.

BEAN AND BACON SALAD IOWA

2 cups cooked, diced green beans
¼ cup cooked, crumbled bacon
1 cup chopped celery
2 tablespoons chopped green pepper
½ cup onion rings
Mayonnaise

Combine beans, bacon, celery, green pepper and onion rings; mix lightly. Add enough mayonnaise to moisten. Serve on salad greens, if desired. Serves 6.

BEET AND CUCUMBER SALAD

1 cup sliced cucumber
½ cup diced, cooked beets
1 teaspoon salt
2 tablespoons vinegar
2 tablespoons minced onion
¾ cup sour cream

Sprinkle cucumber and beets with salt and let stand 1 hour. Add remaining ingredients and mix lightly. Serve with salad greens, if desired. Serves 4.

SHRIMP SALAD

2 cups diced, cooked shrimp
½ cup chopped stuffed olives
⅓ cup chopped sweet pickles
2 tablespoons chopped onion
French dressing

Combine shrimp, olives, pickles and onion. Add enough French dressing to moisten. Serve with salad greens, if desired. Serves 4.

PICKLED BEET SALAD

1 cup diced, cooked beets
¼ cup sweet pickle relish
½ cup diced cucumber
⅛ teaspoon salt
French dressing

Combine beets, pickle relish, cucumber and salt. Add enough French dressing to moisten. Serve on salad greens, if desired. Serves 4.

CABBAGE-CARROT SALAD

1 cup grated carrots
2 cups shredded cabbage
¼ cup chopped sweet pickles
1½ cups shredded turnip
Mayonnaise
Salt and pepper to taste
Salad greens

Combine carrots, cabbage, pickles, turnip and enough mayonnaise to moisten. Season with salt and pepper. Serve on salad greens. Serves 4.

OLD-FASHIONED COLESLAW

⅔ cup heavy cream
¼ cup vinegar
½ teaspoon salt
⅛ teaspoon pepper
3 cups shredded cabbage

Beat cream until stiff gradually adding vinegar. Combine cream mixture with salt, pepper and cabbage. Mix lightly. Chill thoroughly. Serves 4.

CABBAGE-CARROT SLAW

3 cups grated cabbage
¼ cup prepared mustard
2 tablespoons light cream
2 tablespoons lemon juice
1 teaspoon salt
1 cup grated carrots
¼ cup raisins

Combine all ingredients; mix lightly. Serves 4.

RED CABBAGE SALAD

4 cups grated red cabbage
1 large apple, cored and diced
1 cup chopped celery
1 cup heavy cream, whipped
1 tablespoon lemon juice
1 teaspoon grated lemon rind
1 teaspoon salt
1 tablespoon sugar
½ cup chopped walnuts

Combine all ingredients and mix lightly. Serves 4–6.

CARROT-RAISIN SALAD

2 cups grated carrots
½ cup raisins
2 tablespoons salad oil
1 tablespoon vinegar
1 tablespoon honey
⅛ teaspoon salt
⅛ teaspoon pepper
Lettuce
¼ cup mayonnaise

Combine carrots, raisins, oil, vinegar, honey, salt and pepper; mix lightly. Arrange carrot mixture on lettuce. Top with mayonnaise. Serves 4.

BLUE CHEESE TOSSED SALAD

1 small head lettuce
3 tomatoes, cut in wedges
1 cup sliced cucumber
½ cup diced celery
½ cup sliced radishes
½ cup crumbled blue cheese
French dressing

Break lettuce into bite-size pieces. Combine vegetables and cheese in salad bowl. Add enough French dressing to moisten. Toss lightly. Serves 4–6.

MIDWEST CORN AND BEAN SALAD

1 No. 2 can whole kernel corn, drained
1 No. 2 can cut green beans, drained
½ cup chopped celery
1 cup sliced radishes
2 talespoons catsup
½ cup mayonnaise

Combine corn, beans, celery and radishes. Blend catsup with mayonnaise and add to vegetable mixture. Mix lightly. Serve with salad greens, if desired. Serves 6.

COTTAGE CHEESE-STUFFED TOMATO SALAD

6 medium-sized tomatoes
2 cups cottage cheese
½ cup chopped green pepper
1 teaspoon salt
⅛ teaspoon pepper
Salad greens
⅓ cup mayonnaise

Remove stem ends from tomatoes; cut each tomato into quarters without cutting all the way through. Combine cottage cheese, green pepper, salt and pepper. Fill tomato centers with cheese mixture. Arrange tomatoes on greens. Top cheese mixture with mayonnaise. Serves 6.

HOT CHICORY SALAD

4 strips bacon, diced
2 tablespoons white vinegar
1 tablespoon garlic salt
Salt and pepper to taste
½ pound chicory

Cook bacon until crisp; add vinegar, garlic salt, salt and pepper. Pour over chicory. Serves 4.

HOT POTATO SALAD

6 medium sized unpeeled potatoes
4 slices bacon, diced
¼ cup minced onion
1 egg, beaten
½ cup vinegar
1 teaspoon salt
⅛ teaspoon pepper

Cook potatoes until tender. Drain, peel and slice. Cook bacon with onion until onion is tender. Remove bacon and onion; reserve drippings. Gradually add drippings to egg, stirring constantly. Add vinegar, salt and pepper. Combine potatoes, bacon, onion and egg mixture. Heat to serving temperature. Serves 6.

MIXED VEGETABLE SALAD

1 cup cucumber slices
1 cup cooked peas
1 cup cooked diced carrots
¼ cup chopped green pepper
2 tomatoes, diced
¼ cup onion rings
1 teaspoon salt
Salad greens
1 cup mayonnaise
2 tablespoons chili sauce

Combine vegetables and salt; mix lightly. Arrange vegetable mixture on greens. Combine mayonnaise and chili sauce. Top vegetables with mayonnaise mixture. Serves 4–6.

MARINATED TOMATO SALAD

4 large tomatoes
½ cup French dressing
¼ cup chopped chives
2 tablespoons chopped parsley
½ teaspoon salt
¼ teaspoon pepper

Peel and slice tomatoes; pour French dressing over tomatoes and let stand 1 hour. Sprinkle remaining ingredients over tomato mixture. Garnish with greens, if desired. Serves 6.

TOMATO-PEPPER SALAD WITH BACON DRESSING

1 cup chopped green peppers
2 cups diced tomatoes
¼ cup chopped onion
3 cups shredded lettuce
¼ teaspoon salt
4 slices bacon
1 teaspoon chili powder
⅓ cup vinegar

Combine peppers, tomatoes, onion, lettuce and salt. Cook bacon until crisp and crumble. Add chili powder and vinegar to bacon drippings and heat to boiling point. Add bacon and vinegar mixture to vegetable mixture and toss lightly. Serves 6.

VEGETABLE SALAD BOWL

2 cups sliced cucumbers
1 cup sliced radishes
⅓ cup chopped onions
1 small bunch water cress
1 cup chopped celery
1 cup shredded cabbage
1 teaspoon salt
French dressing

Combine vegetables and salt with enough French dressing to moisten. Serves 4–6.

HOT DUTCH POTATO SALAD

6 medium-sized potatoes, cooked and cubed
2 hard-cooked eggs, chopped
4 slices bacon
1 egg, beaten
⅓ cup minced onions
¼ cup vinegar
1 teaspoon salt

Combine potatoes and eggs. Cook bacon until crisp and crumble. Reserve bacon drippings. Add a little of drippings to egg and mix well. Stir into remaining drippings. Add onions, vinegar and salt. Cook, stirring constantly, until thickened. Add to potato mixture. Add bacon and toss lightly. Serves 4.

MARINATED LIMA BEAN SALAD

2 cups cooked lima beans
⅓ cup sour cream
1 clove garlic, minced
2 tablespoons chopped parsley
1 tablespoon vinegar
2 tablespoons salad oil
½ teaspoon sugar
1 teaspoon salt
1 tablespoon grated onion

Combine all ingredients. Mix lightly but thoroughly. Chill several hours. Serve on salad greens, as desired. Serves 6.

SOUR CREAM POTATO SALAD

4 cups diced cooked potatoes
½ cup diced celery
2 tablespoons grated onion
1 teaspoon celery seed
1 teaspoon salt

¼ teaspoon pepper
2 hard-cooked eggs, chopped
½ cup sour cream
2 tablespoons lemon juice
1 tablespoon prepared mustard

Combine potatoes, celery, onion, celery seed, salt and pepper. Mix lightly. Combine remaining ingredients and mix well. Add sour cream mixture to vegetable mixture and mix lightly. Serve with salad greens, as desired. Serves 4–6.

CUCUMBER-SOUR CREAM SALAD

2 large cucumbers
1½ cups sour cream
¼ cup chopped pecans
2 tablespoons grated onion
1 teaspoon lemon juice
½ teaspoon salt
Salad greens

Cut cucumbers into thin slices. Combine sour cream, pecans, onion, lemon juice and salt. Mix well and add to cucumber slices. Arrange on greens. Serves 4–6.

COUNTRY DANDELION GREEN SALAD

2 cups chopped, cooked dandelion greens
¼ cup sliced scallions
¼ cup grated cucumber
½ cup grated carrot
French dressing

Combine greens, scallions, cucumber and carrot. Add enough French dressing to moisten. Serve with salad greens, if desired. Serves 4.

ENDIVE-SOUR CREAM SALAD

1 medium-sized bunch endive
½ cup sour cream
2 tablespoons lemon juice

2 tablespoons horseradish
¼ teaspoon salt

Separate endive into leaves. Combine remaining ingredients and mix well; pour over endive. Serves 6.

CAULIFLOWER SALAD

1 small head cauliflower
1 apple, cored and diced
2 tablespoons lemon juice
¼ cup chopped onion
½ cup chopped parsley
½ cup chopped celery
½ teaspoon salt
⅛ teaspoon pepper
¼ cup vinegar
¼ cup salad oil

Separate cauliflower into small flowerets. Add remaining ingredients and mix lightly. Serves 6.

SPINACH AND EGG SALAD

1 pound fresh spinach, chopped
2 tablespoons chopped onions
2 tablespoons chopped green pepper
2 hard-cooked eggs, chopped
¾ cup French dressing
¼ teaspoon salt

Combine all ingredients; mix lightly. Serves 4–6.

Salad Dressings

UNCOOKED

CERISE CHIFFONADE DRESSING

1 cup French dressing
1 tablespoon chopped parsley
1 tablespoon grated onion
1 hard-cooked egg, chopped
¼ cup cooked chopped beets

Combine all ingredients and shake well. Makes about 1½ cups.

CHIFFONADE DRESSING

1 cup French dressing
2 tablespoons chopped sweet pickles
2 tablespoons grated onion
⅛ teaspoon salt
⅛ teaspoon pepper
2 tablespoons vinegar

Combine all ingredients and shake until thoroughly blended. Serve with salad greens as desired. Makes about 1¼ cups.

WHIPPED CREAM DRESSING

1 cup salad dressing
2 tablespoons lime juice
2 teaspoons sugar
1 cup heavy cream, whipped

Combine salad dressing, lime juice and sugar; mix well. Fold in cream. Serve with fruit salads, as desired. Makes about 2 cups.

CREAMY EGG DRESSING

2 hard-cooked eggs, chopped
2 tablespoons vinegar
1½ cups sour cream
½ teaspoon salt
⅛ teaspoon pepper
Dash cayenne pepper

Combine all ingredients and mix well. Serve with meat, fish and vegetable salads, as desired. Makes about 1¾ cups.

CALIFORNIA SALAD DRESSING

2 medium-sized avocados, sieved
2 tablespoons lemon juice
1 teaspoon grated lemon rind
2 tablespoons onion juice
½ teaspoon salt
⅛ teaspoon pepper

Combine all ingredients and mix well. Serve with meat and vegetable salads as desired. Makes about 1¾ cups.

CHILI SAUCE DRESSING

1 cup chili sauce
¼ cup sugar
¾ cup vinegar
1 cup salad oil
½ teaspoon salt

Combine all ingredients and shake until thoroughly blended. Serve with green and vegetable salads, as desired. Makes about 3 cups.

ANCHOVY-CHIVE DRESSING

8 anchovy fillets, chopped
1 tablespoon minced onion
2 tablespoons minced parsley
2½ cups salad dressing
¼ cup vinegar
¼ cup chopped chives

Combine all ingredients and mix well. Serve with meat and vegetable salads, as desired. Makes about 3 cups.

CREAMY CUCUMBER DRESSING

1 cup diced cucumbers
¾ cup sour cream
2 tablespoons vinegar
½ teaspoon salt
⅛ teaspoon paprika

Combine all ingredients and mix well. Serve with meat, fish, poultry and vegetable salads, as desired. Makes about 1½ cups.

HORSERADISH DRESSING

¾ cup salad oil
1 teaspoon salt
1 teaspoon sugar
3 tablespoons horseradish
1 tablespoon chopped chives
1 teaspoon paprika
⅓ cup vinegar
2 teaspoons dry mustard

⅛ teaspoon pepper
1 teaspoon Worcestershire sauce

Combine all ingredients and shake until thoroughly blended. Serve with meat, fish, poultry and vegetable salads, as desired. Makes about 1¼ cups.

LOW CALORIE DRESSING

1 cup tomato juice
1 teaspoon Worcestershire sauce
1 tablespoon onion juice
1 tablespoon lemon juice
½ teaspoon salt
⅛ teaspoon pepper

Combine all ingredients and shake well. Makes about 1 cup.

MAYONNAISE

1 egg
¼ teaspoon salt
⅛ teaspoon white pepper
⅛ teaspoon paprika
1 tablespoon lemon juice
1 cup salad oil

Combine egg, salt, pepper and paprika; beat well. Add lemon juice and beat well. Add oil, a few drops at a time, beating constantly. Makes about 1¼ cups.

POPPY SEED-ONION DRESSING

⅓ cup sugar
½ teaspoon salt
1 teaspoon dry mustard
1½ teaspoons poppy seeds
½ teaspoon celery seed
1 tablespoon onion juice
1 cup salad oil
¼ cup white vinegar

Combine sugar, salt, mustard, poppy seeds, celery seed and onion juice; mix well. Add oil, a few drops at a time, beating constantly. Add vinegar and mix well. Serve with fruit and vegetable salads, as desired. Makes about 1½ cups.

PINEAPPLE-LEMON DRESSING

⅓ cup pineapple juice
2 tablespoons lemon juice
½ cup salad oil
1 teaspoon grated lemon rind
1 teaspoon sugar
¼ teaspoon salt
½ teaspoon paprika

Combine all ingredients and shake until well blended. Serve with fruit salads, as desired. Makes about 1 cup.

SEA FOOD DRESSING

½ cup mayonnaise
½ cup chili sauce
½ cup chopped tomatoes
1 tablespoon lemon juice
¼ cup chopped green pepper
1 tablespoon onion juice
¼ teaspoon salt
⅛ teaspoon pepper

Combine all ingredients and mix well. Serve with fish salads, as desired. Makes about 1¾ cups.

RUSSIAN DRESSING

1 cup mayonnaise
2 tablespoons chili sauce
1 tablespoon sweet pickle relish
⅛ teaspoon salt
½ teaspoon sugar

Combine all ingredients and mix until well blended. Serve with meat, fish, poultry and vegetable salads, as desired. Makes about 1¼ cups.

FRENCH DRESSING

¼ cup vinegar
½ cup salad oil
¼ teaspoon paprika
1 teaspoon salt
⅛ teaspoon pepper

Combine all ingredients and shake until well blended. Serve with fruit and vegetable salads, as desired. Makes about ¾ cup.

THOUSAND ISLAND DRESSING

1 cup mayonnaise
⅓ cup chili sauce
1 tablespoon catsup
1 tablespoon minced green pepper
2 tablespoons chopped pimiento
1 tablespoon grated onion
½ teaspoon paprika

Combine all ingredients and mix well. Serve with meat, fish, poultry and vegetable salads, as desired. Makes about 1½ cups.

TOMATO DRESSING

½ cup tomato juice
2 tablespoons salad oil
3 tablespoons lemon juice
1 teaspoon salt
1 teaspoon dry mustard
1 tablespoon grated onion
1 tablespoon Worcestershire sauce

Combine all ingredients and shake until well blended. Serve with green, vegetable and meat salads, as desired. Makes about ¾ cup.

WINE DRESSING

½ cup dry white wine
¼ cup white vinegar
¾ cup salad oil
1 teaspoon salt
⅛ teaspoon pepper
1 teaspoon onion juice

Combine all ingredients and shake until well blended. Serve with meat, fish and vegetable salads, as desired. Makes about 1½ cups.

SOUR CREAM DRESSING

1 cup sour cream
2 tablespoons vinegar
1 tablespoon sugar
¼ teaspoon salt

Beat until thoroughly blended. Chill well. Makes about 1¼ cups.

TART CREAM DRESSING

1 cup heavy cream
¼ cup lemon juice
½ teaspoon salt
⅛ teaspoon white pepper

Combine all ingredients and beat until thoroughly blended. Serve with fruit or vegetable salads, as desired. Makes about 1¼ cups.

COOKED DRESSINGS

BOILED SALAD DRESSING

1 tablespoon sugar
1 tablespoon all-purpose flour
1 teaspoon dry mustard
3 eggs, slightly beaten
½ cup vinegar
½ cup water
Dash Tabasco
½ teaspoon salt
2 tablespoons butter or margarine

Combine sugar, flour and mustard; mix well. Add eggs, vinegar, water, Tabasco and salt. Cook over boiling water, stirring constantly, until thickened. Remove from heat and add butter or margarine. Stir until butter or margarine melts. Serve with meat, fish and vegetable salads, as desired. Makes about 1½ cups.

MUSTARD DRESSING

1 tablespoon sugar
1 tablespoon all-purpose flour
1 teaspoon dry mustard
½ teaspoon salt
2 eggs, slightly beaten
¾ cup light cream
½ cup vinegar
½ cup water
1 tablespoon onion juice

Combine sugar, flour, mustard and salt; mix well. Combine eggs and cream; add sugar mixture and mix well. Stir in remaining ingredients. Cook over boiling water, stirring constantly, until thickened. Serve with meat, fish and vegetable salads, as desired. Makes about 2 cups.

HOT BACON DRESSING

4 slices bacon, diced
2 teaspoons grated onion
⅓ cup vinegar
2 teaspoons sugar
½ teaspoon salt
⅛ teaspoon pepper

Cook bacon until crisp. Add remaining ingredients and heat to boiling point, stirring occasionally. Pour over salad greens, as desired. Makes about ¾ cup.

FRUIT SALAD DRESSING

2 eggs
2 tablespoons lemon juice
⅛ teaspoon dry mustard
¼ cup milk
1 cup heavy cream, whipped

Beat eggs with lemon juice and mustard. Add milk and cook over very low heat until thickened, stirring constantly. Cool thoroughly. Fold in cream. Makes about 1½ cups.

COOKED SOUR CREAM DRESSING

3 eggs, slightly beaten
1 cup sour cream
1 cup sugar
¾ cup vinegar
½ teaspoon salt
⅛ teaspoon pepper
1 teaspoon dry mustard
1 teaspoon horseradish

Combine all ingredients and cook over boiling water, stirring until ingredients are well blended. Continue cooking, stirring occasionally, until thickened. Serve with meat, fish, poultry and vegetable salads, as desired. Makes about 3 cups.

SWEET AND SOUR DRESSING

3 eggs, slightly beaten
¾ cup sugar
2 tablespoons all-purpose flour
¼ cup orange juice
1 tablespoon vinegar
1 cup water
2 tablespoons butter

Combine all ingredients and cook over low heat, stirring constantly, until thickened. Serve with fruit salads, as desired. Makes about 2½ cups.

Desserts

FROZEN DESSERTS

ICE CREAM APPLESAUCE PARFAIT

2 cups applesauce
1 pint vanilla ice cream
½ cup chopped walnuts
½ cup heavy cream, whipped

Arrange applesauce, ice cream and nuts alternately in layers in serving glasses. Top with whipped cream. Serves 6–8.

CRANBERRY FLUFF

1 1-pound can cranberry sauce
2 tablespoons sugar
1 tablespoon grated orange rind
1 cup heavy cream, whipped
½ teaspoon almond extract

Beat cranberry sauce with sugar and orange rind until light. Fold cream and almond extract into cranberry mixture. Turn into refrigerator tray and freeze until firm. Stir occasionally during freezing period. Serves 6.

APRICOT-ALMOND SHERBET

2 egg whites
½ cup sugar
½ cup light corn syrup
¼ teaspoon salt
2 tablespoons lemon juice
2 teaspoons grated lemon rind
1 cup apricot puree
1 cup light cream
¼ cup chopped almonds

Beat egg whites until frothy. Gradually add sugar, beating constantly. Continue beating until stiff. Gradually add syrup and salt, beating constantly. Combine remaining ingredients and fold into egg-white mixture. Turn into refrigerator tray and freeze until frozen 1 inch from sides of tray. Turn into chilled bowl and beat until smooth. Turn into refrigerator tray and freeze until firm. Serves 6.

AVOCADO-WALNUT ICE CREAM

1 cup milk
1 cup light cream
½ cup sugar
3 egg yolks, well beaten
¾ cup avocado pulp
¼ cup chopped walnuts

Combine milk, cream and sugar; heat to boiling point, stirring constantly. Pour cream mixture over egg yolks, stirring constantly. Add remaining ingredients and mix well. Cool and turn into refrigerator trays. Freeze until firm. Turn into chilled bowl and beat until smooth. Turn into refrigerator trays and freeze until firm. Serves 10–12.

ICEBOX BANANA WHIP

6 bananas, mashed
¼ cup lemon juice
½ cup orange juice
½ cup sugar
2 egg whites, beaten stiff

Combine bananas, juices and sugar. Turn into refrigerator tray. Freeze until mushy. Fold in egg whites. Freeze until firm. Serves 6.

TOASTED ALMOND ICE CREAM

1 cup toasted almonds
2½ cups milk, scalded
1 cup sugar
1 teaspoon vanilla
1 teaspoon almond extract
1 cup heavy cream, whipped

Grind almonds. Combine milk and sugar; stir until sugar is dissolved. Add almonds, vanilla and almond extract; mix well. Cool thoroughly. Fold in cream. Turn into refrigerator tray and freeze until frozen 1 inch from sides of tray. Beat well. Turn into refrigerator tray and freeze until firm. Serves 6.

FIG RUM FREEZE

2 cups milk
2 cups light cream
6 eggs, separated
1 cup sugar
3 tablespoons rum
4 cups fresh figs, peeled and chopped

Scald milk and cream together. Beat egg yolks with sugar until light. Beat egg whites until stiff. Pour milk mixture over sugar and egg yolks, stirring constantly. Fold in egg whites. Add rum. Add figs. Freeze until firm. Serves 6.

BLUE BAY GINGER FREEZE

¼ pound preserved ginger, chopped
3 cups light cream
½ cup sugar
1 tablespoon ginger syrup

Combine all ingredients. Turn into refrigerator tray. Freeze until firm. Serves 6–8.

CREAMY LEMON SHERBET

1½ cups sugar
¾ cup lemon juice
1 teaspoon grated lemon rind
3 cups milk
1 cup heavy cream
⅛ teaspoon salt

Combine sugar and lemon juice; stir until sugar dissolves. Add remaining ingredients and mix well. Turn into refrigerator trays and freeze until frozen 1 inch from sides of tray. Turn into chilled bowl and beat until smooth. Turn into refrigerator trays and freeze until firm. Serves 6–8.

OLD-FASHIONED MINT FREEZE

1 envelope unflavored gelatin
4 cups milk
2 squares unsweetened chocolate
1 tablespoon all-purpose flour
1½ cups sugar
⅛ teaspoon salt
3 egg yolks, slightly beaten
3 egg whites, stiffly beaten
2 cups heavy cream, whipped
1 teaspoon vanilla
½ teaspoon mint extract
¼ cup crushed peppermint stick candy

Stir gelatin into cold milk to soften. Add chocolate and heat to dissolve gelatin and melt chocolate. Stir until smooth. Mix flour, sugar and salt; add to milk mixture, stirring constantly until mixture begins to thicken. Add a little of hot mixture to egg yolks, return to hot mixture, cook 1 minute, stirring. Chill until slightly thickened, beat until light. Fold in egg whites, cream, vanilla, mint extract and candy. Pour into refrigerator tray. Freeze 1 hour. Beat until smooth. Freeze until firm. Serves 6–8.

CALIFORNIA ORANGE SHERBET

1 cup milk
1 cup sugar
1 teaspoon grated orange rind
½ cup orange juice
1 cup heavy cream, whipped

Combine milk and sugar. Heat to boiling point, stirring until sugar melts. Remove from heat and add orange rind and orange juice. Cool thoroughly. Fold in cream. Turn into refrigerator tray and freeze until mushy. Stir well. Continue freezing until firm. Serves 6.

ORANGE-LIME SHERBET

1 tablespoon unflavored gelatin
¼ cup cold water
1 cup water
1½ cups sugar
1 tablespoon grated orange rind
1 teaspoon grated lemon rind
1¾ cups orange juice
¼ cup lime juice
¼ cup lemon juice

Soften gelatin in cold water. Combine water and sugar. Heat to boiling point, stirring until sugar melts. Add gelatin and stir until dissolved. Cool thoroughly. Add remaining ingredients and turn into refrigerator tray. Freeze until frozen 1 inch from sides of tray. Turn into chilled bowl and beat until smooth. Turn into refrigerator tray and freeze until firm. Serves 10–12.

BUTTER PECAN ICE CREAM

⅔ cup condensed milk
1 tablespoon melted butter
½ cup water
1 teaspoon vanilla
1½ cups heavy cream, whipped
¾ cup toasted chopped pecans

Combine milk and butter; mix well. Add water and vanilla; mix well. Chill thoroughly. Fold in cream. Turn into re-refrigerator tray and freeze until frozen 1 inch from sides of tray. Beat until smooth. Fold in pecans. Turn into refrigerator tray and freeze until firm. Serves 6.

GRAPE MOUSSE

1 envelope unflavored gelatin
1 cup grape juice
1 tablespoon lemon juice
½ cup sugar
½ teaspoon vanilla
1 teaspoon grated orange rind
1½ cups heavy cream, whipped

Soften gelatin in ¼ cup grape juice; dissolve over hot water. Add remaining grape juice, lemon juice, sugar, vanilla and orange rind. Chill until slightly thickened. Fold in cream. Turn into refrigerator tray and freeze until firm. Serves 8–10.

TROPICAL MOUSSE

1½ cups sieved avocado
⅛ teaspoon salt
⅓ cup sugar
1 teaspoon lime juice
1 teaspoon grated lime rind
2 egg whites, stiffly beaten
1 cup heavy cream, whipped

Combine avocado, salt, sugar, lime juice and rind; mix well. Fold in egg whites and cream. Turn into refrigerator tray and freeze until firm. Serves 4–6.

STRAWBERRY CREAM FREEZE

1 cup heavy cream
1 pint vanilla ice cream
1½ quarts sweetened strawberries
3 tablespoons Cointreau

Whip cream until stiff. Soften ice cream slightly and fold into cream. Combine berries and Cointreau. Fold into cream mixture. Freeze until firm. Serves 6–8.

FROZEN STRAWBERRY CREAM

1 quart strawberries
¾ cup sugar
⅛ teaspoon salt
¼ teaspoon vanilla
1 cup heavy cream, whipped

Crush strawberries. Combine berries with remaining ingredients. Turn into refrigerator tray and freeze until frozen 1 inch from sides of tray. Turn into chilled bowl and beat until smooth. Turn into refrigerator tray and freeze until firm. Serves 4–6.

STRAWBERRY ICE

3 cups strawberries
½ pound marshmallows
2 tablespoons lemon juice
½ teaspoon grated lemon rind
⅛ teaspoon salt

Crush berries; reserve ¼ cup juice. Combine strawberry juice and marshmallows; cook over low heat until marshmallows are melted. Cool thoroughly. Fold in remaining ingredients. Turn into refrigerator tray and freeze until frozen 1 inch from sides of tray. Turn into chilled bowl and beat until smooth. Turn into refrigerator tray and freeze until firm. Serves 6.

FROZEN TUTTI-FRUTTI

1 cup mixed candied fruits, chopped
½ cup brandy
2 eggs, slightly beaten
1 cup sugar
⅛ teaspoon salt
½ teaspoon vanilla
2½ cups milk
1 cup heavy cream, whipped

Combine fruits and brandy; let stand 1 hour. Combine eggs, sugar, salt, vanilla and milk. Cook over low heat, stirring constantly, until thickened. Cool. Fold fruits and cream into milk mixture. Turn into refrigerator tray and freeze until frozen 1 inch from sides of tray. Beat well. Turn into refrigerator tray and freeze until firm. Serves 6–8.

SPICED BANANA DESSERT

4 ripe bananas, mashed
½ cup sugar
⅛ teaspoon salt
½ cup apricot nectar
1 teaspoon grated lemon rind
2 tablespoons sherry
1 cup heavy cream, whipped
¼ teaspoon nutmeg
1 teaspoon ginger
¼ teaspoon vanilla

Combine all ingredients and mix lightly. Turn into refrigerator trays. Freeze until firm. Serves 6.

CHOCOLATE MINT MALLOW

16 marshmallows, cut in quarters
1 cup milk
⅛ teaspoon salt
½ teaspoon mint extract
1 cup heavy cream, whipped
¼ cup chopped pecans
½ cup semi-sweet chocolate pieces

Melt marshmallows in milk over hot water. Add salt. Chill until slightly thickened. Add mint extract. Fold in cream, nuts and chocolate pieces. Pour into refrigerator tray and freeze until firm. Serves 6.

PINK PIE PLANT MOUSSE

1 cup cooked and mashed rhubarb
⅔ cup sugar

1 cup heavy cream, whipped
1 teaspoon lemon extract

Combine rhubarb and sugar, mix well. Fold into cream. Add lemon extract. Pour into refrigerator tray. Freeze until firm. Serves 6–8.

CINNAMON-CHOCOLATE ICE CREAM

1 1-ounce square unsweetened chocolate
⅔ cup condensed milk
¾ teaspoon cinnamon
½ teaspoon nutmeg
⅔ cup water
¼ teaspoon vanilla
½ cup heavy cream, whipped

Melt chocolate over very low heat. Add milk, cinnamon and nutmeg; cook, stirring constantly, over low heat 5 minutes. Add water and mix well. Cool thoroughly. Fold in vanilla and cream. Turn into refrigerator tray and freeze until frozen 1 inch from sides of tray. Turn into chilled bowl and beat until smooth. Turn into refrigerator tray and freeze until firm. Serves 6.

WARM DESSERTS

MEXICAN COFFEE PUDDING

2 eggs
¼ cup sugar
1 teaspoon cocoa
⅛ teaspoon salt
1 cup milk
1 cup cold strong coffee

Beat eggs slightly. Add sugar, cocoa, salt, milk and coffee. Pour into greased custard cups. Place in pan with hot water about 1 inch deep. Bake in moderate oven (350° F.) about 1 hour, or until firm. Serves 4.

RASPBERRY BREAD PUDDING

2½ cups small dry bread cubes
4 cups scalded milk
2 eggs
2 eggs, separated
⅓ cup sugar
¼ teaspoon salt
1 teaspoon vanilla
¼ cup melted butter
½ cup raspberry jam
¼ cup sugar

Combine bread cubes and milk. Beat 2 eggs and 2 egg yolks slightly; add the ⅓ cup sugar, salt, vanilla and butter. Mix well. Combine egg mixture with bread-cube mixture. Turn into greased 2-quart baking dish. Bake in moderate oven (350° F.) 25 minutes. Remove from oven and spread evenly with jam. Beat egg whites until foamy. Gradually add the ¼ cup sugar, beating constantly. Continue beating until stiff. Pile meringue over jam. Continue baking 15 minutes. Serves 8.

APPLE BROWN BETTY

¼ cup butter, melted
2 cups soft bread crumbs
3 cups diced apples
⅔ cup firmly packed brown sugar
¼ teaspoon salt
½ teaspoon nutmeg
1 teaspoon cinnamon
½ teaspoon grated lemon rind
2 tablespoons lemon juice
⅓ cup water

Combine butter and crumbs. Combine apples, sugar, salt, nutmeg, cinnamon, and lemon rind. Arrange alternate layers of crumb mixture and apple mixture in greased 1½-quart baking dish, ending with crumb mixture. Combine lemon juice and water; pour over other ingredients. Bake in moderate oven (350° F.). Serve with Hard Sauce (page 382), if desired. Serves 6.

RED CHERRY COBBLER

3 cups pitted sour cherries
1 cup sugar
1 cup water
1 tablespoon cornstarch
1 tablespoon butter
¾ teaspoon cinnamon
2 cups sifted all-purpose flour
3 teaspoons baking powder
1 teaspoon salt
2 tablespoons sugar
⅓ cup shortening
¾ cup milk

Combine cherries, sugar and water; heat to boiling point. Moisten cornstarch with water and add to cherry mixture. Cook, stirring constantly, five minutes. Pour cherry mixture into greased 2-quart baking dish. Dot with butter and sprinkle with cinnamon. Sift flour with baking powder, salt and sugar. Cut in shortening. Add milk and mix lightly. Arrange dough over cherry mixture. Bake in hot oven (400° F.) 25–30 minutes. Serves 6–8.

BRANDIED CHESTNUTS

1¼ cups sugar
½ cup water
¼ teaspoon vanilla
1 pound chestnuts, peeled
⅓ cup brandy

Combine 1 cup of the sugar, water and vanilla. Cook over low heat, stirring until sugar dissolves. Add chestnuts and cook until tender; drain. Arrange chestnuts on serving platter. Sprinkle with remaining ¼ cup sugar. Pour brandy over chestnuts; light. Serves 6.

CHOCOLATE SOUFFLÉ

1½ tablespoons butter or margarine
1½ tablespoons all-purpose flour
½ cup milk
2 squares unsweetened chocolate, melted
3 eggs, separated
⅓ cup sugar
¼ teaspoon vanilla
¼ teaspoon cream of tartar

Melt butter or margarine. Blend in flour. Gradually add milk and cook over low heat, stirring constantly, until thickened. Add chocolate and mix well. Beat egg yolks until thick. Beat in sugar; add vanilla. Gradually add chocolate mixture and mix well. Beat egg whites with cream of tartar until stiff and fold into chocolate mixture. Turn into ungreased 1½-quart baking dish. Place in pan of hot water. Bake in moderate oven (350° F.) 45–50 minutes, or until firm. Serve immediately. Serves 4–6.

COTTAGE PUDDING

1¾ cups sifted cake flour
2½ teaspoons baking powder
¼ teaspoon salt
¼ cup butter or margarine
¾ cup sugar
1 egg
1 teaspoon vanilla
⅔ cup milk

Sift flour, baking powder and salt together. Cream butter or margarine and sugar until light and fluffy. Add egg and

vanilla; mix well. Add sifted ingredients alternately with milk, beating well after each addition. Turn into greased 8″ x 8″ baking pan. Bake in moderate oven (350° F.) 40 minutes or until done. Serve with whipped cream or fruit sauce such as Orange Sauce (page 383), if desired. Serves 6.

LEMON-CHEESE PUDDING

2 tablespoons butter or margarine
¾ cup sugar
1 tablespoon grated lemon rind
3 eggs, separated
1 cup creamed cottage cheese
2 tablespoons all-purpose flour
⅛ teaspoon salt
⅓ cup lemon juice

Cream butter or margarine, sugar and lemon rind together until light and fluffy. Beat egg yolks and cheese together well. Add lemon-rind mixture and mix well. Add flour, salt and lemon juice; mix well. Beat egg whites until stiff and fold into lemon mixture. Turn into 6 greased baking cups. Place in pan of hot water. Bake in moderate oven (350° F.) 30–35 minutes. Serves 6.

RICE CREAM PUDDING

1 cup cooked rice
1 cup sugar
¼ cup raisins
½ cup well-drained canned, crushed pineapple
1 teaspoon grated lemon rind
6 egg yolks
⅛ teaspoon salt
4 cups milk
¼ teaspoon nutmeg
½ teaspoon vanilla
¼ teaspoon cinnamon
2 egg whites
⅛ teaspoon cream of tartar
¼ cup sugar

Combine rice, the 1 cup sugar, raisins, pineapple, lemon rind, egg yolks, salt, milk, nutmeg, vanilla and cinnamon; beat well. Turn into greased 2-quart baking dish. Bake in moderate oven (350° F.) 30 minutes. Remove from oven. Beat egg whites with cream of tartar until frothy. Gradually add the ¼ cup sugar, beating constantly, until stiff. Pile meringue over rice mixture. Bake in moderate oven (350° F.) 12–15 minutes, or until lightly browned. Serves 6.

APPLE-PECAN POLONAISE

6 medium-size apples
1 cup water
¼ cup white wine
3 tablespoons sugar
2 teaspoons grated orange rind
¼ cup chopped pecans
1 envelope unflavored gelatin
½ cup cold water

Pare apples. Add the 1 cup water, wine, sugar and orange rind. Cover and simmer about 25 minutes, or until apples are tender. Remove apples and arrange in serving dishes. Sprinkle with pecans. Soften gelatin in the ½ cup water. Heat apple liquid to boiling point. Add gelatin and stir until dissolved. Chill until slightly thickened. Pour over apples. Chill several hours. Serves 6.

CARAMEL PUDDING

½ cup firmly packed brown sugar
2 tablespoons melted butter or margarine
2 cups milk, scalded
½ cup cold milk
¼ cup all-purpose flour
¼ teaspoon salt
2 eggs, well beaten
½ teaspoon vanilla

Combine sugar and butter or margarine.

Cook over low heat, stirring constantly, 5 minutes. Add scalded milk and stir until sugar dissolves. Combine cold milk, flour and salt. Add flour mixture to sugar mixture and cook over very low heat, stirring constantly, 15 minutes. Add a little of hot mixture to eggs and mix well. Add to hot mixture and cook, stirring constantly, 2 minutes. Add vanilla. Chill. Serves 4.

PINEAPPLE-CHEESE PUDDING

1 cup creamed cottage cheese
½ cup heavy cream, whipped
¼ cup sugar
¾ cup drained, canned crushed pineapple
¼ teaspoon vanilla
½ cup shredded toasted coconut

Combine all ingredients and mix lightly. Serves 4.

COLD DESSERTS

CHOCOLATE ANGEL DESSERT

1 10″ angel food cake
6 tablespoons cocoa
6 tablespoons sugar
¼ teaspoon salt
2 cups heavy cream
½ cup chopped pecans
1 tablespoon chopped maraschino cherries

Cut slice 1 inch thick from top of cake. Remove center from cake leaving shell 1″ thick. Combine cocoa, sugar, salt and cream. Chill 1 hour. Beat cream mixture until stiff. Add pecans and cherries. Fill cake with ⅓ of cream mixture. Place top on cake and frost with remaining mixture. Chill 2 hours. Serves 8–10.

FRENCH CREAM LADYFINGERS

¼ cup all-purpose flour
⅓ cup sugar
½ cup light cream
1 cup milk, scalded
1 egg, slightly beaten
1 teaspoon vanilla
12 ladyfingers, split

Combine flour and sugar; gradually add cream and mix until smooth. Add sugar mixture gradually to milk and cook over hot water, stirring occasionally, 15 minutes. Add a little of hot mixture to egg and mix well. Add to hot mixture and cook, stirring constantly, 2 minutes. Remove from heat and add vanilla. Cool thoroughly. Line serving dishes with ladyfingers. Add cream mixture. Serves 6.

EGG NOG MOLD

1 envelope unflavored gelatin
¼ cup cold water
1¼ cups prepared egg nog
1 cup heavy cream, whipped
½ teaspoon vanilla
½ cup chopped nuts

Soften gelatin in water; dissolve over boiling water. Add egg nog and mix well. Chill until slightly thickened. Fold in remaining ingredients. Turn into 1-quart mold and chill until firm. Serves 4–6.

MOLDED MARSHMALLOW DESSERT

½ pound marshmallows
½ cup milk
¼ cup chopped walnuts
1 medium-sized banana, diced
2 tablespoons lemon juice
1½ cups heavy cream, whipped

Combine marshmallows and milk. Cook over low heat, stirring constantly, until marshmallows are melted. Add walnuts. Combine banana and lemon juice. Combine marshmallow mixture and banana mixture. Fold cream into marshmallow mixture. Turn into 1-quart mold. Chill until firm. Serves 4–6.

LEMON SNOW

1 envelope unflavored gelatin
½ cup cold water
¾ cup boiling water
¾ cup sugar
⅛ teaspoon salt
1½ teaspoons grated lemon rind
¼ cup lemon juice
2 egg whites

Soften gelatin in ½ cup cold water. Add boiling water, sugar and salt and stir until dissolved. Add lemon rind and lemon juice. Chill until slightly thickened. Add egg whites; beat until mixture begins to hold shape. Turn into a 1½-quart mold; chill until firm. Serve with Custard Sauce (page 382). Serves 6.

TAPIOCA PUDDING

¼ cup sugar
⅓ cup quick-cooking tapioca
⅛ teaspoon salt
2 eggs, separated
4 cups milk, scalded
¾ teaspoon vanilla

Combine sugar, tapioca, salt and egg yolks. Gradually add 1 cup of the milk; add remaining 3 cups milk. Cook over hot water, stirring constantly, until thickened. Beat egg whites until stiff. Fold a little of hot mixture into egg whites. Fold egg-white mixture into tapioca mixture. Add vanilla. Chill. Serves 6–8.

MARSHMALLOW CHOCOLATE PUDDING

1 envelope unflavored gelatin
¼ cup milk
1 egg, separated
1¾ cups milk
2 squares unsweetened chocolate, grated
½ cup sugar
⅛ teaspoon salt
1½ cups quartered marshmallows
¼ cup chopped walnuts
½ cup heavy cream, whipped

Stir gelatin into the ¼ cup milk to soften. Beat egg yolk; add the 1¾ cups milk, chocolate, sugar and salt. Cook over low heat, stirring constantly, until slightly thickened. Add gelatin and stir until dissolved. Chill until slightly thickened. Fold in remaining ingredients. Chill until firm. Serves 6–8.

CHOCOLATE MOUSSE

6 ounces semi-sweet chocolate
3 tablespoons black coffee
½ cup butter
⅛ teaspoon salt
⅛ teaspoon cinnamon
6 eggs, separated
½ cup heavy cream
¼ cup confectioners' sugar

Melt chocolate with coffee over low heat. Add butter, salt and cinnamon. Beat egg yolks until light and stir into chocolate mixture. Cool. Beat cream and add sugar. Beat egg whites until stiff. Fold cream and egg whites into chocolate mixture. Chill. Serves 6.

MOCHA DESSERT

½ pound sweet chocolate
¼ cup strong coffee
5 eggs, separated
½ teaspoon vanilla

Grate chocolate; add coffee and cook over low heat, stirring constantly until chocolate melts. Beat egg yolks until thick. Gradually add egg yolks to chocolate mixture and cook over low heat, stirring constantly, until thickened. Cool. Beat egg whites until stiff. Fold egg whites and vanilla into chocolate mixture. Turn into serving dishes and chill. Serves 6.

MOCHA MERINGUE

3 egg whites
¼ teaspoon cream of tartar
⅛ teaspoon salt
¾ cup sugar
¼ teaspoon cinnamon
2 6-ounce packages semi-sweet chocolate morsels
1 tablespoon instant coffee
¼ cup boiling water
½ teaspoon vanilla
1 cup heavy cream, whipped

Beat egg whites until foamy; add cream of tartar and salt; beat until stiff. Gradually add sugar; beat until very stiff. Fold in cinnamon. Cover baking sheet with heavy brown paper. Pile about ⅔ of meringue on paper into a 7" round. Make a depression in the center leaving an inch around sides. Spoon remaining meringue in mounds around edge. Bake in very slow oven (275° F.) 1 hour. Cool. Meanwhile melt chocolate morsels over hot water. Combine instant coffee and boiling water; stir into chocolate. Add vanilla; beat until smooth. Cool thoroughly. Fold in cream; turn into meringue shell. Chill. Serves 8.

ZABAGLIONE

6 egg yolks
¼ cup sugar
½ cup Marsala wine

Beat egg yolks and sugar until very light. Gradually add wine, beating constantly. Cook over hot water until mixture coats spoon. Chill thoroughly. Serves 4.

SARATOGA SHORTCAKE

1 cup sifted cake flour
½ teaspoon salt
5 eggs, separated
1 teaspoon grated lemon rind
1 cup sugar
2 cups crushed sweetened strawberries

Sift flour with ¼ teaspoon of the salt. Beat egg yolks until very thick, add lemon rind. Beat egg whites with remaining ¼ teaspoon salt until stiff but not dry. Gradually add sugar, beating until stiff. Fold in egg yolk mixture. Sift flour gradually over egg white mixture and fold into batter. Turn into 2 ungreased 9″ layer cake pans. Bake in slow over (325° F.) 30–35 minutes. Cool in pans on rack; remove from pans. Spread strawberries between layers. Serve with Custard Sauce (page 382). Serves 6–8.

MERINGUE GLACES

2 cups sugar
¾ cup water
5 egg whites
¼ teaspoon salt
⅛ teaspoon cream of tartar
¾ teaspoon vanilla
¼ teaspoon almond extract

Cook sugar and water to 238° F. Beat egg whites until stiff, add salt and cream of tartar. Pour syrup over egg whites gradually, beating constantly. Beat until cool. Fold in vanilla and almond extract. Shape meringues into cups with pastry tube on wet unglazed paper. Bake in slow oven (275° F.) 1 hour. Cool and fill with ice cream. Top with a Chocolate or Fruit Sauce. Makes about 12.

CURRANT JELLY RICE PUDDING

2 cups milk
2 cups light cream
½ cup uncooked rice
3 tablespoons sugar
¼ teaspoon salt
¼ teaspoon nutmeg
⅛ teaspoon cinnamon
¼ cup currant jelly

Combine milk, cream, rice, sugar, salt and spices. Turn into greased 1½-quart baking dish. Dot with jelly. Bake in slow oven (300° F.) 2½ hours, or until rice is tender. Stir frequently during baking period. Cool thoroughly. Serves 4–6.

SHERRY DESSERT MOLDS

2 envelopes unflavored gelatin
½ cup cold water
1¼ cups boiling water
¾ cup sugar
1 teaspoon grated orange rind
2 tablespoons lemon juice
1 cup sherry wine

Soften gelatin in cold water. Add boiling water and stir until gelatin is dissolved. Add sugar, orange rind and lemon juice; mix well. Cool thoroughly. Add sherry and mix well. Turn into 6 individual molds. Chill until firm. Serves 6.

RAISIN RICE PUDDING

½ cup rice
1 cup milk
1 teaspoon grated lemon rind
¼ cup raisins
1 egg yolk, beaten
Sugar

Cook rice according to package directions. Add milk, lemon rind and raisins.

Cook over low heat 15 minutes. Remove from heat. Add a little of the hot mixture to egg and mix well. Add to hot mixture and cook, stirring constantly, 2 minutes. Remove from heat and season to taste with sugar. Chill. Serves 4–6.

Dessert Sauces

FRESH PEACH SAUCE

6 medium-sized fresh peaches
¾ cup sugar
¼ teaspoon almond extract
1 teaspoon lemon juice

Peel peaches and mash. Fold in remaining ingredients. Serve on ice cream. Makes about 2 cups.

PINEAPPLE SAUCE

1½ cups canned crushed pineapple
1 cup sugar
½ cup water
Few drops mint extract

Combine pineapple, sugar and water. Cook over low heat, stirring occasionally 10 minutes. Cool. Stir in mint extract. Serve on ice cream, unfrosted cake, banana splits. Makes about 2½ cups.

FLUFFY PUDDING SAUCE

1 egg, separated
¾ cup confectioners' sugar
⅛ teaspoon salt
½ cup heavy cream, whipped
2 tablespoons Sherry

Beat egg white until stiff. Gradually add sugar, continuing to beat. Beat in salt and egg yolk; fold in cream and Sherry. Chill thoroughly. Serve on pudding. Makes about 1½ cups.

RASPBERRY SAUCE

1 cup raspberry jam
3 tablespoons hot water
1 tablespoon lemon juice
¼ teaspoon grated lemon rind
⅛ teaspoon salt

Combine all ingredients and cook over low heat, stirring constantly until jam melts. Serve on ice cream, pancakes and waffles. Makes about 1¼ cups.

ST. CROIX RUM SAUCE SUPREME

2 eggs
1 cup confectioners' sugar
1 cup heavy cream, whipped
1 tablespoon rum
½ teaspoon nutmeg

Beat eggs until thick. Gradually add sugar, beating constantly. Fold in cream, rum and nutmeg. Makes about 2½ cups.

CUSTARD SAUCE

2 eggs, slightly beaten
2½ tablespoons sugar
⅛ teaspoon salt
2 cups milk
½ teaspoon vanilla

Combine eggs, sugar and salt in top of double boiler. Gradually stir in milk. Cook over hot water, stirring constantly, until thickened. Add vanilla and cool. Serve on Lemon Snow (page 378); Orange and Grapefruit Cup (page 355); Cake. Makes about 2 cups.

HARD SAUCE

⅓ cup butter
1 cup sifted confectioners' sugar
1 tablespoon cream
½ teaspoon vanilla

Cream butter with sugar until light and fluffy. Add cream and vanilla and beat well. Serve with apple pie, Apple Brown Betty (page 375). Makes about 1¼ cups.

HONEY-ORANGE HARD SAUCE

½ cup butter
½ cup honey
1 tablespoon orange juice
½ teaspoon grated orange rind

Combine all ingredients and beat until light. Chill. Serve with apple pie, bread pudding. Makes about 1 cup.

MIDNIGHT SUPPER SAUCE

½ cup butter or margarine
⅓ cup firmly packed brown sugar
1 tablespoon orange juice
1 teaspoon grated orange rind

Combine all ingredients and cook over low heat, stirring constantly, until sugar melts. Serve with pancakes and waffles, as desired. Makes about ⅔ cup.

CARAMEL SAUCE

1 cup sugar
1 cup boiling water
1 teaspoon vanilla

Melt sugar over low heat, stirring constantly. Remove from heat and gradually stir in water. Cook over low heat 10 minutes. Add vanilla and mix well. Makes about 2 cups.

SHERRY CHEESE SAUCE

1 8-ounce package cream cheese
3 tablespoons sherry
2 tablespoons confectioners' sugar
⅛ teaspoon salt
¼ teaspoon vanilla

Soften cheese. Add remaining ingredients and beat until light and fluffy. Serve with fruit salad. Makes about 1 cup.

CHERRY SAUCE

1½ cups sugar
2 tablespoons all-purpose flour
¼ teaspoon salt
¾ cup sour cherry juice
¼ cup boiling water
1 tablespoon butter or margarine
1 cup canned sour cherries, drained
1 tablespoon lemon juice

Combine sugar, flour and salt. Add cherry juice and water. Cook over low heat, stirring constantly, 5 minutes. Add remaining ingredients and mix well. Serve on ice cream, cake, bread pudding. Makes about 2 cups.

SPEEDY CHOCOLATE SAUCE

2 squares unsweetened chocolate
1⅓ cups sweetened condensed milk
¼ teaspoon vanilla
⅛ teaspoon salt

Melt chocolate over hot water; add remaining ingredients and beat well. Serve on ice cream. Makes about 1¼ cups.

NUTMEG SAUCE

1 cup sugar
2 tablespoons all-purpose flour
2 cups boiling water
1½ tablespoons butter or margarine
1 teaspoon nutmeg
⅛ teaspoon salt

Combine sugar and flour. Gradually add water and cook, stirring constantly until thickened. Add butter or margarine and cook five minutes, stirring occasionally. Add nutmeg and salt. Makes about 2¼ cups.

ORANGE SAUCE

½ cup sugar
1 tablespoon cornstarch
1 cup orange juice
1 tablespoon butter
1 tablespoon grated orange rind
⅛ teaspoon nutmeg
⅛ teaspoon salt

Combine sugar and cornstarch; gradually add orange juice and cook, stirring constantly, until thickened. Add remaining ingredients and mix well. Serve on Cottage Pudding (page 376); bread puddings. Makes about 1¼ cups.

APRICOT CREAM SAUCE

1 cup heavy cream
¼ cup sugar
1 teaspoon vanilla
½ cup apricot jam
1 tablespoon lemon juice

Beat cream until stiff. Fold in remaining ingredients. Chill thoroughly. Serve with angel food cake, gingerbread. Makes about 1½ cups.

BRANDY SAUCE

1 egg, separated
¾ cup confectioners' sugar
⅛ teaspoon salt
½ cup heavy cream, whipped
¼ cup brandy

Beat egg white until stiff, gradually adding sugar. Beat in salt and egg yolk. Fold in cream and brandy. Serve with Chocolate Soufflé (page 376), if desired. Makes about 1½ cups.

RICH BUTTERSCOTCH SAUCE

1½ cups firmly packed brown sugar
⅔ cup light corn syrup
⅓ cup water
⅔ cup evaporated milk

Combine sugar, syrup and water. Cook over low heat, stirring constantly until sugar melts. Continue cooking to soft-ball stage (235° F. on candy thermometer). Cool thoroughly. Gradually add milk and mix well. Serve on ice cream. Makes about 2 cups.

CIDER SAUCE

¼ cup butter or margarine
1 cup confectioners' sugar
¼ cup cider
2 eggs, separated
½ cup evaporated milk

Cream butter or margarine and sugar until light and fluffy. Add cider and beat well. Beat egg yolks until thick and lemon colored. Add to cider mixture; mix well. Gradually add evaporated milk. Cook over low heat, stirring constantly, until thickened. Beat egg whites until stiff. Gradually add hot mixture, beating constantly. Serve with gingerbread. Makes about 1¼ cups.

SHERRY SAUCE

1 cup sugar
1 tablespoon all-purpose flour
2 cups boiling water
2 tablespoons butter
¼ cup Sherry

Combine sugar and flour. Gradually add water and cook, stirring constantly until thickened. Remove from heat and add butter and Sherry. Beat well. Serve on steamed pudding, fruit cake. Makes about 3 cups.

STRAWBERRY SAUCE

1 cup sugar
½ cup water
2 cups crushed strawberries

Combine sugar and water and cook over low heat, stirring until sugar is dissolved. Simmer 10 minutes. Add strawberries and cook 1 minute. Chill. Serve on ice cream, pound cake. Makes about 2½ cups.

Pie

APPLE CRUMB PIE

6 large tart apples
1 unbaked 9″ pastry shell
3 tablespoons granulated sugar
1 teaspoon cinnamon
¼ teaspoon nutmeg
½ cup firmly packed brown sugar
½ cup all-purpose flour
¼ cup butter or margarine

Pare and core apples; cut into thin slices. Arrange apple slices in pastry shell. Combine granulated sugar and spices. Sprinkle spice mixture over apples. Combine brown sugar and flour. Cut in butter or margarine. Sprinkle brown sugar mixture over apple mixture. Bake in hot oven (400° F) 40 minutes. Makes one 9″ pie.

ANGEL PIE

4 eggs, separated
¼ teaspoon salt
¼ teaspoon cream of tartar
1 cup sugar
¾ cup sugar
¼ cup lemon juice
1 teaspoon grated lemon rind
1 cup heavy cream, whipped
Toasted shredded coconut

Beat egg whites until frothy, add salt and cream of tartar. Beat until stiff but not dry. Beat in the 1 cup sugar adding about 2 tablespoons at a time and beating very thoroughly after each addition; continue beating until satiny smooth. Spread over bottom and sides of well-buttered 9″ pie pan. Bake in slow oven

(300° F.) about 1 hour; cool. Beat egg yolks until thick. Gradually beat in the ¾ cup sugar. Add lemon juice and lemon rind. Cook over very low heat, stirring constantly, until thickened. Cool and turn into meringue shell. Spread cream over lemon mixture. Top with coconut. Chill. Makes one 9″ pie.

BUTTERMILK PIE

1 cup sugar
3 tablespoons all-purpose flour
½ teaspoon salt
3 egg yolks
2 cups buttermilk
4 tablespoons butter
3 egg whites
1 9″ pastry shell

Combine the sugar, flour, and salt, blending thoroughly. Beat egg yolks slightly, add the buttermilk and butter which has been melted, then cooled. Add gradually to dry ingredients and blend thoroughly. Fold in stiffly beaten egg whites gently but thoroughly. Pour into pastry shell and bake in a moderate over (375° F.) 45 minutes, or until a silver knife inserted in the center comes out clean. Makes one 9″ pie.

CATSKILL MOUNTAIN APPLE PIE

1 recipe pastry for double-crust 9″ pie
8 large tart apples
¾ cup sugar
⅛ teaspoon salt
½ teaspoon cinnamon
½ teaspoon nutmeg
1 tablespoon lemon juice
2 tablespoons butter or margarine

Roll ½ of pastry out on lightly floured surface to ⅛-inch thickness. Line 9″ pie pan with pastry. Pare and core apples; cut into thin slices. Arrange apples over pastry. Combine sugar, salt, spices and lemon juice. Sprinkle sugar mixture over apples. Dot with butter or margarine. Roll remaining pastry out to ⅛-inch thickness. Place over apple mixture. Seal edges and prick top. Bake in hot oven (400° F.) about 45 minutes. Makes one 9″ pie.

BANANA-CHOCOLATE PIE

1½ squares unsweetened chocolate
2 cups milk
¾ cup sugar
5 tablespoons all-purpose flour
¼ teaspoon salt
2 egg yolks
2 teaspoons butter or margarine
1 teaspoon vanilla
2 medium-sized bananas, sliced
1 baked 9″ pastry shell

Combine chocolate and milk. Cook over low heat, stirring constantly, until chocolate is melted. Combine sugar, flour and salt. Stir into chocolate mixture. Cook over low heat, stirring constantly, until thickened. Cook 5 minutes, stirring occasionally. Add a little of hot mixture to egg yolks and mix well. Stir into hot mixture and cook, stirring constantly, 1 minute. Add butter or margarine and vanilla and mix well. Cool thoroughly. Arrange banana slices over bottom of pastry shell. Pour chocolate mixture over bananas. Serve with whipped cream, if desired. Makes one 9″ pie.

APPLESAUCE-WALNUT PIE

2 eggs
⅓ cup sugar
1 cup light cream
1 cup applesauce
1 teaspoon vanilla
⅛ teaspoon salt
1 cup chopped walnuts
1 9″ unbaked pastry shell

Beat eggs slightly. Add sugar, cream, applesauce, vanilla and salt. Sprinkle walnuts over bottom of shell. Add applesauce mixture. Bake in hot oven (400° F.) 45 minutes. Makes one 9″ pie.

DUTCH APPLE PIE

6 medium-sized apples, pared
    and thinly sliced
1 9″ unbaked pastry shell
½ cup sifted all-purpose flour
1 cup sugar
1 teaspoon cinnamon
¼ teaspoon nutmeg
½ cup sour cream
½ teaspoon vanilla
1 tablespoon butter or margarine

Arrange apples in pastry shell. Combine flour, sugar and spices; sprinkle over apples. Combine sour cream and vanilla. Pour sour cream mixture over apple mixture. Dot with butter or margarine. Bake in moderate oven (350° F.) 35 minutes. Cover and bake 15–20 minutes, or until apples are tender. Make one 9″ pie.

SPICY SCHNITZ PIE

½ pound dried apples
2 cups cold water
¼ cup lemon juice
1 tablespoon grated lemon rind
1 teaspoon cinnamon
1 teaspoon nutmeg
⅛ teaspoon salt
1 cup sugar
1 recipe pastry for 2-crust 9″ pie

Combine apples and water. Cook, covered, over low heat until tender. Add lemon juice, rind, cinnamon, nutmeg, salt and sugar; mix well. Cool. Line 9″ pie pan with pastry. Pour apple mixture over pastry. Cover with remaining pastry. Prick top of pastry. Bake in hot oven (400° F.) 40 to 45 minutes. Makes one 9″ pie.

BANANA CREAM PIE

⅔ cup sugar
⅓ cup all-purpose flour
⅛ teaspoon salt
2 eggs, well beaten
2 cups milk, scalded
½ teaspoon vanilla
3 medium-sized bananas, sliced
1 baked 9″ pastry shell
1 cup heavy cream, whipped

Combine sugar, flour, salt and eggs. Gradually add milk. Cook over low heat, stirring constantly, until thickened. Cool thoroughly. Add vanilla and mix well. Arrange banana slices over bottom of pastry shell. Pour milk mixture over bananas. Top with whipped cream to serve. Makes one 9″ pie.

CHOCOLATE CHIFFON PIE

2 1-ounce squares unsweetened chocolate,
    grated
½ cup boiling water
1 envelope unflavored gelatin
¼ cup cold water
3 eggs, separated
½ cup sugar
⅛ teaspoon salt
½ teaspoon vanilla
½ cup sugar
1 10″ baked pastry shell

Combine chocolate and boiling water. Stir until chocolate melts. Soften gelatin in cold water. Add to chocolate mixture and stir until gelatin dissolves. Beat egg yolks with ½ cup sugar until light. Add gelatin mixture. Add salt and vanilla; cool thoroughly. Beat egg whites until foamy. Gradually add ½ cup sugar, beating constantly until stiff. Fold into chocolate mixture; pour into pastry shell. Chill until firm. Serve with whipped cream, if desired. Makes one 10″ pie.

FRUIT COCKTAIL PIE

1 cup sugar
1 cup chopped Brazil nuts
⅛ teaspoon salt
1 teaspoon grated lemon rind
½ teaspoon cinnamon
½ teaspoon vanilla
¾ cup crumbled soda crackers
3 egg whites, stiffly beaten
½ cup heavy cream, whipped
1 cup drained canned fruit cocktail

Combine sugar, Brazil nuts, salt, lemon rind, cinnamon, vanilla and crackers. Fold egg whites into cracker mixture. Spread cracker mixture over bottom and sides of well greased 8″ pie pan. Bake in moderate oven (350° F.) 25–30 minutes. Cool thoroughly. Combine cream and fruit cocktail. Top pie with fruit mixture. Makes one 8″ pie.

GOOSEBERRY PIE

3 cups gooseberries
1 cup sugar
½ cup water
½ cup sugar
2 tablespoons all-purpose flour
½ teaspoon salt
1 tablespoon lemon juice
⅛ teaspoon nutmeg
1 recipe pastry for double-crust 9″ pie

Combine gooseberries, the 1 cup sugar, and water. Cook over low heat, stirring occasionally until berries are tender. Combine the ½ cup sugar, flour, salt, lemon and nutmeg. Add to gooseberry mixture and mix well. Cool thoroughly.

Roll ½ of pastry out on lightly floured surface to ⅛-inch thickness. Line 9″ pie pan with pastry. Pour gooseberry mixture over pastry. Roll remaining pastry out to ⅛-inch thickness. Place over gooseberry mixture. Seal edges and prick top. Bake in hot oven (400° F.) 35–40 minutes. Makes one 9″ pie.

BOG CRANBERRY AND RAISIN PIE

2½ cups chopped cranberries
1 cup raisins
1 cup sugar
1½ tablespoons all-purpose flour
⅛ teaspoon salt
1 recipe pastry for 9″ double-crust pie
1½ tablespoons butter or margarine

Combine cranberries, raisins, sugar, flour and salt. Roll out ½ of pastry on lightly floured surface to ⅛-inch thickness. Line 9″ pie pan with pastry; pour cranberry mixture over pastry. Dot with butter or margarine. Roll remaining pastry out to ⅛-inch thickness. Place over cranberry mixture. Seal edges and prick top. Bake in hot oven (400° F.) about 40 minutes. Makes one 9″ pie.

OPEN GOOSEBERRY TART

4 cups gooseberries
1 9″ unbaked pastry shell
¾ cup sugar
1 egg yolk
¼ cup sour cream
⅛ teaspoon nutmeg
⅛ teaspoon cinnamon

Turn berries into pastry shell. Sprinkle with sugar. Bake in moderate oven (350° F.) 20 minutes. Combine remaining ingredients and spread over berry mixture. Bake in moderate oven (350° F.) 20 minutes. Makes one 9″ pie.

GRAPE PIE

1 cup seedless white grapes
1 baked 9" pastry shell
4 eggs, separated
1 can sweetened condensed milk
½ cup lemon juice
⅛ teaspoon salt
½ cup sugar

Arrange grapes evenly over bottom of pastry shell. Beat egg yolks until thick; add milk and mix well. Stir in lemon juice and salt. Pour lemon mixture over grapes. Beat egg whites until foamy; gradually add sugar, beating constantly until stiff. Pile meringue over filling. Bake in slow oven (325° F.) about 15 minutes, or until lightly browned. Makes one 9" pie.

GRAPEFRUIT PIE

4 cups grapefruit sections
1 cup firmly packed brown sugar
2 tablespoons all-purpose flour
½ teaspoon cinnamon
1 teaspoon nutmeg
1 recipe pastry for double-crust 9" pie
1 tablespoon butter or margarine

Combine grapefruit sections, sugar, flour and spices. Mix well. Roll ½ of pastry out on lightly floured surface to ⅛-inch thickness. Line 9" pan with pastry. Arrange grapefruit mixture over pastry. Dot with butter or margarine. Roll remaining pastry out to ⅛-inch thickness. Place over grapefruit mixture; seal edges and prick top. Bake in hot oven (400° F.) 35–40 minutes. Makes one 9" pie.

LEMON MERINGUE PIE

1½ cups sugar
2 tablespoons cornstarch
¼ cup all-purpose flour
⅛ teaspoon salt
2 cups boiling water
3 eggs, separated
1 teaspoon grated lemon rind
⅓ cup lemon juice
1½ tablespoons butter or margarine
1 baked 9" pastry shell
6 tablespoons sugar

Combine the 1½ cups sugar, cornstarch, flour and salt. Gradually add boiling water and cook over low heat, stirring constantly, until mixture thickens. Beat egg yolks slightly; add lemon rind and lemon juice. Add to cornstarch mixture and cook over low heat, stirring constantly, 2 minutes. Add butter or margarine and mix well. Cool slightly and turn into pastry shell. Beat egg whites until foamy. Gradually add 6 tablespoons sugar, beating constantly until stiff. Pile meringue over lemon mixture. Bake in moderate oven (350° F.) 12–15 minutes. Makes one 9" pie.

TWO-CRUST LEMON PIE

1 cup sugar
½ cup all-purpose flour
2 tablespoons cornstarch
¼ teaspoon salt
2¼ cups boiling water
3 eggs
½ cup sugar
½ cup lemon juice
2 teaspoons grated lemon rind
1 recipe pastry for double-crust 9" pie

Combine the 1 cup sugar, flour, cornstarch and salt. Gradually add boiling water and cook over low heat, stirring constantly, until thickened. Beat eggs with ½ cup sugar. Pour cornstarch mixture gradually over egg mixture, stirring constantly. Add lemon juice and lemon rind. Cool thoroughly. Roll ½ of pastry out on lightly floured surface. Line 9" pie pan with pastry. Pour lemon mixture over pastry. Roll remaining pastry out to ⅛-inch thickness. Place over lemon mixture. Seal edges and prick top. Bake in hot oven (400° F.) 35–40 minutes. Makes one 9″ pie.

LIME MERINGUE PIE

7 tablespoons cornstarch
⅛ teaspoon salt
1½ cups sugar
2½ cups water
4 eggs, separated
2 tablespoons lemon juice
1 teaspoon grated lemon rind
½ cup lime juice
¼ cup sugar
Green food coloring
1 baked 9″ pastry shell
¼ teaspoon cream of tartar
½ cup sugar

In saucepan combine cornstarch, salt and the 1½ cups sugar. Stir in water; mix until blended. Cook over low heat, stirring constantly, until thickened. Beat egg yolks slightly. Add lemon juice, lemon rind, lime juice and the ¼ cup sugar. Gradually add egg yolk mixture to cornstarch mixture and cook over low heat, stirring constantly, 2 minutes. Add enough green coloring to make mixture light green. Cool thoroughly. Pour into pastry shell. Beat egg whites until foamy. Gradually add cream of tartar and ½ cup sugar, beating constantly until stiff. Pile meringue over lime filling. Bake in hot oven (400° F.) 10 minutes. Cool thoroughly. Makes one 9″ pie.

LEMON SPONGE PIE

4 eggs, separated
½ cup sugar
⅓ cup lemon juice
1 teaspoon grated lemon rind
1 tablespoon butter or margarine
2 tablespoons all-purpose flour
2 tablespoons water
1 baked 9″ pastry shell

Beat egg yolks slightly; add sugar, lemon juice, lemon rind, butter or margarine, flour and water. Cook over low heat, stirring constantly, until thickened. Cool thoroughly. Beat egg whites until stiff and fold into lemon mixture. Turn into pastry shell. Broil 3 or 4 inches from source of heat 4–5 minutes or until lightly browned. Makes one 9″ pie.

OPELOUSAS PECAN PIE

⅓ cup butter or margarine
⅔ cup firmly packed brown sugar
⅛ teaspoon salt
¾ cup dark corn syrup
3 eggs, well beaten
1¼ cups pecan halves
½ teaspoon vanilla
1 unbaked 8″ pastry shell

Cream butter and sugar together until light and fluffy. Add salt, syrup, eggs, pecan halves and vanilla. Mix well. Turn into pastry shell. Bake in hot oven (400° F.) about 40 minutes or until firm. Makes one 8″ pie.

DIXIE PERSIMMON PIE

2 cups persimmon pulp
½ cup sugar
¼ teaspoon cinnamon
1 tablespoon orange juice
1 baked 8″ pastry shell
½ cup heavy cream, whipped

Combine persimmon pulp, sugar, cinnamon and orange juice. Turn into pastry shell. Spread with whipped cream. Makes one 8″ pie.

FRIED GEORGIA PEACH PIES

1 recipe pastry for double-crust pie
2 cups sweetened mashed peaches
1 teaspoon grated orange rind
Fat for frying
Confectioners' sugar

Roll pastry out on lightly floured surface to ⅛-inch thickness. Cut into circles about 5 inches in diameter. Place peach mixture on pastry. Sprinkle with orange rind. Moisten edges and fold to make semicircles. Seal edges and prick tops. Fry in deep hot fat (375° F.) until light brown on all sides. Drain on absorbent paper. Sprinkle with confectioners' sugar. Serves 6.

DE SOTO PECAN PIE

3 eggs, separated
¾ cup sugar
1 tablespoon cornstarch
⅛ teaspoon salt
½ cup chopped pecans
1 cup sour cream
1 8″ unbaked pastry shell
6 tablespoons sugar

Beat egg yolks well. Combine the ¾ cup sugar, cornstarch and salt. Add egg yolks and mix well. Add pecans and sour cream; mix well. Pour into pastry shell and bake in moderate oven (350° F.) 45 minutes or until set. Remove from oven. Cool. Beat egg whites until foamy. Gradually add the 6 tablespoons sugar, beating constantly until stiff. Pile meringue over pecan mixture. Bake in moderate oven (350° F.) 12–15 minutes. Makes one 8″ pie.

MINCEMEAT PIE

¼ cup butter or margarine
½ cup sugar
½ cup molasses
½ teaspoon salt
2 eggs, unbeaten
1 cup prepared mincemeat
½ cup seedless raisins
½ cup chopped nuts
2 tablespoons minced orange rind
1 recipe pastry

Cream together butter and sugar and blend in molasses and salt. Add eggs one at a time, beating thoroughly after each addition. Add mincemeat, raisins, chopped nuts and orange rind. Prepare pastry, and roll out one round of dough to fit a 9″ pie. Roll out remaining dough and cut into strips ¾ of an inch wide. Line pan with pastry, pour in filling and shape pastry strips into lattice on top. Bake in a hot oven (400° F.) 30 to 40 minutes. Makes one 9″ pie.

NESSELRODE PIE

3 eggs, separated
1½ cups milk
⅛ teaspoon salt
⅔ cup sugar
1 envelope unflavored gelatin
¼ cup cold water
1½ tablespoons rum flavoring
½ cup chopped maraschino cherries
1 baked 9″ pastry shell
2 tablespoons grated sweet chocolate

Beat egg yolks slightly. Add milk, salt and ⅓ cup of the sugar. Cook over hot water, stirring constantly, until mixture thickens. Soften gelatin in water. Add to egg yolk mixture and stir until dissolved. Chill until slightly thickened. Beat egg whites until foamy. Gradually add remaining ⅓ cup sugar, beating constantly until stiff. Fold egg white mixture, rum flavoring and cherries into gelatin mixture. Turn into pastry shell. Sprinkle chocolate over filling. Chill until firm. Makes one 9″ pie.

CREAMY MOCHA PIE

1 tablespoon cocoa
¾ cup sugar
5 tablespoons cornstarch
¼ teaspoon salt
1 cup evaporated milk
1 cup strong coffee
1 egg, slightly beaten
½ teaspoon vanilla
1 baked 9″ pastry shell
½ cup heavy cream, whipped

Combine cocoa, sugar, cornstarch and salt. Combine milk and coffee and heat. Add to cornstarch mixture gradually, stirring constantly. Cook over boiling water until thickened, stirring frequently. Add a little of hot mixture to egg and mix well. Stir egg into hot mixture and cook 2 minutes, stirring constantly. Cool. Add vanilla. Turn into pastry shell. Spread with whipped cream. Makes one 9″ pie.

ORANGE CUSTARD PIE

2 egg yolks
1 cup sour cream
⅓ cup orange juice
1 cup sugar
2 tablespoons all-purpose flour
½ teaspoon cloves
¼ teaspoon nutmeg
¼ cup raisins
1 tablespoon grated orange rind
1 unbaked 8″ pastry shell

Beat egg yolks slightly; add sour cream, orange juice, sugar, flour, cloves, nutmeg, raisins and orange rind. Mix well. Turn sour cream mixture into pastry shell. Bake in moderate oven (350° F.) 45 minutes. Makes one 8″ pie.

ORANGE FLUFF PIE

½ pound marshmallows
1 cup orange juice
1 tablespoon lemon juice
1 tablespoon lime juice
½ cup heavy cream, whipped
1 9″ graham cracker shell
1 orange, sliced

Melt marshmallows over low heat. Fold in fruit juices. Cool thoroughly. Fold in cream. Chill until slightly thickened. Turn cream mixture into shell. Chill until firm. Garnish with orange slices. Makes one 9″ pie.

LITTLE PLANTATION PIES

¾ cup rice
3 cups milk
¼ teaspoon salt
4 egg yolks
1 cup sugar
½ teaspoon ginger
1 teaspoon vanilla
¼ cup rum
1 cup heavy cream, whipped
8 individual baked tart shells

Wash rice. Heat milk, add salt and rice, and cook over low heat until rice is tender, stirring occasionally. Beat egg yolks; add sugar. Add rice. Cook over low heat 1 minute, stirring constantly. Cool. Fold in ginger, vanilla, rum and cream. Pour into shells. Makes 8 tarts.

DEEP-DISH PLUM PIE

4 cups diced plums
1 cup sugar
¼ cup all-purpose flour
¼ teaspoon salt
1 tablespoon butter or margarine
½ recipe pastry for double-crust 9″ pie

Arrange plums in 9″ pie pan. Combine sugar, flour and salt. Sprinkle flour mixture over plums. Dot with butter or margarine. Roll pastry out on lightly floured surface to ⅛-inch thickness. Moisten rim of pie pan. Place pastry over plum mixture. Seal edges and prick top. Bake in hot oven (400° F.) 35–40 minutes. Makes one 9″ pie.

SWEET POTATO PIE

2 cups cooked, mashed sweet potatoes
3 eggs, slightly beaten
¼ cup firmly packed brown sugar
¼ teaspoon salt
⅛ teaspoon cinnamon
¼ teaspoon ginger
½ teaspoon allspice
½ cup light cream
¼ cup orange juice
1 tablespoon melted butter or margarine
1 unbaked 9″ pastry shell

Combine sweet potatoes, eggs, sugar, salt, spices, cream, orange juice and butter or margarine. Turn into pastry shell; bake in hot oven (400° F.) about 45 minutes or until firm. Makes one 9″ pie.

HARVEST PUMPKIN PIE

1½ cups cooked, mashed pumpkin
2 eggs, well beaten
¾ cup firmly packed brown sugar
¼ teaspoon ginger
1 teaspoon cinnamon
½ teaspoon nutmeg
¼ teaspoon salt
1½ cups milk
1 9″ unbaked pastry shell

Combine pumpkin, eggs, sugar, spices, salt and milk. Mix well and pour into pastry shell. Bake in hot oven (400° F.) about 35 minutes or until firm. Makes one 9″ pie.

CUSTARD PIE

4 eggs, slightly beaten
¾ cup sugar
¼ teaspoon salt
3 cups milk

½ teaspoon vanilla
1 unbaked 9″ pastry shell

Combine eggs, sugar, salt, milk and vanilla. Mix well. Pour into pastry shell. Bake in hot oven (400° F.) 30–35 minutes or until firm. Makes one 9″ pie.

LOUISIANA STRAWBERRY PIE

1 quart strawberries
1 cup sugar
⅓ cup quick cooking tapioca
⅛ teaspoon salt
1 package pie crust mix
1½ tablespoons butter or margarine

Wash and hull strawberries. Combine strawberries, sugar, tapioca and salt. Prepare pie crust mix according to package directions. Roll ½ of pastry out on lightly floured surface to ⅛-inch thickness. Line 9″ pie pan with pastry. Pour strawberry mixture over pastry. Dot with butter or margarine. Roll remaining pastry out to ⅛-inch thickness. Arrange over strawberry mixture. Seal edges and prick top. Bake in hot oven (400° F.) 40–45 minutes. Makes one 9″ pie.

STRAWBERRY CHIFFON PIE

1 envelope unflavored gelatin
¼ cup cold water
½ cup boiling water
¾ cup sugar
1 cup strawberry pulp
½ cup shredded coconut
⅛ teaspoon salt
2 egg whites
¼ cup sugar
½ cup heavy cream, whipped
1 baked 9″ pastry shell

Soften gelatin in cold water; add boiling water and stir until dissolved. Cool. Add the ¾ cup sugar, strawberry pulp, coconut and salt. Chill until mixture begins to thicken. Beat egg whites until foamy. Gradually add the ¼ cup sugar, beating constantly until stiff. Fold egg white mixture and cream into strawberry mixture. Turn into pastry shell. Chill until firm. Serve with whipped cream, if desired. Makes one 9″ pie.

Combine raisins, cream, sugar, salt, lime juice, spices and eggs. Mix well. Roll ½ of pastry out on lightly floured surface to ⅛-inch thickness. Line 9″ pie pan with pastry. Add raisin mixture. Roll remaining pastry to ⅛-inch thickness. Arrange over raisin mixture. Seal edges; prick top. Bake in hot oven (400° F.) 35–40 minutes. Makes one 9″ pie.

GLAZED STRAWBERRY PIE

¼ cup cornstarch
1¼ cups sugar
½ cup cold water
1 cup boiling water
⅛ teaspoon salt
2 tablespoons lemon juice
Red food coloring
1 quart strawberries
1 baked 9″ pastry shell

Combine cornstarch and sugar. Add cold water and mix well. Add boiling water and cook over low heat, stirring constantly, until mixture is thickened. Add salt, lemon juice and enough food coloring to make mixture a light red. Add strawberries and mix lightly. Cool thoroughly. Turn into pastry shell. Garnish with whipped cream, if desired. Makes one 9″ pie.

TREE OF MUSIC PIE

1 recipe pastry for double-crust 9″ pie
3 cups elderberries
½ cup sugar
⅛ teaspoon salt
2 tablespoons all-purpose flour
1 tablespoon butter or margarine

Roll ½ of pastry out on lightly floured surface to ⅛-inch thickness. Line 9″ pie pan with pastry. Arrange elderberries over pastry. Combine sugar, salt and flour; sprinkle over elderberries. Dot with butter or margarine. Roll remaining pastry out to ⅛-inch thickness. Cut into strips ¼-inch wide. Arrange pastry strips over elderberry mixture, lattice fashion. Bake in hot oven (400° F.) about 35 minutes. Makes one 9″ pie.

THREE FRUIT PIE

1 recipe pastry for double-crust 9″ pie
2 cups fresh strawberries
1 cup diced fresh rhubarb
1 cup diced fresh pineapple
¾ cup sugar
2½ tablespoons minute tapioca
1 teaspoon grated lemon rind

Roll one-half of pastry out on lightly floured surface to ⅛-inch thickness. Line 9″ pie pan with pastry. Combine fruits, sugar, tapioca and lemon rind. Arrange

DIXIE RAISIN PIE

1 cup seeded raisins
1 cup sour cream
¾ cup sugar
¼ teaspoon salt
2 tablespoons lime juice
½ teaspoon ginger
¼ teaspoon allspice
¼ teaspoon nutmeg
2 eggs, well beaten
1 recipe pastry for double-crust 9″ pie

over pastry. Roll remaining pastry out to ⅛-inch thickness and arrange over fruit. Seal edges and prick top. Bake in hot oven (400° F.) 45–50 minutes. Makes one 9″ pie.

RASPBERRY-CHEESE PIE

1 cup sugar
¼ cup cornstarch
⅛ teaspoon salt
½ cup water
2 cups raspberries
1 9″ graham cracker shell
1 3-ounce package cream cheese, softened
1 cup heavy cream, whipped

Combine sugar, cornstarch and salt. Gradually add water and cook, stirring constantly, until thickened. Add raspberries and mix lightly. Cool thoroughly. Dot bottom of graham cracker shell with cream cheese. Pour raspberry mixture over cheese. Chill thoroughly. Top with cream to serve. Makes one 9″ pie.

RHUBARB CUSTARD PIE

1 package frozen rhubarb
2 eggs
¾ cup sugar
2 tablespoons all-purpose flour
1 recipe pastry for double-crust 9″ pie
1½ tablespoons butter or margarine

Thaw rhubarb; beat eggs slightly and add sugar and flour. Add rhubarb and mix well. Roll ½ of pastry out on lightly floured surface to ⅛-inch thickness. Line 9″ pie pan with pastry. Pour rhubarb mixture over pastry. Dot with butter or margarine. Roll remaining pastry out to ⅛-inch thickness. Place over rhubarb mixture. Seal edges and prick top. Bake in moderate oven (375° F.) 50–60 minutes. Makes one 9″ pie.

SHOO FLY PIE

¾ cup dark molasses
¾ cup boiling water
½ teaspoon baking soda
1½ cups sifted all-purpose flour
½ cup brown sugar, firmly packed
¼ cup butter or margarine
1 unbaked 9″ or 10″ pastry shell

Combine molasses, water and baking soda. Combine flour and sugar; cut in butter or margarine. In pastry shell, alternate layers of molasses mixture and flour mixture starting with molasses layer and ending with flour layer. Bake in moderate oven (375° F.) about 30 minutes. Makes one 9″ or 10″ pie.

RASPBERRY CREAM PIE

1 package raspberry flavored gelatin
1¼ cups boiling water
¾ cup sugar
1½ cups raspberries
½ cup heavy cream, whipped
1 baked 8″ pastry shell

Dissolve gelatin in water. Add sugar and raspberries. Chill until slightly thickened. Fold in cream. Pour into pastry shell and chill until firm. Makes one 8″ pie.

Cookies

ROLLED COOKIES

PINWHEEL COOKIES

2 cups sifted all-purpose flour
½ teaspoon baking powder
¼ teaspoon salt
½ teaspoon cinnamon
¼ teaspoon cloves
½ cup shortening
1 cup firmly packed brown sugar
1 egg
1 teaspoon vanilla
1 8-ounce package figs, finely chopped
½ cup granulated sugar
½ cup water
1 teaspoon grated orange rind
¼ cup chopped nuts

Sift flour, baking powder, salt and spices together. Cream shortening and brown sugar together until light and fluffy. Add egg and vanilla and mix well. Gradually add sifted ingredients and mix well. Roll out on lightly floured surface into a rectangle ¼" thick. Combine figs, granulated sugar, water and orange rind. Cook over medium heat, stirring constantly until thickened. Cool thoroughly. Add nuts.

Spread fig mixture over dough and roll up jelly roll fashion. Wrap in waxed paper and chill thoroughly. Cut into slices ¼" thick. Place on greased baking sheets. Bake in moderate oven (375° F.) about 12 minutes. Makes 36–48.

ALMOND CRESCENTS ESPAÑA

½ cup butter or margarine
½ cup sugar
⅛ teaspoon salt
2 egg yolks
⅓ cup finely chopped blanched almonds
1 cup sifted all-purpose flour
1 egg white
1 teaspoon water

Cream butter or margarine and sugar together until light and fluffy. Add salt and egg yolks; beat well. Add almonds and mix well. Gradually blend in flour and mix thoroughly. Chill thoroughly. Roll out on lightly floured surface to ⅛-inch thickness. Cut with floured crescent-shaped cutter. Place on greased baking sheets. Beat egg white with water until frothy. Brush egg-white mixture over cookies. Bake in moderate oven (375° F.) 10–12 minutes. Makes about 18.

MOLASSES CHRISTMAS SNAPS

½ cup shortening
½ cup peanut butter
⅔ cup sugar
½ cup molasses
⅓ cup pineapple juice
3 cups sifted all-purpose flour
1 teaspoon baking soda
1½ teaspoons cinnamon
¼ teaspoon nutmeg
¼ teaspoon salt

Cream shortening, peanut butter and sugar together until light and fluffy. Add molasses and pineapple juice; beat well. Sift flour, baking soda, cinnamon, nutmeg and salt together. Add to molasses mixture and mix well. Roll out to ⅛-inch thickness on lightly floured surface. Cut with floured cutter; place on greased baking sheets. Bake in moderate oven (350° F.) 10–12 minutes. Makes about 48.

VIENNESE CARAWAY SEED COOKIES

1 cup shortening
1 cup sugar
2 eggs
1 tablespoon light cream
1 tablespoon grated lemon rind
1 teaspoon caraway seeds
3 cups sifted cake flour
¼ teaspoon salt
¼ teaspoon baking soda
½ teaspoon ginger

Cream shortening and sugar until light and fluffy. Add eggs; beat well. Add cream, lemon rind and caraway seeds. Mix well. Sift remaining ingredients together and blend into creamed mixture. Chill several hours. Roll dough out on lightly floured surface to ¼-inch thickness. Cut with floured cutter and place on greased baking sheets. Bake in hot oven (400° F.) 10–12 minutes. Makes about 40.

TRUE GINGER SNAPS

1 cup shortening
1 cup molasses
1 egg
½ teaspoon lemon extract
4½ cups sifted all-purpose flour
4 teaspoons ginger
1 teaspoon baking soda
½ teaspoon salt

Melt shortening and cool. Add molasses, egg and lemon extract. Beat well. Sift flour, ginger, baking soda and salt together. Add to molasses mixture and mix thoroughly. Chill. Roll out on lightly floured surface to ⅛-inch thickness. Cut with floured cutter and place on greased baking sheets. Bake in moderate oven (375° F.) about 12 minutes. Makes about 48.

CHINESE ALMOND COOKIES

1¼ cups sifted cake flour
⅓ cup sugar
⅛ teaspoon salt
1 teaspoon baking powder
½ cup shortening
1 egg
1 teaspoon almond flavoring
Blanched almonds

Sift flour, sugar, salt and baking powder together. Cut in shortening. Add egg and almond flavoring. Mix well. Knead until smooth on lightly floured surface. Chill 1 hour. Roll out to ¼-inch thickness on lightly floured surface. Cut with 2" cutter. Place on greased baking sheets. Top each cooky with an almond. Bake in moderate oven (350° F.) about 20 minutes. Makes about 18.

ABERDEEN SHORTBREAD

2 cups butter or margarine
1 cup sugar
3 cups sifted all-purpose flour

Cream butter or margarine until light and fluffy. Gradually add sugar and beat well. Gradually add flour and mix until dough is smooth. Roll out on lightly floured surface to ¼-inch thickness. Cut with floured cutter. Place on ungreased baking sheets. Pierce cookies well with tines of fork. Bake in moderate oven (350°) 15–20 minutes. Makes about 48.

KRINGLES

2 cups sifted all-purpose flour
2 teaspoons baking powder
¼ teaspoon salt
½ cup butter or margarine
1 cup granulated sugar
1 egg, well beaten
2 teaspoons caraway seeds
3 tablespoons brandy
⅓ cup confectioners' sugar

Sift flour, baking powder and salt together. Cream butter or margarine and granulated sugar until light and fluffy. Add egg, caraway seeds and brandy; beat well. Gradually add sifted ingredients and blend thoroughly. Chill. Roll out on lightly floured surface to ⅛-inch thickness. Cut with floured cutter. Place on ungreased baking sheets and sprinkle with confectioners' sugar. Bake in moderate oven (375° F.) 12–15 minutes. Makes about 48.

SUGAR COOKIES

1½ cups sifted all-purpose flour
½ teaspoon baking powder
¼ teaspoon salt
½ teaspoon baking soda
½ cup sugar
½ cup butter or margarine
1 egg
2 tablespoons milk
1 teaspoon vanilla

Sift flour, baking powder, salt, baking soda and sugar together. Cut in butter or margarine until mixture resembles coarse meal. Add egg, milk and vanilla; mix well. Roll out on lightly floured surface to ⅟₁₆-inch thickness. Cut as desired. Place on ungreased baking sheets. Bake in hot oven (400° F.) about 8 minutes. Makes about 60.

RASPBERRY JAMBOREES

1 cup butter or margarine
1 8-ounce package cream cheese
1½ cups sifted all-purpose flour
⅛ teaspoon salt
½ cup raspberry jam (approx.)

Cream butter or margarine, and cheese. Gradually add flour and salt. Chill several hours. Roll out on lightly floured surface to ⅛-inch thickness. Cut in 4″ squares. Place 1 teaspoon jam in center. Fold corners over to center. Place on greased baking sheets. Bake in hot oven (400° F.) 10 minutes. Makes about 24.

DROP COOKIES

ENGLISH BRANDY SNAPS

¾ cup butter or margarine
¾ cup sugar
½ cup molasses
1½ cups sifted all-purpose flour
2½ teaspoons ginger

Combine butter or margarine, sugar and molasses. Cook over low heat, stirring constantly, until ingredients are well blended. Remove from heat. Add flour and ginger. Beat until smooth. Drop by teaspoonfuls onto greased baking sheets 2 inches apart. Bake in slow oven (300° F.) 10–12 minutes. Let stand a minute, then quickly remove cookies from sheet and roll into cone shapes. Makes about 48.

SOUTH PACIFIC ALMOND COOKIES

1 cup sifted all-purpose flour
1 teaspoon baking powder
¼ teaspoon salt
½ cup butter or margarine
⅔ cup sugar
2 egg whites
¼ teaspoon vanilla
¼ teaspoon almond extract
⅔ cup shredded coconut

Sift flour, baking powder and salt together. Cream butter or margarine and sugar together until light and fluffy. Add egg whites, vanilla and almond extract. Beat well. Add coconut and mix well. Blend in sifted ingredients and mix until thoroughly blended. Drop by teaspoonfuls onto greased baking sheets. Bake in moderate oven (375° F.) 12 minutes. Makes about 36.

APPLESAUCE DROPS

1¾ cups sifted all-purpose flour
1 teaspoon baking powder
½ teaspoon salt
½ teaspoon cinnamon
½ teaspoon cloves
½ teaspoon nutmeg
¾ cup shortening
1 cup sugar
1 egg
1 cup applesauce
⅔ cup raisins
1 cup corn flakes

Sift flour, baking powder, salt and spices together. Cream shortening and sugar until light and fluffy. Add egg and beat well. Add sifted ingredients and applesauce alternately to creamed mixture, beating well after each addition. Fold in raisins and corn flakes. Drop by teaspoonfuls 2 inches apart onto greased baking sheets. Bake in hot oven (400° F.) 12–15 minutes. Makes about 48.

BANANA COOKIES

2¼ cups sifted all-purpose flour
1 cup sugar
2 teaspoons baking powder
¼ teaspoon baking soda
¼ teaspoon salt
⅔ cup shortening
2 eggs
1 cup mashed banana
1 teaspoon vanilla
¼ teaspoon nutmeg
1 tablespoon sugar

Sift flour, the one cup sugar, baking powder, baking soda and salt together. Cut in shortening. Add eggs, bananas and vanilla. Beat well. Drop by teaspoonfuls 2 inches apart onto ungreased baking sheets. Combine nutmeg and the one tablespoon sugar. Top each cookie with nutmeg mixture. Bake in hot oven (400° F.) 10–12 minutes. Remove from baking sheets immediately. Makes about 36.

CHOCOLATE MACAROON DROPS

¼ teaspoon salt
2 egg whites
1 cup sifted confectioners' sugar
¼ teaspoon vanilla
¾ cup shredded coconut
2 cups corn flakes
1 6-ounce package semi-sweet
   chocolate morsels

Add salt to egg whites and beat until

frothy. Add sugar gradually and beat until stiff and shiny. Beat in vanilla. Fold in coconut, corn flakes and chocolate morsels. Drop by teaspoonfuls onto well-greased baking sheets. Bake in moderate oven (350° F.) 20 minutes. Makes about 2½ dozen cookies.

CHOCOLATE CHIP COOKIES

½ cup shortening
½ cup granulated sugar
¼ cup firmly packed brown sugar
1 egg, well beaten
1 cup sifted all-purpose flour
¼ teaspoon salt
½ teaspoon baking soda
1 package semi-sweet chocolate pieces
½ cup chopped nuts
1 teaspoon vanilla

Cream shortening and sugars together until light and fluffy. Add egg and beat well. Sift flour, salt and baking soda together. Blend sifted ingredients into creamed mixture. Add remaining ingredients and mix well. Drop by teaspoonfuls onto greased baking sheets 2 inches apart. Bake in moderate oven (350° F.) 10–12 minutes. Makes about 48.

CHOCOLATE COCONUT FLIPS

2 squares unsweetened chocolate
¼ cup water
¾ cup sugar
1½ cups shredded coconut
1 tablespoon all-purpose flour
⅛ teaspoon salt
½ teaspoon vanilla
3 egg whites, stiffly beaten

Combine chocolate and water. Cook over low heat, stirring constantly, until mixture is smooth. Remove from heat and add sugar and coconut; mix well. Stir in flour, salt and vanilla. Fold in egg whites.

Drop by teaspoonfuls 2 inches apart onto greased baking sheets. Bake in moderate oven (350° F.) 12–15 minutes. Makes about 24.

CHOCOLATE DROPS

½ cup butter or margarine
¾ cup sugar
1 square unsweetened chocolate, melted
1 egg, slightly beaten
1 teaspoon vanilla
1¼ cups sifted cake flour
½ teaspoon baking powder
⅛ teaspoon salt

Cream butter or margarine and sugar until light and fluffy. Add chocolate, egg and vanilla. Beat well. Sift remaining ingredients together and blend into chocolate mixture. Drop by teaspoonfuls 2 inches apart onto greased baking sheets. Bake in moderate oven (375° F.) about 15 minutes. Makes about 24.

HERMITS

2 cups sifted cake flour
2 teaspoons baking powder
⅛ teaspoon salt
½ teaspoon nutmeg
1 teaspoon cinnamon
½ teaspoon mace
⅛ cup shortening
½ cup granulated sugar
½ cup firmly packed brown sugar
2 eggs, well beaten
1 cup raisins
¾ cup chopped walnuts

Sift flour, baking powder, salt and spices together. Cream shortening, granulated sugar and brown sugar until light and fluffy. Add eggs and beat well. Add raisins and walnuts; mix well. Gradually add sifted ingredients, blending well. Drop by teaspoonfuls onto greased baking sheets. Bake in moderate oven (350° F.) about 15 minutes. Makes about 24.

CHOCOLATE MOLASSES COOKIES

1 cup shortening
1 cup firmly packed brown sugar
3 eggs
½ cup molasses
2½ cups sifted all-purpose flour
3 teaspoons baking powder
¼ teaspoon salt
1½ teaspoons cinnamon
¼ teaspoon nutmeg
¼ teaspoon baking soda
½ cup milk
1 cup shredded coconut
1 cup semi-sweet chocolate pieces

Cream together shortening and sugar; add eggs, 1 at a time, beating after each addition. Add molasses and beat well. Sift flour, baking powder, salt, cinnamon, nutmeg and baking soda together. Add sifted ingredients alternately with milk, beating well after each addition. Add coconut and chocolate. Drop by teaspoonfuls onto greased baking sheets. Bake in hot oven (400° F.) about 10 minutes. Makes about 48.

COCONUT-ORANGE DROPS

1 cup butter
½ cup sugar
1 egg
1 teaspoon grated orange rind
2 cups sifted all-purpose flour
⅛ teaspoon salt
¾ cup shredded coconut

Cream butter with sugar until light and fluffy. Add egg and beat well. Add rind and mix well. Sift flour and salt together. Gradually add sifted ingredients to creamed mixture, beating well after each addition. Add coconut and mix well. Drop by teaspoonfuls onto ungreased baking sheets. Bake in moderate slow oven (325° F.) 12–15 minutes. Makes 60.

OLD-TIME GINGER COOKIES

1 cup shortening
1 cup sugar
1 egg
2 cups molasses
2 tablespoons vinegar
7 cups sifted all-purpose flour
2 tablespoons ginger
1 teaspoon allspice
½ teaspoon cloves
¼ teaspoon nutmeg
4 teaspoons baking soda
½ teaspoon salt
1 cup boiling water

Cream shortening and sugar together until light and fluffy. Add egg and beat well. Add molasses and vinegar; mix well. Sift flour, spices, baking soda and salt together. Add to creamed mixture and mix well. Add water and mix well. Drop by teaspoonfuls onto greased baking sheets. Bake in moderate oven (350° F.) 8–10 minutes. Makes about 96.

SOUR CREAM NUTMEG COOKIES

2 cups sifted all-purpose flour
1 teaspoon nutmeg
½ teaspoon baking soda
2 teaspoons baking powder
¼ teaspoon salt
½ cup shortening
1 cup sugar
1 egg
½ cup sour cream
½ cup chopped walnuts

Sift flour, nutmeg, baking soda, baking powder and salt together. Cream shortening and sugar until light and fluffy. Add egg and beat well. Add sour cream and sifted ingredients alternately, beating well after each addition. Add walnuts. Drop by teaspoonfuls 2 inches apart onto well-greased baking sheets. Bake in moderate oven (375° F.) 10–12 minutes. Makes about 36.

LONDON LACE COOKIES

1 cup sifted all-purpose flour
1 cup finely chopped walnuts
½ cup light corn syrup
½ cup butter or margarine
⅔ cup firmly packed brown sugar

Combine flour and nuts. Combine syrup, butter or margarine and sugar. Cook over medium heat, stirring constantly, until mixture boils. Remove from heat and add flour mixture, and mix well. Drop by teaspoonfuls 3 inches apart onto greased baking sheets. Bake in slow oven (325° F.) 8–10 minutes. Cool 1 minute. Remove from baking sheet and roll around handle of wooden spoon to shape into cone. Makes about 60.

MARMALADE MUNCHES

3 cups sifted cake flour
½ teaspoon baking soda
¼ teaspoon salt
½ cup shortening
1 cup sugar
2 eggs, well beaten
⅔ cup orange marmalade

Sift flour, baking soda and salt together. Cream shortening with sugar until light and fluffy. Add eggs and beat well. Gradually blend in sifted ingredients. Add marmalade and mix well. Drop by teaspoonfuls 2 inches apart onto greased baking sheets. Bake in moderate oven (350° F.) 10–12 minutes. Remove from baking sheets immediately. Makes about 42.

SPICY NUT DROPS

¾ cup butter or margarine
¾ cup molasses
2 eggs
2¼ cups sifted all-purpose flour
3 teaspoons baking powder
¼ teaspoon salt
½ teaspoon nutmeg
1 teaspoon cinnamon
¼ teaspoon cloves
½ teaspoon baking soda
½ cup milk
½ cup chopped pecans

Melt butter or margarine. Add molasses and eggs and beat well. Sift flour, baking powder, salt, spices and baking soda together. Add sifted ingredients alternately with milk to molasses mixture, beating well after each addition. Add pecans. Drop by teaspoonfuls onto greased baking sheets. Bake in hot oven (400° F.) about 10 minutes. Makes about 48.

GOOBER COOKIES

1 egg, well beaten
¾ cup firmly packed brown sugar
1¼ cups sifted all-purpose flour
½ teaspoon baking soda
¼ teaspoon salt
½ cup cooking oil
1 teaspoon vanilla
¾ cup chopped peanuts

Combine egg and sugar and beat well. Sift flour, baking soda and salt together. Add sifted ingredients alternately with oil to egg mixture, beating well after each addition. Add vanilla and peanuts; mix well. Drop by teaspoonfuls onto greased baking sheets. Bake in moderate oven (375° F.) 8–10 minutes. Makes about 36.

PECAN NUT KISSES

2 egg whites
1¼ cups firmly packed brown sugar
⅛ teaspoon salt
1 teaspoon vanilla
1¼ cups finely chopped pecans

Beat egg whites until frothy. Gradually add sugar, beating constantly until stiff. Fold in remaining ingredients. Drop by teaspoonfuls onto greased baking sheets. Bake in moderate oven (350° F.) 12–15 minutes. Makes about 24.

PINEAPPLE DROPS

½ cup shortening
1 cup firmly packed brown sugar
1 egg
¾ cup canned crushed pineapple, not drained
2 cups sifted all-purpose flour
¼ teaspoon baking soda
1 teaspoon baking powder
⅛ teaspoon salt
½ cup chopped pecans
½ teaspoon vanilla

Cream shortening with sugar until light and fluffy. Add egg and beat well. Add pineapple and mix well. Sift flour, baking soda, baking powder and salt together. Add sifted ingredients gradually to creamed mixture, beating well after each addition. Add pecans and vanilla; beat well. Drop by teaspoonfuls onto greased baking sheets. Bake in moderate oven (375° F.) 12–15 minutes. Makes about 48.

CARAMEL PECAN COOKIES

1½ cups sifted all-purpose flour
¼ teaspoon salt
½ cup shortening
½ cup firmly packed brown sugar
½ cup light corn syrup
1 egg
½ teaspoon vanilla
Pecan halves

Sift flour and salt together; cream shortening and sugar together until light and fluffy. Add syrup and beat well. Add egg and vanilla; beat well. Gradually blend in sifted ingredients. Drop by teaspoonfuls onto greased baking sheets. Top with pecan halves. Bake in hot oven (400° F.) 8–10 minutes. Makes about 48.

SCOTCH OATMEAL COOKIES

1¾ cups sifted all-purpose flour
½ teaspoon baking soda
½ teaspoon salt
½ teaspoon cinnamon
¼ teaspoon nutmeg
¼ teaspoon cloves
¾ cup shortening
½ cup granulated sugar
1 cup firmly packed brown sugar
1 egg
½ cup buttermilk
¼ cup light corn syrup
½ teaspoon vanilla
2 cups rolled oats
1 cup chopped nuts
½ cup raisins

Sift flour, baking soda, salt and spices together. Cream shortening and sugars until light and fluffy. Add egg and beat well. Combine buttermilk, syrup and vanilla. Add buttermilk mixture and sifted ingredients alternately to creamed mixture, beating well after each addition. Add oats, nuts and raisins; mix well. Drop by tablespoonfuls 2 inches apart onto greased baking sheets. Bake in moderate oven (375° F.) about 15 minutes. Makes about 48.

PEANUT COCONUT COOKIES

½ cup peanut butter
1 teaspoon orange juice
⅛ teaspoon salt
1⅓ cups sweetened condensed milk
1½ cups shredded coconut
½ cup chopped dates
½ cup chopped peanuts

Combine peanut butter, orange juice and salt. Mix well. Add remaining ingredients and mix until thoroughly blended. Drop by teaspoonfuls onto greased baking sheets. Bake in moderate oven (375° F.) 10–12 minutes. Makes about 24.

MOLDED COOKIES

MALUCCA CINNAMON ROUNDS

½ cup butter or margarine
1 cup sugar
1 egg, well beaten
½ teaspoon vanilla
1¼ cups sifted all-purpose flour
1 teaspoon baking powder
¼ teaspoon salt
½ cup chopped peanuts
2½ teaspoons cinnamon

Cream butter or margarine and sugar together until light and fluffy. Add egg and vanilla; mix well. Sift flour, baking powder and salt together. Blend sifted ingredients into creamed mixture. Combine peanuts and cinnamon. Shape dough into balls about ½" in diameter. Roll each ball in peanut mixture. Place 2 inches apart on greased baking sheets. Bake in moderate oven (375° F.) about 15 minutes. Remove from baking sheets immediately. Makes about 24.

CORNMEAL COOKIES

3 cups sifted all-purpose flour
1 teaspoon baking powder
½ teaspoon salt
1 cup yellow cornmeal

1 cup butter
1½ cups sugar
2 eggs
¼ cup pineapple juice
½ teaspoon grated lemon rind
1 tablespoon orange juice

Sift flour, baking powder and salt together. Add cornmeal and mix lightly. Cream butter with sugar until fluffy, add eggs and beat well. Add pineapple juice, lemon rind and orange juice. Blend in cornmeal mixture. Shape dough into 1" balls and place on greased baking sheets. Flatten with tines of fork. Bake in moderate oven (375° F.) 12–15 minutes. Makes about 60.

BRAZIL NUT COOKIES

1¾ cups sifted all-purpose flour
½ teaspoon baking powder
¼ teaspoon salt
½ cup shortening
¾ cup sugar
⅓ cup ground Brazil nuts
2 eggs, well beaten
½ teaspoon vanilla

Sift flour, baking powder and salt together. Cream shortening and sugar together until light and fluffy. Add nuts, eggs and vanilla. Beat well. Add sifted ingredients and mix thoroughly. Chill. Shape into small balls and place on greased baking sheets. Bake in hot oven (400° F.) 12–15 minutes. Makes about 36.

LADY FINGERS

½ cup sifted cake flour
⅛ teaspoon salt
⅓ cup confectioners' sugar
3 eggs, separated
⅓ cup confectioners' sugar
¼ teaspoon vanilla

Sift flour, salt and ⅓ cup confectioners' sugar. Beat egg whites until foamy. Gradually add remaining ⅓ cup sugar and beat until stiff. Beat egg yolks until thick and lemon colored. Fold egg yolks and vanilla into egg-white mixture. Gradually fold flour mixture into egg-white mixture. Press through pastry bag onto ungreased baking sheets in 4″ x 1″ strips. Bake in moderate oven (350° F.) about 12 minutes. Makes about 24.

PEANUT BUTTER PLOPS

½ cup shortening
½ cup peanut butter
1½ cups firmly packed brown sugar
½ cup granulated sugar
1 teaspoon vanilla
1 egg
1½ cups sifted all-purpose flour
1 teaspoon baking soda
½ teaspoon salt

Cream shortening, peanut butter and sugars together until light and fluffy. Add vanilla and egg; beat well. Sift flour, baking soda and salt together. Blend into creamed mixture. Shape into 1″ balls. Place on greased baking sheets 2 inches apart. Flatten with tines of fork. Bake in moderate oven (375° F.) 10–12 minutes. Makes about 48.

PENNSYLVANIA DUTCH PFEFFERNUSSE

4½ cups sifted all-purpose flour
¼ teaspoon baking soda
1 teaspoon cloves
½ teaspoon nutmeg
¼ teaspoon cinnamon
½ teaspoon salt
¼ teaspoon black pepper
1½ teaspoons anise seed
4 eggs, slightly beaten
2 cups firmly packed brown sugar
Confectioners' sugar

Sift flour, baking soda, spices, salt and pepper together. Add anise seed. Combine eggs and brown sugar. Add sifted ingredients and mix well. Chill thoroughly. Shape into balls and place on greased baking sheets. Cover and let stand at room temperature several hours. Bake in moderate oven (350° F.) 20–25 minutes. Roll in confectioners' sugar while warm. Makes about 48.

SANTA CLAUS COOKIES

2 cups sifted all-purpose flour
¼ teaspoon salt
1 cup butter or margarine
½ cup confectioners' sugar
2 teaspoons vanilla
1 teaspoon almond extract
½ cup chopped nuts

Sift flour and salt together. Cream butter or margarine, and sugar until light and fluffy. Add vanilla, almond extract and nuts; beat well. Gradually add sifted ingredients and blend well. Shape into small balls and place on ungreased baking sheets. Bake in slow oven (325° F.) about 25 minutes. Makes about 40.

SPRINGERLE

3¾ cups sifted all-purpose flour
¼ teaspoon salt
4 eggs
2 cups sugar
Anise seed

Sift flour and salt together. Beat eggs until thick and lemon colored. Gradually add sugar and continue beating 15 minutes. Fold sifted ingredients into egg mixture. Roll out on lightly floured surface into a rectangle ⅛″ thick. Press springerle board well into dough. Cut cookies. Sprinkle anise seed lightly over ungreased baking sheets. Place cookies on baking sheets. Cover and allow to dry several hours. Bake in moderate oven (375° F.) 5 minutes. Bake in slow oven (300° F.) 25 minutes. Store in airtight container at least 2 weeks before using. Makes about 60.

SPRITZ

1 cup butter
½ cup sugar
1 egg
½ teaspoon salt
½ teaspoon almond extract
2½ cups sifted all-purpose flour

Cream butter and sugar until light and fluffy. Add egg, salt and almond extract; beat well. Gradually blend in flour and mix well. Shape as desired with cooky press. Place on greased baking sheets. Bake in hot oven (400° F.) 8–10 minutes. Makes about 72.

BAR COOKIES

HONDURAS BANANA BARS

½ cup shortening
1 cup sugar
2 eggs, well beaten
½ teaspoon vanilla
1¾ cups sifted cake flour
2 teaspoons baking powder
¼ teaspoon salt
1 cup mashed bananas

Cream shortening and sugar together until light and fluffy. Add eggs and vanilla and beat well. Sift flour, baking

powder and salt together. Add sifted ingredients alternately with bananas to creamed mixture, beating well after each addition. Turn into greased 9″ x 13″ pan. Bake in moderate oven (350° F.) 25–30 minutes. Cool and cut into bars. Makes about 24.

CINNAMON CRISPS

1 cup sifted all-purpose flour
⅛ teaspoon salt
¼ teaspoon cinnamon
⅓ cup butter or margarine
½ cup sugar
1 egg, separated
2 tablespoons milk
¼ teaspoon vanilla
3 tablespoons sugar
¼ teaspoon cinnamon
⅓ cup chopped nuts

Sift flour, salt and ¼ teaspoon cinnamon together. Cream butter or margarine, and ½ cup sugar together until light and fluffy. Add egg yolk, milk and vanilla. Beat well. Add sifted ingredients and beat thoroughly. Spread in ungreased 7″ x 11″ pan. Beat egg white lightly and spread over dough. Combine three tablespoons sugar, ¼ teaspoon cinnamon and nuts; sprinkle over egg white. Bake in moderate oven (350° F.) 25–30 minutes. Cut into bars while warm. Makes about 24.

CHOCOLATE-CHIP HONEY SQUARES

½ cup sifted all-purpose flour
¼ teaspoon baking soda
¼ teaspoon salt
⅓ cup honey
1 egg, well beaten
1 tablespoon melted butter
1 package semi-sweet chocolate pieces
¾ cup chopped nuts
1 teaspoon vanilla

Sift flour, baking soda and salt together. Combine honey and egg; mix well. Add butter, chocolate, nuts and vanilla. Mix well. Add sifted ingredients and beat thoroughly. Turn into greased 8″ x 8″ pan. Bake in moderate oven (350° F.) 30–35 minutes. Cut into squares. Makes about 24.

COCONUT DREAMS

½ cup shortening
¼ teaspoon salt
½ cup firmly packed brown sugar
1 cup sifted cake flour
1 cup brown sugar, firmly packed
1 teaspoon vanilla
2 eggs
2 tablespoons cake flour
½ teaspoon baking powder
⅛ teaspoon salt
1 cup shredded coconut
½ cup chopped walnuts

Cream shortening, salt and ½ cup brown sugar until light and fluffy. Gradually mix in 1 cup cake flour. Press evenly into 8″ x 8″ pan. Bake in hot oven (425° F.) 8 minutes. Remove from oven and reduce heat to 350° F. Mix 1 cup brown sugar, vanilla and eggs. Stir in remaining ingredients. Spread mixture over first mixture. Continue baking in moderate oven (350° F.) 15 minutes. Cut into bars while still warm. Makes about 10.

PECAN STICKS

3 eggs, separated
¾ cups sugar
¾ teaspoon vanilla
¼ cup sifted all-purpose flour
¾ cup finely chopped pecans

Beat egg yolks until thick and lemon colored. Gradually beat in sugar. Add vanilla and mix well. Fold in flour and pecans. Beat egg whites until stiff and fold into pecan mixture. Turn into greased 12″ x 9″ pan. Bake in moderate oven (350° F.) 25–30 minutes. Cut into 4″ x 1″ bars. Makes about 36.

COCONUT-PUMPKIN SQUARES

2 cups sifted all-purpose flour
1 teaspoon baking powder
¼ teaspoon baking soda
½ teaspoon salt
1 teaspoon cinnamon
¾ teaspoon nutmeg
½ cup shortening
1 cup firmly packed brown sugar
1 egg
¾ cup canned pumpkin
2 tablespoons molasses
½ teaspoon vanilla
½ cup shredded coconut

Sift flour, baking powder, baking soda, salt and spices together. Cream shortening and sugar together until light and fluffy. Add egg, pumpkin, molasses and vanilla. Beat well. Gradually add sifted ingredients and beat well. Blend in coconut. Turn into greased 15″ x 10″ pan. Bake in moderate oven (350° F.) 25–30 minutes. Makes about 36.

REFRIGERATOR COOKIES

FILBERT COOKIES

1¼ cups sifted all-purpose flour
⅓ cup sugar

¼ teaspoon ginger
½ cup butter or margarine
1 egg white
½ cup filberts

Sift flour, sugar and ginger together. Cut in butter or margarine. Add egg white and mix until dough is smooth. Add filberts and mix well. Shape into a roll about 1½″ in diameter. Chill 3 hours. Cut into slices ¼″ thick. Place on greased baking sheet. Bake in moderate oven, (350° F.) 12–15 minutes. Makes about 36.

MOLASSES RINGS

½ cup molasses
½ cup shortening
½ cup sugar
1 egg
2½ cups sifted all-purpose flour
¼ teaspoon salt
¼ teaspoon baking soda
⅛ teaspoon allspice
¼ teaspoon nutmeg
½ teaspoon ginger

Combine molasses and shortening. Cook over low heat until shortening melts. Remove from heat and add sugar. Cool. Add egg and beat well. Sift flour, salt, baking soda and spices together; add molasses mixture and mix well. Shape into rolls 2″ in diameter. Wrap in waxed paper and chill thoroughly. Cut into slices ⅛″ thick and place on greased baking sheets. Bake in moderate oven (350° F.) 12–15 minutes. Makes about 60.

BUTTERSCOTCH COOKIES

1½ cups sifted all-purpose flour
1½ teaspoons baking powder
¼ teaspoon salt
½ cup shortening
1¼ cups firmly packed brown sugar
1 egg
½ teaspoon vanilla

Sift flour, baking powder and salt together. Cream shortening and sugar until light and fluffy. Add egg and vanilla and beat well. Gradually add sifted ingredients and mix well. Shape into rolls 2″ in diameter and wrap in waxed paper. Chill thoroughly. Cut into slices ⅛″ thick. Place on ungreased baking sheets. Bake in hot oven (400° F.) 8–10 minutes. Makes about 50.

BUTTERSCOTCH BITES

1 cup shortening
2 cups firmly packed brown sugar
1 teaspoon vanilla
2 eggs
3½ cups sifted all-purpose flour
½ teaspoon salt
1 teaspoon baking soda
¾ cup chopped nuts

Cream shortening and sugar together until light and fluffy. Add vanilla and beat well. Add eggs and mix well. Sift flour, salt and baking soda together. Add sifted ingredients to creamed mixture and mix well. Add nuts and beat well. Shape into rolls two inches in diameter and wrap in waxed paper. Chill thoroughly. Cut into slices ⅛″ thick. Place on ungreased baking sheets. Bake in moderate oven (375° F.) 12 minutes. Makes about 96.

Cakes

APPLESAUCE CAKE

1 cup sugar
1 teaspoon cinnamon
½ teaspoon allspice
¼ teaspoon nutmeg
½ cup shortening
1 egg
1 cup thick applesauce (unsweetened)
1 teaspoon vanilla
2 cups sifted all-purpose flour
½ teaspoon salt
1 teaspoon baking soda
1 teaspoon baking powder
¾ cup chopped raisins
1 cup broken walnuts

Mix sugar and spices; add gradually to shortening, creaming thoroughly. Add egg and beat well. Stir in applesauce and vanilla. Add flour sifted with salt, baking soda, and baking powder; beat smooth. Add raisins and walnuts. Bake in two well-greased 8″ layer cake pans in moderate oven (350° F.) about 35 minutes. Makes two 8″ layers.

BLACK BLIZZARD CAKE

2 eggs, separated
1 cup sugar
1 cup sour cream
1½ cups sifted cake flour
1 teaspoon baking powder
1 teaspoon baking soda
¼ teaspoon salt
½ teaspoon nutmeg
½ teaspoon cinnamon
⅛ teaspoon allspice
½ cup chopped pecans

Beat egg yolks until thick, add sugar and sour cream. Sift flour, baking powder, baking soda, salt and spices together. Add pecans and mix lightly. Fold flour mixture into egg yolk mixture. Beat egg whites until stiff and fold into batter. Turn batter into waxed-paper-lined, greased 8″ x 8″ pan. Bake in moderate oven (350° F.) about 45 minutes. Serves 6–8.

CLASSIC ANGEL FOOD

1¼ cups sifted cake flour
¾ cup sugar
1½ cups egg whites
1 teaspoon cream of tartar
¼ teaspoon salt
1 cup sugar
1 teaspoon vanilla

Sift flour with ¾ cup sugar 3 times. Beat egg whites with cream of tartar and salt until foamy. Gradually add 1 cup sugar, beating constantly. Continue beating until stiff. Gradually fold in flour-sugar mixture. Fold in vanilla. Pour into ungreased 10" tube pan. Bake in moderate oven (375° F.) 30–35 minutes. Makes one 10" tube cake.

CHEESE CAKE

6-ounce package zwieback
2 tablespoons sugar
½ cup softened butter
½ cup sugar
2 tablespoons flour
¼ teaspoon salt
1 pound cream cheese
2 tablespoons lemon juice
1 teaspoons grated lemon rind
4 eggs separated
1 cup sour cream

Crush zwieback into fine crumbs. With fingers mix crumbs with the 2 tablespoons sugar and softened butter. Reserve ½ cup crumbs. Press remaining crumbs on bottom and a little over halfway up the sides of 9" spring form pan. Combine the ½ cup sugar, flour and salt and blend into cream cheese. Add lemon juice and rind. Beat in egg yolks one at a time. Blend in sour cream. Beat egg whites until stiff but not dry and fold into cheese mixture. Turn into crumb-lined pan. Bake in a slow oven (325° F.) 1 hour and 30 minutes. When cake is done, turn off oven, open door and leave cake in oven until thoroughly cool. Garnish with extra crumbs. Makes one 9" cake.

OLD-FASHIONED CHOCOLATE CAKE

2 cups sifted cake flour
2 teaspoons baking powder
¾ teaspoon baking soda
¼ teaspoon salt
½ cup butter or margarine
1 cup sugar
2 eggs, well beaten
2 squares unsweetened chocolate, melted
½ cup milk
½ cup sour cream
¼ teaspoon vanilla
¼ teaspoon almond extract
½ cup chopped toasted almonds

Sift flour, baking powder, baking soda and salt together. Cream butter or margarine with sugar. Add eggs and chocolate; beat well. Add sifted ingredients, milk and sour cream alternately. Beat well after each addition. Add vanilla and almond extract. Add almonds. Turn into 2 greased 9" layer cake pans. Bake in moderate oven (350° F.) 45–50 minutes. Makes two 9" layers.

CHERRY-COCONUT CAKE

½ cup shortening
1½ cups sugar
2⅓ cups sifted cake flour
3 teaspoons baking powder
¼ teaspoon salt
¼ cup maraschino cherry liquid
½ cup milk
1 teaspoon vanilla
16 maraschino cherries, cut fine
½ cup chopped nuts
4 egg whites
1 cup shredded coconut

Cream shortening and sugar until fluffy. and light. Sift together flour, baking powder and salt. Combine cherry liquid, milk and vanilla. Add flour mixture in thirds, alternating with milk mixture, to the creamed shortening and sugar, beating smooth after each addition. Fold in cherries and nuts. Beat egg whites until stiff and fold into cake mixture. Fold in coconut. Bake in 2 greased 9" layer cake pans in moderate oven (375° F.) 30–35 minutes. Makes two 9" layers.

CHOCOLATE ANGEL FOOD

¾ cup sifted cake flour
¼ cup cocoa
1¼ cups egg whites
¼ teaspoon salt
1 teaspoon cream of tartar
1¼ cups sifted sugar
1 teaspoon vanilla
¼ teaspoon almond extract

Sift flour and cocoa together 3 times. Beat egg whites and salt until foamy. Add cream of tartar and beat until stiff. Fold in sugar gradually. Fold in vanilla and almond extract. Sift flour over egg-white mixture gradually. Fold in quickly. Turn batter into ungreased 10″ tube pan. Cut through batter with spatula. Bake in moderate oven (375° F.) 30–35 minutes. Invert pan and cool. Makes one 10″ tube cake.

DENVER RED CHOCOLATE CAKE
(Adapted for ordinary altitudes)

4 cups sifted cake flour
2 teaspoons baking soda
1½ teaspoons salt
1 cup shortening
2½ cups sugar
4 eggs
6 squares unsweetened chocolate, melted
½ cup vinegar
1½ cups milk
2 teaspoons vanilla

Sift flour, baking soda and salt together. Cream shortening with sugar until light and fluffy. Add eggs, 1 at a time, and beat well after each addition. Add chocolate and mix well. Combine vinegar, milk and vanilla. Add milk mixture and sifted ingredients alternately to chocolate mixture; beat well after each addition. Turn into 3 greased 9″ layer cake

pans. Bake in moderate oven (350° F.) about 30 minutes, or until cake tests done. Makes three 9″ layers.

PECAN CHOCOLATE TORTE

1 egg
6 eggs, separated
¾ cup sugar
1¾ cups very finely chopped or grated pecans
1 square unsweetened chocolate, grated
½ cup fine dry cake crumbs
1 teaspoon vanilla

Beat egg and egg yolks until lemon colored. Add sugar, pecans, chocolate and crumbs; beat well. Add vanilla. Beat egg whites until stiff; fold into pecan mixture. Turn into 2 well-greased and lightly floured 9″ layer cake pans. Bake in moderate oven (350° F.) 20–25 minutes. Cool thoroughly. Fill and frost, as desired. Makes 12 servings.

PECAN DEVIL'S FOOD CAKE

⅓ cup shortening
1¼ cups brown sugar, firmly packed
2 eggs, well beaten
½ cup hot black coffee
2 squares unsweetened chocolate
1½ cups sifted cake flour
1 teaspoon baking soda
1 teaspoon baking powder
½ teaspoon salt
¾ cup finely chopped pecans
½ cup buttermilk
1 teaspoon vanilla

Cream shortening; add sugar gradually, and cream until light and fluffy. Add eggs and beat well. Meanwhile pour coffee over chocolate; stir over low heat until smooth and thick; cool, add to egg mixture, mixing thoroughly. Sift flour, baking soda, baking powder and salt together; add pecans. Combine buttermilk and vanilla, and add alternately with dry ingredients to the chocolate mixture, beating after each addition until smooth. Turn into well-greased and lightly floured 8″ x 8″ x 2″ pan and bake in moderate oven (350° F.) 50–60 minutes. Makes one 8″ square cake.

CITRON CAKE

2 cups sifted cake flour
½ teaspoon baking soda
¼ teaspoon nutmeg
¼ teaspoon allspice
¼ teaspoon salt
⅓ cup shortening
1 cup sugar
2 eggs
1 tablespoon grated orange rind
¾ cup orange juice
2 tablespoons chopped citron

Sift flour, baking soda, spices and salt together. Cream shortening with sugar until fluffy. Beat eggs until thick; add to shortening mixture. Add orange rind and beat well. Add sifted ingredients and orange juice alternately, beating thoroughly after each addition. Add citron. Pour into greased 8″ x 8″ x 2″ pan. Bake in moderate oven (350° F.) 50 minutes. Makes one 8″-square cake.

FAVORITE ONE-EGG SQUARE

2 cups sifted cake flour
2½ teaspoons baking powder
¼ teaspoon salt
¼ cup butter or margarine
1 cup sugar
1 egg
1 teaspoon vanilla
¾ cup milk

Sift flour, baking powder and salt together. Cream butter or margarine with sugar. Add egg and vanilla; beat well. Add sifted ingredients and milk alternately, beating well after each addition. Pour into greased 8″ x 8″ x 2″ pans. Bake in moderate oven (350° F.) 50 minutes. Makes one 8″-square cake.

MIDNIGHT FRUIT CAKE

4 pounds seeded raisins, chopped
1 cup citron, chopped
2 cups dried apricots, chopped
1 cup chopped candied pineapple
¼ cup chopped candied lemon rind
¼ cup chopped candied orange rind
½ cup grape juice
½ cup orange juice
2 cups chopped walnuts
2½ cups sifted cake flour
2 cups shortening
1 pound brown sugar
12 eggs
1 cup molasses
1 teaspoon cloves
4 teaspoons allspice
1½ teaspoons mace
½ teaspoon baking soda
½ teaspoon salt
4 squares unsweetened chocolate, melted
2 tablespoons brandy

Combine fruits, grape juice and orange juice. Let stand several hours. Drain; reserve liquid. Combine fruits, walnuts and 1 cup flour; mix lightly. Cream shortening and sugar until fluffy. Add eggs, 1 at a time, to creamed mixture. Beat well after each addition. Add molasses and mix well. Combine remaining 1½ cups flour with spices, baking soda and salt. Add spice mixture alternately with grape-juice mixture and fruit mixture to egg mixture. Beat well after each addition. Add chocolate and brandy. Mix well. Pour into greased waxed-paper lined 7″ x 3″ loaf pans. Steam 2 hours. Bake in slow oven (300° F.) about 1½ hours. Cool slightly and remove paper. Makes about 7 loaves.

HOLIDAY FRUIT CAKE

4 cups sifted cake flour
1 teaspoon mace
¼ teaspoon nutmeg
2 teaspoons cinnamon
½ teaspoon baking soda
6 cups currants
4 cups raisins
1 pound citron, sliced
½ cup candied orange rind
½ cup chopped candied cherries
1 cup blanched almonds, slivered
1 cup chopped pecans
2 cups shortening
2 cups brown sugar, firmly packed
9 eggs, separated
¾ cup cold coffee
¼ cup rum or brandy

Sift flour, spices and baking soda together. Add fruits and nuts; mix lightly. Cream shortening with sugar until light. Beat egg yolks until thick. Beat egg whites until stiff. Add egg yolks and egg whites to sugar mixture; mix lightly. Add fruit mixture alternately with coffee and rum or brandy. Pour into 4 greased wax-paper lined 9″ x 5″ x 3″ pans (or bake 1 or 2 at a time, keeping remaining batter in bowl). Bake in slow oven (275° F.) 1½–2 hours, or until top of cake looks dry. Makes about four 2-pound cakes.

YANKEE DOODLE FRUIT CAKE

5½ cups sifted cake flour
2½ teaspoons baking powder
¼ teaspoon mace
1 cup shortening
2 cups brown sugar, firmly packed
3 eggs, well beaten
1 teaspoon vanilla
3¼ cups raisins
½ cup sliced candied orange rind
¼ cup sliced candied cherries
¼ cup sliced candied pineapple
1 cup chopped pecans
1 cup cranberry juice

Sift flour, baking powder and mace together. Cream shortening with sugar until fluffy. Add eggs and beat well. Add vanilla, fruits and pecans; mix well. Add sifted ingredients and cranberry juice alternately. Beat well after each addition. Turn into greased, lined 10″ tube pan. Bake in slow oven (300° F.) 2–2¼ hours. Makes one 10″ tube cake.

ALEPPO HONEY CAKE

1 cup molasses
2 cups honey
¾ cup sugar
½ teaspoon nutmeg
1½ teaspoons ginger
3 tablespoons grated lemon rind
4½ cups sifted cake flour
4½ teaspoons baking powder
¼ teaspoon salt
¾ cup milk
½ cup chopped crystallized ginger
½ cup chopped pistachio nuts

Combine molasses, honey, sugar, spices and lemon rind. Sift flour with baking powder and salt. Add sifted ingredients and milk alternately to molasses mixture, beating well after each addition. Add crystallized ginger and nuts; mix well; pour into 2 greased 8″ x 8″ x 2″ pans. Bake in moderate oven (350° F.) for 1 hour. Makes two 8″-square cakes.

JELLY CAKE

2 cups sifted cake flour
1½ teaspoons baking powder
⅛ teaspoon salt
⅔ cup shortening
1¼ cups sugar
1 teaspoon vanilla
¼ teaspoon almond flavoring
3 eggs, separated
½ cup milk
¾ cup raspberry jam
Confectioners' sugar

Sift flour, baking powder and salt together. Cream shortening with the 1¼ cups sugar until light and fluffy. Add vanilla and almond flavoring; mix well. Beat egg yolks until thick and add to sugar mixture; beat well. Gradually add sifted ingredients and milk alternately; beat well after each addition. Beat egg whites until stiff and fold into batter. Turn into 2 greased 9″ layer cake pans. Bake in moderate oven (350° F.) about 25 minutes. Cool thoroughly. Spread jam between layers. Sprinkle confectioners' sugar over top. Makes one 9″ layer cake.

LORD BALTIMORE CAKE

2½ cups sifted cake flour
½ teaspoon salt
3 teaspoons baking powder
¾ cup shortening
1¼ cups sugar
8 egg yolks
¾ cup milk
½ teaspoon almond extract
½ teaspoon grated orange rind

Sift flour, salt and baking powder together. Cream shortening and sugar until light. Beat egg yolks until thick. Add to shortening mixture and beat thoroughly. Add sifted ingredients alternately with milk. Beat well after each addition. Add almond extract and orange rind; beat well. Pour into 3 greased 8″ layer cake pans. Bake in moderate oven (375° F.) about 20 minutes. Fill and frost with Lord Baltimore Filling and Frosting (page 419). Makes three 8″ layers.

VERMONT MAPLE CAKE

⅓ cup shortening
½ cup sugar
¾ cup maple syrup
2¼ cups sifted cake flour
3 teaspoons baking powder
¼ teaspoon salt
½ cup milk
3 egg whites
1 teaspoon lemon extract

Cream shortening with sugar until light and fluffy. Add syrup and beat well. Sift flour, baking powder and salt together. Add sifted ingredients alternately with milk to syrup mixture, beating well after each addition. Beat egg whites until stiff and fold into batter. Add lemon extract. Turn into 2 greased 9″ layer cake pans. Bake in moderate oven (350° F.) 25–30 minutes. Makes two 9″ layers.

DRIED PRUNE-APRICOT UPSIDE-DOWN CAKE

1¼ cups sifted cake flour
1½ teaspoons baking powder
¼ teaspoon salt
½ cup granulated sugar
1 egg, well beaten
½ cup milk
½ teaspoon almond extract
¼ cup melted shortening
3 tablespoons butter or margarine
¼ cup firmly packed brown sugar
8 canned apricot halves, well-drained
8 cooked prunes, well-drained
½ cup shredded coconut, toasted

Sift flour, baking powder, salt and granulated sugar. Combine egg, milk and almond extract. Gradually add flour mixture. Mix well after each addition. Stir in shortening; beat vigorously 1 minute. Melt butter or margarine in 8″ x 8″ pan. Add brown sugar and stir until sugar is dissolved. Arrange apricot halves and prunes in sugar mixture. Pour batter over fruits. Bake in moderate oven (350° F.) 40–50 minutes. Cool slightly and turn out of pan. Top with coconut. Makes one 8″-square cake.

RASPBERRY JELLY ROLL

1 cup sifted cake flour
¼ teaspoon salt
5 eggs, separated
1 cup sugar
2 tablespoons orange juice
Confectioners' sugar
1 cup raspberry jelly

Sift flour with salt. Beat egg whites until almost stiff. Add ½ cup sugar gradually, beating constantly until very stiff. Beat egg yolks until thick; add remaining ½ cup sugar gradually, beating constantly, until thick. Add orange juice. Fold egg-yolk mixture into egg whites. Fold flour mixture gradually into egg mixture. Line 11″ x 16″ pan with waxed paper; grease paper. Turn batter into pan. Bake in moderate oven (350° F.) about 15 minutes. Turn out on towel sprinkled with confectioners' sugar. Remove paper and trim crusts. Roll up and cool. Unroll; spread with jelly and roll. Makes 1 jelly roll.

STATE OF MAINE FUDGE CAKE

1 cup shortening
2 cups sugar
4 eggs, separated
1 cup grated raw potato
2½ cups sifted cake flour
¼ teaspoon salt
3 teaspoons baking powder
1 teaspoon cinnamon
¾ cup chopped pecans
½ cup milk
2 squares unsweetened chocolate, melted
1 tablespoon grated lemon rind

Cream shortening with sugar until light and fluffy. Add egg yolks and beat well. Add potato and beat. Sift flour with salt, baking powder and cinnamon. Add pecans to sifted ingredients and mix lightly.

Add nut mixture and milk alternately to creamed mixture, beating well after each addition. Add chocolate and lemon rind. Beat egg whites until stiff and fold into chocolate mixture. Turn into greased 13″ x 9″ x 2″ pan. Bake in moderate oven (350° F.) for about 1 hour. Makes 1 loaf.

NEW ENGLAND GINGERBREAD

2 cups sifted all-purpose flour
1 teaspoon baking soda
¼ teaspoon salt
1¼ teaspoons ginger
½ teaspoon allspice
¼ teaspoon nutmeg
½ cup firmly packed light brown sugar
2 eggs, beaten
½ cup molasses
1 cup buttermilk
½ cup shortening, melted

Sift dry ingredients together. Combine eggs, molasses, buttermilk and shortening. Gradually add to flour mixture; beat well. Turn into greased 8″ x 8″ pan. Bake in moderate oven (350° F.) 35–40 minutes. Serves 6.

MARASCHINO WALNUT CAKE

2 cups sifted cake flour
¼ teaspoon salt
2½ teaspoons baking powder
½ cup shortening
1¼ cups sugar
2 eggs, separated
⅓ cup maraschino syrup (drained from cherries)
⅓ cup milk
½ teaspoon lemon juice
1 5-ounce bottle maraschino cherries
½ cup chopped walnuts

Sift flour, salt, baking powder. Cream shortening and sugar, stir in egg yolks. Add liquids and dry ingredients, alternately, to creamed mixture. Fold in stiffly beaten egg whites. Divide batter into 2 bowls. Add chopped maraschino cherries (floured) to half of batter and chopped walnuts (floured) to other half. Bake in two greased 8″ x 8″ x 2″ pans in moderate oven (375° F.) about 25 minutes. Makes two 8″-square layers.

BRAZIL NUT CAKE

½ cup shortening
1 cup sugar
2 egg yolks
2 cups sifted cake flour
1 teaspoon baking soda
¼ teaspoon salt
¼ teaspoon ginger
½ teaspoon nutmeg
¾ cup ground Brazil nuts
1 cup buttermilk

Cream shortening with sugar until light and fluffy. Add egg yolks and beat well. Sift flour with baking soda, salt, ginger and nutmeg. Add Brazil nuts and mix lightly. Add nut mixture and buttermilk alternately to creamed mixture, beating well after each addition. Turn into greased 8″ x 8″ x 2″ pan. Bake in moderate oven (350° F.) about 45 minutes. Makes one 8″-square cake.

SPECIAL NUT TORTE

2½ cups very finely chopped or grated
    Cashew nuts or walnuts
1½ cups sugar
¼ teaspoon salt
8 eggs, separated
1¼ teaspoons vanilla
½ teaspoon almond extract

Combine nuts, sugar and salt. Beat egg yolks until thick; add nut mixture and mix well. Beat egg whites until stiff; fold into nut mixture. Fold in vanilla and almond extract. Turn into 3 well-greased 9″ layer cake pans. Bake in slow oven (325° F.) 30–35 minutes. Cool thoroughly. Fill and frost with whipped cream, raspberry jam, or as desired. Makes 12 servings.

OLD-TIME PORK CAKE

1 cup hot coffee
1 cup brown sugar, firmly packed
1 egg, beaten
1 teaspoon baking soda
½ cup molasses
½ pound fat salt pork, ground fine
½ pound white raisins
¾ cup currants
½ cup nuts, chopped
1 teaspoon cinnamon
½ teaspoon allspice
½ teaspoon cloves
¼ teaspoon nutmeg
3 cups sifted all-purpose flour

Combine coffee, sugar, egg, baking soda and molasses. Blend well. Stir in pork. Combine remaining ingredients, except flour, and add to coffee mixture. Sift in flour. Mix well. Pour into 2 greased and floured 9″ x 5″ loaf pans, and bake in moderate oven (350° F.) 1 hour. Wrap in heavy waxed paper. Place in air-tight container for 1 week. Slice and serve. Makes 2 loaves.

CLASSIC POUND CAKE

1 cup butter
1 cup sugar
5 eggs, separated
2 cups sifted cake flour
½ teaspoon nutmeg
¼ teaspoon salt
1 teaspoon vanilla

Cream butter with sugar until very light and fluffy. Beat egg yolks until thick and lemon colored. Add egg yolks to butter mixture and beat well. Sift flour with nutmeg and salt. Add sifted ingredients gradually to sugar mixture, beating well after each addition. Beat until batter is smooth. Beat egg whites until stiff and fold into batter. Fold in vanilla. Turn into greased 9" x 5" x 3" pan. Bake in slow oven (325° F.) for about 1 hour. Makes one 9" loaf.

ELECTION DAY CAKE

1½ cups warm, not hot, water (lukewarm for compressed yeast)
2 teaspoons sugar
2 packages active dry yeast, or 2 cakes compressed yeast
4½ cups sifted all-purpose flour
¾ cup butter or margarine
1 cup sugar
2 eggs
1 teaspoon salt
1½ teaspoons cinnamon
¼ teaspoon cloves
1 teaspoon grated orange rind
½ cup candied orange peel
½ teaspoon nutmeg
1½ cups raisins
½ cup chopped pecans

Measure water into a mixing bowl (warm, not hot, for active dry yeast; lukewarm for compressed). Add and stir in 2 teaspoons sugar. Sprinkle or crumble in yeast; stir until dissolved. Add 1½ cups of the flour and beat well. Cover with a cloth and let rise in a warm place, free from draft, until very bubbly, about 30 minutes. Cream butter or margarine with 1 cup sugar. Add and beat in eggs. Combine with bubbly yeast mixture. Sift together salt, spices and remaining 3 cups flour, and add to yeast mixture. Beat until smooth. Add and stir in fruits and nuts. Turn into a greased, lightly

floured 10" tube pan or into 2 well-greased loaf pans (9" x 5" x 3") or two well-greased 1½-quart casseroles. Cover with a cloth. Let rise in a warm place, free from draft, until doubled in bulk, about 1½ hours. Bake tube cake in a moderate oven (375° F.) for 1 hour; bake loaves or casseroles in a moderate oven (350° F.) 60–70 minutes. Cool cake in pans 5 minutes. Turn out on cake rack. Cool.

MOCHA LAYER CAKE

2 squares unsweetened chocolate melted
1 cup boiling coffee
½ cup salad oil
2 cups sugar
¼ teaspoon salt
2 cups sifted all-purpose flour
1½ teaspoons baking soda
½ cup buttermilk
2 eggs, beaten

Combine chocolate, coffee and oil. Add remaining ingredients. Beat 2 minutes. Pour batter into 2 greased 9" layer cake pans. Bake in moderate oven (350° F.) 30–35 minutes. Makes two 9" layers.

BABKA

¾ cup milk
1 package active dry yeast, or 1 cake compressed yeast
¼ cup warm, not hot, water (lukewarm for compressed yeast)
¼ cup butter or margarine
½ cup sugar
1 teaspoon salt
½ teaspoon ground cardamon
2 egg yolks
2½ cups sifted all-purpose flour
½ cup raisins
¼ cup chopped candied cherries
¼ cup chopped nuts
Soft butter or margarine
Fine dry bread crumbs

Scald milk; cool to lukewarm. Sprinkle or crumble yeast into water (warm, not hot, water for active dry yeast; lukewarm water for compressed yeast), stir until dissolved. Cream butter or margarine. Mix in sugar, salt, cardamon and egg yolks. Beat until light. Stir yeast into lukewarm milk; add alternately with sifted flour to sugar-egg yolk mixture. Beat until smooth. Add fruits and nuts. Turn out on floured board and knead until light and springy. Place in greased bowl and grease top of dough. Cover and let stand in warm place until double in bulk. Punch down. Rub butter or margarine in a 1-quart mold, dust with bread crumbs. Place dough in crumb lined pan. Grease top of dough. Cover, let rise in warm place until double in bulk. Bake in moderate oven (350° F.) 40 minutes. Makes 1 cake.

SPICE CAKE

2½ cups sifted cake flour
2½ teaspoons baking powder
¼ teaspoon salt
½ teaspoon cinnamon
½ teaspoon nutmeg
½ teaspoon cloves
½ cup shortening
1 cup sugar
2 eggs
⅓ cup molasses
¾ cup milk

Sift flour, baking powder, salt and spices together. Cream shortening and sugar thoroughly, and add eggs one at a time, beating thoroughly after each addition. Blend in molasses and add sifted ingredients alternately with milk. Beat well. Pour into 2 greased 9″ layer cake pans. Bake in moderate oven (375° F.) for 25 minutes. Makes two 9″ layers.

WALNUT SPICE CAKE

½ cup shortening
1 cup granulated sugar
1 egg, beaten
3 cups sifted cake flour
1½ teaspoons baking soda
1 teaspoon allspice
¾ teaspoon cloves
1½ teaspoons cinnamon
½ teaspoon nutmeg
½ teaspoon salt
1 cup buttermilk
½ cup seedless raisins
½ cup chopped walnuts

Cream shortening; add sugar gradually, creaming well. Add egg and beat. Sift together 2¾ cups flour, baking soda, allspice, cloves, cinnamon, nutmeg and salt, and add alternately in thirds with buttermilk to sugar mixture. Add raisins and walnuts dredged with remaining ¼ cup of flour, and mix. Bake in 10″ greased tube pan in moderate oven (350° F.) 50–60 minutes. Makes one 10″ tube cake.

TUTTI-FRUTTI HONEY CAKE

2 cups sifted cake flour
2 teaspoons baking powder
¼ teaspoon salt
⅔ cup butter or margarine
½ cup sugar
½ cup honey
3 eggs
¼ cup milk
1 cup candied fruits
1 teaspoon vanilla

Sift flour, baking powder and salt together. Cream butter or margarine, sugar and honey until light and fluffy. Add ¼ of the dry ingredients and blend until smooth. Beat egg whites until stiff, then fold into batter. Add remaining dry ingredients and milk alternately. Add fruits and vanilla. Turn into greased 9″ x 5″ x 3″ pan. Bake in slow oven (325° F.) about 1 hour and 25 minutes. Makes 1 loaf.

SEMINOLE ORANGE CAKE

½ cup shortening
1 cup sugar
2 eggs, well beaten
2 cups sifted cake flour
3 teaspoons baking powder
½ teaspoon salt
¾ cup milk
⅔ cup candied orange peel
¼ teaspoon lemon extract

Cream shortening with sugar until light and fluffy. Add eggs and beat well. Sift flour with baking powder and salt. Add sifted ingredients and milk, alternately, to creamed mixture, beating well after each addition. Fold in orange peel and lemon extract. Turn into 2 greased 8″ layer cake pans. Bake in moderate oven (375° F.) 25–30 minutes. Makes two 8″ layers.

ORANGE-COCONUT CAKE

4 eggs, separated
1½ cups sugar
1 cup butter
1 teaspoon salt
2 tablespoons grated orange rind
1¼ teaspoons orange extract
3 cups sifted cake flour
3 teaspoons baking powder
1¼ cups milk
1 cup shredded coconut

Beat egg whites until stiff. Cream sugar, butter, salt, rind and orange extract. Add egg yolks and beat. Sift flour with baking powder and add, alternately, with milk. Fold egg whites into mixture; fold in coconut. Turn into 3 greased 8″ layer cake pans. Bake in moderate oven (350° F.) 25–30 minutes. Makes three 8″ layers.

Frostings and Fillings

FILLINGS

APPLESAUCE-DATE FILLING

1 cup thick applesauce
½ cup chopped dates
¼ teaspoon cinnamon
⅛ teaspoon nutmeg

Combine all ingredients and mix well. Makes about 1½ cups.

LORD BALTIMORE FILLING AND FROSTING

1 recipe Seven-Minute Frosting
¼ cup chopped figs
¼ cup raisins
¼ cup chopped candied cherries
¼ cup chopped pecans
¼ teaspoon orange extract

To ⅓ cup of the Seven-Minute Frosting, add remaining ingredients. Spread between Lord Baltimore cake layers. Frost top and sides of cake with remaining frosting.

NUT CREAM FILLING

2 tablespoons sugar
1 tablespoon cornstarch
⅛ teaspoon salt
1 egg yolk, beaten
1 cup sour cream
½ teaspoon grated lemon rind
½ cup chopped walnuts or almonds

Combine sugar, cornstarch, salt and egg yolk. Add sour cream and cook over very low heat, stirring constantly, until mixture coats spoon. Stir in lemon rind and nuts. Cool thoroughly. Makes about 1½ cups.

MISSION ORANGE FILLING

1 tablespoon all-purpose flour
¾ cup sugar
⅛ teaspoon salt
½ cup water
3 egg yolks, well beaten
⅔ cup orange juice
½ teaspoon lemon extract
1 tablespoon orange rind

Combine flour, sugar, salt and water. Add egg yolks and mix well. Add remaining ingredients and cook over low heat, stirring constantly, until thickened. Cool thoroughly.

CUSTARD FILLING

⅓ cup sugar
3 tablespoons cornstarch
¼ teaspoon salt
2 egg yolks
2 cups milk, scalded
2 tablespoons butter
2 teaspoons rum

Combine sugar, cornstarch and salt. Add egg yolks and beat well. Add a little milk slowly, mix and return mixture to remaining hot milk. Cook over boiling water, stirring constantly until mixture thickens. Add butter; cool. Add rum. Makes about 2½ cups.

DATE-CREAM CHEESE FILLING

2 8-ounce packages cream cheese
3 tablespoons light cream
¾ cup chopped dates
½ cup chopped pecans
⅛ teaspoon salt
¼ teaspoon vanilla

Cream cheese with cream until light and fluffy. Add remaining ingredients and mix well.

PINEAPPLE-FIG FILLING

2 cups dried figs
1 cup crushed pineapple
3 cups pineapple juice
¼ teaspoon salt
2 cups sugar
½ teaspoon vanilla

Rinse figs in hot water and drain. Cut figs into thin strips. Combine with pineapple and juice; cook 10 minutes. Add salt and sugar. Cook, stirring occasionally, until figs are tender (about 15 minutes). Cool. Add vanilla. Makes about 5 cups.

JANICE'S PINEAPPLE FILLING

½ cup sifted all-purpose flour
1 cup sugar
⅛ teaspoon salt
2 eggs
2 cups scalded milk
½ teaspoon lemon extract
½ teaspoon grated lemon rind
½ teaspoon grated orange rind
1½ cups canned crushed pineapple

Combine flour, sugar, salt and eggs. Add milk and stir until smooth. Cook over very low heat, stirring constantly, until thickened. Cool thoroughly. Add remaining ingredients and mix well. Makes about 4 cups.

BROWN BUTTER FILLING

½ cup butter
¼ cup cocoa
⅛ teaspoon cinnamon
2 egg whites
2 cups confectioners' sugar
1 teaspoon vanilla

Melt butter; add cocoa and cinnamon; mix well. Beat whites until stiff; fold in sugar. Fold cocoa mixture into egg-white mixture. Add vanilla and mix lightly. Makes about 3 cups.

PEANUT FILLING

½ cup peanut butter
¼ cup orange juice
¼ cup honey
¼ cup chopped peanuts
1 teaspoon grated orange rind

Combine all ingredients and mix well. Makes about 1¼ cups.

FROSTINGS

RASPBERRY FROSTING

1 teaspoon unflavored gelatin
3 tablespoons cold water
1 cup sugar
¼ cup hot water
2 egg whites
1 cup red raspberries

Soften gelatin in cold water. Combine sugar and hot water. Cook over low heat to soft-ball stage (236° F. on candy thermometer). Add gelatin and stir until dissolved. Beat egg whites until stiff. Gradually add gelatin mixture, beating constantly. Cook over boiling water, stirring occasionally, until very thick. Remove from heat. Stir until cool. Fold in raspberries. Makes about 2¼ cups.

RUM MOCHA FROSTING

5 squares unsweetened chocolate
½ cup butter
3½ cups sifted confectioners' sugar
⅛ teaspoon salt
2 tablespoons rum
2 tablespoons coffee

Melt chocolate; add butter and beat well. Add remaining ingredients and beat until light and fluffy. Makes about 4½ cups.

SNOW FROSTING

1 cup heavy cream
¼ teaspoon vanilla
¼ teaspoon lemon extract

¼ cup confectioners' sugar
1½ cups grated coconut

Beat cream until stiff. Fold in remaining ingredients. Makes about 3 cups.

ORANGE BLOSSOM FROSTING

2 egg whites
¾ cup sugar
⅓ cup light corn syrup
2 tablespoons orange juice
¼ teaspoon cream of tartar
⅛ teaspoon salt
2 teaspoons grated lemon rind

Combine all ingredients in top of double boiler. Place over boiling water. Beat with rotary beater until mixture stands in stiff peaks. Remove from heat. Beat until slightly cooled. Cool thoroughly. Makes about 2 cups.

PINEAPPLE-CHEESE FROSTING

1 3-ounce package cream cheese
2 tablespoons butter
3 cups sifted confectioners' sugar
1 tablespoon drained crushed pineapple
3 tablespoons pineapple juice
1 teaspoon lemon juice

Cream cheese with butter until light. Add remaining ingredients and beat until fluffy. Makes about 4 cups.

IN-THE-OVEN FROSTING

1 egg white
¼ teaspoon baking powder
¾ cup firmly packed brown sugar
½ cup chopped pecans

Beat egg white until frothy. Add baking powder and beat until stiff. Gradually add sugar. Beat well. Spread over 8″ x 8″ cake and top with chopped nuts. Bake in moderate oven (350° F.) about 10 minutes. Makes about 1½ cups.

SIMPLE BUTTER FROSTING

¾ cup butter
4 cups confectioners' sugar
2 egg whites
⅛ teaspoon salt
1 teaspoon vanilla

Cream butter until soft. Add 2 cups of the sugar and beat well. Add egg whites and blend. Add salt and remaining sugar. Beat until light and fluffy. Add vanilla and mix well. Makes about 5 cups.

BUTTERSCOTCH FROSTING

1 cup firmly packed brown sugar
⅓ cup butter
⅛ teaspoon salt
¼ cup milk
1½ cups sifted confectioners' sugar

Combine brown sugar, butter and salt. Cook over low heat until mixture boils, stirring constantly. Add milk and cook, stirring constantly, three minutes. Remove from heat and cool thoroughly. Add confectioners' sugar and beat until well blended. Makes about 2½ cups.

VERMONT CARAMEL FROSTING

3 cups sifted confectioners' sugar
1 cup firmly packed brown sugar
⅓ cup hot water
½ cup butter
½ teaspoon vanilla
½ teaspoon maple flavoring

Combine sugars and water. Cream butter until soft. Add sugar mixture and beat until light and fluffy. Add vanilla and maple flavoring; beat well. Makes about 4 cups.

VELVET CHOCOLATE FROSTING

1 egg yolk, beaten
1 cup sugar
¼ cup light cream
⅛ teaspoon salt
2½ squares unsweetened chocolate
1 tablespoon butter
1 teaspoon vanilla

Combine egg yolk, sugar, cream, salt and chocolate. Cook over hot water until thickened, stirring occasionally. Remove from heat. Add butter and vanilla. Beat until thick. Makes about 1½ cups.

JERSEY STRAWBERRY FROSTING

1 cup fresh strawberries
2 egg whites
⅛ teaspoon salt
1 teaspoon lemon juice
¼ teaspoon cream of tartar
½ cup sugar

Force berries through sieve. Beat egg whites with salt, lemon juice and cream of tartar until foamy. Gradually add sugar, beating constantly. Continue beating until stiff. Fold in berries. Makes about 2¼ cups.

CHOCOLATE CREAM FROSTING

1 square unsweetened chocolate
2 tablespoons milk
⅓ cup sugar
1 egg
1 cup heavy cream, whipped
½ teaspoon vanilla
½ cup shredded coconut

Melt chocolate over hot water. Add milk and sugar; mix well. Cool. Add egg and beat well. Fold cream into chocolate mixture. Fold in vanilla and coconut. Fill and frost cake. Chill thoroughly. Makes about 2 cups.

CHOCOLATE PUFF FROSTING

½ cup butter
2 squares unsweetened chocolate, melted
2½ cups confectioners' sugar
1 egg, beaten
1 teaspoon vanilla
⅛ teaspoon salt
1 cup chopped walnuts
1 cup shredded coconut

Cream butter until soft. Add chocolate and mix well. Add remaining ingredients and beat until light and fluffy. Makes about 4½ cups.

CHOCOLATE PECAN FROSTING

¼ pound sweet chocolate
½ cup chopped pecans
1 cup heavy cream, whipped

Melt chocolate over hot water. Add nuts and mix well; cool. Fold in cream. Makes about 2 cups.

COFFEE FROSTING

¼ cup butter
1½ cups sifted confectioners' sugar
¼ cup strong coffee
⅛ teaspoon salt

Combine all ingredients and beat until light and fluffy. Makes about 2 cups.

Candy

CARAMEL APPLES

1 cup sugar
¾ cup dark corn syrup
1 cup light cream
1½ tablespoons butter or margarine
½ teaspoon vanilla
6 medium-sized red apples
¾ cup chopped nuts

Combine sugar, syrup, cream, and butter or margarine. Cook over low heat to hard-ball stage (260° F. on candy thermometer). Remove from heat and add vanilla. Meanwhile stick wooden skewers into stem ends of apples. Dip apples into sugar mixture and roll in nuts. Cool thoroughly. Makes 6.

CANDY-COATED BRAZIL NUTS

1½ cups sugar
¼ cup orange juice
1 teaspoon grated orange rind
¼ cup water
1½ cups Brazil nuts

Combine sugar, orange juice, rind and water. Cook over low heat, stirring until sugar melts. Cook over low heat to soft-ball stage (236° F. on candy thermometer). Remove from heat and add Brazil nuts. Stir until creamy. Turn out on waxed paper. Makes about 2½ cups.

CARIBBEAN CONFECTION

3 cups gingersnap crumbs
1 cup chopped almonds
1½ cups confectioners' sugar
¼ cup honey
¼ cup cocoa
2½ tablespoons melted butter or margarine
¼ cup rum
Powdered sugar

Combine crumbs, almonds, confectioners' sugar, honey, cocoa, butter or margarine, and rum. Mix well and shape into 1" balls. Roll in powdered sugar. Makes about 48.

STUFFED DATES

1 cup pitted dates
½ cup marshmallow halves (approx.)
½ cup pecans (approx.)
Granulated sugar

Stuff dates with marshmallows and pecans. Roll in sugar. Makes about 24.

DIVINITY

3 cups sugar
1 cup light corn syrup
½ cup water
1 teaspoon vinegar
2 egg whites, stiffly beaten
1 teaspoon vanilla
1 cup chopped walnuts

Combine sugar, syrup, water and vinegar. Cover and cook over low heat 5 minutes. Cook, uncovered, to hard-ball stage (265° F. on candy thermometer). Cool slightly. Pour gradually over egg whites. Beat until stiff. Cool, stirring occasionally, until mixture reaches 100° F. Add vanilla and nuts. Drop by teaspoonfuls onto waxed paper. Makes about 60.

CHOCOLATE ALMOND CANDY

2 cups sugar
1 cup light cream
2 tablespoons butter or margarine
¼ cup cocoa
¾ cup chopped almonds
3 tablespoons marshmallow cream
½ teaspoon almond extract
10 marshmallows, quartered

Combine sugar, cream, butter or margarine, and cocoa. Cook over low heat to soft-ball stage (236° F. on candy thermometer). Remove from heat; add almonds, marshmallow cream and almond extract. Beat until mixture begins to thicken. Arrange marshmallows on greased baking sheet. Pour chocolate mixture over marshmallows. Cool thoroughly. Cut into pieces. Makes about 24.

CHOCOLATE CARAMELS

1 square unsweetened chocolate
1 cup sugar
1 cup light corn syrup
⅛ teaspoon salt
3 tablespoons butter or margarine
1 cup light cream
1 teaspoon vanilla
½ cup chopped nuts

Melt chocolate; add sugar, syrup and salt. Bring to boil, stirring constantly. Add butter or margarine. Gradually add cream so that mixture does not stop boiling. Cook, stirring constantly, until mixture reaches firm-ball stage (242° F. on candy thermometer). Add vanilla and nuts. Pour into greased shallow pan. Do not scrape sides of pan. Cool thoroughly. Makes about 1 pound.

CHOCOLATE COCONUT ALMONDS

1 6-ounce package semi-sweet chocolate morsels
2½ cups blanched almonds
1 cup shredded coconut

Melt chocolate; cool to lukewarm. Dip almonds in chocolate and roll in coconut. Makes about 4 cups.

COCOA FUDGE

2 cups sugar
½ cup cocoa
1 cup light cream
2 tablespoons butter or margarine
1 teaspoon vanilla
¾ cup chopped nuts

Combine sugar, cocoa and cream. Cook over low heat, stirring until sugar dissolves. Cook until mixture reaches soft-ball stage (236° F. on candy thermometer). Add butter or margarine, and vanilla. Cool to lukewarm. Beat until mixture holds shape. Add nuts. Turn into greased shallow pan. Cut into squares. Makes about 24.

FUDGE ROLL

2 squares unsweetened chocolate
2 cups sugar
¼ cup light corn syrup
½ cup light cream
1 tablespoon butter or margarine
½ teaspoon vanilla
¾ cup chopped nuts
½ cup shredded coconut

Melt chocolate; add sugar, syrup, cream, and butter or margarine. Cook over low heat, stirring until sugar dissolves. Cook until mixture reaches soft-ball stage (234° F. on candy thermometer). Cool to lukewarm. Add vanilla, nuts and coconut. Beat until mixture holds shape. Shape into a roll and cool thoroughly. Slice. Makes about 24.

QUICK FUDGE

2 6-ounce packages semi-sweet chocolate
   morsels
⅔ cup sweetened condensed milk
½ teaspoon vanilla

Melt semi-sweet chocolate morsels over hot water. Remove from heat; stir in milk and vanilla. Mix well. Turn into greased shallow pan. Let stand several hours. Makes about 1¼ pounds.

BLACK WALNUT FUDGE

1 tablespoon instant coffee
1 cup boiling water
3 cups firmly packed brown sugar
1½ tablespoons butter
1 teaspoon vanilla
1 cup chopped black walnuts

Combine coffee and water; stir to dissolve coffee. Add sugar and cook over low heat, stirring constantly, until mixture reaches soft-ball stage (236° F. on candy thermometer). Add butter and cool to lukewarm. Beat until creamy. Add vanilla and walnuts. Mix well. Turn into greased shallow pan and cool. Cut into squares. Makes about 36.

CANDIED GRAPEFRUIT PEEL

2 large grapefruit
1 cup sugar
½ cup water
3 tablespoons light corn syrup
Granulated sugar

Remove skins from grapefruits in quarters. Cook, covered, in boiling salted water 20 minutes. Drain and cover with fresh water. Cook 30 minutes. Cool and cut into thin strips. Combine 1 cup sugar, water and syrup. Heat to boiling point; add grapefruit peel. Cook over low heat until liquid is absorbed. Cool and separate strips. Roll in granulated sugar and dry. Makes about 2 cups.

NOUGAT SQUARES

1 cup sugar
⅓ cup light corn syrup
⅓ cup honey
¼ cup water
⅛ teaspoon salt
2 egg whites
½ teaspoon vanilla
¾ cup chopped walnuts

Combine sugar, corn syrup, honey and water. Cook over low heat to hard-ball stage (260° F. on candy thermometer). Combine salt and egg whites. Beat until stiff. Gradually add sugar mixture, beating constantly. Add vanilla and beat until mixture is thickened. Add nuts. Cook over hot water until mixture dries, stirring constantly. Turn into greased shallow pans. Cover with pan or board. Press with heavy weight at least 12 hours. Cut into squares and wrap in waxed paper. Makes about 36.

NUT MINTS

¼ cup sweetened condensed milk
1¼ cups confectioners' sugar
½ teaspoon mint extract
⅔ cup pecans (approx.)

Combine milk and sugar; mix well. Add mint extract. Shape into balls ½" in diameter. Top with pecans. Makes about 36.

MARZIPAN

2 egg whites
1 cup almond paste
1 teaspoon vanilla
1 cup confectioners' sugar

Beat egg whites and almond paste until well blended. Add vanilla and sugar; mix well. Let stand 24 hours. Form into fruit shapes, or other shapes, as desired. Makes about 1 pound.

MOCHA ALMOND BALLS

¼ pound unsweetened chocolate, grated
¼ cup confectioners' sugar
⅓ cup almond paste
2 tablespoons coffee
1 teaspoon butter or margarine
½ teaspoon vanilla
¼ cup cocoa
1 teaspoon nutmeg

Combine chocolate, sugar, almond paste, coffee, butter or margarine, and vanilla; mix until smooth. Shape into ½″ balls. Combine cocoa and nutmeg. Roll balls in cocoa mixture. Makes about 24.

SUGARED PEANUTS

1½ cups sugar
¼ cup light corn syrup
½ cup water
½ teaspoon vanilla
2 cups shelled peanuts

Combine sugar, syrup and water. Cook over low heat to firm-ball stage (242° F. on candy thermometer). Remove from heat and add vanilla. Stir until creamy. Add peanuts and mix well. Turn out on waxed paper. Cool and break into pieces. Makes about 24.

PECAN CREAMS

3 cups firmly packed brown sugar
1 cup evaporated milk
1 teaspoon vanilla
1 tablespoon butter or margarine
1½ cups chopped pecans

Combine sugar and milk. Cook over low heat stirring until sugar melts. Cook until mixture reaches soft-ball stage (234° F. on candy thermometer). Cool to lukewarm. Add remaining ingredients. Beat until creamy. Drop by spoonfuls onto waxed paper. Makes about 48.

CLASSIC PENUCHE

3 cups firmly packed brown sugar
1 cup milk
1½ tablespoons butter or margarine
1 teaspoon vanilla
⅛ teaspoon salt
¾ cup chopped walnuts

Combine sugar and milk. Cook over low heat, stirring constantly, until mixture reaches soft-ball stage (236° F. on candy thermometer). Remove from heat; add butter or margarine, and salt. Cool. Beat until mixture will hold shape. Add walnuts. Turn into greased shallow pan. Cut into squares. Makes about 24.

CORN SYRUP POPCORN BALLS

1 cup sugar
¼ cup light corn syrup
1 cup water
⅛ teaspoon salt
1 teaspoon vanilla
3 quarts popped corn

Combine sugar, syrup and water. Cook over low heat, stirring until sugar melts. Cook over low heat until mixture reaches soft-ball stage (236° F. on candy thermometer). Remove from heat; add salt and vanilla. Cool. Pour syrup mixture over popped corn and mix lightly. Shape into balls. Makes about 24.

APRICOT TURKISH DELIGHT

3 cups sugar
¼ teaspoon salt
2 envelopes unflavored gelatin
1 cup water
1 cup cold water
¼ cup apricot nectar
2 tablespoons lemon juice
½ cup chopped pistachio nuts
½ cup confectioners' sugar

In a saucepan combine the 3 cups sugar, salt and gelatin. Add water, bring to boil and simmer 20 minutes. Remove from heat and add apricot nectar and lemon juice. Chill until slightly thickened. Stir in nuts. Turn into 8" x 4" pan that has been rinsed in cold water. Chill until firm. Turn out of pan onto board lightly covered with confectioners' sugar. Cut into cubes. Roll in confectioners' sugar. Makes about 50 ¾" cubes.

PRALINES

1 cup firmly packed brown sugar
1 cup granulated sugar
½ cup light cream
2 tablespoons butter or margarine
¾ cup pecans

Combine sugars and cream. Cook over low heat, stirring until sugar melts. Cook until mixture spins a thread (228° F. on candy thermometer). Add butter or margarine, and pecans. Cook until mixture reaches soft-ball stage (236° F. on candy thermometer). Cool. Beat until mixture begins to thicken. Drop by spoonfuls onto greased baking sheets. Cool thoroughly. Makes about 12.

MAPLE POPCORN

4 quarts popped corn
2 cups granulated sugar
2 cups maple syrup
1 teaspoon vinegar
2 tablespoons butter
1 cup chopped peanuts

Combine sugar, syrup and vinegar and cook over low heat, stirring until sugar dissolves. Cook to 275° F. on candy thermometer. Remove from heat; add butter and stir until melted. Add peanuts and pour over popcorn; blend well.

WALNUT ROLL

2 cups granulated sugar
1 cup firmly packed brown sugar
½ cup light corn syrup
1 cup light cream
1 teaspoon vanilla
1¼ cups chopped walnuts

Combine sugars, syrup and cream. Cook over low heat, stirring constantly until sugar dissolves. Cook over low heat to soft-ball stage (236° F. on candy thermometer). Remove from heat and cool until mixture reaches 110° F. Add vanilla. Beat until mixture holds shape. Cool and knead until firm. Shape into rolls 1½" in diameter. Roll in walnuts. Chill until firm and cut into slices ½" thick. Makes about 24.

MOLASSES TAFFY

4 cups molasses
1 cup firmly packed brown sugar
½ cup water
3 tablespoons butter or margarine
½ teaspoon baking soda

Combine molasses, sugar and water. Cook over low heat until mixture reaches soft-crack stage (272° F. on candy thermometer). Remove from heat; add butter or margarine, and baking soda. Turn into shallow pan. Let stand until cool enough to handle. Gather into a ball and pull until firm. Cut into pieces. Makes about 48.

OLD-FASHIONED TAFFY

2 cups sugar
½ cup light corn syrup
½ cup water
1¼ teaspoons vanilla

Combine sugar, syrup and water. Cook over low heat to soft-crack stage (272° F. on candy thermometer). Remove from heat and add vanilla. Turn out on greased baking sheet. When mixture is cool enough to handle, pull until firm. Cut into pieces. Makes about 24.

ENGLISH NUT TOFFEE

2½ cups sugar
¼ teaspoon salt
½ cup water
1¼ cups butter or margarine
1 cup chopped nuts

Combine sugar, salt, water, and butter or margarine. Heat to boiling point. Add nuts. Cook, stirring constantly, to soft-crack stage (285° F. on candy thermometer). Pour into greased shallow pan. Cool thoroughly and break into pieces. Makes about 36.

Jams—Jellies—Relishes

JAMS,

PRESERVES,

CONSERVES

SPICED BLUEBERRY JAM

2 quarts blueberries
½ cup lemon juice
1 teaspoon cinnamon
1 teaspoon nutmeg
½ teaspoon allspice
2 cups sugar

Crush berries and combine with lemon juice and spices; simmer 30 minutes. Add sugar and simmer until thickened, stirring occasionally. Pour into hot sterilized jars and seal. Makes about 2 pints.

GUAVA JAM

4 cups sugar
1 cup water
5½ pounds guavas
¼ cup grated lemon rind

Combine sugar and 1 cup water and cook over low heat to 238° F. Cut guavas in half and remove stones; cook in small amount of water until tender.

Put through sieve. Strain and add to sugar mixture. Cook until thickened. Add lemon rind. Pour into hot sterilized jars and seal. Makes about 6 6-ounce glasses.

PAPAYA-LIME JAM

6 cups papaya pulp
⅓ cup lime juice
2 tablespoons pineapple juice
5 cups sugar

Press papaya through coarse sieve. Cook over medium heat until thickened. Add remaining ingredients and cook until thickened, stirring frequently. Pour into hot sterilized jars and seal. Makes about 5 pints.

PEACH CONSERVE

4 pounds peaches
2 oranges, peeled and chopped
Rind of 1 orange, sliced
3 pounds (6¾ cups) sugar
1 cup broken walnuts

Cut peaches into ½″ cubes. Mix peaches, oranges, orange rind and sugar. Cook, stirring occasionally, until mixture is thick. Remove from heat and add nuts. Turn into hot sterilized jars and seal. Makes 8–10 6-ounce glasses.

HAWAIIAN PEACH JAM

1 pound dried peaches
1 fresh pineapple
Sugar
½ tablespoon grated lemon rind
1 tablespoon grated lime rind
1 tablespoon grated orange rind

Soak peaches in water overnight. Pare and core pineapple. Drain peaches. Put peaches and pineapple through food chopper. Reserve juice. Measure fruit

and juice into a saucepan. Add ¾ cup sugar for each cup peach mixture. Stir over low heat until sugar is dissolved. Add lemon, lime and orange rinds. Heat to boiling point. Cook over low heat 25–35 minutes, stirring occasionally. Pour into hot sterilized jars and seal. Makes about 3 pints.

QUINCE NECTAR

7 cups peeled, cored and ground quinces
6 cups pared, cored and ground apples
2 oranges, ground
6 cups sugar

Put fruits in a saucepan and add enough water to cover. Heat to boiling, cover and simmer 15 minutes. Add sugar and cook over low heat until dissolved, stirring constantly. Pour into hot sterilized jars and seal. Makes about 8 pints.

RED RASPBERRY CONSERVE

5 cups red raspberries
2 cups currants
4½ cups sugar
¼ cup orange juice

Wash and drain raspberries. Crush currants. Cook currants over low heat until juice runs. Add raspberries and heat to boiling. Add sugar and orange juice; cook over medium heat until thickened. Pour into hot sterilized jars and seal. Makes about 6 pints.

GOOSEBERRY JAM

4½ cups gooseberries
4 cups sugar
1 tablespoon cinnamon

Wash and drain berries. Mash and heat to boiling point, stirring constantly. Add sugar and stir until sugar is dissolved. Cook over low heat 20 minutes, stirring frequently. Add cinnamon. Pour into hot sterilized jars and seal. Makes about 6 6-ounce glasses.

STRAWBERRY JAM

3 cups crushed strawberries
5 cups sugar
1 package powdered pectin
1 cup water

Mix strawberries and sugar and let stand 20 minutes, stirring occasionally. Dissolve pectin in water; bring to a boil and boil 1 minute. Add to fruit-sugar mixture and stir 2 minutes. Spoon into hot sterilized jars to about ½ inch of top; cover and let stand until jellied (24–48 hours). Seal with hot paraffin and a metal lid or heavy aluminum foil. Freeze or refrigerate. Jam keeps in refrigerator a few months and in freezer 1 year. Makes 9 6-ounce jars.

TANGERINE CONSERVE

4½ cups ground carrots
2 tangerines, ground
1 lemon, ground
4 cups sugar

Cook carrots in small amount of salted boiling water until all water has evaporated. Add tangerines, lemon and sugar. Cook over low heat, stirring occasionally, until thickened. Pour into hot sterilized jars and seal. Makes about 4 pints.

SPICED TOMATO PRESERVES

6 pounds green tomatoes
2 pounds red tomatoes
5 pounds granulated sugar
1 teaspoon whole cloves
1 3-inch stick cinnamon
4 lemons, sliced

Scald tomatoes; peel and cut into quarters. Add sugar, spices and lemons. Heat to boiling point. Cook over low heat until thickened. Pour into hot sterilized jars and seal. Makes about 8 pints.

DAMASCUS FIG PRESERVES

3½ pounds ripe black figs
Water
¾ cup vinegar
1 tablespoon orange juice
3 cups sugar
1½ teaspoons whole cloves
1 cinnamon stick

Stem figs. Cover with water. Heat to boiling point. Simmer 20 minutes. Drain. Combine vinegar, orange juice, sugar and spices. Heat to boiling. Cook until syrup spins a fine thread. Add figs and cook 10 minutes. Remove spices. Turn into hot sterilized jars and seal. Makes about 6 pints.

GREEN GRAPE CONSERVE

1 orange
2 lemons
1 lime
1½ cups water
3 cups sugar
3 cups cut seeded green grapes
1 tablespoon white raisins

Chop orange, lemons and lime. Add water and cook, covered, 10 minutes. Add sugar, grapes and raisins. Cook, uncovered, until thickened. Pour into hot sterilized jars and seal. Makes about 4 pints.

RHUBARB-ORANGE JAM

4 pounds rhubarb
4 pounds sugar
2 tablespoons grated orange rind
1½ cups orange juice

½ teaspoon nutmeg
1 teaspoon allspice

Wash rhubarb and cut into 1" pieces. Add sugar and let stand several hours. Add remaining ingredients. Heat to boiling point. Simmer until thickened, stirring frequently. Pour into hot sterilized glasses and seal. Makes about 4 pints.

JELLIES

GRAPE JELLY

5 pounds Concord grapes
¼ cup lemon juice
¼ cup water
7 cups sugar
½ cup commercial liquid pectin

Wash and stem grapes. Crush grapes and add lemon juice and water. Cook, covered, over low heat 15 minutes. Drip grape mixture through jelly bag. Measure 4 cups juice. Combine grape juice and sugar. Cook over high heat until mixture boils. Add pectin, stirring constantly. Heat to boiling point. Cook 1 minute, stirring constantly. Remove from heat and skim. Pour into hot sterilized glasses. Cover with paraffin. Makes about 10 6-ounce glasses.

LEMON-MINT JELLY

¾ cup lemon juice
¾ cup water
½ cup mint leaves
Green food coloring
3 cups sugar
½ cup commercial liquid pectin

Combine lemon juice, water and mint leaves. Add enough food coloring to tint mixture a light green. Add sugar and mix well. Cook over high heat until mixture boils. Add pectin, stirring constantly. Heat to boiling point and cook 30 seconds, stirring constantly. Strain and pour into hot sterilized glasses. Cool thoroughly and cover with paraffin. Makes about 4 8-ounce glasses.

PINEAPPLE-ORANGE JELLY

1½ cups unsweetened pineapple juice
1½ cups orange juice
¼ cup grated orange rind
2 tablespoons grated lemon rind
6 cups sugar
1 cup commercial liquid pectin

Combine pineapple juice, orange juice, orange rind, lemon rind and sugar. Cook over high heat until mixture boils. Add pectin, stirring constantly. Heat to boiling point. Cook 1 minute, stirring constantly. Strain and pour into hot sterilized glasses. Cover with paraffin. Makes about 12 6-ounce glasses.

RHUBARB-RASPBERRY JELLY

1 pound rhubarb
2 quarts red raspberries
8 cups sugar
1 cup commercial liquid pectin

Grind rhubarb. Crush raspberries. Drip rhubarb and raspberries through jelly bag. Measure 3½ cups juice. Add sugar and mix well. Cook over high heat until mixture boils. Add pectin, stirring constantly. Heat to boiling point and cook 30 seconds, stirring constantly. Remove from heat and skim. Pour into hot sterilized glasses. Cover with paraffin. Makes about 9 8-ounce glasses.

BLACK RASPBERRY JELLY

3 quarts black raspberries
7 cups sugar
2 tablespoons lemon juice
1 cup commercial liquid pectin

Crush raspberries and drip through jelly bag. Measure 4 cups juice. Combine raspberry juice, sugar and lemon juice. Cook over high heat until mixture boils. Add pectin, stirring constantly. Remove from heat and skim. Pour into hot sterilized glasses. Cover with paraffin. Makes about 10 8-ounce glasses.

BUTTERS

AND MARMALADES

TROPICAL MARMALADE

1 pineapple
1 grapefruit
2 limes
Water
Sugar
2 tablespoons grated orange rind

Pare and core pineapple and chop. Cut grapefruit and limes in fourths lengthwise. Slice very thin crosswise and remove seeds. Measure fruit including juice and add 1½ cups water for each cup fruit. Let stand several hours. Simmer, covered, over low heat about 2 hours or until tender. Measure and add an equal amount of sugar. Add orange rind. Cook over medium heat until mix-

ture sheets when dropped from spoon. Pour into hot sterilized glasses and seal. Makes about 9 6-ounce glasses.

WATERMELON MARMALADE

4 cups water
4 cups thinly sliced watermelon rind, ⅛″ thick and ¾″ long
4½ cups sugar
¾ cup orange juice
Rind from 2 oranges, coarsely ground
1 cup raisins

Pour water over watermelon rind and soak 24 hours. Add sugar, orange juice, orange rind and raisins. Cook, stirring frequently, until syrup sheets from spoon. Pour into hot sterilized jars and seal. Makes about 2 pints.

COUNTRY-STYLE APPLE BUTTER

10 pounds apples
Cider
Sugar
1 tablespoon allspice
1 teaspoon nutmeg
1 tablespoon cloves

Pare, core and slice apples. Measure apples and add an equal amount of cider. Cook over low heat until tender. Press through sieve. For each cup of pulp, add ½ cup sugar. Add remaining ingredients and cook over low heat until thickened. Turn into hot sterilized jars and seal. Makes about 12 pints.

CARROT-RAISIN MARMALADE

3 oranges
4 cups water
1 cup coarsely grated carrots
¼ cup lemon juice
4 cups sugar
1 cup raisins

Peel oranges. Cut peel in very thin strips and cook in water until tender. Add carrots and boil 10 minutes. Cut oranges into very small pieces and add to carrot mixture. Add other ingredients. Boil, stirring frequently, until syrup sheets from spoon. Pour into hot sterilized jars and seal. Makes 2½ pints.

ORANGE MARMALADE

7 large oranges
Water
Sugar
1 tablespoon lime juice
2 tablespoons lemon juice
1 tablespoon grated lemon rind

Wash oranges and cut in fourths lengthwise. Slice very thin crosswise, remove seeds. Measure fruit including juice and add 1½ cups water for each cup fruit and let stand 24 hours. Simmer covered over low heat about 2 hours or until tender. Measure fruit; add 1 cup sugar for each cup fruit. Add lime juice, lemon juice and lemon rind; cook until mixture sheets when dropped from spoon. Pour into hot sterilized glasses and seal. Makes about 8 6-ounce glasses.

PEACH BUTTER

4 cups peach puree
½ cup lemon juice
1 tablespoon grated lemon rind
2 cups sugar

Combine all ingredients. Cook over low heat, stirring constantly, until sugar melts. Cook until mixture is thickened, stirring frequently. Pour into clean hot sterilized glasses. Cover with paraffin. Makes about 5 8-ounce glasses.

PRUNE BUTTER

Wash prunes and cook in a small amount of water until soft. Rub through a colander, then through a fine wire strainer. If pulp is quite juicy, boil until thick. Add 1 cup sugar for each 2 cups pulp. If a tart butter is desired, use less sugar. Cook slowly until butter is the desired thickness. Stir in cinnamon, allspice, and cloves to taste. Pour boiling hot butter into hot sterilized jars. Cover with paraffin.

RELISHES

AND PICKLES

DUTCH PICKLED CHERRIES

5 quarts sour cherries
Vinegar
¼ cup grated lemon rind
Sugar

Remove pits from cherries, cover with vinegar and let stand 24 hours. Add lemon rind. Drain; put in layers in hot sterilized jars, sprinkling each layer with 2 teaspoons sugar. Seal. Makes about 6 quarts.

PICKLED CARROTS

1 cup vinegar
1 cup water
1 cup sugar
½ teaspoon salt
2 quarts hot diced cooked carrots

Boil vinegar, water, sugar and salt 2 minutes and pour over carrots. Let stand several hours. Seal in hot sterilized jars. Makes about 2 quarts.

CATSUP

2½ quarts (15 to 17 medium-sized) sliced
    tomatoes
1 cup chopped onions
3″ piece stick cinnamon
1 large garlic clove, chopped
1 teaspoon whole cloves
1 cup cider vinegar
½ cup sugar
½ teaspoon ground ginger
1¼ teaspoons salt
1 teaspoon paprika
Dash cayenne pepper

Simmer together tomatoes and onion for 30 minutes; press through sieve. Put cinnamon, garlic and cloves loosely in clean, thin, white cloth; tie top tightly; add to vinegar and simmer 30 minutes. Remove spices. Boil tomatoes rapidly until ½ original volume. Stir frequently. Add vinegar, sugar, ginger, salt, paprika and cayenne pepper to tomato mixture. Boil rapidly, stirring constantly, about 10 minutes or until slightly thickened. Pour into hot sterilized jars and seal. Makes about 2 pints.

SPICED RED CABBAGE

4 quarts shredded red cabbage
½ cup salt
6 cups vinegar
1 cup sugar
1 cup chopped celery
½ teaspoon pepper
1 teaspoon mustard seed
½ teaspoon allspice
½ teaspoon nutmeg

Sprinkle cabbage with salt. Let stand overnight. Drain. Combine remaining in-gredients. Boil 5 minutes and pour over cabbage. Turn into hot sterilized jars and seal. Makes about 4 quarts.

CHILI SAUCE

4 quarts peeled and chopped tomatoes
1¾ cups chopped sweet red pepper
2½ cups chopped onions
½ teaspoon Tabasco
1 tablespoon mustard seed
1 teaspoon whole cloves
1 teaspoon ginger
1 teaspoon nutmeg
2 3″ pieces stick cinnamon
1 cup firmly packed brown sugar
3 cups vinegar
2 tablespoons salt

Combine tomatoes, sweet pepper, chopped onions and Tabasco. Add mustard seed, cloves, ginger, nutmeg and cinnamon. Boil slowly about 2 hours, stirring often. Add sugar, vinegar and salt. Cook, stirring constantly, 5 minutes or until desired thickness. Turn into hot sterilized jars. Seal. Makes about 3 quarts.

TOMATO-APPLE CHUTNEY

3 quarts (18 to 20 medium-sized) chopped
    tomatoes
3 quarts (12 to 15 medium-sized) chopped
    apples
1½ cups chopped green pepper
3 cups chopped onions
2 cups seedless raisins
4 teaspoons salt
4 cups firmly packed brown sugar
4 cups cider vinegar
½ cup preserved ginger
⅓ cup whole mixed pickle spices

Combine tomatoes, apples, green pepper, onions, raisins, salt, sugar, vinegar and ginger. Put spices loosely in clean, thin, white cloth; tie top tightly; add to tomato mixture. Bring to a boil; simmer 1½ hours; stir frequently. Remove spices. Pack chutney into hot sterilized jars and seal. Makes about 3 quarts.

CORN RELISH

15 medium-sized ears of corn
2½ cups diced sweet red peppers
2 cups diced green peppers
4 cups chopped celery
1 cup sliced onions
1 cup sugar
4 cups vinegar
2 tablespoons salt
2 teaspoons celery seed
2 tablespoons dry mustard
¼ cup all-purpose flour
½ cup water

Remove husks and silks from corn. Place in boiling water. Simmer 10 minutes. Drain; cut corn from cob. Combine red peppers, green peppers, celery, onions, sugar, vinegar, salt and celery seed. Boil 15 minutes. Mix mustard and flour; blend with water. Add with corn to pepper mixture. Stir and simmer 5 minutes. Turn into hot sterilized jars and seal. Makes about 7 pints.

CUCUMBER CRISPS

10 pounds medium-sized cucumbers
1 cup salt
2¼ quarts vinegar
½ cup lemon juice
3 cups sugar
⅓ cup mixed pickling spices

Wash and cut cucumbers into slices ¼ inch thick. Combine cucumbers and salt. Let stand several hours. Drain. Rinse in cold water. Combine vinegar, lemon juice, sugar and spices. Boil 1 minute. Add cucumbers and simmer 5 minutes. Turn into hot sterilized jars and seal. Makes about 12 pints.

TANGY CUCUMBER SAUCE

1 quart ground cucumbers
1 tablespoon salt
½ cup grated onions
1 cup vinegar
1 cup lemon juice
½ teaspoon black pepper
½ teaspoon cayenne
½ teaspoon ground cloves
½ teaspoon dry mustard
¼ cup brown sugar, firmly packed

Mix cucumbers and salt thoroughly. Let stand 30 minutes. Drain. Combine cucumbers and onions. Combine vinegar, lemon juice, spices and sugar. Heat to boiling point. Simmer 5 minutes. Add vegetables and remaining ingredients. Heat to boiling; simmer 5 minutes. Seal in hot sterilized jars. Makes about 3 pints.

SPICED CURRANTS

2 quarts currants
1 cup lemon juice
2 cups sugar
1 teaspoon allspice
¼ teaspoon cloves
½ teaspoon nutmeg

Stem and wash currants. Combine lemon juice, sugar and spices. Heat to boiling point. Cook over high heat about 5 minutes. Add currants and cook over low heat until thickened. Turn into hot sterilized jars and seal. Makes about 5 pints.

DUTCH RED EGGS

2½ cups small beets
¼ cup brown sugar, firmly packed
1 cup lemon juice
½ teaspoon salt
4 cloves
6 hard-cooked eggs

Cook beets until tender. Drain and peel. Combine sugar, lemon juice, salt and cloves; pour over beets and cook over low heat 10 minutes. Add eggs; chill. Makes 1½ pints.

CAPE COD KETCHUP

2½ pounds cranberries
Vinegar
2½ cups sugar
1 tablespoon cinnamon
1 teaspoon nutmeg
1¼ teaspoons ground cloves
¼ teaspoon powdered ginger
¼ teaspoon paprika

Wash cranberries; cover with vinegar. Heat to boiling point. Cook until berries are tender. Press through sieve. Add remaining ingredients. Cook over low heat until thickened. Turn into hot sterilized jars. Makes about 6 pints.

PICKLED PEACHES

8 pounds medium-sized peaches
2½ tablespoons whole cloves
8 2″ pieces stick cinnamon
2 pounds sugar
1 quart cider vinegar
¼ cup grated lemon rind

Wash and pare peaches. Put cloves and cinnamon loosely in clean, thin, white cloth and tie top tightly. Cook together spices, sugar and vinegar 10 minutes. Add peaches and lemon rind; cook until tender. Let stand several hours. Remove spices. Drain syrup from peaches; boil syrup until thickened. Pack peaches in hot sterilized jars. Pour syrup over peaches. Seal. Makes about 6 pints.

RED AND GREEN RELISH

4½ cups finely chopped onions
2 cups finely chopped sweet red peppers
2 cups finely chopped green peppers
1 cup sugar
1 quart vinegar
1 tablespoon salt

Combine all ingredients and heat to boiling point. Cook until slightly thickened. Pour into hot sterilized jars and seal. Makes about 8 pints.

PICCALILLI

4 cups chopped green tomatoes
2 medium-sized sweet red peppers, chopped
2 medium-sized green peppers, chopped
3 large mild onions, chopped
1 small head cabbage, chopped
½ cup salt
3 cups vinegar
1 pound (2 cups firmly packed) brown sugar
2 tablespoons mixed pickle spices

Combine vegetables; mix with salt. Let stand overnight. Drain and press in clean, thin, white cloth to remove all liquid possible. Combine vinegar and sugar. Place spices loosely in thin, white cloth; tie top tightly. Add to vinegar mixture; bring to boil. Add vegetables and simmer about 30 minutes. Remove spice bag. Pack into hot sterilized jars and seal. Makes about 4 pints.

SPICED PRUNES

1 pound prunes, cooked
1 cup lemon juice
1 cup sugar
1 cup water
1 teaspoon nutmeg
1 teaspoon cinnamon

Combine prunes, lemon juice, sugar, water and spices. Heat to boiling point and cook 1 minute. Turn into hot sterilized jars and seal. Makes about 2 pints.

WATERMELON PICKLE

4 pounds prepared thick watermelon rind
Limewater made with 2 quarts of cold water and 1 tablespoon of lime (calcium oxide, purchased from drugstore)
2½ tablespoons whole allspice
1 tablespoon ginger root, chopped
2 tablespoons whole cloves
10 2" pieces stick cinnamon
1 quart cider vinegar
1 quart water
4 pounds sugar

Select thick rind from firm, not overripe melon. To prepare, trim off green skin and pink flesh. Weigh 4 pounds of remaining portion and cut in 1" pieces. Soak 1 hour in limewater. Drain, cover with fresh water, and cook 1½ hours, or until tender. Add more water as needed. Drain. Put spices loosely in a clean, thin, white cloth; tie top tightly. Bring to boiling spices, vinegar, 1 quart water and sugar. Add watermelon rind and simmer 2 hours. Remove spice bag. Pack rind in hot sterilized jars. Fill jars to top with hot syrup and seal. Makes about 6 pints.

RED PEAR RELISH

2½ cups chopped tomatoes
2½ cups diced pears
½ cup chopped green pepper
½ cup chopped onions
1 cup sugar
½ cup vinegar
1 teaspoon salt
½ teaspoon ginger
½ teaspoon dry mustard
¼ cup chopped canned pimiento

Combine tomatoes, pears, green pepper, onions, sugar, vinegar, salt, ginger and mustard. Cook over low heat 1 hour, stirring occasionally. Add pimiento. Turn into hot sterilized jars and seal. Makes about 2 pints.

SPICY PICKLED PEARS

7 pounds pears
3½ pounds (6¾ cups) sugar
4 cups vinegar
6 3" sticks cinnamon

Peel pears. Combine remaining ingredients; heat to boiling point. Add pears and cook, over low heat, until pears are tender. Remove pears. Continue cooking syrup until reduced ½ in volume. Pack pears into hot sterilized jars. Pour syrup over pears and seal. Makes about 9 pints.

TOMATO-PEPPER RELISH

2 quarts ripe tomatoes
1½ cups chopped onions
1 cup sugar
½ cup salt
2 green peppers, chopped
1 cup diced carrots
1 tablespoon prepared mustard
2 cups white vinegar
¼ cup horseradish

Peel tomatoes and chop; drain. Add remaining ingredients. Pour into hot sterilized jars and seal. Makes about 3 quarts.

RED TOMATO SPREAD

2 pounds tart apples, pared and sliced
5 pounds tomatoes, peeled and chopped
1 cup vinegar
6 cups sugar
1 teaspoon mace
1 teaspoon whole cloves
1 teaspoon nutmeg
½ teaspoon allspice

Combine apples, tomatoes, vinegar and sugar. Add spices. Simmer about 3½ hours, until thickened. Turn into hot sterilized jars and seal. Makes about 12 pints.

INDEX

Index

NOTES

NOTES

NOTES

NOTES

NOTES

NOTES

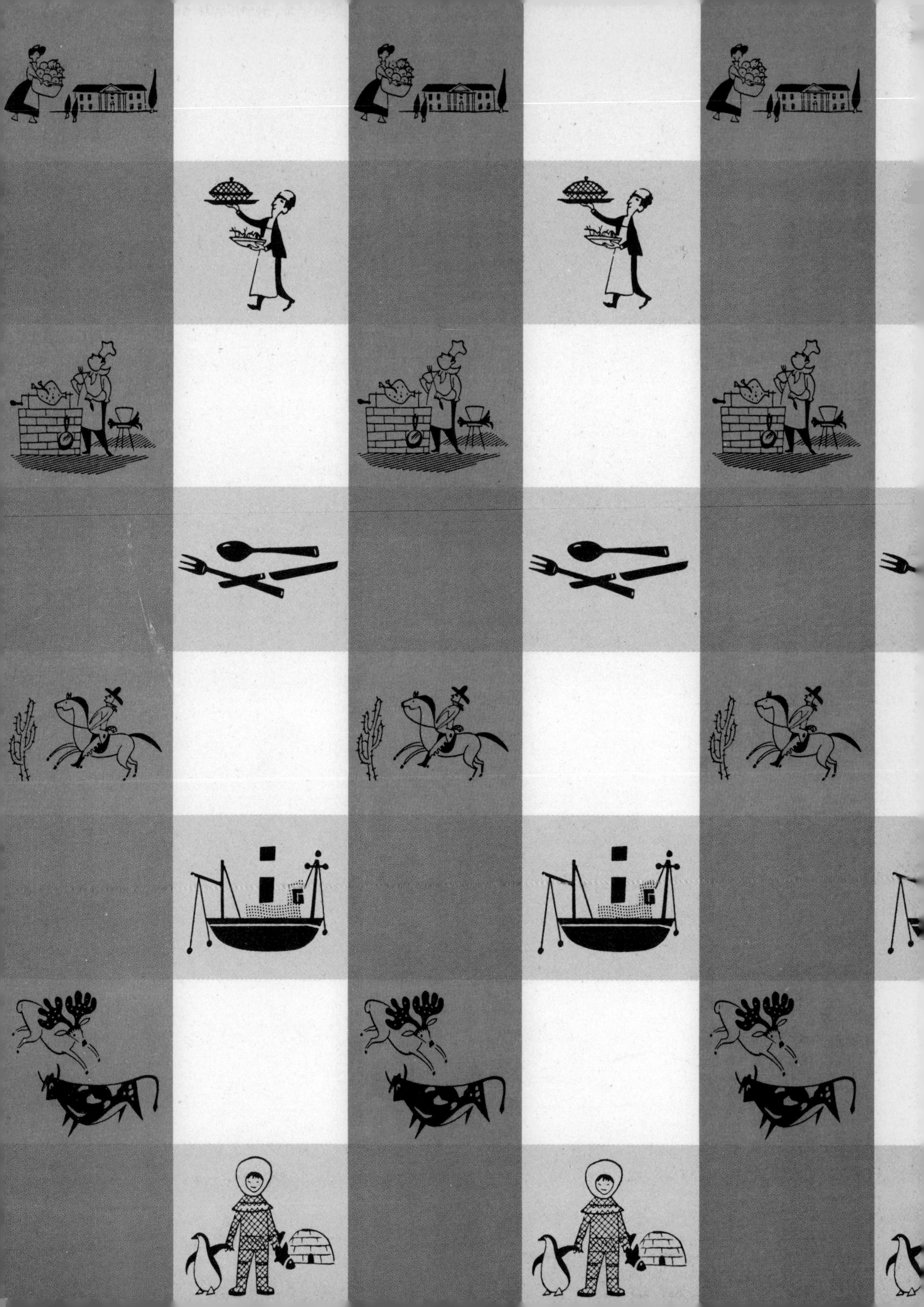